Macintosh™ Revealed

Volume Two: Programming with the Toolbox

Stephen Chernicoff

HAYDEN BOOK COMPANY
a division of Hayden Publishing Company, Inc.
Hasbrouck Heights, New Jersey and Berkeley, California

Apple believes that good books are important to successful computing. The Apple Press imprint is your assurance that this book has been published with the support and encouragement of Apple Computer Inc., and is the type of book we would be proud to publish ourselves.

For

Ann,

who likes the one with the mouse.

Acquisitions Editor: MICHAEL MCGRATH
Consulting Editor: SCOT KAMINS
Production Editors: MARY PICKLUM, RONNIE GROFF
Editorial Production Service: GANIS & HARRIS, INC.: CLAIRE MCKEAN
Cover design: JIM BERNARD
Cover photo: LOU ODOR
Composition: MCFARLAND GRAPHICS & DESIGN, INC.
Printed and bound by: COMMAND WEB OFFSET, INC.

Library of Congress Cataloging in Publication Data
(Revised for vol. 2)

Chernicoff, Stephen.
    Macintosh revealed.

    Includes bibliographical references and index.
    Contents: v. 1. Unlocking the toolbox.—v. 2.
Programming with the toolbox.
    1. Macintosh (Computer)   I. Title.
QA76.8.M3C48 1985   005.2'65   85-8611
ISBN 0-8104-6561-2

Printed in the United States of America

1	2	3	4	5	6	7	8	9	Printing
85	86	87	88	89	90	91	92	93	Year

Preface

If you're reading this book, you probably don't need to be told that Apple Computer's Macintosh is an extraordinary personal computer. It does things you may never have seen a computer do before, in ways you may never have imagined. If you've wondered what goes on behind the scenes to make the magic happen, this book is for you. By the time you've finished it, the inner workings of the Macintosh will stand revealed before your eyes, and you'll be able to use the User Interface Toolbox built into the Macintosh to perform the same magic in your own programs.

You should realize, though, that the Toolbox is for experienced programmers, not beginners. To get the most out of this book, you should have some previous experience (the more the better) in at least one high-level programming language. The programming examples given here are written in Pascal, but their general principles are applicable in other languages as well. If Pascal isn't your native programming tongue, you should at least be able to pick up enough of it to follow the logic of the programming examples and apply them in your own preferred language. The book will offer a few hints to help you over the rough spots, but in general it's assumed that you're already acquainted with the syntax and semantics of standard Pascal. (For hard-core bit bangers, there's also information on how to use the Toolbox in assembly language.)

The only other assumption is that you want to know how the Macintosh user interface works from the inside. Whether you're a professional software developer, a college student, a midnight hacker, or just the kind of person who likes to take watches apart and see what makes them tick, read on and behold the Macintosh revealed.

STEPHEN CHERNICOFF
Belmont, California

iii

Acknowledgments

No book is ever the product of one person working alone—especially a book of the size and complexity of this one. These are some of the people who have helped me bring the book to completion, and to whom I owe a special debt of gratitude and appreciation:

First and forever, to my wife, **Helen**, whose love and understanding through the ordeal of living with an author have brought new meaning to the word "patience"; and to my parents, **Murray and Annette Chernicoff**, for their unwavering encouragement and support.

To **Chris Espinosa**, manager of Macintosh User Education, and **Mike Murray**, manager of Macintosh Marketing, who graciously afforded me the freedom to pursue this project as an independent agent.

To **Mike McGrath**, **Ronnie Groff**, **Mary Picklum**, and **Nancy Ragle** of Hayden Book Company, professionals all in the noblest sense of the word, whose contributions were manifold and invaluable.

To **David Casseres** of Apple Computer, for his indispensable assistance with the programming examples and his wise and thoughtful counsel throughout.

To **Scott Knaster** of Apple, for his thorough technical review of the manuscript.

To the redoubtable **Scot Kamins** of Technology Translated, Inc., whose candid judgment and incisive suggestions have helped make this a better book in countless ways.

To **Steven Smith** of CommuniTree Group, who executed the illustrations with imagination and panache.

To **Claire McKean** of Ganis & Harris, Inc., and **Charles Andrews** of McFarland Graphics & Design, Inc., for their skillful services in production, and to **Doug Henwood and Chris Bratton** for their professionalism in compiling the index.

And finally, to the men and women of Apple Computer's Macintosh Division, as talented and creative a group of people as I have ever been privileged to work with; and to **Steven Jobs**, chairman of the board of Apple Computer and general manager of the Macintosh Division, who provided the vision and inspiration for these remarkable people to bring Macintosh to reality.

Contents

Chapter 3   **Windows on the World**   65

CHAPTER

1

All the Tools You Need

What sets the Macintosh apart from other personal computers is its revolutionary *user interface*. In plain English, the word *interface* means a junction or boundary where two things meet. In computerese, it refers to the set of rules and conventions by which one part of an organized system (like the Macintosh) communicates with another. Wherever two components of the system come together, they exchange information by way of an interface.

The Macintosh system consists of hardware (physical components such as chips, circuits, and other electronic and mechanical devices) and of software (programs). The most important component of all is the human being peering at the screen and fiddling with the mouse and keyboard. This flesh-and-blood component of the system is known, in technical parlance, as the *user*. So the user interface is the set of conventions that allow the human user to communicate with the rest of the system.

In the past, user interfaces were typically based on a screen full of text characters (usually displayed in garish green) and a keyboard for typing those characters. To tell the computer what to do, you had to memorize a complex command language, so you could press exactly the right keys in exactly the right order. If your actions didn't conform to what the computer expected of you, it would tell you so in terms ranging from curt to unintelligible. On the whole, it was sometimes hard to tell that the human was the boss and the computer, the servant.

The Macintosh changes all that. In place of the time-honored character screen and keyboard, it uses a high-resolution, "bit-mapped" display and a hand-held pointing device, called a mouse. This results in a whole new way of communicating between people and computers. The bit-mapped screen can present information in vivid visual form, using pictorial "icons," elaborate graphical effects, and varied patterns and textures. Text can be depicted exactly as it will appear on the printed page—in black characters on a white background, with a variety of typefaces, sizes, and styles. The mouse provides a direct, natural way of giving commands. This is done by using the mouse to point and manipulate images directly on the screen instead of typing arcane command sequences using the keyboard. The programmers at Apple have put a great deal of thought and effort into taking advantage of these features to produce a user interface that feels natural and comfortable. The result of their efforts is the User Interface Toolbox, 64 kilobytes of tightly engineered, hand-crafted machine-language code that's built into every Macintosh in *read-only memory (ROM)*. With it, you can write programs that use overlapping windows, pull-down menus, scroll bars, dialog boxes, and all the other wonders you see on the Macintosh screen. This book will teach you how.

Strictly speaking, the Macintosh ROM is divided into three parts: the Macintosh Operating System, which handles low-level tasks such as memory management, disk input/output, and serial communications; the QuickDraw graphics routines, which are responsible for everything displayed on the screen; and the User Interface Toolbox, which implements the higher-level constructs of the user interface, such as windows and menus. As a rule, we'll be using the term "Toolbox" to refer loosely to the entire body of built-in code that's available to a running program; only occasionally will we use it in the narrower sense of the user-interface code alone, to distinguish it from the Operating System and QuickDraw.

How This Book Is Organized

The book is divided into two volumes. Volume One, *Unlocking the Toolbox,* presents the foundations of the Toolbox: basic conventions and utilities, memory management, QuickDraw graphics, resources (one of the corner-stones of the Macintosh software design), program startup, and text display. Once you've mastered these fundamentals, you're ready for Volume Two, *Programming with the Toolbox.* Here you'll learn about the various parts of the Macintosh user interface and how they work:

• Chapter 2, "Keeping Up with Events," introduces the concept of events, the basic mechanism for monitoring the user's actions with the mouse and keyboard, and shows how to structure a program around them.

- Chapter 3, "Windows on the World," tells how to maintain and manipulate overlapping windows on the screen.
- Chapter 4, "What's on the Menu?," deals with pull-down menus and how to use them to accept commands from the user.
- Chapter 5, "Scissors and Paste," describes the facilities built into the Toolbox for simple cut-and-paste text editing.
- Chapter 6, "At the Controls," discusses controls that the user can manipulate directly with the mouse, such as on-screen "pushbuttons" and scroll bars.
- Chapter 7, "Meaningful Dialogs," covers alert and dialog boxes, used to display status messages and to request information or instructions from the user.
- Chapter 8, "Files at Your Fingertips," is about disk files and how to work with them.

Because the Toolbox includes such a broad range of facilities and features, it's impossible to cover them all in this book. Unavoidably, some topics were left out because of time and space limitations. But we've included those features most programmers need for most applications. The ultimate, comprehensive source of information on the Toolbox is Apple's own forthcoming *Inside Macintosh* manual.

A central feature of this second volume is a fully worked example program, a simple interactive text editor named **MiniEdit**. As each part of the Toolbox is discussed, its use is illustrated in detail by examining the relevant routines of the example program: those dealing with events in Chapter 2, windows in Chapter 3, and so on. A complete listing of the program is given for reference and study in Appendix H.

The example program serves two purposes. First, it illustrates concretely how to use the Toolbox's various parts. Second, once you understand how it works, you can use it as a "shell" within which to develop your own application programs. The **MiniEdit** program already includes all the Toolbox calls needed to implement the standard features of the user interface—for instance, to display pull-down menus when the user presses the mouse in the menu bar, or move windows around on the screen when the user drags them by their title bars—so it can save you from having to "reinvent the wheel" every time you write a program of your own. By returning the mail-order form included with this volume, you can order a software disk containing the source code of the **MiniEdit** program. Then instead of writing your own programs from scratch, you can modify the existing program for whatever application you choose.

Beware, however: although the program has been tested and found to work, it is offered with no guarantees. A well-known programmer's axiom states that testing can reveal the presence of bugs, but not their absence. Please report any bugs and suggested corrections to the author, in care of the Hayden Book Company.

How to Use This Book

With the exception of Chapter 1, each chapter in the book consists of two complementary parts: the basic text of the chapter and the subsequent reference sections. They are designed to be used in parallel. For an overview of the Toolbox and how to use it, you should read the text sections from beginning to end. Cross-references enclosed in square brackets, such as [2.1.1], indicate the relevant parts of the reference sections, where you'll find detailed descriptions of individual Toolbox procedures, functions, constants, variables, and data types. When you encounter one of these for the first time, follow the cross-reference to the reference section for the details. Together, the text and reference sections will teach you step by step how to use the Toolbox in your own programs.

After you've learned the basic concepts, you'll find the reference sections useful on their own for refreshing your memory or looking up specific facts and details. The reference sections are organized for quick reference rather than sequential reading. Although their structure generally parallels that of the text sections, they don't always treat topics in exactly the same order or build logically on what's gone before. Thus you may find some of the material in the reference sections hard to understand at first, because it refers to topics you haven't yet learned. Try not to let this bother you—just skip the parts that don't make sense and come back to them later when you're better prepared to understand them. You'll also find some subjects covered in the reference section that aren't discussed in the text sections at all; once you've acquired a working knowledge of the Toolbox, you can pick up these extra topics by browsing the reference sections on your own.

What's in the Reference Sections

Each reference section is headed by a set of Pascal declarations defining the Toolbox entities—procedures, functions, constants, variables, and data types—that are discussed in that section. The declarations give the names of the entities being defined, plus other practical information, such as the number, order, and types of a procedure's parameters, the type of value a function returns, or the names and types of a record's fields. Following the declarations are a series of notes explaining the meaning and use of the Toolbox entities being discussed. Finally, most reference sections end with a data box containing further information of interest only to assembly-language programmers.

For readers unfamiliar with Pascal, let's look at examples of the reference declarations and discuss how to read them. Program 1-1 shows a Pascal declaration typical of those you'll find in the reference sections. (This particular one, in fact, is taken from section [2.1.1].) The declaration says that **EventRecord** is the name of a record type with five components, or *fields*. The first field is named **what** and holds a value of type **INTEGER**; the second, **message**, and the third, **when**, both hold values of type **LONGINT**; the fourth is named **where** and is of type **Point**; and the fifth, **modifiers**, is of type **INTEGER**. To the right of each field definition is a comment (enclosed in the Pascal comment brackets { and }) describing the meaning of that field: for instance, field **when** represents the time on the system clock when the event occurred. (We'll be learning about events and the system clock in Chapter 2.) If **theEvent** is the name of a record in your program of type **EventRecord,** the expression

theEvent.when

denotes a value of type **LONGINT** giving the time of the event on the system clock.

```
type
   EventRecord = record
                 what      : INTEGER;          {Event type}
                 message   : LONGINT;          {Type-dependent information}
                 when      : LONGINT;          {Time of event on system clock}
                 where     : Point;            {Mouse position in global coordinates}
                 modifiers : INTEGER           {State of modifier keys and mouse button}
                 end;
```

Program 1-1 A type declaration

Program 1-2 shows an example of a procedure declaration, taken from reference section [3.2.4]. This declaration defines the procedure **SetWTitle**, used to set the title of a window. The procedure accepts two parameters named **theWindow** and **newTitle**, of types **WindowPtr** and **Str255**, respectively. As the explanatory comments state, the first parameter is a pointer to the window whose title is to be changed and the second is the new title, a string of up to 255 characters. (The Toolbox utility data type

Str255 was introduced in Volume One, Chapter 2.) If your program has a window pointer named **thisWindow**, the statement

    SetWTitle (thisWindow, 'Our Founder')

will give the title **'Our Founder'** to the window it points to.

```
procedure SetWTitle
            (theWindow : WindowPtr;              {Pointer to the window}
             newTitle  : Str255);               {New title}
```
Program 1-2 A procedure declaration

Program 1-3 shows the declaration for the Toolbox function **GetCtlValue**, taken from reference section [6.2.4]. This function reports the current setting of a control, such as the position of the scroll box within the "shaft" of a scroll bar. Like the procedure declaration we just looked at, a function declaration defines the names and types of the parameters the function expects you to supply. In addition, it also specifies the type of value the function returns as a result, following the colon (**:**) on the declaration's last line. In this case the function accepts one parameter named **theControl**, of type **ControlHandle**, and returns a result of type **INTEGER**. You might call this function with a statement such as

    scrollPos := GetCtlValue (theScrollBar)

where **scrollPos** is a variable of type **INTEGER** declared in your program, and **theScrollBar** is of type **ControlHandle**.

```
function GetCtlValue
            (theControl : ControlHandle)        {Handle to the control}
              : INTEGER;                         {Current setting}
```
Program 1-3 A function declaration

If you compare the procedure and function declarations shown in the reference sections with those given in Apple's *Inside Macintosh* manual, you'll find that the parameter names are often different. Since you don't actually use the parameter names when you call a routine in your program, the names given in the declaration don't affect the way the routine is used. Because of that we've taken the liberty of changing many of the names to suggest more clearly the meaning or purpose of the parameters.

Names that you *do* use directly in your own program, such as those of constants and variables or of the fields in a record, are, of course, listed the same way in the reference sections as in the Apple documentation. Even here, however, you may notice slight variations in capitalization style; these make no difference, since Apple's Pascal compiler doesn't distinguish between corresponding upper- and lowercase letters. Similarly, the compiler uses only the first eight characters of any name, so variations occurring after the eighth character have no significance.

Some Terms and Conventions

Before we start, we'll explain some of the terms and conventions we'll be using. The Macintosh's microprocessor (the Motorola MC68000, usually referred to simply as the "68000") works with data items of three different sizes: *bytes* of 8 bits each, *words* of 16 bits (2 bytes), and *long words* of 32 bits (2 words, or 4 bytes). All memory addresses are long words, 32 bits in length, of which only the last 24 bits are significant. Each address designates a single 8-bit byte in memory. As a rule, word-length and long-word data items in memory must begin at an even-numbered byte address, known as a *word boundary*.

Throughout the book, we use a **bold** or ***italic bold*** typeface as a kind of implicit quotation mark to distinguish actual program code from ordinary body text. In displayed program lines we use an alternate

```
computer-voice typeface
```

for the same purpose. The computer voice is also used occasionally for characters typed on the Macintosh keyboard or displayed on the screen.

In keeping with the convention used in many programming languages, including Apple's versions of Pascal and assembly language for the Macintosh, we use a dollar sign ($) to denote hexadecimal (base-16) constants. For instance, the constant **$43** represents the same numerical value as decimal **67** (4 sixteens plus 3). As usual, the letters **A** to **F** stand for hexadecimal digits with numerical values from **10** to **15**—so the hexadecimal constant **$BD** stands for 11 sixteens plus 13, or decimal **189**.

We've already mentioned that section numbers enclosed in square brackets, such as [2.1.1], denote cross-references to the designated reference section. References to Volume One are prefixed with a Roman numeral I and a colon: for instance, [I:2.1.1] refers to Volume One, section 2.1.1.

Throughout the text sections of this book, you'll see shaded boxes like this one. These "by-the-way" boxes enclose side comments, helpful hints, exceptional cases, and other material subordinate to the main discussion.

Several chapters end with a section titled "Nuts and Bolts." This section is for miscellaneous topics that don't fit anywhere else in the chapter—the little unclassified odds and ends rattling around in the bottom of the Toolbox. In general these are minor points of only limited interest, or things that are useful only in unusual or high specialized circumstances.

That does it for the preliminaries, so now it's time to get to the business at hand. If you're ready to see the Macintosh revealed, proceed to the next page and let's get started.

CHAPTER

2

Keeping Up with Events

One of the cornerstones of the Macintosh philosophy is that *people* should tell *computers* what to do and not the other way around. Too often it has seemed that using a computer has been an exercise in catering to the machine, and it's the computer that has given the orders:

    Please type a file name

or

    Answer Y or N

or

    Press any key to continue

If you didn't type just the right incantation, the computer would beep angrily and spew some cryptic error message out across your screen.

Macintosh is dedicated to the principle that the *user*, not the *computer*, should be in control. Instead of giving the user instructions about what should happen next, a Macintosh program accepts instructions *from* the user about the next step. The user controls the program's behavior by clicking the mouse or typing on the keyboard; each such action constitutes an *event* for the program to respond to. The program spends most of its time idling, waiting for an event to occur. Then it responds and waits for the next one.

A program that works this way is said to be *event-driven*. By way of illustration, we'll be developing an example event-driven program over the remaining chapters of this book, a simple interactive text editor named **MiniEdit**. Program 2-1 shows the program's high-level structure. This is

```
program MiniEdit;

  { Skeleton program to illustrate event-driven structure. }

  var
    Finished : BOOLEAN;                          {Flag to signal end of main event loop}
    . . . ;


  procedure Initialize;

    { Do one-time-only initialization [Prog. 2-6]. }

    begin {Initialize}
      Finished := FALSE;                         {Initialize quit flag}
      . . .
    end; {Initialize}


  procedure DoEvent; forward;

  procedure MainLoop;

    { Execute one pass of main program loop [Prog. 2-2]. }

    begin {MainLoop}
      . . . ;
      DoEvent                                    {Get and process one event}
    end; {MainLoop}


  procedure DoEvent;

    { Get and process one event [Prog. 2-3]. }

    begin {DoEvent}
      . . .
    end; {DoEvent}
```

Program 2-1 Skeleton of an event-driven program

```
begin {MiniEdit}

    Initialize;                           {Do one-time-only initialization}

    repeat
        MainLoop                          {Execute one pass of main loop}
    until Finished

end.  {MiniEdit}
```

Program 2-1 (*continued*)

simply a skeleton outline, of course; as we learn more about the Toolbox in the chapters to come, we'll gradually add flesh to the bare bones. You'll find a complete listing of the **MiniEdit** program in Appendix H.

The program begins by calling a procedure named **Initialize** to handle the one-time preliminaries needed to start things. Then it enters its *main event loop*, in which it repeatedly calls the procedure **MainLoop**. This continues until the global flag **Finished**, set to **FALSE** by the **Initialize** routine, becomes **TRUE**. After a few routine housekeeping chores (not shown in the example), **MainLoop** calls another procedure named **DoEvent** to check whether or not there's an event waiting to be processed and, if so, respond to it as appropriate. Sooner or later an event will occur (such as the user's choosing the **Quit** menu command) that will set the **Finished** flag to **TRUE**, thereby terminating the program. We'll define the **Initialize**, **MainLoop**, and **DoEvent** procedures later in this chapter. But first, let's talk about events in general and how the Toolbox handles them.

The Event Queue

At the lowest level, events are detected and recorded by an *interrupt* mechanism. When the user presses the mouse button or a key on the keyboard, an electrical impulse is sent to the Macintosh's processor, causing it to temporarily suspend whatever it's doing and immediately execute a special *interrupt handler* routine. The interrupt handler doesn't respond to the event right away. Instead, it records the circumstances of the event for later processing: when it occurred, where on the screen the mouse was pressed, which key was typed on the keyboard, and so forth. Then it returns control to the running program, which resumes execution right from the point of suspension as though nothing had happened. Later, when the program is ready to process the event, it can retrieve the recorded information through the Toolbox and take whatever action is called for in response.

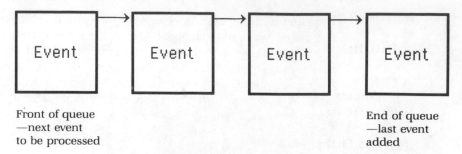

Front of queue
—next event
to be processed

End of queue
—last event
added

Figure 2-1 The event queue

The list in which events are recorded for later processing is called the *event queue* (see Figure 2-1). Each item in the queue is an *event record* representing one single event. When an event occurs, the interrupt handler stores all the pertinent information about the event into a new event record and adds it to the end of the queue. (This is called *posting* the event.) When the running program calls for the next event to be processed, it receives the first event record from the *front* of the queue. Events move through the queue in "FIFO" order—first in, first out—so that they're eventually processed in the same order they occurred. The event queue is a device for collecting events that can happen at unpredictable times and feeding them to your program to be processed in an orderly way.

The System Clock

While the Macintosh is running, its video circuitry continually reads out the contents of the screen buffer in memory and paints them onto the screen. Sixty times a second, when it reaches the bottom of the screen, it must pause and wait for the display tube's electron beam to return to the top and start over again. Each time this happens, the video circuitry sends a special interrupt signal to the processor.

This regularly recurring *vertical retrace interrupt* (sometimes called the "vertical blanking" or "VBL" interrupt) is the heartbeat of the Macintosh system. Since nothing has to be read out of the screen buffer while the electron beam is in transit from the bottom of the screen back to the top, a little extra processor time is available for other purposes. This makes the vertical retrace a convenient time to take care of routine "housekeeping" chores that have to be performed periodically, such as checking for mouse movement and updating the position of the cursor on the screen.

The time interval between "heartbeats," one sixtieth of a second, is called a *tick*, and is the basic unit of time on the *system clock*. The clock is restarted from zero every time the system is started up, and then increases by one at each vertical retrace interrupt. Thus it always registers the elapsed time in ticks since the system was last started. Whenever a new event is posted (added to the event queue), it's "time-stamped" with the current time on the system clock. Your program can read the system clock at any time with the **TickCount** function [2.7.1]; in assembly language, you can read it directly as a long-word global variable named **Ticks**.

Don't confuse the system clock with the real-time clock chip discussed in Volume One, Chapter 2. The system clock operates only while the Macintosh is turned on, and gets restarted from zero whenever the system is started up. The real-time clock is battery-powered and continues to record the current date and time even when the rest of the system is switched off.

Living with Desk Accessories

Something to remember when writing application programs for the Macintosh is that your program may not have the system all to itself. Don't forget that the Macintosh software environment includes "desk accessories" like the Alarm Clock, Calculator, and Scrapbook, which can coexist on the screen with any other application. The desk accessories aren't automatically available, however: if you want your user to have access to them, you have to take the proper steps in your program to make them available. Later on, in Chapter 4, we'll see how to set up an "Apple menu" listing the various desk accessories, and how to start up an accessory when the user chooses it from the menu. If you offer such a menu, there are certain other things you have to do as well to support the desk accessories.

Some of the desk accessories have tasks that they must perform periodically so they will work properly. For instance, when the Alarm Clock is active it has to update the time displayed on the screen once a second. It's up to you to make sure the desk accessories get the processor time they need to carry out such periodic tasks. You do this by calling the Toolbox procedure **SystemTask** [2.7.2]. This gives each active accessory a chance to check the system clock, see how much time has elapsed since it last executed its periodic task, and perform the task again if necessary.

To keep the desk accessories functioning smoothly, you should ideally call **SystemTask** at least once per tick, or 60 times a second. The easiest way to do this is to call it on each pass of your main event loop, as shown in our **MiniEdit** program's **MainLoop** routine (Program 2-2). This is

```
procedure MainLoop;

   { Execute one pass of main program loop.  }

   begin {MainLoop}

      FixCursor;                          {Adjust cursor for region of screen [Prog. 2-8]}
      SystemTask;                         {Do system idle processing [2.7.2]}

      {Perform any other periodic tasks};

      DoEvent                             {Get and process one event [Prog. 2-3, 2-5]}

   end;   {MainLoop}
```

Program 2-2 Main event loop

also a convenient time to take care of other "housekeeping" chores that need to be performed regularly. For instance, **MiniEdit** uses this opportunity to call one of its routines named **FixCursor**, which adjusts the appearance of the mouse cursor according to the part of the screen the user has moved it into. (We'll look at the definition of **FixCursor** in the section on cursor display later in this chapter.) After seeing to all such periodic chores (including calling **SystemTask**), **MainLoop** calls the program's **DoEvent** procedure to get and process the next available event.

> To make sure the desk accessories get the processor time they need, you should also call **SystemTask** from time to time during particularly time-consuming operations when control won't be returning to your main loop for a while.

Event Types

There are sixteen possible *event types*, identified by integer codes from **0** to **15** [2.1.2]. The important ones fall into the following general categories:

- *Mouse events:* The user pressed the mouse button (a *mouse-down* event) or released it (a *mouse-up* event).
- *Keyboard events:* The user pressed a key on the keyboard (a *key-down* event), held it down until it began to repeat automatically (an *auto-key* event), or released it (a *key-up* event).
- *Disk-inserted events:* The user inserted a disk into a disk drive.

- *Window events:* The user deactivated a window (a *deactivate* event), activated it (an *activate* event), or exposed a new part of it to view on the screen (an *update* event). We'll discuss these when we talk about windows in Chapter 3.
- *Null events:* You asked the Toolbox for an event and there weren't any to report.

These are all the event types you should normally have to deal with; *I/O driver* and *network* events are used internally by the Macintosh system, and needn't concern you directly. There are also four *application event* types that you can use any way you like. These allow you to send a "signal to yourself" that will be received and processed on a later pass through the event loop; they're useful for synchronizing your program's internal communications and control to the overall flow of events.

Keyboard Events

Keyboard events, in particular, require more discussion. As we learned in Volume One, Chapter 8, every keyboard event includes both a *key code* [I:8.1.3] identifying the physical key that was pressed or released and a *character code* [I:8.1.1] identifying the character that key represents, under whatever keyboard configuration is currently in effect. You can use either of these pieces of information, depending on your program's needs. Usually you want to know what character was typed—you don't particularly care which key the user pressed to produce it. So you'll normally want to look at the character code for a keyboard event, rather than the "raw" key code.

Recall from Volume One, Chapter 8, that the keys on the Macintosh keyboard are divided into *character keys* and *modifier keys*. Keyboard events deal only with character keys. The modifier keys (shift, caps lock, option, and command) don't generate any events of their own: you'll never receive an event telling you that the user pressed the shift key. However, the modifier keys affect the events that you *do* receive in two ways. First, as we'll see in the next section, every event includes information on which of the modifier keys, if any, were down at the time the event was posted. (This information is actually given for all events, not just keyboard events.) Second, the keyboard configuration takes the modifier keys into account in deciding what character to generate for a given key. An event's key code is never affected by the modifier keys, but the character code generally is: for instance, under any reasonable keyboard configuration, the same key that produces a lowercase letter **d** when pressed all by itself will produce a capital **D** if the shift or caps lock key is held down at the same time.

When the user presses and holds down any character key, the Toolbox automatically generates auto-key events to make the key repeat continually until released. There's a certain *initial delay* from the time the key is pressed until the first auto-key event, then a different (usually shorter) *repeat interval* between the auto-key events themselves. The standard settings are 24 ticks (four tenths of a second) for the initial delay and 6 ticks (10 repeats per second) for the repeat interval; the user can adjust these settings if desired with the Control Panel desk accessory.

Event Records

Everything your program needs to know about an event is summarized in an *event record* [2.1.1]. The fields of the record tell what type of event it was, when it occurred, where on the screen the mouse was at the time, and so forth. By analyzing the information in the event record, your program can determine what the event means and how to respond.

The most important information about an event is its event type, contained in the **what** field of the event record. The **message** field contains an *event message* giving further information about the event. Each type of event can use the event message in its own way [2.1.4]. For instance, window events store a pointer to the window in this field; for keyboard events, it contains both the key code and the character code for the key that was pressed or released.

The rest of the information in the event record is filled in the same way for all events, regardless of type. The **when** field gives the time on the system clock when the event was posted, the **where** field gives the screen coordinates of the mouse, and the **modifiers** field gives the state of the mouse button and modifier keys. Each modifier key, as well as the mouse button, corresponds to a bit in the **modifiers** field [2.1.5]: **1** if the key was down at the time the event was posted, **0** if it wasn't. You can examine these bits directly and interpret them in any way that's appropriate for your program.

Unfortunately, there's no way to distinguish between the two shift keys or the two option keys. The shift or option bit in the **modifiers** field is set to **1** if *either* of the corresponding keys is down.

The **when**, **where**, and **modifiers** fields are even filled in for null events. A null event tells you that, for instance, "at **52014** ticks on the system clock, with the mouse at screen coordinates (**279**, **136**) and the caps lock key down, nothing happened."

Event Masks

Some of the Toolbox routines dealing with events expect you to supply an *event mask* as a parameter, stating which specific event types the operation should apply to. The event mask is a 16-bit integer, with 1 bit for each of the possible event types [2.1.3]. A **1** bit in a given position includes the corresponding type in the operation; a **0** excludes it.

The Toolbox defines a set of mask constants for referring to each individual bit within the mask [2.1.3]. You can combine these with **BitAnd**, **BitOr**, **BitXOr**, and **BitNot** [I:2.2.2] to construct any mask you need. For example, the expression

    BitOr (MDownMask, MUpMask)

yields a mask referring to all mouse events, and

    BitNot (AutoKeyMask)

refers to all except auto-key events. The mask constant **EveryEvent** denotes the mask **$FFFF**, which refers to all events regardless of type.

Event Reporting

The usual way you find out about events is by calling **GetNextEvent** [2.2.1]. You supply a mask parameter specifying which types of event you're interested in. The Toolbox finds the next event of any of those types, removes it from the event queue, and returns it to you. All other types are ignored. If there are no pending events of the requested types, you'll get back a null event instead; null events can never be "masked out."

Not all events have the same priority. As we'll see in Chapter 3, window events are treated specially. They're never actually placed in the event queue, but are detected in other ways instead. When you ask for an event with **GetNextEvent**, the Toolbox checks for activate or deactivate events *before* looking in the event queue, and for update events only *after* looking in the queue and finding no events of the types you've requested. So activate and deactivate events have *higher* priority and update events *lower* priority than all others.

Auto-key events are also special. Instead of placing them in the queue whenever the appropriate time interval has elapsed, the Toolbox waits for you to explicitly request an event. Then, if there aren't any events in the queue of the requested types (and no activate or deactivate events), it checks to see whether the user is holding down a character key and whether the required interval has elapsed since the last event for that key.

If all the appropriate conditions are met, the Toolbox generates an auto-key event and returns it in response to your request. Otherwise it goes on to check for update events.

Putting all this together, the priority ranking for all events is as follows:

1. Deactivate events
2. Activate events
3. All except window, auto-key, and null events, in the order posted
4. Auto-key events
5. Update events, in front-to-back order of the windows on the screen
6. Null events

Null events have the lowest priority, since they're generated only if there are no other events to report.

Intercepted Events

Not every event you receive is actually of interest to your program. If you're supporting the use of desk accessories, you must remember that your program may be sharing the screen with one or more *system windows* containing accessories. Some of the user's actions with the mouse and keyboard may be directed to a desk accessory and not to your program itself.

Each time the Toolbox reports an event, it checks to see whether the event is directed to an active desk accessory. If so, it "intercepts" the event and passes it along to the desk accessory to handle. Then it reports the event to your program, just like any other. But by the time you receive the event, it will already have been handled by the desk accessory—so you can just ignore it and move on to the next event. To let you know whether the event is your responsibility, **GetNextEvent** returns a Boolean result: **TRUE** if you have to respond to the event, **FALSE** if it's already been intercepted and processed.

For instance, window events (activate, deactivate, and update) are your responsibility only if they're directed to one of your windows; those that apply to a system window are intercepted and handled by the desk accessory displayed in that window. Similarly, whenever a system window is active—that is, frontmost on the screen—all keyboard events are intercepted and fed to the window's desk accessory for action. The Toolbox also intercepts all I/O driver and network events, which are strictly for its private use; and, of course, there's nothing for you to do in response to a null event. So in all these cases, **GetNextEvent** will return a result of **FALSE** when reporting the event, telling you to ignore it.

Mouse-up events are also intercepted when a system window is active, but mouse-down events are not. The Toolbox doesn't check whether the mouse was pressed in a system window: it simply reports the event to you with a Boolean result of **TRUE**, telling you to handle the event yourself. As we'll see in Chapter 3, the first thing you do with a mouse-down event is find out which window it occurred in. If it was in a system window, it's then up to you to pass the event along to the appropriate desk accessory.

This exceptional treatment for mouse-down events only may seem arbitrary, but there's a good reason for it. Even if the Toolbox were to check every mouse-down event and intercept those that occur in system windows, you would still have to repeat the check yourself for every event that *wasn't* intercepted, to find out which of your windows the mouse was pressed in so you could respond appropriately. To avoid going through the same motions twice, the Toolbox simply leaves it to you to perform the check in the first place.

Before reporting a disk-inserted event, **GetNextEvent** automatically does some preliminary housekeeping to prepare the disk for use, such as reading its directory into memory. This operation is known as *mounting* the disk, and we'll have more to say about it in Chapter 8. **GetNextEvent** then copies the result code returned by the mounting operation into the disk event's **message** field and returns it to you with a function result of **TRUE**, in case you want to take any further action of your own. (For instance, if the disk was unreadable, you might want to offer the user the option of initializing it.) Usually there's nothing more to do and you can simply ignore the event, in spite of the **TRUE** result from **GetNextEvent**.

One other Toolbox routine worth mentioning is **EventAvail** [2.2.1], which works like **GetNextEvent** except that it doesn't remove the reported event from the queue. This is sometimes useful when you want to "peek" at the event queue for a particular type of event, but still leave the event in the event queue for later processing. Since it's assumed that the event will eventually be dealt with later, **EventAvail** makes no attempt to intercept and respond to system events. The only time it returns **FALSE** is for a null event, meaning that there are no events available of the types specified by the mask parameter. If there *is* an event available, **Event-Avail** returns **TRUE** and passes back the event in the variable parameter **theEvent**, just the same way **GetNextEvent** does.

Responding to Events

The routine that forms the heart of our event-driven example program is **DoEvent**. As we've seen, this routine is called repeatedly from the program's main event loop. Each time it's called, its job is to retrieve a single event from the Toolbox and respond to that event.

Program 2-3 shows a preliminary version of the **DoEvent** routine. It begins by calling **GetNextEvent** with a mask parameter of **EveryEvent**, asking for the next available event of any type. If **GetNextEvent** returns a Boolean result of **FALSE**, then our program isn't responsible for handling this event, so **DoEvent** simply returns to the main loop without taking any action in response. If **GetNextEvent** returns **TRUE**, **DoEvent** next looks at the **what** field of the event record to find out the event type, and uses a *case* statement to call the appropriate **MiniEdit** routine to respond to that type of event. We'll be defining all of these other routines in due course in the coming chapters.

Notice that our **DoEvent** routine makes a few assumptions about how certain events are to be handled. For instance, since it makes no difference to our program whether the user is pressing a key for the first time or holding down a repeating key, we call the same procedure, named **Do-Keystroke** (Program 4-4) to handle both key-down and auto-key events. If for some reason we wanted to distinguish between these two event types, we could, of course, handle them with separate **DoKeyDown** and **DoAutoKey** procedures. Mouse-up and key-up events are meaningless for our purposes, so our **DoEvent** routine simply ignores them; it also ignores disk-inserted events. Again, we could easily add the appropriate clauses to the *case* statement if we wanted to respond to these events in some way.

Under the straightforward arrangement shown in Program 2-1, event processing continues until an event occurs that causes the global flag **Finished** to be set to **TRUE**. At this point the program falls out of its main loop and terminates. We've already mentioned that the event that causes this to happen is the user's choosing the **Quit** command from one of the program's menus; presumably the response to this command consists of the single statement

```
Finished := TRUE
```

causing the program to terminate forthwith.

```
{ Global variables }

var
    TheEvent : EventRecord;                          {Current event [2.1.1]}
    Quitting : BOOLEAN;                              {Closing up shop?}
    Finished : BOOLEAN;                              {All closed?}


procedure DoEvent;

    { Get and process one event. }

    begin {DoEvent}

        if GetNextEvent (EveryEvent, TheEvent) then      {Get next event [2.2.1]}

            case TheEvent.what of

                MouseDown:
                    DoMouseDown;                     {Handle mouse-down event [Prog. 3-7]}

                KeyDown, AutoKey:
                    DoKeystroke;                     {Handle keystroke [Prog. 4-4]}

                UpdateEvt:
                    DoUpdate;                        {Handle update event [Prog. 3-6, 5-3]}

                ActivateEvt:
                    DoActivate;                      {Handle activate/deactivate event [Prog. 3-5, 5-14]}

                otherwise
                    {Do nothing}

                end {case}

    end; {DoEvent}
```

Program 2-3 Get and process one event

The trouble with that approach is that the user can lose valuable work without warning. For example, if there are windows on the screen whose contents have been edited and not yet saved to the disk, all the changes made in those windows will be lost if the program simply shuts down immediately on receiving a **Quit** command. We would like to give the user an opportunity to save the contents of such "dirty" windows before quitting. We'll see later that our program does, in fact, offer this option routinely, via a dialog box on the screen, before closing any window; so all we need to do after a **Quit** command is close each window on the screen, one by one, just as if the user had chosen the **Close** menu command or clicked the mouse in the window's close box. Only when all windows have been properly disposed of in this way will we terminate the program.

However, as we'll learn in Chapter 3, the Toolbox itself uses the event mechanism—specifically the category known as window events (activate, deactivate, and update)—to coordinate the changes that take place on the screen as windows are manipulated. As we start closing down windows in response to a **Quit** command, we have to see to it that window events continue to be processed normally, so that what's happening will be reflected visually on the screen in the proper way.

The way we arrange this is by introducing a second global flag, named **Quitting**, in addition to the **Finished** flag already mentioned. Instead of setting **Finished** to TRUE when the user chooses the **Quit** command, we'll set **Quitting** to TRUE instead, as shown in our **DoQuit** routine, Program 2-4. (We'll see when we talk about menus in Chapter 4 how this routine gets called by way of **DoEvent** when the **Quit** command is chosen.)

```
{ Global variable }

var
   Quitting : BOOLEAN;                      {Closing up shop?}


procedure DoQuit;

   { Handle Quit command. }

   begin {DoQuit}

      Quitting := TRUE                       {Start closing up shop}

   end; {DoQuit}
```

Program 2-4 Handle **Quit** command

Now we can modify our **DoEvent** routine to take the **Quitting** flag into account (see Program 2-5). When that flag is set, we will continue to process activate and update events, but will ignore mouse and keyboard events. On receiving a null event, meaning that nothing else is happening that needs a response, we will call our program's **DoClose** routine (Program 3-3) to close the frontmost window on the screen, just as if the user had chosen the **Close** command from the menu. If the window has been edited and not yet saved to the disk, **DoClose** will post a dialog box allowing the user to save the window's contents before closing. When there *is* no frontmost window—that is, when the screen is empty—then we will finally set the **Finished** flag to **TRUE**, causing the program to terminate.

```
{ Global variables }

var
   TheEvent : EventRecord;                          {Current event [2.1.1]}
   Quitting : BOOLEAN;                              {Closing up shop?}
   Finished : BOOLEAN;                              {All closed?}


procedure DoEvent;

   { Get and process one event. }

   begin {DoEvent}

      if GetNextEvent (EveryEvent, TheEvent) then   {Get next event [2.2.1]}

         case TheEvent.what of

            MouseDown:
               if not Quitting then
                  DoMouseDown;                       {Handle mouse-down event [Prog. 3-7]}

            KeyDown, AutoKey:
               if not Quitting then
                  DoKeystroke;                       {Handle keystroke [Prog. 4-4]}

            UpdateEvt:
               DoUpdate;                             {Handle update event [Prog. 3-6, 5-3]}

            ActivateEvt:
               DoActivate;                           {Handle activate/deactivate event [Prog. 3-5, 5-14]}

            otherwise
               {Do nothing}

         end {case}
```

Program 2-5 Get and process one event

```
    else if Quitting and (TheEvent.what = NullEvent) then  {Closing up shop after a Quit command?}
      begin
        if FrontWindow <> NIL then                {Any windows on the screen? [3.3.3]}
          DoClose                                 {Close the frontmost [Prog. 3-3]}
        else
          Finished := TRUE                        {Signal end of program}
      end {if}

  end; {DoEvent}
```

Program 2-5 (*continued*)

Posting and Removing Events

Ordinarily the system puts events into the event queue and you take them out one by one (via **GetNextEvent**) and respond to them. Occasionally, though, you may have some reason to place an event in the queue yourself. (For instance, if you're using any of the four application event types, you need some way of getting them into the queue.) In these cases, you can use the Toolbox routine **PostEvent** [2.3.2]. You supply the event type and the contents of the **message** field; the rest of the event record is filled in automatically when the event is posted.

You can also "turn off" the processing of certain event types by preventing them from ever getting posted in the first place. You do this by setting the *system event mask*, which controls exactly which types of event can be posted. A **0** bit in any position of the mask prevents events of that type from being placed in the queue. The mask is initially set to allow all but key-up events to be posted (since they're meaningless for most applications). If necessary, you can change this setting with **SetEvent-Mask** [2.3.2]. For instance, you might want to turn off keyboard repeat by disabling auto-key events. In general, it's a good idea to disable any type of event you know your program has no use for. This measure conserves space in the event queue—the queue has a limited, fixed capacity.

Since window events are treated in special ways and are never placed in the event queue, the system event mask has no effect on them. Never attempt to post a window event yourself; let the Toolbox handle them in its own way.

The Toolbox routine **FlushEvents** [2.3.1] is used to remove events from the queue without processing them. It takes two mask parameters: the first tells which event types to remove from the queue, the second tells which types should stop the search. For example, the call

```
FlushEvents (AutoKeyMask, KeyDownMask)
```

would remove all auto-key events from the beginning of the queue up to the first key-down event.

Another common use for **FlushEvents** is to clear out the event queue at the program's beginning, in case there are any unprocessed events left from a previous program:

```
FlushEvents (EveryEvent, 0)
```

The first parameter, **EveryEvent**, says to remove all events from the queue, regardless of type; the **0** for the second parameter says not to stop until the entire queue has been flushed. Because this has to be done only once, at the beginning of the program, we can put it in our one-time-only **Initialize** routine (Program 2-6).

Since our example program attaches no special meaning to mouse-up events, we may as well set the system event mask to ignore them; the **Initialize** routine is the natural place to do this, too. The **Initialize** procedure shown here also performs a few other initialization calls that are needed at the beginning of every program. We've already learned about **InitGraf** and **InitFonts** in Volume One (Chapters 4 and 8 respectively); the others will be covered later in this volume (**InitWindows** in Chapter 3, **InitMenus** in Chapter 4, **TEInit** in Chapter 5, and **InitDialogs** in Chapter 7). **Initialize** also calls a couple of other program routines to set up the menus and cursors **MiniEdit** will be using and to open any document files the user may have selected in starting up the program from the Finder. The **SetUpCursors** routine is defined later in this chapter, **SetUpMenus** in Chapter 4, and **DoStartup** in Chapter 8.

```
{ Global variables }

var
    Quitting : BOOLEAN;                                     {Closing up shop?}
    Finished : BOOLEAN;                                     {All closed?}


procedure Initialize;

    { Do one-time-only initialization. }

    var
        theMask : INTEGER;                                  {New value for system event mask [2.1.3]}

    begin {Initialize}

        InitGraf (@ThePort);                                {Initialize QuickDraw [I:4.3.1]}
        InitFonts;                                          {Initialize fonts [I:8.2.4]}
        InitWindows;                                        {Initialize windows [3.2.1]}
        InitMenus;                                          {Initialize menus [4.2.1]}
        TEInit;                                             {Initialize text editing [5.2.1]}
        InitDialogs (NIL);                                  {Initialize dialogs [7.2.1]}

        theMask := EveryEvent - KeyUpMask - MUpMask;        {Disable key-up and mouse-up events [2.1.3]}
        SetEventMask (theMask);                             {Set the mask [2.3.2]}
        FlushEvents  (EveryEvent, 0);                       {Clear out event queue [2.3.1]}

        SetUpMenus;                                         {Create program's menus [Prog. 4-2]}
        SetUpCursors;                                       {Get standard cursors [Prog. 2-8]}

        DoStartup;                                          {Process Finder startup information [Prog. 8-7]}

        {Perform any other needed initialization};

        Quitting := FALSE;                                  {Initialize quitting flags}
        Finished := FALSE

    end; {Initialize}
```

Program 2-6 One-time initialization

The sequence of Toolbox initialization calls shown in Program 2-6, from **InitGraf** through **FlushEvents**, form a kind of magical incantation that you should faithfully intone at the beginning of each program. Even if you don't use a particular part of the Toolbox, you should still initialize them all in case they're needed by other parts of the Toolbox itself. For instance, even a program that never displays any text on the screen must still call **InitFonts**, so that the Toolbox can find its own fonts for window titles, menu items, alert messages, and so forth. Even the order of the calls is critical: **InitGraf** must precede **InitFonts** must precede **InitWindows**, and so on. Wouldn't it be easier if there were just one routine named **InitToolbox** that you could call and be done with it?

Reading the Mouse and Keyboard

Movements of the mouse are not reported to your program as events in themselves: you receive a mouse event only when the user presses or releases the button. If you want to follow the mouse's movements, you can use the Toolbox routine **GetMouse** [2.4.1], which returns a point representing the current mouse position. Unlike the **where** field of an event record, which gives the mouse position in global (screen) coordinates, **GetMouse** gives it in the *local* coordinate system of the current graphics port (usually the currently active window). There's also a Boolean function named **Button** [2.4.2] that allows you to read the state of the mouse button directly, rather than indirectly through mouse-down and mouse-up events.

A mouse-down event tells you where and when the user pressed the mouse button. If the button is still down by the time you begin processing the event, then the user is ''dragging'' the mouse (moving it while holding down the button), and you may want to respond in some special way. But to find this out, it isn't enough just to call **Button**: this function only gives the state of the button at the instant you call it, so it will return **TRUE** even if the user has released the button and pressed it again since the original mouse-down event. To find out whether the button is still down from the original event, use the Toolbox function **StillDown** [2.4.2] instead. **StillDown** returns **TRUE** only if the mouse button is down *and* there are no further mouse events pending in the event queue. This guarantees that the button hasn't been released and pressed again since the original press.

If **StillDown** reports that the user is dragging the mouse, you'll typically want to loop until the button is released, by following the mouse's movements and performing some repeated action such as displaying visual feedback to the user on the screen. When the button is released, you'll take some final action and then return to the main loop for the next event. The loop can be controlled with **WaitMouseUp** [2.4.2]. This function is similar to **StillDown**, except that if it finds a mouse-up event in the queue, it removes the event before returning **FALSE**. Your routine to respond to mouse-down events should contain a sequence like the following to handle mouse dragging:

```
if StillDown then
  begin
    while WaitMouseUp do
      begin
        {Code to track mouse while button is down}
      end;
    {Code to "finalize" drag when button is released}
  end;
else
  begin
    {Code to handle mouse-down events other than drags}
  end
```

Occasionally you may want to read the state of the keyboard directly, instead of waiting for it to be reported as keyboard events. You can do this with the Toolbox routine **GetKeys** [2.6.1]. **GetKeys** returns a *key map*, a Boolean array containing one element for every key on the keyboard (and also on the optional numeric keypad). A **TRUE** value for any element of the array means that the corresponding key was down at the time of the call.

Cursor Display

The positioning of the cursor on the screen to reflect the mouse's movements is handled for you automatically. At every tick of the system clock, the Toolbox checks to see whether the mouse has been moved since the last tick, and it repositions the cursor accordingly. Cursor positioning is under system control: there's no way you can force the cursor to a specific location on the screen. However, you can control whether it's visible or invisible and what it looks like.

Hot spot

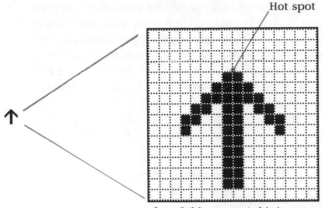

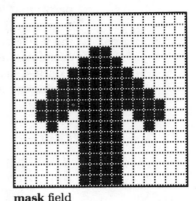

data field—cursor's bit image   **mask** field

The **mask** field in this example is constructed
so that there will always be a border of
white around the black arrow.

Figure 2-2 Cursor definition

The cursor's appearance is defined by a *cursor record* [2.5.1]. The
data field of the record gives the cursor's actual bit image, a 16-by-16-bit
array (see Figure 2-2). The **mask** field defines which bits of the image
actually "count" as part of the cursor. Where the mask has a **1** bit, the
corresponding bit of the image, white (**0**) or black (**1**), will be copied
directly to the screen as part of the cursor. Where the mask has a **0** bit,
the image normally has a **0** also: this makes the cursor "transparent" at
that position, so that the corresponding pixel already on the screen will
be left unchanged.

In Figure 2-2, for instance, the mask extends 1 pixel beyond the edge
of the cursor image in all directions. This gives the cursor a border of
white pixels for better visibility against black or patterned backgrounds.
Outside this border, the cursor is transparent, with **0** bits in both the
image and the mask.

The last combination, a **0** in the mask and a **1** in the image, has the
exotic effect of *inverting* existing pixels on the screen, from black to
white or white to black, as the cursor passes over them. Someday
you may think of a good use for this.

The last field of the cursor record defines the cursor's *hot spot,* the point that aligns with the actual mouse position on the screen. It's expressed in the cursor's own coordinate system, with (**0, 0**) designating the top-left corner of the cursor. As usual on the Macintosh, the vertical coordinate is given first. For example, the cursor shown in Figure 2-2 has its hot spot at coordinates (**4, 8**). Notice that the hot spot is a point on the coordinate grid, not a pixel of the cursor itself.

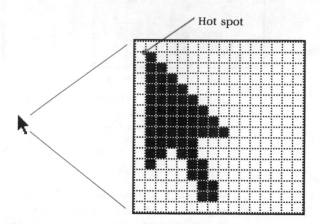

Figure 2-3 Standard cursor

Normally, you display a cursor on the screen by passing its cursor record to the Toolbox routine **SetCursor** [2.5.2]. (The one exceptional case is the standard cursor shown in Figure 2-3, the familiar arrow pointing upward at an angle of "eleven o'clock." There's a special routine, **Init-Cursor** [2.5.2], for displaying the arrow cursor; you should always use this routine instead of **SetCursor**.) The recommended way of defining cursors for a program is to store them in a resource file under the resource type '**CURS**' [2.9.1] and read them into memory with **GetCursor** [2.5.2]. You supply the resource ID and receive a handle to the cursor record in memory; you can then pass the record to **SetCursor** to display the cursor on the screen.

A number of commonly used cursors (other than the arrow cursor) are available in the system resource file; their resource IDs are defined as Toolbox constants [2.5.2]. Our **MiniEdit** program will use two of these, the I-beam for text selection and the wristwatch to signal a delay. Program 2-7 (**SetUpCursors**) is the routine that reads them from the resource file for use; it's called from the one-time **Initialize** routine that we looked at earlier (Program 2-6). **SetUpCursors** simply reads in the cursors that the program will use and stores their handles into global variables of type **CursHandle**, where they'll be available when needed. Then it calls **Init-Cursor** to start off with the standard arrow cursor.

```
{ Global variables }

var
    IBeam : CursHandle;                    {Handle to I-beam cursor [2.5.1]}
    Watch : CursHandle;                    {Handle to wristwatch cursor [2.5.1]}


procedure SetUpCursors;

    { Set up program's cursors. }

    begin {SetUpCursors}

        IBeam := GetCursor (IBeamCursor);     {Get cursors from system resource file [2.5.2]}
        Watch := GetCursor (WatchCursor);

        InitCursor                            {Set standard arrow cursor [2.5.2]}

    end;  {SetUpCursors}
```

Program 2-7 Set up cursors

If you want the cursor to change its form in different areas of the screen, it's up to you to check the mouse location periodically and set the cursor as appropriate. The natural place to do this is in the main event loop. In our example program, the main loop calls procedure **FixCursor** (Program 2-8) to do the job. By Macintosh convention, we want the cursor to change to an I-beam whenever it's within the text area of an active application window. (In Program 2-8, the test for the cursor's location is shown in schematic form; we'll be able to spell it out in more detail when we talk about text editing in Chapter 5.) If the cursor isn't in the window's text area, or if the screen is empty, the **FixCursor** routine calls **InitCursor** to set the cursor to the standard arrow shape. If a system window is active, our routine does nothing: we just leave it to the desk accessory contained in the window to set the cursor as appropriate. As we'll see later, our program will also be using the "wristwatch" cursor to notify the user whenever a time-consuming operation (such as disk I/O) is in progress. In this case there's no need to set the cursor back when the operation is finished; it'll be reset by **FixCursor** the next time through the main event loop.

```
{ Global variable }

var
   IBeam : CursHandle;                          {Handle to I-beam cursor [2.5.1]}


procedure FixCursor;

   { Adjust cursor for region of screen.  }

   var
      mousePoint : Point;                       {Current mouse position in window coordinates [I:4.1.1]}
      textRect   : Rect;                        {Active window's text rectangle [I:4.1.2]

   begin {FixCursor}

      if {screen is empty} then
         InitCursor                             {Set arrow cursor [2.5.2]}

      else if {an application window is active} then
         begin

            GetMouse (mousePoint);              {Get mouse position [2.4.1]}

            if {mousePoint in window's text area} then
               SetCursor (IBeam^^)              {Set I-beam cursor [2.5.2]}
            else
               InitCursor                       {Set arrow cursor [2.5.2]}

         end {if}

      else                                      {A system window is active:      }
         {Do nothing}                           {  let desk accessory set cursor}

   end; {FixCursor}
```

Program 2-8 Adjust cursor for region of screen

To keep track of the cursor's visibility on the screen, the Toolbox maintains a number called the *cursor level.* A cursor level of **0** makes the cursor appear on the screen; any negative value makes it invisible. Calling **InitCursor** makes the cursor visible by setting the cursor level to **0**; **HideCursor** [2.5.3] reduces the cursor level by **1**, making the cursor invisible (if it wasn't already). **ShowCursor** [2.5.3] increases the cursor level by **1**, undoing the effects of the last call to **HideCursor**; when the cursor level returns to **0**, the cursor becomes visible again. Thus calls to **Hide-Cursor** and **ShowCursor** can be paired and nested to any depth. (The cursor level can never go above **0**; if it's already **0**, **ShowCursor** has no effect.)

Two more Toolbox routines, **ObscureCursor** and **ShieldCursor** [2.5.4], also make the cursor temporarily invisible. **ObscureCursor** makes it disappear until the next time the mouse is moved; **ShieldCursor** removes it from the screen if any part of it lies within a specified *shield rectangle*. Notice that **ObscureCursor** doesn't affect the cursor level, so it should *not* be balanced by a call to **ShowCursor**.

REFERENCE

2.1 Internal Representation of Events

2.1.1 Event Records

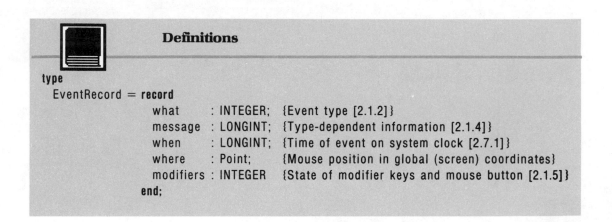

Definitions

```
type
  EventRecord = record
              what     : INTEGER;   {Event type [2.1.2]}
              message  : LONGINT;   {Type-dependent information [2.1.4]}
              when     : LONGINT;   {Time of event on system clock [2.7.1]}
              where    : Point;     {Mouse position in global (screen) coordinates}
              modifiers : INTEGER   {State of modifier keys and mouse button [2.1.5]}
            end;
```

Notes

1. All fields are filled in for every event, regardless of type.
2. **where** and **modifiers** give the location of the mouse and the state of the modifier keys and mouse button [2.1.5] *at the time the event was posted.*
3. The mouse location is given in global (screen) coordinates.
4. The contents of **message** vary with the type of event; see [2.1.4].
5. In assembly language, the high- and low-order bytes of **modifiers** are separately accessible with the offset constants **evtMeta** and **evtMBut** (see the following table).

Assembly-Language Information

Field offsets in an event record:

(Pascal) Field name	(Assembly) Offset name	Offset in bytes
what	**evtNum**	**0**
message	**evtMessage**	**2**
when	**evtTicks**	**6**
where	**evtMouse**	**10**
modifiers	**evtMeta**	**14**
	evtMBut	**15**

Assembly-language constants:

Name	Value	Meaning
EvtBlkSize	**16**	Size of event record in bytes
EvtMax	**30**	Maximum number of events in queue

2.1.2 Event Types

Definitions

```
const
    NullEvent   =  0;      {Nothing happened}
    MouseDown   =  1;      {Mouse button pressed}
    MouseUp     =  2;      {Mouse button released}
    KeyDown     =  3;      {Key pressed}
    KeyUp       =  4;      {Key released}
    AutoKey     =  5;      {Automatic keyboard repeat}
    UpdateEvt   =  6;      {Window must be redrawn}
    DiskEvt     =  7;      {Disk inserted}
    ActivateEvt =  8;      {Window activated or deactivated}
    NetworkEvt  = 10;      {Network event (reserved for system use)}
    DriverEvt   = 11;      {I/O driver event (reserved for system use)}
    App1Evt     = 12;      {Available for application use}
    App2Event   = 13;      {Available for application use}
    App3Evt     = 14;      {Available for application use}
    App4Evt     = 15;      {Available for application use}
```

Notes

1. A null event is generated when the application asks for an event and there's nothing to report.

2. *Mouse events* include mouse-down and mouse-up.

3. *Keyboard events* include key-down, key-up, and auto-key.

4. *Window events* include activate, deactivate, and update; these are discussed further in Chapter 3.

5. Event type **9** is no longer used.

6. Network and I/O driver events are reserved for use by the system.

7. The last four event types are reserved as *application events,* to be used for any purpose the application program chooses. They're useful for synchronizing communication and control within the program to the overall flow of events.

Assembly-Language Information

Event types:

Name	Value	Meaning
NullEvt	0	Nothing happened
MButDwnEvt	1	Mouse button pressed
MButUpEvt	2	Mouse button released
KeyDwnEvt	3	Key pressed
KeyUpEvt	4	Key released
AutoKeyEvt	5	Automatic keyboard repeat
UpdatEvt	6	Window must be redrawn
DiskInsertEvt	7	Disk inserted
ActivateEvt	8	Window activated or deactivated
NetworkEvt	10	Network event (reserved for system use)
IODrvrEvt	11	I/O driver event (reserved for system use)
App1Evt	12	Available for application use
App2Evt	13	Available for application use
App3Evt	14	Available for application use
App4Evt	15	Available for application use

2.1.3 Event Masks

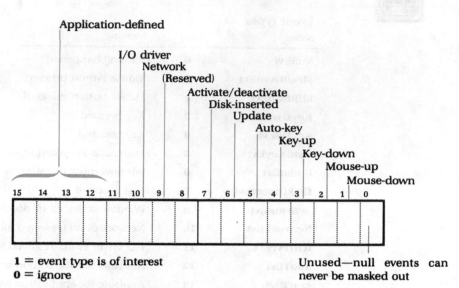

1 = event type is of interest
0 = ignore

Unused—null events can never be masked out

An event mask specifies which events an operation applies to.

Event mask

Definitions

```
const
    MDownMask    = $0002;    {Mouse-down event}
    MUpMask      = $0004;    {Mouse-up event}
    KeyDownMask  = $0008;    {Key-down event}
    KeyUpMask    = $0010;    {Key-up event}
    AutoKeyMask  = $0020;    {Auto-key event}
    UpdateMask   = $0040;    {Update event}
    DiskMask     = $0080;    {Disk-inserted event}
    ActivMask    = $0100;    {Activate/deactivate event}
    NetworkMask  = $0400;    {Network event (reserved for system use)}
    DriverMask   = $0800;    {I/O driver event (reserved for system use)}
    App1Mask     = $1000;    {Application-defined event}
    App2Mask     = $2000;    {Application-defined event}
    App3Mask     = $4000;    {Application-defined event}
    App4Mask     = $8000;    {Application-defined event}
    EveryEvent   = $FFFF;    {Any event}
```

Notes

1. Event masks are used as parameters to some event-related routines, to specify which specific event types an operation applies to.

2. The event mask has one bit for each possible event type. A **1** bit in any position includes the corresponding type in the mask; a **0** bit excludes the type.

3. The mask constants shown can be combined with **BitAnd, BitOr, BitXOr,** and **BitNot** [I:2.2.2] to form any combination of event types you need.

4. The mask **EveryEvent** includes all possible event types.

2.1.4 Event Messages

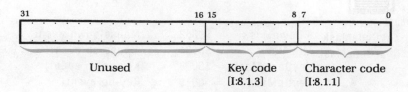

Unused

Key code
[I:8.1.3]

Character code
[I:8.1.1]

The key code tells which physical key
was pressed; the character code tells
what character the key represents.

Message format for keyboard events

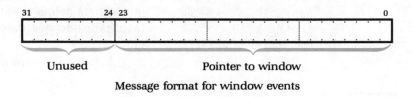

Unused

Pointer to window

Message format for window events

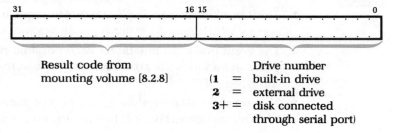

Result code from
mounting volume [8.2.8]

Drive number
(**1** = built-in drive
2 = external drive
3+ = disk connected
through serial port)

Message format for disk events

Definitions

```
const
  KeyCodeMask  = $0000FF00;   {Mask for extracting key code from keyboard event}
  CharCodeMask = $000000FF;   {Mask for extracting character code from keyboard event}
```

Notes

1. For keyboard events, the event message identifies the key involved, along with the corresponding character as determined by the keyboard configuration currently in effect. Key codes and character codes are listed in [I:8.1.3] and [I:8.1.1], respectively, as well as in Appendix D.

2. The key code and character code can be extracted from the message field with **BitAnd** [I:2.2.2], using the mask constants **KeyCodeMask** and **CharCodeMask**.

3. For window events, the event message contains a window pointer [3.1.1] to the window involved.

4. For disk events, the Toolbox will already have attempted to mount the newly inserted volume before reporting the event to the program. The event message contains the result code returned by this mounting operation. Mounting of volumes is discussed in Chapter 8.

5. For mouse and null events, the message field is meaningless; for network and I/O driver events, its contents are private to the system.

6. For application events, the event message can be used any way the application chooses.

2.1.5 Event Modifiers

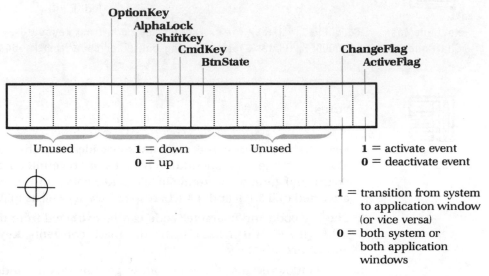

Modifier bits

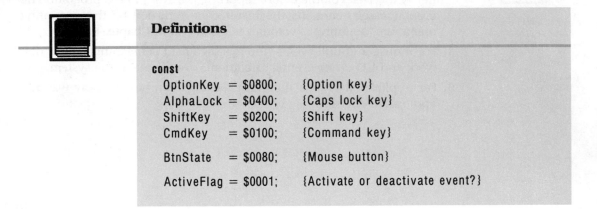

Definitions

```
const
    OptionKey  = $0800;     {Option key}
    AlphaLock  = $0400;     {Caps lock key}
    ShiftKey   = $0200;     {Shift key}
    CmdKey     = $0100;     {Command key}

    BtnState   = $0080;     {Mouse button}

    ActiveFlag = $0001;     {Activate or deactivate event?}
```

Notes

1. The state of the modifier keys is recorded for all events, not just keyboard events.

2. No distinction is made between the left and right shift keys or the left and right option keys.

3. Bit 0 (**ActiveFlag**) distinguishes activate (**1**) from deactivate (**0**) events. See Chapter 3 for further discussion.

4. For activate/deactivate events, bit 1 is supposed to be set to **1** when control passes from an application window to a system window or vice versa; **0** if the windows being deactivated and activated are both system or both application windows. However, this bit is not always set reliably; see Chapter 3 for further discussion.

5. The assembly-language constants (following) are bit numbers within the **modifiers** field, for use with the **BTST**, **BSET**, **BCLR**, and **BCHG** instructions.

Assembly-Language Information

Bit numbers in the **modifiers** field:

Name	Value	Meaning
OptionKey	11	Option key
AlphaLock	10	Caps lock key
ShiftKey	9	Shift key
CmdKey	8	Command key
BtnState	7	Mouse button
ActiveFlag	0	Activate or deactivate?

2.2 Event Reporting

2.2.1 Retrieving Events

Definitions

function GetNextEvent
        (mask   : INTEGER;   {Mask designating event types of interest [2.1.3]}
        var theEvent : EventRecord)   {Returns information about event}
            : BOOLEAN;   {Should application respond to event?}

function EventAvail
        (mask   : INTEGER;   {Mask designating event types of interest [2.1.3]}
        var theEvent : EventRecord)   {Returns information about event}
            : BOOLEAN;   {Should application respond to event?}

Notes

1. Both of these routines check for the next available event of any of the types designated by the **mask** parameter. Event types excluded by the mask are ignored.

2. An event record describing the event is returned in the variable parameter **theEvent**.

3. **GetNextEvent** removes the reported event from the queue; **EventAvail** doesn't, and can be used to "peek" at an event while leaving it in the queue for later processing.

4. Events are reported in order of priority, as follows:
    1. Deactivate events
    2. Activate events
    3. All except window, auto-key, and null events, in the order posted
    4. Auto-key events
    5. Update events, in front-to-back order of the windows on the screen
    6. Null events

5. If no event of the requested types is available, a null event is returned. Null events are never affected by the **mask** parameter.

6. The function result tells whether the event must be handled by your program. If **FALSE**, you should simply ignore the event.

7. **GetNextEvent** intercepts certain events involving desk accessories and passes them to the accessory for processing. If the accessory accepts the event, **GetNextEvent** returns **FALSE**, indicating that your program need not respond to it; in the unlikely case that the accessory refuses the event, **GetNextEvent** returns **TRUE**, asking you to handle it yourself if appropriate.

8. Events intercepted by **GetNextEvent** include all keyboard and window events directed to a system window (one containing a desk accessory).

9. Mouse-up events directed to a system window are also intercepted, but mouse-down events are not. You must check all mouse-down events yourself with **FindWindow** [3.5.1] and pass those involving system windows to the appropriate desk accessory for action.

10. Only **GetNextEvent** intercepts events involving desk accessories; **EventAvail** never does.

11. For disk-inserted events, **GetNextEvent** mounts the new volume but still returns **TRUE**. This allows you to take further action if appropriate, based on the result code returned by the mounting operation. (Mounting of volumes is discussed in Chapter 8.) **EventAvail** doesn't attempt to mount the volume.

12. For null events, both **GetNextEvent** and **EventAvail** always return **FALSE**.

Assembly-Language Information

Trap macros:

(Pascal) Routine name	(Assembly) Trap macro	Trap word
GetNextEvent	**_GetNextEvent**	**$A970**
EventAvail	**_EventAvail**	**$A971**

2.3 Posting and Removing Events

2.3.1 Emptying the Event Queue

Definitions

```
procedure FlushEvents
        (whichMask : INTEGER;      {Event types to be flushed}
         stopMask   : INTEGER);    {Event types on which to stop}
```

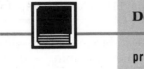

Notes

1. **FlushEvents** removes events from the event queue.

2. **whichMask** tells which event types are to be removed.

3. **stopMask** tells which event types are to stop the search. After the first such event is encountered, no further events are flushed from the queue.

4. A **stopMask** of **0** flushes the entire queue of the event types designated by **whichMask**.

5. Call

   FlushEvents (EveryEvent, 0)

   to clear out the event queue at the beginning of the program.

6. When called from assembly language, **FlushEvents** is register-based: see the following register usage information.

Assembly-Language Information

Trap macro:

(Pascal) Routine name	(Assembly) Trap macro	Trap word
FlushEvents	**_FlushEvents**	**$A032**

Register usage:

Routine	Register	Contents
FlushEvents	**D0.L** (in)	high word: **stopMask** low word: **whichMask**
	D0.W (out)	event type that stopped search (**0** if none)

2.3.2 Posting Events

Definitions

```
function   PostEvent
              (eventType : INTEGER;      {Type of event}
               message   : LONGINT)      {Event message}
               : OSErr;                  {Result code}

procedure  SetEventMask
              (newMask : INTEGER);       {New setting of system event mask}
```

Notes

1. **PostEvent** places a new event in the event queue.

2. **eventType** and **message** give the new event's type and the contents of its **message** field.

3. The event's **when**, **where**, and **modifiers** fields will be set to reflect conditions at the time the event is posted.

4. **SetEventMask** sets the system event mask, which controls which types of event can be posted into the event queue. A **0** bit in any position prevents events of the corresponding type from being posted.

5. The system event mask is initially set to allow all but key-up events to be posted.

6. Window events (activate, deactivate, update) are treated specially and are never actually placed in the event queue. Do not attempt to post such events with **PostEvent**. Window events are also unaffected by the system event mask.

7. When called from assembly language, **PostEvent** is register-based: see the following register usage information.

Assembly-Language Information

Trap macro:

(Pascal) Routine name	(Assembly) Trap macro	Trap word
PostEvent	**_PostEvent**	**$A02F**

Register usage:

Routine	Register	Contents
PostEvent	**A0.W** (in)	**eventType**
	D0.L (in)	**message**
	D0.W (out)	result code

Assembly-language global variable:

Name	Address	Meaning
SysEvtMask	**$144**	System event mask

2.4 The Mouse

2.4.1 Reading the Mouse Position

Definitions

procedure GetMouse
      (**var** mouseLoc : Point);   {Returns mouse location in local (window) coordinates}

Notes

1. **GetMouse** returns the current location of the mouse via the variable parameter **mouseLoc**.

2. The mouse location is expressed in the *local coordinates* of the current graphics port (typically the currently active window.) Notice that the **where** field of an event record [2.1.1] is in *global* (screen) coordinates.

Assembly-Language Information

Trap macro:

(Pascal) Routine name	(Assembly) Trap macro	Trap word
GetMouse	**_GetMouse**	**$A972**

2.4.2 Reading the Mouse Button

Definitions

```
function Button
        : BOOLEAN;        {Is mouse button down?}

function StillDown
        : BOOLEAN;        {Is mouse button still down from previous press?}

function WaitMouseUp
        : BOOLEAN;        {Is mouse button still down from previous press?}
```

Notes

1. **Button** returns **TRUE** if the mouse button is currently down, otherwise **FALSE**.

2. Both **StillDown** and **WaitMouseUp** return **TRUE** if the mouse button is currently down and there are no pending mouse events in the event queue. This implies that the button is still down from the last reported mouse-down event, and can't have been released and pressed again.

3. If the event queue does contain a pending mouse-up event, **WaitMouseUp** removes the event from the queue before returning **FALSE**; **StillDown** leaves the event pending.

4. In assembly language, the global variable **MBState** is a single byte whose low-order bit (bit 0) gives the current state of the mouse button.

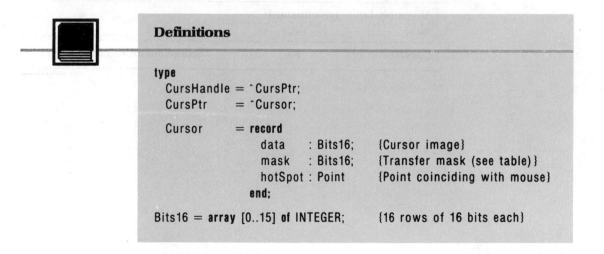

Assembly-Language Information

Trap macros:

(Pascal) Routine name	(Assembly) Trap macro	Trap word
Button	**_Button**	**$A974**
StillDown	**_StillDown**	**$A973**
WaitMouseUp	**_WaitMouseUp**	**$A977**

Assembly-language global variable:

Name	Address	Meaning
MBState	**$172**	State of mouse button

2.5 The Cursor

2.5.1 Cursor Records

Definitions

```
type
  CursHandle = ^CursPtr;
  CursPtr    = ^Cursor;

  Cursor     = record
                 data    : Bits16;   {Cursor image}
                 mask    : Bits16;   {Transfer mask (see table)}
                 hotSpot : Point     {Point coinciding with mouse}
               end;

Bits16 = array [0..15] of INTEGER;   {16 rows of 16 bits each}
```

Mask bit	Data bit	Result
1	1	Black
1	0	White
0	1	Invert screen
0	0	Invisible

Notes

1. **data** contains the cursor's bit image, 16 by 16 bits.

2. **mask** is another bit image, also 16 by 16 bits, that defines how the **data** image is transferred to the screen (see table).

3. **hotSpot** defines the point in the cursor that coincides with the mouse position on the screen.

4. The hot spot designates a point on the coordinate grid, not a pixel of the cursor. The top-left corner of the cursor has coordinates (**0, 0**).

Assembly-Language Information

Field offsets in a cursor record:

(Pascal) Field name	(Assembly) Offset name	Offset in bytes
data	**data**	**0**
mask	**mask**	**32**
hotSpot	**hotSpot**	**64**

Assembly-language constant:

Name	Value	Meaning
CursRec	**68**	Size of cursor record in bytes

2.5.2 Setting the Cursor

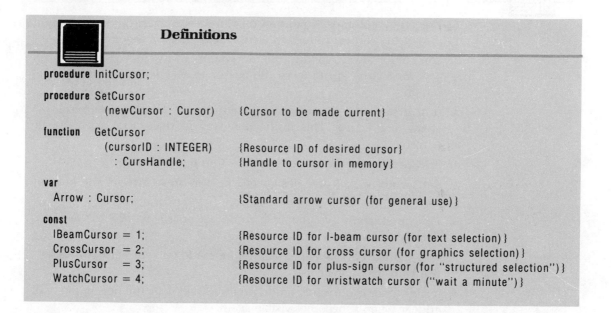

Definitions

procedure InitCursor;

procedure SetCursor
        (newCursor : Cursor)   {Cursor to be made current}

function GetCursor
        (cursorID : INTEGER)   {Resource ID of desired cursor}
        : CursHandle;   {Handle to cursor in memory}

var
  Arrow : Cursor;   {Standard arrow cursor (for general use)}

const
  IBeamCursor = 1;   {Resource ID for I-beam cursor (for text selection)}
  CrossCursor = 2;   {Resource ID for cross cursor (for graphics selection)}
  PlusCursor = 3;   {Resource ID for plus-sign cursor (for "structured selection")}
  WatchCursor = 4;   {Resource ID for wristwatch cursor ("wait a minute")}

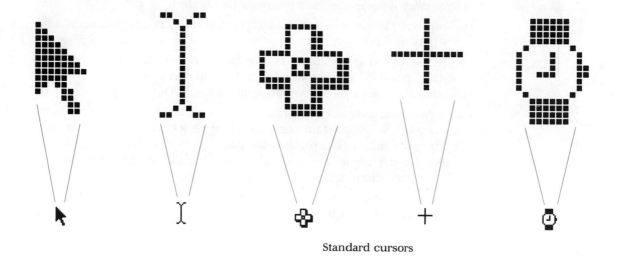

Standard cursors

Notes

1. The current cursor is painted on the screen at the mouse location during the vertical retrace interrupt, sixty times a second.

2. The cursor always follows the movements of the mouse. There is no way for a program to force the cursor to a specific position on the screen.

3. **InitCursor** sets the current cursor to the standard "eleven-o'clock" arrow (see figure). This is the *only* way to make the arrow cursor current.

4. **InitCursor** sets the cursor level [2.5.3] to **0** (visible).

5. **SetCursor** makes the designated cursor (**newCursor**) the current cursor.

6. The **newCursor** parameter is an actual cursor record [2.5.1], not a pointer or handle.

7. The standard arrow cursor cannot be made current with **SetCursor**; use **InitCursor** instead.

8. If the cursor is currently hidden (cursor level < **0**), the new cursor will appear when it becomes visible again.

9. **GetCursor** gets a cursor record from a resource file, reads it into memory if necessary, and returns a handle to it.

10. **cursorID** is the resource ID of the desired cursor; its resource type is 'CURS' [2.9.1].

11. The standard arrow cursor is kept in the global variable **Arrow**. The other standard cursors are available from the system resource file, using the constants shown for their resource IDs.

12. **Arrow** is actually a QuickDraw global variable [I:4.3.1]. To access it in assembly language, find the pointer to QuickDraw's globals at the address contained in register **A5**, then locate the variable relative to that pointer using the offset constant **Arrow** (see table). See [I:4.3.1] for further discussion.

13. The cursor record defining the current cursor is kept in the assembly-language global variable **TheCrsr**. There is no straightforward way to access the current cursor from the Pascal level.

Assembly-Language Information

Trap macros:

(Pascal) Routine name	(Assembly) Trap macro	Trap word
InitCursor	**_InitCursor**	**$A850**
SetCursor	**_SetCursor**	**$A851**
GetCursor	**_GetCursor**	**$A9B9**

Assembly-language constants:

Name	Value	Meaning
IBeamCursor	**1**	Resource ID of I-beam cursor
CrossCursor	**2**	Resource ID of cross cursor
PlusCursor	**3**	Resource ID of plus-sign cursor
WatchCursor	**4**	Resource ID of wristwatch cursor

Assembly-language global variable:

Name	Address	Meaning
TheCrsr	**$844**	Current cursor record

QuickDraw global variable:

Name	Offset in bytes
Arrow	**−108**

2.5.3 Showing and Hiding the Cursor

Definitions

procedure HideCursor;

procedure ShowCursor;

Notes

1. These routines control the cursor's visibility on the screen by manipulating the *cursor level*.

2. The cursor is displayed on the screen if the cursor level is **0**, hidden if the cursor level is negative.

3. The cursor level is set to **0** (visible) by **InitCursor** [2.5.2].

4. **HideCursor** removes the cursor from the screen and decrements the cursor level by **1**.

5. **ShowCursor** undoes the effects of **HideCursor** and restores the cursor's visibility to its previous state. It increments the cursor level by **1**; if the cursor level becomes **0**, the cursor is redisplayed on the screen.

6. The cursor level never becomes greater than **0**. If it's already **0** (visible), **ShowCursor** leaves it unchanged.

7. Calls to **HideCursor** and **ShowCursor** may be nested to any depth. Every call to **HideCursor** should be balanced by a corresponding call to **ShowCursor**.

Assembly-Language Information

Trap macros:

(Pascal) Routine name	(Assembly) Trap macro	Trap word
HideCursor	**_HideCursor**	**$A852**
ShowCursor	**_ShowCursor**	**$A853**

2.5.4 Obscuring and Shielding the Cursor

Definitions

procedure ObscureCursor;

procedure ShieldCursor;
    (shieldRect   : Rect;   {Shield rectangle}
    globalOrigin : Point);   {Origin of coordinate system in global (screen) coordinates}

Notes

1. **ObscureCursor** temporarily removes the cursor from the screen; it will reappear the next time the mouse is moved.

2. **ShieldCursor** removes the cursor from the screen if any part of it lies within the designated shield rectangle.

3. The shield rectangle may be expressed in any convenient coordinate system. **globalOrigin** establishes the coordinate system relative to global (screen) coordinates. If **shieldRect** is expressed in screen coordinates, **globalOrigin** should be (**0, 0**); if it's in the local coordinates of some graphics port (such as a window), **globalOrigin** should be the origin of the port's boundary rectangle.

4. **ShieldCursor** decrements the current cursor level and so must be balanced eventually with a call to **ShowCursor** [2.5.3]. **ObscureCursor** doesn't affect the current cursor level and must *not* be balanced with **ShowCursor**.

Assembly-Language Information

Trap macros:

(Pascal) Routine name	(Assembly) Trap macro	Trap word
ObscureCursor	**_ObscureCursor**	**$A856**
ShieldCursor	**_ShieldCursor**	**$A855**

2.6 The Keyboard

2.6.1 Reading the Keyboard

Definitions

```
procedure GetKeys
           (var keys : KeyMap);   {Returns current state of keyboard}
type
   KeyMap = packed array [0..127] of BOOLEAN;
```

Second hexadecimal digit

First hexadecimal digit

	$7	$6	$5	$4	$3	$2	$1	$0	$F	$E	$D	$C	$B	$A	$9	$8
$0	X	Z	G	H	F	D	S	A	R	E	W	Q	B		V	C
$1	5	6	4	3	2	1	T	Y	0	]	O	8	-	7	9	=
$2	'	J	L	Return	P	I	[	U	.	M	N	/	,	\	;	K
$3	⌘			Enter	Back-space	`	space bar	Tab						Option	Caps Lock	Shift
$4	Clear	+				*	.			-	/	Enter				,
$5	5	4	3	2	1	0						9	8		7	6
$6																
$7																

Shaded boxes are map
entries for keypad keys.

The routine **GetKeys** returns a 128-bit
result (many bits are unused). Key map
shows the state of every key on the
keyboard and keypad: **1** = down; **0** = up.

Key map format

Notes

1. **GetKeys** returns a *key map* representing the current state of the key-board and the optional numeric keypad.

2. The key map is a packed array in which each Boolean element occu-pies a single bit of memory. A value of **TRUE** (**1**) means that the corres-ponding key was down at the time of the call; **FALSE** (**0**) means it wasn't.

3. At most two character keys will be reported down simultaneously, along with any combination of the modifier keys shift, caps lock, option, and command.

4. No distinction is made between the left and right shift keys or the left and right option keys.

5. At the assembly-language level, although the bytes of the key map read normally from left to right, the bits within each byte read from right to left (see figure).

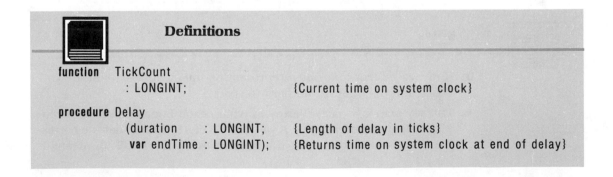

Assembly-Language Information

Trap macro:

(Pascal) Routine name	(Assembly) Trap macro	Trap word
GetKeys	**_GetKeys**	**$A976**

Assembly-language global variables:

Name	Address	Meaning
KeyMap	**$174**	System keyboard map
KeypadMap	**$17C**	System keypad map

2.7 The System Clock

2.7.1 Reading the System Clock

Definitions

```
function TickCount
        : LONGINT;                    {Current time on system clock}

procedure Delay
        (duration    : LONGINT;       {Length of delay in ticks}
        var endTime : LONGINT);       {Returns time on system clock at end of delay}
```

Notes

1. **TickCount** returns the time in ticks (sixtieths of a second) since the system was started up.

2. **Delay** suspends program execution for a specified number of ticks.

3. The delay is only approximate; it is usually (but not always) accurate to within one tick of the number specified by the **duration** parameter.

4. The variable parameter **endTime** returns the actual time on the system clock when the delay ends.

5. In assembly language, the system clock is accessible directly as the long-word global variable **Ticks**.

6. When called from assembly language, **Delay** is register-based: see the register usage information that follows.

Assembly-Language Information

Trap macros:

(Pascal) Routine name	(Assembly) Trap macro	Trap word
TickCount	**_TickCount**	**$A975**
Delay	**_Delay**	**$A03B**

Register usage:

Routine	Register	Contents
Delay	A0.L (in)	**duration**
	D0.L (out)	**endTime**

Assembly-language global variable:

Name	Address	Meaning
Ticks	**$16A**	System clock

2.7.2 Performing Periodic Tasks

Definitions

procedure SystemTask;

Notes

1. **SystemTask** performs any periodic tasks associated with active desk accessories, under the control of the system clock.

2. Each accessory's periodic task is executed only if the appropriate interval has elapsed on the system clock since the task was last performed.

3. You should call **SystemTask** at least once per tick (60 times per second) to ensure that all desk accessories receive the processor time they need. This is normally done by calling it once on every pass of the program's main event loop; it may have to be called more often during time-consuming operations.

Assembly-Language Information

Trap macro:

(Pascal) Routine name	(Assembly) Trap macro	Trap word
SystemTask	**_SystemTask**	**$A9B4**

2.8 The Speaker

2.8.1 Beeping the Speaker

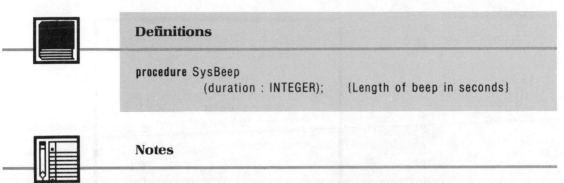

Definitions

procedure SysBeep
        (duration : INTEGER);   {Length of beep in seconds}

Notes

1. **SysBeep** emits a beep from the Macintosh's speaker.

2. The **duration** parameter gives the length of the beep in seconds.

3. The speaker volume is controlled by the user with the Control Panel desk accessory. If the volume is set to **0**, the menu bar flashes instead.

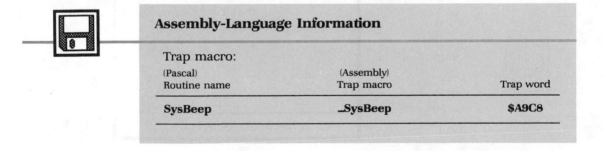

Assembly-Language Information

Trap macro:

(Pascal) Routine name	(Assembly) Trap macro	Trap word
SysBeep	**_SysBeep**	**$A9C8**

2.9 Event-Related Resources

2.9.1 Resource Type 'CURS'

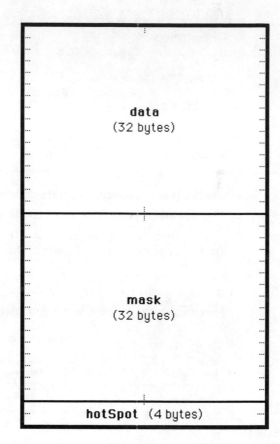

Format of resource type **'CURS'**

Notes

1. A resource of type **'CURS'** contains a cursor record [2.5.1].

2. Use **GetCursor** [2.5.2] to load a resource of this type.

CHAPTER

3

Windows on the World

Anyone who's used a Macintosh knows all about windows. From your program's point of view, they serve as a two-way channel of communication with the user: the program conveys information to the user by displaying it in a window, and the user tells the program what to do by clicking the mouse at strategic places in the window.

Windows can be of various types, each with its own characteristic appearance and structure. All windows, regardless of type, are expected to behave in certain standard ways, spelled out in the Macintosh User Interface Guidelines (part of Apple's *Inside Macintosh* documentation). The User Interface Toolbox includes all the facilities you need to display and manipulate windows in accordance with the Guidelines, but it's up to you to call the right Toolbox routines at the right times to make it all happen. In this chapter we'll see how.

Window Fundamentals

There can be any number of windows on the screen, and they can overlap in any order. Some windows belong to your program, and are called *application windows*; others are put there by the Macintosh system itself, and are known as *system windows*. (Examples of system windows are those that display desk accessories like the Calculator, the Control Panel, and the Alarm Clock.)

a. Document window

b. Alert box

c. Dialog box

d. Accessory window

Figure 3-1 Standard windows

A window's front-to-back position on the screen is called its *plane*. Each window has its own plane on the screen. When two windows overlap, the one in front gets drawn, covering the other behind it. A window that's completely obscured from view by other windows is said to be *covered*; if any part of the window is not obscured from view, the window is *exposed*. You can also make a window logically *visible* or *invisible*: to actually appear on the screen, it must be both visible and exposed. Your program controls whether a window is visible or invisible; whether it's covered or exposed depends on where the user places it in relation to other windows on the screen. Making a window invisible is called *hiding* the window, making it visible is called *showing* it.

The frontmost window at any given time is called the *active window*. All the user's menu choices and keyboard actions are directed to the active window, as are all mouse clicks inside the window. A click in any other window causes that window to come to the front and become the active window. It's your program's responsibility to respond to user actions directed to its own application windows, and to refer those directed to system windows to the appropriate Toolbox routines to be acted upon.

Certain types of window are built into the Macintosh system, and are automatically available for your program to use:

- *Document windows* (Figure 3-1a) are the standard type of window that you normally see on your screen. Their appearance and behavior are discussed briefly in the following section, and are described fully in the Macintosh Owner's Guide and the User Interface Guidelines.

- *Alert boxes* (Figure 3-1b) and *dialog boxes* (Figure 3-1c) report errors, issue warnings, and request specific information from the user. We'll be discussing them in detail in Chapter 7.

- *Accessory windows* (Figure 3-1d) display desk accessories and are recognizable by their rounded corners.

For the vast majority of applications, these standard window types are all you will need. If you're adventurous, you might want to define an octagonal window for the viewport of your starship. The *Inside Macintosh* manual contains complete information on how to "roll your own" window types; in this book we'll confine ourselves to the standard types only.

Anatomy of a Window

Figure 3-2 shows the structure of a standard document window. At the top of the window is the *title bar,* which displays the window's title. When the window is active, the title bar is *highlighted,* as shown in Figure 3-3; when it's inactive, the highlighting is removed. Clicking anywhere within an inactive window activates it, making it come to the front of the screen and highlight its title bar.

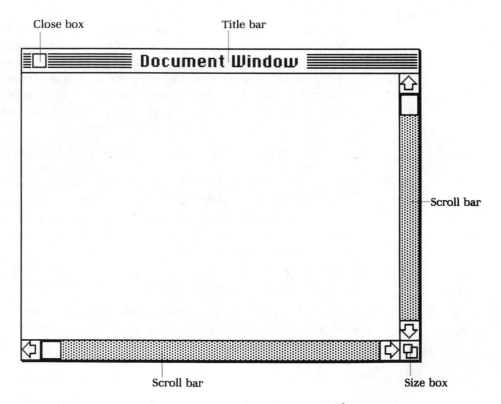

Figure 3-2 Parts of a document window

Inactive window   Active window

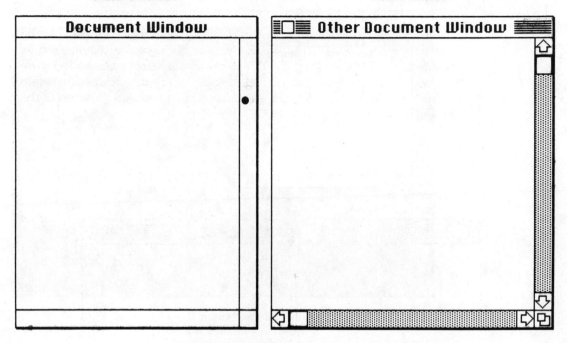

The active window highlights its title bar and displays
its close box, size box, and scroll bars.

Figure 3-3 Highlighting of a document window

Pressing and dragging inside a window's title bar causes an outline of
the window to appear and follow the mouse's movements (Figure 3-4).
When the button is released, the window moves to its new location on
the screen. Inside the title bar, at the left, is the window's *close box*. Clicking inside the close box closes the window and erases it from the screen
(Figure 3-5). A window that can't be closed by the user has no close box.

a.

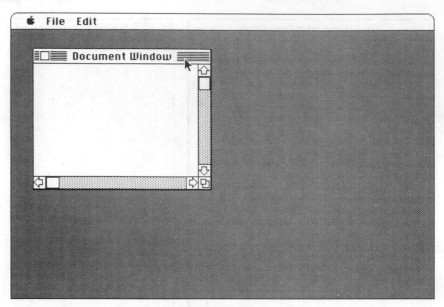

Before: Mouse button about to be
pressed in window's title bar.

b.

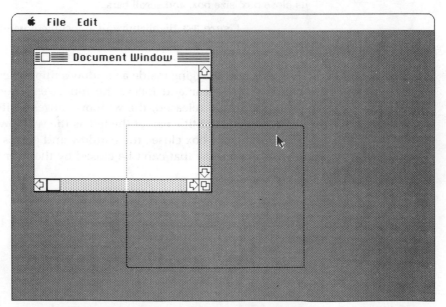

During: Dotted outline of window follows mouse.

Figure 3-4 Moving a document window

c.

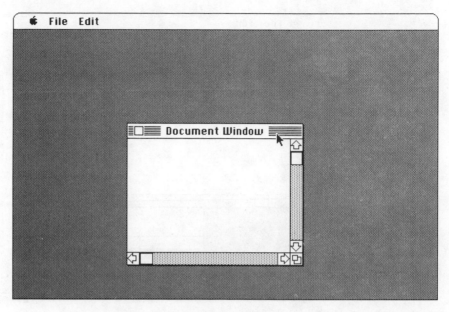

After: When mouse button is released,
window moves to new location.

Figure 3-4 (*continued*)

a.

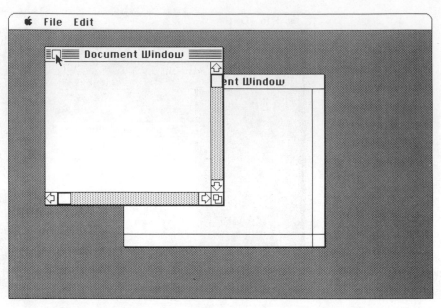

Before: Mouse button about to be pressed
in window's close box

b.

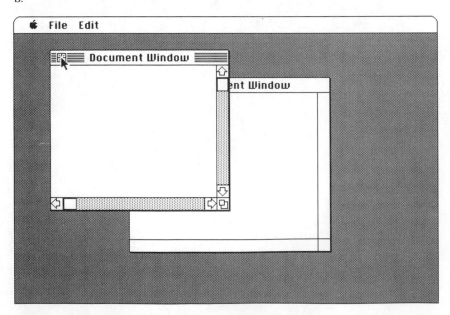

During: Close box indicates that window is about to vanish.

Figure 3-5 Closing a document window

c.

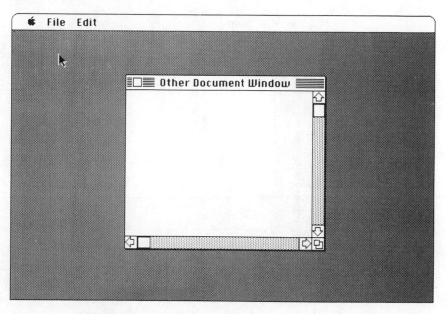

After: When mouse button is released, window goes away; next-frontmost window becomes active.

Figure 3-5 *(continued)*

a.

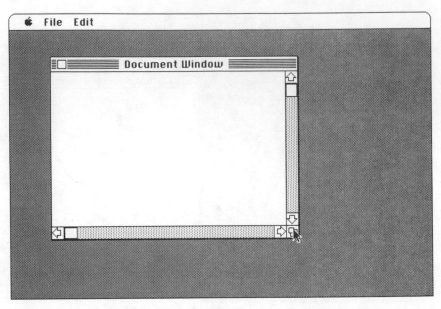

Before: Mouse button about to be pressed
in window's size box.

b.

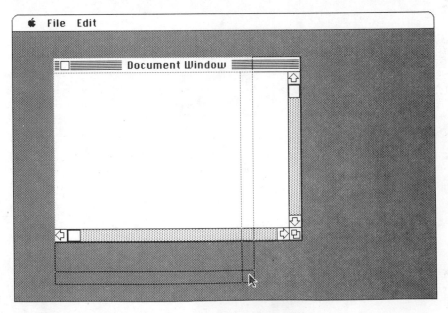

During: Bottom-right corner of window outline
follows mouse; top-left corner remains fixed.

Figure 3-6 Sizing a document window

c.

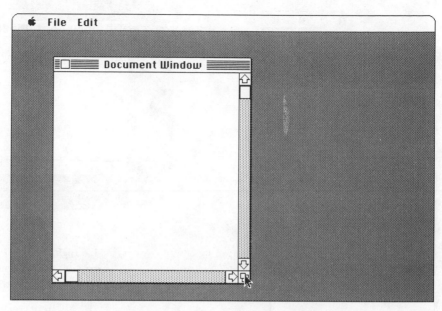

After: When mouse button is released,
window changes to new size.

Figure 3-6 (*continued*)

At the bottom-right corner of the window is the *size box*, used to adjust the window's size. When the user presses and drags the mouse inside the size box, an outline of the window appears with its top-left corner "anchored" and its bottom-right corner following the mouse (Figure 3-6). The window is redrawn to its new size when the button is released. A window that can't be resized has no size box.

A window may also contain *controls* of various types, such as the "pushbuttons" and "checkboxes" commonly used in dialog boxes. The most familiar examples of controls are the *scroll bars* along a window's right and bottom edges. (Not all windows have scroll bars. Normally a window will have a scroll bar in a given direction—vertical or horizontal—only if it can actually be scrolled in that direction.) Controls, including scroll bars, are discussed in Chapter 6.

A window's outline on the screen (including the title bar, if any) is called its *frame*. The Toolbox draws the frame for you; what's inside the frame (the window's *content*) is your responsibility. The area inside the window that you can draw into is called the *content region*. Together, the content region and the frame make up the window's *structure region*, the total area occupied by the window (see Figure 3-7). Notice that these are

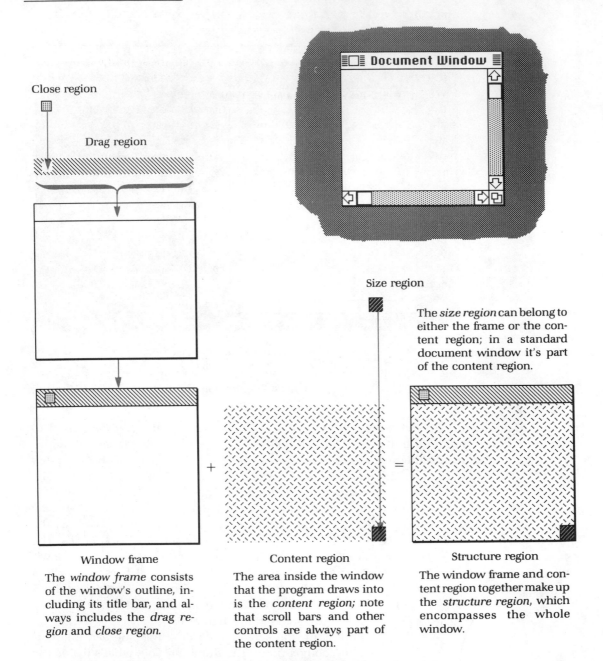

Close region

Drag region

Size region

The *size region* can belong to either the frame or the content region; in a standard document window it's part of the content region.

Window frame

The *window frame* consists of the window's outline, including its title bar, and always includes the *drag region* and *close region.*

Content region

The area inside the window that the program draws into is the *content region;* note that scroll bars and other controls are always part of the content region.

Structure region

The window frame and content region together make up the *structure region,* which encompasses the whole window.

Figure 3-7 Regions of a window

QuickDraw regions, and can be any shape—for a standard document window, they just happen to be rectangular.

A window can also have a *drag region* for moving the window, a *close region* (also called the "go-away region") for closing it, and a *size region* (also called the "grow region") for changing its size. (For a document window, the drag region is the title bar minus the close box, the close region is the close box, and the size region is the size box.) The drag and close regions are always part of the window's frame, meaning that the Toolbox draws them for you automatically. The size region, on the other hand, may belong to either the frame or the content region: in a standard document window, in fact, it lies within the content region, which means you have to draw it for yourself whenever necessary. The same goes for a window's controls (including scroll bars), which are *always* part of the content region.

Two other important regions associated with a window are its visible region, discussed in the next section, and its update region, which is used in connection with update events and is discussed later under "Window Events."

Window Records

Internally, each window is represented by a *window record* [3.1.1] summarizing all the needed information pertaining to the window. The first item in the window record is a graphics port for drawing into the window. This is actually a complete record of type **GrafPort** [I:4.2.2] embedded in the window record—not just a pointer to one. One way to think of a window record is as an extended graphics port with some extra fields added at the end to describe its window-specific properties. To draw a window's contents on the screen, you just use the window as a graphics port and draw into it with QuickDraw.

As the user moves windows around on the screen, the Toolbox keeps track of each window's *visible region*, the portion of the window that's exposed to view at any given time. A handle to the visible region is kept in the **visRgn** field of the window's port, and anything you draw in the window is automatically clipped to this region. This means that if your application calls for it, you can draw into a window even when it isn't frontmost on the screen, and only the part that's exposed to view will actually be drawn. Notice that the Toolbox itself takes full responsibility for maintaining a window's visible region: you should never attempt to manipulate this field of the window record yourself.

Like the graphics port it's based on, a window record is a nonrelocatable object and is referred to by a pointer rather than a handle. Actually, there are two different types of window pointer [3.1.1], one for treating the window as a window and one for treating it as a port. To use a window as a port, you refer to it with a pointer of type **WindowPtr**. This is equivalent to a **GrafPtr** [I:4.2.2]: that is, a pointer to a graphics port. So you can give this type of pointer to any QuickDraw routine that expects a **GrafPtr** as an argument. Since the window record and the graphics port in its first field both start at the same address, QuickDraw will find all the port's fields at the correct locations and everything will work as it should. The other type of window pointer is called a **WindowPeek**. This is defined as a pointer to a window record (not to a graphics port), so you can use it to "peek" at the window-specific fields beyond the end of the port record.

Even though a **WindowPtr** and a **WindowPeek** point to the same place in memory, Pascal considers them different types and won't let you use one where the other is expected. To illustrate the difference, suppose you have two variables, declared as

```
var
  wPtr  : WindowPtr;
  wPeek : WindowPeek;
```

that both point to the same window record. You can refer to the window's port rectangle as either

```
wPtr^.portRect
```

or

```
wPeek^.port.portRect
```

You can refer to its content region as

```
wPeek^.contRgn
```

but there's no way to refer to the content region by means of **wPtr**. You can make the window the current port with

```
SetPort(wPtr)
```

and draw into it with QuickDraw, but you can't do the same with **wPeek**.

When you create a new window, what you get back from the Toolbox is a **WindowPtr**. It's up to you to convert it to a **WindowPeek** if that's what you need. You can convert one type of pointer to the other with the Pascal "typecasting" feature:

```
wPeek := WindowPeek(wPtr)
```

or

```
wPtr   := WindowPtr(wPeek)
```

All windows in existence at any time (whether visible or not) are chained together into a single *window list*, ordered from front to back according to their plane on the screen. The beginning of the list is kept in the system global **WindowList**, which always points to the frontmost window on the screen. Each window's **nextWindow** field points to the next window behind it; the last window in the list has a **nextWindow** of **NIL**. Each window also has its own *control list*, beginning in the **control-List** field of the window record; we'll have more to say about this in Chapter 6.

Each window record includes a 4-byte (long integer) field reserved for use by your program. This field is called **refCon**, for "reference constant," even though it's really not a constant but a variable. You can use it optionally to hold any special information you want to associate with a window. (If you need more than 4 bytes, you can allocate the needed space from the heap and store a handle to it as the window's reference constant. You'll have to typecast the handle to a long integer in order to store it into the **refCon** field, and back to a handle when you want to use it. This is the technique we'll be using in our example program.)

Creating and Destroying Windows

Before you can create any windows, you have to initialize QuickDraw with **InitGraf** [I:4.3.1], font handling with **InitFonts** [I:8.2.4], and windows themselves with **InitWindows** [3.2.1]. (We've already done all this in our earlier **Initialize** routine, Program 2-6.) You can then create any windows you need with **NewWindow** or **GetNewWindow**, and destroy them when you're finished with them by calling **DisposeWindow** or **CloseWindow**.

NewWindow [3.2.2] creates a new window and returns a **WindowPtr** to it. You supply the window's title, its position and plane on the screen, its window type, and its reference constant, and specify whether it's initially visible or invisible and whether it has a close region. The window's position is expressed as a rectangle in global (screen) coordinates, which becomes its port rectangle. You specify the window's plane by giving a pointer to the window immediately in front of it; the new window will be inserted right after this one in the window list. (A value of **NIL** for this **behindWindow** parameter places the new window behind all others on the screen; a value of **WindowPtr**(−**1**) places it in front of all others, making it the active window.) The new window's type is identified with an integer called a *window definition ID*, which we'll discuss later.

You can also provide a pointer, **wStorage**, to the storage to be used for the new window record. You can pass a value of **NIL** for **wStorage**, asking the Toolbox to allocate the storage for you from the heap, but you may instead want to declare a variable of type **WindowRecord** on the stack and use the @ operator (Volume One, Chapter 2) to pass a pointer to it. This avoids fragmenting the heap with nonrelocatable objects (remember, window records are based on graphics ports and are referred to with pointers instead of handles). Bear in mind, though, that any variable residing on the stack will be deallocated on exit from the routine in which it's declared: to avoid dangling pointers, be sure to destroy the window with **CloseWindow** before returning from the routine.

Program 3-1 (**DoNew**) shows one way our example program **MiniEdit** might create a new window on the screen. (We'll see in the next chapter how this routine gets called when the user chooses the **New** menu command.) Our program will be using the window's reference constant to hold a handle to a "window data record" containing various pieces of information it needs about the window. Later we'll define a record type, **WindowData**, to represent this record, and a handle type, **WDHandle**, to point to it. We're not ready yet to look at the complete definition, but we can say that the window data record will contain the following information:

• A handle to the window's *edit record*, used for editing text in the window (Chapter 5)

• A handle to the window's scroll bar (Chapter 6)

• The reference number of the file associated with the window, if any (Chapter 8)

• A flag telling whether the window's text has been changed since it was last read from or written to the disk

```
{ Global variable }

var
   TheWindow : WindowPtr;                          {Pointer to currently active window [3.1.1]}


procedure DoNew;

   { Handle New command. }

   const
      windowTop    = 70;                            {Top edge of window in screen coordinates}
      windowLeft   = 50;                            {Left edge of window in screen coordinates}
      windowBottom = 270;                           {Bottom edge of window in screen coordinates}
      windowRight  = 350;                           {Right edge of window in screen coordinates}

   var
      windowRect : Rect;                            {New window's port rectangle [I:4.1.2]}
      theData    : WDHandle;                        {Handle to window's data record [Prog. 5-1]}
      dataHandle : Handle;                          {Untyped handle for creating data record [I:3.1.1]}

   begin {DoNew}

      SetRect (windowRect, windowLeft, windowTop,   {Set up port rectangle [I:4.1.2]}
                      windowRight, windowBottom);
      dataHandle := NewHandle (SIZEOF(WindowData));  {Allocate window data record [I:3.2.1, Prog. 5-1]}

      TheWindow := NewWindow (NIL, windowRect, 'untitled',     {Make new window from scratch [3.2.2]}
                      TRUE, DocumentProc, WindowPtr(-1),
                      TRUE, LONGINT(dataHandle));

      SetPort  (TheWindow);                         {Get into the window's port [I:4.3.3]}
      TextFont (Geneva);                            {Set text font [I:8.3.2, I:8.2.1]}

      HLock (dataHandle);                           {Lock data record [I:3.2.4]}

        theData := WDHandle(dataHandle);            {Convert to typed handle [Prog. 5-1]}
        with theData^^ do
           {Initialize fields of data record};

        {Set global handles to scroll bar and edit record};

      HUnlock (dataHandle)                          {Unlock data record [I:3.2.4]}

   end; {DoNew}
```

Program 3-1 Make new window from scratch

Our **DoNew** routine allocates space for the window data record from the heap, typecasts the resulting handle to a long integer, and supplies it to **NewWindow** as the window's reference constant. Then it goes on to initialize the fields of the data record; in Chapter 5 we'll look at a more detailed version of **DoNew** that shows exactly how this is done.

Don't confuse what we're calling the window data record with the window record itself. The window record is a Toolbox data structure, and always contains the same items of information for every window; the window data record is strictly a creature of our example program, and holds additional information that this particular program needs to maintain about each window it creates. A different program might define the contents of the window data record differently, or might use the window's reference constant for a different purpose entirely, or might not use the reference constant at all (in which case you would just set it to **0** and forget about it).

Notice that **DoNew** stores the pointer to the newly created window into a global variable of the **MiniEdit** program named **TheWindow**. Whenever one of our own application windows is frontmost on the screen, **TheWindow** will hold a pointer to it; when a system window is frontmost, **TheWindow** will be set to **NIL**. As we'll see, many of **MiniEdit**'s routines rely on this variable to be set up properly. Since we're placing the new window in front of all others on the screen, it will become the active window—so we have to see to it that **TheWindow** is set to point to it. (The program also maintains global handles to the active window's scroll bar and edit record; our later version of **DoNew** will show how these are set up as well.)

Finally, some of the program's routines assume that the active window is also the current graphics port, so our **DoNew** routine must call **SetPort** [I:4.3.3] to "get into" the window's port. We'll also use this opportunity to set the typeface for displaying text in the window with **TextFont** [I:8.3.2].

Instead of creating a new window "from scratch" with **NewWindow**, you can use **GetNewWindow** [3.2.2] to create one from a predefined *window template*. The template is a resource of type **'WIND'** [3.7.1], typically stored in the program's application resource file. It contains most of the same information you would have supplied to **NewWindow** as parameters; with **GetNewWindow**, you just give the resource ID of the template instead. The only information you still have to provide explicitly is the **behindWindow** parameter defining the window's plane (since the identity of the other windows on the screen can't be known ahead of time) and the optional storage pointer; all the rest comes from the template. Window templates are handy because they save code and allow you to change the properties of your windows without changing your program; like all other resources, their use is encouraged. Our **MiniEdit** program actually creates its windows from a template in its resource file rather than from scratch, using the version of the **DoNew** routine shown in Program 3-2.

Of course, before you can create windows from a template, you first have to create the template itself and place it in a resource file for your program to use. As discussed in Volume One, Chapter 6, the only software officially available from Apple for such purposes as this book goes to press runs on a Lisa rather than directly on the Macintosh. A Mac-based resource editor will soon be available, however, as part of Apple's planned Macintosh software development system. Preliminary versions of the resource editor are already widely available—both by mail order from Apple as part of the Macintosh Software Supplement and unofficially through Macintosh user groups and "bulletin boards"—and in fact all of the resources for our **MiniEdit** program were created with it.

When you're finished with a window, use **CloseWindow** or **DisposeWindow** [3.2.3] to destroy it. **DisposeWindow** frees all storage associated with the window, including that occupied by the window record itself. Use it if you had the Toolbox allocate the window record for you (that is, if you set the **wStorage** parameter to **NIL** when you created the window). If you supplied your own storage for the window record, use **CloseWindow** to destroy the window instead. This frees the storage occupied by the window's auxiliary data structures (such as its structure, content, and update regions), but not by the window record itself. If you've been using the window's **refCon** field to hold a handle to some

```
{ Global variable }

var
   TheWindow : WindowPtr;                            {Pointer to currently active window [3.1.1]}


procedure DoNew;

   { Handle New command. }

   const
      windowID = 1000;                               {Resource ID for window template [3.7.1]}

   var
      theData    : WDHandle;                         {Handle to window's data record [Prog. 5-1]}
      dataHandle : Handle;                           {Untyped handle for creating data record [I:3.1.1]}

   begin {DoNew}

      TheWindow := GetNewWindow (windowID, NIL, WindowPtr(-1));  {Make new window from template [3.2.2]}

      SetPort  (TheWindow);                          {Get into the window's port [I:4.3.3]}
      TextFont (Geneva);                             {Set text font [I:8.3.2, I:8.2.1]}

      dataHandle := NewHandle (SIZEOF(WindowData));  {Allocate window data record [I:3.2.1, Prog. 5-1]}
      SetWRefCon (TheWindow, LONGINT(dataHandle));   {Store as reference constant [3.2.4]}

      HLock (dataHandle);                            {Lock data record [I:3.2.4]}

         theData := WDHandle(dataHandle);            {Convert to typed handle [Prog. 5-1]}
         with theData^^ do
            {Initialize fields of data record};

         {Set global handles to scroll bar and edit record};

      HUnlock (dataHandle)                           {Unlock data record [I:3.2.4]}

   end; {DoNew}
```

Program 3-2 Make new window from template

data on the heap (such as the window data record we're using in our example program), it's up to you to explicitly dispose of whatever the handle points to before you destroy the window.

As we'll see later, whenever the user clicks in a window's close box or chooses the **Close** menu command, our **MiniEdit** program calls one of its routines named **DoClose**, shown in Program 3-3. **DoClose**, in turn, calls either **CloseAppWindow** (shown here) or **CloseSysWindow** (shown in Chapter 4), depending on whether an application or system window is frontmost on the screen.

```
{ Global variable }

var
   TheWindow : WindowPtr;                 {Pointer to currently active window [3.1.1]}


procedure DoClose;

   { Handle Close command. }

   begin {DoClose}

      if FrontWindow = TheWindow then     {Is the active window one of ours? [3.3.3]}
         CloseAppWindow                   {Close application window [Prog. 3-4, 7-2]}
      else
         CloseSysWindow                   {Close system window [Prog. 4-7]}

   end; {DoClose}
```

Program 3-3 Handle **Close** command

CloseAppWindow (Program 3-4) begins by calling the Toolbox routine **GetWRefCon** [3.2.4] to get the active window's reference constant. It typecasts the reference constant from a long integer to a handle, then uses the handle to gain access to the fields of the window data record. After disposing of the data record's contents, it proceeds to dispose of the data record itself and then of the whole window. (Notice that it isn't necessary to explicitly dispose of the window's scroll bar, since **DisposeWindow** automatically disposes of all of a window's controls.)

```
{ Global variable }

var
   TheWindow : WindowPtr;                                {Pointer to currently active window [3.1.1]}


procedure CloseAppWindow;

   { Skeleton procedure to close application window. }

   var
      theData   : WDHandle;                              {Handle to window's data record [Prog.5-1]}
      dataHandle : Handle;                               {Untyped handle for destroying data record [I:3.1.1]}
      thisWindow : WindowPtr;                            {Pointer to window being closed [3.1.1]}

   begin {CloseAppWindow}

      dataHandle := Handle(GetWRefCon(TheWindow));       {Get window data [3.2.4]}

      HLock (dataHandle);                                {Lock data record [I:3.2.4]}
         theData := WDHandle(dataHandle);                {Convert to typed handle [Prog. 5-1]}
         with theData^^ do
            begin

               {Allow user to save window's text if necessary};

               {Close window's file, if any};

               {Dispose of window's edit record}

            end; {with}
      HUnlock (dataHandle);                              {Unlock data record [I:3.2.4]}

      thisWindow := TheWindow;                           {Save window pointer (DoActivate will change TheWindow)}
      HideWindow (TheWindow);                            {Force deactivate event [3.3.1]}

      if GetNextEvent (ActivateEvt, TheEvent) then       {Get deactivate event [2.2.1, 2.1.2]}
         DoActivate;                                     {   and handle it [Prog. 3-5, 5-14] }
      if GetNextEvent (ActivateEvt, TheEvent) then       {Get activate event [2.2.1, 2.1.2] }
         DoActivate;                                     {   and handle it [Prog. 3-5, 5-14]}

      DisposHandle  (dataHandle);                        {Dispose of window data record [I:3.2.2]}
      DisposeWindow (thisWindow)                         {Dispose of window [3.2.3]}

   end;  {CloseAppWindow}
```

Program 3-4 Close application window

There's a hitch, however. As we'll see in a minute, changing the window that's active (frontmost) on the screen ordinarily generates a pair of events to handle any special "housekeeping" associated with the transition: a deactivate event for the window becoming inactive and an activate event for the one becoming active. But when a window is destroyed with **CloseWindow** or **DisposeWindow**, the usual deactivate event never occurs (since the window it would refer to no longer exists). To make sure all the needed housekeeping is taken care of, we have to resort to a bit of chicanery.

First we hide the window we're about to destroy, bringing the next window behind it to the front of the screen and forcing a pair of deactivate/activate events to be generated. Then, using **GetNextEvent** [2.2.1] with an event mask [2.1.2] specifying activate/deactivate events only, we retrieve the two events and process them immediately instead of waiting to handle them later in the normal way, via our **DoEvent** routine. Once the window we're closing has been duly deactivated, we can safely dispose of it. (Notice, however, that in responding to the two events we will have changed the global variable **TheWindow** to point to the other window becoming active—so we have to save the original window pointer in a local variable, **thisWindow**, where it will still be available when the time comes to destroy the window.) Does all this strike you as an awful lot of work for so common a task as closing a window? You're right!

Window Types and Definition Functions

Each type of window has its own structure and appearance, which are determined by a *window definition function*. The Toolbox calls the definition function whenever it needs to perform type-dependent operations on a window, such as drawing it on the screen or testing which of its regions the mouse was pressed in.

Window definition functions are normally kept in a resource file. When you create a new window, you specify its type by giving a *window definition ID*, either as the **windowType** parameter to **NewWindow** or as part of a window template to **GetNewWindow**. The definition ID is a coded integer that includes the resource ID of the definition function, along with some additional information. The Toolbox loads the definition function into memory from the resource file and stores a handle to it into the **windowDefProc** field of the window record.

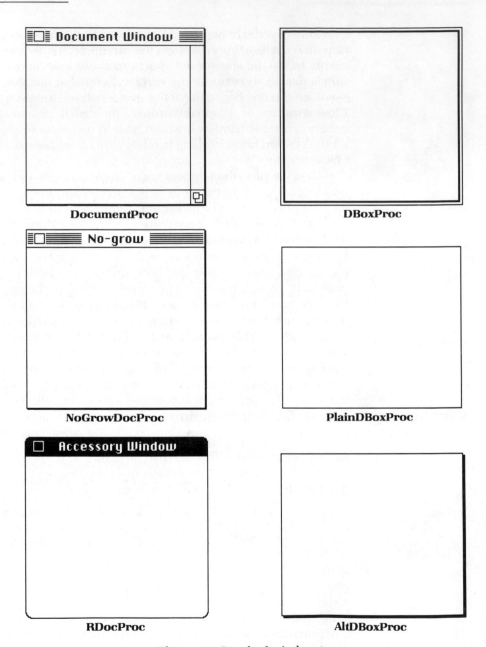

Figure 3-8 Standard window types

Definition functions for the standard window types are kept in the system resource file, where they're available for any program to use. Unless you're defining your own window types, all you need to know are the definition IDs for the standard types. These are available as predefined constants [3.2.2], producing the standard window types shown in Figure 3-8:

- **DocumentProc** for a standard document window
- **NoGrowDocProc** for a document window with no size box
- **DBoxProc** for an alert or dialog box with a double border
- **PlainDBoxProc** for an alert or dialog box with a plain border
- **AltDBoxProc** for an alert or dialog box with a two-pixel "shadow"
- **RDocProc** for an accessory window (a "rounded document window")

If you use these built-in constants, the proper definition functions will be loaded and used automatically. If you want to write your own window definition functions, see *Inside Macintosh* for further information.

Window Events

As the user manipulates windows on the screen, the Toolbox tracks the changes and reports them to your program via special *window events*. For instance, when the user clicks in an inactive window to bring it to the front, you get a *deactivate event* for the window that was previously active, followed by an *activate event* for the window becoming active. When part of a window that was previously covered becomes exposed on the screen, you get an *update event* telling you to redraw the newly exposed part of the window's content region. Window events are detected in special ways and are never placed in the event queue like ordinary user events. However, they're reported through the normal event mechanism, and you receive them just like any other event, by calling **GetNextEvent** [2.2.1].

Activate and Deactivate Events

Activate and deactivate events normally occur in pairs—one window gets deactivated and another activated at the same time. Pointers to the two windows are kept in a pair of system globals named **CurActivate** and **CurDeactivate**. When you ask the Toolbox for an event, it looks in these special locations and returns an activate or deactivate event if it finds either of them nonempty.

> The Toolbox checks for activate and deactivate events *before* looking
> in the event queue, so these events take priority over all others.
> Since there's only one memory location for each of the two types of
> event, there can never be more than one activate and one deactivate
> pending at the same time. If there's one of each, the deactivate is
> reported first, so one window will become inactive before the other
> becomes active.

Actually, activate and deactivate events both have the same event
type (**activateEvt**) in the **what** field of the event record [2.1.1]. You can tell
them apart by looking at the low-order bit (bit 0) of the event's **modifiers**
field, corresponding to the Toolbox mask constant **ActiveFlag** [2.1.5]. This
bit will be **0** for a deactivate event or **1** for an activate event. The event's
message field [2.1.4] contains a pointer to the window affected.

Program 3-5 (**DoActivate**) shows how our example program handles
activate and deactivate events. For both types of event, it gets the window
pointer from the event record and makes sure that window is the current
port. Then it calls the Toolbox procedure **DrawGrowIcon** [3.3.4] to redraw the window's size region. (Recall that in a standard document window the size box is part of the content region, so redrawing it is your
responsibility.)

```
{ Global variables }

var
   TheEvent  : EventRecord;              {Current event [2.1.1]}
   TheWindow : WindowPtr;                {Pointer to currently active window [3.1.1]}


procedure DoActivate;

   { Skeleton procedure to handle activate or deactivate event. }

   const
      changeFlag = $0002;                {Mask for extracting "change bit" from event modifiers}
```

Program 3-5 Handle activate or deactivate event

```
var
   whichWindow : WindowPtr;                        {Pointer to the window [3.1.1]}

begin {DoActivate}

   with TheEvent do
      begin
         whichWindow := WindowPtr(message);        {Convert long integer to pointer [3.1.1]}
         SetPort (whichWindow);                     {Make window the current port [I:4.3.3]}

         DrawGrowIcon (whichWindow);                {Highlight or unhighlight size box [3.3.4]}

         if BitAnd(modifiers, ActiveFlag) <> 0 then {Test activate/deactivate bit [I:2.2.2, 2.1.5]}
            begin
               TheWindow := whichWindow;            {Set global pointer}

               {Set global handles to scroll bar and edit record};

               {Activate window's scroll bar, text selection, etc.};

               if BitAnd(modifiers, changeFlag) <> 0 then  {Coming from a system window? [I:2.2.2, 2.1.5]}
                  {Take special action on return from a system window}
            end {then}
         else
            begin
               TheWindow := NIL;                    {Clear global pointer}

               {Clear global handles to scroll bar and edit record};

               {Deactivate window's scroll bar, text selection, etc.};

               if BitAnd(modifiers, changeFlag) <> 0 then  {Exiting to a system window? [I:2.2.2, 2.1.5]}
                  {Take special action on exit to a system window}
            end {else}
      end {with}

end; {DoActivate}
```

Program 3-5 (*continued*)

The size region is drawn differently depending on whether the window is active or inactive (actually, on whether it's highlighted or not). An active document window displays the standard "grow icon" in its size box, while an inactive one just shows the outline of an empty box (see Figure 3-3). By calling **DrawGrowIcon** whenever a window is activated or deactivated, you allow the size region to change its appearance in step with the state of the window. Notice that you call **DrawGrowIcon** the same way for both activate and deactivate events: it always draws the size region according to the current state of the **hilited** flag in the window record.

Next, **DoActivate** examines the **ActiveFlag** bit of the event's **modifiers** field [2.1.5] to see whether the event is an activate or a deactivate. At this point you can take any further steps your application may call for. In the case of our example application, we set our global variables to point to the newly activated window (and its scroll bar and edit record), activate the scroll bar, and highlight the text selection. (A later version of **DoActivate** will show all these steps in detail.) On deactivating a window, of course, we do the reverse.

You might also want to take some special actions, such as enabling or disabling menu items, when control passes from one of your own windows to a system window or vice versa. Bit 1 (the next-to-last bit) of the **modifiers** field tells you when this happens. When one window is deactivated and another activated at the same time, the Toolbox sets this bit to **1** if one of the windows is a system window and the other belongs to the application, or to **0** if they're both system or both application windows. Program 3-5 shows how to test this bit and do any special processing that may be required. (Of course you can leave this test out if there's nothing special to do on the transition between system and application windows.)

Just as this book was going to press, Apple released a new version of the Toolbox interface in which the mask constant for testing the system/application transition bit, **ChangeFlag**, had been removed. The reason given was that the Toolbox had been discovered not to be setting this bit reliably in all cases. Since no such problem has ever been detected with **MiniEdit**, we haven't removed the test on this bit from our **DoActivate** routine—although we now have to define the mask constant **changeFlag** for ourselves. Be advised, however, that programs that rely on this bit may occasionally run into trouble.

Update Events

Whenever the user closes, moves, or sizes a window, the Toolbox checks to see which parts of this or other windows have been exposed to view and need to be updated (redrawn) on the screen. The Toolbox itself redraws the window's frame, but the content region is your responsibility. So the Toolbox generates an *update event* to notify your program when part of a window's content region needs redrawing.

To keep track of what needs updating, the Toolbox maintains an *update region* for each window. When part of a window is exposed to view, the Toolbox draws the exposed part of the frame and adds the exposed part of the content region into the update region (see Figure 3-9). Then, when you ask for an event with **GetNextEvent** [2.2.1], it scans down the window list looking for a window whose update region is nonempty. If it finds one, it reports an update event for that window.

The Toolbox checks the event queue first and scans for updates only if the queue is empty, so all other events take priority over update events. Notice also that since the window list is scanned from the beginning, windows get updated in front-to-back order on the screen.

Update events have an event type of **updateEvt** in the **what** field of the event record [2.1.1] and a pointer to the window to be updated in the **message** field [2.1.4]. Program 3-6 (**DoUpdate**) shows the normal way of responding to such an event: make the window the current port, call **BeginUpdate**, redraw the window's contents, and finally call **EndUpdate** [3.4.1]. **BeginUpdate** saves a copy of the window's visible region, then temporarily restricts the visible region by intersecting it with the update region (see Figure 3-10). When you draw the window's contents, Quick-Draw will automatically clip to this restricted region, so that only the part that really needs to be updated will actually be drawn on the screen. (You could just redraw the update region, but it's usually more convenient to draw the whole content region and let QuickDraw take care of the clipping.) For normal document windows, don't forget that the size box and scroll bars are part of the content region and must be included in your redrawing operation, as in the example.

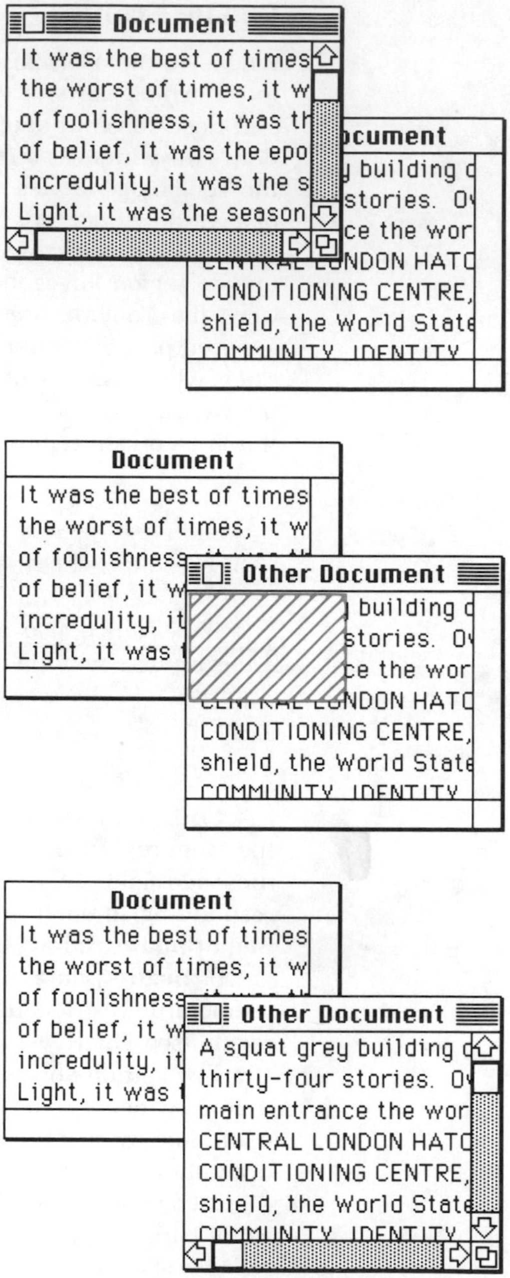

Before: Window in back is about to come to front; overlapping portion will have to be updated (redrawn).

During: Toolbox draws exposed part of frame; exposed part of content region [colored box] is accumulated into update region, causing an update event.

After: Program finishes the job by drawing contents of update region.

Figure 3-9 Update region

```
{ Global variable }

var
   TheEvent : EventRecord;                          {Current event [2.1.1]}


procedure DoUpdate;

   { Skeleton procedure to handle an update event. }

   var
      savePort    : GrafPtr;                        {Pointer to previous current port [I:4.2.2]}
      whichWindow : WindowPtr;                      {Pointer to window to be updated [3.1.1]}

   begin {DoUpdate}

      GetPort (savePort);                           {Save previous port [I:4.3.3]}

         whichWindow := WindowPtr(TheEvent.message); {Convert long integer to pointer [3.1.1]}
         SetPort (whichWindow);                     {Make window the current port [I:4.3.3]}

         BeginUpdate (whichWindow);                 {Restrict visible region to update region [3.4.1]}

            EraseRect (whichWindow^.portRect);      {Clear update region [I:5.3.2]}

            DrawGrowIcon (whichWindow);             {Redraw size box [3.3.4]}
            {Draw window's controls};

            {Draw window's contents};

         EndUpdate (whichWindow);                   {Restore original visible region [3.4.1]}

      SetPort (savePort)                            {Restore original port [I:4.3.3]}

   end;  {DoUpdate}
```

Program 3-6 Handle update event

After you're finished redrawing, **EndUpdate** restores the window's original visible region and empties the update region. This has the effect of "clearing" the update event, so that it won't be reported again the next time you call **GetNextEvent**. (Also notice in the example that **DoUpdate** is careful to save the previous current port on entry and restore it again before returning, since the window being updated isn't necessarily the active window.)

> Be sure to balance every call to **BeginUpdate** with a corresponding call to **EndUpdate** when you're finished redrawing the window.

Sometimes you need to manipulate a window's update region yourself instead of letting the Toolbox do it. The routines **InvalRect** and **InvalRgn** [3.4.2] allow you to declare a rectangle or an arbitrary region of a window "invalid" (that is, not correctly displayed on the screen) by adding it to the update region to be redrawn. This is useful, for instance, for resizing a window: we'll see an example later in this chapter. Similarly, **ValidRect** and **ValidRgn** [3.4.2] declare a rectangle or a region to be already "valid" and remove it from the update region. (Perhaps you've already redrawn the region for some reason and it doesn't have to be drawn again.)

> Another option that's sometimes handy is that of supplying a *window picture* instead of redrawing the window with update events. Recall that a picture is a "transcript" of a series of calls to Quick-Draw. A window picture consists of all the QuickDraw calls needed to draw the window's contents. If a window has a window picture, the Toolbox uses the picture to redraw the window when necessary, instead of generating an update event asking you to do it. This can save both space and time if the picture occupies less memory than the code and data needed to redraw the window yourself. A handle to the window picture, if any, is kept in the **windowPic** field of the window record; you can access it with **GetWindowPic** and change it with **SetWindowPic** [3.4.3].

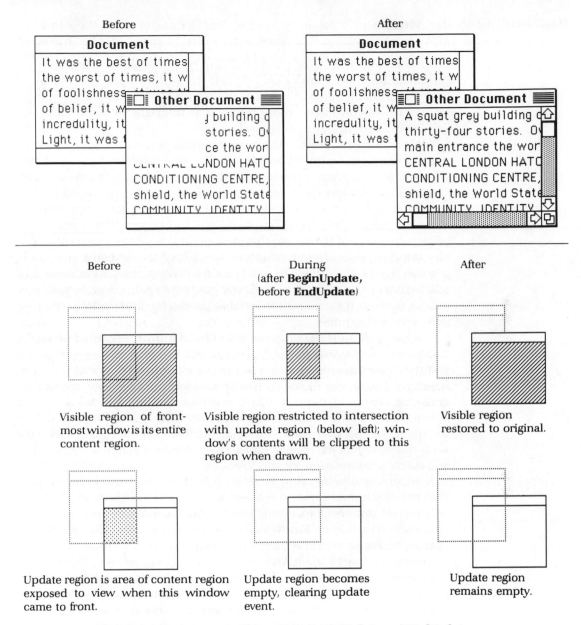

Figure 3-10 BeginUpdate and EndUpdate

Responding to the Mouse

Responding to the user's actions with the mouse is entirely your responsibility. The Toolbox provides all the routines you need to make your windows operate according to the standard Macintosh conventions, but it's up to you to call those routines at the right times to make the windows do what they're supposed to.

When the user presses the mouse button, you will receive a mouse-down event from **GetNextEvent** [2.2.1]. The first thing to do is call **FindWindow** [3.5.1] to find out where on the screen the button was pressed. You tell **FindWindow** the point where the mouse event occurred (in global coordinates, the same form in which you receive it in the **where** field of the event record). **FindWindow** gives back an integer called a *part code*, telling what part of the screen the given point lies in: the menu bar, a system window, one of your windows, or simply the screen's gray background (the desktop). If it's in one of your windows, the part code further tells whether it was in the window's content region, drag region, size region, or close region, and the variable parameter **theWindow** returns a pointer to the window.

What to do next depends on what **FindWindow** reveals about where the mouse button was pressed. The Toolbox provides routines for all the standard cases except for a click in the content region of one of your own windows. This is up to you to handle in whatever way your application calls for. Many of these Toolbox routines "track" the mouse, maintaining control for as long as the user holds down the button and following the mouse's movements with visual feedback on the screen. When the button is released, the routine either takes standard action in response or passes back information for you to act on.

All this is illustrated in Program 3-7 (**DoMouseDown**), the routine that handles mouse-down events for our example program **MiniEdit**. We use a *case* statement to decide what action to take, depending on the part code returned by **FindWindow**. If the part code is **InDesk**, there's nothing to do, so we return without taking any action. Mouse presses in the menu bar (part code **InMenuBar**) are passed along to a **MiniEdit** routine named **DoMenuClick**, which we'll look at in Chapter 4. To handle a part code of **InSysWindow**, we call the Toolbox routine **SystemClick** [3.5.3]. This routine does whatever is needed to respond to a mouse press in a system window; typically it just passes the event on to the desk accessory displayed in the window to handle in its own way.

Any other part code means that the mouse was pressed somewhere in one of our own windows; how we respond depends on which window and which part of the window it was in. A part code of **InContent** means that the mouse press was in the window's content region: we'll postpone this case until our discussion of controls in Chapter 6, at which time we'll look at the **MiniEdit** procedure for such events, **DoContent**. For presses

```
{ Global variable }

var
   TheEvent : EventRecord;                          {Current event [2.1.1]}


procedure DoMouseDown;

   { Handle mouse-down event. }

   var
      whichWindow : WindowPtr;                       {Window that mouse was pressed in [3.1.1]}
      thePart     : INTEGER;                         {Part of screen where mouse was pressed [3.5.1]}

   begin {DoMouseDown}

      thePart := FindWindow (TheEvent.where, whichWindow); {Where on the screen was mouse pressed? [3.5.1]}

      case thePart of

         InDesk:
            {Do nothing};

         InMenuBar:
            DoMenuClick;                             {Handle click in menu bar [Prog. 4-3]}

         InSysWindow:
            SystemClick (TheEvent, whichWindow);     {Handle click in system window [3.5.3]}

         InContent:
            DoContent (whichWindow);                 {Handle click in content region [Prog. 6-1]}

         InDrag:
            DoDrag (whichWindow);                    {Handle click in drag region [Prog. 3-8]}

         InGrow:
            DoGrow (whichWindow);                    {Handle click in size region [Prog. 3-9]}

         InGoAway:
            DoGoAway (whichWindow)                   {Handle click in close region [Prog. 3-10]}

         end {case}

   end; {DoMouseDown}
```

Program 3-7 Handle mouse-down event

in the drag, size, and close regions, we call the **MiniEdit** procedures **DoDrag**, **DoGrow**, and **DoGoAway** which are shown in the following programs.

Program 3-8 (**DoDrag**) shows the response to a mouse press in a window's drag region (part code **InDrag**). Basically this routine calls the Toolbox routine **DragWindow** [3.5.4], after some preliminary work to set up one of its parameters. **DragWindow** keeps control for as long as the button is held down and displays an outline of the window that the user can drag with the mouse, as shown earlier in Figure 3-4. When the button is released, **DragWindow** moves the window to its new location on the screen, generating all the needed update events for this and other windows. Since the window is moved automatically, there's no need to call **MoveWindow** [3.3.2] explicitly on return from **DragWindow**.

```
{ Global declarations }

const
    ScreenWidth   = 512;              {Width of screen in pixels}
    ScreenHeight  = 342;             {Height of screen in pixels}
    MenuBarHeight = 20;              {Height of menu bar in pixels}
    ScreenMargin  =  4;              {Width of "safety margin" around edge of screen}

var
    TheEvent : EventRecord;          {Current event [2.1.1]}


procedure DoDrag (whichWindow : WindowPtr);

    { Handle mouse-down event in drag region. }

    var
        limitRect : Rect;             {Limit rectangle for dragging [I:4.1.2]}

    begin {DoDrag}

        SetRect   (limitRect, 0, MenuBarHeight, ScreenWidth, ScreenHeight);
                                          {Set limit rectangle [I:4.1.2]}
        InsetRect (limitRect, ScreenMargin, ScreenMargin);  {Inset by screen margin [I:4.4.4]}

        DragWindow (whichWindow, TheEvent.where, limitRect) {Let user drag the window [3.5.4]}

    end;  {DoDrag}
```

Program 3-8 Mouse-down event in drag region

If the window being dragged is inactive, **DoDrag** will automatically activate it by calling **SelectWindow** [3.5.2]. This unhighlights the previously active window, brings the one being activated to the front of the screen, highlights it, and generates all the needed deactivate, activate, and update events. However, in keeping with the Macintosh User Interface Guidelines, **DragWindow** first checks the state of the command key and doesn't activate the window if the key is down.

The **limitRect** parameter to **DragWindow** limits the window's movement on the screen. If the user moves the mouse outside this rectangle, the window's outline disappears from the screen; releasing the button at such a time cancels the drag operation and leaves the window where it was. If the mouse returns inside the limit rectangle while the button is still down, the window outline reappears and **DragWindow** continues to track. In Program 3-8, the limit rectangle is set up to include the entire desktop (excluding the menu bar), minus a 4-pixel margin around the edges. This prevents the user from dragging a window completely off the desktop, and guarantees that at least that many pixels of the window remain visible at all times, both horizontally and vertically. (The width of the screen margin can easily be adjusted by changing a single constant definition in the program.)

The response to a mouse press in a window's size region (part code **InGrow**) is shown in Program 3-9 (**DoGrow**). First we test whether the window is active, and if not, just activate it with **SelectWindow** [3.5.2]. If the window is already active, we call the Toolbox function **GrowWindow** [3.5.4] to track the mouse as the user drags it. Like **DragWindow**, **Grow-Window** keeps control until the mouse button is released, displaying an outline of the window that follows the mouse's movements. In this case, however, the outline's top-left corner remains "anchored" while its size region (for a document window, the size box at the bottom-right) follows the mouse, as shown earlier in Figure 3-6.

The **sizeRect** parameter tells **GrowWindow** the limits on the window's dimensions. This rectangle's **left** and **right** fields give the window's minimum and maximum width, respectively, and **top** and **bottom** give the minimum and maximum height. **GrowWindow** will "pin" the window outline at these limits as the user drags it with the mouse. The minimum and maximum dimensions chosen in the example are arbitrary, of course; you can use whatever values make sense for your application.

```
{ Global declarations }

const
   MinWidth      = 80;                    {Minimum width of window in pixels}
   MinHeight     = 80;                    {Minimum height of window in pixels}
   ScreenWidth   = 512;                   {Width of screen in pixels}
   ScreenHeight  = 342;                   {Height of screen in pixels}
   MenuBarHeight = 20;                    {Height of menu bar in pixels}

var
   TheEvent : EventRecord;                {Current event [2.1.1]}


procedure DoGrow (whichWindow : WindowPtr);

   { Handle mouse-down event in size region. }

   var
      sizeRect  : Rect;                   {Minimum and maximum dimensions of window [I:4.1.2]}
      newSize   : LONGINT;                {Coded representation of new dimensions}
      newWidth  : INTEGER;                {New width of window}
      newHeight : INTEGER;                {New height of window}

   begin {DoGrow}

      if whichWindow <> FrontWindow then  {Is it an inactive window? [3.3.3]}

         SelectWindow (whichWindow)       {If so, just activate it [3.5.2]}

      else

         begin

            SetRect (sizeRect, MinWidth, MinHeight, ScreenWidth, (ScreenHeight - MenuBarHeight) );
                                          {Set size rectangle [I:4.1.2]}
            newSize := GrowWindow (whichWindow, TheEvent.where, sizeRect);
                                          {Let user drag size region [3.5.4]}

            if newSize <> 0 then           {Was size changed?}
               begin

                  EraseRect (whichWindow^.portRect);   {Clear window to white [I:5.3.2]}
```

Program 3-9 Mouse-down event in size region

```
newWidth  := LoWord(newSize);        {Extract width from low word [I:2.2.3]}
newHeight := HiWord(newSize);        {Extract height from high word [I:2.2.3]}
SizeWindow (whichWindow, newWidth, newHeight, TRUE);
                                     {Adjust size of window [3.3.2]}

InvalRect (whichWindow^.portRect);   {Force update of window's contents [3.4.2]}

FixScrollBar;                        {Resize scroll bar [Prog. 6-10]}
FixText                              {Resize text rectangle [Prog. 6-11]}

   end {if}

end {else}

end; {DoGrow}
```

Program 3-9 (*continued*)

When the button is released, **GrowWindow** returns a coded long integer representing the window's new size, with the height in the high-order word and the width in the low. (This is actually a point record masquerading as a long integer because of Pascal's silly restrictions on function result types.) **GrowWindow** doesn't actually adjust the window's size for you, just tells you the new size the user has requested (or **0** for no change). It's up to you to do the actual resizing by calling **SizeWindow** [3.3.2] explicitly, as shown in the example. After resizing the window, a couple of **MiniEdit** utility routines, **FixScrollBar** and **FixText**, are called to adjust the window's scroll bar and contents to match the new size. These routines will be discussed in Chapter 6.

Resizing a window sometimes produces annoying visual effects on the screen. These effects are caused by various parts of the window's contents being redrawn at different times or in an inconvenient order. Program 3-9 shows one way to avoid these problems and ensure a visually "clean" transition. First we use **EraseRect** [I:5.3.2] to clear the entire port rectangle to the window's background pattern (normally white). Then, after resizing the window, we force its contents to be redrawn by adding the port rectangle into the window's update region with **InvalRect** [3.4.2]. Notice that the order of the calls is critical: the **EraseRect** must come *before* the call to **SizeWindow**, so that the *old* port rectangle will be cleared, while the **InvalRect** must come *after* **SizeWindow**, so that the *new* port rectangle will be redrawn.

Finally, a mouse press in a window's close region (part code **InGoAway**) is handled by **MiniEdit**'s **DoGoAway** routine (Program 3-10). Again, if the window is inactive, we just call **SelectWindow** [3.5.2] to activate it; if it's already active, we pass control to the Toolbox routine **TrackGoAway** [3.5.4]. This tracks the mouse for as long as the user holds down the button, highlighting and unhighlighting the close region as the mouse moves into and out of it. (Exactly what it means to "highlight" the close region depends on the type of window, and is determined by the window definition function. For the standard document window, the close box appears to "pop" like a bubble when the mouse is pressed inside it, as shown earlier in Figure 3-5.)

```
{ Global variable }

var
   TheEvent : EventRecord;                              {Current event [2.1.1]}


procedure DoGoAway (whichWindow : WindowPtr);

   { Handle mouse-down event in close region.  }

   begin {DoGoAway}

      if whichWindow <> FrontWindow then                {Is it an inactive window? [3.3.3]}
         SelectWindow (whichWindow)                     {If so, just activate it [3.5.2]}

      else if TrackGoAway (whichWindow, TheEvent.where) then {Otherwise, track mouse in close region [3.5.4]}
         DoClose                                        {   and close window [Prog. 3-3]          }

   end; {DoGoAway}
```

Program 3-10 Mouse-down event in close region

When the button is released, **TrackGoAway** returns **TRUE** or **FALSE**, depending on whether it was released inside or outside the close region. If the result is **TRUE**, we call our **DoClose** routine (Program 3-3) to close the active window, just as if the user had chosen **Close** from the menu. Since an application window is active, this will in turn call the **CloseAppWindow** routine that we looked at earlier (Program 3-4).

Nuts and Bolts

One shortcoming of the **DoNew** routine we looked at earlier (Programs 3-1 and 3-2) is that every new window it creates will come up in exactly the same place on the screen. To keep them all from "stacking up" in that one spot, it's better to offset each new window a small distance horizontally and vertically from the one before, so that they don't overlap completely (see Figure 3-11). The method for doing this is simple in principle but a little trickier than you might imagine in practice.

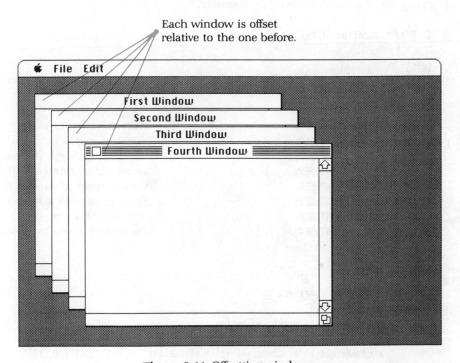

Figure 3-11 Offsetting windows

Program 3-11 (**OffsetWindow**) is the **MiniEdit** routine that offsets the location of each new window relative to the one before. (We'll add a line to our **DoNew** routine to call **OffsetWindow** immediately after creating the window with **NewWindow** or **GetNewWindow**.) **OffsetWindow** gets the window's dimensions from its port rectangle and performs a few straightforward calculations to find the maximum number of windows of that size that it can offset horizontally and vertically before running off the screen's edge. Next it increments its running count of new windows

```
{ Global declarations }

const
    ScreenWidth    = 512;                    {Width of screen in pixels}
    ScreenHeight   = 342;                    {Height of screen in pixels}
    MenuBarHeight  = 20;                     {Height of menu bar in pixels}
    TitleBarHeight = 18;                     {Height of window title bar in pixels}

var
    WindowCount : INTEGER;                   {Number of windows opened so far}


procedure OffsetWindow (whichWindow : WindowPtr);

    { Offset location of new window.  }

    const
        offset = 20;                         {Screen offset from previous window, in pixels}

    var
        windowWidth  : INTEGER;              {Width of window in pixels}
        windowHeight : INTEGER;              {Height of window in pixels}
        hExtra       : INTEGER;              {Excess screen width in pixels}
        vExtra       : INTEGER;              {Excess screen height in pixels}
        hMax         : INTEGER;              {Maximum number of windows horizontally}
        vMax         : INTEGER;              {Maximum number of windows vertically}
        windowLeft   : INTEGER;              {Left edge of window in global coordinates}
        windowTop    : INTEGER;              {Top edge of window in global coordinates}

    begin {OffsetWindow}

        with whichWindow^.portRect do
          begin
            windowWidth  := right  - left;         {Get window dimensions from }
            windowHeight := bottom - top;          {   port rectangle [I:4.2.2]}
            windowHeight := windowHeight + TitleBarHeight    {Adjust for title bar}
          end;

        hExtra := ScreenWidth  - windowWidth;            {Find excess screen width}
        vExtra := ScreenHeight - (windowHeight + MenuBarHeight);  {   and height          }
        hMax   := (hExtra div offset) + 1;               {Find maximum number of windows horizontally}
        vMax   := (vExtra div offset) + 1;               {   and vertically                }
```

Program 3-11 Offset new window

```
WindowCount := WindowCount + 1;                          {Increment window count}
windowLeft  := (WindowCount mod hMax) * offset;          {Calculate offsets}
windowTop   := (WindowCount mod vMax) * offset;
windowTop   := windowTop + TitleBarHeight + MenuBarHeight;  {Adjust for title bar and menu bar}

MoveWindow (whichWindow, windowLeft, windowTop, FALSE)    {Move window to new location [3.3.2]}

end;  {OffsetWindow}
```

Program 3-11 (*continued*)

created since the program was started up, which it keeps in a global program variable (**WindowCount**) so that the count will be preserved from
one execution of **OffsetWindow** to the next. Each new window's location
on the screen is calculated modulo the horizontal and vertical maximum
found earlier, so that on reaching the edge of the screen the windows will
"wrap around" to the opposite edge and continue to offset. Finally the
new window is moved to its offset location with **MoveWindow** [3.3.2].

The tricky part is that we don't want each new window to come up
first at the original location and then jump visibly to its new, offset location. So we have to make the window initially invisible by setting the **visible** parameter to **NewWindow** (or the corresponding field of the window
template supplied to **GetNewWindow**) to **FALSE**. Then, after calling the
OffsetWindow routine to move the window to its offset location, we can
make it visible with **ShowWindow** [3.3.1], causing it to appear for the first
time at the proper location on the screen:

```
TheWindow := GetNewWindow ( . . . );
OffsetWindow (TheWindow);
ShowWindow (TheWindow)
```

This is the actual series of calls we use in our final version of the
DoNew routine (Program 5-2).

REFERENCE

3.1 Internal Representation of Windows

3.1.1 Window Records

Definitions

```
type
  WindowPtr    = GrafPtr;                          {For drawing into window}
  WindowPeek   = ^WindowRecord;                    {For accessing window-specific fields}

  WindowRecord = record
                    port         : GrafPort;       {Graphics port for this window}
                    windowKind   : INTEGER;        {Window class (see notes 3-6)}
                    visible      : BOOLEAN;        {Is window visible?}
                    hilited      : BOOLEAN;        {Is window highlighted?}
                    goAwayFlag   : BOOLEAN;        {Does window have close region?}
                    spareFlag    : BOOLEAN;        {Reserved for future use}
                    strucRgn     : RgnHandle;      {Handle to structure region}
                    contRgn      : RgnHandle;      {Handle to content region}
                    update Rgn   : RgnHandle;      {Handle to update region}
                    windowDefProc : Handle;        {Handle to window definition function}
                    dataHandle   : Handle;         {Handle to definition function's data}
                    titleHandle  : StringHandle;   {Handle to window's title}
                    titleWidth   : INTEGER;        {Private}
                    controlList  : ControlHandle;  {Handle to start of control list}
```

```
          nextWindow    : WindowPeek;        {Pointer to next window in window list}
          windowPic     : PicHandle;         {Handle to QuickDraw picture representing}
                                             {  window's contents (see note 15)}
          refCon        : LONGINT            {Reference constant (see note 9)}
     end;

const
   DialogKind = 2;          {Window class for dialog and alert boxes}
   UserKind   = 8;          {Window class for application-created windows}
```

Notes

1. Use a **WindowPtr** to refer to the window as a graphics port (to draw into it with QuickDraw), a **WindowPeek** to refer to it as a window (to access the remaining fields of the window record).

2. **port** is a complete graphics port record [I:4.2.2] embedded within the window record (not just a pointer).

3. The window class (**windowKind**) is set by the Toolbox when the window is created. Negative values denote system windows, positive values those belonging to your program.

4. Positive window classes from **1** to **7** are reserved for windows created for you by the Toolbox. In particular, your own dialog or alert boxes have a window class of **2** (**DialogKind**).

5. Any positive window class above **7** denotes a window you've created for yourself with **NewWindow** or **GetNewWindow** [3.2.2]. Such windows initially have **windowKind = 8** (**UserKind**), but you can change this for your own purposes to any value greater than **8**.

6. For system windows containing desk accessories, **windowKind** is the accessory's driver reference number [I:7.5.5], which is always negative.

7. The **visible** flag tells whether the window is *logically* visible, even though it may be covered by other windows.

8. The handle to the window definition function (**windowDefProc**) is obtained when the definition function is read into memory from a resource file.

9. **dataHandle** is reserved for use by the window definition function in any way it chooses. **refCon** is for your program's own use.

10. All windows are kept in a window list, linked together through their **nextWindow** fields in front-to-back order as they appear on the screen.

11. The last (rearmost) window in the window list has **nextWindow = NIL**.

12. In assembly language, the beginning of the window list is accessible in the global variable **WindowList**.

13. Each window has a control list beginning in its **controlList** field and linked through the **nextControl** fields of the control records [6.1.1].

14. A window with no controls has **controlList = NIL**.

15. If **windowPic ≠ NIL**, the Toolbox will use this picture to redraw the window's contents when its image on the screen needs updating, instead of generating an update event.

Assembly-Language Information

Field offsets in a window record:

(Pascal) Field name	(Assembly) Offset name	Offset in bytes
port	**windowPort**	**0**
windowKind	**windowKind**	**108**
visible	**wVisible**	**110**
hilited	**wHilited**	**111**
goAwayFlag	**wGoAway**	**112**
strucRgn	**structRgn**	**114**
contRgn	**contRgn**	**118**
updateRgn	**updateRgn**	**122**
windowDefProc	**windowDef**	**126**
dataHandle	**wDataHandle**	**130**
titleHandle	**wTitleHandle**	**134**
titleWidth	**wTitleWidth**	**138**
controlList	**wControlList**	**140**
nextWindow	**nextWindow**	**144**
windowPic	**windowPic**	**148**
refCon	**wRefCon**	**152**

Assembly-language constants:

Name	Value	Meaning
WindowSize	**156**	Size of window record in bytes
DialogKind	**2**	Window class for application's dialog and alert boxes
UserKind	**8**	Window class for windows created by application

Assembly-language global variable:

Name	Address	Meaning
WindowList	**$9D6**	Pointer in first window in window list

3.2 Creating and Destroying Windows

3.2.1 Initialing the Toolbox for Windows

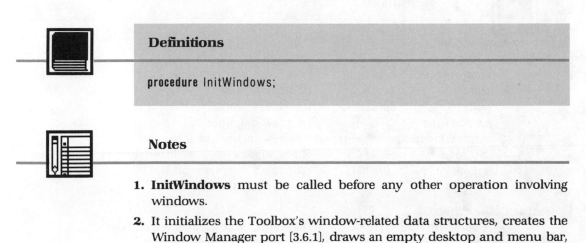

Definitions

procedure InitWindows;

Notes

1. **InitWindows** must be called before any other operation involving windows.

2. It initializes the Toolbox's window-related data structures, creates the Window Manager port [3.6.1], draws an empty desktop and menu bar, and starts an empty window list.

3. Before calling **InitWindows**, you must first call **InitGraf** [I:4.3.1] and **InitFonts** [I:8.2.4].

Assembly-Language Information

Trap macro:

(Pascal) Routine name	(Assembly) Trap macro	Trap word
InitWindows	**_InitWindows**	**$A912**

3.2.2 Creating Windows

Definitions

```
function NewWindow
        (wStorage        : Ptr;              {Storage for window record}
        windowRect       : Rect;             {Window's port rectangle in screen coordinates}
        title            : Str255;           {Window's title}
        visible          : BOOLEAN;          {Is window initially visible?}
        windowType       : INTEGER;          {Window definition ID}
        behindWindow     : WindowPtr;        {Window in front of this one}
        hasClose         : BOOLEAN;          {Does window have a close region?}
        refCon           : LONGINT)          {Window's reference constant}
         : WindowPtr;                        {Pointer to new window}

function GetNewWindow
        (templateID      : INTEGER;          {Resource ID of window template}
        wStorage         : Ptr;              {Storage for window record}
        behindWindow     : WindowPtr)        {Window in front of this one}
         : WindowPtr;                        {Pointer to new window}

const                                        {Standard window definition IDs: }
   DocumentProc  = 0;                         {Standard document window}
   DBoxProc      = 1;                         {Standard dialog or alert box}
   PlainDBoxProc = 2;                         {Dialog or alert box with plain border}
   AltDBoxProc   = 3;                         {Dialog or alert box with "shadow"}
   NoGrowDocProc = 4;                         {Document window with no size box}
   RDocProc      = 16;                        {Accessory window}
```

Notes

1. **NewWindow** and **GetNewWindow** both create a new window, enter it in the window list, and return a pointer to it.

2. **NewWindow** takes its initialization information as parameters, **GetNewWindow** gets it from a window template in a resource file.

3. Both routines return a **WindowPtr**; to access the fields of the new window record, you can convert this pointer to a **WindowPeek** [3.1.1] by typecasting (Volume One, Chapter 2).

4. **templateID** is the resource ID of a window template, resource type **'WIND'** [3.7.1].

5. **wStorage** is a pointer to the storage for the new window record; use **CloseWindow** [3.2.3] to destroy the window when no longer needed. If **wStorage** = **NIL**, storage will be allocated from the heap; use **DisposeWindow** [3.2.3] to destroy.

6. **behindWindow** determines the new window's plane on the screen. It will be inserted in the window list immediately following the designated window.

7. if **behindWindow** = **NIL**, the window goes behind all other windows; if **behindWindow** = **WindowPtr(−1)**, it goes in front of all others and becomes the active window.

8. **windowRect** is expressed in global (screen) coordinates, and will become the port rectangle of the new window's graphics port. The port's coordinate system is adjusted to place the top-left corner of this rectangle at local coordinates (**0, 0**).

9. **title** is the new window's title, and will appear in its title bar.

10. All other fields of the window's graphics port are given the standard initial values [I:4.3.2], except that its text font is the application font instead of the system font.

11. **visible** tells whether the new window is *logically* visible, even though it may be obscured by other windows. The window will be drawn on the screen if visible and exposed.

12. **windowType** is a coded integer (a *window definition ID*) that includes the resource ID of the window definition function. The definition function is read into memory from its resource file and a handle to it is placed in the **windowDefProc** field of the window record [3.1.1].

13. Use the built-in constants **DocumentProc**, **DBoxProc**, **PlainDBox-Proc**, **AltDBoxProc**, **NoGrowDocProc**, and **RDocProc** for the standard window types.

14. The new window's class (field **windowKind** of the window record [3.1.1]) will be set to **UserKind**, meaning that it was created directly by the application. You can then change this to a different value if appropriate.

15. **hasClose** specifies whether the new window has a close box (or close region).

16. **refCon** is the initial value of the window's reference constant.

Assembly-Language Information

Trap macros:

(Pascal) Routine name	(Assembly) Trap macro	Trap word
NewWindow	**_NewWindow**	**$A913**
GetNewWindow	**_GetNewWindow**	**$A9BD**

Standard window definition IDs:

Name	Value	Meaning
DocumentProc	**0**	Standard document window
DBoxProc	**1**	Standard dialog or alert box
PlainDBoxProc	**2**	Dialog or alert box with plain border
AltDBoxProc	**3**	Dialog or alert box with "shadow"
NoGrowDocProc	**4**	Document window with no size box
RDocProc	**16**	Accessory window

3.2.3 Destroying Windows

Definitions

```
procedure CloseWindow
          (theWindow : WindowPtr);    {Window to destroy}
procedure DisposeWindow
          (theWindow : WindowPtr);    {Window to destroy}
```

Notes

1. Both routines destroy a window and remove it from the screen and the window list.

2. **DisposeWindow** frees all storage associated with the window; **CloseWindow** frees all except the window record itself.

3. Use **DisposeWindow** if you let the Toolbox allocate the window record (**wStorage = NIL**) when creating the window [3.2.2, note 5]. If you allocated your own storage for the window record, use **CloseWindow** and then dispose of the window record yourself if appropriate.

4. If you're using the window's reference constant (**refCon**) to hold a handle to auxiliary information about the window [3.2.4, note 4], be sure to dispose of the auxiliary information before destroying the window itself.

5. Both routines automatically destroy all controls associated with the window.

6. If this window covered any others on the screen, they will be updated. If it was the active (frontmost) window, the next-frontmost window will be activated. All needed update and activate events are generated automatically.

7. No deactivate event is generated for the window being destroyed, since the window no longer exists.

8. The trap macro for **DisposeWindow** is spelled **_DisposWindow**.

Assembly-Language Information

Trap macros:

(Pascal) Routine name	(Assembly) Trap macro	Trap word
CloseWindow	**_CloseWindow**	**$A92D**
DisposeWindow	**_DisposWindow**	**$A914**

3.2.4 Setting Window Properties

Definitions

```
procedure SetWTitle
          (theWindow : WindowPtr;      {Pointer to the window}
           newTitle  : Str255);        {New title}

procedure GetWTitle
          (theWindow : WindowPtr;      {Pointer to the window}
           var theTitle : Str255);     {Returns current title}

procedure SetWRefCon
          (theWindow : WindowPtr;      {Pointer to the window}
           newRefCon : LONGINT);       {New reference constant}

function   GetWRefCon
          (theWindow : WindowPtr)      {Pointer to the window}
           : LONGINT;                  {Returns current reference constant}
```

Notes

1. **SetWTitle** sets a window's title; **GetWTitle** returns its current title via parameter **theTitle**. Always use these routines instead of manipulating the window's **titleHandle** field directly.

2. **SetWRefCon** sets a window's reference constant; **GetWRefCon** returns its current reference constant.

3. The reference "constant" (really a variable) is for your program's optional private use. You can give it any 4-byte value that makes sense to your program.

4. If you need more than 4 bytes of private data per window, allocate space for the data from the heap and store a handle to it as the reference constant. (Don't forget to deallocate this space before destroying the window.)

Assembly-Language Information

Trap macros:

(Pascal) Routine name	(Assembly) Trap macro	Trap word
SetWTitle	_SetWTitle	$A91A
GetWTitle	_GetWTitle	$A919
SetWRefCon	_SetWRefCon	$A918
GetWRefCon	_GetWRefCon	$A917

3.3 Window Display

3.3.1 Showing and Hiding Windows

Definitions

```
procedure HideWindow
        (theWindow : WindowPtr);     {Window to hide}

procedure ShowWindow
        (theWindow : WindowPtr);     {Window to show}

procedure ShowHide
        (theWindow : WindowPtr;      {Window to show or hide}
         showFlag  : BOOLEAN);       {Show or hide?}
```

Notes

1. **HideWindow** makes a window invisible; **ShowWindow** makes it visible; **ShowHide** makes it visible if **showFlag = TRUE**, invisible if **FALSE**.

2. Always use these routines to make a window visible or invisible, instead of storing directly into the **visible** field of the window record.

3. Appropriate update events are generated for newly exposed parts of any windows.

4. Hiding an already invisible window or showing an already visible one has no effect.

5. The window's position and plane are unaffected. (*Exception:* Hiding the active (frontmost) window with **HideWindow** deactivates it and activates the next-frontmost window, if any. The activated window is highlighted automatically and the appropriate activate and deactivate events are generated. The activated window is brought to the front of the window list; if the hidden window is later shown again without being activated, it will no longer be frontmost.)

6. **ShowHide** never generates activate or deactivate events or changes the plane or highlighting of any window. Unless you're doing something unusual, you should normally use **HideWindow** and **ShowWindow** instead.

Assembly-Language Information

Trap macros:

(Pascal) Routine name	(Assembly) Trap macro	Trap word
HideWindow	**_HideWindow**	**$A916**
ShowWindow	**_ShowWindow**	**$A915**
ShowHide	**_ShowHide**	**$A908**

3.3.2 Moving and Sizing Windows

Definitions

procedure MoveWindow
    (theWindow : WindowPtr;   {Pointer to the window}
    hGlobal   : INTEGER: {New horizontal position in screen coordinates}
    vGlobal   : INTEGER;   {New vertical position in screen coordinates}
    activate   : BOOLEAN);   {Activate the window?}

procedure SizeWindow
    (theWindow : WindowPtr;   {Pointer to the window}
    newWidth   : INTEGER;   {New width}
    newHeight : INTEGER;   {New height}
    update   : BOOLEAN);   {Update the window?}

Notes

1. **MoveWindow** moves a window to a new location on the screen; **SizeWindow** changes its size.

2. All coordinates apply to the window's port rectangle.

3. For **MoveWindow**, **hGlobal** and **vGlobal** give the new location of the window's top-left corner, in *global* (*screen*) *coordinates*. The window's size remains the same.

4. For **SizeWindow**, **newWidth** and **newHeight** give the window's new dimensions in pixels. The location of the top-left corner remains the same.

5. If **activate** = **TRUE**, **MoveWindow** activates the window (brings it to the front); if **FALSE**, the window's plane is unchanged. **SizeWindow** never changes the window's plane.

6. If **update** = **TRUE** (the usual case), **SizeWindow** generates all needed update events by adding the newly exposed parts of any window's content region (including this one) to the window's update region. If **update** = **FALSE**, you have to handle the updating yourself, for instance by calling **InvalRect** or **InvalRgn** [3.4.2].

7. **SizeWindow** makes all needed adjustments in the window's structure, content, and visible regions.

8. Don't startle the user with sudden jumps in a window's location or size. Ordinarily you should move and size windows only in response to the user's mouse actions, with **DragWindow** and **GrowWindow** [3.5.4].

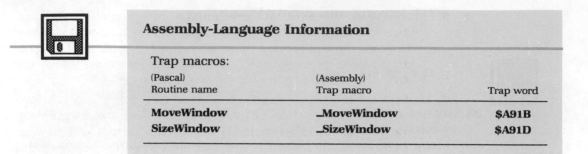

Assembly-Language Information

Trap macros:

(Pascal) Routine name	(Assembly) Trap macro	Trap word
MoveWindow	**_MoveWindow**	**$A91B**
SizeWindow	**_SizeWindow**	**$A91D**

3.3.3 Front-to-Back Ordering

Definitions

function FrontWindow
: WindowPtr;   {The currently active window}

procedure BringToFront
(theWindow   : WindowPtr);   {Window to bring to front}

procedure SendBehind
(theWindow   : WindowPtr;   {Window to demote}
behindWindow : WindowPtr);   {Window to send it behind}

Notes

1. **FrontWindow** returns a pointer to the active window, the frontmost visible window on the screen.

2. **BringToFront** brings a window to the front of the window list and redraws it on the screen in front of all other windows; **SendBehind** "demotes" a window (sends it behind another) and redraws all portions of other windows that are exposed as a result.

3. If **behindWindow** = **NIL**, **theWindow** is sent behind all other windows on the screen.

4. Both **BringToFront** and **SendBehind** generate update events asking you to redraw the needed portions of all affected windows' content regions.

5. If you demote the active window, **SendBehind** generates the appropriate events to deactivate it and activate the next-frontmost window, and adjusts the highlighting of both windows accordingly. **BringTo-Front**, however, never generates any activate or deactivate events and doesn't affect the highlighting of any window.

6. Explicit manipulation of the plane (front-to-back ordering) of windows normally isn't needed. Usually you activate a window by calling **Select-Window** [3.5.2], which automatically brings the designated window to the front, sends the previously active window behind it, and generates all the needed window events.

Assembly-Language Information

Trap macros:

(Pascal) Routine name	(Assembly) Trap macro	Trap word
FrontWindow	**_FrontWindow**	**$A924**
BringToFront	**_BringToFront**	**$A920**
SendBehind	**_SendBehind**	**$A921**

3.3.4 Window Highlighting

Definitions

```
procedure HiliteWindow
        (theWindow : WindowPtr;      {Window to highlight}
         onOrOff    : BOOLEAN);      {Highlight or unhighlight?}
procedure DrawGrowIcon
        (theWindow : WindowPtr);     {Window to draw size region for}
```

Notes

1. **HiliteWindow** highlights a window if **onOrOff** = **TRUE**, unhighlights it if **FALSE**.

2. **DrawGrowIcon** draws a window's size region ("grow icon"), which may vary in appearance depending on whether the window is high-lighted or unhighlighted.

3. Call **DrawGrowIcon** when responding to an activate or deactivate event, to redraw the window's size region to reflect the change.

4. When responding to an update event, call **DrawGrowIcon** if the window's size region is part of the content region (as it is for stan-dard document windows). If the size region is part of the window's frame, it's redrawn automatically.

5. Both routines call the window definition function to do the actual drawing. The definition function determines the window's appearance and the shape, location, and appearance of its size region, depending on the value of its **hilited** flag [3.1.1].

6. Explicit highlighting and unhighlighting of windows normally isn't needed. Activating a window with **SelectWindow** [3.5.2] automatically highlights the window and unhighlights the one that was previously active.

Assembly-Language Information

Trap macros:

(Pascal) Routine name	(Assembly) Trap macro	Trap word
HiliteWindow	**_HiliteWindow**	**$A91C**
DrawGrowIcon	**_DrawGrowIcon**	**$A904**

3.4 Updating Windows

3.4.1 Update Processing

Definitions

procedure BeginUpdate
        (theWindow : WindowPtr);   {Window being updated}
procedure EndUpdate
        (theWindow : WindowPtr);   {Window being updated}

Notes

1. **BeginUpdate** and **EndUpdate** bracket a series of QuickDraw calls for redrawing a window's update region in response to an update event.

2. **BeginUpdate** saves the window's visible region, then restricts the visible region by intersecting it with the update region. Subsequent drawing with QuickDraw will be clipped to this restricted region.

3. **EndUpdate** restores the window's original visible region and sets the update region to empty, clearing the update event.

4. It's sufficient just to redraw the window's update region, but it's usually more convenient to redraw the entire content region and let QuickDraw take care of the clipping.

5. Make sure every call to **BeginUpdate** is balanced by a corresponding call to **EndUpdate**.

Assembly-Language Information

Trap macros:

(Pascal) Routine name	(Assembly) Trap macro	Trap word
BeginUpdate	**_BeginUpdate**	**$A922**
EndUpdate	**_EndUpdate**	**$A923**

3.4.2 Manipulating the Update Region

Definitions

```
procedure InvalRect
          (badRect    : Rect);        {Rectangle to add to update region}

procedure InvalRgn
          (badRegion  : RgnHandle);   {Region to add to update region}

procedure ValidRect
          (goodRect   : Rect);        {Rectangle to remove from update region}

procedure ValidRgn
          (goodRegion : RgnHandle);   {Region to remove from update region}
```

Notes

1. These routines manipulate a window's update region by adding or removing a specified rectangle or region.

2. All operations apply to the window that's the current graphics port. Make sure the current port is a window!

3. The rectangle or region is expressed in local (window) coordinates.

4. **InvalRect** and **InvalRgn** declare a rectangle or region to be invalid—that is, its appearance on the screen doesn't reflect the true state of the desktop. The designated area is added to the window's update region so that it will be redrawn when the window is updated.

5. **ValidRect** and **ValidRgn** declare a rectangle or region to be valid—its appearance on the screen correctly reflects the true state of the desktop. The designated area is removed from the window's update region, since it doesn't need to be redrawn.

Assembly-Language Information

Trap macros:

(Pascal) Routine name	(Assembly) Trap macro	Trap word
InvalRect	**_InvalRect**	**$A928**
InvalRgn	**_InvalRgn**	**$A927**
ValidRect	**_ValidRect**	**$A92A**
ValidRgn	**_ValidRgn**	**$A929**

3.4.3 Window Pictures

Definitions

```
procedure  SetWindowPic
             (theWindow : WindowPtr;        {Pointer to the window}
              thePicture : PicHandle);      {Handle to its new window picture}

function   GetWindowPic
             (theWindow : WindowPtr)        {Pointer to the window}
              : PicHandle;                  {Handle to its current window picture}
```

Notes

1. **SetWindowPic** sets a window's window picture; **GetWindowPic** returns its current picture.

2. The window picture is an alternative to update events for updating a window on the screen. If a window has a picture (**windowPic ≠ NIL** in the window record [3.1.1]), the Toolbox uses the picture to redraw the window when necessary, instead of generating an update event.

3. A window picture is more efficient than using update events if the picture occupies less memory space than the code and data needed to redraw the window yourself.

4. Always use these routines instead of manipulating the **windowPic** field yourself.

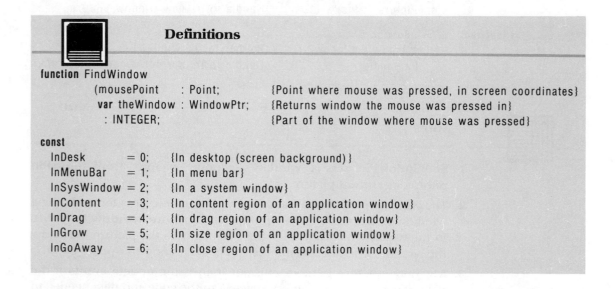

Assembly-Language Information

Trap macros:

(Pascal) Routine name	(Assembly) Trap macro	Trap word
SetWindowPic	**_SetWindowPic**	**$A92E**
GetWindowPic	**_GetWindowPic**	**$A92F**

Assembly-language global variables:

Name	Address	Meaning
CurActivate	**$A64**	Pointer to window awaiting activate event
CurDeactivate	**$A68**	Pointer to window awaiting deactivate event

3.5 Responding to the Mouse

3.5.1 Locating Mouse Clicks

Definitions

```
function FindWindow
          (mousePoint   : Point;        {Point where mouse was pressed, in screen coordinates}
           var theWindow : WindowPtr;    {Returns window the mouse was pressed in}
           : INTEGER;                    {Part of the window where mouse was pressed}

const
  InDesk      = 0;    {In desktop (screen background)}
  InMenuBar   = 1;    {In menu bar}
  InSysWindow = 2;    {In a system window}
  InContent   = 3;    {In content region of an application window}
  InDrag      = 4;    {In drag region of an application window}
  InGrow      = 5;    {In size region of an application window}
  InGoAway    = 6;    {In close region of an application window}
```

Notes

1. **FindWindow** finds which window (or what other part of the screen) contains a given point, normally the point where the mouse button was pressed.

2. **mousePoint** should give the location of a mouse-down event, in *global (screen) coordinates*. This is the form in which the point is reported in the **where** field of the event record [2.1.1].

3. The variable parameter **theWindow** returns a pointer to the window the given point is in, if any.

4. If the point is in the menu bar or the desktop, **theWindow** is set to **NIL**.

5. The function result is a *part code* telling what part of the screen, or of a particular window, contains the given point.

6. **FindWindow** will never return a part code of **InGoAway** for a window that has no close region. However, it may return **InGrow** even for a window with no size region: your program should consider this equivalent to **InContent**.

Assembly-Language Information

Trap macro:

(Pascal) Routine name	(Assembly) Trap macro	Trap word
FindWindow	_FindWindow	$A92C

Part codes:

Name	Value	Meaning
InDesk	0	In desktop (screen background)
InMenuBar	1	In menu bar
InSysWindow	2	In a system window
InContent	3	In content region of an application window
InDrag	4	In drag region of an application window
InGrow	5	In size region of an application window
InGoAway	6	In close region of an application window

3.5.2 Window Selection

Definitions

```
procedure SelectWindow
        (theWindow : WindowPtr);     {Window to activate}
```

Notes

1. **SelectWindow** activates the designated window, after deactivating the one that was previously active.

2. The selected window is redrawn in front of all others on the screen, the highlighting of both windows is adjusted, and the appropriate deactivate and activate events are generated.

3. Call this routine when **FindWindow** reports that the mouse button was pressed inside an inactive window.

Assembly-Language Information

Trap macro:

(Pascal) Routine name	(Assembly) Trap macro	Trap word
SelectWindow	**_SelectWindow**	**$A91F**

3.5.3 Click in a System Window

Definitions

procedure SystemClick
       (theEvent   : EventRecord;   {Event to be processed}
       theWindow : WindowPtr);   {System window affected}

Notes

1. **SystemClick** processes a mouse-down event in a system window. Call it when **FindWindow** [3.5.1] returns a part code of **InSysWindow**.

2. **SystemClick** does all necessary processing to respond to the event, such as activating the window if it's inactive or tracking the mouse in its drag or close region.

3. If the window belongs to a desk accessory, mouse clicks in the content region are passed to the accessory for processing.

Assembly-Language Information

Trap macro:

(Pascal) Routine name	(Assembly) Trap macro	Trap word
SystemClick	**_SystemClick**	**$A9B3**

3.5.4 Drag, Size, and Close Regions

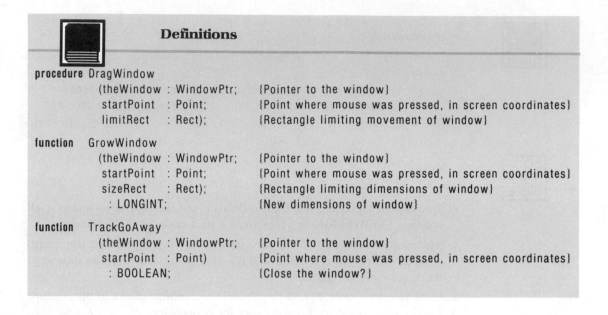

Definitions

```
procedure  DragWindow
             (theWindow : WindowPtr;      {Pointer to the window}
              startPoint : Point;         {Point where mouse was pressed, in screen coordinates}
              limitRect  : Rect);         {Rectangle limiting movement of window}

function   GrowWindow
             (theWindow : WindowPtr;      {Pointer to the window}
              startPoint : Point;         {Point where mouse was pressed, in screen coordinates}
              sizeRect   : Rect);         {Rectangle limiting dimensions of window}
               : LONGINT;                 {New dimensions of window}

function   TrackGoAway
             (theWindow : WindowPtr;      {Pointer to the window}
              startPoint : Point)         {Point where mouse was pressed, in screen coordinates}
               : BOOLEAN;                 {Close the window?}
```

Notes

1. All of these routines keep control for as long as the user holds down the mouse button, tracking the movements of the mouse and providing visual feedback on the screen, then perform some action when the button is released.

2. Call **DragWindow** when **FindWindow** [3.5.1] reports that the mouse button was pressed in a window's drag region (part code **InDrag**); **GrowWindow** if it was pressed in the size region (**InGrow**); **TrackGoAway** if it was pressed in the close region (**InGoAway**).

3. **startPoint** should give the location of a mouse-down event, in *global (screen) coordinates*. This is the form in which the point is reported in the **where** field of the event record [2.1.1].

4. **DragWindow** follows the mouse with an outline of the window. When the button is released, the window is moved to the new location: you needn't call **MoveWindow** [3.3.2].

5. If the window being moved isn't the active window, **DragWindow** activates it and brings it to the front unless the user is holding down the command key.

6. **limitRect** is a rectangle in global coordinates. If the mouse leaves this rectangle, the window outline disappears from the screen; it will reappear if the mouse re-enters the rectangle while the button is still down. If the button is released outside the rectangle, the window's position and plane are left unchanged.

7. **GrowWindow** displays an outline of the window with its size region following the mouse's movements. When the button is released, **GrowWindow** returns a long integer giving the new dimensions of the window.

8. The high-order word of the function result gives the new height of the window in pixels; the low-order word gives its width.

9. A result of **0** means the window's size is to be left unchanged.

10. **GrowWindow** doesn't actually adjust the window's size for you; you have to do it yourself by calling **SizeWindow** [3.3.2].

11. **sizeRect** sets limits on the window's dimensions. The **left** and **right** fields of this rectangle give the window's minimum and maximum width in pixels; **top** and **bottom** give its minimum and maximum height. As the user moves the mouse, the window's outline will "pin" at these size limits.

12. **TrackGoAway** highlights and unhighlights the window's close region as the user moves the mouse into and out of the region (while holding down the button). The exact appearance of the close region when highlighted and unhighlighted is determined by the window definition function.

13. When the button is released, **TrackGoAway** returns **TRUE** if the mouse is inside the close region, **FALSE** if it isn't. If **TRUE**, you can then make the window invisible with **HideWindow** [3.3.1] or destroy it with **CloseWindow** or **DisposeWindow** [3.2.3], depending on the needs of your application; **TrackGoAway** doesn't do any of this for you.

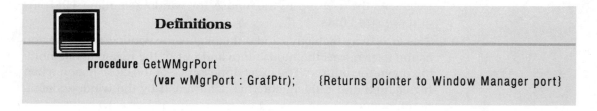

Assembly-Language Information

Trap macros:

(Pascal) Routine name	(Assembly) Trap macro	Trap word
DragWindow	**_DragWindow**	**$A925**
GrowWindow	**_GrowWindow**	**$A92B**
TrackGoAway	**_TrackGoAway**	**$A91E**

3.6 Nuts and Bolts

3.6.1 Nuts and Bolts

Definitions

```
procedure GetWMgrPort
          (var wMgrPort : GrafPtr);    {Returns pointer to Window Manager port}
```

Notes

1. **GetWMgrPort** returns a pointer to the Window Manager port, the graphics port in which the Toolbox draws all window frames. The port rectangle of this port is the entire screen.

2. In assembly language, a pointer to the Window Manager port is available in the global variable **WMgrPort**. Another full-screen port is available for general-purpose use as **DeskPort**. Global variable **GrayRgn** holds a handle to the rounded-corner region defining the gray desktop within these ports.

Assembly-Language Information

Trap macro:

(Pascal) Routine name	(Assembly) Trap macro	Trap word
GetWMgrPort	**_GetWMgrPort**	**$A910**

Assembly-language global variables:

Name	Address	Meaning
WMgrPort	**$9DE**	Pointer to Window Manager port
DeskPort	**$9E2**	Pointer to general-purpose full-screen port
GrayRgn	**$9EE**	Handle to region defining gray desktop

3.7 Window-Related Resources

3.7.1 Resource Type 'WIND'

```
┌─────────────────────────────────────────┐
│                                         │
│              windowRect                 │
│              (8 bytes)                  │
│                                         │
├─────────────────────────────────────────┤
│          windowType (2 bytes)           │
├─────────────────────────────────────────┤
│           visible (2 bytes)             │
├─────────────────────────────────────────┤
│          hasClose (2 bytes)             │
├─────────────────────────────────────────┤
│                refCon                   │
│              (4 bytes)                   │
├──────────────────┬──────────────────────┤
│ Length of title  │                      │
├──────────────────┴──────────────────────┤
│                                         │
│                                         │
│                 title                   │
│          (indefinite length)            │
│                                         │
│                                         │
└─────────────────────────────────────────┘
```

Format of resource type 'WIND'

Notes

1. A resource of type **'WIND'** contains a window template.

2. All fields of the window template are in the same form as the corresponding parameters to **NewWindow** [3.2.2].

3. The window title is in Pascal string form, with a 1-byte length count followed by the characters of the title. The overall size of the window template depends on the length of the title string.

4. To create a window from a window template, call **GetNewWindow** [3.2.2] with the template's resource ID.

CHAPTER

4

What's on the Menu?

Macintosh's "pull-down" menus are in keeping with the overall Macintosh philosophy of keeping the user in control. Macintosh menus don't take over the screen and demand attention; they wait patiently, hidden under the menu bar, ready to spring to life at a click of the mouse. They free the user from having to remember cryptic command sequences to be typed from the keyboard. They're easy to back out of if you change your mind. And they serve as an on-screen reminder of what operations are available from moment to moment.

Naturally, the User Interface Toolbox includes a full set of facilities for working with menus. In this chapter, you'll learn how to define your own menus, display them on the screen, and put them at the user's disposal to control the operation of your program.

Anatomy of a Menu

Most of the time, all that's visible to the user in the way of menus is the *menu bar* at the top of the screen, listing the titles of the available menus. By pressing and holding down the mouse button over one of these titles, the user can "pull down" the menu itself, which offers a list of *items* to choose from. Dragging the mouse down the menu with the button still down causes one item after another to become highlighted on the screen. When the button is released, the currently highlighted item will take effect; this is called *choosing* an item. (Notice that choosing is not the same as selecting in Macintosh terminology: you select something to work on, then choose an operation to apply to it.) If no item is highlighted when the button is released—for instance, if the mouse has moved outside the frame of the menu—then the menu just vanishes harmlessly from the screen.

Like windows, menus can come in various types. The appearance and behavior of any given type of menu are defined by a *menu definition procedure*, which the Toolbox calls whenever it needs to draw the menu on the screen or make it respond to the mouse. Menu definition procedures are kept in resource files under resource type '**MDEF**'. Unless you're doing something very unusual, you'll just want to use the standard type of *text menu*, whose definition procedure is found in the system resource file; the Toolbox will always assume you want a text menu unless you explicitly tell it otherwise. All descriptions in this chapter apply specifically to standard text menus; if you want to define other menu types for special needs, see the *Inside Macintosh* manual.

Figure 4-1 shows a typical text menu. Each item consists of a separate line of text, displayed in the standard system font. Items that aren't applicable at any given moment are "dimmed" (displayed in gray instead of black) to show that they can't be chosen. Such items are said to be *disabled*, and don't highlight when pointed at with the mouse; those that can be chosen are *enabled*. For example, the menu shown in the figure has the **Cut** and **Copy** items disabled, presumably because there is nothing currently selected to cut or copy.

A program can define an optional *keyboard alias* for any menu item, for the convenience of users who are fast with their fingers. This is a combination of the command key together with some other key, with which the user can invoke the item from the keyboard instead of choosing it with the mouse. The alias, if there is one, is displayed to the right of the item on the menu, preceded by the "cloverleaf" command symbol. For instance, in Figure 4-1 the **Undo** command has the keyboard alias Command-**Z**, while **Show Clipboard** has no alias.

Figure 4-1 Standard menu

Keyboard aliases are purely an added convenience for the user, and are strictly optional. They're especially useful in keyboard-intensive applications such as word processing, to reduce the amount of hand motion between keyboard and mouse. The command key should never be the only way to perform an operation; the user should always have the option of choosing the command from the menu in the usual way.

Although the text of a menu item is always shown in the standard system font, you can vary its appearance with character style attributes such as bold, italic, or outline (see Figure 4-2). You can also mark any item with a *check mark*, as in the figure. This is useful for items that control a two-way, on-or-off setting of some kind; the presence or absence of a check mark displays the current setting visually on the screen. (Actually you can mark an item with any character you like, but the check mark is by far the most common.)

One last capability that's available, though seldom used, is to associate a 32-by-32-bit icon with any menu item. If an item has an icon, it appears to the left of the item's text on the menu; the check mark, if any, goes to the left of the icon.

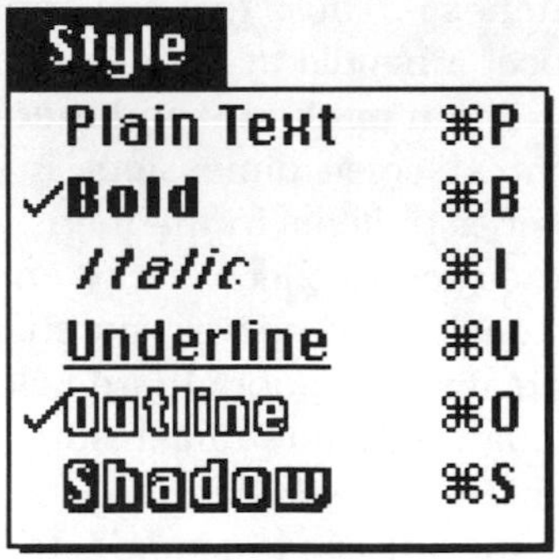

Figure 4-2 Character style and check marks

Menu Records

To define a new menu, you can either build one up "from scratch," starting with an empty menu and adding items one by one, or you can read in a predefined menu from a resource file. In either case, the Toolbox allocates heap space for a *menu record* [4.1.1] and gives you back a handle to it. The fields of this record hold all the information about one particular menu. In general, you should use Toolbox routines to read or change the information in a menu record, rather than manipulate the record's fields directly. (The one exception is the **menuProc** field, as described below.)

Every menu has an identifying number called a *menu ID*, kept in the **menuID** field of the menu record. You supply the menu ID when you create a new menu. Once assigned, the ID for a given menu should never change: don't ever attempt to store a new value into the **menuID** field. If you follow the recommended practice of predefining your menus and reading them in as resources, the menu ID is simply the resource ID of the menu (under resource type 'MENU' [4.8.1]) in the resource file. For menus that your program builds for itself, you can choose any positive number you like for the menu ID. (Negative IDs are reserved for menus belonging to desk accessories; a menu ID of **0** isn't allowed.) Needless to say, no two menus should ever have the same menu ID.

The Toolbox maintains a private data structure representing the menu bar, containing handles to all menus currently available to the user. (Technically this is called the *menu list*, but it's usually just referred to as "the menu bar.") Not all menus have to be in the menu bar at all times. A menu in the menu bar is said to be *active*; if it isn't in the menu bar, it's *inactive*. Toolbox routines that apply specifically to active menus generally accept a menu ID as an argument and scan the menu bar for a menu that matches it. Those that can apply to any menu, whether active or inactive, expect a handle to the menu in memory rather than an ID number.

The **menuWidth** and **menuHeight** fields of the menu record give the menu's screen dimensions in pixels. These dimensions depend on the number of items in the menu, their length, whether they have keyboard aliases, icons, check marks, and so on. The Toolbox itself recalculates the dimensions whenever you change the contents of the menu, so you can normally just ignore these fields. If for some reason you ever want to recalculate a menu's dimensions explicitly, you can use the Toolbox routine **CalcMenuSize** [4.7.1].

menuProc is a handle to the menu definition procedure, which will almost always be the one for the standard type of text menu. When you read in a menu from a resource file, the Toolbox also reads in the definition procedure (if it isn't already in memory) and stores a handle to it into this field. When you create an empty menu to build from scratch, **menu-Proc** is automatically set to the standard definition procedure; in those rare cases where you want to use some other definition procedure instead, you have to store its handle into this field yourself after creating the menu.

enableFlags is a 32-bit field that controls whether the items on the menu are enabled or disabled. Each bit except the first corresponds to a single item: **1** if the item is enabled, **0** if it's disabled. (This means that each menu is limited to a maximum of 31 items.) The first (high-order) bit applies to the menu as a whole rather than any single item. When this bit is **0**, it overrides all the others: every item on the menu is disabled, regardless of its own individual enable flag.

> Always use the Toolbox routines **EnableItem** and **DisableItem** [4.6.2] instead of manipulating the enable flags yourself.

The most important field of a menu record is **menuData**, which defines the text and other properties of all the items in the menu [4.1.1]. From the Pascal point of view, the **menuData** field just looks like a string giving the title of the menu, with a 1-byte character count followed by the characters of the title itself. The information defining the individual menu items is "hidden" beyond the end of the title string, where only the Toolbox can get at it. The only way to access or change this information is to call the appropriate Toolbox routines and let the Toolbox do it for you.

> *Never* store a menu title directly into the **menuData** field; this will destroy the "hidden" information about the items the menu contains.

Building Menus

The first step in using menus is to define your menus and install them in the menu bar. As we've already mentioned, there are two ways of doing this. In this section, we'll learn how to build up menus "from scratch"; later we'll see how to read them in as predefined resources.

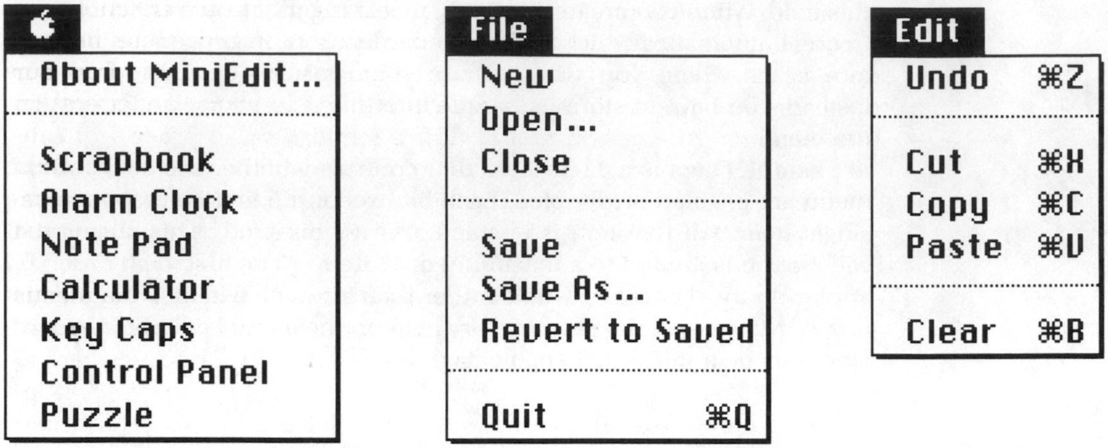

Figure 4-3 MiniEdit menus

Figure 4-3 shows the menus used by our example program **MiniEdit**. These three menus are considered standard; by convention, it's recommended that every Macintosh application start with these same three menus (or something like them) at the beginning of the menu bar. The first is the "Apple menu," containing the names of all available desk accessories. Then come the **File** menu, with commands for opening and closing windows and reading and writing documents, and the **Edit** menu, which includes the standard editing commands **Cut**, **Copy**, **Paste**, **Clear**, and **Undo**. Any application that supports desk accessories must include these editing commands even if it doesn't use them itself, since some of the accessories expect them to be available. (We'll see later how such menu commands get passed to the desk accessory whenever one is active.) After the Apple, **File**, and **Edit** menus, you can add any others you may need for your own purposes.

Starting the menu bar with the three standard menus is only a general recommendation, not an ironclad rule. If they don't make sense for a particular application, you can of course leave them out: a program that doesn't support desk accessories or use any of the standard filing operations might omit them all.

In our **MiniEdit** program, the job of defining the menus is handled by a procedure named **SetUpMenus**. The menus only have to be defined once, at the beginning of the program, so **SetUpMenus** is called from our one-time **Initialize** routine (Program 2-6). Before attempting any operation involving menus, you first have to call the initialization procedure **Init-Menus** [4.2.1], which in turn must be preceded by calls to **InitGraf** [I:4.3.1], **InitFonts** [I:8.2.4], and **InitWindows** [3.2.1]. Our **Initialize** procedure will already have taken care of these preliminary calls by the time it calls **SetUpMenus**.

Program 4-1 shows a version of **SetUpMenus** that builds the menus from scratch. The Apple menu is atypical and requires somewhat special treatment, so we'll discuss the **File** and **Edit** menus first and come back to the Apple menu later. After defining these three standard menus, **SetUp-Menus** could of course go on to build any further menus a particular application might need.

To build a menu from scratch, we begin by creating a brand-new, empty menu with **NewMenu** [4.2.2], then add the items to it one by one. **NewMenu** accepts an integer menu ID and a string defining the menu's title; it allocates heap space for a new menu record and returns a handle to it. As mentioned earlier, menus that a program builds for itself can have any positive ID number. By convention, the Apple menu has an ID of **1**, so we might as well use IDs **2** and **3** for the **File** and **Edit** menus, respectively.

Once you've created a new menu, you can use **AppendMenu** [4.3.1] to add items to it. New items are always added at the end; there's no way to insert an item at the beginning or in the middle of a menu. There's also no way to delete an item once it's been appended, or to reorder the items within a menu (short of rebuilding the whole menu from scratch).

Along with a handle to the menu, **AppendMenu** accepts a *defining string* describing the item to be added. In its simplest form, the defining string is just the text of the item as you want it to appear on the menu. For example, in Program 4-1, the statement

```
AppendMenu (FileMenu, 'New')
```

adds an item to the **File** menu consisting of the word **New**, initially enabled, with no icon, check mark, keyboard alias, or fancy character style.

```
{ Global constants and variables }

const
    AppleID = 1;                                {Menu ID for Apple menu}
    FileID  = 2;                                {Menu ID for File menu}
    EditID  = 3;                                {Menu ID for Edit menu}

var
    AppleMenu  : MenuHandle;                    {Handle to Apple menu [4.1.1]}
    FileMenu   : MenuHandle;                    {Handle to File menu [4.1.1]}
    EditMenu   : MenuHandle;                    {Handle to Edit menu [4.1.1]}


procedure SetUpMenus;

    { Procedure to set up menus by direct definition. }

    var
        appleTitle : Str255;                    {Title for Apple menu [I:2.1.1]}

    begin {SetUpMenus}

        appleTitle    := 'a';                   {Set up title for Apple menu        }
        appleTitle[1] := CHR(AppleMark);        {   with special Apple symbol [I:8.1.1]}

        AppleMenu := NewMenu (AppleID, appleTitle);  {Make Apple menu [4.2.2]}
        AppendMenu (AppleMenu, 'About MiniEdit...');  {Add items [4.3.1]}
        AppendMenu (AppleMenu, '(------------------');
        AddResMenu (AppleMenu, 'DRVR');         {Add names of available desk accessories [4.3.3]}
        InsertMenu (AppleMenu, 0);              {Install at end of menu bar [4.4.1]}

        FileMenu := NewMenu (FileID, 'File');   {Make File menu [4.2.2]}
        AppendMenu (FileMenu, 'New');           {Add items [4.3.1]}
        AppendMenu (FileMenu, 'Open...');
        AppendMenu (FileMenu, 'Close');
        AppendMenu (FileMenu, '(---------------');
        AppendMenu (FileMenu, 'Save');
        AppendMenu (FileMenu, 'Save As...');
        AppendMenu (FileMenu, 'Revert to Saved');
        AppendMenu (FileMenu, '(---------------');
        AppendMenu (FileMenu, 'Quit/Q');
        InsertMenu (FileMenu, 0);               {Install at end of menu bar [4.4.1]}
```

Program 4-1 Set up menus by direct definition

```
EditMenu := NewMenu (EditID, 'Edit');          {Make Edit menu [4.2.2]}
AppendMenu (EditMenu, 'Undo/Z');               {Add items [4.3.1]}
AppendMenu (EditMenu, '(-------');
AppendMenu (EditMenu, 'Cut/X');
AppendMenu (EditMenu, 'Copy/C');
AppendMenu (EditMenu, 'Paste/V');
AppendMenu (EditMenu, '(-------');
AppendMenu (EditMenu, 'Clear/B');
InsertMenu (EditMenu, 0);                       {Install at end of menu bar [4.4.1]}

{Insert code here to define any other needed menus};

DrawMenuBar                                     {Show new menu bar on screen [4.4.3]}

end;   {SetUpMenus}
```

Program 4-1 (*continued*)

> The text of a menu item must always include at least one character;
> the null string is not allowed. If you want to leave a completely
> blank line in a menu, you have to use an item consisting of one or
> more space characters:
>
> ```
> AppendMenu (anyMenu, ' ')
> ```

To exercise more control over an item's properties, you can include
modifier characters [4.3.2] in the defining string you give to **Append-
Menu**. For instance, a left parenthesis as the first character of the defining
string tells the Toolbox that the item you're defining should be
disabled rather than enabled. In Program 4-1, the statement

```
AppendMenu (FileMenu, '(--------------')
```

defines an item consisting simply of a row of dashes, to serve as a separator between different sections of the menu. Since this is not intended to
be a meaningful menu item in itself, we use a left parenthesis as a
modifier character to disable it; this makes the item appear "dimmed"
on the menu that prevents the user from choosing it with the mouse.

Similarly, the modifier character / (slash) introduces a keyboard alias for the item being defined. The statement

```
AppendMenu (EditMenu, 'Cut/X')
```

defines a menu item whose text is the word **Cut**, with Command-**X** as a keyboard alias. The alias will be displayed to the right of the item on the menu, preceded by the command symbol, as we saw earlier in Figure 4-1.

As shown in Program 4-1, the first four keys in the bottom row of the keyboard (**ZXCV** in the standard American layout) are reserved by convention as keyboard aliases for the standard editing commands **Undo**, **Cut**, **Copy**, and **Paste**, respectively. To conform to the Macintosh User Interface Guidelines, any program that includes these commands should also provide these standard aliases. (The next key in the same row, **B**, is sometimes used for the **Clear** command, but this is not part of the official convention and some programs use it for other purposes instead. Command-**Q** for **Quit** is another common alias whose use is strongly encouraged but not officially required.)

You can define two or more menu items in one call to **AppendMenu** by separating them with semicolons (;) in the defining string. For instance, Program 4-1 could have combined the **Cut**, **Copy**, and **Paste** commands into a single definition

```
AppendMenu (EditMenu, 'Cut/X;Copy/C;Paste/V')
```

instead of using three separate statements. There are other modifier characters that you can use as well; they're summarized in [4.3.2], and we'll be discussing some of them further in the section titled "Controlling Menu Items," later in this chapter.

Sometimes a menu command needs further information from the user in order to operate: for instance, the **Open** command needs to know what document to open. The normal way to get such extra information from the user is with a dialog box; we'll learn how in Chapter 7. The only point to notice here is that menu items that open a dialog box are conventionally supposed to end with three dots, like **Open...** and **SaveAs...** in Program 4-1.

After you've added all the items you want to a menu, you have to place it in the menu bar with **InsertMenu** [4.4.1]. Unlike appending items to a menu, you can insert a menu in the menu bar anywhere you like, by giving the ID of the menu it precedes (or **0** to put it at the end). Also unlike items in a menu, menus can be deleted from the menu bar as well as added. However, accepted user interface style is to avoid changing the contents of the menu bar "on the fly." Appearing and disappearing menus can be disconcerting to the user; it's better to leave all your menus in the menu bar all the time and disable those that aren't applicable at any given moment.

One thing to watch out for is that changes you make in the menu bar don't take place automatically on the screen. After inserting or deleting a menu, you have to redraw the menu bar explicitly with **DrawMenuBar** [4.4.3] to make the change visible to the user.

Listing Resources on a Menu

Now that we've seen how to set up the **File** and **Edit** menus, let's go back and look at the Apple menu. This menu is atypical in several ways. First of all, the Apple symbol that's used for its title is one of those special Macintosh characters (along with the check mark and the "cloverleaf" command symbol) that can be displayed on the screen but can't be typed from the keyboard [I:8.1.1]. Since Pascal won't let us store a "raw" character directly into a string variable, we have to create a one-character dummy string for the menu's title and store the Apple symbol into it "by hand":

```
appleTitle    := '@';
appleTitle[1] := CHR(AppleMark);

appleMenu := NewMenu (appleID, appleTitle)
```

(The @ character used here is just a placeholder; it doesn't matter what character you use.)

The Apple menu conventionally starts with an "**About**" item. This item brings up a dialog or alert box (Chapter 7) containing identifying information about the program, such as the author's name, a copyright notice, the version number and date, and so forth. If you're so inclined, you can liven up your "about" box with fancy layout and graphics, or show additional information such as the amount of free disk space available. Some applications even use it to offer the user on-screen documentation or "help" facilities. Since the **About** item opens a dialog box, it should end with the usual three dots:

AppendMenu (AppleMenu, 'About MiniEdit...')

The rest of the Apple menu lists the available desk accessories that the user can open while running our program. We can't define these items with **AppendMenu** in the program itself, because we don't know what desk accessories will be available on the disk when the program is run. Recall that desk accessories are actually a special kind of input/output driver, and reside in the system resource file under resource type **'DRVR'** [I:7.5.5]. To list them on a menu, we need to use **AddResMenu** [4.3.3]. This routine accepts a menu handle and a resource type; it searches all open resource files for resources of the given type and adds their resource names to the menu.

> Not all **'DRVR'** resources are desk accessories, however: some of them are bona fide I/O drivers, and shouldn't appear on the Apple menu. To keep such resources off the menu, they're conventionally given names beginning with a period, such as **.Sound** and **.Print**. **AddResMenu** ignores all names of this form and doesn't add them to the menu.

You can use **AddResMenu** to create menus of any resource type that can be identified by name as well as ID number—in fact, this is precisely the reason resources have names in the first place. Another common use of **AddResMenu** is to set up a menu of available fonts (resource type **'FONT'** [I:8.4.5]). There's also a routine called **InsertResMenu** [4.3.3], which works similarly to **AddResMenu**. The difference is that it allows you to insert the list of resources before any designated item in the menu, rather than only at the end. For some reason, however, **InsertResMenu** adds items to the menu in the opposite order from **AddResMenu**; it's recommended that you use **AddResMenu** whenever possible, so that all applications will list their desk accessories (or fonts, or whatever) in the same order.

Menus as Resources

The alternative (and recommended) way to set up your program's menus is by reading them in as resources. A resource of type **'MENU'** [4.8.1] consists of a complete menu record, including the "hidden" data in the

menuData field describing the individual items. In the resource file, the record's **menuWidth** and **menuHeight** are set to **0**; these fields will be filled in with their correct values when the menu is read into memory. In the **menuProc** field, in place of the handle to the menu definition procedure, is a resource ID for finding the definition procedure in a resource file under resource type 'MDEF'. (The resource ID is in the first 2 bytes of the 4-byte field, with **0** in the last 2 bytes; the standard menu definition procedure has resource ID **0**, so for most menu resources the **menuProc** field is just a 4-byte **0**.)

Program 4-2 shows an alternative version of our **SetUpMenus** procedure that reads the program's menus from a resource file instead of building them from scratch. Instead of creating the menus with **NewMenu**, this time we use **GetMenu** [4.2.2] to read them in under the appropriate resource IDs, which also become their menu IDs. **GetMenu** calculates each menu's screen dimensions and stores them into its **menuWidth** and **menuHeight** fields. It also uses the resource ID given in the **menuProc** field of the menu resource to locate the menu definition procedure, loads the procedure into memory if necessary, and stores its handle into the **menuProc** field of the menu record in memory.

The **File** and **Edit** menus are ready to insert in the menu bar just the way we find them in the resource file. For the Apple menu, however, the menu resource defines only the first two items, the **About MiniEdit...** item and the disabled separator line. Before inserting the menu in the menu bar, we have to add the names of all the available desk accessories with **AddResMenu**, as before.

> If you need to dispose of a menu in mid-program, use **Dispose-Menu** [4.2.3] if you originally created the menu from scratch with **NewMenu**, or **ReleaseResource** [I:6.3.2] if you read it from a resource file with **GetMenu**.

It's also possible to read in a whole menu bar from a resource file, with resource type 'MBAR' [4.8.2]. This resource type is just a list of the resource IDs of the menus in the menu bar. You use **GetNewMBar** [4.4.2] to read it in and convert it to a menu bar in memory. This automatically locates all the needed menus in the resource file, loads them into memory, and inserts them in the new menu bar. The new menu bar doesn't automatically replace the current one, however; you have to remember to call **SetMenuBar** [4.4.4] if you want to make it current, followed by **DrawMenuBar** [4.4.3] to show it on the screen.

```
{ Global constants and variables }

const
    AppleID = 1;                                {Menu ID for Apple menu}
    FileID  = 2;                                {Menu ID for File menu}
    EditID  = 3;                                {Menu ID for Edit menu}


var
    AppleMenu : MenuHandle;                     {Handle to Apple menu [4.1.1]}
    FileMenu  : MenuHandle;                     {Handle to File menu [4.1.1]}
    EditMenu  : MenuHandle;                     {Handle to Edit menu [4.1.1]}


procedure SetUpMenus;

    { Procedure to set up menus using resources. }

    begin {SetUpMenus}

        AppleMenu := GetMenu (AppleID);         {Get Apple menu from resource file [4.2.2]}
        AddResMenu (AppleMenu, 'DRVR');         {Add names of available desk accessories [4.3.3]}
        InsertMenu (AppleMenu, 0);              {Install at end of menu bar [4.4.1]}

        FileMenu := GetMenu (FileID);           {Get File menu from resource file [4.2.2]}
        InsertMenu (FileMenu, 0);               {Install at end of menu bar [4.4.1]}

        EditMenu := GetMenu (EditID);           {Get Edit menu from resource file [4.2.2]}
        InsertMenu (EditMenu, 0);               {Install at end of menu bar [4.4.1]}

        {Insert code here to read in any other needed menus};

        DrawMenuBar                             {Show new menu bar on screen [4.4.3]}

    end;  {SetUpMenus}
```

Program 4-2 Set up menus using resources

Choosing from a Menu

The user can invoke a menu item in either of two ways: by choosing it with the mouse or by typing its keyboard alias using the command key. You find out about the first by receiving a mouse-down event in the menu bar, the second by receiving a key-down event with the **CmdKey** bit on in the **modifiers** field [2.1.5]. Both user actions are considered equivalent, and your program should respond to both in exactly the same way.

In our **MiniEdit** program, recall that all events are processed by the procedure **DoEvent** (Program 2-5), which is called repeatedly from the program's main loop. That procedure asks the Toolbox for the next event and then calls the appropriate routine to handle the event, depending on its type. In the case of mouse-down events, it calls **DoMouseDown** (Program 3-7), which in turn calls the Toolbox routine **FindWindow** [3.5.1] to find out what part of the screen the mouse button was pressed in. If it was in the menu bar, **DoMouseDown** will call a routine named **Do-MenuClick**, which is shown here as Program 4-3.

```
{ Global variable }

var
    TheEvent : EventRecord;                    {Current event [2.1.1]}


procedure DoMenuClick;

    { Handle mouse-down event in menu bar. }

    var
        menuChoice : LONGINT;                  {Menu ID and item number}

    begin {DoMenuClick}

        menuChoice := MenuSelect (TheEvent.where);   {Track mouse [4.5.1]}
        DoMenuChoice (menuChoice)                    {Handle user's menu choice [Prog. 4-5]}

    end;  {DoMenuClick}
```

Program 4-3 Mouse-down event in the menu bar

DoMenuClick is only two statements long: all it does is call the Toolbox routine **MenuSelect** [4.5.1] to handle the menu interaction with the user, then pass along the resulting information about the user's menu choice for another **MiniEdit** routine named **DoMenuChoice** to respond to. We'll be looking at **DoMenuChoice** in a minute; it's separated out as an independent procedure so that it can be called in response to command keystrokes as well as menu choices with the mouse.

MenuSelect needs to know where on the screen, in global coordinates, the mouse button was originally pressed. It then tracks the mouse for as long as the button is held down, showing and hiding menus and highlighting and unhighlighting individual items as the user rolls the mouse over them. When the button is released, it flashes the chosen item a few times and then hides the menu, but leaves its title highlighted in the menu bar as a signal that the item is still being processed. Finally, it returns a long integer identifying the chosen item, consisting of the menu ID in the high-order word and an *item number* in the low-order word. The item number is just the sequential position of the chosen item within the menu, counting the first item as number **1**. If the user released the button over a disabled item, or outside of any menu, the long integer result returned by **MenuSelect** will be **0**.

In addition to your program's menus, an active desk accessory can insert a whole menu of its own in the menu bar. The Toolbox recognizes menus belonging to desk accessories by their negative menu IDs. When the user chooses an item from such a menu, **MenuSelect** automatically relays the choice to the desk accessory for action, then returns **0** to your program, telling you to ignore the event.

When our **DoEvent** routine (Program 2-5) receives a key-down or auto-key event, it calls **DoKeystroke** (Program 4-4) to process the event. Here we begin by extracting from the event's **message** field the character code identifying which character was typed on the keyboard. Then we examine the command bit in the event's **modifiers** field to see whether the user held down the command key while typing the character. If not, we pass the character to the routine **DoTyping** (defined in the next chapter) to handle as an ordinary keystroke.

```
{ Global variable }

var
    TheEvent : EventRecord;                                  {Current event [2.1.1]}


procedure DoKeystroke;

  { Handle keystroke. }

  var
    chCode     : INTEGER;                                    {Character code from event message [I:8.1.1]}
    ch         : CHAR;                                       {Character that was typed}
    menuChoice : LONGINT;                                    {Menu ID and item number for keyboard alias}

  begin {DoKeystroke}

    with TheEvent do
      begin

          chCode := BitAnd (message, CharCodeMask);          {Get character code from event message [I:2.2.2, 2.1.4]}
          ch := CHR(chCode);                                 {Convert to a character}

          if BitAnd (modifiers, CmdKey) <> 0 then            {Command key down? [I:2.2.2, 2.1.5]}
            begin
                if what <> AutoKey then                      {Ignore repeats with Command key down [2.1.1, 2.1.2]}
                  begin
                      menuChoice := MenuKey (ch);            {Get menu equivalent [4.5.1]}
                      DoMenuChoice (menuChoice)             {Handle as menu choice [Prog. 4-5]}
                  end
            end
          else
            DoTyping (ch)                                    {Handle as normal character [Prog. 5-6]}

      end {with}

  end; {DoKeystroke}
```

Program 4-4 Process keystroke

If the command key *was* down, we next check the type of the event (field **what** of the event record) to see whether it was a key-down or an auto-key event. (Command-key combinations aren't supposed to repeat when held down, so we simply ignore auto-key events in this case.) For true key-down events only, we call the Toolbox routine **MenuKey** [4.5.1] to convert the command combination into an equivalent menu item. **MenuKey** returns a long integer consisting of a menu ID and item number, just the same as **MenuSelect**, or **0** if the given command combination hasn't been defined as a keyboard alias for any menu item. We can then pass this result to our **DoMenuChoice** routine just as if it had come from **MenuSelect** instead of **MenuKey**. (Notice that this mechanism guarantees that every meaningful command keystroke is just an alias for a menu item that could have been chosen with the mouse instead.)

As we've just seen, both the user's menu choices with the mouse and the equivalent command keystrokes get passed to our **MiniEdit** program's **DoMenuChoice** routine (Program 4-5) for processing. **DoMenuChoice** first checks to see if the result received from **MenuSelect** or **MenuKey** is **0**, in which case there's nothing to do: the user has moved out of the menu before releasing the button, or chosen a disabled menu item, or typed an invalid keyboard alias. If the menu choice is nonzero, we extract the menu ID and item number with the utility routines **HiWord** and **LoWord** [I:2.2.3]; then we use a *case* statement to call the appropriate **MiniEdit** routine for handling choices from that menu, passing the item number as a parameter. (We'll be defining routines below for the Apple, **File**, and **Edit** menus; you can, of course, add more routines to handle any other menus your program may need.) After we're finished responding to the menu choice, we call the Toolbox routine **HiliteMenu** [4.5.4] to unhighlight the menu's title, which will have been left highlighted in the menu bar by **MenuSelect** or **MenuKey**. This signals that the processing of the menu choice is complete, and the user can continue with the next action.

Program 4-6 (**DoAppleChoice**) shows how we handle a choice from the Apple menu. If the item chosen was **About MiniEdit...**, we call the routine **DoAbout** (defined later in Chapter 7) to open an alert box displaying identifying information about the program. Otherwise, the user has chosen an item representing a desk accessory; we use **GetItem** [4.6.1] to get the name of the accessory (which is simply the text of the chosen menu item), then **OpenDeskAcc** [4.5.2] to activate the accessory on the screen. This opens a system window for the accessory if there isn't one already, or brings its existing window to the front. The accessory's driver reference number (which is always negative) will automatically be stored in the **windowKind** field of the window record [3.1.1] for reference.

```
{ Global constants }

const
    AppleID = 1;                            {Menu ID for Apple menu}
    FileID  = 2;                            {Menu ID for File menu}
    EditID  = 3;                            {Menu ID for Edit menu}

procedure DoMenuChoice (menuChoice : LONGINT);

    { Handle user's menu choice. }

    var
        theMenu : INTEGER;                  {Menu ID of selected menu}
        theItem : INTEGER;                  {Item number of selected item}

    begin {DoMenuChoice}

        if menuChoice <> 0 then             {Nothing to do if 0}
            begin

                theMenu := HiWord(menuChoice);   {Get menu ID [I:2.2.3]}
                theItem := LoWord(menuChoice);   {Get item number [I:2.2.3]}

                case theMenu of

                    AppleID:
                        DoAppleChoice (theItem);    {Handle choice from Apple menu [Prog. 4-6]}

                    FileID:
                        DoFileChoice  (theItem);    {Handle choice from File menu [Prog. 4-8]}

                    EditID:
                        DoEditChoice  (theItem);    {Handle choice from Edit menu [Prog. 4-9]}

                    {Insert code here to handle any other menus}

                    end; {case}

                HiliteMenu(0)               {Unhighlight menu title [4.5.4]}

            end {if}

    end; {DoMenuChoice}
```

Program 4-5 Process menu choice

```
{ Global constant and variable }

const
   AboutItem = 1;                           {Item number for About MiniEdit... command}

var
   AppleMenu : MenuHandle;                  {Handle to Apple menu [4.1.1]}


procedure DoAppleChoice (theItem : INTEGER);

   { Handle choice from Apple menu. }

   var
      accName   : Str255;                   {Name of desk accessory [I:2.1.1]}
      accNumber : INTEGER;                  {Reference number of desk accessory}

   begin {DoAppleChoice}

      case theItem of

         AboutItem:
            DoAbout                         {Handle About MiniEdit... command [Prog. 7-1]}

         otherwise
            begin
               GetItem (AppleMenu, theItem, accName);  {Get accessory name [4.6.1]}
               accNumber := OpenDeskAcc (accName)      {Open desk accessory [4.5.2]}
            end

      end {case}

   end; {DoAppleChoice}
```

Program 4-6 Handle choice from Apple menu

When the user clicks the mouse in the close box of an active system window, our **DoMouseDown** routine (Program 3-7) will receive a part code of **InSysWindow** from **FindWindow** [3.5.1], and will call the Toolbox routine **SystemClick** [3.5.3] to handle the event. **SystemClick** will detect that the click was in the close box, and will automatically close the system window for us. However, if the user chooses **Close** from the **File** menu when a system window is active, it's our responsibility to close the system window ourselves.

The **DoClose** routine that we looked at in the last chapter (Program 3-3) checks to see whether an application or a system window is active. If it's an application window, **DoClose** closes it by calling the routine **Close-AppWindow**, which we've already looked at (Program 3-4); if a system window is active, it calls the **CloseSysWindow** routine shown here as Program 4-7. This routine simply gets the reference number of the window's desk accessory from the **windowKind** field [3.1.1] and calls the Toolbox routine **CloseDeskAcc** [4.5.2] to close the accessory, removing its window from the screen.

Program 4-8 (**DoFileChoice**) shows how **MiniEdit** handles a choice from the **File** menu. Here we just use a *case* statement to dispatch to the appropriate routine for responding to the chosen item. (We've seen a couple of these routines already; we'll define the rest when we learn about filing in Chapter 8.) Any further routines that you add to your program to handle additional menus will typically have this same form.

As shown in Program 4-9 (**DoEditChoice**), the **Edit** menu requires a bit of special treatment. We mentioned earlier that some of the desk accessories use the standard editing commands **Cut**, **Copy**, **Paste**, **Clear**, and **Undo**, and expect these commands to be available whenever the accessory is active. When the user chooses one of these commands, you have to call the Toolbox routine **SystemEdit** [4.5.3] to relay the command to the active desk accessory if there is one.

```
procedure CloseSysWindow;

  { Close system window. }

var
    whichWindow : WindowPeek;           {Pointer for access to window's fields [3.1.1]}
    accNumber   : INTEGER;              {Reference number of desk accessory [I:7.5.5]}

begin {CloseSysWindow}

    whichWindow := WindowPeek(FrontWindow);    {Convert to a WindowPeek [3.1.1, 3.3.3]}

    accNumber := whichWindow^.windowKind;   {Get reference number of desk accessory [3.1.1]}
    CloseDeskAcc (accNumber)                 {Close desk accessory [4.5.2]}

end;  {CloseSysWindow}
```

Program 4-7 Close system window

```
{ Global constants  }

const
    NewItem    = 1;                          {Item number for New command}
    OpenItem   = 2;                          {Item number for Open... command}
    CloseItem  = 3;                          {Item number for Close command}
    SaveItem   = 5;                          {Item number for Save command}
    SaveAsItem = 6;                          {Item number for Save As... command}
    RevertItem = 7;                          {Item number for Revert to Saved command}
    QuitItem   = 9;                          {Item number for Quit command}


procedure DoFileChoice (theItem : INTEGER);

  { Handle choice from File menu.  }

  begin {DoFileChoice}

    case theItem of

        NewItem:
          DoNew;                             {Handle New command [Prog. 3-2, 5-2]}

        OpenItem:
          DoOpen;                            {Handle Open... command [Prog. 8-5]}

        CloseItem:
          DoClose;                           {Handle Close command [Prog. 3-3]}

        SaveItem:
          DoSave;                            {Handle Save command [Prog. 8-2]}

        SaveAsItem:
          DoSaveAs;                          {Handle Save As... command [Prog. 8-8]}

        RevertItem:
          DoRevert;                          {Handle Revert to Saved command [Prog. 8-4]}

        QuitItem:
          DoQuit;                            {Handle Quit command [Prog. 2-4]}

      {Insert code here to handle any other File menu commands}

      end {case}

  end; {DoFileChoice}
```

Program 4-8 Handle choice from **File** menu

```
{ Global constants }

const
    UndoItem  = 1;                      {Item number for Undo command}
    CutItem   = 3;                      {Item number for Cut command}
    CopyItem  = 4;                      {Item number for Copy command}
    PasteItem = 5;                      {Item number for Paste command}
    ClearItem = 7;                      {Item number for Clear command}


procedure DoEditChoice (theItem : INTEGER);

    { Handle choice from Edit menu. }

    begin {DoEditChoice}

        case theItem of

            UndoItem:
                if not SystemEdit (UndoCmd) then
                    SysBeep(1);         {Undo command not implemented [2.8.1]}

            CutItem:
                if not SystemEdit (CutCmd) then
                    DoCut;              {Handle Cut command [Prog. 5-8]}

            CopyItem:
                if not SystemEdit (CopyCmd) then
                    DoCopy;             {Handle Copy command [Prog. 5-9]}

            PasteItem:
                if not SystemEdit (PasteCmd) then
                    DoPaste;           {Handle Paste command [Prog. 5-10]}

            ClearItem:
                if not SystemEdit (ClearCmd) then
                    DoClear;           {Handle Clear command [Prog. 5-11]}

            {Insert code here to handle any other Edit menu commands}

        end {case}

    end; {DoEditChoice}
```

Program 4-9 Handle choice from **Edit** menu

The argument to **SystemEdit** tells it which of the standard commands was chosen, and must be one of the Toolbox constants **CutCmd**, **CopyCmd**, **PasteCmd**, **UndoCmd**, or **ClearCmd** [4.5.3]. (Notice that these are not necessarily the same as the item numbers of the corresponding commands in your **Edit** menu. Be sure to use the built-in constants when calling **SystemEdit**, not your own item numbers!) If the active window is a system window containing a desk accessory, **SystemEdit** will pass the given command along to the accessory to handle, and will return a Boolean result of **TRUE**. This tells you that the command has been successfully relayed to a desk accessory, so you can just ignore it; a result of **FALSE** means that no accessory is currently active (or that the active accessory isn't prepared to accept the command), so you have to respond to the command yourself. You can add other commands to your **Edit** menu if your application requires them, but only the five standard editing commands should ever be passed to **SystemEdit** for handling by a desk accessory.

The constants **UndoCmd**, **CutCmd**, **CopyCmd**, **PasteCmd**, and **ClearCmd** were dropped from Apple's officially supported Toolbox interface just before this book went to press. You must now either define these constants for yourself (as in the final version of our **MiniEdit** program shown in Appendix H) or arrange your **Edit** menu in such a way that the proper argument values to **SystemEdit** can be derived from the item numbers of the standard editing commands.

Notice, though, that the **SystemEdit** argument values start from **0** (for the **Undo** command), whereas the item numbers within a menu always start from **1**. The best you can do is give each standard editing command an item number *one greater than* the corresponding argument value, then remember to subtract **1** back from the item number before passing it on to **SystemEdit**. Isn't that convenient?

Controlling Menu Items

There are two ways to control the properties of a menu item (such as its icon or character style, or whether it's enabled or disabled). One way is to set the properties at the time you define the item, by including modifier characters in the defining string that you give to **AppendMenu** [4.3.1]. We've already seen how to use the modifier character ((left parenthesis) to disable an item and / (slash) to give it a keyboard alias. In this section we'll talk about the remaining modifier characters and how to use them.

The second way to control an item's properties is by calling Toolbox routines to read or change them "on the fly," after the item has already been defined. In general, these routines expect you to identify the item by giving a handle to the menu it resides in, along with an item number representing its sequential position within the menu. The first item in a menu always has item number **1**; in some cases, an item number of **0** refers to the menu as a whole, rather than any individual item.

Text of an Item

To read or change the text of an item, use **GetItem** and **SetItem** [4.6.1]. **SetItem** is useful for "toggling" or alternating menu items. For instance, the **Show Clipboard** command in our earlier Figure 4-1 might change to **Hide Clipboard** when the Clipboard is visible on the screen, then revert to **Show Clipboard** when it's hidden again. Another example of changing the text of an item is the way MacWrite changes its **Undo** command to, for instance, **Undo Cut** or **Undo Typing** or **Can't Undo**, depending on the last operation the user performed.

One more use for **SetItem** is to include any of **AppendMenu**'s modifier characters as part of an item's text. A statement like

```
AppendMenu (anyMenu, 'Wow!')
```

won't work properly, because **AppendMenu** will interpret the exclamation point as a modifier character for marking the item on the menu. (We'll talk about marking items in a minute.) Instead, you have to do something like this:

```
AppendMenu (anyMenu, 'Dummy');
SetItem     (anyMenu, itemNumber, 'Wow!')
```

where **itemNumber** is the appropriate item number for this item. Unlike **AppendMenu**, **SetItem** attaches no special significance to the exclamation point or any of the other modifier characters: it simply treats them as text characters like any other.

Character Style

Items in a standard text menu are always displayed in the system font and the standard size; there's no way to ask for a different typeface or size. However, you can specify character styles such as bold, italic, or outline. When you define a menu item with **AppendMenu**, you can give it any one style attribute by including the modifier character $<$ in the defining string, followed by a letter standing for the desired attribute: **B** for bold,

I for italic, **U** for underline, **O** for outline, **S** for shadow. For instance, the statement

```
AppendMenu (anyMenu, 'Italic<I')
```

defines an item that will be displayed on the menu in italic.

To specify a combination of two or more style attributes, such as bold italic, or to change character styles on the fly, use **SetItemStyle** [4.6.3]. This routine accepts any desired character style in the form of a Quick-Draw **Style** set [I:8.3.1]:

```
SetItemStyle (anyMenu, itemNumber, [Bold, Italic])
```

You can find out the current character style of a menu item with **GetItemStyle** [4.6.3].

Enabling and Disabling Items

As we've already seen, you can disable a menu item at the time you define it, by using a left parenthesis as the first character of the defining string. This is useful mainly for items that are permanently disabled, such as a blank line or a row of dashes that you're using to separate sections of a menu. The Toolbox routines **DisableItem** and **EnableItem** [4.6.2] allow you to disable and enable items dynamically to reflect changing conditions as your program runs. In general, you should disable an item whenever it's inapplicable in a particular situation: for instance, if your program uses the standard editing commands, you might disable **Cut** and **Copy** whenever there's no current selection (nothing to cut or copy), and **Paste** when the Clipboard is empty (nothing to paste).

You can also disable or enable an entire menu by supplying an item number of **0**. Disabling a menu disables all of its items, overriding their individual enable flags in the menu record. The menu's title appears dimmed in the menu bar. (As usual when you make any change in the menu bar, you have to remember to call **DrawMenuBar** to make the change visible on the screen.) The user can still pull down a disabled menu and look at its contents, but all of its items will be dimmed and none can be chosen. When you enable the menu again, the items will be restored to their previous state according to their individual enable flags.

Marking Items

For menu items that control a two-way, on-or-off setting of some kind, you can use a *mark character* (usually a check mark) to display the item's current setting on the menu. (For instance, both MacWrite and MacPaint use check marks in their **Style** menus to show which character style options are in effect.) The usual way of checking or unchecking an item is with **CheckItem** [4.6.4]. The Boolean parameter **checked** tells whether to mark the item with a check mark (**TRUE**) or unmark it (**FALSE**).

The check mark is another of the special, screen-only Macintosh characters, and its character code is defined as a Toolbox constant named **CheckMark** [I:8.1.1]. Actually, you can mark an item with any character you like, although the check mark is by far the most common. To mark an item with some other character, use **SetItemMark**; you can find out an item's current mark character with **GetItemMark** [4.6.4]. The null character (character code **0**, defined as the Toolbox constant **NoMark** [4.6.4]) denotes an unmarked item. **GetItemMark** returns a null character if the designated item is unmarked; **SetItemMark** accepts a null mark character

```
SetItemMark (anyMenu, itemNumber, CHR(NoMark))
```

and unmarks the item.

> You can also use **CheckItem** to unmark an item, even if it's marked with something other than a check mark. The statement
>
> ```
> CheckItem (anyMenu, itemNumber, FALSE)
> ```
>
> removes any mark character the item may have, whether it's a check mark or something else.

You can mark a character at the time you define it by using the modifier character ! (exclamation point) in the defining string, followed by the desired mark character:

```
AppendMenu (CalcMenu, 'Calculate Percentage!%')
```

Notice, though, that this won't work for a check mark (the usual case), since you can't type it into your program from the keyboard. You could store the check mark into the defining string by hand,

```
defString    := 'Normal!*';
defString[8] := CHR(CheckMark);
AppendMenu (OptionsMenu, defString)
```

but it's usually simpler just to create the item unmarked and then check it separately with **CheckItem**:

```
AppendMenu (OptionsMenu, 'Normal');
CheckItem    (OptionsMenu, itemNumber)
```

where **itemNumber** is the sequential position of the **Normal** item on the **Options** menu.

Item Icons

Any menu item can be given an icon, which will appear to the left of the item on the menu. Like all icons, this is a 32-by-32-bit image that's read in from a resource file, where it's stored under resource type 'ICON' [I:5.5.3]. By convention, icons used in menus have resource IDs from **257** to **511**. However, instead of using the resource ID directly, Toolbox routines that deal with menu icons refer to them with an *icon number* that's **256** less than the resource ID. In other words, icon number **1** is understood to refer to the icon with resource ID **257**, icon number **2** corresponds to resource ID **258**, and so on.

> This use of an icon number **256** less than the resource ID applies only to Toolbox routines related to menus. In the rest of the Toolbox, icons are identified directly by their actual resource IDs.

You can associate an icon with a menu item by calling **SetItemIcon** [4.6.5]. As usual, you identify the item with a menu handle and an item number within the menu, and the icon with an icon number. The Toolbox will add **256** to the given icon number to arrive at the icon's resource ID, then load the icon from a resource file. An icon number of **0** removes any previous icon the item may have had. **GetItemIcon** [4.6.5] returns an item's current icon number, or **0** if it has none.

You can also specify an icon in an item's defining string, using the modifier character ˆ followed by a one-digit icon number. For instance, the statement

    AppendMenu (ChessMenu, 'White Bishopˆ4')

defines an item named **White Bishop** with icon number **4** (resource ID **260**). One-digit icon numbers are sufficient as long as you don't need more than ten menu icons altogether. In the unlikely event that you need more than ten, you can use icon numbers higher than **9** (resource IDs higher than **265**) by creating an item without an icon and then using **SetItemIcon** to give it one.

If you want to get tricky, you can actually define icon numbers greater than **9** in the defining string. **AppendMenu** takes the single character following the modifier ˆ and converts it to a resource ID by adding **208** to its character code. For example, the digit **1**, with character code **$31** (decimal **49**) denotes icon number **1**, or resource ID **257**. Thus characters that lie beyond the digit **9** in the Macintosh character set (I:8.1.1] stand for resource IDs greater than **265**. The statement

    AppendMenu (ChessMenu, 'Black Bishopˆ:')

defines an item with icon number **10** (resource ID **266**), since the character **:** (colon) immediately follows the digit **9** in the character set, with character code **$3A** (decimal **58**). This method is tricky, though, and error-prone—it's usually better to use **SetItemIcon** instead.

REFERENCE

4.1 Internal Representation of Menus

4.1.1 Menu Records

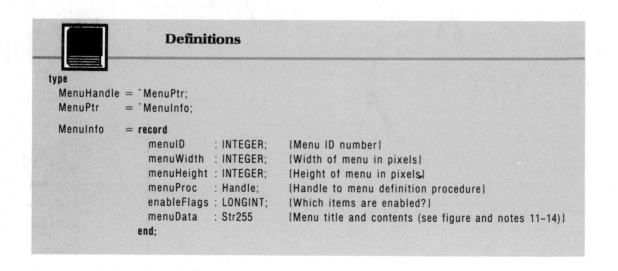

Definitions

```
type
  MenuHandle = ^MenuPtr;
  MenuPtr    = ^MenuInfo;

  MenuInfo   = record
                 menuID     : INTEGER;   {Menu ID number}
                 menuWidth  : INTEGER;   {Width of menu in pixels}
                 menuHeight : INTEGER;   {Height of menu in pixels}
                 menuProc   : Handle;    {Handle to menu definition procedure}
                 enableFlags : LONGINT;  {Which items are enabled?}
                 menuData   : Str255     {Menu title and contents (see figure and notes 11–14)}
               end;
```

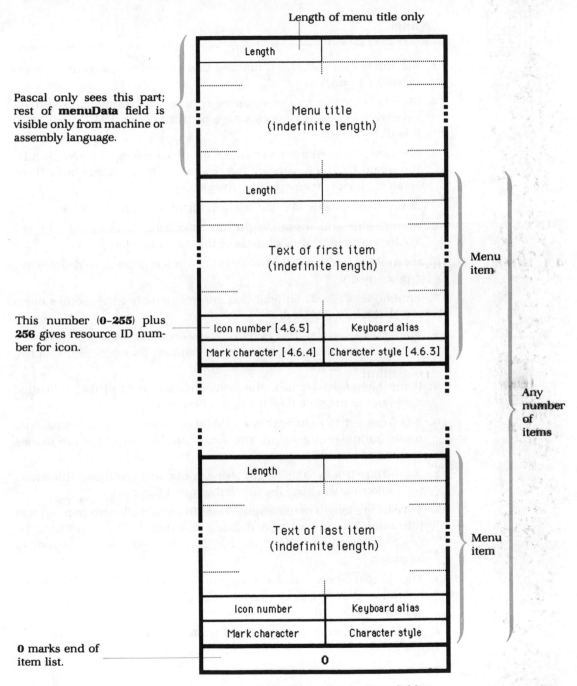

Length of menu title only

Pascal only sees this part; rest of **menuData** field is visible only from machine or assembly language.

This number (**0–255**) plus **256** gives resource ID number for icon.

Length

Menu title (indefinite length)

Length

Text of first item (indefinite length)

| Icon number [4.6.5] | Keyboard alias |
| Mark character [4.6.4] | Character style [4.6.3] |

Menu item

Any number of items

Length

Text of last item (indefinite length)

Icon number	Keyboard alias
Mark character	Character style
0	

Menu item

0 marks end of item list.

Format of **menuData** field

Notes

1. **menuID** is an identifying number that should be different for every menu in a program.

2. Menus belonging to the application have positive menu IDs; those belonging to desk accessories have negative menu IDs. A menu ID of **0** is not allowed.

3. For menus loaded from a resource file (resource type '**MENU**' [4.8.1]), the menu ID is the same as the resource ID; for menus built "from scratch," it can be any positive integer.

4. Never store directly into the **menuID** field of a menu record.

5. **menuWidth** and **menuHeight** are calculated automatically by the Toolbox whenever the contents of the menu change.

6. **menuProc** is a handle to the menu definition procedure defining the type of menu.

7. **enableFlags** is a 32-bit field that controls whether the menu's items are enabled or disabled.

8. The first (high-order) bit of **enableFlags** enables or disables the entire menu. When this bit is **0**, the menu and all its items are disabled, overriding all of the remaining flag bits.

9. If the high-order bit is **1**, the remaining bits control the individual items in the menu: **1** if enabled, **0** if disabled.

10. Bits from left to right within **enableFlags** correspond to items from top to bottom on the menu. The size of **enableFlags** limits all menus to a maximum of 31 items.

11. **menuData** is a variable-length string containing the menu title along with information about the items the menu contains.

12. The string's length count (**menuData[0]**) gives the length of the menu title only. The information defining the menu's items is "hidden" beyond the end of the title, and is accessible only in assembly language.

13. The format shown is for the standard text menu. Nonstandard definition procedures can redefine the "hidden data" at the end of the menu record in any way they like.

14. Never store directly into the **menuData** field, as this will destroy the hidden data beyond the end of the title string.

Assembly-Language Information

Field offsets in a menu record:

(Pascal) Field name	(Assembly) Offset name	Offset in bytes
menuID	**menuID**	**0**
menuWidth	**menuWidth**	**2**
menuHeight	**menuHeight**	**4**
menuProc	**menuDefHandle**	**6**
enableFlags	**menuEnable**	**10**
menuData	**menuData**	**14**

Assembly-language constant:

Name	Value	Meaning
MenuBlkSize	**14**	Size of menu record in bytes, excluding **menuData**

4.2 Creating and Destroying Menus

4.2.1 Initializing the Toolbox for Menus

Definitions

procedure InitMenus;

Notes

1. **InitMenus** must be called before any other operation involving menus.

2. It initializes the Toolbox's menu-related data structures, starts an empty menu bar, and draws the menu bar on the screen.

3. Before calling **InitMenus**, you must first call **InitGraf** [I:4.3.1], **Init-Fonts** [I:8.2.4], and **InitWindows** [3.2.1].

Assembly-Language Information

Trap macro:

(Pascal) Routine name	(Assembly) Trap macro	Trap word
InitMenus	**_InitMenus**	**$A930**

4.2.2 Creating Menus

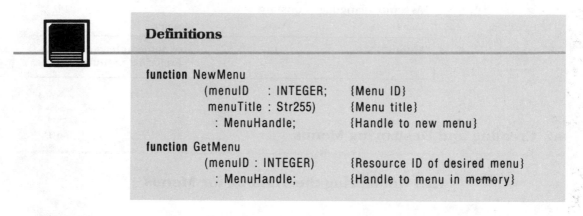

Definitions

```
function NewMenu
        (menuID    : INTEGER;      {Menu ID}
         menuTitle : Str255)       {Menu title}
          : MenuHandle;            {Handle to new menu}
function GetMenu
        (menuID : INTEGER)         {Resource ID of desired menu}
          : MenuHandle;            {Handle to menu in memory}
```

Notes

1. **NewMenu** and **GetMenu** both allocate heap space for a new menu record and return a handle to it.

2. **NewMenu** creates a brand-new menu, initially empty; it can then be filled with **AppendMenu** [4.3.1], **AddResMenu**, and **InsertResMenu** [4.3.3].

3. **GetMenu** loads a predefined menu from a resource file.

4. The menu ID supplied to **GetMenu** gives the resource ID for the desired menu; its resource type is 'MENU' [4.8.1]. If the menu is already in memory, **GetMenu** just returns a handle to it.

5. For **NewMenu**, the menu ID can be any positive integer, provided that no two menus have the same ID. The menu ID should never be **0** or negative.

6. The new menu is not inserted in the menu bar; this must be done explicitly with **InsertMenu** [4.4.1].

7. **GetMenu** also loads the menu's definition procedure from the resource file, if necessary, and stores a handle to it in the menu record. **NewMenu** always stores a handle to the menu definition procedure for standard text menus; for nonstandard menu types, you can replace this with a handle to a different definition procedure.

8. Use **DisposeMenu** [4.2.3] to deallocate menus created with **NewMenu**; use **ReleaseResource** [I:6.3.2] to deallocate those read in with **GetMenu**.

9. The trap macro for **GetMenu** is spelled **_GetRMenu**.

Assembly-Language Information

Trap macros:

(Pascal) Routine name	(Assembly) Trap macro	Trap word
NewMenu	**_NewMenu**	**$A931**
GetMenu	**_GetRMenu**	**$A9BF**

4.2.3 Destroying Menus

Definitions

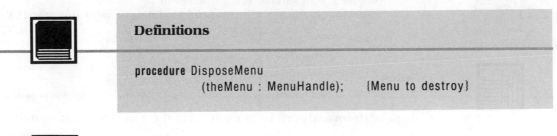

```
procedure DisposeMenu
        (theMenu : MenuHandle);    {Menu to destroy}
```

Notes

1. **DisposeMenu** deallocates the space occupied by a menu record. All existing handles to the menu are left "dangling" and can no longer be used.

2. The menu is not removed from the menu bar; remember to remove it explicitly with **DeleteMenu** [4.4.1] before disposing of it.

3. If the menu was originally read in from a resource file with **GetMenu** [4.2.2], dispose of it with **ReleaseResource** [I:6.3.2] instead of **DisposeMenu**.

4. The trap macro for **DisposeMenu** is spelled **_DisposMenu**.

Assembly-Language Information

Trap macro:

(Pascal) Routine name	(Assembly) Trap macro	Trap word
DisposeMenu	**_DisposMenu**	**$A932**

4.3 Building Menus

4.3.1 Adding Menu Items

Definitions

```
procedure AppendMenu
          (theMenu  : MenuHandle;      {Handle to the menu}
           defString : Str255);        {String defining item(s) to append}
```

Notes

1. **AppendMenu** adds one or more items to the end of an existing menu.

2. **defString** consists of the text of the item, along with optional modifiers [4.3.2] to define the item's properties.

3. A menu needn't be in the menu bar to append items to it.

4. Items cannot be removed or reordered once appended to a menu. There's no way to insert a new item anywhere except at the end of the menu.

5. The null string is not allowed as the text of a menu item. To leave a blank line in a menu, use an item consisting of one or more space characters. By convention, such blank items should always be disabled.

6. Menu items that invoke a dialog conventionally end with three periods:

AppendMenu (FileMenu, 'Open...')

7. Modifier characters [4.3.2] in the defining string are not considered part of the item itself. To incorporate any of these characters in the text of an item, use **SetItem** [4.6.1] to redefine the text after appending the item to the menu.

Assembly-Language Information

Trap macro:

(Pascal) Routine name	(Assembly) Trap macro	Trap word
AppendMenu	**_AppendMenu**	**$A933**

4.3.2 Modifier Characters

Modifier character	Meaning
;	Item separator
(	Disable item [4.6.2]
/	Keyboard alias
<	Character style [4.6.3]
!	Mark item [4.6.4]
^	Icon [4.6.5]

Notes

1. These modifier characters can be included in the defining string supplied to **AppendMenu** [4.3.1] to define an item's properties.

2. Modifier characters in the defining string are not considered part of the item itself. To incorporate any of these characters in an item's text, use **SetItem** [4.6.1] to redefine the text after appending the item to the menu.

3. The modifier (precedes the text of an item; all other modifiers follow the text, in any order.

4. To define two or more items at once, separate their definitions with semicolons in the defining string:

   AppendMenu (FileMenu, 'Open...;Close')

5. All properties of an item except its keyboard alias can be changed "on the fly" with the routines described in [4.6]. The keyboard alias, if any, must be defined with a modifier character when the item is first appended to the menu.

6. To give an item a keyboard alias, use the modifier / followed by the alias character:

   AppendMenu (EditMenu, 'Copy/C')

   The user can then invoke this menu item by typing the alias character with the command key down.

7. The alias character will appear to the right of the item on the menu, preceded by the "cloverleaf" command symbol.

8. If the alias is a letter of the alphabet, an uppercase (capital) letter is used to define it. The user can then type the alias in either upper- or lowercase; both will be recognized as equivalent aliases.

4.3.3 Adding Resource Names to a Menu

Definitions

procedure AddResMenu
       (theMenu : MenuHandle; {Handle to the menu}
       rsrcType : ResType);   {Resource type to be added}

procedure InsertResMenu
       (theMenu : MenuHandle; {Handle to the menu}
       rsrcType : ResType;   {Resource type to be added}
       afterItem : INTEGER);   {Number of item to insert after}

Notes

1. These routines search all open resource files for resources of a given type, and add their names to an existing menu.

2. **rsrcType** can be any resource type [I:6.1.1] whose members have names as well as ID numbers. The most common are **'DRVR'** (input/output drivers, including desk accessories [I:7.5.5]) and **'FONT'** [I:8.4.5].

3. **AddResMenu** adds the resources at the end of the menu; **InsertResMenu** adds them after a specified item.

4. If **afterItem** is **0**, the resources are inserted at the beginning of the menu; if it's greater than the number of items in the menu, they're inserted at the end.

5. Resource names beginning with a period (.) are suppressed and are not added to the menu.

6. All items added to the menu are enabled and unmarked, in the normal character style, with no icon or keyboard alias. These properties can then be changed if necessary with the routines described in [4.6].

7. **AddResMenu** and **InsertResMenu** list the resources in opposite orders. For consistency, it's recommended that you use **AddResMenu** whenever possible.

8. To get the names of items added by these routines, use **GetItem** [4.6.1].

9. The menu of desk accessories conventionally has menu ID **1** and a one-character title consisting of the Apple symbol (character code **$14**). To give it this title, define a one-character "placeholder" string (any character will do) and store the Apple symbol into it, using the Toolbox constant **AppleMark** [I:8.1.1]:

```
appleTitle    := '@';
appleTitle[1] := CHR(AppleMark);
appleMenu     := NewMenu (1, appleTitle)
```

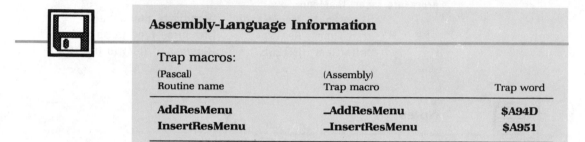

Assembly-Language Information

Trap macros:

(Pascal) Routine name	(Assembly) Trap macro	Trap word
AddResMenu	**_AddResMenu**	**$A94D**
InsertResMenu	**_InsertResMenu**	**$A951**

4.3.4 Counting Menu Items

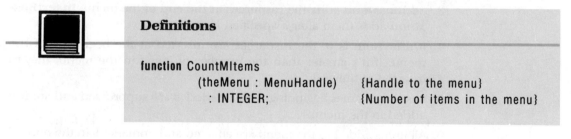

Definitions

```
function CountMItems
        (theMenu : MenuHandle)      {Handle to the menu}
            : INTEGER;              {Number of items in the menu}
```

Notes

1. **CountMItems** returns the number of items in a menu.

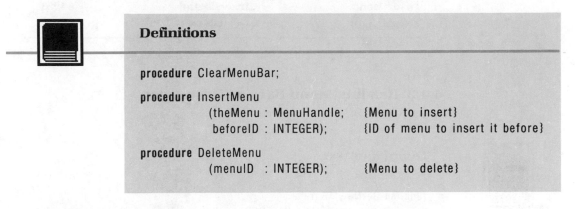

Assembly-Language Information

Trap macro:

(Pascal) Routine name	(Assembly) Trap macro	Trap word
CountMItems	**_CountMItems**	**$A950**

4.4 Building the Menu Bar

4.4.1 Adding and Removing Menus

Definitions

procedure ClearMenuBar;

procedure InsertMenu
       (theMenu : MenuHandle;   {Menu to insert}
       beforeID : INTEGER);   {ID of menu to insert it before}

procedure DeleteMenu
       (menuID : INTEGER);   {Menu to delete}

Notes

1. **ClearMenuBar** makes the menu bar empty, deleting any menus it may previously have contained.

2. **ClearMenuBar** is called automatically at the beginning of a program by **InitMenus** [4.2.1].

3. **InsertMenu** adds a menu to the menu bar; **DeleteMenu** removes one.

4. To add a menu at the end of the menu bar, set **beforeID** to **0**. The new menu is also added at the end if there's no menu in the menu bar with the specified ID, **beforeID**.

5. Menus deleted by **DeleteMenu** and **ClearMenuBar** aren't deallocated, just removed from the menu bar. All handles to a deleted menu remain valid.

6. Changes in the menu bar are *not* reflected automatically on the screen. Call **DrawMenuBar** [4.4.3] to redisplay the menu bar explicitly after the change.

7. If the designated menu is already in the menu bar, **InsertMenu** does nothing. If there's no menu with the given ID, **DeleteMenu** does nothing.

Assembly-Language Information

Trap macros:

(Pascal) Routine name	(Assembly) Trap macro	Trap word
ClearMenuBar	**_ClearMenuBar**	**$A934**
InsertMenu	**_InsertMenu**	**$A935**
DeleteMenu	**_DeleteMenu**	**$A936**

4.4.2 Reading Menu Bars as Resources

Definitions

```
function GetNewMBar
        (menuBarID : INTEGER)      {Resource ID of desired menu bar}
        : Handle;                  {Handle to menu bar in memory}
```

Notes

1. **GetNewMBar** loads a menu bar into memory from a resource file and returns a handle to it.

2. The resource type for a menu bar is 'MBAR' [4.8.2].

3. All needed menus are loaded from the resource file and inserted in the new menu bar.

4. The new menu bar is *not* automatically made current. You can do this explicitly with **SetMenuBar** [4.4.4]. Don't forget to follow this with a call to **DrawMenuBar** [4.4.3] to display the new menu bar on the screen.

5. To deallocate the menu bar when you're through with it, use **Release-Resource** [I:6.3.2].

Assembly-Language Information

Trap macro:

(Pascal) Routine name	(Assembly) Trap macro	Trap word
GetNewMBar	**_GetNewMBar**	**$A9C0**

4.4.3 Drawing the Menu Bar

Definitions

procedure DrawMenuBar;

Notes

1. **DrawMenuBar** redisplays the menu bar on the screen according to its current composition.

2. If any menu title is highlighted, it will remain highlighted when re-drawn.

3. Call this routine after any change in the contents of the menu bar, to reflect the change on the screen.

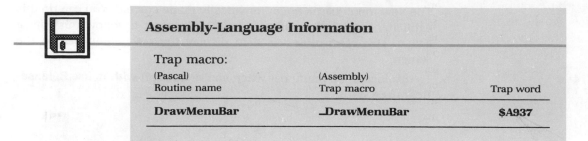

Assembly-Language Information

Trap macro:

(Pascal) Routine name	(Assembly) Trap macro	Trap word
DrawMenuBar	**_DrawMenuBar**	**$A937**

4.4.4 Changing Menu Bars

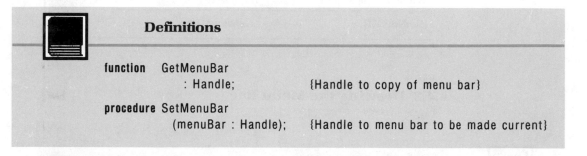

Definitions

function	GetMenuBar	
	: Handle;	{Handle to copy of menu bar}
procedure	SetMenuBar	
	(menuBar : Handle);	{Handle to menu bar to be made current}

Notes

1. **GetMenuBar** makes a copy of the current menu bar and returns a handle to it; **SetMenuBar** makes a designated menu bar current.

2. **GetMenuBar** copies only the menu bar itself, not the menus it contains. Both the original and the copy contains handles to the same underlying menus. Be careful not to deallocate any of the menus as long as either copy still points to it.

3. Use **DisposHandle** [I:3.2.2] to destroy a menu bar created with **GetMenuBar**.

4. **SetMenuBar** doesn't display the new current menu bar on the screen; do it explicitly with **DrawMenuBar** [4.4.3].

5. To make temporary changes in the menu bar, use **GetMenuBar** to save a copy, then make the changes in the original. You can later undo the changes by making the copy current with **SetMenuBar**.

Assembly-Language Information

Trap macros:

(Pascal) Routine name	(Assembly) Trap macro	Trap word
GetMenuBar	**_GetMenuBar**	**$A93B**
SetMenuBar	**_SetMenuBar**	**$A93C**

Assembly-language global variable:

Name	Address	Meaning
MenuList	**$A1C**	Handle to current menu bar

4.4.5 Getting Menus from the Menu Bar

Definitions

```
function GetMHandle
        (menuID : INTEGER)      {Menu ID}
          : MenuHandle;         {Handle to the menu}
```

Notes

1. GetMHandle accepts the menu ID of a menu in the menu bar and returns a handle to the menu in memory.

2. If there's no menu in the menu bar with the given ID, the handle returned is **NIL**.

Assembly-Language Information

Trap macro:

(Pascal) Routine name	(Assembly) Trap macro	Trap word
GetMHandle	**_GetMHandle**	**$A949**

4.5 Responding to the Mouse and Keyboard

4.5.1 Choosing Menu Items

 Definitions

```
function MenuSelect
        (startPoint : Point)      {Point where mouse was pressed, in screen coordinates}
          : LONGINT;             {Menu item chosen}

function MenuKey
        (ch : CHAR)               {Character typed with command key}
          : LONGINT;             {Menu item chosen}
```

Menu ID (16 bits)	Item number (16 bits)

Result of **MenuSelect** and **MenuKey**

 Notes

1. These functions allow the user to choose a menu item: **MenuSelect** with the mouse, **MenuKey** with the command key.

2. Both functions return a long integer identifying the item that was chosen. The high-order word gives the menu ID, the low-order word the item number within the menu.

3. If no menu item is chosen, both functions return **0**.

4. When an item is chosen from a menu belonging to a desk accessory (negative menu ID), both functions automatically intercept the choice, pass it to the desk accessory for action, and return a result of **0**.

5. Call **MenuSelect** after a mouse-down event, when **FindWindow** [3.5.1] reports that the mouse was pressed in the menu bar (part code **InMenuBar**).

6. **startPoint** should give the location of the mouse-down event, in *global (screen) coordinates*. This is the form in which the point is reported in the **where** field of the event record [2.1.1].

7. **MenuSelect** keeps control for as long as the user holds down the mouse button, tracking the movements of the mouse and providing visual feedback on the screen. This includes highlighting menu titles, "pulling down" menus, and highlighting individual menu items.

8. When the button is released, the chosen item (if any) flashes several times, the menu vanishes from the screen, and **MenuSelect** returns, identifying the item that was chosen.

9. If the button is released over a disabled item, or outside of any menu, **MenuSelect** returns **0**.

10. Call **MenuKey** after a key-down event if the event's **modifiers** field [2.1.5] shows that the command key was down at the time of the event.

11. **ch** is the character that was typed with the command key down, taken from the low-order byte of the event record's **message** field [2.1.4]. If this character isn't an alias for any existing menu item, or if the item is disabled, **MenuKey** returns **0**.

12. According to Macintosh user interface conventions, command keystrokes do not repeat when the key is held down. Auto-key events with the command key down should be ignored.

13. Both **MenuSelect** and **MenuKey** leave the title of the chosen menu highlighted. After responding to the chosen item, you must unhighlight the menu title yourself by calling **HiliteMenu(0)** [4.5.4].

Assembly-Language Information

Trap macros:

(Pascal) Routine name	(Assembly) Trap macro	Trap word
MenuSelect	**_MenuSelect**	**$A93D**
MenuKey	**_MenuKey**	**$A93E**

4.5.2 Opening and Closing Desk Accessories

Definitions

function	OpenDeskAcc	
	(accName : Str255)	{Name of desk accessory to open}
	: INTEGER;	{Reference number of desk accessory}
procedure	CloseDeskAcc	
	(refNum : INTEGER)	{Reference number of desk accessory to close}

Notes

1. **OpenDeskAcc** opens a desk accessory and displays it on the screen. Call it when **MenuSelect** [4.5.1] reports that the user has chosen a desk accessory from the Apple menu.

2. Use **GetItem** [4.6.1] to get the name of the desk accessory to open.

3. If the accessory isn't already on the screen, a new system window is opened to display it in.

4. The reference number of the desk accessory (always negative) is stored into the **windowKind** field of the new window record [3.1.1].

5. The accessory's window comes to the front and becomes the active window.

6. **OpenDeskAcc** returns the desk accessory's reference number; if the accessory can't be opened, it returns **0**.

7. **CloseDeskAcc** closes a desk accessory and removes its window from the screen.

8. Desk accessories are usually closed for you by **SystemClick** [3.5.3] when the user clicks in the close box of a system window, or automatically when your program terminates. You'll rarely need to call **CloseDeskAcc** explicitly.

Assembly-Language Information

Trap macros:

(Pascal) Routine name	(Assembly) Trap macro	Trap word
OpenDeskAcc	**_OpenDeskAcc**	**$A9B6**
CloseDeskAcc	**_CloseDeskAcc**	**$A9B7**

4.5.3 Editing in Desk Accessories

Definitions

```
function SystemEdit
          (editCmd : INTEGER)      {Command to relay}
              : BOOLEAN;           {Handled by desk accessory?}

const
  UndoCmd  = 0;                    {Edit code for Undo command}
  CutCmd   = 2;                    {Edit code for Cut command}
  CopyCmd  = 3;                    {Edit code for Copy command}
  PasteCmd = 4;                    {Edit code for Paste command}
  ClearCmd = 5;                    {Edit code for Clear command}
```

Notes

1. **SystemEdit** relays an editing command chosen from a menu to the active desk accessory, if any, for action. Call it whenever the user chooses any of the standard editing commands.

2. The parameter **editCmd** must be one of the constants shown.

3. These constants were inexplicably removed from Apple's Toolbox interface just before this book went to press. To use them, you must now either define them for yourself as program constants or arrange your **Edit** menu so that the standard commands have item numbers one greater than the corresponding constant values (as shown above). In the latter case, don't forget to subtract **1** back from a chosen item number before passing it on to **SystemEdit**.

4. The Boolean result of **SystemEdit** is **TRUE** if the command was successfully relayed to a desk accessory and can be ignored by the application.

5. If the result is **FALSE**, the command is your responsibility to handle. This will happen if the active window doesn't contain a desk accessory, or if the active accessory isn't prepared to handle the given command.

6. Make sure the five standard editing commands are available and enabled whenever a desk accessory is active.

7. The trap macro for **SystemEdit** is spelled **_SysEdit**.

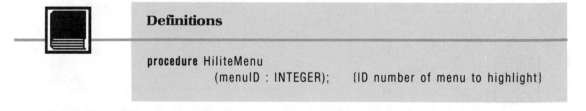

Assembly-Language Information

Trap macro:

(Pascal) Routine name	(Assembly) Trap macro	Trap word
SystemEdit	**_SysEdit**	**$A9C2**

4.5.4 Highlighting Menu Titles

Definitions

```
procedure HiliteMenu
        (menuID : INTEGER);    {ID number of menu to highlight}
```

Notes

1. **HiliteMenu** highlights a menu title in the menu bar.

2. Any previously highlighted menu title becomes unhighlighted.

3. If **menuID** is **0** or doesn't correspond to any menu in the menu bar, the previous title is unhighlighted but no new title is highlighted in its place.

4. Call **HiliteMenu(0)** after you finish responding to any menu item, to unhighlight the menu title which will have been left highlighted by **MenuSelect** or **MenuKey**.

5. The assembly-language global variable **TheMenu** always contains the menu ID of the currently highlighted menu, or **0** if none.

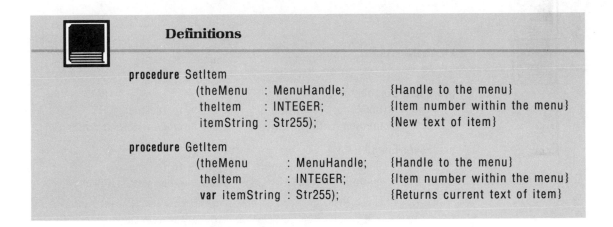

Assembly-Language Information

Trap macro:

(Pascal) Routine name	(Assembly) Trap macro	Trap word
HiliteMenu	**_HiliteMenu**	**$A938**

Assembly-language global variable:

Name	Address	Meaning
TheMenu	**$A26**	Menu ID of currently highlighted menu

4.6 Controlling Menu Items

4.6.1 Text of an Item

Definitions

```
procedure SetItem
        (theMenu    : MenuHandle;        {Handle to the menu}
         theItem    : INTEGER;           {Item number within the menu}
         itemString : Str255);           {New text of item}

procedure GetItem
        (theMenu        : MenuHandle;    {Handle to the menu}
         theItem        : INTEGER;       {Item number within the menu}
         var itemString : Str255);       {Returns current text of item}
```

Notes

1. **SetItem** changes the text of an existing menu item; **GetItem** returns the current text of an item.

2. The modifier characters used with **AppendMenu** [4.3.1] have no special significance to **SetItem**; they're considered part of the item's text, just like any other character. The string returned by **GetItem** doesn't include modifiers describing the item's properties.

3. The null string is not allowed as the text of a menu item. To make an item appear blank, use a string consisting of one or more space characters. Such blank items should always be disabled.

Assembly-Language Information

Trap macros:

(Pascal) Routine name	(Assembly) Trap macro	Trap word
SetItem	**_SetItem**	**$A947**
GetItem	**_GetItem**	**$A946**

4.6.2 Enabling and Disabling Items

Definitions

```
procedure DisableItem
          (theMenu : MenuHandle;    {Handle to the menu}
           theItem  : INTEGER);     {Item number within the menu}

procedure EnableItem
          (theMenu : MenuHandle;    {Handle to the menu}
           theItem  : INTEGER);     {Item number within the menu}
```

Modifier character	Meaning
(	Disable item

Notes

1. These routines are used to disable or enable an existing menu item.

2. Disabled items appear "dimmed" on the menu and can't be chosen with the mouse.

3. An item number of **0** disables or enables the entire menu. The menu title isn't automatically dimmed or undimmed on the screen; call **DrawMenuBar** [4.4.3] explicitly to make the change visible to the user.

4. An item should be disabled whenever it's inapplicable in a particular situation (for instance, **Paste** when the Clipboard is empty). Items not intended to be chosen, such as separator lines, should always be disabled.

5. To disable an item when defining it with **AppendMenu** [4.3.1], precede the text of the item in the defining string with the modifier character (:

   AppendMenu (anyMenu, '(----------')

Assembly-Language Information

Trap macros:

(Pascal) Routine name	(Assembly) Trap macro	Trap word
DisableItem	**_DisableItem**	**$A93A**
EnableItem	**_EnableItem**	**$A939**

4.6.3 Character Style of Menu Items

Definitions

```
procedure SetItemStyle
        (theMenu : MenuHandle;          {Handle to the menu}
         theItem  : INTEGER;            {Item number within the menu}
         theStyle : Style);             {New character style}

procedure GetItemStyle
        (theMenu     : MenuHandle;      {Handle to the menu}
         theItem     : INTEGER;         {Item number within the menu}
     var theStyle : Style);             {Returns current character style}
```

Modifier character	Argument character	Meaning
<	**B**	Bold
<	**I**	Italic
<	**U**	Underline
<	**O**	Outline
<	**S**	Shadow

Notes

1. **SetItemStyle** sets the character style for an existing menu item; **Get-ItemStyle** returns an item's current style.

2. The character style is represented as a QuickDraw **Style** set [I:8.3.1].

3. Items in standard text menus are always displayed in the system font and the standard size; only the character style can be changed.

4. To set the character style when defining a new item with **Append-Menu** [4.3.1], use the modifier character $<$ in the defining string, followed by a single letter specifying the style (see table): for example,

AppendMenu (styleMenu, 'Shadow$<$S')

To specify two or more separate style attributes for the same item, you must use **SetItemStyle**.

5. The trap macros for **SetItemStyle** and **GetItemStyle** are spelled **_SetItmStyle** and **_GetItmStyle**.

Assembly-Language Information

Trap macros:

(Pascal) Routine name	(Assembly) Trap macro	Trap word
SetItemStyle	**_SetItmStyle**	**$A942**
GetItemStyle	**_GetItmStyle**	**$A941**

4.6.4 Marking Items

Definitions

```
procedure CheckItem
        (theMenu  : MenuHandle;         {Handle to the menu}
         theItem  : INTEGER;            {Item number within the menu}
         checked  : BOOLEAN);           {Check or uncheck?}

procedure SetItemMark
        (theMenu  : MenuHandle;         {Handle to the menu}
         theItem  : INTEGER;            {Item number within the menu}
         markChar : CHAR);              {Character to mark item with}

procedure GetItemMark
        (theMenu     : MenuHandle;      {Handle to the menu}
         theItem     : INTEGER;         {Item number within the menu}
    var  markChar    : CHAR);           {Returns character item is currently marked with}

const
  NoMark — 0;                           {Item is unmarked}
```

Modifier character	Argument character	Meaning
!	Mark character	Mark item

Notes

1. **CheckItem** checks or unchecks a menu item.

2. If **checked** is **TRUE**, the item is marked with the standard check mark symbol; if **FALSE**, any character marking the item is removed. The character removed can be any mark character, not necessarily a check mark.

3. **SetItemMark** marks an item with any desired character; **GetItemMark** returns the item's current mark character.

4. **SetItemMark** accepts a null mark character, **CHR(NoMark)**, and removes the item's mark character, if any, leaving the item unmarked. **GetItemMark** returns a null mark character for an unmarked item.

5. An item's mark character appears on the menu to the left of the item and its icon, if any.

6. To mark an item when defining it with **AppendMenu** [4.3.1], use the modifier character ! in the defining string, followed by the mark character.

7. For the standard check mark, use the Toolbox constant **CheckMark** [I:8.1.1] to store it into the defining string "by hand"

```
defString    := 'Normal!*';
defString[8] := CHR(CheckMark);
AppendMenu (OptionsMenu, defstring)
```

or create the item unmarked and then check it separately with **CheckItem**.

8. The trap macros for **SetItemMark** and **GetItemMark** are spelled **_SetItmMark** and **_GetItmMark**.

Assembly-Language Information

Trap macros:

(Pascal) Routine name	(Assembly) Trap macro	Trap word
CheckItem	**_CheckItem**	**$A945**
SetItemMark	**_SetItmMark**	**$A944**
GetItemMark	**_GetItmMark**	**$A943**

4.6.5 Item Icons

Definitions

```
procedure SetItemIcon
          (theMenu : MenuHandle;        {Handle to the menu}
           theItem  : INTEGER;          {Item number within the menu}
           iconNum : Byte);             {New icon number}

procedure GetItemIcon
          (theMenu    : MenuHandle;     {Handle to the menu}
           theItem     : INTEGER;       {Item number within the menu}
           var iconNum : Byte);         {Returns current icon number}
```

Modifier character	Argument character	Meaning
^	One-digit icon number	Define icon

Notes

1. **SetItemIcon** sets the icon associated with a menu item; **GetItemIcon** returns an item's current icon.

2. The icon is a 32-by-32-bit image, stored in a resource file under resource type 'ICON' [I:5.5.3]. It appears on the menu to the left of the item, but to the right of the mark character, if any.

3. By convention, icons used in menus have resource IDs from **257** to **511**. The icon number used by **SetItemIcon** and **GetItemIcon** is the resource ID minus **256**.

4. **SetItemIcon** accepts an icon number of **0** and removes the item's icon, if any. **GetItemIcon** returns an icon number of **0** for an item with no icon.

5. To give an item an icon when defining it with **AppendMenu** [4.3.1], use the modifier character ^ in the defining string, followed by a one-digit icon number:

```
AppendMenu (ChessMenu, 'White Bishop^4')
```

6. Since the icon's resource ID is **256** more than the icon number, it is **208** more than the character code of the corresponding digit in **AppendMenu**'s defining string. (For example, the digit **1**, with character code **$31**—decimal **49**—denotes icon number **1**, or resource ID **257**). For icon numbers greater than **9** (resource IDs greater than **265**), you can use a character in the defining string that lies beyond the digit **9** in the ASCII character set [I:8.1.1]:

AppendMenu (ChessMenu, 'Black Bishop^:')

7. The trap macros for **SetItemIcon** and **GetItemIcon** are spelled **_SetItmIcon** and **_GetItmIcon**.

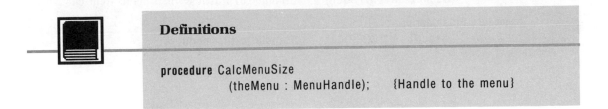

Assembly-Language Information

Trap macros:

(Pascal) Routine name	(Assembly) Trap macro	Trap word
SetItemIcon	**_SetItmIcon**	**$A940**
GetItemIcon	**_GetItmIcon**	**$A93F**

4.7 Nuts and Bolts

4.7.1 Menu Dimensions

Definitions

```
procedure CalcMenuSize
          (theMenu : MenuHandle);    {Handle to the menu}
```

Notes

1. **CalcMenuSize** recalculates a menu's screen dimensions in pixels, based on its current contents.

2. The dimensions are stored into the **menuWidth** and **menuHeight** fields of the menu record [4.1.1].

3. **CalcMenuSize** is called automatically whenever the contents of the menu are changed. It should never be necessary to call it explicitly.

Assembly-Language Information

Trap macro:

(Pascal) Routine name	(Assembly) Trap macro	Trap word
CalcMenuSize	**_CalcMenuSize**	**$A948**

4.7.2 Flashing Menu Items

Definitions

```
procedure SetMenuFlash
         (flashCount : INTEGER);     {Number of flashes when menu item chosen}
procedure FlashMenuBar
         (menuID : INTEGER);         {Handle to the menu}
```

Notes

1. **SetMenuFlash** sets the number of times a menu item flashes when chosen with the mouse.

2. A flash count of **0** specifies no flash at all; the standard flash count is **2**.

3. The user can set a preferred flash count with the Control Panel desk accessory. You should normally honor this setting and not call **Set-MenuFlash** yourself.

4. **FlashMenuBar** inverts a menu's title in the menu bar.

5. If the designated menu ID is **0** or doesn't correspond to any menu in the menu bar, the entire menu bar is inverted.

6. The trap macro for **SetMenuFlash** is spelled **_SetMFlash**.

Assembly-Language Information

Trap macros:

(Pascal) Routine name	(Assembly) Trap macro	Trap word
SetMenuFlash	**_SetMFlash**	**$A94A**
FlashMenuBar	**_FlashMenuBar**	**$A94C**

Assembly-language global variable:

Name	Address	Meaning
MenuFlash	**$A24**	Current flash count for menu items

4.8 Menu-Related Resources

4.8.1 Resource Type 'MENU'

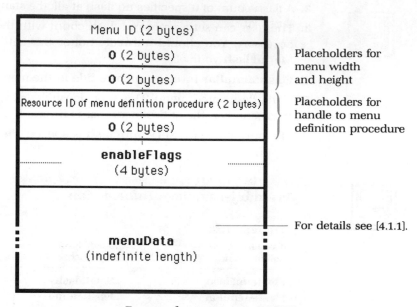

Format of resource type '**MENU**'

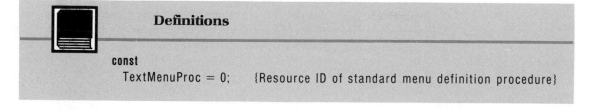

Definitions

```
const
    TextMenuProc = 0;     {Resource ID of standard menu definition procedure}
```

Notes

1. A resource of type '**MENU**' contains a complete menu record [4.1.1], including the "hidden" data at the end defining the menu's items.

2. The handle to the menu definition procedure (field **menuProc**) is replaced by the definition procedure's resource ID in the high-order word of the field, with **0** in the low-order word.

3. The resource type of the menu definition procedure is **'MDEF'**. The standard definition procedure has resource ID **0**.

4. Use **GetMenu** [4.2.2] to read in a resource of this type.

Assembly-Language Information

Assembly-language constant:

Name	Value	Meaning
TextMenuProc	**0**	Resource ID of standard menu definition procedure

4.8.2 Resource Type 'MBAR'

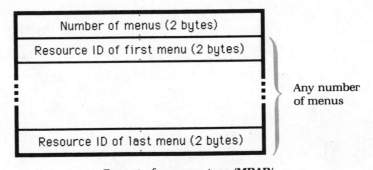

Format of resource type **'MBAR'**

Notes

1. A resource of type **'MBAR'** defines the contents of a menu bar.

2. Use **GetNewMBar** [4.4.2] to read in a resource of this type.

CHAPTER 5

Scissors and Paste

Just about any Macintosh application program, whether it's directly concerned with text or not, will have occasion to do simple text editing at one time or another. The Macintosh User Interface Guidelines prescribe certain standard conventions for text selection and editing, based on a "cut-and-paste" metaphor. In this chapter we'll learn to use the Toolbox to do on-screen text editing in accordance with the Guidelines. For purposes of illustration, we've chosen text editing as the application for our example program, **MiniEdit**.

The Toolbox's text-editing facilities are known collectively by the name TextEdit—just as the graphics facilities are called QuickDraw. Text-Edit just offers basic text editing, without any frills or fancy refinements. It works with text in the form of a straight sequence of characters, with no internal structure or formatting information of any kind. This means it can only display text in a single typeface, size, and style: it won't let you change fonts in the middle or set just a word or phrase in bold or italic. A real, professional word processing program would naturally offer more advanced capabilities, such as multiple fonts and type styles, paragraph structure, and "rulers" or other apparatus for setting margins and tabs. TextEdit is just designed to let you do the bare essentials in a simple, straightforward way.

Edit Records

Just as a graphics port is a self-contained drawing environment for QuickDraw, TextEdit's operating environment is an *edit record* of type **TERec**. (**TE** for TextEdit, of course.) Edit records are relocatable objects

201

residing in the heap, and are referred to by handles of type **TEHandle**. The definition of the edit record [5.1.1] may look imposing, but many of its fields are for TextEdit's private use, so you needn't worry about them. For the most part, those that you do need to understand present no great conceptual difficulties.

Each edit record has its own text to edit, kept in the heap and located by way of a *text handle*, **hText**, in the edit record. The text itself is just a packed array of characters of any length, like the resource data of a **'TEXT'** resource [I:8.4.1]. It is *not* a Pascal string, and doesn't begin with a length byte; its length is given by the **teLength** field of the edit record. **teLength** is an *unsigned* 16-bit integer, so the text can be up to 65,535 characters long.

Every edit record is associated with a particular graphics port, normally a window in which text editing is to be done. When you create a new edit record, whatever port is current at the time of creation becomes the port for that record. TextEdit places a pointer to the port in the new record's **inPort** field, and also copies the port's text characteristics (**txFont**, **txFace**, **txMode**, and **txSize** [I:8.3.1]) into the corresponding fields of the edit record. Then, every time you perform any editing operation involving that edit record, TextEdit will copy the text characteristics back *from* the record *to* the current port. You can change any of the text characteristics by just storing a new value directly into the appropriate field of the edit record; changing the text characteristics of the port itself, with **TextFont**, **TextSize**, **TextFace**, or **TextMode** [I:8.3.2], won't do the trick.

> TextEdit does *not* automatically set the current port to match the edit record you're working with. It's up to you to make sure the proper port is current before invoking any text editing operation.

Destination and View Rectangles

Two very important fields of the edit record are its *destination rectangle* and *view rectangle*. Both rectangles are expressed in the local coordinate system of the edit record's port—in other words, in window-relative coordinates. The destination rectangle marks the boundaries within which the text will be set; the view rectangle defines the portion of the window (or other port) in which the text will actually be displayed (see Figure 5-1). The two rectangles need not coincide, and in general, they won't. As we'll see later, the way TextEdit performs scrolling in an edit record is by shifting the destination rectangle while holding the view rectangle fixed.

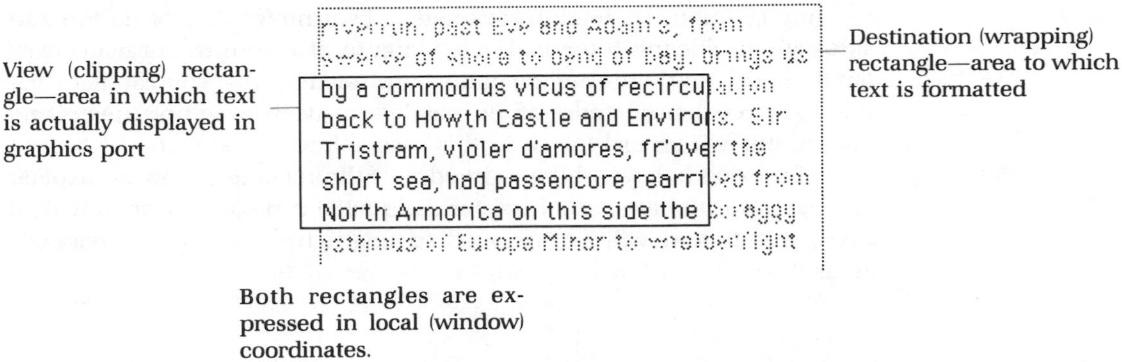

View (clipping) rectangle—area in which text is actually displayed in graphics port

Destination (wrapping) rectangle—area to which text is formatted

Both rectangles are expressed in local (window) coordinates.

Figure 5-1 Destination and view rectangles

In normal operation, TextEdit will never allow text to run outside the boundaries of the destination rectangle. When the text reaches the right edge of the rectangle, it automatically "wraps" to the next line. (Because of this, the destination and view rectangles are sometimes referred to as the "wrapping" and "clipping" rectangles.) Instead of breaking a line in the middle of a word, TextEdit carries the entire word forward to the next line; a word is never broken in the middle unless it's too long to fit on a single line by itself. This particular method of wrapping text is known as *word wrap*.

TextEdit defines a word as any sequence of non-space characters, surrounded by spaces (or ASCII control characters such as tabs or carriage returns). This means, for example, that punctuation marks are considered part of the adjoining word, and that a hyphenated word will never be broken at the hyphen. The Macintosh character set also includes a "sticky space" character (character code **$CA**) that looks just like a blank space but isn't considered a word break. If you don't like TextEdit's definition, you can redefine what constitutes a word by installing your own *word-break routine* [5.6.2] in a field of the edit record. We'll discuss word-break routines further in the "Nuts and Bolts" section at the end of this chapter.

Actually, the destination rectangle is "bottomless": only its top and sides are significant. If the text is too long to fit within the specified rectangle, it just continues out the bottom and keeps going. You can tell Text-Edit to ignore the right edge of the rectangle as well, by setting the **crOnly** field of the edit record to −**1**. In this case, a line of text won't be broken even if it extends beyond the right edge of the rectangle; only an explicit carriage return character (character code **$0D**) can cause a line break. If **crOnly** = **0**, text will be wrapped to the right edge of the rectangle as usual.

> **0** and −**1** are the only meaningful values for the **crOnly** field. Only the Shadow knows why it's defined as an integer and not a Boolean.

The vertical spacing of text within the destination rectangle is controlled by the edit record's **fontAscent** and **lineHeight** fields. As shown in Figure 5-2, **fontAscent** determines the vertical placement of the first baseline, measured from the top of the destination rectangle; **lineHeight** is the vertical distance from each baseline to the next one below it. A brand-new edit record is set up for single spacing in the font designated by its **txFont** and **txSize** fields: its first baseline is initialized to the font's ascent, and its line height to the font's character height (ascent plus descent) plus leading [I:8.2.2]. You can then adjust the vertical spacing as needed by storing new values directly into the **fontAscent** and **lineHeight** fields. To produce double spacing, for instance, you would add the original value of **lineHeight** to both fields.

> TextEdit uses the values of **fontAscent** and **lineHeight** to calculate the height of the inverted rectangle representing a text selection or of the blinking vertical bar marking an insertion point in the text. Changing one of these fields and not the other will produce strange-looking selections and insertion points, so be careful always to adjust both fields simultaneously by the same amount.

fontAscent and **lineHeight** aren't updated automatically when you change an edit record's typeface (**txFont**) or point size (**txSize**). You have to remember to update them yourself: use **GetFontInfo** [I:8.2.6] to get the characteristics of the new font.

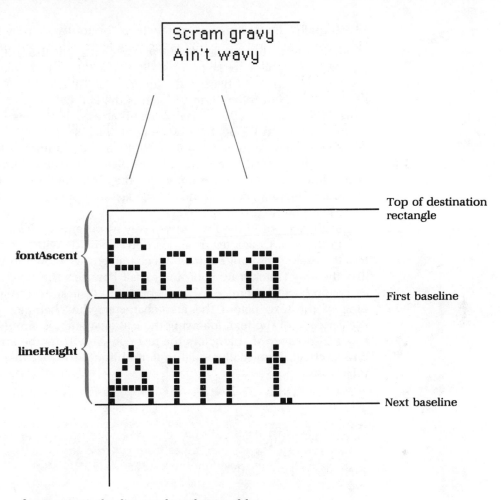

fontAscent is the distance from the top of the destination rectangle to the first baseline; **lineHeight** is the distance from one baseline to the next.

Figure 5-2 Line height and font ascent

Line Starts

Given the destination rectangle, the text to be displayed, and the typeface, type size, and character style, TextEdit can calculate how many lines the text will take up and where all the line breaks will fall. It keeps this information in the **lineStarts** array, which is the last field of the edit record. Since Pascal doesn't allow variable-length arrays, **lineStarts** is nominally indexed from **0** to **16000**. In reality it contains just as many entries as are actually needed, running from **0** up to the actual number of text lines as specified by the edit record's **nLines** field. The first element of the array, **lineStarts[0]**, corresponds to the first line of text; the last, **lineStarts[nLines]**, corresponds to the last line plus one, and marks the overall end of the text.

Each element of the **lineStarts** array represents a *character position* within the text. Character positions don't coincide with the text characters themselves, but fall *between* the characters, as shown in Figure 5-3—just the way QuickDraw coordinates fall between the pixels instead of coinciding with them. Character position **0** lies at the very beginning of the text, before the first character; the character position at the very end of the text, following the last character, is simply **teLength**, the total number of characters the text contains. Thus the array element **lineStarts[0]** is normally equal to **0**, and **lineStarts[nLines]** is equal to **teLength**.

> Like **teLength** itself, all character positions are interpreted as *unsigned* integers. Negative values from −**32768** to −**1** actually denote positive character positions from **32768** to **65535**.

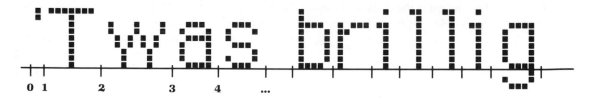

Character positions lie *between* characters.

Figure 5-3 Character positions

TextEdit automatically rewraps (or *recalibrates*) the text after any editing operation that may affect the line breaks, such as a cut, paste, or type-in from the keyboard. However, the line breaks can also be affected by non-editing operations such as changes in the edit record's text characteristics or in the width of its destination rectangle. In these cases you have to force a recalibration yourself by explicitly calling the TextEdit routine **TECalText** [5.3.1].

Preparation for Editing

Like many other parts of the Toolbox, TextEdit has a one-time initialization routine, **TEInit** [5.2.1], to set up its internal data structures. You call this routine only once, at the beginning of your program, after calling **InitGraf** [I:4.3.1] and **InitFonts** [I:8.2.4] and before attempting any other TextEdit operation. In our example program, we've already included a call to **TEInit** in our **Initialize** routine (Program 2-6).

To prepare a window for text editing, you need an edit record for that window. Make sure the window is the current port, then call **TENew** [5.2.2] to create an edit record. You supply the destination and view rectangles, in window coordinates, and get back a handle to the new edit record. As already noted, the record's text characteristics will be copied from those of the window (the current port) at the time it's created.

The text of a new edit record is initially empty: its text handle, **hText**, is set to point to a zero-length block in the heap, and its **teLength** field is set to **0**. In some cases you can just leave the text empty until the user types some in from the keyboard; at other times you'll want to set up the edit record to work on some pre-existing text (for instance, to read a file into a window for editing). There are two ways of doing this. One is to call **TESetText** [5.2.3], giving it a pointer to the text you want to edit. **TESetText** will make a copy of the text in the heap and store a handle to the copy into the edit record. From then on, any editing performed with that edit record will affect the *copy*, not the original text. If you later want to reflect the changes back to the original (for instance, to save a file back to the disk after editing), you can get a handle to the edited copy with **TEGetText** [5.2.3].

Notice that **TESetText** expects to receive a simple pointer to the text to be edited, *not* a handle! If your original copy of the text is relocatable, you have to dereference its handle and pass the underlying master pointer to **TESetText**. As always, remember to lock the handle before dereferencing it and unlock it again when you're finished:

```
HLock   (textHandle);
  TESetText (textHandle^, textLength, editRec);
HUnlock (textHandle)
```

The second way of setting an edit record's text is to store your own text handle into its **hText** field. This avoids the overhead (in both time and space) of making a copy; the edit record will just operate directly on the original text. However, you must remember to call **TECalText** [5.3.1] after storing the new text handle, to wrap the text to the destination rectangle. (When you use the first method, **TESetText** wraps the text for you automatically.) Also, don't forget to set the **teLength** field to the length of the new text.

When you're finished with an edit record, you can destroy it with **TEDispose** [5.2.2]. Beware, however: **TEDispose** disposes of the edit record's text as well as the record itself. If you're still holding a handle to the text (such as one you've received from **TEGetText**), the handle will become invalid. If you still need to refer to the text after destroying the edit record, you must either make a copy of the text and continue to work with the copy, or else hold onto the original text handle and clear the **hText** field to **NIL** before destroying the edit record, so that the text won't be destroyed at the same time.

If your program supports more than one text editing window at a time, you'll want each window to have its own edit record. You can keep a handle to the edit record in the window's reference constant field or, as in our **MiniEdit** program, make it part of a larger window data record and keep a handle to *that* as the reference constant. We've already seen (Program 3-2) how **MiniEdit**'s **DoNew** procedure allocates a window data record when creating a new window, but we glossed over the details of the record's internal structure. Now it's time to go back and fill in the gaps.

Program 5-1 shows the type definition for **MiniEdit**'s window data record. (Don't forget that this definition is just a part of our own program, *not* a Toolbox data structure!) The **editRec** field holds a handle to the window's edit record; the **dirty** flag is also connected with text editing, and we'll have more to say about it in a minute. The remaining fields have to do with topics we aren't yet ready to discuss, so we'll come back

```
type

WDHandle   = ^WDPtr;
WDPtr      = ^WindowData;

WindowData = record
                  editRec    : TEHandle;        {Handle to edit record}
                  scrollBar  : ControlHandle;   {Handle to scroll bar}
                  dirty      : BOOLEAN;          {Document changed since last saved?}
                  padding    : Byte;            {Extra byte for padding}
                  volNumber  : INTEGER;         {Volume reference number}
                  fileNumber : INTEGER          {File reference number}
             end;
```

Program 5-1 Window data record

to them later: **scrollBar** holds a handle to the window's scroll bar (Chapter 6), and **volNumber** and **fileNumber** are the volume and file reference numbers (Chapter 8) for the window's disk file. Notice that we also need a byte of padding following the 1-byte **dirty** field, to keep the fields that follow it aligned on even word boundaries.

The purpose of the **dirty** flag is to protect the user from inadvertently losing valuable work. A window is considered "dirty" if it contains editing changes that haven't yet been saved to the disk. **MiniEdit** will check a window's **dirty** flag before doing anything that would permanently destroy the window's contents (such as closing the window, reverting to an earlier version of a file, or quitting the program). If the window is dirty, **MiniEdit** will warn the user with an alert box. The user can then choose whether to proceed with the operation anyway, save the window's contents to the disk first, or cancel the operation altogether. The **dirty** flag is set to **FALSE** when the window is created; it becomes **TRUE** whenever the window's contents are changed by an editing operation (including typing in text from the keyboard), and **FALSE** again after any operation that leaves it in agreement with the disk, such as **Save**, **Save As...**, or **Revert to Saved**. (Again, notice carefully that all this is a function of our **MiniEdit** program itself, not a service provided automatically by the Toolbox.)

Program 5-2 shows the complete version of our **DoNew** procedure, which we looked at in skeleton form in Chapter 3. This version includes the code needed to initialize the components of the window's data record, including its edit record. The edit record's view (clipping) rectangle is based on the window's port rectangle, but is shortened at the right and bottom to allow room for the window's scroll bar and size box. The width of the scroll bar (global constant **SBarwidth**) is 16 pixels, but the view rectangle is actually shortened by 1 pixel less than that, since the scroll bar's

```
{ Global declarations }

const
    SBarWidth  = 16;                              {Width of scroll bars in pixels}
    TextMargin = 4;                               {Inset from window to text rectangle}

var
    TheWindow    : WindowPtr;                     {Pointer to currently active window [3.1.1]}
    TheScrollBar : ControlHandle;                 {Handle to active window's scroll bar [6.1.1]}
    TheText      : TEHandle;                       {Handle to active window's edit record [5.1.1]}


procedure DoNew;

    { Handle New command. }

    const
        windowID = 1000;                          {Resource ID for window template [3.7.1]}
        scrollID = 1000;                          {Resource ID for scroll bar template [6.5.1]}

    var
        theData    : WDHandle;                    {Handle to window's data record [Prog. 5-1]}
        dataHandle : Handle;                      {Untyped handle for creating data record [I:3.1.1]}
        destRect   : Rect;                        {Wrapping rectangle for window's text [I:4.1.2]}
        viewRect   : Rect;                        {Clipping rectangle for window's text [I:4.1.2]}

    begin {DoNew}

        TheWindow := GetNewWindow (windowID, NIL, WindowPtr(-1));   {Make new window from template [3.2.2]}

        OffsetWindow (TheWindow);                 {Offset from location of previous window [Prog. 3-11]}
        ShowWindow   (TheWindow);                 {Make window visible [3.3.1]}

        SetPort  (TheWindow);                     {Get into the window's port [I:4.3.3]}
        TextFont (Geneva);                        {Set text font [I:8.3.2, I:8.2.1]}

        with TheWindow^.portRect do               {Set up clipping rectangle [I:4.2.2]}
            SetRect (viewRect, 0, 0, right - (SBarWidth - 1), bottom - (SBarWidth - 1));
        destRect := viewRect;
        InsetRect (destRect, TextMargin, TextMargin);   {Inset wrapping rectangle by text margin [I:4.4.4]}
```

Program 5-2 Make new window

```
    dataHandle := NewHandle (SIZEOF(WindowData));      {Allocate window data record [I:3.2.1, Prog.5-1]}
    SetWRefCon (TheWindow, LONGINT(dataHandle));       {Store as reference constant [3.2.4]}

    HLock (dataHandle);                                {Lock data record [I:3.2.4]}
       theData := WDHandle(dataHandle);                {Convert to typed handle [Prog. 5-1]}
       with theData^^ do
          begin

             editRec    := TENew (destRect, viewRect);           {Make edit record [5.2.2]}
             scrollBar  := GetNewControl (scrollID, TheWindow);  {Make scroll bar [6.2.1]}
             dirty      := FALSE;                                 {Document is initially clean}
             fileNumber := 0;                                     {Window has no associated file}
             volNumber  := 0;                                     {   or volume              }

             SetClikLoop (@AutoScroll, editRec);     {Install auto-scroll routine [5.6.1, Prog. 6-9]}

             TheScrollBar := scrollBar;              {Set global handles}
             TheText      := editRec

          end; {with}
    HUnlock (dataHandle);                          {Unlock data record [I:3.2.4]}

    EnableItem (FileMenu, CloseItem)               {Enable Close command on menu [4.6.2]}

end; {DoNew}
```

Program 5-2 (*continued*)

right border will overlap with that of the window itself. The destination (wrapping) rectangle is inset a few extra pixels for legibility. (The size of the inset is defined as a program constant, **TextMargin**, so that it can easily be adjusted by changing just one declaration.)

After storing a handle to the new edit record into the **editRec** field, the procedure goes on to initialize the remaining fields of the window data record. The window's scroll bar is created from a template in a resource file using the Toolbox routine **GetNewControl**, which we'll learn about in the next chapter. The **dirty** flag is initialized to **FALSE**, since the user hasn't yet typed anything into the window that would require saving to the disk; the volume and file reference numbers are set to **0** to show that the window is not yet associated with any disk file.

Once the window data record is initialized, **DoNew** calls the TextEdit routine **SetClikLoop** to install a *click-loop routine* in the new window's edit record. (When we discuss click-loop routines later in this chapter, we'll see that this step is needed in order to provide "automatic scrolling" when the mouse is dragged outside the window during text selection, as called for in the User Interface Guidelines.) Next, since the new window will immediately become the active window, **DoNew** sets the global handles **TheText** and **TheScrollBar** to point to its edit record and scroll bar; other **MiniEdit** routines will expect to find these handles properly set up for the currently active window. Finally, since there's now an active window on the screen, **DoNew** makes sure the **Close** command on the **File** menu is enabled. (If the screen was previously empty, the **Close** command will have been disabled, since there was nothing to close.)

Text Display

The basic routine for displaying the text of an edit record is **TEUpdate** [5.3.2]. Along with a handle to the edit record, you supply an *update rectangle* as a parameter. **TEUpdate** draws the edit record's text, wrapped to the destination rectangle and clipped to the intersection of the given update rectangle, the view rectangle, and the window's visible region.

As the name implies, **TEUpdate** is intended to be used in responding to an update event for a window, to redraw the window's text as part of the overall job of redrawing the content region. Program 5-3 is the complete version of **MiniEdit**'s **DoUpdate** routine, which handles update events for the program's windows. The only difference between this and our earlier skeleton version of the same routine (Program 3-6) is that we can now show the step that actually redraws the window's text:

```
with theData^^ do
   TEUpdate (editRec^^.viewRect, editRec)
```

This gets the edit record handle from the window's data record and uses it to update the edit record. To avoid unnecessary drawing, we could have set our update rectangle to the bounding box of the window's update region—

```
whichWindow^.updateRgn^^.rgnBBox
```

—but it's simpler (though perhaps a bit less efficient) to use the edit record's view rectangle instead.

```
{ Global variable }

var
    TheEvent : EventRecord;                              {Current event [2.1.1]}


procedure DoUpdate;

    { Handle update event. }

    var
        savePort    : GrafPtr;                           {Pointer to previous current port [I:4.2.2]}
        whichWindow : WindowPtr;                         {Pointer to window to be updated [3.1.1]}
        theData     : WDHandle;                          {Handle to window's data record [Prog. 5-1]}
        dataHandle  : Handle;                            {Untyped handle for locking data record [I:3.1.1]}

    begin {DoUpdate}

        GetPort (savePort);                              {Save previous port [I:4.3.3]}

            whichWindow := WindowPtr(TheEvent.message);  {Convert long integer to pointer [3.1.1]}
            SetPort (whichWindow);                       {Make window the current port [I:4.3.3]}

            BeginUpdate (whichWindow);                   {Restrict visible region to update region [3.4.1]}

                EraseRect (whichWindow^.portRect);       {Clear update region [I:5.3.2]}

                DrawGrowIcon (whichWindow);              {Redraw size box [3.3.4]}
                DrawControls (whichWindow);              {Redraw scroll bar [6.3.1]}

                dataHandle := Handle(GetWRefCon(whichWindow)); {Get window data [3.2.4]}
                HLock (dataHandle);                      {Lock data record [I:3.2.4]}
                    theData := WDHandle(dataHandle);     {Convert to typed handle [Prog. 5-1]}
                    with theData^^ do
                        TEUpdate (editRec^^.viewRect, editRec); {Redraw the text [5.3.2]}
                HUnlock (dataHandle);                    {Unlock data record [I:3.2.4]}

            EndUpdate (whichWindow);                     {Restore original visible region [3.4.1]}

        SetPort (savePort)                               {Restore original port [I:4.3.3]}

    end; {DoUpdate}
```

Program 5-3 Handle update event

The use of **TEUpdate** isn't confined to update events only. You can use it whenever you need to redraw the text of an edit record for any reason. However, all the standard editing and scrolling operations redraw the text for you automatically, so you needn't worry about it in those cases. Notice also that **TEUpdate** automatically rewraps the text to the destination rectangle before drawing it, so there's no need to explicitly call **TECalText** [5.3.1] first.

Another routine that's sometimes useful is **TextBox** [5.3.2]. It allows you to display non-editable text anywhere you want within a window, without constructing an edit record for displaying it. (Actually, **TextBox** constructs an edit record for you, uses it to display the text, and then immediately disposes of it.)

The Toolbox can *justify* the text it displays in any of three ways: flush left (that is, aligned with the left edge of the destination rectangle), centered, or flush right. The **just** field of the edit record specifies which method of justification to use, and should always contain one of the three built-in constants **TEJustLeft**, **TEJustCenter**, or **TEJustRight** [5.1.1]. You can set the justification for an edit record with **TESetJust** [5.3.1]; this doesn't automatically redisplay the text with the new justification, however, so be sure to call **TEUpdate** afterward.

The Toolbox text editing routines don't support "full justification" to both the left and right margins simultaneously. This form of justification is more complicated than the others, since the widths of the spaces within a line must be adjusted to make the margins come out even. If you want full justification, you'll have to produce it yourself by manipulating the **spExtra** field of the graphics port [I:8.3.1].

Before   After

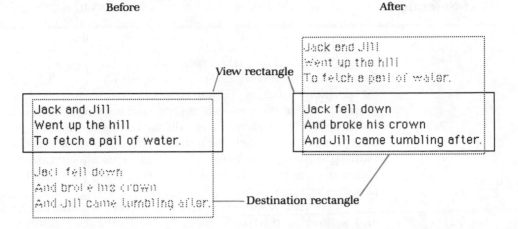

View rectangle

Destination rectangle

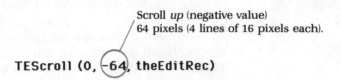

Scroll *up* (negative value)
64 pixels (4 lines of 16 pixels each).

TEScroll (0, -64, theEditRec)

Scrolling is done by changing the coordinates
of the destination rectangle while leaving the
view rectangle fixed.

Figure 5-4 Scrolling in an edit record

To scroll text within the view rectangle, use **TEScroll** [5.3.3]. The
horiz and **vert** parameters tell how far to scroll in each direction, in pixels. As mentioned earlier, scrolling is done by offsetting the destination
rectangle by the specified amounts horizontally and vertically, while leaving the view rectangle fixed. The effect is to shift the text relative to the
window (see Figure 5-4). Positive parameter values shift the text in the
direction of increasing QuickDraw coordinates: down and to the right.
Negative values scroll up and to the left. We'll see how **MiniEdit** uses
TEScroll when we talk about scroll bars in the next chapter.

Text Selection

Every edit record has a *selection range* marking where in the text the next editing operation will take effect. The selection range is defined by two fields of the edit record, **selStart** and **selEnd** [5.1.1]. These denote character positions—that is, points between characters, not the characters themselves. The text between the two character positions is the *selection*, and appears highlighted when displayed on the screen. A zero-length selection (**selStart** = **selEnd**) is called an *insertion point*, and appears as a blinking vertical bar between characters. (This blinking bar is sometimes called the "caret," even though it doesn't really look like the traditional proofreader's caret mark.)

When **TENew** creates a new edit record, it initializes both **selStart** and **selEnd** to **0**. (That's the only valid character position, since the record's text is initially empty.) When you assign text to the record with **TESetText**, both ends of the selection are automatically set to the length of the text, denoting an insertion point immediately following the last character. However, if you bypass **TESetText** and store a text handle directly into the edit record's **hText** field, you must set the selection range yourself.

The routine you use for this is named **TESetSelect** [5.4.2]. If you specify the ends of the selection range out of order (**selStart** > **selEnd**), **TESetSelect** will automatically exchange them for you; if you try to set either or both beyond the end of the text, it will force them to the actual text length. (However, remember that **selStart** and **selEnd**, like all character positions, are unsigned integers. If you give a negative value for either, it will be interpreted as a large positive value and forced to the end of the text, not to the beginning as you might expect.)

Tracking the Mouse

Most of the time, though, instead of setting the selection range yourself, you'll let the user do it by clicking or dragging with the mouse. When a mouse-down event occurs in the text rectangle of one of your windows (that is, in the view rectangle of the window's edit record), you should respond by calling **TEClick** [5.4.1], giving it the point where the mouse was pressed *in window coordinates*. Like other mouse-tracking routines that we've already encountered (such as **DragWindow** [3.5.4], **GrowWindow** [3.5.4], and **MenuSelect** [4.5.1]), **TEClick** keeps control until the mouse button is released, following the mouse's movements and giving visual feedback on the screen. (In this case the feedback is to highlight the selected text as the mouse is dragged through it.) When the user finalizes the selection by releasing the button, **TEClick** sets the edit record's **selStart** and **selEnd** fields accordingly, then returns control to your program.

TEClick remembers the time and location of the last mouse click and compares them with those of the current click. If both clicks occurred at the same character position and within a certain time interval, they're considered a *double click.* In this case, **TEClick** will select text by word rather than by character, in accordance with the User Interface Guidelines. The Guidelines also call for extending or shortening an existing selection, rather than starting a new one, when the mouse button is pressed with the shift key down. **TEClick** provides for this feature by accepting a Boolean parameter (**extend**) to tell it whether to extend or start a new selection.

The length of the double-click interval is a matter of individual preference that the user can set with the Control Panel desk accessory; the standard setting is 32 ticks, or about half a second. You can find out the current setting by calling **GetDblTime** [5.4.1], but there's no straightforward way to change it in Pascal. (In assembly language, you can just store the desired value directly into the system global **DoubleTime**.)

Program 5-4 (**DoSelect**) shows how **MiniEdit** tracks the user's text selections with the mouse. When our **DoMouseDown** procedure (Program 3-7) learns from **FindWindow** [3.5.1] that the mouse was pressed in the content region of an application window, it calls the **MiniEdit** routine **DoContent** to handle the event. Since, among other things, **DoContent** must handle mouse clicks in the window's scroll bar (or other controls, if any), we'll postpone discussing it until we talk about controls in Chapter 6. But if the click turns out *not* to be in a control, **DoContent** next checks whether it was in the window's text rectangle and, if so, calls the **DoSelect** routine shown here.

DoSelect first checks the appropriate bit in the event's **modifiers** field [2.1.5] to see whether the shift key was down at the time of the click, and sets the **extend** flag accordingly. Then it calls **TEClick** to track the mouse and set the selection. Finally, it has to examine the result and enable or disable the **Cut**, **Copy**, and **Clear** commands on the **Edit** menu, depending on whether the new selection is nonempty. (We want the commands to be disabled if the selection is just an insertion point, since there's nothing to cut, copy, or clear.) This last task is performed by the **MiniEdit** utility procedure **FixEditMenu**, shown in Program 5-5.

```
{ Global variables }

var
   TheEvent : EventRecord;                    {Current event [2.1.1]}
   TheText  : TEHandle;                       {Handle to active window's edit record [5.1.1]}


procedure DoSelect (thePoint : Point);

   { Handle mouse-down event in text rectangle. }

   var
      extend : BOOLEAN;                        {Extend existing selection (Shift-click)?}

   begin {DoSelect}

      with TheEvent do
         extend := (BitAnd(modifiers, ShiftKey) <> 0);  {Shift key down? [I:2.2.2, 2.1.5]}

      TEClick (thePoint, extend, TheText);     {Do text selection [5.4.1]}

      FixEditMenu                              {Enable/disable menu items [Prog. 5-5]}

   end;  {DoSelect}
```

Program 5-4 Mouse-down event in text rectangle

Selection Display

According to the User Interface Guidelines, a window is supposed to high-light its text selection or display its insertion point only when active, and hide them again when it becomes inactive. The TextEdit routines **TEActivate** and **TEDeactivate** [5.4.3] handle this job for you. They're intended to be called as part of the response to an activate or deactivate event; we'll see an example later in this chapter, when we look at the final version of **MiniEdit**'s **DoActivate** routine.

To make the insertion caret blink on the screen, the Toolbox has to check the system clock periodically and show or hide the caret if the required interval has elapsed since the last change. This task is handled by a TextEdit routine named **TEIdle** [5.4.3]. Just as you must call **SystemTask** [2.7.2] at least once per tick to allow the desk accessories to perform their periodic tasks, you have to call **TEIdle** that often to keep the caret blinking at a steady rate. Again, the natural place to do it is in the program's main event loop; so we'll just add a call to **TEIdle** to our earlier **MainLoop** procedure (Program 2-2), producing the final version shown in Appendix H.

```
{ Global variable }

var
    TheText : TEHandle;                             {Handle to active window's edit record [5.1.1]}


procedure FixEditMenu;

    { Enable/disable editing commands.  }

    begin {FixEditMenu}

        DisableItem (EditMenu, UndoItem);            {Disable Undo command [4.6.2]}

        HLock (Handle(TheText));                      {Lock edit record [I:3.2.4]}
            with TheText^^ do
                if selStart = selEnd then             {Is selection empty? [5.1.1]}
                    begin
                        DisableItem (EditMenu, CutItem);   {Disable menu items that operate   }
                        DisableItem (EditMenu, CopyItem);  {  on a nonempty selection [4.6.2]}
                        DisableItem (EditMenu, ClearItem)
                    end  {then}
                else
                    begin
                        EnableItem (EditMenu, CutItem);    {Enable menu items that operate   }
                        EnableItem (EditMenu, CopyItem);   {  on a nonempty selection [4.6.2]}
                        EnableItem (EditMenu, ClearItem)
                    end; {else}
            HUnlock (Handle(TheText));                 {Unlock edit record [I:3.2.4]}

        if TEGetScrapLen = 0 then                      {Is scrap empty? [5.5.4]}
            DisableItem (EditMenu, PasteItem)          {Disable Paste command [4.6.2]}
        else
            EnableItem  (EditMenu, PasteItem)          {Enable Paste command [4.6.2]}

    end;  {FixEditMenu}
```

Program 5-5 Enable/disable editing commands

Like the double-click interval discussed earlier, the caret's blink interval can be controlled by the user with the Control Panel desk accessory. The initial setting is 32 ticks, or about two blinks per second. You can read the current setting in Pascal by calling **GetCaretTime** [5.4.3], and read or change it in assembly language via the system global **CaretTime**.

Keyboard Input

The routine that handles the user's keyboard input is **TEKey** [5.5.1]. It accepts one character typed from the keyboard and inserts it into the text of an edit record at the current insertion point. If there's a nonempty selection instead of an insertion point, the typed character replaces the entire selection; the text it replaces is permanently lost and cannot be recovered. In either case, **TEKey** leaves the selection as an insertion point following the inserted character, marking the point where the next character typed will go. Then it rewraps the text to the destination rectangle and redisplays it within the view rectangle, causing the text to "bubble forward" on the screen as the user types.

TEKey also does the right thing when the user types a backspace or a carriage return. If you give it a carriage return character (character code **$0D**), it will wrap the text to a new line at that point, even if it isn't at the right edge of the destination rectangle. If you give it a backspace character (**$08**), it will "back up" the insertion point one position, deleting the immediately preceding character. (If the selection is nonempty, the backspace character simply deletes the selected text permanently from the document.) However, **TEKey** doesn't do any special formatting in response to a tab character (**$09**), since TextEdit has no notion of tab stops and doesn't provide a way to set them.

Program 5-6 (**DoTyping**) is the routine of our example program that handles the user's typing from the keyboard. This routine gets called from **DoKeystroke** (Program 4-4) when the **modifiers** field of the event record shows that the command key was not being held down at the time of the keystroke. The heart of the **DoTyping** routine is the call to **TEKey**; all the rest is merely housekeeping. First of all, we have to bring the current selection or insertion point into view, in case the user has scrolled it out of the window. This is done by a utility routine of our program named **Scroll-ToSelection**, which we'll be looking at in the next chapter. Then, after calling **TEKey** to insert the typed character, we call two more utility routines, **AdjustScrollBar** and **AdjustText**, to adjust the setting of the window's scroll bar as the length of the text changes and rescroll the

```
procedure DoTyping (ch : CHAR);

   { Handle character typed from keyboard.  }

begin {DoTyping}

      ScrollToSelection;                      {Make sure insertion point is visible [Prog. 6-13]}

      TEKey (ch, TheText);                     {Process character [5.5.1]}

      AdjustScrollBar;                         {Adjust scroll bar to length of text [Prog. 6-5]}
      AdjustText;                              {Adjust text to match scroll bar [Prog. 6-7]}
      ScrollToSelection;                       {Keep insertion point visible [Prog. 6-13]}

      DisableItem (EditMenu, CutItem);         {Disable menu items that operate   }
      DisableItem (EditMenu, CopyItem);        {  on a nonempty selection [4.6.2]}
      DisableItem (EditMenu, ClearItem);

      WindowDirty (TRUE)                       {Mark window as dirty [Prog. 5-7]}

end;  {DoTyping}
```

Program 5-6 Handle character typed from keyboard

window's text to match the new scroll bar setting. (These routines, too, are discussed in detail in the next chapter.) The second call to **ScrollTo-Selection** makes sure the insertion point stays visible as the user types; if the typing goes past the end of the window, **ScrollToSelection** will scroll the text up one line to bring it back into view.

Since **TEKey** always leaves an insertion point—that is, an empty selection—we next have to disable those editing commands that operate on a nonempty selection. Finally, since we've just changed the window's text, we have to mark the window as dirty, so that we can alert the user to save its contents before closing it or quitting the program. This is done by the utility routine **WindowDirty** (Program 5-7).

In addition to setting the **dirty** flag in the window data record, our **WindowDirty** routine also enables a couple of **File** menu commands that apply to dirty windows only. We always want to enable the **Save** command when the active window is dirty, allowing the user to save the changes to a disk file. **Revert to Saved**, on the other hand, is applicable only if the window is associated with a file, so we enable it only if the window's file reference number is nonzero. When a dirty window becomes clean after a file operation, we'll again call **WindowDirty**, but this time with a **FALSE** value for the **isDirty** parameter, to mark the window as clean rather than dirty. In this case the routine disables both the **Save** and **Revert** commands, since the window's contents are now in agreement with the version on the disk.

```
procedure WindowDirty (isDirty : BOOLEAN);

   { Mark window dirty or clean. }

   var
      theData   : WDHandle;                         {Handle to window's data record [Prog. 5-1]}
      dataHandle : Handle;                          {Untyped handle for locking data record [I:3.1.1]}

   begin {WindowDirty}

      dataHandle := Handle(GetWRefCon(TheWindow));  {Get window data [3.2.4]}
      HLock (dataHandle);                           {Lock data record [I:3.2.4]}

         theData := WDHandle(dataHandle);           {Convert to typed handle [Prog. 5-1]}
         with theData^^ do
            begin

               dirty := isDirty;                    {Set flag in data record [Prog. 5-1]}

               if isDirty then                      {Is window becoming dirty or clean?}
                  begin
                     EnableItem (FileMenu, SaveItem);   {Enable Save command [4.6.2]}
                     if fileNumber <> 0 then        {Is window associated with a file? [Prog. 5-1]}
                        EnableItem (FileMenu, RevertItem)  {Enable Revert command [4.6.2]}
                  end {then}

               else
                  begin
                     DisableItem (FileMenu, SaveItem);   {Disable menu items [4.6.2]}
                     DisableItem (FileMenu, RevertItem)
                  end {else}

            end {with}

      HUnlock (dataHandle);                         {Unlock data record [I:3.2.4]}

   end; {WindowDirty}
```

Program 5-7 Mark window dirty or clean

Cutting and Pasting

TextEdit has built-in routines for performing all the standard cut-and-paste editing operations: **TECut**, **TECopy**, and **TEPaste** [5.5.2]. They all operate on an edit record's current selection and transfer text by way of a private *text scrap* that TextEdit maintains in the heap. **TECut** deletes the selected characters from the edit record's text to the scrap; **TECopy** copies the selection to the scrap without deleting it; **TEPaste** copies the scrap into the text, replacing the current selection if it's nonempty. There's just one scrap, which is shared in common among all edit records; this allows the user to cut or copy text from one window and paste it down in another.

The Macintosh user manuals talk about cutting and pasting via the "Clipboard," but *scrap*, the term programmers usually use, seems more descriptive. Back in the typewriter era, when people actually composed written documents on something called "paper," the thing that you would cut out of one place and paste in somewhere else was undeniably a scrap. Why would you want to stick the scrap on a clipboard before pasting it back into the document?

Programs 5-8 to 5-10 are the **MiniEdit** routines for handling the standard editing commands. As you can see, they all do the same general kind of housekeeping as the **DoTyping** routine we looked at in the last section (Program 5-6), but with minor variations from one operation to another. All three routines scroll the current selection into view before performing the operation; but since **TECopy** doesn't change the existing text or selection in any way, **DoCopy** needn't scroll to the selection again afterward, nor does it have to recalibrate the scroll bar or mark the window as dirty. Menu commands that operate on a nonempty selection must be disabled after **TECut** or **TEPaste**, since they both leave the selection empty, but again this isn't necessary after **TECopy**. On the other hand, we have to enable the **Paste** command after either **TECut** or **TECopy**, since they both leave the scrap nonempty, but not after **TEPaste**, which has no effect on the previous state of the scrap. The purpose of the global flag **ScrapDirty** will become clear in the next section.

```
procedure DoCut;

   { Handle Cut command. }

   begin {DoCut}

      ScrollToSelection;                        {Make sure selection is visible [Prog. 6-13]}

      TECut (TheText);                          {Cut the selection [5.5.2]}

      AdjustScrollBar;                          {Adjust scroll bar to length of text [Prog. 6-5]}
      AdjustText;                               {Adjust text to match scroll bar [Prog. 6-7]}
      ScrollToSelection;                        {Keep insertion point visible [Prog. 6-13]}

      DisableItem (EditMenu, CutItem);          {Disable menu items that operate   }
      DisableItem (EditMenu, CopyItem);         {   on a nonempty selection [4.6.2]}
      DisableItem (EditMenu, ClearItem);

      EnableItem  (EditMenu, PasteItem);        {Enable Paste command [4.6.2]}

      ScrapDirty := TRUE;                       {Mark scrap as dirty}
      WindowDirty (TRUE)                        {Mark window as dirty [Prog. 5-7]}

   end;  {DoCut}
```

Program 5-8 Handle **Cut** command

```
procedure DoCopy;

   { Handle Copy command. }

   begin {DoCopy}

      ScrollToSelection;                        {Make sure selection is visible [Prog. 6-13]}

      TECopy (TheText);                         {Copy the selection [5.5.2]}

      EnableItem (EditMenu, PasteItem);         {Enable Paste command [4.6.2]}

      ScrapDirty := TRUE                        {Mark scrap as dirty}

   end;  {DoCopy}
```

Program 5-9 Handle **Copy** command

```
procedure DoPaste;

    { Handle Paste command. }

    begin {DoPaste}

        ScrollToSelection;                      {Make sure selection is visible [Prog. 6-13]}

        TEPaste (TheText);                       {Paste the scrap [5.5.2]}

        AdjustScrollBar;                         {Adjust scroll bar to length of text [Prog. 6-5]}
        AdjustText;                              {Adjust text to match scroll bar [Prog. 6-7]}
        ScrollToSelection;                       {Keep selection visible [Prog. 6-13]}

        DisableItem (EditMenu, CutItem);         {Disable menu items that operate  }
        DisableItem (EditMenu, CopyItem);        {  on a nonempty selection [4.6.2]}
        DisableItem (EditMenu, ClearItem);

        WindowDirty (TRUE)                       {Mark window as dirty [Prog. 5-7]}

    end; {DoPaste}
```

Program 5-10 Handle **Paste** command

There is also a pair of "scrapless" editing routines, **TEDelete** and **TEInsert** [5.5.3]. **TEInsert** inserts text that you specify directly, instead of taking it from the scrap; you supply a pointer to the text and a length count. **TEDelete** deletes the current selection without copying it to the scrap, meaning that it can't be recovered. The contents of the scrap aren't affected in any way. Program 5 11 shows how our example program uses **TEDelete** to implement the standard **Clear** command.

Notice, however, that TextEdit doesn't include a built-in **Undo** command: there is no routine named **TEUndo**. Once again, if you want your program to provide this feature you have to "roll your own." We haven't included it in our **MiniEdit** program, because it would have introduced an extra level of complexity without adding anything useful to our understanding of the Toolbox. The **MiniEdit** routine **DoUndo** (Appendix H) just beeps the speaker and does nothing; it can never actually be called anyway, since the **Undo** command on the menu is permanently disabled. If you're so inclined, you can try adding a true **Undo** command as an exercise.

```
procedure DoClear;

   { Handle Clear command.  }

   begin {DoClear}

      ScrollToSelection;                          {Make sure selection is visible [Prog. 6-13]}

      TEDelete (TheText);                          {Delete the selection [5.5.3]}

      AdjustScrollBar;                             {Adjust scroll bar to length of text [Prog. 6-5]}
      AdjustText;                                  {Adjust text to match scroll bar [Prog. 6-7]}
      ScrollToSelection;                           {Keep insertion point visible [Prog. 6-13]}

      DisableItem (EditMenu, CutItem);             {Disable menu items that operate   }
      DisableItem (EditMenu, CopyItem);            {  on a nonempty selection [4.6.2]}
      DisableItem (EditMenu, ClearItem);

      WindowDirty (TRUE)                           {Mark window as dirty [Prog. 5-7]}

   end; {DoClear}
```

Program 5-11 Handle **Clear** command

Access to the Scrap

It's important to distinguish between the Toolbox text scrap and the *desk scrap* that we learned about in Volume One, Chapter 7. The Toolbox scrap is used internally by TextEdit for your program's text editing operations; the desk scrap is used for passing information *between* one application program and another, or between an application and a desk accessory. If you want your program to be able to pass or receive information by cutting and pasting, you must make special arrangements to transfer text between the desk scrap and the internal TextEdit scrap.

TextEdit keeps a handle to its current text scrap, along with a long integer giving the length of the scrap, in a pair of special locations in the Toolbox globals area of memory. In assembly language, you can simply access these locations directly under the names **TEScrpHandle** and **TEScrpLength**. In Pascal, you can use the routines **TEScrapHandle**, **TEGetScrapLen**, and **TESetScrapLen** [5.5.4] to access their contents; as for the desk scrap, we've already seen in Volume One how to read and write it with the Toolbox routines **GetScrap** and **PutScrap** [I:7.4.3]. But the easiest way to transfer text between the two scraps is with the special-purpose transfer routines **TEFromScrap** and **TEToScrap** [5.5.5].

Our **MiniEdit** program uses these facilities in a pair of utility routines for keeping the Toolbox and desk scraps coordinated: **ReadDeskScrap** to copy the desk scrap into the Toolbox scrap, and **WriteDeskScrap** to do the reverse. At the very beginning of the program, the **Initialize** routine calls **ReadDeskScrap,** as you can see in the final version of the routine in Appendix H. If the previous application has left an item of resource type 'TEXT' [I:8.4.1] in the desk scrap, this will copy the text into the Toolbox scrap to make it available to our user for editing.

As the program runs, whenever control passes from one of its application windows to a system window containing a desk accessory, we call **WriteDeskScrap** to transfer the Toolbox scrap to the desk scrap, making the text available to the accessory. When control returns *from* a desk accessory *to* an application window, we call **ReadDeskScrap** again to copy the desk scrap back to the Toolbox scrap, allowing the user to cut text from the accessory and paste it into an editing window. Finally, at the very end of the program we have to call **WriteDeskScrap** one last time, to allow text to be passed via the scrap to the next application the user starts up.

The **ReadDeskScrap** and **WriteDeskScrap** routines are shown in Programs 5-12 and 5-13. Recall from Volume One, Chapter 7, that the Toolbox maintains a *scrap count,* accessible via the **InfoScrap** function [I:7.4.2], that's used to detect when the contents of the desk scrap have changed. Every time our **WriteDeskScrap** routine writes anything to the desk scrap, it first calls **ZeroScrap** [I:7.4.3] to change the value of the scrap count, and saves the new count in a global program variable named **ScrapCompare**. Then, when control returns from the desk accessory, **ReadDeskScrap** compares **ScrapCompare** with the current scrap count; if they're the same, then the accessory hasn't changed the desk scrap, so we know the two scraps are still in agreement and there's no need to copy one to the other.

If the scrap count *has* changed, **ReadDeskScrap** reads the desk scrap into the Toolbox scrap and saves the new count in **ScrapCompare**, to show that the desk scrap has already been read. Before calling **ReadDeskScrap** the first time, we have to initialize **ScrapCompare** to a value known to be different from the scrap count:

```
ScrapCompare := InfoScrap^.scrapCount + 1
```

(See the final version of **Initialize** in Appendix H.) This guarantees that **ReadDeskScrap** will copy in the desk scrap the first time it's called.

```
{ Global variable }

var
   ScrapCompare   : INTEGER;                        {Previous scrap count for comparison}


procedure ReadDeskScrap;

   { Read desk scrap into Toolbox scrap. }

   var
      scrapLength : LONGINT;                         {Length of desk text scrap in bytes}
      ignore      : LONGINT;                         {Dummy variable for scrap offset}
      result      : OSErr;                           {Result code from scrap transfer [I:3.1.2]}

   begin {ReadDeskScrap}

      if ScrapCompare <> InfoScrap^.scrapCount then  {Has scrap count changed? [I:7.4.2]}
         begin

            scrapLength := GetScrap (NIL, 'TEXT', ignore);  {Check desk scrap for a text item [I:7.4.3]}

            if scrapLength >= 0 then                  {Is there a text item?}
               begin
                  result := TEFromScrap;             {Transfer desk scrap to Toolbox scrap [5.5.5]}
                  if result <> NoErr then             {Was there an error? [I:3.1.2]}
                     scrapLength := result            {Make sure scrap length is negative}
               end; {if}

            if scrapLength > 0 then                   {Was scrap nonempty?}
               EnableItem (EditMenu, PasteItem)       {Enable Paste command [4.6.2]}
            else
               begin
                  TESetScrapLen (0);                  {Mark Toolbox scrap as empty [5.5.4]}
                  DisableItem (EditMenu, PasteItem)   {Disable Paste command [4.6.2]}
               end; {else}

            ScrapCompare := InfoScrap^.scrapCount     {Save scrap count for later comparison [I:7.4.2]}

         end {if}

   end; {ReadDeskScrap}
```

Program 5-12 Read desk scrap into Toolbox scrap

```
{ Global variables }

var
    ScrapCompare : INTEGER;                    {Previous scrap count for comparison}
    ScrapDirty   : BOOLEAN;                    {Has scrap been changed?}


procedure WriteDeskScrap;

    { Write Toolbox scrap to desk scrap. }

    var
        result : OSErr;                        {Result code from scrap transfer [I:3.1.2]}

    begin {WriteDeskScrap}

        if ScrapDirty then                     {Has scrap changed since last read?}
            begin

                ScrapCompare := ZeroScrap;     {Change scrap count, save for comparison [I:7.4.3]}

                result := TEToScrap;           {Transfer Toolbox scrap to desk scrap [5.5.5]}

                ScrapDirty := FALSE            {Toolbox and desk scraps now agree}

            end {if}

    end; {WriteDeskScrap}
```

Program 5-13 Write Toolbox scrap to desk scrap

Similarly, there's no need for **WriteDeskScrap** to copy the scrap in the other direction unless we've changed the Toolbox scrap since the last time it was known to agree with the desk scrap. This is the purpose of the global program flag **ScrapDirty.** We initialize this flag to **FALSE** at the beginning of the program and again whenever we copy the Toolbox scrap to the desk scrap; then we set it to **TRUE** after any editing operation that affects the Toolbox scrap (as we've already seen in Programs 5-8 and 5-9). If the **WriteDeskScrap** routine finds **ScrapDirty** set to **FALSE**, it knows that two scraps already agree, so no copying is necessary.

Now that we've defined **ReadDeskScrap** and **WriteDeskScrap**, we're finally ready to look at the complete version of our **DoActivate** routine (Program 5-14). Whenever we activate or deactivate one of our windows, we test the **ChangeFlag** bit of the event record's **modifiers** field [2.1.5] to see if control is coming from or exiting to a system window. If so, we call **ReadDeskScrap** or **WriteDeskScrap** to copy text in the appropriate direction from one scrap to the other.

```
{ Global variables }

var
   TheEvent     : EventRecord;              {Current event [2.1.1]}
   TheWindow    : WindowPtr;                {Pointer to currently active window [3.1.1]}
   TheScrollBar : ControlHandle;            {Handle to active window's scroll bar [6.1.1]}
   TheText      : TEHandle;                 {Handle to active window's edit record [5.1.1]}


procedure DoActivate;

   { Handle activate (or deactivate) event. }

   const
      active  =   0;                        {Highlighting code for active scroll bar [6.3.3]}
      inactive = 255;                       {Highlighting code for inactive scroll bar [6.3.3]}

      changeFlag = $0002;                   {Mask for extracting "change bit" from event modifiers}

   var
      whichWindow : WindowPtr;              {Pointer to the window [3.1.1]}
      theData     : WDHandle;               {Handle to window's data record [Prog. 5-1]}
      dataHandle  : Handle;                 {Untyped handle for locking data record [I:3.1.1]}

   begin {DoActivate}

      with TheEvent do
         begin

            whichWindow := WindowPtr(message);        {Convert long integer to pointer [3.1.1]}
            SetPort (whichWindow);                    {Make window the current port [I:4.3.3]}

            DrawGrowIcon (whichWindow);               {Highlight or unhighlight size box [3.3.4]}

      dataHandle := Handle(GetWRefCon(whichWindow));  {Get window data [3.2.4]}
      HLock (dataHandle);                             {Lock data record [I:3.2.4]}

         theData := WDHandle(dataHandle);             {Convert to typed handle [Prog. 5-1]}
         with theData^^ do
            if BitAnd(modifiers, ActiveFlag) <> 0 then   {Test activate/deactivate bit [I:2.2.2, 2.1.5]}
```

Program 5-14 Handle activate and deactivate events

```
begin

    TheWindow    := whichWindow;         {Set global pointers/handles}
    TheScrollBar := scrollBar;
    TheText      := editRec;

    HiliteControl (scrollBar, active);   {Activate scroll bar [6.3.3]}
    TEActivate (editRec);                {Highlight selection [5.4.3]}

    if BitAnd(modifiers, changeFlag) <> 0 then {Coming from a system window? [I:2.2.2, 2.1.5]}
        ReadDeskScrap;                   {Copy desk scrap to Toolbox scrap [Prog. 5-12]}

    FixEditMenu;                         {Enable/disable editing commands [Prog. 5-5]}

    EnableItem (FileMenu, SaveAsItem);   {Enable Save As... command [4.6.2]}
    if dirty then                        {Is document dirty? [Prog.5-1]}
        EnableItem (FileMenu, SaveItem); {Enable Save command [4.6.2]}
    if dirty and (fileNumber <> 0) then  {Is there a file to revert to? [Prog. 5-1]}
        EnableItem (FileMenu, RevertItem) {Enable Revert command [4.6.2]}

    end {then}

else

    begin

        TheWindow    := NIL;             {Clear global pointers/handles}
        TheScrollBar := NIL;
        TheText      := NIL;

        TEDeactivate (editRec);          {Unhighlight selection [5.4.3]}
        HiliteControl (scrollBar, inactive); {Deactivate scroll bar [6.3.3]}

        if BitAnd(modifiers, changeFlag) <> 0 then  {Exiting to a system window? [I:2.2.2, 2.1.5]}
            begin
                WriteDeskScrap;          {Copy Toolbox scrap to desk scrap [Prog. 5-13]}

                EnableItem (EditMenu, UndoItem); {Enable standard editing commands}
                EnableItem (EditMenu, CutItem);  (   for desk accessory [4.6.2]   )
                EnableItem (EditMenu, CopyItem);
                EnableItem (EditMenu, PasteItem);
                EnableItem (EditMenu, ClearItem)
            end; {if}
```

Program 5-14 (*continued*)

```
            DisableItem (FileMenu, SaveItem);        {Disable filing commands for desk  }
            DisableItem (FileMenu, SaveAsItem);      {   accessory or empty desk [4.6.2] }
            DisableItem (FileMenu, RevertItem)

      end; {else}

    HUnlock (dataHandle)                             {Unlock data record [I:3.2.4]}

  end {with}

end; {DoActivate}
```

Program 5-14 (continued)

One last bit of housekeeping that **DoActivate** must do is to enable and disable all the proper menu commands for the window becoming active. When an application window is activated, we call our earlier **FixEditMenu** routine (Program 5-5) to fix up the **Edit** menu as needed, depending on the window's current selection and the contents of the scrap; there are also a few **File** commands—**Save**, **Save As...**, and **Revert to Saved**—that we need to enable if the conditions are appropriate.

On exiting to a system window, we enable all the standard editing commands. (Remember that some desk accessories use these commands; it's up to us to make sure they're available whenever an accessory gets control.) Also, *whenever* we deactivate an application window, we disable the three **File** commands, just in case we happen to be closing the last window on the screen, leaving nothing but an empty desktop. (If the screen *isn't* becoming empty, then another window will immediately be activated and these commands will be enabled again if appropriate.)

Nuts and Bolts

Search and Replace

In any program that does text editing, a useful feature to include is a search-and-replace capability. The Toolbox supports search and replace with a very versatile utility routine that goes by the inelegant name of **Munger** [5.5.6] (rhymes with plunger, not hunger). This routine accepts three different pieces of text to operate on: the *destination text* to be searched, the *target text* to search for, and the *replacement text* to replace it with. All three are specified as straight sequences of characters, without the usual Pascal length count in the first byte.

In the most straightforward case, **Munger** searches the destination text, beginning at a designated starting character position, for the first occurrence of the given target text and replaces it with the replacement text. However, by varying the way you specify the target and replacement text, you can produce a variety of other effects instead. For instance, if you supply a **NIL** pointer for the replacement text, **Munger** will just find the first occurrence of the target text and return its character position within the destination text, without performing any replacement. If you give a non-**NIL** replacement pointer but specify a length of **0** for the replacement text, it will just delete the target from the destination text, in effect replacing it with nothing at all.

Similarly, if you give a target length of **0**, the specified replacement text will simply be inserted in the destination text at the designated starting position without replacing anything. If you give a **NIL** target pointer with a positive target length, the replacement text will replace the specified number of characters beginning at the starting position, regardless of what they contain. Finally, if you give a **NIL** target pointer and a negative target length, the replacement text will replace everything from the given starting position to the end of the destination text. In all cases, **Munger** returns as its function result the character position in the destination text marking the end of the text it found or inserted. If it can't find an instance of the target text within the destination (beginning at the given starting position), it will return a negative value as its result.

Automatic Scrolling

One feature of the standard interface that TextEdit doesn't provide is *automatic scrolling*. When the user, while selecting, drags the mouse out of the window without releasing the button, the window's contents are supposed to scroll continuously in the opposite direction, extending the selection as they go. As we mentioned earlier, if you want to provide this feature you have to implement it for yourself by installing a pointer to a *click-loop routine* [5.6.1] in the **clikLoop** field of the edit record [5.1.1].

If there is a click-loop routine, **TEClick** [5.4.1] will call it repeatedly while tracking the mouse, for as long as the button remains down. The click-loop routine accepts no parameters and returns a Boolean result telling **TEClick** whether to continue tracking normally (**TRUE**) or stop tracking and return immediately to the caller (**FALSE**). Under normal circumstances, the routine should just do whatever it has to do and then unconditionally return **TRUE**: it's hard to think of a convincing example in which you would want to stop tracking the mouse prematurely while the user is still holding down the button.

To implement automatic scrolling, our **MiniEdit** program uses a click-loop routine named **AutoScroll**. We've already seen in Program 5-2 how we install a pointer to this routine in the edit record of each new window we create. The routine checks the position of the mouse and, if it's outside the currently active window (more precisely, outside the view rectangle of the window's edit record), scrolls the window's text one line in the appropriate direction. When called repeatedly, it causes the text to scroll continuously, a line at a time, for as long as the button is held down outside the window. We'll look at the code of the **AutoScroll** routine when we discuss scrolling in the next chapter (Program 6-9).

When **TEClick** calls a click-loop routine, it expects to get back the Boolean result in a register, **D0**. This is no problem if the routine is written in assembly language, but if you write it in Pascal it will return its result on the stack instead of in a register. To install a Pascal click-loop routine, you have to use **SetClikLoop** [5.6.1], as we did in Program 5-2.

SetClikLoop actually stores a pointer to a special "glue routine" into the edit record. The glue routine, in turn, calls your Pascal click-loop routine and then transfers the result from the stack to register **D0** for **TEClick** to find. A click-loop routine written in Pascal won't work (and in fact will quickly crash your program) if you bypass **SetClikLoop** and store the routine pointer directly into the edit record's **clikLoop** field. Conversely, an assembly-language click-loop routine *must* be installed directly, and will just as surely blow up your program if you *do* use **SetClikLoop**.

Word-Break Routines

As we mentioned earlier, you can change TextEdit's definition of what constitutes a word by installing your own *word-break routine* in the **wordBreak** field of the edit record [5.1.1]. The word-break routine is called by **TEClick** [5.4.1] to find the beginning and end of a word when the user double-clicks the mouse, and by **TECalText** [5.3.1] to decide where to break a line when wrapping text to the destination rectangle. The routine accepts a pointer (*not* a handle!) to the text and an integer character position, and returns a Boolean result telling whether a word break falls at that position. If you don't supply a word-break routine of your own, the standard one will break a word at any space, tab, carriage return, or any other ASCII control character with a character code [I:8.1.1] of **$20** or less.

Like the click-loop routine, the word-break routine is assumed to be register-based. If you write it in Pascal, you have to use **SetWord-Break** [5.6.2] to install it in the edit record; this sets up a "glue routine" to convert the register-based call to Pascal stack-based conventions. If your word-break routine is written in assembly language, bypass **SetWordBreak** and just store the routine pointer directly into the edit record's **wordBreak** field.

Customized Text Selection

TextEdit routines such as **TEClick** [5.4.1], **TEActivate**, **TEDeactivate**, and **TEIdle** [5.4.3] ordinarily display a nonempty text selection by black-to-white inversion and an empty one (an insertion point) with a blinking vertical bar. If you wish, you can change the appearance of the selection or insertion point by installing pointers to your own drawing routines in the **highHook** and **caretHook** fields of the edit record [5.1.1]. You might use this feature, for instance, to underline the selection instead of inverting it, or to display a true caret mark at the insertion point instead of a vertical bar. The drawing routines are register-based and can only be written in assembly language; see *Inside Macintosh* for details.

REFERENCE

5.1 The Editing Environment

5.1.1 Edit Records

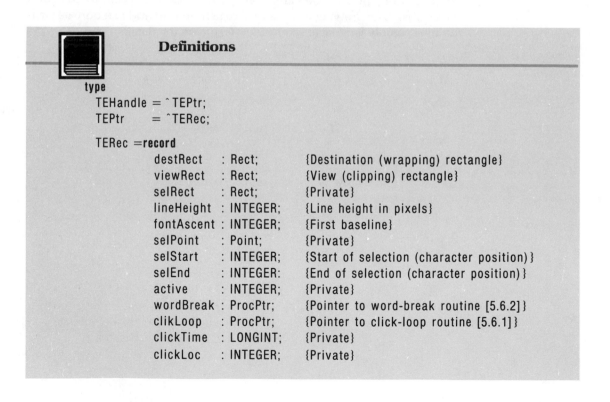

Definitions

```
type
   TEHandle = ^TEPtr;
   TEPtr    = ^TERec;

   TERec = record
           destRect   : Rect;      {Destination (wrapping) rectangle}
           viewRect   : Rect;      {View (clipping) rectangle}
           selRect    : Rect;      {Private}
           lineHeight : INTEGER;   {Line height in pixels}
           fontAscent : INTEGER;   {First baseline}
           selPoint   : Point;     {Private}
           selStart   : INTEGER;   {Start of selection (character position)}
           selEnd     : INTEGER:   {End of selection (character position)}
           active     : INTEGER;   {Private}
           wordBreak  : ProcPtr;   {Pointer to word-break routine [5.6.2]}
           clikLoop   : ProcPtr;   {Pointer to click-loop routine [5.6.1]}
           clickTime  : LONGINT;   {Private}
           clickLoc   : INTEGER;   {Private}
```

```
            caretTime   : LONGINT;        {Private}
            caretState  : INTEGER;        {Private}
            just        : INTEGER;        {Justification}
            teLength    : INTEGER;        {Length of text in characters}
            hText       : Handle;         {Handle to text}
            recalBack   : INTEGER;        {Private}
            recalLines  : INTEGER;        {Private}
            clikStuff   : INTEGER;        {Private}
            crOnly      : INTEGER;        {Break line at carriage returns only?}
            txFont      : INTEGER;        {Font number of typeface [I:8.3.1]}
            txFace      : Style;          {Character style [I:8.3.1]}
            txMode      : INTEGER;        {Transfer mode for text [I:8.3.1]}
            txSize      : INTEGER;        {Type size in points [I:8.3.1]}
            inPort      : GrafPtr;        {Pointer to graphics port [I:4.2.2]}
            highHook    : ProcPtr;        {Pointer to "custom" highlighting routine}
            caretHook   : ProcPtr;        {Pointer to "custom" insertion point routine}
            nLines      : INTEGER;        {Number of lines of text}
            lineStarts  : array [0..16000] of INTEGER
                                          {Character positions of line starts}
        end;

 const
   TEJustLeft   =  0;               {Left justification}
   TEJustCenter =  1;               {Center justification}
   TEJustRight  = -1;               {Right justification}
```

Notes

1. Fields marked "private" are for TextEdit's internal use, and are of no concern to the application.

2. **inPort** is a pointer to the graphics port in which text is to be edited, normally a window. This field is set to the port that was current when the edit record was created.

3. **hText** is a handle to the text being edited. The text is just a sequence of from 0 to 32000 characters; its length is given by **teLength**.

4. The destination rectangle (**destRect**) marks the boundaries within which text will be set; the view rectangle (**viewRect**) defines the boundaries within which the text will be displayed in the port.

5. Both rectangles are expressed in local (window) coordinates.

6. The bottom edge of the destination rectangle is ignored; text may extend downward indefinitely.

7. Text will automatically "wrap" to the next line on reaching the right edge of the destination rectangle, provided that the **crOnly** field is set to **0**. If **crOnly** = −**1**, a new line is begun only on encountering an explicit carriage return character (character code **$0D**) in the text. These are the only values **crOnly** should ever have.

8. **lineStarts** is an array of indefinite length giving the beginning character position for each line of text. Its true length is given by **nLines**.

9. **lineStarts[0]** gives the beginning of the first line of text, which is presumably character position **0**; the last element of the array, **lineStarts[nLines]**, gives the character position just beyond the end of the last line (presumably **teLength**).

10. Never store directly into the **lineStarts** array; always use the TextEdit routine **TECalText** [5.3.1] to calculate the line starts for you.

11. **selStart** and **selEnd** define the *selection range*, the character positions at the beginning and end of the current text selection.

12. If **selStart** = **selEnd**, the selection range is just an insertion point at the designated character position.

13. All character positions (**teLength**, **selStart**, **selEnd**, **lineStarts**) are expressed as *unsigned* integers: negative values from −**32768** to −**1** actually denote positive character positions from **32768** to **65535**.

14. **txFont**, **txFace**, **txMode**, and **txSize** are the QuickDraw text characteristics [I:8.3.1] for displaying text, copied from the graphics port when the edit record is created.

15. **fontAscent** is the vertical distance, in pixels, from the top of the destination rectangle to the baseline for the first line of text. **lineHeight** is the vertical distance from one baseline to the next.

16. **just** denotes the style of text justification to be used, and should be one of the constants **TEJustLeft**, **TEJustCenter**, or **TEJustRight**. Full justification (both left and right) is not supported.

17. **wordBreak** and **clikLoop** are pointers to the edit record's optional word-break and click-loop routines [5.6.2, 5.6.1], or **NIL** for the standard routines built into the Toolbox.

18. **highHook** and **caretHook** are pointers to optional drawing routines for "customizing" the appearance of the text selection and insertion point. See [5.4.3, note 7] and *Inside Macintosh* for more information.

Assembly-Language Information

Field offsets in an edit record:

(Pascal) Field name	(Assembly) Offset name	Offset in bytes
destRect	teDestRect	0
viewRect	teViewRect	8
lineHeight	teLineHite	24
fontAscent	teAscent	26
selStart	teSelStart	32
selEnd	teSelEnd	34
wordBreak	teWordBreak	38
clikLoop	teClikProc	42
just	teJust	58
teLength	teLength	60
hText	teTextH	62
crOnly	teCROnly	72
txFont	teFont	74
txFace	teFace	76
txMode	teMode	78
txSize	teSize	80
inPort	teGrafPort	82
highHook	teHiHook	86
caretHook	teCarHook	90
nLines	teNLines	94
lineStarts	teLines	96

Assembly-language constants:

Name	Value	Meaning
TERecSize	104	Size of edit record in bytes, excluding line starts
TEJustLeft	0	Left justification
TEJustCenter	1	Center justification
TEJustRight	−1	Right justification

5.1.2 Text Representation

Definitions

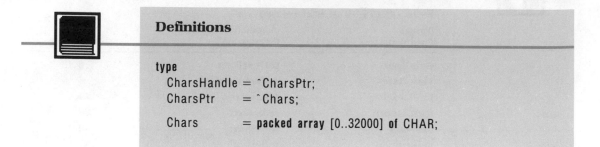

```
type
  CharsHandle = ^CharsPtr;
  CharsPtr    = ^Chars;

  Chars       = packed array [0..32000] of CHAR;
```

Notes

1. A **CharsHandle** is the form in which the text of an edit record is returned by **TEGetText** [5.2.3].

2. The underlying **Chars** array can be any length; the upper bound of **32000** used in the definition is only a dummy value. To get the actual length of the array, use **GetHandleSize** [I:3.2.3].

5.2 Preparation for Text Editing

5.2.1 Initializing the Toolbox for Text Editing

Definitions

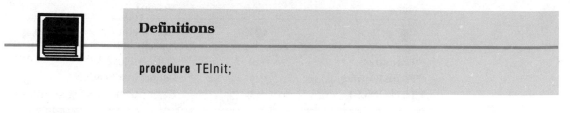

```
procedure TEInit;
```

Notes

1. **TEInit** must be called before any other text editing operation, to initialize the Toolbox's internal text scrap.

2. Before calling **TEInit**, you must first call **InitGraf** [I:4.3.1] and **InitFonts** [I:8.2.4].

3. Don't call **TEInit** more than once in the same program.

Assembly-Language Information

Trap macro:

(Pascal) Routine name	(Assembly) Trap macro	Trap word
TEInit	**_TEInit**	**$A9CC**

5.2.2 Creating and Destroying Edit Records

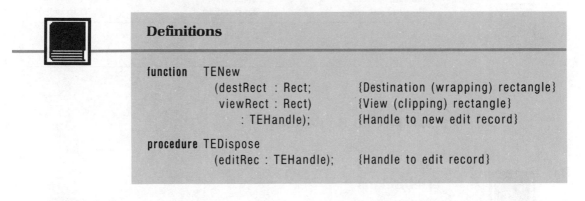

Definitions

```
function  TENew
            (destRect : Rect;        {Destination (wrapping) rectangle}
             viewRect : Rect)        {View (clipping) rectangle}
                : TEHandle);         {Handle to new edit record}

procedure TEDispose
            (editRec : TEHandle);    {Handle to edit record}
```

Notes

1. **TENew** creates a new edit record; **TEDispose** destroys an existing one.

2. The text of a new edit record is initially empty. You can give it text to edit with **TESetText** [5.2.3] or by storing directly into its **hText** and **teLength** fields [5.1.1].

3. The destination and view rectangles are expressed in the local coordinates of the current port, normally a window in which text is to be edited. This port becomes the new edit record's graphics port.

4. The edit record's text characteristics are set to those of the current port [I:8.3.1].

5. The **fontAscent** field is initialized to the ascent of the font designated by the port's **txFont** and **txSize** fields; the **lineHeight** field is initialized to the font's character height (ascent plus descent) plus leading [I:8.2.2]. This produces the effect of "single spacing." If you want, you can then change the spacing by adjusting the values of **fontAscent** and **lineHeight**.

6. The **just** field is initially set for left justification. You can change this setting with **TESetJust** [5.3.1].

7. **selStart** and **selEnd** are both initialized to **0**, representing an insertion point at the beginning of the text.

8. Disposing of an edit record with **TEDispose** also automatically disposes of its text.

Assembly-Language Information

Trap macros:

(Pascal) Routine name	(Assembly) Trap macro	Trap word
TENew	**_TENew**	**$A9D2**
TEDispose	**_TEDispose**	**$A9CD**

5.2.3 Text to Be Edited

Definitions

```
procedure TESetText
            (textPtr   : Ptr;          {Pointer to text}
             textLength : LONGINT;     {Length of text in characters}
             editRec   : TEHandle);    {Handle to edit record}

function    TEGetText
            (editRec : TEHandle);      {Handle to edit record}
              : CharsHandle;           {Handle to text}
```

Notes

1. **TESetText** sets the text to be edited by an edit record; **TEGetText** returns a handle to the record's text.

2. **textPtr** is a pointer to the text to be edited and **textLength** is its length in characters.

3. **TESetText** makes a copy of the designated text in the heap and stores a handle to the *copy* in the edit record's **hText** field [5.1.1]; the **teLength** field is set to **textLength**. Editing done with the edit record will affect the copy only, not the original text.

4. Instead of using **TESetText**, you can store your own text handle directly into the **hText** field. (Don't forget to set **teLength** properly as well.) In this case, editing with the edit record *will* affect the original text.

5. **TESetText** automatically wraps the new text to the destination rectangle, calculating its **lineStarts** and **nLines** [5.1.1], and sets the selection range to an insertion point at the end of the text. If you set the **hText** field directly, you must also set the selection range yourself and call **TECalText** [5.3.1] to wrap the text.

6. The new text is not automatically displayed on the screen; call **TEUpdate** [5.3.2] to display it.

7. **TEGetText** returns a **CharsHandle** [5.1.2] to the edit record's actual text, *not* a copy.

8. If you later dispose of the edit record with **TEDispose** [5.2.2], the handle you received from **TEGetText** will become invalid, since the text it points to will be deallocated from the heap. If you still need to refer to the text, be sure to make a copy of it before disposing of the edit record.

Assembly-Language Information

Trap macros:

(Pascal) Routine name	(Assembly) Trap macro	Trap word
TESetText	**_TESetText**	**$A9CF**
TEGetText	**_TEGetText**	**$A9CB**

5.3 Text Display

5.3.1 Wrapping and Justification

Definitions

```
procedure TECalText
        (editRec : TEHandle);   {Handle to edit record}

procedure TESetJust
        (just    : INTEGER;    {Justification (see [5.1.1, note 16])}
         editRec : TEHandle);   {Handle to edit record}
```

Notes

1. **TECalText** wraps an edit record's text to its destination rectangle, calculating its **lineStarts** and **nLines** [5.1.1].

2. Call **TECalText** after changing any of an edit record's properties that affect the location of the line breaks, such as its text, typeface, type size, character style, **crOnly** setting, or the width of its destination rectangle.

3. Each new line begins at a word boundary, normally defined as a space, tab, carriage return, or any other ASCII control character with a character code [I:8.1.1] of **$20** or less. You can change this definition if you wish by installing your own word-break routine [5.6.2] in the edit record.

4. **TESetJust** sets an edit record's justification.

5. The **just** parameter is designed to be one of the built-in constants **TEJustLeft**, **TEJustCenter**, or **TEJustRight** [5.1.1].

6. Neither **TECalText** nor **TESetJust** redisplays the record's text on the screen. Call **TEUpdate** [5.3.2] to redisplay the text with the new line breaks or justification.

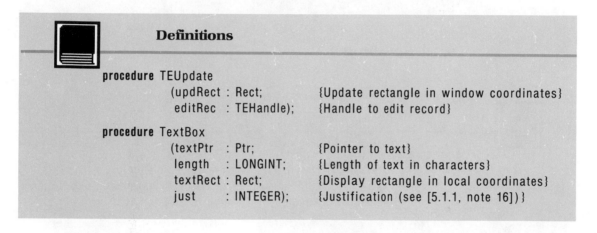

Assembly-Language Information

Trap macros:

(Pascal) Routine name	(Assembly) Trap macro	Trap word
TECalText	**_TECalText**	**$A9D0**
TESetJust	**_TESetJust**	**$A9DF**

5.3.2 Displaying Text on the Screen

Definitions

```
procedure TEUpdate
        (updRect : Rect;        {Update rectangle in window coordinates}
         editRec  : TEHandle);  {Handle to edit record}

procedure TextBox
        (textPtr  : Ptr;        {Pointer to text}
         length   : LONGINT;    {Length of text in characters}
         textRect : Rect;       {Display rectangle in local coordinates}
         just     : INTEGER);   {Justification (see [5.1.1, note 16])}
```

Notes

1. **TEUpdate** draws an edit record's text in its graphics port. Use it in responding to an update event for the record's window, or after any operation that changes the appearance of the text on the screen.

2. **updRect** is a rectangle in the local coordinates of the record's port (usually a window). The text to be drawn will be clipped to the intersection of this rectangle with the record's view rectangle.

3. The record's text is automatically rewrapped to its destination rectangle before drawing; there's no need to call **TECalText** [5.3.1] first.

4. **TEUpdate** is called automatically after any editing [5.5] or scrolling [5.3.3] operation.

5. **TextBox** displays text on the screen within a specified rectangle, without returning an edit record for editing the text.

6. **textRect** is a rectangle in the local coordinates of the current graphics port. If you want to use screen-relative coordinates, make the Window Manager port [3.6.1] current before calling **TextBox**.

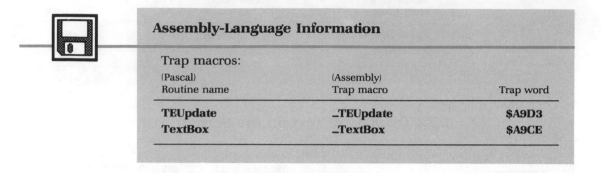

Assembly-Language Information

Trap macros:

(Pascal) Routine name	(Assembly) Trap macro	Trap word
TEUpdate	**_TEUpdate**	**$A9D3**
TextBox	**_TextBox**	**$A9CE**

5.3.3 Scrolling

Definitions

```
procedure TEScroll
        (horiz  : INTEGER;     {Horizontal scroll distance in pixels}
         vert   : INTEGER;     {Vertical scroll distance in pixels}
         editRec : TEHandle);  {Handle to edit record}
```

Notes

1. **TEScroll** scrolls text within an edit record's view rectangle.

2. The destination rectangle is offset by the number of pixels specified by **horiz** and **vert**; the view rectangle is unchanged.

3. Positive values for **vert** scroll the text down, negative values scroll up; positive values for **horiz** scroll to the right, negative values to the left.

4. The text is automatically updated on the screen to reflect the new scroll position.

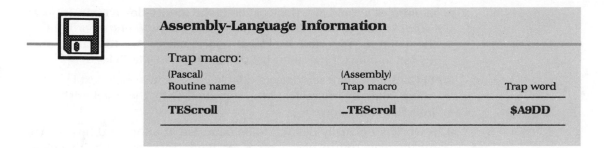

Assembly-Language Information

Trap macro:

(Pascal) Routine name	(Assembly) Trap macro	Trap word
TEScroll	**_TEScroll**	**$A9DD**

5.4 Text Selection

5.4.1 Selection with the Mouse

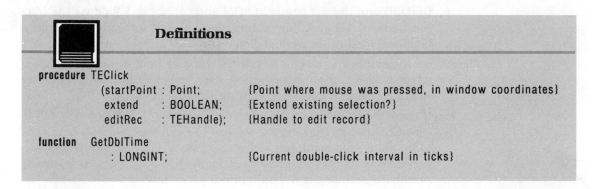

Definitions

```
procedure TEClick
         (startPoint : Point;        {Point where mouse was pressed, in window coordinates}
          extend     : BOOLEAN;      {Extend existing selection?}
          editRec    : TEHandle);    {Handle to edit record}

function  GetDblTime
              : LONGINT;             {Current double-click interval in ticks}
```

Notes

1. Call **TEClick** after a mouse-down event in an edit record's view rectangle. This allows the user to set an insertion point or select text by clicking or dragging with the mouse.

2. **TEClick** keeps control for as long as the user holds down the mouse button. It unhighlights the previous selection on the screen and then tracks the movements of the mouse, highlighting the new selection and adjusting the edit record's selection range (**selStart** and **selEnd**) accordingly.

3. If the new selection is an insertion point (**selStart** = **selEnd**), it's displayed on the screen as a blinking vertical bar.

4. **startPoint** should give the location of the mouse-down event, in *local* (*window*) *coordinates*. In the **where** field of the event record [2.1.1], the point is reported in *global* coordinates. Use **GlobalToLocal** [I:4.4.2] to convert the point before passing it to **TEClick**.

5. **TEClick** automatically detects double clicks and selects text by word rather than by character, in accordance with the Macintosh User Interface Guidelines.

6. A word is normally defined to be bounded at either end by a space, tab, carriage return, or any other ASCII control character with a character code [I:8.1.1] of **$20** or less. You can change this definition by installing your own word-break routine [5.6.2] in the edit record.

7. The maximum time interval defining a double click is set by the user with the Control Panel desk accessory. **GetDblTime** returns the current setting in ticks (sixtieths of a second). The standard setting is 32 ticks.

8. **GetDblTime** doesn't reside in ROM and cannot be called via the trap mechanism. To find. the current double-click interval in assembly language, look in the system global **DoubleTime**.

9. Set the **extend** parameter to **TRUE** if the user held down the shift key while pressing the mouse button. This tells **TEClick** to extend the existing selection instead of starting a new one.

10. If the edit record has a click-loop routine [5.6.1], **TEClick** will call it repeatedly while tracking the mouse. You can use this feature to provide "automatic scrolling" when the user drags the mouse outside the view rectangle, as prescribed in the User Interface Guidelines. Automatic scrolling is *not* built into the Toolbox.

Assembly-Language Information

Trap macro:

(Pascal) Routine name	(Assembly) Trap macro	Trap word
TEClick	**_TEClick**	**$A9D4**

Assembly-language global variable:

Name	Address	Meaning
DoubleTime	**$2F0**	Current double-click interval in ticks

5.4.2 Selection Control

Definitions

```
procedure TESetSelect
            (selStart : LONGINT;    {Start of selection (character position)}
             selEnd   : LONGINT;    {End of selection (character position)}
             editRec  : TEHandle);  {Handle to edit record}
```

Notes

1. **TESetSelect** sets an edit record's selection range directly, rather than in response to the mouse.

2. **selStart** and **selEnd** are interpreted as *unsigned* integers: negative values from **−32768** to **−1** actually denote positive character positions from **32768** to **65535**.

3. If the endpoints are specified out of order (**selStart > selEnd**), their values are automatically reversed.

4. If either endpoint is specified beyond the end of the edit record's text, it's set to the actual end of text.

5. The previous selection is unhighlighted on the screen and the new one is highlighted.

6. If **selStart = selEnd**, the new selection is an insertion point and is represented on the screen by a blinking vertical bar.

Assembly-Language Information

Trap macro:

(Pascal) Routine name	(Assembly) Trap macro	Trap word
TESetSelect	**_TESetSelect**	**$A9D1**

5.4.3 Selection Display

Definitions

procedure TEActivate
         (editRec : TEHandle);   {Handle to edit record}

procedure TEDeactivate
         (editRec : TEHandle);   {Handle to edit record}

procedure TEIdle
         (editRec : TEHandle);   {Handle to edit record}

function   GetCaretTime
          : LONGINT;   {Current blink interval in ticks}

Notes

1. **TEActivate** and **TEDeactivate** should be called as part of the response to an activate or deactivate event for a text editing window.

2. **TEActivate** highlights the edit record's selection or displays a blinking bar at the insertion point; **TEDeactivate** does the reverse.

3. **TEIdle** reads the system clock [2.7.1] and periodically blinks the edit record's insertion point on and off.

4. When a text editing window is active, you should call **TEIdle** at least once per tick (sixtieth of a second) to keep the insertion point blinking constantly. This is normally done by calling it once on every pass of the program's main event loop. It may have to be called more often during time-consuming operations.

5. The time interval between blinks is set by the user with the Control Panel desk accessory. **GetCaretTime** returns the current setting in ticks. The standard setting is 32 ticks.

6. **GetCaretTime** doesn't reside in ROM and can't be called via the trap mechanism. To find the current blink interval in assembly language, look in the system global **CaretTime**.

7. It's possible to "customize" the appearance of the selection and insertion point by installing pointers to your own drawing routines in the **highHook** and **caretHook** fields of the edit record [5.1.1]. The drawing routines can only be written in assembly language; see *Inside Macintosh* for details.

Assembly-Language Information

Trap macros:

(Pascal) Routine name	(Assembly) Trap macro	Trap word
TEActivate	**_TEActivate**	**$A9D8**
TEDeactivate	**_TEDeactivate**	**$A9D9**
TEIdle	**_TEIdle**	**$A9DA**

Assembly-language global variable:

Name	Address	Meaning
CaretTime	**$2F4**	Current blink interval in ticks

5.5 Editing Operations

5.5.1 Keyboard Input

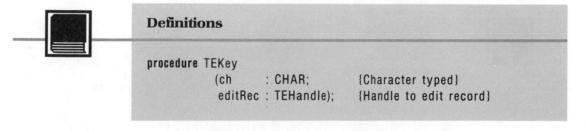

Definitions

```
procedure TEKey
          (ch      : CHAR;        {Character typed}
           editRec : TEHandle);   {Handle to edit record}
```

Notes

1. **TEKey** accepts a character typed from the keyboard and inserts it into the text of an edit record.

2. If there is a nonempty text selection, the character replaces it; if the selection is empty (an insertion point), the character is inserted at that point.

3. If the character is a backspace (character code **$08**) and the selection is nonempty, the selected text is deleted from the document; if the selection is an insertion point, the character preceding it is deleted.

4. A deleted or replaced selection or a backspaced character is *not* copied to the scrap and cannot be recovered.

5. If the character is a carriage return (character code **$0D**), it forces a new line beginning with the next character in the document.

6. After the insertion the text is automatically rewrapped to the destination rectangle and redisplayed within the view rectangle.

7. An insertion point is left following the inserted character.

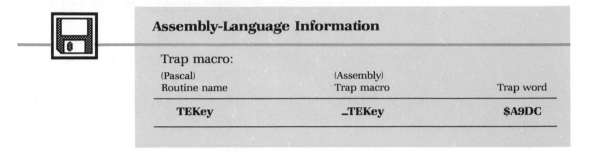

Assembly-Language Information

Trap macro:

(Pascal) Routine name	(Assembly) Trap macro	Trap word
TEKey	**_TEKey**	**$A9DC**

5.5.2 Cutting and Pasting

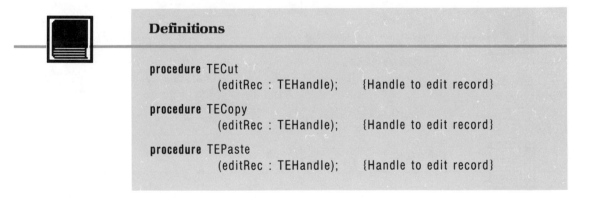

Definitions

```
procedure TECut
        (editRec : TEHandle);    {Handle to edit record}
procedure TECopy
        (editRec : TEHandle);    {Handle to edit record}
procedure TEPaste
        (editRec : TEHandle);    {Handle to edit record}
```

Notes

1. These routines perform standard cut-and-paste editing on the text of an edit record via the Toolbox's private text scrap.

2. **TECut** deletes the current selection from the text and places it in the scrap; **TECopy** copies the current selection to the scrap without deleting it from the text.

3. In both cases, the previous contents of the scrap are lost and cannot be recovered.

4. If the current selection is empty (an insertion point), the scrap is emptied.

5. **TECut** leaves an insertion point at the point of the cut; **TECopy** leaves the selection range unchanged.

6. **TEPaste** copies the current contents of the scrap into the edit record's text.

7. If the current selection is nonempty, it's replaced by the pasted text; if it's an insertion point, the scrap is pasted at that point.

8. If the scrap is currently empty, the selection is simply deleted.

9. An insertion point is left at the end of the pasted text.

10. The contents of the scrap are unaffected.

11. **TECut** and **TEPaste** automatically rewrap the text to the destination rectangle and redisplay it within the view rectangle.

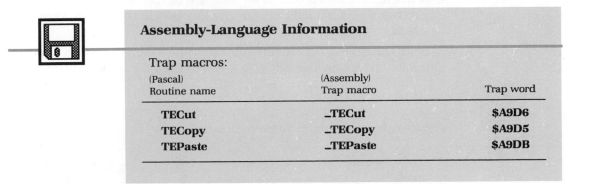

Assembly-Language Information

Trap macros:

(Pascal) Routine name	(Assembly) Trap macro	Trap word
TECut	**_TECut**	**$A9D6**
TECopy	**_TECopy**	**$A9D5**
TEPaste	**_TEPaste**	**$A9DB**

5.5.3 Scrapless Editing

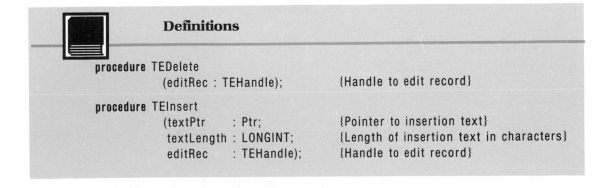

Definitions

```
procedure TEDelete
          (editRec : TEHandle);        {Handle to edit record}

procedure TEInsert
          (textPtr    : Ptr;           {Pointer to insertion text}
           textLength : LONGINT;       {Length of insertion text in characters}
           editRec    : TEHandle);     {Handle to edit record}
```

Notes

1. These routines operate on the text of an edit record without affecting the Toolbox's private text scrap.

2. **TEDelete** deletes the current selection; the deleted text is not copied to the scrap and cannot be recovered.

3. An insertion point is left at the point of the deletion.

4. If the selection is empty (an insertion point), nothing happens.

5. **TEInsert** inserts text at the beginning of the current selection, but without replacing the selection. If the selection is an insertion point, the text is inserted at that point.

6. The selection range is adjusted by the length of the insertion, so that the same characters remain selected after the operation as before.

7. **textPtr** is a pointer to the text to be inserted; **textLength** is its length in characters.

8. **textLength** is interpreted as an *unsigned* integer: negative values from **−32768** to **−1** actually denote positive text lengths from **32768** to **65535**.

9. Both **TEDelete** and **TEInsert** automatically rewrap the text to the destination rectangle and redisplay it within the view rectangle.

Assembly-Language Information

Trap macros:

(Pascal) Routine name	(Assembly) Trap macro	Trap word
TEDelete	**_TEDelete**	**$A9D7**
TEInsert	**_TEInsert**	**$A9DE**

5.5.4 Scrap Access

Definitions

function	TEScrapHandle : Handle;	{Handle to Toolbox scrap}
function	TEGetScrapLen : LONGINT;	{Current length of Toolbox scrap in characters}
procedure	TESetScrapLen (newLength : LONGINT);	{New length of Toolbox scrap in characters}

Notes

1. **TEScrapHandle** returns a handle to the current Toolbox text scrap; **TEGetScrapLen** returns its current length in characters; **TESet-ScrapLen** sets its length to a new value.

2. These routines do not reside in ROM and cannot be called via the trap mechanism. In assembly language, you can access the Toolbox scrap handle and length directly in the global variables **TEScrpHandle** and **TEScrpLength**.

Assembly-Language Information

Assembly-language global variables:

Name	Address	Meaning
TEScrpHandle	**$AB4**	Handle to text scrap
TEScrpLength	**$AB0**	Length of text scrap in characters

5.5.5 Scrap Transfer

Definitions

```
function TEFromScrap
            : OSErr;      {Result code}

function TEToScrap
            : OSErr;      {Result code}
```

Notes

1. These routines transfer text between the desk scrap [I:7.4] and the Toolbox's internal scrap.

2. **TEFromScrap** transfers a text item, if there is one, from the desk scrap to the Toolbox scrap.

3. If there is no desk scrap, or if it doesn't contain an item of type 'TEXT' [I:8.4.1], **TEFromScrap** returns an error code of **NoScrapErr** or **NoTypeErr** [I:7.4.3] and leaves the Toolbox scrap unaffected.

4. **TEToScrap** transfers the contents of the Toolbox scrap to the desk scrap as an item of type 'TEXT'.

5. If the Toolbox scrap is empty, an empty text item will be written to the desk scrap.

6. Always clear the previous contents of the desk scrap by calling **Zero-Scrap** [I:7.4.3] before transferring text to it with **TEToScrap**. **TEToScrap** does *not* take care of this automatically.

7. **TEFromScrap** and **TEToScrap** do not reside in ROM and cannot be called via the trap mechanism; in assembly language you have to carry out the transfer for yourself. Use the Toolbox routines **GetScrap** and **PutScrap** [I:7.4.3] to access the desk scrap and the system globals **TEScrpLength** and **TEScrpHandle** [5.5.4] to access the Toolbox scrap.

5.5.6 Search and Replace

Definitions

```
function Munger
        (textHandle   : Handle;           {Handle to destination text}
        startAt       : LONGINT;          {Character position at which to start search}
        targetText    : Ptr;              {Pointer to target text}
        targetLength  : LONGINT;          {Length of target text}
        replaceText   : Ptr;              {Pointer to replacement text}
        replaceLength : LONGINT)          {Length of replacement text}
        : LONGINT;                        {Character position at end of operation}
```

Notes

1. This routine searches character text for a given target string and optionally replaces it with a given replacement string.

2. **textHandle** is a handle to the *destination text*, the text to be operated on; **startAt** is the character position at which the search is to begin.

3. **startAt** must not be greater than the actual length of the destination text designated by **textHandle**.

4. **targetText** is a pointer to the *target text*, the text to be searched for; **targetLength** is its length. The target text is the first **targetLength** characters beginning at the location pointed to by **targetText**.

5. **replaceText** is a pointer to the *replacement text*, the text that is to replace the target text; **replaceLength** is its length. The replacement text is the first **replaceLength** characters beginning at the location pointed to by **replaceText**.

6. The destination, target, and replacement text all consist of straight ASCII text, *not* a Pascal-style string. None of the three carries a leading length-count byte.

7. In the normal case, when **targetText**, **targetLength**, **replaceText**, and **replaceLength** are all positive, the first occurrence of the target text found in the destination text, starting from character position **startAt**, is replaced by the replacement text. The function result is the character position following the replacement.

8. If a partial match for the target text is found, running from character position **startAt** to the end of the destination text, it is replaced by the replacement text.

9. If no occurrence of the target text is found, the function result is negative.

10. If no target text is specified (**targetText** = **NIL**) and **targetLength** > **0**, the text replaced is the first **targetLength** characters in the destination text, beginning at character position **startAt**. The function result is the character position following the replacement.

11. If no target text is specified (**targetText** = **NIL**) and **targetLength** < **0**, the text replaced is all characters from character position **startAt** to the end of the destination text. The function result is the character position following the replacement.

12. If **targetLength** = **0**, the replacement text is simply inserted in the destination text at character position **startAt**. The function result is the character position following the insertion.

13. If no replacement text is specified (**replaceText** = **NIL**), the target string is found but not replaced. The function result is the character position following the first occurrence of the target text within the destination text, starting from character position **startAt**.

14. If **replaceText** ≠ **NIL** and **replaceLength** = **0**, the first occurrence of the target text, starting from character position **startAt**, is deleted from the destination text. The function result is the character position at which the deletion took place.

Assembly-Language Information

Trap macro:

(Pascal) Routine name	(Assembly) Trap macro	Trap word
Munger	**_Munger**	**$A9E0**

5.6 Nuts and Bolts

5.6.1 Click-Loop Routine

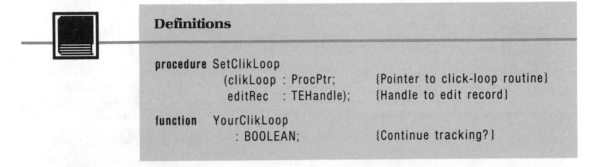

Definitions

```
procedure SetClikLoop
          (clikLoop : ProcPtr;        {Pointer to click-loop routine}
           editRec  : TEHandle);      {Handle to edit record}

function  YourClikLoop
              : BOOLEAN;              {Continue tracking?}
```

Notes

1. **SetClikLoop** installs a *click-loop routine* in an edit record. The click-loop routine will be called repeatedly by **TEClick** [5.4.1] while tracking the mouse.

2. The most common use of the click-loop routine is to provide "automatic scrolling" when the mouse is dragged outside the view rectangle during text selection, as prescribed in the Macintosh User Interface Guidelines.

3. The function heading shown above is a model for your click-loop routine. You can give your routine any name you like; there is no Toolbox routine named **YourClikLoop**.

4. The Toolbox has no built-in click-loop routine. If you don't install one of your own, **TEClick** will highlight the text selection while tracking the mouse, without taking any other special action.

5. The Boolean result returned by the click-loop routine tells **TEClick** whether to continue tracking the mouse (**TRUE**) or stop tracking and return immediately (**FALSE**). Normally your click-loop routine should unconditionally return **TRUE**.

6. All calls issued by **TEClick** to the click-loop routine are register-based (see "Register usage," following). **SetClikLoop** sets up a special "glue routine" to intercept these calls and convert them to Pascal stack-based calling conventions. Always use **SetClikLoop** to install your click-loop routine if it's written in Pascal.

7. For click-loop routines written in assembly language, *don't* use **Set-ClikLoop**: just store a pointer to the routine directly into the edit record's **clikLoop** field [5.1.1].

8. Because of a bug in **TEClick**, assembly-language click-loop routines must preserve the contents of register **D2**.

Assembly-Language Information

Register usage:

Routine	Register	Contents
YourClikLoop	**D0.L** (out)	function result
		1: continue tracking
		0: return immediately
	D2.L (out)	same as **D2.L** (in)

5.6.2 Word-Break Routine

Definitions

```
procedure SetWordBreak
          (wordBreak : ProcPtr;        {Pointer to word-break routine}
           editRec   : TEHandle);      {Handle to edit record}

function  YourWordBreak
          (theText   : Ptr;            {Pointer to text}
           charPos   : INTEGER)        {Character position within text}
           : BOOLEAN;                  {Is there a word break at that position?}
```

Notes

1. **SetWordBreak** installs a *word-break routine* in an edit record, defining where the word breaks fall in the edit record's text.

2. The word-break routine is called by **TECalText** [5.3.1] to decide where to start a new line when wrapping text, and by **TEClick** [5.4.1] to find the word boundaries when selecting text by word after a double click.

3. The function heading shown above is a model for your word-break routine. You can give your routine any name you like; there is no Toolbox routine named **YourWordBreak**.

4. The standard word-break routine, used if you don't install one of your own, breaks at a space, tab, carriage return, or any other ASCII control character with a character code [I:8.1.1] of **$20** or less.

5. All calls issued by **TECalText** or **TEClick** to the word-break routine are register-based (see "Register usage," below). **SetWordBreak** sets up a special "glue routine" to intercept these calls and convert them to Pascal stack-based calling conventions. Always use **SetWordBreak** to install your word-break routine if it's written in Pascal.

6. For word-break routines written in assembly language, *don't* use **SetWordBreak**: just store a pointer to the routine directly into the edit record's **wordBreak** field [5.1.1].

7. Assembly-language word-break routines return their result via the 68000 processor's **Z** (zero) condition flag. Notice that the setting of the flag is inverted: **0** for a word break at the designated character position, **1** for no break.

Assembly-Language Information

Register usage:

Routine	Register	Contents
YourWordBreak	**A0.L** (in)	**theText**
	D0.W (in)	**charPos**
	Z flag	function result **0**: break **1**: no break

C H A P T E R

6

At the Controls

In keeping with the Macintosh user interface philosophy, *controls* give the user a way to choose options or make things happen by direct manipulation with the mouse. The most familiar examples of controls are the "pushbuttons" and "checkboxes" that you see in dialog and alert boxes, and the scroll bars along the right and bottom edges of a document window. In this chapter we'll see how such controls work and how you can use them in your own programs.

Standard Control Types

Like windows (Chapter 3), controls are implemented by a two-tiered software structure. The Toolbox, built into the Macintosh ROM, includes all of the general facilities needed to create and manipulate them, while the specific behavior of each particular type of control is defined by a *control definition function* that's read from the disk as a resource. When you create a control, you identify its type with a coded integer called a *control definition ID*. The definition ID includes the resource ID of the definition function (its resource type is '**CDEF**'), along with some further information that the Toolbox uses internally. The Toolbox finds the definition function on the disk and loads it into memory; then it calls the definition function whenever it needs to perform a type-dependent operation such as displaying the control on the screen or detecting mouse clicks inside it.

Certain standard control types are predefined for you. Their definition functions are built into the standard **System** resource file that's included on all Macintosh software disks, and their definition IDs are defined as Toolbox constants [6.2.1]. You can use the standard control types just by supplying one of these standard IDs when you create a control. If the standard types don't meet your needs, you can "roll your own" control types by writing your own definition functions for them; Apple's *Inside Macintosh* manual tells how to do this. Here we'll just concentrate on the standard control types.

Controls fall into two general categories, buttons and dials. Buttons have just two states—on and off—and can be "pressed" by clicking with the mouse. Figure 6-1 shows the three standard types of button:

- *Pushbuttons* make something happen immediately. The action may occur continuously for as long as the button is "held down" with the mouse, or just instantaneously when the button is released.

- *Checkboxes* retain an on-or-off setting that affects the way something will happen at a later time. Clicking with the mouse alternately turns the checkbox on and off, independently of any other control.

- *Radio buttons* are like interdependent checkboxes that are grouped together to offer a multiple choice. They work like the selector buttons on your car radio: pressing any one button makes all the others in the group "pop out," so that only one button at a time can be in the "on" position.

From the point of view of the Toolbox, all three types of button are equivalent; they differ only in the way they appear on the screen, as determined by their definition functions. The differences in appearance are meant to suggest the different forms of behavior described above, but it's entirely up to you to make them behave as described. Later in this chapter we'll see how.

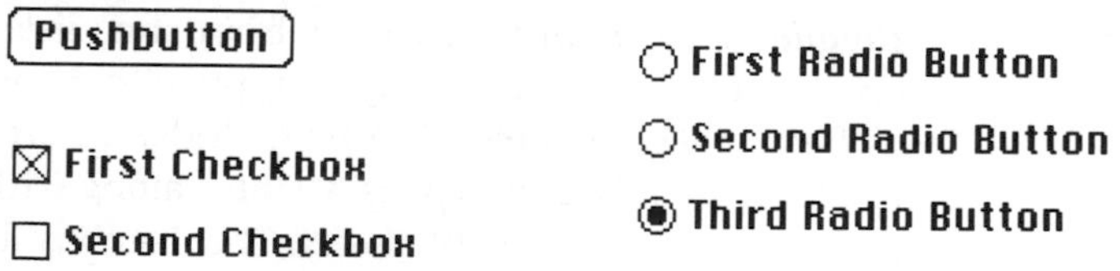

Figure 6-1 Standard buttons

Dials (Figure 6-2) offer a whole range of settings instead of just a simple on-or-off. They typically have a moving *indicator* of some kind that displays the current setting and can be manipulated with the mouse. The only predefined type of dial is the standard scroll bar, whose indicator (the *scroll box*) shows the relative position of a window's visible contents with respect to the entire document it's displaying. We'll be discussing scroll bars at length later on.

A dial has a moving indicator
and can take on a range of settings.

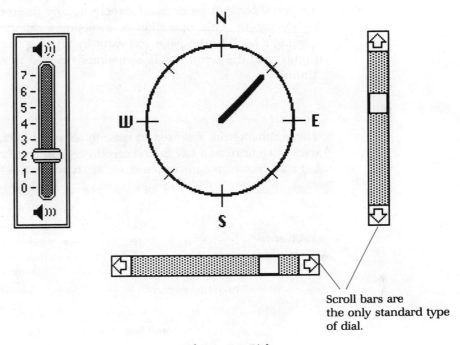

Scroll bars are
the only standard type
of dial.

Figure 6-2 Dials

Part Codes

One important point to notice about scroll bars is that they are made up of several parts that produce different effects when manipulated with the mouse, (see Figure 6-3):

- The *up arrow* scrolls the window's contents upward a line at a time.
- The *down arrow* scrolls downward a line at a time.
- The *page-up region* scrolls upward one windowful ("page") at a time.
- The *page-down region* scrolls downward one "page" at a time.
- The *scroll box* can be dragged directly to any desired position within the document. This operation is sometimes called "thumbing" (like opening a book to the page you want by flipping the pages with your thumb), and the scroll box is sometimes referred to as the scroll bar's "thumb."

These same terms are used to refer to all scroll bars, horizontal as well as vertical. In a horizontal scroll bar, "up" really means to the left and "down" means to the right, as shown in the figure.

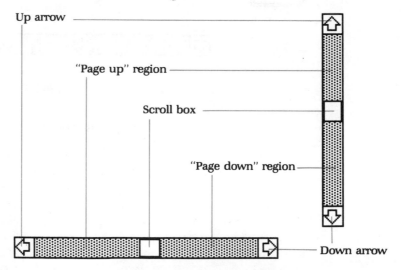

Figure 6-3 Parts of a scroll bar

In general, a control can have any number of parts it needs to do its job. The various parts are identified by integer *part codes* analogous to the ones that **FindWindow** [3.5.1] uses for the parts of a window. Unlike windows, however, in controls the number and nature of the parts can vary from one type of control to another. So each type of control must have its own set of part codes, assigned by the definition function for that particular control type.

Part codes are always 1-byte integers between **0** and **255**. Certain specific values—**0**, **128**, and **255**—have special meanings, which we'll be learning about later. All the rest are available for the definition function to use as ordinary part codes; the only other restriction is that the moving indicator of a dial (such as the scroll box or "thumb" of the scroll bar) must have a part code of **129** or greater, while all other parts must have codes between **1** and **127.**

The part codes for the standard control types are predefined as Toolbox constants [6.4.1]. Simple buttons have just one part each, denoted by the part code **InButton** for pushbuttons, **InCheckbox** for both checkboxes and radio buttons. For scroll bars, the part codes are named **InUpButton**, **InDownButton**, **InPageUp**, **InPageDown**, and **InThumb**.

Creating and Destroying Controls

The internal representation of a control is a relocatable *control record*, referred to by means of a *control handle* [6.1.1]. Like windows, controls can be created either by supplying the needed descriptive information directly or by reading it from a *control template* in a resource file. As usual, the recommended method is to use a predefined template, of resource type '**CNTL**' [6.5.1]. You just pass the template's resource ID to the Toolbox routine **GetNewControl** [6.2.1]; all the information needed to create the control comes from the template (with one exception, which we'll get to in a minute). Alternatively, you can supply the same information explicitly as parameters to **NewControl** [6.2.1]. In either case, the Toolbox will allocate heap space for a new control record, fill it with the specified information, and return a control handle that you can use from then on to refer to the control.

Every control belongs to exactly one window, called its *owner* or *owning window*. The control will appear on the screen as part of the owning window's content region, and will operate specifically on that window or its contents. The owning window is the one piece of descriptive information that can't be included in a control template, since the window doesn't yet exist at the time the template is created. So that's the only piece of information you still have to supply explicitly as a parameter when you create a control with **GetNewControl**. We've already seen an example of this in Program 5.2 (**DoNew**), where we created the scroll bar for a new window (named **TheWindow**) with the statement

```
scrollBar := GetNewControl (scrollID, TheWindow)
```

All of a given window's controls are kept in a *control list*, and new controls are added to the front of this list as they're created. The **control-List** field of the window record [3.1.1] holds a handle to the first control in the list; each control then points to the next via a handle in the control record's **nextControl** field. A **NIL** handle marks the end of the list.

All coordinates pertaining to a control are expressed in the local coordinate system of its owning window. In particular, the control's size and location within its window are defined by an *enclosing rectangle* in window-relative coordinates. When the user moves the window to a new location on the screen, the control will be redrawn at this same relative position within the window. You specify the enclosing rectangle when you create a control, and can later change it if necessary with **MoveControl** and **SizeControl** [6.3.2].

The coordinates of a control's enclosing rectangle are always defined relative to the window's top-left corner, on the assumption that that point lies at local coordinates (**0**, **0**). If you change the window's coordinate system with **SetOrigin** [I:4.3.4], the control's enclosing rectangle will *not* be adjusted to compensate, and the control won't be drawn properly on the screen. You'll be absolutely safe if you just never change the window's origin at all; but if you must change the origin, be sure to set it back to (**0**, **0**)—at least temporarily—before drawing any of the window's controls or performing any other control-related operation.

Besides the owning window and enclosing rectangle, the information needed to create a new control includes the control's title and type. As already noted, the control type is specified by an integer called the *control definition ID*, which includes the resource ID of the control definition function, along with some further identifying information. The definition IDs for the standard control types are defined as Toolbox constants: **PushbutProc**, **CheckboxProc**, **RadioButProc**, and **ScrollBarProc** [6.2.1]. If all you need are the standard types, you can just use these constants without worrying about the exact structure of the coded information they contain.

How a control's title is displayed depends on the type of control. For pushbuttons, the title is centered within the button itself; for checkboxes and radio buttons, it's displayed next to the box or button (see Figure 6-1). Some controls, such as scroll bars, don't display any title at all; in this case you can just pass an empty string for the title. If the title will actually be displayed, make sure the control's enclosing rectangle is big enough to include it all; otherwise it will be truncated at one or both ends, depending on the type of control. The Toolbox routines **GetCTitle** and **SetCTitle** [6.2.3] allow you to access or change a control's title at any time. You should always use these routines instead of manipulating the control's **contrlTitle** field directly.

> The title of a control is normally displayed in the standard system font, 12-point **Chicago**. If you like, you can instead use the typeface and size currently associated with the control's owning window [I:8.3.1]. To specify this option, add the constant **UseWFont** [6.2.1] to the control definition ID when you create the control.

In creating a new control, you also have to specify its initial setting and range and whether it's initially visible; we'll be discussing these properties in the next few sections. Finally, you give the initial value of the control's *reference constant*. Like that of a window, a control's reference constant really isn't a constant at all, but a variable—you can change its value any time you want with the Toolbox routine **SetCRefCon**, or find out its current value with **GetCRefCon** [6.2.3]. It's simply an extra 4-byte (long integer) field that's included in the control record for your program to use in any way you want. Just as with a window, you can use a control's reference constant to hold a handle to an auxiliary data record if the extra information you need to associate with the control is more than 4 bytes long.

When you're all through with a control, you use **DisposeControl** [6.2.2] to destroy it. (If you're using the control's reference constant to hold a handle to an auxiliary data record, it's your responsibility to dispose of the auxiliary record before destroying the control itself.) There's also a routine named **KillControls** [6.2.2] that destroys all controls belonging to a given window; however, the Toolbox routines **CloseWindow** and **DisposeWindow** [3.2.3] take care of this for you automatically, so you don't normally need to call **KillControls** for yourself before destroying a window.

Control Display

Like a window, a control can be logically *visible* or *invisible*. These properties are under your program's control, and are independent of whether the control happens to be covered or exposed on the screen. That is, a control may be logically "visible" and still not appear on the screen, because it is partially or completely obscured by overlapping windows or other objects; the control is actually drawn on the screen only if it's both visible and exposed. When you create a new control, you specify whether it's initially visible—either with a Boolean parameter that you pass to **NewControl** or with a flag contained in the control template you supply to **GetNewControl**. Once the control is created, you can make it invisible with **HideControl** or visible with **ShowControl** [6.3.1].

The Toolbox routine **DrawControls** [6.3.1] draws all of a window's controls on the screen (more precisely, all those that are currently visible and exposed). The most common use for this routine is in responding to update events. Recall that on receiving an update event for a window, you have to redraw the window's entire content region, using **BeginUpdate** and **EndUpdate** [3.4.1] to clip your drawing to the region that actually needs updating. Since the window's controls are part of its content region, you should always include a call to **DrawControls** as part of the update process, as we've already seen in our earlier **DoUpdate** routine (Program 5-3).

Notice a subtle but important difference in meaning between **ShowControl** and **DrawControls**. **ShowControl** makes a control *logically* visible; if the control happens to be completely or partially exposed to view, it will be redrawn on the screen as a side effect. **DrawControls**, on the other hand, has no effect on a control's visibility: it simply redraws those controls that are *already* visible (and exposed).

Another aspect of a control's appearance is its *highlighting*. All or part of a control may be highlighted: the **contrlHilite** field of the control record holds a 1-byte integer part code that identifies which part of the control is highlighted (or **0** if none). To make sure all changes in a control's highlighting state are reflected visibly on the screen, always use the Toolbox routine **HiliteControl** [6.3.3] instead of storing directly into the **contrlHilite** field.

The usual purpose of highlighting is to provide visual feedback when the user manipulates a control with the mouse. As we'll see later, the Toolbox automatically handles the highlighting for you in this case, so you don't usually have to set a control's highlighting for yourself. Normally the only time you need to call **HiliteControl** is to make a control active or inactive, as described below.

The actual appearance of a highlighted control is determined by its definition function. Inverting colors (white to black and vice versa) is one common convention, but the definition function can use any method that makes sense for a particular type of control. Figure 6-4 shows the forms of highlighting used for the standard control types. Pushbuttons use color inversion, while checkboxes and radio buttons are drawn with a heavier outline. For scroll bars, only the up and down arrows exhibit visible highlighting on the screen: the arrow becomes solid black instead of just an outline. Highlighting other parts of the scroll bar produces no visible effect.

One special use of highlighting that's particularly important is to make a control *inactive*. An inactive control remains visible on the screen, but doesn't respond to the mouse. The control is normally displayed in some special way to show that it's inactive: for instance, standard buttons become "dimmed," and scroll bars hide their scroll box and turn its "shaft" white instead of gray (see Figure 6-5). You make a control inactive by setting its highlighting state to a special part code of **255**. The control will then behave as though it were completely invisible; when the mouse is pressed in that control, the Toolbox will report that it was in no control at all.

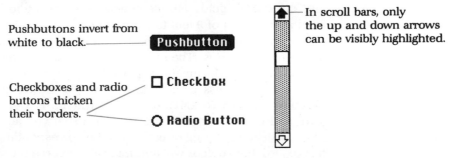

Figure 6-4 Highlighting of standard controls

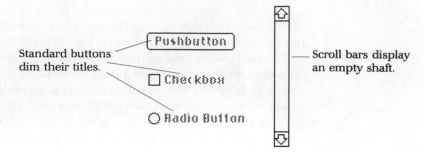

Standard buttons dim their titles.

Scroll bars display an empty shaft.

Figure 6-5 Inactive controls

Macintosh user interface conventions call for a window's scroll bar to appear inactive whenever the window itself is inactive. Accordingly, our **DoActivate** routine (Program 5-14) calls **HiliteControl** to activate or deactivate the scroll bar as part of the process of activating or deactivating the window itself. A control should always become inactive when it doesn't apply in a particular situation: for instance, the **Find Next** pushbutton in MacWrite's **Find...** dialog becomes inactive when there's nothing specified to find. A window's scroll bar should become inactive when the window's contents are small enough to be displayed all at once without scrolling; we'll see how this is done when we look at our example program's scrolling routines later in this chapter.

Setting and Range of a Control

Except for pushbuttons, which produce an immediate effect, the essence of a control is that it retains a *setting* that the user can set with the mouse. The setting is an integer held in the **contrlValue** field of the control record; the range of values it can assume is defined by the **contrlMin** and **contrlMax** fields. Simple checkboxes and radio buttons just range from a minimum of **0** (off) to a maximum of **1** (on). Scroll bars and other dials can cover a wider range of settings, and the range can vary with changing conditions. (The range of a scroll bar, for instance, depends on the length of the document displayed in its window.)

You can access or change a control's setting and range with the Toolbox routines **GetCtlValue** and **SetCtlValue**, **GetCtlMin** and **SetCtlMin**, and **GetCtlMax** and **SetCtlMax** [6.2.4]. If you always use these routines, instead of storing directly into the corresponding fields of the control record, the Toolbox will automatically enforce the specified range and won't let the control's setting stray outside it. For instance, if you try to give the control a setting greater than the maximum, the actual setting will be forced equal to the maximum to keep it in range. Similarly, if you reduce the maximum to a value less than the current setting, the setting will be adjusted downward to equal the new maximum. Analogous precautions are taken at the other end of the range, to prevent the setting from going below the specified minimum.

Any time you change a control's setting or range, it's automatically redrawn on the screen to reflect the change (provided, of course, that it's visible and exposed). This means you needn't bother with details like how to reposition a dial's indicator to represent its new setting. You simply specify the setting with **SetCtlValue**, and the Toolbox (with help from the control definition function) takes care of the redrawing for you.

Responding to the Mouse

We've already seen in Chapter 3 how the **MiniEdit** program's **DoMouse-Down** routine (Program 3-7) responds to mouse-down events by calling **FindWindow** [3.5.1] to find out where on the screen the mouse button was pressed. Since a window's controls are part of its content region, **FindWindow** will return the part code **InContent** for a mouse press in a control. **DoMouseDown** will then call the **DoContent** routine shown here (Program 6-1) to handle the event.

If the mouse was pressed in an inactive window, all that's needed is to activate the window with **SelectWindow** [3.5.2]. If the window is already active, **DoContent** has to find out what part of its content region the click was in. It does this by passing the point where the mouse was pressed, along with a pointer to the window itself, to the Toolbox routine **FindControl** [6.4.1].

First, however, the point has to be converted into the window's local coordinate system. Until now we didn't know which window the mouse point was in (if any), so we've been dealing with the point in screen-relative (global) coordinates, just the way we found it in the **where** field of the event record [2.1.1]. Now that we've identified the window, all further operations on the point will be in window coordinates. So before passing the point to **FindControl**, we have to convert it from screen to window coordinates with **GlobalToLocal** [I:4.4.2]. (Notice that we're assuming implicitly that the window in question is already the current port. Since we know at this point that it's the active window, our **DoActivate** routine (Program 5-14) will have made it the current port when it was activated.)

```
{ Global variables }

var
   TheEvent     : EventRecord;              {Current event [2.1.1]}
   TheScrollBar : ControlHandle;            {Handle to active window's scroll bar [6.1.1]}
   TheText      : TEHandle;                 {Handle to active window's edit record [5.1.1]}


procedure DoContent (whichWindow : WindowPtr);

   { Handle mouse-down event in content region of active window. }

   var
      thePoint  : Point;                    {Location of mouse click in window coordinates [I:4.1.1]}
      theControl : ControlHandle;           {Handle to control [6.1.1]}
      thePart   : INTEGER;                  {Part of control where mouse was pressed [6.4.1]}

   begin {DoContent}

      if whichWindow <> FrontWindow then    {Is it an inactive window? [3.3.3]}
         SelectWindow (whichWindow)         {If so, just activate it [3.5.2]}

      else
         begin

            thePoint := TheEvent.where;     {Get point in screen coordinates [2.1.1]}
            GlobalToLocal (thePoint);       {Convert to window coordinates [I:4.4.2]}

            thePart := FindControl (thePoint, whichWindow, theControl);
                                            {Was mouse pressed in a control? [6.4.1]}

            if theControl = TheScrollBar then   {Was it in the scroll bar?}
               DoScroll (thePart, thePoint)     {Go scroll the window [Prog. 6-6]}

            {else if theControl = (some other control) then
               respond to that control}

            else if theControl = NIL then       {Not in a control?}

               if PtInRect (thePoint, TheText^^.viewRect) then  {Was it in the text rectangle? [I:4.4.3]}
                  DoSelect (thePoint)           {Go handle text selection [Prog. 5-4]}
               {else do nothing}

         end {else}

   end; {DoContent}
```

Program 6-1 Mouse-down event in content region

FindControl tests whether the given point lies in one of the window's visible controls. If so and the control is active, **FindControl** returns a handle to the control via the variable parameter **theControl**; its function result is a part code identifying the part of the control that the point is in. If the control is inactive, or if the mouse point isn't in any visible control, **FindControl** will return **NIL** for the control handle and **0** for the part code. In that case our **DoContent** routine will next test whether the point lies in the window's text rectangle (**TheText^ .viewRect**). If it does, then the user is making a text selection, so we call the **MiniEdit** routine **DoSelect** (Program 5-4) to handle the response.

When the mouse is pressed in a visible, active control, what happens next depends on the type of control. The only controls **MiniEdit** uses are scroll bars, which we'll be getting to in the next section; but first, let's talk about how to handle pushbuttons, checkboxes, and radio buttons.

Pushbuttons

Since a pushbutton is designed to produce an immediate action, you might think the appropriate response would be just to perform the indicated action as soon as you find out the mouse was pressed inside the pushbutton:

```
if theControl = aPushbutton then
  {Perform the action}
```

Actually, though, the action shouldn't be quite *that* immediate. One mark of a friendly user interface is that users can change their minds and "back out" of an action without any penalty. In the case of a pushbutton, this means you have to track the mouse for as long as the button remains down, and take the indicated action only when it's *released* inside the control; if it's released outside the control, nothing happens.

The Toolbox routine for tracking mouse actions in a control is **TrackControl** [6.4.2]. Program 6-2 (**DoPushButton**) is a hypothetical, skeleton routine illustrating how you might use it to respond to a mouse click in a pushbutton:

```
if theControl = aPushbutton then
  DoPushbutton (aPushbutton, thePoint)
```

```
procedure DoPushbutton (theControl : ControlHandle; startPoint : Point);

   {  Skeleton procedure to handle mouse-down event in a pushbutton.  }


   var
      thePart : INTEGER;                              {Part of control where mouse was released}


   begin {DoPushbutton}

      thePart := TrackControl (theControl, startPoint, NIL);
                                                      {Track mouse with no action procedure [6.4.2]}

      if thePart = InButton then                      {Was it released in the pushbutton? [6.4.1]}

         {Take appropriate action to respond to mouse click in pushbutton}

      {else do nothing}

   end;  {DoPushbutton}
```

Program 6-2 Mouse-down event in a pushbutton

TrackControl accepts a handle to the control, along with the point where the mouse was pressed in *window coordinates*. It finds which part of the control contains the given point, then focuses its attention only on that part. (In the case of a simple button, of course, the entire control consists of just one "part.") Like other tracking routines, **TrackControl** keeps control for as long as the mouse button is held down, following the mouse's movements and providing visual feedback: in this case, highlighting and unhighlighting the selected part of the control as the mouse moves into and out of it. When the mouse is released, **TrackControl** returns either the part code of the selected part or **0**, depending on whether the mouse was inside or outside the original part when the user released the button. You can then use this result to decide whether to perform the indicated action or do nothing, as shown in Program 6-2.

TrackControl also accepts a third parameter, a pointer to an *action procedure* that it will execute repeatedly while tracking the mouse. You can use this to perform some continuous action while a push-button is "held down," or to provide additional visual feedback beyond the usual highlighting and unhighlighting of the selected control part. In Program 6-2, we just pass **NIL** for the action procedure parameter; when we get to scroll bars later in the chapter, we'll actually be using an action procedure to produce continuous scrolling.

Checkboxes and Radio Buttons

Program 6-3 (**DoCheckbox**) shows the response to a mouse click in a checkbox. Again we call **TrackControl** to track the mouse, and take action only if it's released inside the same control it was originally pressed in. In the case of a checkbox, the action is to reverse the control's setting, from **0** to **1** or vice versa. We do this by getting the current setting with **GetCtlValue** [6.4.2], subtracting it from **1** to reverse it, then calling **SetCtlValue** to set the control to the result.

Radio buttons are a little more complicated than checkboxes, because user actions in one button can affect the settings of others as well. In Program 6-4 (**DoRadioButton**), we define a group of related radio buttons as an array of control handles named **TheButtons**. When the mouse is pressed and released in one of them, we have to run through the entire array, turning that button on and all the others off. (Of course, if we had more than one group of radio buttons to keep track of, we'd have to be sure to operate on the right array for a given button. We'd probably want to keep a pointer or handle to the relevant array as the button's reference constant.)

Notice that both checkboxes and radio buttons have the same part code, named **InCheckbox** [6.4.1].

```
procedure DoCheckbox (theControl : ControlHandle; startPoint : Point);

   { Handle mouse-down event in a checkbox.  }


   var
      thePart  : INTEGER;                         {Part of control where mouse was released}
      oldValue : INTEGER;                         {Previous setting of checkbox}


   begin {DoCheckbox}

      thePart := TrackControl (theControl, startPoint, NIL);
                                                  {Track mouse with no action procedure [6.4.2]}

      if thePart = InCheckbox then                {Was it released in the checkbox? [6.4.1]}

         begin
            oldValue := GetCtlValue (theControl);  {Get old setting [6.2.4]}
            SetCtlValue (theControl, 1 - oldValue) {Toggle the setting [6.2.4]}
         end

      {else do nothing}

   end; {DoCheckbox}
```

Program 6-3 Mouse-down event in a checkbox

```
{ Global declarations }

const
   NButtons = {whatever};                         {Number of radio buttons in group}

var
   TheButtons : array [1..NButtons] of ControlHandle;    {Group of related radio buttons}


procedure DoRadioButton (theControl : ControlHandle; startPoint : Point);

   { Handle mouse-down event in a radio button.  }
```

Program 6-4 Mouse-down event in a radio button

```
var
   thePart     : INTEGER;                              {Part of control where mouse was released}
   whichButton : 1..NButtons;                          {Index into array of radio buttons}
   thisButton  : ControlHandle;                        {Handle to a radio button [6.1.1]}


begin {DoRadioButton}

   thePart := TrackControl (theControl, startPoint, NIL);
                                                       {Track mouse with no action procedure [6.4.2]}


   if thePart = InCheckbox then                        {Was it released in the same button? [6.4.1]}

      for whichButton := 1 to NButtons do              {Iterate through array of radio buttons}
         begin

            thisButton := TheButtons[whichButton];     {Get button from array}

            if thisButton = theControl then            {Is this the button that was clicked?}
               SetCtlValue (thisButton, 1)             {Turn button on [6.2.4]}
            else
               SetCtlValue (thisButton, 0)             {Turn button off [6.2.4]}

         end

   {else do nothing}

end; {DoRadioButton}
```

Program 6-4 (*continued*)

Scrolling

At long last, we come to the subject of scrolling and scroll bars. As we've already noted, a scroll bar is a form of *dial*—that is, a control that can assume a whole range of settings, depending on the position of a moving *indicator*. In this case, the indicator is the scroll box or "thumb" that slides within the gray "shaft" of the scroll bar. The basic idea is to use the control's setting to denote the relative vertical or horizontal positioning of the associated window's contents.

For the sake of simplicity, our example program **MiniEdit** does vertical scrolling only: since it always "wraps" text to the actual width of the window, there's no need to scroll horizontally. After you've learned how vertical scrolling works, you might want to check your understanding by working out for yourself how to add horizontal scroll bars to the program.

In the case of **MiniEdit**, what's displayed in a window is a text document that we're operating on by means of an edit record. The natural way to indicate the document's vertical position is with a line number representing the first line of text that's visible in the window. The **nLines** field of the edit record [5.1.1] gives us the total number of lines in the document; the lines are numbered from **0** to **nLines** − **1**. So we can use these limits to define the minimum and maximum settings the scroll bar can take on.

When our **DoNew** procedure (Program 5-2) creates a brand-new, empty window, it calls **GetNewControl** [6.2.1] to create the window's scroll bar from a control template in the application resource file. The scroll bar's initial setting and range come from the template. Since a new window's text is initially empty, the template just specifies values of **0** for the minimum, maximum, and current setting. From then on, whenever anything happens that might change the number of lines in the window's text, we have to readjust the range of the scroll bar to match the new text length.

We accomplish this task with a utility routine named **AdjustScroll-Bar**, shown in Program 6-5. When we discuss files in Chapter 8, we'll see that this routine gets called when we read a file into the window from the disk, to calibrate the scroll bar to the length of the file's text. We also call it whenever the user types text into a window from the keyboard (**DoTyping**, Program 5-6) or issues a **Cut**, **Paste**, or **Clear** command (**DoCut**, Program 5-8; **DoPaste**, 5-10; **DoClear**, 5-11), since all of these operations can change the length of the window's text. Finally, we have to call it when we adjust a window's text rectangle after resizing the window (**FixText**, Program 6-11), since the number of lines changes when the text is rewrapped to the new rectangle.

```
{ Global variables }

var
    TheScrollBar : ControlHandle;           {Handle to active window's scroll bar [6.1.1]}
    TheText      : TEHandle;                {Handle to active window's edit record [5.1.1]}


procedure AdjustScrollBar;

    { Adjust scroll bar to length of document. }

    const
        active   =   0;                     {Highlighting code for active scroll bar [6.3.3]}
        inactive = 255;                     {Highlighting code for inactive scroll bar [6.3.3]}

    var
        windowHeight : INTEGER;             {Height of text rectangle in lines}
        maxTop       : INTEGER;             {Maximum value for top line in window}

    begin {AdjustScrollBar}

        with TheText^^, viewRect do
            begin
                windowHeight := (bottom - top) div lineHeight; {Get window height [5.1.1]}
                maxTop       := nLines - windowHeight          {Avoid white space at bottom [5.1.1]}
            end; {with}

        if maxTop <= 0 then                 {Is text smaller than window?}
            begin
                maxTop := 0;                {Show all of text}
                HiliteControl (TheScrollBar, inactive)   {Disable scroll bar [6.3.3]}
            end {then}
        else
            HiliteControl (TheScrollBar, active);        {Enable scroll bar [6.3.3]}

        SetCtlMax (TheScrollBar, maxTop)    {Adjust range of scroll bar [6.2.4]}

    end;  {AdjustScrollBar}
```

Program 6-5 Adjust scroll bar to length of document

Actually, if we allow the scroll bar's setting to run from **0** up to **nLines** − **1**, we can end up with just the last line of text showing at the top of an otherwise empty window. What we really want is for the text to stop scrolling when the last line reaches the *bottom* of the window; this will allow the user to see the last full windowful of text by dragging the scroll box all the way to the bottom. So our **AdjustScrollBar** routine has to set the scroll bar's maximum setting (that is, the highest line number that can be scrolled to the top of the window) to the total number of text lines (**nLines**) *minus* the number of lines that will fit in the window. First we find the height of the window's text rectangle in lines, by subtracting the rectangle's top and bottom coordinates and dividing by the line height in pixels.

windowHeight := (bottom − top) **div** lineHeight

Then we subtract the result from the total number of lines to arrive at the maximum setting for the scroll bar:

maxTop := nLines − windowHeight

If the total amount of text is one windowful or less, this calculation will produce a zero or negative value for **maxTop**. In that case we force **maxTop** to **0** (to scroll the first line of text to the top of the window) and deactivate the scroll bar by setting its highlighting state to **255** (since there's room to display all the text at once without scrolling). Conversely, if **maxTop** is positive, then the text can't all fit in the window at once; so we make sure the scroll bar is active by setting its highlighting state to **0**. Finally, in either case, we set the scroll bar's maximum range to the value of **maxTop** we've just calculated.

Dragging the Scroll Box

Mouse presses in a scroll bar, like those for simple buttons that we discussed earlier, are handled by the Toolbox routine **TrackControl** [6.4.2]. In the case of scroll bars and other dials, however, **TrackControl** works a bit differently. We said before that **TrackControl** focuses its attention only on the particular part of a control that the mouse was originally pressed in. If that part turns out to be the moving indicator of a dial (identified by a part code greater than **128**), **TrackControl** treats it in a special way. Instead of just highlighting and unhighlighting the part in response to the mouse's movements, as described earlier, it drags an outline of the indicator around to follow the mouse on the screen. Then, when the mouse button is finally released, it redraws the control with the indicator in its new position and *adjusts the control's setting* accordingly. This all happens automatically, without your having to supply an action procedure or intervene in any other way.

In the specific case of a scroll bar, this means that when the mouse is pressed in the scroll box, **TrackControl** will slide an outline of the scroll box up and down the shaft to follow the mouse's movements. When the mouse is released, the routine will redraw the actual scroll box, compare its new position with the overall height of the scroll bar in pixels, and adjust the scroll bar's setting proportionally between the current minimum and maximum. You needn't worry about doing this interpolation for yourself: **TrackControl** handles it automatically (with some help from the control definition function for scroll bars). Notice, though, that **TrackControl** *doesn't* actually scroll the contents of the window for you. It just translates the user's mouse actions into a new scroll bar setting; it's up to you to reposition the window's contents to match that new setting.

Program 6-6 (**DoScroll**) shows how **MiniEdit** makes use of this mechanism. This routine gets called from our earlier **DoContent** routine (Program 6-1) when **FindControl** reports that the mouse was pressed in a window's scroll bar. **DoScroll** in turn calls **TrackControl** to track the mouse, but in one of two different ways depending on whether the original press was in the indicator (the scroll box) or in some other part of the control. We'll see in the next section what happens when it's in another part; if it was in the scroll box (part code **InThumb** [6.4.1]), we just call **TrackControl** with no action procedure, to adjust the scroll bar's setting as described above, then **AdjustText** (Program 6-7) to reposition the text according to the new setting.

In the last chapter we saw how to position text within a window with the Toolbox routine **TEScroll** [5.3.3], which adjusts the relationship between the destination and view rectangles of an edit record. To do this, however, we first have to figure out how many pixels to scroll the text up or down from its current position. First we find the window's current scroll position by comparing the top coordinates of the destination and view rectangles:

    oldScroll := viewRect.top − destRect.top

Then we calculate the position we want to end up in by multiplying the current scroll bar setting by the line height in pixels:

    newScroll := GetCtlValue (TheScrollBar) * lineHeight

The difference between these two numbers

    oldScroll − newScroll

gives the relative scroll distance we need to pass to **TEScroll**.

```
{ Global variable }

var
   TheScrollBar : ControlHandle;                    {Handle to active window's scroll bar [6.1.1]}


procedure DoScroll (thePart : INTEGER; thePoint : Point);

   { Handle mouse-down event in scroll bar. }

   begin {DoScroll}

      if thePart = InThumb then                     {Dragging the indicator? [6.4.1]}

         begin
            thePart := TrackControl (TheScrollBar, thePoint, NIL);
                                                     {Track mouse with no action procedure [6.4.2]}
            AdjustText                               {Adjust text to new setting [Prog. 6-7]}
         end {then}

      else

         thePart := TrackControl (TheScrollBar, thePoint, @ScrollText)
                                                     {Track mouse with continuous scroll [6.4.2, Prog. 6-8]}

   end; {DoScroll}
```

Program 6-6 Mouse-down event in scroll bar

Continuous Scrolling

When the mouse is pressed in any part of a scroll bar other than the scroll box, the window is supposed to scroll continuously for as long as the button is held down. The direction and speed of the scrolling depend on which part of the scroll bar is involved: the up and down arrows scroll one line at a time, the page-up and page-down regions a whole windowful at a time. To make the window scroll continuously, our **DoScroll** routine (Program 6-6) uses an action procedure in its call to **TrackControl:**

```
TrackControl (TheScrollBar, thePoint, @ScrollText)
```

The action procedure **ScrollText** is shown in Program 6-8. **Track-Control** will call this procedure repeatedly until the mouse button is released. Remember that **TrackControl** focuses only on the part of the control where the mouse was originally pressed. Each time it calls the action procedure, it checks whether the mouse is still inside that original part. If so, it passes the corresponding part code to the action procedure (along with a handle to the control itself); otherwise it passes a part code

```
{ Global variables }

var
    TheScrollBar : ControlHandle;        {Handle to active window's scroll bar [6.1.1]}
    TheText      : TEHandle;             {Handle to active window's edit record [5.1.1]}


procedure AdjustText;

    { Adjust text within window to match scroll bar setting. }

    var
        oldScroll : INTEGER;             {Old text offset in pixels}
        newScroll : INTEGER;             {New text offset in pixels}

    begin {AdjustText}

        HLock (Handle(TheText));         {Lock edit record [I:3.2.4]}
            with TheText^^ do
                begin

                    oldScroll := viewRect.top - destRect.top;          {Get current offset [5.1.1]}
                    newScroll := GetCtlValue (TheScrollBar) * lineHeight;  {Scroll bar gives new offset [6.2.4]}

                    TEScroll (0, (oldScroll - newScroll), TheText)     {Scroll by difference [5.3.3]}

                end; {with}
        HUnlock (Handle(TheText))         {Unlock edit record [I:3.2.4]}

    end;  {AdjustText}
```

Program 6-7 Adjust text to scroll bar setting

of **0**. Our **ScrollText** routine uses this part code to decide how many lines to scroll and in which direction; then it gets the scroll bar's current setting, adjusts it by the desired amount, and calls **AdjustText** to reposition the window's text accordingly. Notice that for the page-up and page-down regions, we actually scroll by *one less than* the number of lines in the window, so that one line will remain visible both before and after the operation: either the top line will scroll to the bottom or the bottom line will scroll to the top. Notice also that if **ScrollText** receives a part code of **0** (meaning that the mouse has moved outside the original part), it will do nothing at all.

```
{ Global variable }

var
   TheText : TEHandle;                              {Handle to active window's edit record [5.1.1]}


procedure ScrollText (theControl: ControlHandle; thePart : INTEGER);

   { Scroll text within window. }

   var
      delta    : INTEGER;                           {Amount to scroll by, in lines}
      oldValue : INTEGER;                           {Previous setting of scroll bar}

   begin {ScrollText}

      case thePart of

         inUpButton:
            delta := -1;                             {Scroll up one line at a time}

         inDownButton:
            delta := +1;                             {Scroll down one line at a time}

         inPageUp:
            with TheText^^, viewRect do
               delta := (top - bottom) div lineHeight + 1;  {Scroll up by height of text rectangle [5.1.1]}

         inPageDown:
            with TheText^^, viewRect do
               delta := (bottom - top) div lineHeight - 1;  {Scroll down by height of text rectangle [5.1.1]}

         otherwise
            {Do nothing}

         end; {case}

      if thePart <> 0 then                          {Is mouse still in the original part?}
         begin
            oldValue := GetCtlValue (theControl);    {Get old setting [6.2.4]}
            SetCtlValue (theControl, oldValue + delta); {Adjust by scroll amount [6.2.4]}

            AdjustText                               {Scroll text to match new setting [Prog. 6-7]}
         end

   end; {ScrollText}
```

Program 6-8 Scroll text within window

Automatic Scrolling

One more form of scrolling that we have to take care of is the "automatic" kind that happens when the user drags the mouse outside a window while making a selection. We saw in the last chapter how to install a *click-loop routine* in an edit record for this purpose, to be called repeatedly by the TextEdit routine **TEClick** [5.4.1] while tracking the mouse during the selection. Program 6-9 on page 288 shows the code of **Mini-Edit**'s click-loop routine, **AutoScroll**.

In principle, all **AutoScroll** has to do is get the current mouse position and compare its vertical coordinate with the top and bottom edges of the window's text rectangle. If the mouse is above the top of the rectangle, we call our **ScrollText** routine (Program 6-8) with the part code **InUpButton.** This will scroll the contents of the window up one line, just as if the mouse had been pressed in the up arrow of the scroll bar. If the mouse is below the bottom of the text rectangle, we of course use a part code of **InDownButton**, to scroll down one line instead of up; if neither case applies, we just do nothing. When the **AutoScroll** routine is called repeatedly by **TEClick**, the result will be to scroll the window continuously for as long as the mouse remains outside the text rectangle with the button still down.

As you may have guessed, though, there's a hitch. Every time we change the setting of the scroll bar, the Toolbox will automatically redraw it on the screen, updating the position of its scroll box. However, because **AutoScroll** is called from within a TextEdit routine (**TEClick**), it will find the active window's clipping region restricted to the TextEdit clipping (view) rectangle—what we've been calling the window's text rectangle. Since the scroll bar lies outside this rectangle, the Toolbox's attempts to redraw it will be "clipped out" and will have no visible effect on the screen. For the scroll bar to be updated properly, **AutoScroll** has to reset the clipping region to include the window's entire port rectangle. Naturally, it first has to save the original clipping region and then restore it later before returning. When it's all through it returns a function result of **TRUE**, signaling **TEClick** to continue tracking the mouse.

Resizing a Window

When the user resizes a window on the screen, both its scroll bar and its text rectangle must be adjusted to match. **MiniEdit** handles these chores with the routines **FixScrollBar** and **FixText**, both of which are called from the **DoGrow** routine that we looked at in Chapter 3 (Program 3-9).

```
{ Global declarations }

var
   TheScrollBar : ControlHandle;                    {Handle to active window's scroll bar [6.1.1]}
   TheText      : TEHandle;                          {Handle to active window's edit record [5.1.1]}


function AutoScroll : BOOLEAN;

   { Handle automatic scrolling during text selection. }

   var
      mousePoint : Point;                            {Mouse location in local (window) coordinates [I:4.1.1]}
      textRect   : Rect;                             {Active window's text rectangle [I:4.1.2]}
      saveClip   : RgnHandle;                        {Original clipping region on entry [I:4.1.5]}

   begin {AutoScroll}

      saveClip := NewRgn;                            {Create temporary region [I:4.1.6]}
      GetClip  (saveClip);                           {Set it to existing clipping region [I:4.3.6]}
      ClipRect (TheWindow^.portRect);                {Clip to entire port rectangle [I:4.3.6, I:4.2.2]}

         GetMouse (mousePoint);                      {Find mouse location [2.4.1]}
         textRect := TheText^^.viewRect;             {Get text rectangle [5.1.1]}

         if mousePoint.v < textRect.top then         {Above top of rectangle? [I:4.1.1, I:4.1.2]}
            ScrollText (TheScrollBar, InUpButton)     {Scroll up one line [Prog. 6-8, 6.4.1]}

         else if mousePoint.v > textRect.bottom then {Below bottom of rectangle? [I:4.1.1, I:4.1.2]}
            ScrollText (TheScrollBar, InDownButton)    {Scroll down one line [Prog. 6-8, 6.4.1]}

         {else do nothing};

      SetClip    (saveClip);                         {Restore original clipping region [I:4.3.6]}
      DisposeRgn (saveClip);                         {Dispose of temporary region [I:4.1.6]}

      AutoScroll := TRUE                             {Continue tracking mouse [5.6.1]}

   end; {AutoScroll}
```

Program 6-9 Handle automatic scrolling

In principle, **FixScrollBar** (Program 6-10) is fairly straightforward: it hides the scroll bar, moves it to its proper position and size in the window, and shows it again. However, a word of explanation is in order about the calculations used to arrive at the scroll bar's new position and size. The standard vertical scroll bar is a strip 16 pixels wide running along the right edge of its window; **MiniEdit** defines a global constant, **SBarWidth**,

```
{ Global declarations }

const
    SBarWidth = 16;                            {Width of scroll bar in pixels}

var
    TheScrollBar : ControlHandle;             {Handle to active window's scroll bar [6.1.1]}


procedure FixScrollBar;

    { Resize window's scroll bar. }

    begin {FixScrollBar}

        HideControl (TheScrollBar);            {Hide scroll bar [6.3.1]}

        with TheWindow^.portRect do
            begin

                MoveControl (TheScrollBar,      {Move top-left corner [6.3.2]}
                        right - (SBarWidth - 1), {Allow for 1-pixel overlap at right}
                        -1);                     {Overlap window top by 1 pixel}

                SizeControl (TheScrollBar,       {Adjust bottom-right corner [6.3.2]}
                        SBarWidth,
                        (bottom + 1) - (top - 1) - (SBarWidth - 1) )
                                                 {Allow room for size box}

            end; {with}

        ShowControl (TheScrollBar);            {Redisplay scroll bar [6.3.1]}

        ValidRect (TheScrollBar^^.contrlRect)  {Avoid updating again [3.4.2]}

    end;  {FixScrollBar}
```

Program 6-10 Resize scroll bar

to represent this standard width. Instead of running from the top of the window all the way to the bottom, the scroll bar stops 16 pixels short of the bottom edge to allow room for the size box in the window's bottom-right corner. (A horizontal scroll bar would naturally occupy an analogous position along the window's bottom edge.)

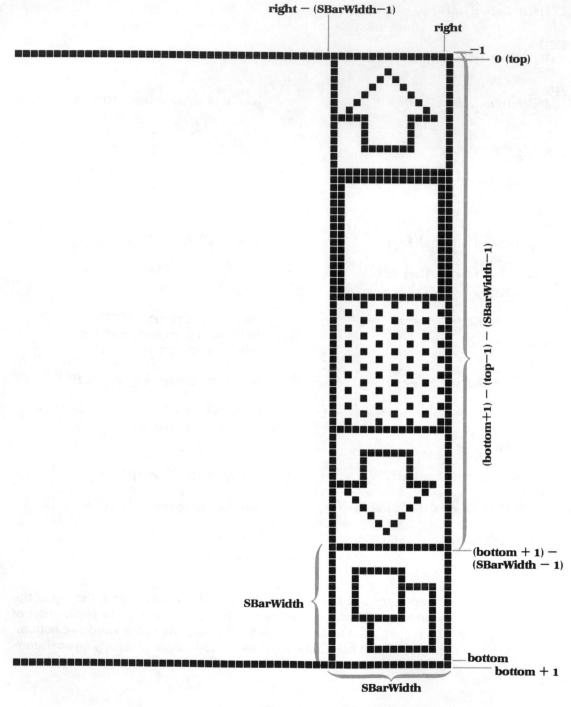

Figure 6-6 Scroll bar positioning

At first glance, all this would seem to suggest that the scroll bar's enclosing rectangle should have its top-left corner at window coordinates

    right − SBarWidth

horizontally and **0** vertically, and should be **SBarWidth** pixels wide by

    (bottom − top) − SBarWidth

high (where **right**, **bottom**, and **top** are the edges of the window's port rectangle). For the sake of appearance, however, we want the edges of the scroll bar to overlap those of the window itself by 1 pixel, so it will fit snugly into the window's frame. So we have to offset the top, right, and bottom edges of the enclosing rectangle by 1 pixel to account for the overlap (see Figure 6-6). This yields an origin of

    right − (SBarWidth − 1)

horizontally and **−1** vertically, with a width of **SBarWidth** pixels and a height of

    (bottom + 1) − (top − 1) − (SBarWidth − 1)

as shown in the program. Finally, since there's always an update event pending when this routine is called, we remove the scroll bar from the window's update region with **ValidRect** to avoid unnecessary redrawing.

   FixText (Program 6-11) is the routine that readjusts a window's text rectangle when the window is resized. Changing the size of the text rectangle requires rewrapping the text to the new width and changing all the line breaks. We begin by finding the first text character currently visible in the window, so we can scroll it back to the top after the text is rewrapped. The current scroll bar setting tells us which line is at the top of the window. We then look in the edit record's **lineStarts** array [5.1.1] to get the character position at the beginning of that line.

   We calculate the coordinates of the new view rectangle by starting with the window's port rectangle and insetting for the scroll bars and size box at the right and bottom. (We also truncate the text rectangle to a whole number of line heights to avoid displaying a partial line of characters at the bottom of the window.) The wrapping rectangle is inset another few pixels from the edges of the view rectangle for legibility. After recalibrating the line starts with **TECalText** [5.3.1], we call **AdjustScroll-Bar** (Program 6-5) to adjust the scroll bar's range to the new number of lines. Finally we have to scroll the old first character back to the top of the window; this is done by calling the utility routine **ScrollCharacter**, shown in Program 6-12.

```
{ Global declarations }

const
   SBarWidth  = 16;                          {Width of scroll bar in pixels}
   TextMargin = 4;                           {Inset from window to text rectangle}

var
   TheWindow    = WindowPtr;                 {Pointer to currently active window [3.1.1]}
   TheScrollBar = ControlHandle;             {Handle to active window's scroll bar [6.1.1]}
   TheText      = TEHandle;                   {Handle to active window's edit record [5.1.1]}

   Watch        = CursHandle;                {Handle to wristwatch cursor [2.5.1]}


procedure FixText;

   { Resize window's text rectangle. }

      var
         topLine   : INTEGER;                {First line visible in window}
         firstChar : INTEGER;                {Character position of first character in window}
         maxTop    : INTEGER;                {Maximum value for top line in window}

   begin {FixText}

      SetCursor (Watch^^);                   {Indicate delay [2.5.2]}

      HLock (Handle(TheText));               {Lock edit record [I:3.2.4]}
         with TheText^^ do
            begin

               topLine  := GetCtlValue (TheScrollBar); {Get previous first line [6.2.4]}
               firstChar := lineStarts[topLine];       {Find first character previously visible [5.1.1]}

               viewRect := TheWindow^.portRect;        {Display text in window's port rectangle [3.1.1]}
               with viewRect do
                  begin
                     right  := right  - (SBarWidth - 1);  {Exclude scroll bar, allowing for 1-pixel overlap}
                     bottom := bottom - (SBarWidth - 1);  {Leave space for scroll bar at bottom}
                     bottom := (bottom div lineHeight) * lineHeight
                                                        {Truncate to a whole number of lines [5.1.1]}
                  end;
```

Program 6-11 Resize text rectangle

```
        destRect := viewRect;                    {Wrap to same rectangle [5.1.1]}
        InsetRect (destRect, TextMargin, TextMargin);  {Inset by text margin [I:4.4.4]}

        TECalText (TheText);                      {Recalibrate line starts [5.3.1]}
        AdjustScrollBar;                          {Adjust scroll bar to new length [Prog. 6-5]}

        ScrollCharacter (firstChar, FALSE)        {Scroll same character to top of window [Prog. 6-12]}

      end; {with}
  HUnlock (Handle(TheText))                       {Unlock edit record [I:3.2.4]}

end; {FixText}
```

Program 6-11 *(continued)*

ScrollCharacter scrolls a designated character position to the top or bottom of the active window. First it scans through the edit record's **lineStarts** array until it finds the line containing the given character position. Then it sets the window's scroll bar to that line number and calls **AdjustText** (Program 6-7) to reposition the text to the new setting. (If it's asked to scroll the character to the bottom of the window instead of the top, it adjusts for the height of the window before setting the scroll bar.)

ScrollToSelection (Program 6-13) does one last bit of useful housekeeping, scrolling the current text selection into view. The editing routines of Chapter 5 call this routine to keep the selection visible before and after any editing operation or typing from the keyboard. If the entire text is small enough to fit in the window at once, **ScrollToSelection** calls **AdjustText** to make sure that it's all visible. Otherwise, if any part of the selection is already visible, no scrolling is needed. If the whole selection is out of view beyond the top of the window, **ScrollToSelection** calls **ScrollCharacter** (Program 6-12) to scroll the beginning of the selection to the top of the window; if the entire selection is beyond the bottom, it scrolls the end of the selection to the bottom. This guarantees that as much as possible of the selection will become visible.

```
{ Global variable }

var
   TheText : TEHandle;                              {Handle to active window's edit record [5.1.1]}


procedure ScrollCharacter (theCharacter : INTEGER; toBottom : BOOLEAN);

   { Scroll character into view. }

   var
      theLine    : INTEGER;                         {Number of line containing character}
      windowHeight : INTEGER;                       {Height of text rectangle in lines}

   begin {ScrollCharacter}

      HLock (Handle(TheText));                       {Lock edit record [I:3.2.4]}
         with TheText^^ do
            begin

               theLine := 0;                         {Start search at first line}
               while lineStarts[theLine+1] <= theCharacter do
                  theLine := theLine + 1;            {Find line containing character [5.1.1]}

               if toBottom then                       {Scrolling to bottom of window?}
                  begin
                     with viewRect do
                        windowHeight := (bottom - top) div lineHeight;  {Get window height}
                     theLine := theLine - (windowHeight - 1)            {Offset for window height}
                  end; {if}

               SetCtlValue (TheScrollBar, theLine);   {Adjust setting of scroll bar [6.2.4]}
               AdjustText                             {Scroll text to match new setting [Prog. 6-7]}

            end; {with}
         HUnlock (Handle(TheText))                    {Unlock edit record [I:3.2.4]}

   end; {ScrollCharacter}
```

Program 6-12 Scroll character into view

```
{ Global variable }

var
   TheText : TEHandle;                        {Handle to active window's edit record [5.1.1]}


procedure ScrollToSelection;

   { Scroll current selection into view. }

   var
      topLine      : INTEGER;                 {First line visible in window}
      bottomLine   : INTEGER;                 {First line beyond bottom of window}
      windowHeight : INTEGER;                 {Height of text rectangle in lines}

   begin {ScrollToSelection}

      HLock (Handle(TheText));                {Lock edit record [I:3.2.4]}
         with TheText^^, viewRect do
            begin

               topLine      := GetCtlValue (TheScrollBar); {Get current top line [6.2.4]}
               windowHeight := (bottom - top) div lineHeight; {Get window height [5.1.1]}
               bottomLine   := topLine + windowHeight;    {Find line beyond bottom}

               if GetCtlMax (TheScrollBar) = 0 then       {Not enough text to fill the window? [6.2.4]}
                  AdjustText                              {Start of text to top of window [Prog. 6-7]}

               else if selEnd < lineStarts[topLine] then  {Whole selection above window top? [5.1.1]}
                  ScrollCharacter (selStart, FALSE)       {Start of selection to top of window [Prog. 6-12]}

               else if selStart >= lineStarts[bottomLine] then {Whole selection below window bottom? [5.1.1]}
                  ScrollCharacter (selEnd, TRUE)          {End of selection to bottom of window [Prog. 6-12]}

            end; {with}
         HUnlock (Handle(TheText))            {Unlock edit record [I:3.2.4]}

   end;  {ScrollToSelection}
```

Program 6-13 Scroll current selection into view

REFERENCE

6.1 Internal Representation of Controls

6.1.1 Control Records

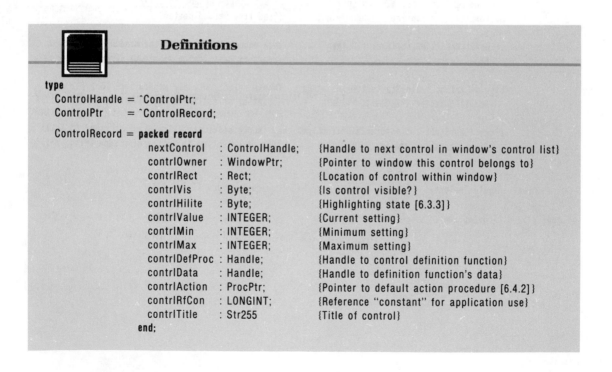

Definitions

```
type
  ControlHandle = ^ControlPtr;
  ControlPtr    = ^ControlRecord;

  ControlRecord = packed record
                    nextControl  : ControlHandle;    {Handle to next control in window's control list}
                    contrlOwner  : WindowPtr;         {Pointer to window this control belongs to}
                    contrlRect   : Rect;              {Location of control within window}
                    contrlVis    : Byte;              {Is control visible?}
                    contrlHilite : Byte;              {Highlighting state [6.3.3]}
                    contrlValue  : INTEGER;           {Current setting}
                    contrlMin    : INTEGER;           {Minimum setting}
                    contrlMax    : INTEGER;           {Maximum setting}
                    contrlDefProc : Handle;           {Handle to control definition function}
                    contrlData   : Handle;            {Handle to definition function's data}
                    contrlAction : ProcPtr;           {Pointer to default action procedure [6.4.2]}
                    contrlRfCon  : LONGINT;           {Reference "constant" for application use}
                    contrlTitle  : Str255             {Title of control}
                  end;
```

Notes

1. **contrlOwner** is a pointer to the window that "owns" this control.

2. **nextControl** is a handle to the next control in the window's control list. The beginning of the control list is in the **controlList** field of the window record [3.1.1].

3. A **nextControl** value of **NIL** marks the end of the control list.

4. **contrlRect** is the control's *enclosing rectangle*, which defines its location and dimensions in local (window) coordinates.

5. **contrlVis** is nominally defined as a 1-byte integer for packing purposes, but is really a Boolean flag telling whether the control is visible. Use **HideControl** and **ShowControl** [6.3.1] to manipulate this field instead of storing into it yourself.

6. **contrlVis** tells whether the control is *logically* visible, independently of whether it's exposed to view or covered by overlapping objects.

7. **contrlHilite** is an integer from **0** to **255** denoting the control's highlighting state. See **HiliteControl** [6.3.3] for further information.

8. **contrlValue** is the control's current setting; **contrlMin** and **contrlMax** define the minimum and maximum values the setting can take.

9. The handle to the control definition function (**contrlDefProc**) is obtained when the definition function is read into memory from a resource file.

10. The high-order byte of the **contrlDefProc** field contains some additional identifying information to distinguish between different types of control that share the same definition function. The Toolbox stores this additional information into the field automatically when the control is created.

11. **contrlData** is reserved for use by the control definition function in any way it chooses. **contrlRfCon** is for your program's own use.

12. **contrlAction** is a pointer to the control's default *action procedure*, used by the **TrackControl** routine; see [6.4.2] for details.

13. **contrlTitle** is the title of the control, in Pascal string format (1-byte character count followed by the characters themselves). The actual length of this field (and hence of the control record itself) is just enough to include the characters of the title.

Assembly-Language Information

Field offsets in a control record:

(Pascal) Field name	(Assembly) Offset name	Offset in bytes
nextControl	nextControl	0
contrlOwner	contrlOwner	4
contrlRect	contrlRect	8
contrlVis	contrlVis	16
contrlHilite	contrlHilite	17
contrlValue	contrlValue	18
contrlMin	contrlMin	20
contrlMax	contrlMax	22
contrlDefProc	contrlDefHandle	24
contrlData	contrlData	28
contrlAction	contrlAction	32
contrlRfCon	contrlRfCon	36
contrlTitle	contrlTitle	40

Assembly-language constant:

Name	Value	Meaning
ContrlSize	40	Size of control record in bytes, excluding title

6.2 Creating and Destroying Controls

6.2.1 Creating Controls

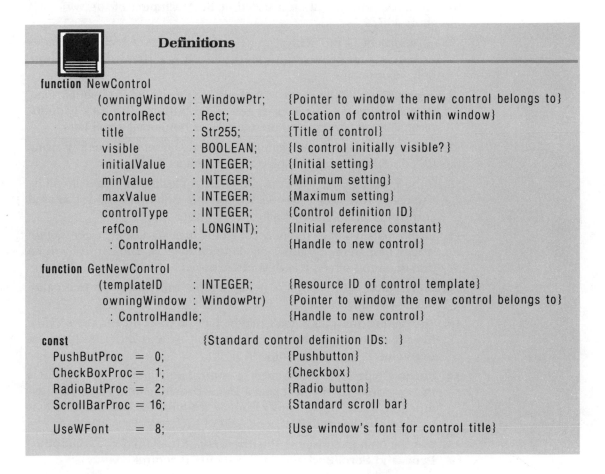

Definitions

```
function NewControl
        (owningWindow : WindowPtr;      {Pointer to window the new control belongs to}
         controlRect  : Rect;           {Location of control within window}
         title        : Str255;         {Title of control}
         visible      : BOOLEAN;        {Is control initially visible?}
         initialValue : INTEGER;        {Initial setting}
         minValue     : INTEGER;        {Minimum setting}
         maxValue     : INTEGER;        {Maximum setting}
         controlType  : INTEGER;        {Control definition ID}
         refCon       : LONGINT);       {Initial reference constant}
       : ControlHandle;                 {Handle to new control}

function GetNewControl
        (templateID   : INTEGER;        {Resource ID of control template}
         owningWindow : WindowPtr)      {Pointer to window the new control belongs to}
       : ControlHandle;                 {Handle to new control}

const                      {Standard control definition IDs:  }
  PushButProc  =  0;                    {Pushbutton}
  CheckBoxProc =  1;                    {Checkbox}
  RadioButProc =  2;                    {Radio button}
  ScrollBarProc = 16;                   {Standard scroll bar}

  UseWFont     =  8;                    {Use window's font for control title}
```

Notes

1. **NewControl** and **GetNewControl** both create a new control, enter it in its window's control list, and return a handle to it.

2. Before creating any controls, you must first call **InitGraf** [I:4.3.1], **InitFonts** [I:8.2.4], and **InitWindows** [3.2.1].

3. **NewControl** takes initialization information as parameters, **GetNewControl** gets it from a control template in a resource file.

4. **templateID** is the resource ID of a control template; its resource type is '**CNTL**' [6.5.1].

5. **owningWindow** is a pointer to the window that the new control will belong to.

6. The new control will be inserted at the beginning of the window's control list.

7. **controlRect** is the control's enclosing rectangle, which determines its size and location within the window. It is expressed in *local (window) coordinates*.

8. **controlRect** will be at least 20 pixels high for standard pushbuttons, 16 pixels high for checkboxes and radio buttons, 16 pixels wide for vertical scroll bars, and 16 pixels high for horizontal scroll bars.

9. **title** is the title of the new control, and may be set to the empty string for controls that don't display a title (such as scroll bars).

10. If the title is too long to fit in the given enclosing rectangle, it will be truncated at the right for checkboxes and radio buttons, or centered and truncated at both ends for pushbuttons.

11. **visible** tells whether the new control is *logically* visible, even though it may be covered by other overlapping objects. The control will be drawn on the screen if visible and exposed.

12. **initialValue** is the control's initial setting; **minValue** and **maxValue** define its initial range.

13. The setting and range don't matter for standard pushbuttons, since they don't retain a setting. For checkboxes and radio buttons, set **minValue = 0** and **maxValue = 1**.

14. **controlType** is a coded integer (a *control definition ID*) that includes the resource ID of the control definition function. The definition function is read into memory from its resource file and a handle to it is placed in the **contrlDefProc** field of the control record.

15. Use the built-in constants **PushbutProc**, **CheckboxProc**, **RadioButProc**, and **ScrollBarProc** for the standard control types.

16. A control's title is normally displayed in the standard system font (12-point **Chicago**). Adding the constant **UseWFont** to the control type causes it to use the owning window's current typeface and size [I:8.3.1] instead.

17. **refCon** is the initial value of the control's reference constant (**contrlRfCon**).

18. The new control will initially have no highlighting (**contrlHilite = 0**) and no default action procedure (**contrlAction = NIL**); you can change these attributes if necessary with **HiliteControl** [6.3.3] and **SetCtlAction** [6.4.2].

Assembly-Language Information

Trap macros:

(Pascal) Routine name	(Assembly) Trap macro	Trap word
NewControl	**_NewControl**	**$A954**
GetNewControl	**_GetNewControl**	**$A9BE**

Standard control definition IDs:

Name	Value	Meaning
PushbutProc	**0**	Pushbutton
CheckboxProc	**1**	Checkbox
RadioButProc	**2**	Radio button
ScrollBarProc	**16**	Standard scroll bar
UseWFont	**8**	Use window font for title

6.2.2 Destroying Controls

Definitions

procedure DisposeControl
         (theControl : ControlHandle);   {Control to be destroyed}

procedure KillControls
         (theWindow : WindowPtr);   {Window whose controls are to be destroyed}

Notes

1. **DisposeControl** destroys a designated control; **KillControls** destroys all controls belonging to a given window.

2. Destroying a control removes it from the screen and from its window's control list.

3. If you're using the control's reference constant (**contrlRfCon**) to hold a handle to auxiliary information about the control, it's up to you to dispose of it before destroying the control itself. All other storage associated with the control is released automatically.

4. Destroying a window with **CloseWindow** or **DisposeWindow** [3.2.3] automatically destroys all of its controls; there's no need to call **Kill-Controls** explicitly.

5. The trap macro for **DisposeControl** is spelled **_DisposControl**.

Assembly-Language Information

Trap macros:

(Pascal) Routine name	(Assembly) Trap macro	Trap word
DisposeControl	**_DisposControl**	**$A955**
KillControls	**_KillControls**	**$A956**

6.2.3 Setting Control Properties

Definitions

```
procedure   SetCTitle
                (theControl  : ControlHandle;     {Handle to the control}
                 newTitle    : Str255);           {New title}

procedure   GetCTitle
                (theControl  : ControlHandle;     {Handle to the control}
             var theTitle    : Str255);           {Returns current title}

procedure   SetCRefCon
                (theControl  : ControlHandle;     {Handle to the control}
                 newRefCon   : LONGINT);          {New reference constant}

function    GetCRefCon
                (theControl  : ControlHandle)     {Handle to the control}
                  : LONGINT;                      {Current reference constant}
```

Notes

1. **SetCTitle** sets a control's title; **GetCTitle** returns its current title via parameter **theTitle**. Always use these routines instead of manipulating the **contrlTitle** field directly.

2. **SetCTitle** redisplays the control on the screen with its new title.

3. **SetCRefCon** sets a control's reference constant; **GetCRefCon** returns its current reference constant.

4. The reference "constant" (really a variable) is for your program's optional private use. You can give it any 4-byte value that makes sense to your program.

5. If you need more than 4 bytes of private data per control, allocate space for the data from the heap and store a handle to it as the reference constant. (Don't forget to deallocate this space before destroying the control!)

Assembly-Language Information

Trap macros:

(Pascal) Routine name	(Assembly) Trap macro	Trap word
SetCTitle	**_SetCTitle**	**$A95F**
GetCTitle	**_GetCTitle**	**$A95E**
SetCRefCon	**_SetCRefCon**	**$A95B**
GetCRefCon	**_GetCRefCon**	**$A95A**

6.2.4 Control Setting and Range

Definitions

```
procedure SetCtlValue
        (theControl : ControlHandle;      {Handle to the control}
         newValue   : INTEGER);           {New setting}

function  GetCtlValue
        (theControl : ControlHandle)      {Handle to the control}
         : INTEGER                        {Current setting}

procedure SetCtlMin
        (theControl : ControlHandle;      {Handle to the control}
         newMin     : INTEGER);           {New minimum setting}

function  GetCtlMin
        (theControl : ControlHandle)      {Handle to the control}
         : INTEGER                        {Current minimum setting}

procedure SetCtlMax
        (theControl : ControlHandle;      {Handle to the control}
         newMax     : INTEGER);           {New maximum setting}

function  GetCtlMax
        (theControl : ControlHandle)      {Handle to the control}
         : INTEGER                        {Current maximum setting}
```

Notes

1. **SetCtlValue** gives a control a new setting; **GetCtlValue** returns its current setting.

3. **SetCtlMin** and **SetCtlMax** set the range of values a control's setting can assume; **GetCtlMin** and **GetCtlMax** return its current range.

3. A control's setting is never permitted to go outside the current range. If the value specified to **SetCtlValue**, **SetCtlMin**, or **SetCtlMax** would place the setting out of range, it is automatically forced to the nearest endpoint (minimum or maximum) of the range.

4. **SetCtlValue**, **SetCtlMin**, and **SetCtlMax** all redisplay the control on the screen to reflect its new setting and range.

5. The trap macros for **SetCtlMin** and **GetCtlMin** are spelled **_SetMinCtl** and **_GetMinCtl**; those for **SetCtlMax** and **GetCtlMax** are spelled **_SetMaxCtl** and **_GetMaxCtl**.

Assembly-Language Information

Trap macros:

(Pascal) Routine name	(Assembly) Trap macro	Trap word
SetCtlValue	**_SetCtlValue**	**$A963**
GetCtlValue	**_GetCtlValue**	**$A960**
SetCtlMin	**_SetMinCtl**	**$A964**
GetCtlMin	**_GetMinCtl**	**$A961**
SetCtlMax	**_SetMaxCtl**	**$A965**
GetCtlMax	**_GetMaxCtl**	**$A962**

6.3 Control Display

6.3.1 Showing and Hiding Controls

Definitions

```
procedure HideControl
        (theControl : ControlHandle);     {Handle to the control}

procedure ShowControl
        (theControl : ControlHandle);     {Handle to the control}

procedure DrawControls
        (theWindow : WindowPtr);          {Pointer to the window}
```

Notes

1. **HideControl** makes a control invisible; **ShowControl** makes it visible.

2. The **contrlVis** field of the control record [6.1.1] is nominally defined as a 1-byte integer instead of a Boolean, so that it will be packed into a single byte of the record. Always use **ShowControl** or **HideControl** to make a control visible or invisible, instead of storing directly into the **contrlVis** field.

3. **HideControl** erases the control by filling its enclosing rectangle (**contrlRect**) with the owning window's background pattern. The rectangle is also added to the window's update region, causing anything previously obscured by the control to be redisplayed.

4. **ShowControl** makes the control *logically* visible; it will actually appear on the screen only if not obscured by other objects.

5. Hiding an already invisible control or showing an already visible one has no effect.

6. **DrawControls** draws all of a window's visible controls on the screen.

7. Always call **DrawControls** as part of your response to an update event for a window. The window's controls are *not* redrawn automatically by **ShowWindow** [3.3.1], **SelectWindow** [3.5.2], or **BringToFront** [3.3.3].

Assembly-Language Information

Trap macros:

(Pascal) Routine name	(Assembly) Trap macro	Trap word
HideControl	**_HideControl**	**$A958**
ShowControl	**_ShowControl**	**$A957**
DrawControls	**_DrawControls**	**$A969**

Assembly-language constant:

Name	Value	Meaning
SBarPatID	**17**	Resource ID of pattern for scroll bar shaft

6.3.2 Moving and Sizing Controls

Definitions

```
procedure MoveControl
        (theControl : ControlHandle;    {Handle to the control}
         hLocal     : INTEGER;          {New horizontal coordinate}
         vLocal     : INTEGER);         {New vertical coordinate}

procedure SizeControl
        (theControl : ControlHandle;    {Handle to the control}
         newWidth   : INTEGER;          {New width}
         newHeight  : INTEGER);         {New height}
```

Notes

1. **MoveControl** moves a control to a new location within its window; **SizeControl** changes its size.

2. If the control is visible, it is erased and redrawn in its new location or size.

3. All coordinates apply to the control's enclosing rectangle (**contrlRect**).

4. For **MoveControl**, **hLocal** and **vLocal** give the new location of the control's top-left corner, in *local (window) coordinates*. The control's size remains the same.

5. For **SizeControl**, **newWidth** and **newHeight** give the control's (that is, the enclosing rectangle's) new dimensions in pixels. The location of the top-left corner remains the same.

Assembly-Language Information

Trap macros:

(Pascal) Routine name	(Assembly) Trap macro	Trap word
MoveControl	**_MoveControl**	**$A959**
SizeControl	**_SizeControl**	**$A95C**

6.3.3 Control Highlighting

Definitions

```
procedure HiliteControl
              (theControl : ControlHandle;      {Handle to the control}
               hiliteState : INTEGER);          {Part of the control to be highlighted}
```

Notes

1. **HiliteControl** specifies the way a control is highlighted on the screen and redraws it accordingly.

2. **hiliteState** is a 1-byte integer (**0–255**) denoting the control's new highlighting state.

3. A highlighting state of **0** stands for no highlighting at all.

4. A highlighting state of **255** marks the control as *inactive*. Such a control is displayed in some distinctive way and behaves as if it were invisible; **TestControl** and **FindControl** [6.4.1] will not report mouse clicks in the control.

5. For historical reasons, a highlighting state of **254** is invalid and should not be used.

6. Any other highlighting state (**1–253**) is a *part code* [6.4.1] identifying which part of the control is highlighted.

7. The actual appearance of a control in any given highlighting state is determined by its control definition function.

Assembly-Language Information

Trap macro:

(Pascal) Routine name	(Assembly) Trap macro	Trap word
HiliteControl	**_HiliteControl**	**$A95D**

6.4 Responding to the Mouse

6.4.1 Locating Mouse Clicks

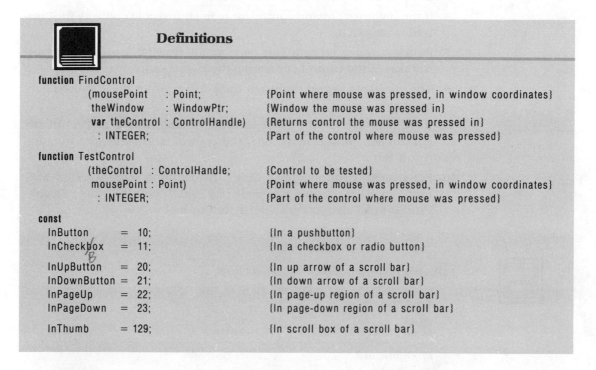

Definitions

```
function FindControl
        (mousePoint    : Point;          {Point where mouse was pressed, in window coordinates}
         theWindow     : WindowPtr;      {Window the mouse was pressed in}
         var theControl : ControlHandle) {Returns control the mouse was pressed in}
         : INTEGER;                      {Part of the control where mouse was pressed}

function TestControl
        (theControl  : ControlHandle;    {Control to be tested}
         mousePoint : Point)             {Point where mouse was pressed, in window coordinates}
         : INTEGER;                      {Part of the control where mouse was pressed}

const
  InButton      = 10;                    {In a pushbutton}
  InCheckbox    = 11;                    {In a checkbox or radio button}

  InUpButton    = 20;                    {In up arrow of a scroll bar}
  InDownButton  = 21;                    {In down arrow of a scroll bar}
  InPageUp      = 22;                    {In page-up region of a scroll bar}
  InPageDown    = 23;                    {In page-down region of a scroll bar}

  InThumb       = 129;                   {In scroll box of a scroll bar}
```

Notes

1. **FindControl** finds which of a window's controls (if any), and which part of the control, contains a given point. This is normally a point where the mouse button was pressed; call **FindControl** after **Find-Window** [3.5.1] reports that the point lies in the window's content region.

2. **TestControl** tests whether a given point lies inside a given control, and if so, in which part of the control.

3. For both routines, **mousePoint** should give the location of a mouse-down event, in *local (window) coordinates*. In the **where** field of the event record [2.1.1], the point is reported in *global* coordinates. Use **GlobalToLocal** [I:4.4.2] to convert the point before passing it to either of these routines.

4. For **FindControl**, the parameter **theWindow** identifies the window in whose coordinate system the point is expressed; for **TestControl**, the window is the one the given control (**theControl**) belongs to.

5. **FindControl** returns a handle to the control containing the given point in the variable parameter **theControl**.

6. If the point isn't in any control (or is in an invisible control), **theControl** is set to **NIL**.

7. Both functions return a *part code* as the function result, identifying the part of the control containing the given point.

8. The constants shown represent the part codes for the standard control types.

9. If the point isn't in the given control (for **testControl**) or isn't in any control (for **FindControl**), or if the control is invisible, the function result is **0**.

10. For inactive controls (those with a highlighting state [6.3.3] of **255**), both functions return a part code of **0** as if the control were invisible; **FindControl** also sets parameter **theControl** to **NIL**.

Assembly-Language Information

Trap macros:

(Pascal) Routine name	(Assembly) Trap macro	Trap word
FindControl	**_FindControl**	**$A96C**
TestControl	**_TestControl**	**$A966**

Part codes for standard controls:

Name	Value	Meaning
InButton	**10**	Pushbutton
InCheckbox	**11**	Checkbox or radio button
InUpButton	**20**	Scroll bar up arrow
InDownButton	**21**	Scroll bar down arrow
InPageUp	**22**	Scroll bar page-up region
InPageDown	**23**	Scroll bar page-down region
InThumb	**129**	Scroll box

6.4.2 Tracking the Mouse

Definitions

```
function   TrackControl
               (theControl : ControlHandle;      {Handle to the control}
                startPoint  : Point;             {Point where mouse was pressed, in window coordinates}
                actionProc  : ProcPtr)           {Repeated action while tracking}
                : INTEGER;                       {Part of control affected}

procedure  SetCtlAction
               (theControl : ControlHandle;      {Handle to the control}
                newAction  : ProcPtr);           {New action procedure}

function   GetCtlAction
               (theControl : ControlHandle)      {Handle to the control}
                : ProcPtr;                       {Current action procedure}
```

Notes

1. Call **TrackControl** after a mouse-down event in a control, to track the mouse's movements and respond accordingly.

2. **startPoint** should give the location of the mouse-down event, in *local* (*window*) *coordinates*. In the **where** field of the event record [2.1.1], the point is reported in *global* coordinates. Use **GlobalToLocal** [I:4.4.2] to convert the point before passing it to **TrackControl**.

3. **TrackControl** keeps control for as long as the user holds down the mouse button, tracking the mouse's movements and providing visual feedback on the screen.

4. All actions are limited to the part of the control that contains the original starting point.

5. If the mouse was pressed in the indicator of a dial, an outline of the indicator follows the mouse as long as the button remains down. When the button is released, the control is redrawn with the indicator at its new position and its setting is adjusted accordingly. You should then do whatever is appropriate to respond to the new setting.

6. If **theControl** is not a dial, or if the mouse was pressed in a part of a dial other than the indicator, the selected part is highlighted and unhighlighted as the mouse moves into and out of it. When the mouse is released, the part is unhighlighted.

7. If the mouse is released in the same part of the control where it was originally pressed, **TrackControl** returns the corresponding part code as its function result; otherwise it returns **0**.

8. While the mouse button is down, **TrackControl** performs some continuous action by repeatedly calling the specified *action procedure* (**actionProc**).

9. For tracking the indicator of a dial, the action procedure should take no parameters; for any other control part, it should be of the form

```
procedure Action (theControl : ControlHandle;
                  thePart     : INTEGER);
```

10. Each time the action procedure is called, the value passed for parameter **thePart** will be either the part code of the part where the mouse was originally pressed (if the mouse is still within that part) or **0** (if it isn't). The procedure should normally do nothing on receiving a part code of **0**.

11. If **actionProc** is **NIL**, no continuous action will be performed while tracking, other than highlighting and unhighlighting the selected control part.

12. If **actionProc** is **ProcPtr(−1)**, the control's default action procedure (**contrlAction**) will be used. The default action procedure can be set with **SetCtlAction** or read with **GetCtlAction**.

Assembly-Language Information

Trap macros:

(Pascal) Routine name	(Assembly) Trap macro	Trap word
TrackControl	**_TrackControl**	**$A968**
SetCtlAction	**_SetCtlAction**	**$A96B**
GetCtlAction	**_GetCtlAction**	**$A96A**

6.4.3 Dragging a Control

Definitions

```
procedure DragControl
            (theControl : ControlHandle;      {Handle to the control}
             startPoint : Point;              {Point where mouse was pressed}
             limitRect  : Rect;               {Rectangle limiting movement}
             trackRect  : Rect;               {Rectangle limiting tracking}
             axis       : INTEGER);           {Axis constraint}

const
   BothAxes  = 0;                             {Both axes}
   HAxisOnly = 1;                             {Horizontal only}
   VAxisOnly = 2;                             {Vertical only}
```

Notes

1. **DragControl** allows the user to drag a control with the mouse to a new position in its window.

2. This is an unusual operation; the normal way of responding to a mouse event in a control is with **TrackControl** [6.4.2].

3. **startPoint** should give the location of a mouse-down event, in *local* (*window*) *coordinates*. In the **where** field of the event record [2.1.1], the point is reported in *global* coordinates. Use **GlobalToLocal** [I:4.4.2] to convert the point before passing it to **DragControl**.

4. **DragControl** keeps control for as long as the user holds down the mouse button, following the mouse's movements on the screen with an outline of the control. When the button is released, the control is moved to the new location: you needn't call **MoveControl** [6.3.2] yourself.

5. **limitRect** limits the movement of the control's outline on the screen. If the mouse leaves this rectangle, the outline "pins" at the edge of the rectangle and will not travel any further.

6. **trackRect** limits the tracking of the mouse. If the mouse leaves this rectangle, the control outline disappears from the screen; it will reappear if the mouse re-enters the rectangle while the button is still down. If the button is released outside this rectangle, the control's position is left unchanged.

7. Both rectangles are expressed in *local (window) coordinates*.

8. limitRect should lie entirely within both **trackRect** and the window's content region. To allow the user some margin of error in dragging the control, **trackRect** should be slightly larger than **limitRect**.

9. axis allows the motion of the control to be limited to horizontal motion only (**HAxisOnly**), vertical only (**VAxisOnly**), or both (**BothAxes**).

Assembly-Language Information

Trap macro:

(Pascal) Routine name	(Assembly) Trap macro	Trap word
DragControl	**_DragControl**	**$A967**

Assembly-language constants:

Name	Value	Meaning
NoConstraint	**0**	Both axes
HAxisOnly	**1**	Horizontal only
VAxisOnly	**2**	Vertical only

6.5 Control-Related Resources

6.5.1 Resource Type 'CNTL'

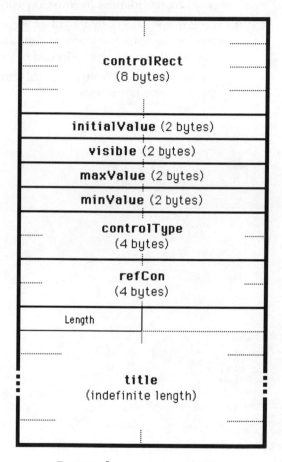

Format of resource type **'CNTL'**

Notes

1. A resource of type '**CNTL**' contains a control template.

2. All fields of the control template are in the same form as the corresponding parameters to **NewControl** [6.2.1].

3. The control title is in Pascal string form, with a 1-byte length count followed by the characters of the title. The overall size of the control template depends on the length of the title string.

4. To create a control from a control template, call **GetNewControl** [6.2.1] with the template's resource ID.

CHAPTER

7

Meaningful Dialogs

Generally speaking, Macintosh commands take effect as soon as the user invokes them, whether through a menu or by typing a keyboard alias with the command key. Often the command operates on information that's already available at the time it's invoked, such as the currently active window or the current selection. Sometimes, though, some further information is needed before the command can be carried out: for instance, a command that does disk input or output may need the name of a file to operate on, or a **Find** command may need to know what string of characters to search for. In these cases the program can ask the user for the needed information by opening a *dialog box* on the screen. Dialog boxes are also useful for conveying important information *to* the user, such as error messages or progress reports, or for pausing to let the user perform some preliminary action, such as inserting a piece of paper in the printer.

There are actually three different levels of dialogs, differing in how much interaction they permit with the user and how long they remain on the screen. (Throughout this chapter, the term "dialog box," or just "dialog," refers equally to all three kinds unless explicitly stated otherwise.) At the lowest level are *alerts*, normally used to display error messages or other status information (see Figure 7-1). When an alert box is visible, it's always the frontmost window on the screen. The only meaningful action the user can take is to *dismiss* the alert, usually by clicking the mouse in a pushbutton; all other actions are ignored.

The next level up from alerts are *modal dialogs* (Figure 7-2), so called because they put the system in a "mode" that restricts the user's freedom of action: only the dialog box will respond to the mouse and keyboard. Like an alert box, a modal dialog remains frontmost on the screen until the user dismisses it by clicking a pushbutton. As long as it's visible, no

Figure 7-1 Alert box

other window can be brought to the front; mouse clicks outside the dialog box produce no response except a beep from the speaker. Unlike an alert, however, a modal dialog allows the user to do other things than just dismiss it, such as manipulate controls with the mouse or type text from the keyboard.

Finally there are *modeless dialogs* (Figure 7-3), which don't restrict the user's actions in any way. A modeless dialog box behaves just like an ordinary document window: it can be activated, deactivated, and moved around freely on the screen. The user can activate other windows and work in them—type, edit, change the selection, and so forth—then reactivate the dialog window and continue to use it. When it's no longer needed, the user dismisses it by clicking the mouse in its close box or choosing **Close** from the **File** menu, just like any other window.

As usual, there's a one-time initialization routine, **InitDialogs** [7.2.1], that you have to call before performing any dialog-related operation. It must be preceded in turn by **InitGraf** [I:4.3.1], **InitFonts** [I:8.2.4], **InitWindows** [3.2.1], **InitMenus** [4.2.1], and **TEInit** [5.2.1].

Quality:	● High	○ Standard	○ Draft	OK
Page Range:	● All	○ From:	To:	
Copies:	1			
Paper Feed:	○ Continuous	● Cut Sheet		Cancel

Figure 7-2 Modal dialog box

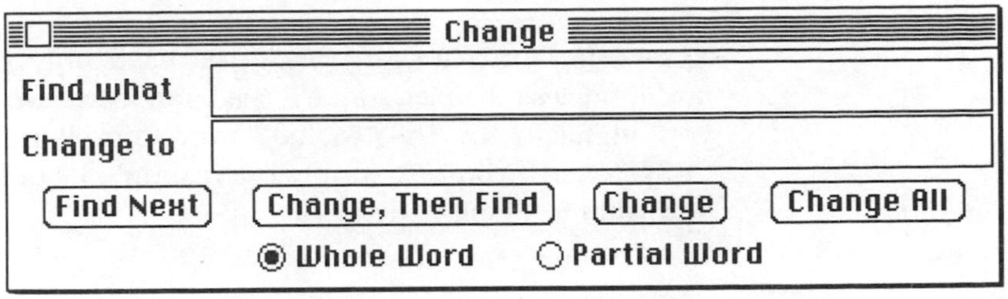

Figure 7-3 Modeless dialog box

Creating and Destroying Dialogs

From the point of view of the Toolbox, a dialog box is just another window on the screen that happens to have some unusual extra properties. A *dialog record* [7.1.1], the internal data structure representing a dialog or alert box, has a complete window record embedded within it as its first field, just the way a window record in turn contains a complete graphics port. Just as you can think of a window as an extended graphics port, a dialog is an extended window.

The most important piece of extra information in the dialog record is a handle to the dialog's *item list*. The item list in turn contains handles to each of the individual items. A dialog can have any number of items, which may include text, icons, pictures, controls of any kind, and text boxes where the user can type in information such as a file name or a search string.

There are two ways of creating a new dialog box, analogous to the two ways of creating a window. You can either supply all the needed information as parameters to **NewDialog** [7.2.2] or use a predefined template (resource type 'DLOG' [7.6.2]) and pass its resource ID to **GetNewDialog** [7.2.2]. The Toolbox needs exactly the same information to create a dialog as to create a window, plus an item list to define the dialog's contents. The item list is normally taken from a resource file, under resource type 'DITL' ("dialog item list") [7.6.3]. The template you provide to **GetNewDialog** includes the resource ID of the item list, which the Toolbox will read in for you from the resource file. When you use **NewDialog** instead, you have to read in the item list yourself with **GetResource** [I:6.3.1] and pass its handle as a parameter.

NewDialog and **GetNewDialog** are used only for creating modal and modeless dialogs. As we'll see later, alerts are always created for you implicitly by the Toolbox from templates of resource type 'ALRT' [7.6.1]. You just supply the resource ID of the template when you want to display the alert.

A dialog window's **windowKind** field is set automatically on creation to the constant **DialogKind** [3.1.1], to identify it as a dialog box and not an ordinary application window. Just as when you create a window, you can either allocate your own space for the dialog record and pass a pointer to it as the **dStorage** parameter, or pass **NIL** for **dStorage** to have the Toolbox allocate the space for you. When the time comes to destroy the dialog record, you'll use **CloseDialog** [7.2.3] if you supplied your own storage, **DisposDialog** [7.2.3] if you let the Toolbox allocate it for you.

You specify the overall appearance of your dialog box by passing one of the standard window definition IDs [3.2.2] as the **windowType** parameter to **NewDialog**, or in the corresponding field of the dialog template to **GetNewDialog**. (Refer back to Figure 3-8 for the appearance of the standard window types.) Alert boxes always use window type **DBoxProc**, the standard double-bordered dialog window. Modal dialogs can use either the double border, a plain border (**PlainDBoxProc**), or a two-pixel "shadow" (**AltDBoxProc**). Modeless dialogs should have a title bar so the user can drag them around on the screen; they're usually of window type **NoGrowDocProc**, the standard document window with no size box.

Dialog Pointers

Since a dialog record is ultimately based on a graphics port, it's a non-relocatable object and is referred to with a pointer instead of a handle. Just as there are two kinds of window pointers, a **WindowPtr** for treating a window as a graphics port and a **WindowPeek** for treating it specifically as a window, so are there two kinds of dialog pointer. A **DialogPtr** is defined to be equivalent to a **WindowPtr** [3.1.1], which in turn is equivalent to a **GrafPtr**—a pointer to a **GrafPort** [I:4.2.2]. On the other hand, a **DialogPeek** is defined as a pointer to a **DialogRecord**, so you can use it to "peek" at the record's dialog-specific fields.

When you create a new dialog box with **NewDialog** or **GetNewDialog**, you get back a **DialogPtr**. Since this is equivalent to both a **GrafPtr** and a **WindowPtr**, you can pass it to any Toolbox routine that operates on ports or windows, as well as those that operate exclusively on dialogs. If necessary, you can use typecasting to convert the **DialogPtr** to a **WindowPeek** in order to access its window-related fields, or to a **DialogPeek** to access those specific to dialogs. For example, suppose you declare

```
var
    dPtr   : DialogPtr;
    wPeek  : WindowPeek;
    dPeek  : DialogPeek;
```

then create a new dialog record and convert the resulting **DialogPtr** by typecasting:

```
dPtr   := GetNewDialog ( . . . );
wPeek := WindowPeek(dPtr)
dPeek := DialogPeek (dPtr)
```

You can now pass the **DialogPtr** to any routine that operates on graphics ports

```
SetPort (dPtr)
```

or on windows

```
ShowWindow (dPtr)
```

or on dialogs

```
DrawDialog (dPtr)
```

You can access the fields of the dialog's graphics port with any of the three types of pointer

```
dPtr^.portRect
```

```
wPeek^.port.portRect
```

```
dPeek^.window.port.portRect
```

—those of its window with the **WindowPeek** or the **DialogPeek**

```
wPeek^.updateRgn
```

```
dPeek^.window.updateRgn
```

—and those specific to the dialog itself with the **DialogPeek** only

```
dPeek^.textH
```

Item Lists

As noted earlier, a dialog's item list is normally defined by a resource of type 'DITL' [7.6.3]. This item list resource begins with a word-length (2-byte) integer giving the number of items in the list minus 1; this is followed by the list entries describing the items themselves. The list entry for each item contains the following information:

- An empty 4-byte field that will be filled with an *item handle* when the list is copied into memory
- A *display rectangle* giving the item's size and location in the local coordinate system of the dialog window
- A 1-byte integer code (from **0** to **255**) identifying the *item type* [7.1.2]
- One additional piece of descriptive information, depending on the type of item

The length of the additional descriptive information, and hence the overall length of the item list entry itself, can vary from one item to another. (The only restriction is that the length must be even, so it will align on word boundaries in memory.) So each list entry also contains a length count giving the length of the descriptive information in bytes. When you create a dialog box, the Toolbox uses the descriptive information in each entry of the item list to create the corresponding item itself, then stores (in most cases) a handle to the item into the field reserved for it in the list entry. (The one exception is discussed later, in the section "User Items.") Finally, it places a handle to the resulting item list into the **items** field of the new dialog record.

When you create a dialog box from a template with **GetNewDialog**, the Toolbox makes a *copy* of the item list and uses the copy from then on. Once the copy is made, the original is no longer needed in memory. Always be sure to make the item list a purgeable resource, so it can be removed from the heap to make room for something else.

On the other hand, when you use **NewDialog** to create a dialog from scratch (rather than from a template), the item list you supply is *not* copied; the **items** field of the dialog record will hold a handle to the original item list itself. So in this case the item list must be *unpurgeable*.

To access or change the properties of individual items, you can use the Toolbox routines **GetDItem** and **SetDItem** [7.3.1]. You identify the item you want by giving a pointer to the dialog it belongs to, along with the *item number* of the individual item. (The item number is simply the index of the item within the dialog's item list: the first item in the list is item number **1**, the second is item number **2**, and so on.) **GetDItem** returns the item type, item handle, and display rectangle through variable parameters; **SetDItem** accepts these same three pieces of information and modifies the item accordingly. After getting the item handle from **GetDItem**, you can use it to perform any needed operation on the item. For example, to hide a control that's an item in a dialog, you might do something like this:

```
GetDItem (theDialog, itemNumber, itemType, itemHandle, dispRect);
ctrlHandle := ControlHandle(itemHandle);
HideControl (ctrlHandle)
```

Item Types

Item types fall into two broad categories, which we can call *static* and *interactive*. Static items are those that are displayed purely to convey information *to* the user, such as non-editable text, icons, and pictures; interactive items are those that gather information *from* the user via the mouse and keyboard, such as controls of any kind and text boxes in which text can be entered from the keyboard.

Static Text

Static text items have an item type of **StatText**, to distinguish them from editable text boxes that the user can type into. The item list resource contains the actual text of the item. When the item list is copied into memory, a copy of this text is made in the heap and a handle to the copy becomes the item handle. The item's display rectangle is used for both the destination and view rectangles of the edit record used to display the text; this means that the text will be both wrapped and clipped to this same rectangle.

Sometimes the text of an item can't be completely defined ahead of time. For instance, you may want your **Find** command to display a message such as

Can't find string "Rutabaga"

when it can't find the string the user has asked to search for. A static text item can include as many as four such variable strings, to be substituted in at the time the dialog is displayed. They're represented in the text of the item by the special placeholders ^**0**, ^**1**, ^**2**, and ^**3**; you specify the actual text to be substituted for the placeholders by calling the Toolbox routine **ParamText** [7.4.6]. This routines takes four strings as parameters, one for each of the four placeholders. (If you're not using all four, you can just pass null strings for the ones you don't need.) For example, to display the message shown above, you would define a static text item with the text

Can't find string "^0"

and substitute the user's search string into the text by calling

ParamText (searchString, '', '', '')

before displaying the dialog.

Icon and Picture Items

A dialog's item list can include icons (item type **IconItem**) and Quick-Draw pictures of arbitrary complexity (**PicItem**). The descriptive information in the item list resource is the resource ID of the icon or picture (resource type 'ICON' [I:5.5.3] or 'PICT' [I:5.5.5]). The Toolbox will read in the designated resource from the resource file and store its handle into the item list in memory as the item handle. When drawn in the dialog box, the icon or picture will be scaled to the display rectangle specified for the item.

a. Note

b. Caution

c. Stop

Figure 7-4 Standard alert icons

The Toolbox provides three standard *alert icons*, shown in Figure 7-4. These are intended to denote alerts of differing levels of severity:

- A *note alert* (Figure 7-4a) merely calls some possibly useful information to the user's attention, such as

    Memory space is running low.
    Consider splitting your document into smaller pieces.

    It doesn't necessarily mean that an actual error has occurred, and implies that it's probably safe to proceed with the original operation.

- A *caution alert* (Figure 7-4b) reports a more serious error or anomaly, or asks the user for additional instructions about how to proceed:

    Save changes to file "Term Paper" before quitting?

- A *stop alert* (Figure 7-4c) reports a serious error or problem that makes it impossible to complete the requested operation, or warns the user of potentially dangerous or irrevocable consequences: for example,

    Are you sure you want to erase that disk?

The standard alert icons don't have to be included explicitly in an alert's item list. Instead, you can request any of the three icons implicitly by displaying the alert box with one of the Toolbox routines **NoteAlert**, **CautionAlert**, or **StopAlert** instead of just **Alert** [7.4.2]. The icon will always be displayed at a standard position within the alert box, running from local coordinates (**10, 20**) at the top left to (**42, 52**) at the bottom right. (If you want to put it somewhere else instead, you can define an explicit item of type **IconItem**, giving one of the constants **NoteIcon**, **CautionIcon**, or **StopIcon** [7.4.2] as the resource ID.)

Control Items

The item type for a control item is formed by adding the constant **CtrlItem** to another constant denoting the specific type of control: **BtnCtrl** for a pushbutton, **ChkCtrl** for a checkbox, or **RadCtrl** for a radio button. For example, the item type for a simple pushbutton is

    CtrlItem + BtnCtrl

For these three standard button types, the descriptive information in the item list resource is just the text of the button's title. The Toolbox will automatically create a control of the specified type with that title, using the item's display rectangle as the enclosing rectangle for the control. For any other type of control, the item type is

    CtrlItem + ResCtrl

("resource control"), and the additional descriptive information is the resource ID of a control template (resource type 'CNTL' [6.5.1]). The template in turn will include a control definition ID specifying the control type. For both standard and resource controls, the item handle is simply a handle to the control in memory.

An alert or modal dialog box should always include at least one pushbutton for dismissing the dialog from the screen. (A modeless dialog doesn't need such a button, since it's dismissed with the close box like an ordinary window.) Often there will be two or more pushbuttons that dismiss the dialog in different ways: for instance, an **OK** button to proceed with the original command and a **Cancel** button to rescind it. In any case, one pushbutton is singled out for special treatment as the *default button*. While the alert or dialog box is visible, the Toolbox will interpret a press of the return or enter key as equivalent to a mouse click in the default button. To signal this fact to the user, it will automatically outline the button on the screen with a heavy black double border, as shown in Figure 7-5.

For modal dialogs, the first item in the item list (item number **1**) is always assumed to be the default button, so you should set up your item list accordingly. For alerts, the alert template can specify either of the first two items as the default button. These first two items are commonly used for an **OK** and a **Cancel** button; so commonly, in fact, that the Toolbox defines constants by those names to stand for the item numbers **1** and **2** [7.1.1]. The item number of the default button is kept in the **aDefItem** field of the dialog record [7.1.1].

The default button has a heavy, double border.

Figure 7-5 Default button

By convention, the default button should be the "safest" way of dismissing a dialog box—that is, the one that results in the least loss of data. For instance, if you're asking the user whether to save or discard the contents of a window before closing it, the **Save** button would be the safest choice and should be the default.

Text Boxes

A dialog box can contain one or more *text boxes* for entering text from the keyboard. Text boxes automatically support selection with the mouse, extended selection with the shift key, point-and-type insertion or replacement, and character deletion with the backspace key. If you want, you can also arrange to have them support the standard editing commands **Cut**, **Copy**, **Paste**, and **Clear**, or their command-key equivalents: later we'll see an example of how to do this.

The item type for text boxes is **EditText** ("editable text"). The item list in the resource file gives the text to be used for the initial contents of the text box; in memory, this will be converted into an item handle to the box's current contents in the heap. You can obtain the item handle with **GetDItem** [7.3.1] and pass it to **GetIText** [7.3.2] to get the box's contents in Pascal string form, or to **SetIText** [7.3.2] to change the contents. You can also set the box's selection range with **SelIText** [7.3.2].

A dialog can have any number of text boxes, but only one of them is *current* at any given time. Only the current text box displays an insertion point or selection; all characters typed from the keyboard are directed to that text box. The Toolbox automatically advances from one text box to the next (or from the last back to the first) when the user presses the tab key. The **editField** field of the dialog record [7.1.1] always identifies the current text box by giving its item number minus **1**. The **textH** field holds a handle to the edit record the Toolbox uses to display the box's contents on the screen; just as for a static text item, the edit record uses the text box's display rectangle for both wrapping and clipping.

User Items

There's also a catchall item type named **UserItem**, which you can use to include any kind of object you want as an item in a dialog box. In this case, instead of a handle to the item itself, the item list holds a pointer to a procedure you supply for drawing the item on the screen. You can use **SetDItem** [7.3.1] to store this procedure pointer into the item list in place of an item handle.

The drawing procedure for a user item should be of the form

```
procedure DrawItem (theWindow  : WindowPtr;
                    itemNumber : INTEGER);
```

where **theWindow** is a pointer to the dialog window and **itemNumber** is the number of the item to be drawn (that is, its index within the window's item list). Everything this procedure draws will be clipped to the item's display rectangle. You can safely assume that the given dialog window (**theWindow**) will already be the current port at the time the procedure is called.

Error Sounds and Staged Alerts

In addition to displaying an alert box on the screen, an alert (but not a modal or modeless dialog) can also emit sounds from the Macintosh speaker. There can be as many as four different *error sounds* available for use with alerts, identified by *sound numbers* from **0** to **3**. The standard sound built into the Toolbox for each sound number is just the corresponding number of short beeps, from none to three. If you want, you can replace these with any other sounds you like by writing your own *sound procedure* and installing it with **ErrorSound** [7.5.1]. See the *Inside Macintosh* manual for details on how to produce sounds through the speaker.

Another special property of alerts is that they can be *staged* to behave differently each time they occur. For instance, the first time the user attempts some questionable action you might just want to beep once without displaying an alert box; the second time, beep twice and display an alert box with a suitable error message, and with the **Cancel** button outlined as the recommended (default) action; beginning with the third time, don't beep at all and make **OK** the default button, on the assumption that the user is doing it (whatever "it" is) deliberately.

You can define as many as four stages for a given alert: one stage for each of the first three times in a row that the alert occurs, and the last stage for the fourth and all subsequent times. The alert's behavior at each stage is defined by a *stage list* in the alert template [7.1.3], which consists of four 4-bit fields packed into a single memory word. For each stage, the stage list tells the Toolbox whether to display an alert box, which button to treat as the default, and how many times to beep (or more precisely, which of the four currently defined error sounds to emit). If you don't need four distinct stages, you can define some or all of them to behave the same way.

For reasons best known to Apple's programmers, the fields of the stage list are stored backwards: the last field defines stage 1 of the alert and the first defines stage 4.

If you need to, you can also find out what stage an alert is currently up to with the Toolbox function **GetAlrtStage**, or reset the alert back to stage 1 with **ResetAlrtStage** [7.5.2]. Both of these routines apply implicitly to the last alert that was displayed on the screen; all other alerts are, of course, at stage 1 by definition. **GetAlrtStage** returns an integer from **0** to **3** that's *one less than* the stage at which the last alert occurred.

In assembly language, you can find the resource ID and stage of the last alert in the system globals **ANumber** and **ACount**, respectively. To reset the alert to stage 1, store **−1** into **ACount**.

Using Alerts

Alerts are the simplest form of dialog to use, because they require no active intervention on your part. An alert normally consists of nothing but static items (text, icons, pictures) and simple pushbuttons for dismissing the alert. (Other interactive items, such as checkboxes, radio buttons, and text boxes, are meaningful only in modal and modeless dialogs.) When you display an alert, you relinquish control to the Toolbox and don't get it back until after the alert has been dismissed; there's no opportunity to interact directly with the user while the alert is on the screen. The only information you get about the user's actions is after the fact: the item number of the pushbutton that was clicked to dismiss the alert.

Actually, you can arrange for any item to dismiss the alert when clicked, not just pushbuttons. Every item, regardless of type, can be either *enabled* or *disabled*; the alert will be dismissed when the user clicks the mouse in an enabled item. An item is always assumed to be enabled unless you specify otherwise by adding the constant **ItemDisable** [7.1.2] to its item type when you create it. Ordinarily you'll want to disable all static items, so that mouse clicks in them will be ignored; but you can leave them enabled if you want the alert box to disappear when they're clicked.

The basic Toolbox routine for putting up an alert box on the screen is **Alert** [7.4.2]. The alternate routines **NoteAlert**, **CautionAlert**, and **Stop-Alert** work exactly the same way; the only difference is that they automatically include one of the standard icons of Figure 7-4 in the alert box when they display it on the screen. In each case, you supply the resource ID of an alert template, along with an optional *filter function* that we'll be discussing later. (For now, we can assume that you just pass **NIL** for the **filter** parameter.)

The **Alert** routine retains control and monitors the user's actions for as long as the alert remains on the screen. It just ignores mouse presses in disabled items, or those that don't fall within any item's display rectangle. (If the mouse is pressed outside the alert box entirely, **Alert** will emit error sound number **1**, normally a single beep.) When the user finally presses the mouse in an enabled item, **Alert** will remove the alert box from the screen, dispose of it, and return as its function result the item number of the item that was clicked.

In the case of a control item such as a pushbutton, **Alert** first calls the Toolbox routine **TrackControl** [6.4.2] to track the mouse until it's released. **Alert** will dismiss the alert box and return the control's item number only if the mouse is released inside the same control it was originally pressed in; otherwise it will treat the mouse press as if it were in a disabled item and just ignore it. Notice that disabling a control item isn't the same as deactivating it with **HiliteControl** [6.3.3]. An inactive control doesn't respond to the mouse at all; one that's active but disabled responds to the mouse but doesn't dismiss the alert box.

Program 7-1 (**DoAbout**) illustrates the straightforward use of an alert box. This routine is called from the **MiniEdit** routine **DoAppleChoice** (Program 4-6) when the user chooses the **About MiniEdit...** item from the Apple menu. All it does is display the alert shown in Figure 7-6 and return when the user dismisses the alert. Since there's only one enabled item (the **OK** button), the item number returned by the Toolbox **Alert** routine doesn't convey any useful information in this case, so **DoAbout** just ignores it.

A more interesting example arises when the user attempts to close a "dirty" window (one containing changes that haven't yet been saved to the disk). When this happens, our **CloseAppWindow** routine displays the alert shown in Figure 7-7, offering the user three choices:

• Save the window's contents before closing.
• Discard the contents; just close the window.
• Cancel the operation; don't close the window.

Figure 7-6 About alert

```
{ Global declaration }

const
    AboutID = 1000;                         {Resource ID for About alert}


procedure DoAbout;

    { Handle About MiniEdit... command. }

    var
        ignore : INTEGER;                   {Item number for About alert}

    begin {DoAbout}

        ignore := Alert (AboutID, NIL)      {Post alert [7.4.2]}

    end;  {DoAbout}
```

Program 7-1 Handle **About Miniedit...** command

Recall that **CloseAppWindow** is called by **DoClose** (Program 3-3), which in turn can be called by way of **DoFileChoice** (Program 4-8) when the user chooses the **Close** command from the **File** menu, via **DoGoAway** (Program 3-10) when the mouse is clicked in a window's close box, or via **DoEvent** (Program 2-5) after the user chooses the **Quit** command or types command-Q. In the earlier discussion of **CloseAppWindow** in Chapter 3, we glossed over a few steps that we weren't yet ready to discuss; now we're in a position to look at the complete version of the routine (Program 7-2).

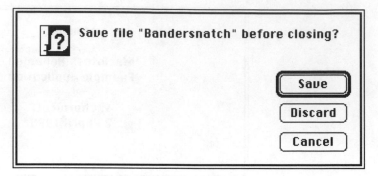

Figure 7-7 Save alert

```
{ Global variables }

var
   TheWindow : WindowPtr;                    {Pointer to currently active window [3.1.1]}
   TheEvent  : EventRecord;                  {Current event [2.1.1]}
   ErrorFlag : BOOLEAN;                      {I/O error flag}
   Quitting  : BOOLEAN;                      {Quit command in effect?}


procedure CloseAppWindow;

   { Close application window. }

   const
      saveID = 1001;                         {Resource ID for Save alert}

      saveItem    = 1;                       {Item number for Save button}
      discardItem = 2;                       {Item number for Discard button}
      cancelItem  = 3;                       {Item number for Cancel button}

   var
      theData    : WDHandle;                 {Handle to window's data record [Prog. 5-1]}
      dataHandle : Handle;                   {Untyped handle for destroying data record [I:3.1.1]}
      theTitle   : Str255;                   {Title of window [I:2.1.1]}
      theItem    : INTEGER;                  {Item number for Save alert}
      resultCode : OSErr;                    {I/O error code [I:3.1.2]}
      thisWindow : WindowPtr;                {Pointer to window being closed [3.1.1]}
```

Program 7-2 Close application window

```
begin {CloseAppWindow}

    dataHandle := Handle(GetWRefCon(TheWindow));     {Get window data [3.2.4]}
    HLock (dataHandle);                              {Lock data record [I:3.2.4]}

      theData := WDHandle(dataHandle);               {Convert to typed handle [Prog. 5-1]}
      with theData^^ do
        begin

            if dirty then                            {Have window contents been changed? [Prog. 5-1]}
              begin

                GetWTitle (TheWindow, theTitle);     {Get window title [3.2.4]}
                ParamText (theTitle, '', '', '');    {Substitute into alert text [7.4.6]}

                theItem := CautionAlert (saveID, NIL);  {Post alert [7.4.2]}
                case theItem of

                  saveItem:
                    begin
                      DoSave;                         {Save window contents to disk [Prog. 8-2]}
                      if ErrorFlag then               {Check for I/O error}
                        begin
                          HUnlock (dataHandle);       {Unlock data record [I:3.2.4]}
                          EXIT (CloseAppWindow)       {Exit to main event loop}
                        end {if}
                    end;

                  discardItem:
                    {Do nothing};

                  cancelItem:
                    begin
                      Quitting := FALSE;              {Cancel Quit command, if any}
                      HUnlock (dataHandle);           {Unlock data record [I:3.2.4]}
                      EXIT (CloseAppWindow)           {Exit to main event loop}
                    end

                end {case}

            end; {if}
```

Program 7-2 (*continued*)

```
         if fileNumber <> 0 then                  {Is window associated with a file? [Prog. 5-1]}
            begin
               resultCode := FSClose (fileNumber);  {Close file [8.2.2]}
               IOCheck (resultCode);                {Check for error [Prog. 8-1]}
               if ErrorFlag then                    {Error detected?}
                  begin
                     HUnlock (dataHandle);          {Unlock data record [I:3.2.4]}
                     EXIT (CloseAppWindow)          {Exit to main event loop}
                  end {if}
            end; {if}

         TEDispose (editRec);                      {Dispose of edit record [5.2.2]}

         TheScrollBar := NIL;                      {Clear global handles}
         TheText     := NIL

      end; {with}

   HUnlock (dataHandle);                           {Unlock data record [I:3.2.4]}

   thisWindow := TheWindow;                        {Save window pointer (DoActivate will change TheWindow)}
   HideWindow (TheWindow);                         {Force deactivate event [3.3.1]}

   if GetNextEvent (ActivateEvt, TheEvent) then    {Get deactivate event [2.2.1, 2.1.2]}
      DoActivate;                                  {   and handle it [Prog. 5-14]     }
   if GetNextEvent (ActivateEvt, TheEvent) then    {Get activate event [2.2.1, 2.1.2]}
      DoActivate;                                  {   and handle it [Prog. 5-14]     }

   DisposHandle  (dataHandle);                     {Dispose of window data record [I:3.2.2]}
   DisposeWindow (thisWindow)                      {Dispose of window [3.2.3]}

end; {CloseAppWindow}
```

Program 7-2 (*continued*)

The first thing we have to do in **CloseAppWindow** (after getting the active window's data record and locking it down in the heap) is check whether the window's contents have been changed since the last **Save**. If the **dirty** flag in the data record is **FALSE**, there's no need for an alert; if it's **TRUE**, we get the window's title and substitute it into the text of the Save alert with **ParamText** [7.4.6], then call **CautionAlert** to display the alert with the standard caution icon. Next we use a *case* statement on the item number we get back, to decide how to proceed depending on which pushbutton the user clicked to dismiss the alert. If it was the **Save** button, we call the **MiniEdit** routine **DoSave** to save the window's contents, just as if the user had chosen **Save** from the menu. We'll be looking at **DoSave** in detail when we talk about filing operations in Chapter 8; we'll also discuss the **MiniEdit** global variable **ErrorFlag** at that time.

If the alert was dismissed with the **Discard** button, then the user doesn't want to save the window's contents and there's nothing to do. If the user clicked the **Cancel** button, we take an immediate exit from **CloseAppWindow** back to our program's main event loop. (In case the window is being closed as part of a **Quit** sequence, we also take the precaution of clearing the global **Quitting** flag, discussed earlier in Chapter 2, to cancel the **Quit** command.)

Assuming we've gotten through the *case* statement without heading for the exit, the next step is to close the disk file associated with the window, if there is one. (The Toolbox routine for this purpose, **FSClose**, will be covered in the next chapter, as well as the **MiniEdit** routine **IOCheck**, which checks for errors during an input/output operation.) Finally, we dispose of the window's edit record with **TEDispose** [5.2.2] and clear **MiniEdit**'s global handles **TheScrollBar** and **TheText** to **NIL**. The rest of the **CloseAppWindow** routine has already been discussed in Chapter 3.

Using Modal Dialogs

Modal dialogs are a bit more complicated to use than alerts, because they call for intervention by your program while the dialog box is still on the screen. For one thing, you have to create the dialog for yourself with **NewDialog** or **GetNewDialog** and put it up on the screen with **Show-Window** [3.1.1], instead of letting the Toolbox do it all for you as it does with the **Alert** routine. Once the dialog is on the screen, you repeatedly call the Toolbox routine **ModalDialog** [7.4.3] to handle the user's mouse and keyboard actions.

Like **Alert**, **ModalDialog** intercepts all user events in a dialog box and reports back to you by item number those that involve an enabled item. However, it doesn't automatically dismiss the dialog when the user clicks an enabled item; it leaves it on the screen to allow further interaction. It's up to you to decide, depending on the item number you receive, whether to dismiss the dialog with **HideWindow** [3.3.1] or leave it up and call **ModalDialog** again to continue processing events. Also like **Alert**, **ModalDialog** ignores mouse presses in a disabled item, as well as those that aren't in any item at all. It responds with a single beep (or whatever is currently defined as sound number **1**) if the mouse is pressed outside the dialog box entirely. Only those mouse events that involve an enabled item are reported back to you.

ModalDialog automatically handles all window events (activate, deactivate, and update) directed to the dialog window. When the mouse is pressed in a control, it calls **TrackControl** [6.4.2] to track the mouse, and reports the event to you only if the mouse is released inside the same control. Since the dialog box doesn't go away when an enabled item is clicked, its controls aren't limited to simple pushbuttons that cause an immediate action, like those of an alert: a modal dialog can include checkboxes, radio buttons, and even adjustable dials such as scroll bars if they make sense. Of course, on receiving back the item number of such a control, it's up to you to do whatever is appropriate in response, such as turning a checkbox on or off or turning off one radio button when another is clicked.

If the dialog includes editable text boxes, **ModalDialog** will also take care of all mouse selection and keyboard type-in for you. It passes all mouse presses in a text box to the TextEdit routine **TEClick** [5.4.1], to track the mouse and perform standard text selection; this includes double-click word selection and extended selection with the shift key. Characters typed from the keyboard are inserted into the current text box with **TEKey** [5.5.1], which also handles character deletion with the back-space key. When the user presses the tab key, **ModalDialog** automatically advances to the next text box and selects its entire contents, so that they can be replaced just by typing from the keyboard.

> However, **ModalDialog** does *not* handle command-key combinations automatically; it just ignores the command key and treats them as ordinary characters. If you want to interpret such combinations as commands, you have to do it yourself with a filter function; we'll see how in a minute.

If a text box is enabled, **ModalDialog** will report its item number back to you after every mouse press or typed character directed to it. Normally, though, there's nothing more you need to do, since the standard point-and-type selection and editing conventions will already have been taken care of. All you really care about are the final contents of the text box, which you can get with **GetIText** [7.3.2] after the dialog is finally dismissed. So you'll usually want to disable all your text boxes by giving them an item type of

    EditText + ItemDisable

ModalDialog will still handle events in the text box as described; it just won't bother to tell you about them.

Using Modeless Dialogs

Modeless dialogs require even more active intervention on your part than modal ones. This is because a modeless dialog can coexist with other active windows on the screen. Events outside the dialog box aren't ignored, as they are when an alert or a modal dialog is active; so you can't just rely on a Toolbox routine like **Alert** or **ModalDialog** to intercept and handle all events for you until the dialog is dismissed. Instead you just carry on with your normal event processing, but pick out those events directed to the dialog and pass them through to the Toolbox to handle.

The Toolbox routine **IsDialogEvent** [7.4.4] helps you decide which events are dialog-related. It accepts an event record as a parameter and returns **TRUE** if the event pertains to a dialog window, **FALSE** if it doesn't. Whenever there's a modeless dialog box on the screen (even when it isn't the frontmost window), you should pass each event you receive from **GetNextEvent** [2.2.1] to **IsDialogEvent**. If the result you get back is **FALSE**, then the event is your responsibility to handle; if the result is **TRUE**, then the event is directed to a dialog box and you should pass it to the Toolbox routine **DialogSelect** for processing.

DialogSelect [7.4.4] handles a single dialog-related event. You pass it an event record and it responds to the event in exactly the same way **ModalDialog** would. That is, it activates, deactivates, and updates dialog windows, tracks the mouse in controls and text boxes with **TrackControl** or **TEClick**, and inserts typed characters into the current text box with **TEKey**. But whereas **ModalDialog** calls **GetNextEvent** for itself, **Dialog-Select** expects *you* to get the event and pass it in as a parameter. And whereas **ModalDialog** will continue to get and process events until it gets one for an enabled dialog item, **DialogSelect** always handles just one single event; it returns a Boolean result to let you know whether an enabled item was involved. In other words, if **ModalDialog** would have notified you of the event, **DialogSelect** returns **TRUE**; if **ModalDialog** would have suppressed the event and kept on processing, **DialogSelect** returns **FALSE**. When it does return **TRUE**, it identifies the item affected by passing back a dialog pointer and an item number as variable parameters. You can then respond with whatever action the item calls for, which may or may not include dismissing the dialog box from the screen.

Filter Functions

Both **Alert** and **ModalDialog** accept a pointer to an optional *filter function* [7.4.5] as a parameter. As the Toolbox routine gets and processes events, it will pass each event to the filter function before responding to it. This gives you a chance to intercept the event and handle it your own way or modify its meaning before it's acted upon by the Toolbox.

If you supply a filter function, it should be of the form

```
function Filter (theDialog    : DialogPtr;
                 var theEvent    : EventRecord;
                 var itemNumber : INTEGER)
                     : BOOLEAN;
```

The Toolbox will pass you a dialog pointer and an event record. You can either handle the event yourself, leave it alone for the Toolbox to handle, or change it into some other event. (Notice that **theEvent** is declared as a variable parameter, so that you can modify the fields of the event record and send it back to the Toolbox for processing in altered form.) A function result of **FALSE** tells the Toolbox to go ahead and process the event in the normal way; **TRUE** tells it to report the event as if it were a mouse click in the item identified by variable parameter **itemNumber**. The standard Toolbox filter function (which you get if you pass **NIL** for the **filter** parameter to **Alert** or **ModalDialog**) uses this feature to convert a press of the return or enter key into a click of the dialog's default button.

Program 7-3 shows an example of a filter function to provide the standard cut-and-paste editing operations as command-key combinations in a dialog text box. First we check the event type to see if it's a key-down event; if not, we simply return **FALSE** from the filter function to let the Toolbox handle the event in the normal way. For key-down events, we get the key code, character code, and command bit from the event record and start checking for keystrokes that require special handling.

As with the standard filter function, we want to translate the return or enter key into a click of the dialog's default button. We do this by returning a function result of **TRUE** along with the item number **OK**, denoting the first item in the dialog's item list. (Recall that in a modal dialog the default button is always item number **1**.) As an added feature, we'll also interpret the tidle key (top-left on the keyboard) as an alias for the dialog's **Cancel** button. Notice that these tests are based on the event's key code rather than its character code; this makes them depend only on the key's physical position on the keyboard, regardless of what character it represents under the current keyboard configuration.

```
function EditFilter (theDialog     : DialogPtr;        {Pointer to dialog}
                     var theEvent   : EventRecord;      {Event to be processed}
                     var itemNumber : INTEGER)          {Item number to report}
                       : BOOLEAN;                       {Bypass normal event processing?}


{ Filter function to allow Command-key aliases for standard editing operations. }

const
    returnCode = $24;                                   {Key code for Return key}
    enterCode  = $34;                                   {Key code for Enter key}
    cancelCode = $32;                                   {Key code for Cancel (tilde) key}

var
    keyCode : INTEGER;                                  {Key code}
    chCode  : INTEGER;                                  {Character code}
    ch      : CHAR;                                     {Character that was typed}
    cmdDown : BOOLEAN;                                  {Command key down?}

begin {EditFilter}

    with theEvent do

        if what <> keyDown then                         {Was it a key-down event? [2.1.2]}
            EditFilter := FALSE                         {Not a keystroke, handle as a normal event}

        else
            begin


                EditFilter := TRUE;                     {Initialize function result to bypass normal processing}


                keyCode := BitAnd (message, KeyCodeMask);   {Get key code from event message [I:2.2.2, 2.1.4]}
                keyCode := BitShift (-8, keyCode);          {Shift to low-order byte [I:2.2.2]}

                chCode  := BitAnd (message, CharCodeMask);  {Get character code [I:2.2.2, 2.1.4]}
                ch      := CHR(chCode);                     {Convert to a character}

                cmdDown := (BitAnd (modifiers, CmdKey) <> 0);  {Command key down? [2.1.5]}


                if keyCode in [returnCode, enterCode] then  {Return or Enter key?}
                    itemNumber := OK                        {Masquerade as OK button [7.1.1]}


                else if keyCode = cancelCode then           {Tilde key?}
                    itemNumber := Cancel                    {Masquerade as Cancel button [7.1.1]}
```

Program 7-3 Filter function for keyboard editing

```
        else if not cmdDown then          {Command key down?}
            EditFilter := FALSE           {Ordinary keystroke, handle as a normal event}

        else
            begin

                itemNumber := theDialog^^.editField + 1;  {Return item number of current text box [7.1.1]}

                case ch of
                    'X':
                        DlgCut (theDialog);       {Command-X means Cut [7.4.7]}

                    'C':
                        DlgCopy (theDialog);      {Command-C means Copy [7.4.7]}

                    'V':
                        DlgPaste (theDialog);     {Command-V means Paste [7.4.7]}

                    'B':
                        DlgDelete (theDialog);    {Command-B means Clear [7.4.7]}

                {Other Command-key equivalents, if any}

                    otherwise
                        {Do nothing}          {Ignore meaningless Command combinations}

                    end {case}

            end {else}

        end {else}

end; {EditFilter}
```

Program 7-3 (*continued*)

If the keystroke wasn't an alias for the **OK** or **Cancel** button, we next check for a command-key combination. If the command key wasn't down, then the event is an ordinary keystroke and we again pass it through with a **FALSE** function result to be handled normally. For command combinations, we'll return **TRUE** along with the item number of the current text box, which we get from the dialog record; if the text box is an enabled item, **ModalDialog** will in turn report this item number back to the calling program.

We can now proceed to check for the standard editing commands and respond to them with the Toolbox calls **DlgCut**, **DlgCopy**, **DlgPaste**, and **DlgDelete** [7.4.7]. Each of these performs the corresponding editing operation on a dialog's current text box. At this point we can also check for any other command combinations we might want to add. For unrecognizable combinations, we just report back the item number of the text box and otherwise ignore the event.

Another important use of filter functions is for mouse tracking in interactive dials or nonstandard (user) items. Your filter function can intercept mouse events in these items and do whatever is needed in response, such as redrawing the dial's indicator to follow the mouse or performing some continuous action while the mouse button is held down. You can also use a filter function to check for and respond to disk-inserted events while a dialog box is active. (The **Alert** and **ModalDialog** routines mask out disk events in their **GetNextEvent** calls, so it's up to you to detect and handle them if your application requires it.)

You may have noticed that although **Alert** and **ModalDialog** accept a filter function parameter, the Toolbox routine for modeless dialogs, **DialogSelect**, doesn't. This is because in a modeless dialog you yourself request the events from **GetNextEvent** and feed them one by one to **DialogSelect**. If there's any filtering to be done, you can do it yourself instead of supplying a filter function for the Toolbox to do it with.

Nuts and Bolts

If you want, you can change the typeface used in dialogs and alerts with the Toolbox routine **SetDAFont** [7.5.1]. (Ordinarily the system font is used.) The typeface you specify will be used from that time on for all static text items and editable text boxes in dialogs and alerts. Control titles, however, are always displayed in the system font and are unaffected by **SetDAFont**.

One problem that can sometimes arise is for a dialog's resources to be inaccessible when they're needed because the disk they're on has been ejected from the disk drive. When this happens, the Toolbox will automatically eject the disk that's currently in the drive and put up an alert of its own asking the user to insert the disk it needs. You can minimize this problem by using the Toolbox routines **CouldDialog** and **CouldAlert** [7.5.3] before beginning any operation that may involve disk swapping. You give the resource ID of a dialog or alert that you know might occur during the swapping operation; all resources associated with that dialog or alert will be read into the heap and made unpurgeable, so that they're guaranteed to be available if needed. When the operation is finished and the disk containing the resources is back in the drive, you can call **FreeDialog** or **FreeAlert** [7.5.3] to reclaim the heap space occupied by the resources.

REFERENCE

7.1 Internal Representation of Dialogs

7.1.1 Dialog Records

Definitions

```
type
  DialogPtr    = WindowPtr;              {For treating as a window}
  DialogPeek   = ^DialogRecord;          {For accessing dialog-specific fields}

  DialogRecord = record
                   window   : WindowRecord;  {Dialog window}
                   items    : Handle;        {Handle to item list}
                   textH    : TEHandle;      {Handle to edit record for current text box}
                   editField : INTEGER;      {Item number of current text box minus 1}
                   editOpen : INTEGER;       {Private}
                   aDefItem : INTEGER        {Item number of default button}
                 end;

const
  OK     = 1;                             {Item number of OK button}
  Cancel = 2;                             {Item number of Cancel button}
```

Notes

1. **window** is a complete window record (not just a pointer) embedded within the dialog record. Use a **DialogPtr** to refer to the dialog as a window or as a graphics port (to draw into it with QuickDraw); use a **DialogPeek** to refer to it specifically as a dialog (to access the fields of the dialog record).

2. A dialog window's class (field **windowKind** of the window record [3.1.1]) is **DialogKind**.

3. **items** is a handle to the dialog's item list in memory. This is the Toolbox's own private copy of the item list; its structure differs somewhat from that of the item list resource [7.6.3] supplied when the dialog was created.

4. Use **SetDItem** and **GetDItem** [7.3.1], **SetIText** and **GetIText** [7.3.2] to access the contents of the item list, rather than accessing it directly through the item list handle.

5. If the dialog includes any editable text boxes, **editField** is one less than the item number of the current text box, and **textH** is a handle to the text box's edit record. **editOpen** is used privately by the Toolbox and is of no concern to the application.

6. If the dialog has no text boxes, **editField** is −1 and **textH** is undefined.

7. **aDefItem** is the item number of the dialog's *default button*. Pressing the return or enter key will (normally) be considered equivalent to clicking the mouse in this button.

8. The default button is boldly outlined on the screen. The outline is 3 pixels thick and extends 4 pixels beyond the button's display rectangle in each direction.

9. For modal dialogs, the default button is always the **OK** button (item number **1**); for alerts, it can be either **OK** (**1**) or **Cancel** (**2**). Modeless dialogs have no default button.

Assembly-Language Information

Field offsets in a dialog record:

(Pascal) Field name	(Assembly) Offset name	Offset in bytes
window	**dWindow**	**0**
items	**items**	**156**
textH	**teHandle**	**160**
editField	**editField**	**164**
editOpen	**editOpen**	**166**
aDefItem	**aDefItem**	**168**

Assembly-language constants:

Name	Value	Meaning
DWindLen	**170**	Length of dialog record in bytes
OKButton	**1**	Item number of OK button
CancelButton	**2**	Item number of Cancel button

7.1.2 Item Types

Definitions

```
const
    UserItem   =  0;        {Application-defined item}
    CtrlItem   =  4;        {Control}
        BtnCtrl    =  0;        {Pushbutton}
        ChkCtrl    =  1;        {Checkbox}
        RadCtrl    =  2;        {Radio button}
        ResCtrl    =  3;        {Other, defined by control template resource}
    StatText   =  8;        {Static text}
    EditText   = 16;        {Editable text box}
    IconItem   = 32;        {Icon}
    PicItem    = 64;        {Picture}

    ItemDisable = 128;      {Item is disabled}
```

Notes

1. The item type for a control item is formed by adding together the constant **CtrlItem** and a second constant (**BtnCtrl**, **ChkCtrl**, **RadCtrl**, or **ResCtrl**) for the specific control type.

2. Static text items and editable text boxes are limited to a maximum length of 241 characters.

3. A user item is defined by a drawing procedure of the form

   ```
   procedure DrawUserItem
            (theDialog  : DialogPtr;
             itemNumber : INTEGER);
   ```

   to draw the item within its dialog window.

4. The constant **ItemDisable** added to any item type specifies that the item is *disabled*; without this constant, the item is *enabled*. This affects the reporting of events involving the item by the alert routines [7.4.2], **ModalDialog** [7.4.3], and **DialogSelect** [7.4.4].

Assembly-Language Information

Item types:

Name	Value		Meaning
UserItem	0		Application-defined item
CtrlItem	4		Control
BtnCtrl		0	Pushbutton
ChkCtrl		1	Checkbox
RadCtrl		2	Radio button
ResCtrl		3	Other control
StatText	8		Static text
EditText	16		Editable text box
IconItem	32		Icon
PicItem	64		Picture
ItemDisable	128		Item is disabled

7.1.3 Alert Templates

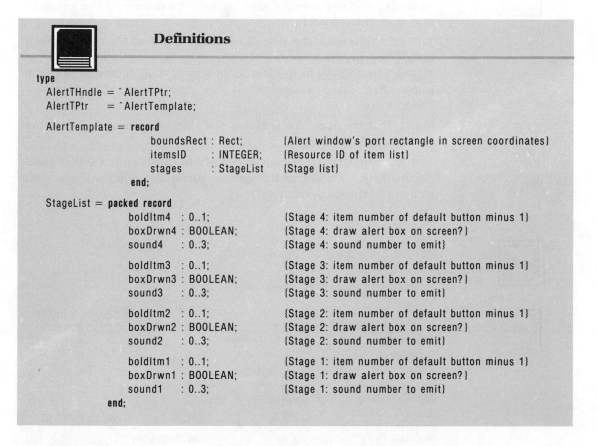

Definitions

```
type
    AlertTHndle = ^AlertTPtr;
    AlertTPtr   = ^AlertTemplate;

    AlertTemplate = record
                    boundsRect : Rect;        {Alert window's port rectangle in screen coordinates}
                    itemsID    : INTEGER;     {Resource ID of item list}
                    stages     : StageList    {Stage list}
                  end;

    StageList = packed record
                    boldItm4 : 0..1;          {Stage 4: item number of default button minus 1}
                    boxDrwn4 : BOOLEAN;       {Stage 4: draw alert box on screen?}
                    sound4   : 0..3;          {Stage 4: sound number to emit}

                    boldItm3 : 0..1;          {Stage 3: item number of default button minus 1}
                    boxDrwn3 : BOOLEAN;       {Stage 3: draw alert box on screen?}
                    sound3   : 0..3;          {Stage 3: sound number to emit}

                    boldItm2 : 0..1;          {Stage 2: item number of default button minus 1}
                    boxDrwn2 : BOOLEAN;       {Stage 2: draw alert box on screen?}
                    sound2   : 0..3;          {Stage 2: sound number to emit}

                    boldItm1 : 0..1;          {Stage 1: item number of default button minus 1}
                    boxDrwn1 : BOOLEAN;       {Stage 1: draw alert box on screen?}
                    sound1   : 0..3;          {Stage 1: sound number to emit}
                  end;
```

Notes

1. **AlertTemplate** represents the structure of an alert template, as stored in a resource file under resource type 'ALRT' [7.6.1].

2. **boundsRect** defines the alert window's port rectangle, in global (screen) coordinates.

3. **boundsRect** should have a top coordinate of at least **25**, to allow for the height of the menu bar and the border of the alert box itself.

4. **itemsID** is the resource ID of the alert's item list, resource type 'DITL' [7.6.3].

5. **stages** is a *stage list* defining the behavior of the alert at each of four consecutive stages.

6. The stage list identifies the default button at each stage of the alert (for example, **boldItm1** for the first stage), the sound to be emitted (**sound1**), and whether the alert box is to be drawn on the screen at that stage (**boxDrwn1**).

7. The value given for the default button is *one less than* the button's actual item number.

8. Stages 1 to 3 apply to the first three consecutive occurrences of the same alert; stage 4 implies to the fourth and all subsequent occurrences.

9. Notice that the stage list specifies the stages in *reverse order*, from stage 4 down to stage 1.

10. The assembly-language constants **VolBits**, **AlBit**, and **OKDismissal** are masks for extracting the various subfields within a single 4-bit element of the stage list word.

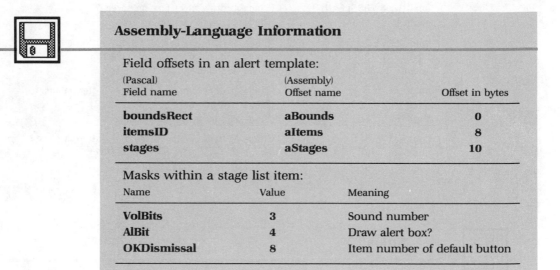

Assembly-Language Information

Field offsets in an alert template:

(Pascal) Field name	(Assembly) Offset name	Offset in bytes
boundsRect	**aBounds**	**0**
itemsID	**aItems**	**8**
stages	**aStages**	**10**

Masks within a stage list item:

Name	Value	Meaning
VolBits	**3**	Sound number
AlBit	**4**	Draw alert box?
OKDismissal	**8**	Item number of default button

7.1.4 Dialog Templates

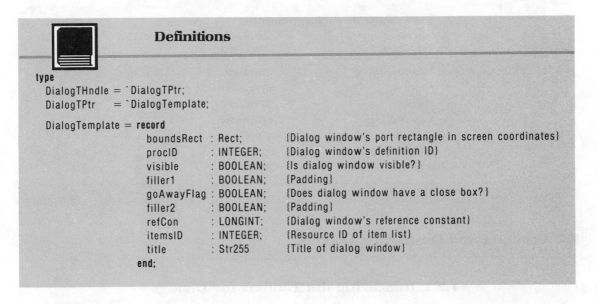

Definitions

```
type
  DialogTHndle = ^DialogTPtr;
  DialogTPtr   = ^DialogTemplate;

  DialogTemplate = record
                     boundsRect : Rect;      {Dialog window's port rectangle in screen coordinates}
                     procID     : INTEGER;   {Dialog window's definition ID}
                     visible    : BOOLEAN;   {Is dialog window visible?}
                     filler1    : BOOLEAN;   {Padding}
                     goAwayFlag : BOOLEAN;   {Does dialog window have a close box?}
                     filler2    : BOOLEAN;   {Padding}
                     refCon     : LONGINT;   {Dialog window's reference constant}
                     itemsID    : INTEGER;   {Resource ID of item list}
                     title      : Str255     {Title of dialog window}
                   end;
```

Notes

1. **DialogTemplate** represents the structure of a dialog template, as stored in a resource file under resource type **'DLOG'** [7.6.2].

2. **boundsRect** defines the dialog window's port rectangle, in global (screen) coordinates.

3. **boundsRect** should have a top coordinate of at least **25** for a modal dialog or **40** for a modeless one, to allow for the height of the menu bar and the border or title bar of the dialog window itself.

4. **procID** is the window type (window definition ID [3.2.2]) of the dialog window.

5. **itemsID** is the resource ID of the dialog's item list, resource type **'DITL'** [7.6.3].

6. All remaining fields of the dialog template (except the "padding" fields **filler1** and **filler2**) contain the same information as the corresponding parameters to **NewWindow** [3.2.2] or **NewDialog** [7.2.2].

Assembly-Language Information

Field offsets in a dialog template:

(Pascal) Field name	(Assembly) Offset name	Offset in bytes
boundsRect	dBounds	0
procID	dWindProc	8
visible	dVisible	10
goAwayFlag	dGoAway	12
refCon	dRefCon	14
itemsID	dItems	18
title	dTitle	20

7.2 Creating and Destroying Dialogs

7.2.1 Initializing the Toolbox for Dialogs

Definitions

```
procedure InitDialogs
            (restartProc : ProcPtr);    {Pointer to restart procedure}
```

Notes

1. **InitDialogs** must be called before any other dialog-related operation, to initialize the Toolbox's internal data structures pertaining to dialogs and alerts.

2. Before calling **InitDialogs**, you must first call **InitGraf** [I:4.3.1], **Init-Fonts** [I:8.2.4], **InitWindows** [3.2.1], **InitMenus** [4.2.1], and **TEInit** [5.2.1].

3. **restartProc** is a pointer to a parameterless procedure that can be used to restart your program after a system error, or **NIL** if there is no such procedure.

4. A pointer to the restart procedure is kept in the assembly-language global variable **RestProc**.

Assembly-Language Information

Trap macro:

(Pascal) Routine name	(Assembly) Trap macro	Trap word
InitDialogs	**_InitDialogs**	**$A97B**

Assembly-language global variable:

Name	Address	Meaning
RestProc	**$A8C**	Pointer to restart procedure

7.2.2 Creating Dialogs

Definitions

```
function NewDialog
        (dStorage      : Ptr;           {Storage for dialog record}
        windowRect     : Rect;          {Dialog window's port rectangle in screen coordinates}
        title          : Str255;        {Title of dialog window}
        visible        : BOOLEAN;       {Is dialog window initially visible?}
        windowType     : INTEGER;       {Dialog window's definition ID}
        behindWindow   : WindowPtr;     {Window in front of this one}
        goAwayFlag     : BOOLEAN;       {Does dialog window have a close box?}
        refCon         : LONGINT;       {Dialog window's reference constant}
        itemList       : Handle)        {Handle to item.list}
          : DialogPtr;                  {Pointer to new dialog record}

function GetNewDialog
        (templateID    : INTEGER;       {Resource ID of dialog template}
        dStorage       : Ptr;           {Storage for dialog record}
        behindWindow   : WindowPtr)     {Window in front of this one}
          : DialogPtr;                  {Pointer to new dialog record}
```

Notes

1. **NewDialog** and **GetNewDialog** both create a new dialog record, enter it in the window list, and return a pointer to it.

2. These routines are for creating modal and modeless dialogs only; alerts are always created implicitly by the alert routines [7.4.2].

3. **NewDialog** takes its initialization information as parameters; **Get-NewDialog** gets it from a dialog template in a resource file.

4. Both routines return a **DialogPtr**; to access the fields of the new dialog record, you can convert this pointer to a **DialogPeek** [7.1.1] by typecasting.

5. The new dialog window's class (field **windowKind** of the window record [3.1.1]) is set to **DialogKind**.

6. **NewDialog** accepts a handle to the dialog's item list. The item list is normally taken from a resource file (resource type 'DITL' [7.6.3]); you have to read it in yourself with **GetResource** [I:6.3.1] and pass the resulting handle to **NewDialog**.

7. **GetNewDialog** accepts the resource ID of a dialog template (resource type 'DLOG' [7.6.2]), which in turn contains the resource ID of the item list. In this case the item list will be read in automatically; you needn't call **GetResource** to read it in yourself.

8. After reading the item list from the resource file, **GetNewDialog** makes a *copy* for use in the dialog record. The original item list should be a purgeable resource, so that it can be discarded after the copy is made. **NewDialog** uses the original item list you give it, *not* a copy—so make sure the item list is unpurgeable.

9. **dStorage** is a pointer to the storage for the new dialog record; use **CloseDialog** [7.2.3] to destroy the dialog when no longer needed. If **dStorage = NIL**, storage will be allocated from the heap; use **DisposDialog** [7.2.3] to destroy.

10. The remaining parameters are identical to those for **NewWindow** and **GetNewWindow** [3.2.2].

11. **windowRect** should have a top coordinate of at least **25** for a modal dialog or **40** for a modeless one, to allow for the height of the menu bar and the border or title bar of the dialog window itself.

12. Modal dialog windows normally have no title bar; pass the empty string for the **title** parameter.

13. Use window type **DBoxProc**, **PlainDBoxProc**, or **AltDBoxProc** [3.2.2] for a modal dialog, **NoGrowDocProc** for a modeless one.

Assembly-Language Information

Trap macros:

(Pascal) Routine name	(Assembly) Trap macro	Trap word
NewDialog	**_NewDialog**	**$A97D**
GetNewDialog	**_GetNewDialog**	**$A97C**

7.2.3 Destroying Dialogs

Definitions

```
procedure CloseDialog
            (theDialog : DialogPtr);     {Dialog to destroy}

procedure DisposDialog
            (theDialog : DialogPtr);     {Dialog to destroy}
```

Notes

1. Both **CloseDialog** and **DisposDialog** destroy a dialog and remove it from the screen and the window list.

2. If this dialog window covered any others on the screen, they will be updated. If it was the active (frontmost) window, the next-frontmost will be activated. All needed update and activate events are generated automatically.

3. **DisposDialog** frees *all* storage associated with the dialog. Use it if you let the Toolbox allocate the space (**dStorage = NIL**) when you created the dialog [7.2.2, note 9].

4. **CloseDialog** frees all of the dialog's storage *except* the item list and the dialog record itself. Use it if you allocated your own storage for the dialog record (**dStorage ≠ NIL**). You must then dispose of the dialog record and item list yourself if they reside in the heap.

5. If you're using the dialog window's reference constant (**refCon**) to hold a handle to auxiliary information about the window [3.2.4, note 4], be sure to dispose of the auxiliary information before destroying the dialog itself.

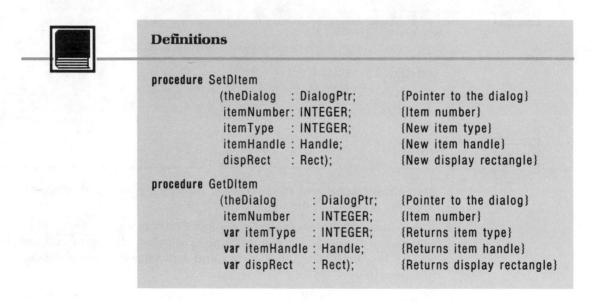

Assembly-Language Information

Trap macros:

(Pascal) Routine name	(Assembly) Trap macro	Trap word
CloseDialog	**_CloseDialog**	**$A982**
DisposDialog	**_DisposDialog**	**$A983**

7.3 Manipulating Items

7.3.1 Access to Items

Definitions

```
procedure SetDItem
        (theDialog  : DialogPtr;      {Pointer to the dialog}
        itemNumber: INTEGER;          {Item number}
        itemType   : INTEGER;         {New item type}
        itemHandle : Handle;          {New item handle}
        dispRect   : Rect);           {New display rectangle}

procedure GetDItem
        (theDialog     : DialogPtr;   {Pointer to the dialog}
        itemNumber     : INTEGER;     {Item number}
        var itemType   : INTEGER;     {Returns item type}
        var itemHandle : Handle;      {Returns item handle}
        var dispRect   : Rect);       {Returns display rectangle}
```

Notes

1. **SetDItem** sets the properties of an item in a dialog's item list; **Get-DItem** returns the item's current properties.

2. The item is identified by a pointer to the dialog and an item number within the item list.

3. Use typecasting to convert between the untyped item handle and whatever specific handle type is appropriate. For control items, the item handle is equivalent to a **ControlHandle** [6.1.1]; for picture items, a **PicHandle** [I:5.4.1]; for text items, a **CharsHandle** [5.1.2]. For icon items, it's a handle to the icon in the heap.

4. For an editable text box, the item handle leads to the current contents of the box. Pass this handle to **GetIText** or **SetIText** [7.3.2] to get or change the item's text; don't attempt to change the text directly with **SetDItem**.

5. For user items, the "item handle" is actually a *pointer* (not a handle) to the item's drawing procedure [7.1.2, note 3].

6. **SetDItem** doesn't redraw the item on the screen after changing its properties.

Assembly-Language Information

Trap macros:

(Pascal) Routine name	(Assembly) Trap macro	Trap word
SetDItem	**_SetDItem**	**$A98E**
GetDItem	**_GetDItem**	**$A98D**

7.3.2 Text of an Item

Definitions

```
procedure SetIText
        (itemHandle : Handle;          {Handle to text item}
         theText    : Str255);         {New text}

procedure GetIText
        (itemHandle : Handle;          {Handle to text item}
     var theText : Str255);            {Returns current text}

procedure SelIText
        (theDialog   : DialogPtr;      {Pointer to dialog}
         itemNumber : INTEGER;         {Item number}
         selStart    : INTEGER;        {Start of selection (character position)}
         selEnd      : INTEGER);       {End of selection (character position)}
```

Notes

1. **SetIText** sets the text of a text item; **GetIText** returns the item's current text.

2. The item is identified by a handle, obtained from **GetDItem** [7.3.1]. It may be either static text or an editable text box.

3. Text items are limited to a maximum length of 241 characters.

4. **SelIText** sets the selection range in an editable text box. The previous selection is unhighlighted on the screen and the new one is highlighted.

5. The text box is identified by a pointer to the dialog and an item number within the item list.

6. **selStart** and **selEnd** are character positions (points between characters, not the characters themselves) designating the beginning and end of the new selection range.

7. **selStart** and **selEnd** have the same meanings as for **TESetSelect** [5.4.2]. In particular, if they're equal, they designate an insertion point represented by a blinking vertical bar at the given character position.

Assembly-Language Information

Trap macros:

(Pascal) Routine name	(Assembly) Trap macro	Trap word
SetIText	**_SetIText**	**$A98F**
GetIText	**_GetIText**	**$A990**
SetIText	**_SelIText**	**$A97E**

7.4 Using Alerts and Dialogs

7.4.1 Static Display

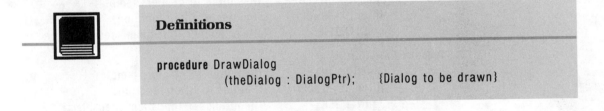

Definitions

```
procedure DrawDialog
            (theDialog : DialogPtr);    {Dialog to be drawn}
```

Notes

1. **DrawDialog** draws the contents of a dialog window on the screen. Its main use is in responding to an update event for the window.

2. Only the window's contents are drawn, not its frame. The Toolbox will already have drawn the frame by the time the update event is processed.

3. It's generally unnecessary to call this routine, since the alert routines [7.4.2], **ModalDialog** [7.4.3], and **DialogSelect** [7.4.4] handle a dialog window's update events automatically.

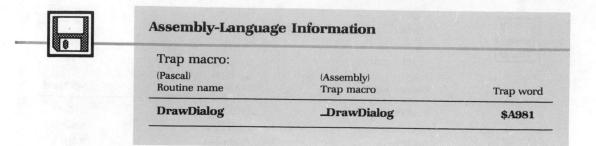

Assembly-Language Information

Trap macro:

(Pascal) Routine name	(Assembly) Trap macro	Trap word
DrawDialog	**_DrawDialog**	**$A981**

7.4.2 Using Alerts

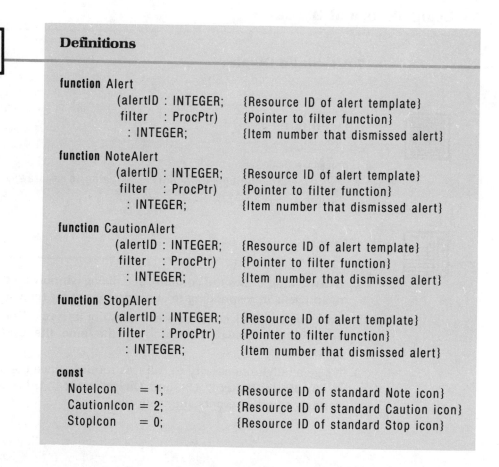

Definitions

function Alert

(alertID : INTEGER;	{Resource ID of alert template}
filter : ProcPtr)	{Pointer to filter function}
: INTEGER;	{Item number that dismissed alert}

function NoteAlert

(alertID : INTEGER;	{Resource ID of alert template}
filter : ProcPtr)	{Pointer to filter function}
: INTEGER;	{Item number that dismissed alert}

function CautionAlert

(alertID : INTEGER;	{Resource ID of alert template}
filter : ProcPtr)	{Pointer to filter function}
: INTEGER;	{Item number that dismissed alert}

function StopAlert

(alertID : INTEGER;	{Resource ID of alert template}
filter : ProcPtr)	{Pointer to filter function}
: INTEGER;	{Item number that dismissed alert}

const

NoteIcon = 1;	{Resource ID of standard Note icon}
CautionIcon = 2;	{Resource ID of standard Caution icon}
StopIcon = 0;	{Resource ID of standard Stop icon}

a. Note

b. Caution

c. Stop

Standard alert icons

Notes

1. These routines display an alert box on the screen and handle all user activity until it's dismissed.

2. **alertID** is the resource ID of an alert template (resource type 'ALRT' [7.6.1]).

3. An alert box should normally contain only static items (item types **StatText**, **IconItem**, **PicItem** [7.1.2]) and simple pushbuttons (**Ctrl-Item + BtnCtrl**). Other interactive items (checkboxes, radio buttons, text boxes) are intended for use in modal and modeless dialogs only.

4. **Alert** displays the alert box exactly as defined; **NoteAlert**, **Caution-Alert**, and **StopAlert** display it with one of the three standard icons added (see figure).

5. The standard icons appear within the alert window in a display rectangle 32 pixels wide by 32 high, with its top-left corner at coordinates (**10**, **20**).

6. If you want, you can override the standard icons by including 'ICON' resources [I:5.5.3] in your own application resource file under the same resource IDs.

7. After displaying the alert box on the screen, each alert routine gets and processes all events until the user clicks the mouse in an enabled item. It then removes the box from the screen, disposes of it, and returns the corresponding item number as its function result.

8. Mouse clicks in a disabled item, or in no item at all, are ignored.

9. Mouse clicks outside the alert box produce error sound number **1** [7.5.1], normally a single beep or a flash of the menu bar.

10. If the mouse is pressed in an enabled control item, **TrackControl** [6.4.2] is called to track its movements until it's released. If the mouse is released inside the same control, the alert routine dismisses the alert and returns the control's item number; if it's released outside the original control, the event is ignored.

11. All keyboard events are ignored.

12. Disk-inserted events are masked out. If you want to respond to them while the alert is on the screen, you have to check for them yourself in your filter function (see below).

13. The alert routines take care of calling **SystemTask** [2.7.2] periodically to perform any needed tasks associated with active desk accessories.

14. If the alert's stage list specifies that the alert box is not to be drawn on the screen at the current stage, the alert routines simply emit the error sound called for in the stage list and return an item number of −1.

15. **filter** is a pointer to an optional *filter function* [7.4.5]. All events are passed to the filter function for preprocessing before being handled by the alert routines.

16. If the filter function returns **TRUE**, the alert routine immediately dismisses the alert and returns the item number it receives from the filter function. If the filter function returns **FALSE**, the alert routine handles the event in the normal way.

17. A **NIL** value for the **filter** parameter specifies the standard filter function, which converts a press of the return or enter key into a click of the alert's default button.

Assembly-Language Information

Trap macros:

(Pascal) Routine name	(Assembly) Trap macro	Trap word
Alert	**_Alert**	**$A985**
NoteAlert	**_NoteAlert**	**$A987**
CautionAlert	**_CautionAlert**	**$A988**
StopAlert	**_StopAlert**	**$A986**

Resource IDs of standard alert icons:

Name	Value	Meaning
NoteIcon	**1**	Note icon
CtnIcon	**2**	Caution icon
StopIcon	**0**	Stop icon

7.4.3 Using Modal Dialogs

Definitions

```
procedure ModalDialog
          (filter          : ProcPtr;      {Pointer to filter function}
      var itemNumber : INTEGER);           {Returns item number of reported item}
```

Notes

1. **ModalDialog** handles user activity in a modal dialog box.

2. The dialog box must already be on the screen as the frontmost window. Use **NewDialog** or **GetNewDialog** [7.2.2] to create it and **ShowWindow** [3.3.1] to display it before calling **ModalDialog**.

3. **ModalDialog** gets and processes all events until the user clicks the mouse in an enabled item or types a character into an enabled text box. It then returns the corresponding item number in the variable parameter **itemNumber**.

4. The dialog box remains visible on the screen for further interaction with the user.

5. All window events (activate, deactivate, and update) for the dialog box are handled automatically.

6. Mouse clicks in a disabled item, or in no item at all, are ignored.

7. Mouse clicks outside the dialog box produce error sound number **1** [7.5.1], normally a single beep or a flash of the menu bar.

8. If the mouse is pressed in an enabled control item, **TrackControl** [6.4.2] is called to track its movements until it's released. If the mouse is released inside the same control, **ModalDialog** returns the control's item number; if it's released outside the original control, the event is ignored.

9. If the mouse is pressed in a text box, **TEClick** [5.4.1] is called to track its movements and perform text selection. Extended selection with the shift key and double-click word selection are handled properly. If the text box is enabled, **ModalDialog** returns its item number; otherwise it just goes on to process the next event.

10. If the dialog includes any text boxes, keyboard events are directed to the current text box via **TEKey** [5.5.1]. If the text box is enabled, **ModalDialog** returns its item number; otherwise it just goes on to process the next event. If there are no text boxes, keyboard events are ignored.

11. The command key is ignored on all keyboard events. If you want to allow command combinations in a dialog box, you must recognize and response to them yourself in your filter function (see below).

12. Disk-inserted events are masked out. If you want to respond to them while a modal dialog is on the screen, you must check for them yourself in your filter function.

13. **ModalDialog** takes care of calling **SystemTask** [2.7.2] periodically to perform any needed tasks associated with active desk accessories.

14. **filter** is a pointer to an optional *filter function* [7.4.5]. All events are passed to the filter function for preprocessing before being handled by **ModalDialog**.

15. If the filter function returns **TRUE** for an event, **ModalDialog** immediately returns the item number it receives from the filter function. If the filter function returns **FALSE**, **ModalDialog** handles the event in the normal way.

16. A **NIL** value for the **filter** parameter specifies the standard filter function, which converts a press of the return or enter key into a click of the dialog's default button.

Assembly-Language Information

Trap macro:

(Pascal) Routine name	(Assembly) Trap macro	Trap word
ModalDialog	**_ModalDialog**	**$A991**

7.4.4 Using Modeless Dialogs

Definitions

```
function IsDialogEvent
        (theEvent : EventRecord)          {Event to be handled}
        : BOOLEAN;                        {Is event dialog-related?}

function DialogSelect
        (theEvent      : EventRecord;     {Event to be handled}
        var theDialog   : DialogPtr;      {Returns pointer to dialog affected}
        var itemNumber : INTEGER)         {Returns item number of reported item}
        : BOOLEAN;                        {Response needed?}
```

Notes

1. **IsDialogEvent** tells whether a given event is directed to a dialog window.

2. Call this routine for every event you receive when a modeless dialog box is on the screen (whether active or not). If it returns **TRUE**, pass the event on to **DialogSelect** to be processed; if **FALSE**, handle the event yourself in the normal way.

3. **IsDialogEvent** returns **TRUE** for the following types of event:

   - Window events involving a dialog window
   - Mouse presses in an active dialog window's content region
   - All other types of event when a dialog window is active

   For all other events it returns **FALSE**.

4. **DialogSelect** handles user activity in a modeless dialog box.

5. **theEvent** should be a dialog-related event (one for which **IsDialog-Event** returned **TRUE**); **DialogSelect** just processes that one event. This differs from the alert routines [7.4.2] and **ModalDialog** [7.4.3], which get events for themselves and continue to get and process them until they receive one involving an enabled item.

6. The dialog box remains visible on the screen for further interaction with the user.

7. The function result tells whether the event involved an enabled dialog item: **TRUE** if it did, **FALSE** if it didn't.

8. If the function result is **TRUE**, the variable parameters **theDialog** and **itemNumber** identify the item affected by the event. You can then do whatever is needed to respond to that item. If the result is **FALSE**, the values returned in the variable parameters are undefined.

9. For window events (activate, deactivate, and update) involving a dialog window, **DialogSelect** responds to the event as appropriate and returns a result of **FALSE**.

10. For mouse clicks in a disabled item, or in no item at all, **DialogSelect** returns **FALSE**.

11. If the mouse is pressed in an enabled control item, **TrackControl** [6.4.2] is called to track its movements until it's released. If the mouse is released inside the same control, **DialogSelect** returns **TRUE**; if it's released outside the original control, **DialogSelect** returns **FALSE**.

12. If the mouse is pressed in a text box, **TEClick** [5.4.1] is called to track its movements and perform text selection. Extended selection with the shift key and double-click word selection are handled properly. **DialogSelect** then returns **TRUE** if the text box is enabled, **FALSE** if it's disabled.

13. If the dialog includes any text boxes, keyboard events are directed to the current text box via **TEKey** [5.5.1]. **DialogSelect** then returns **TRUE** if the text box is enabled, **FALSE** if it's disabled (or if there are no text boxes).

14. The command key is ignored on all keyboard events. If you want to allow command combinations in a dialog box, you have to recognize and respond to them yourself instead of passing the event to **Dialog-Select.**

15. Disk-inserted events are ignored. If you want to respond to them while a modeless dialog box is active, you have to check for them and handle them yourself.

16. Unlike the alert routines and **ModalDialog**, **DialogSelect** doesn't accept a filter function [7.4.5] as a parameter. Any preprocessing that the filter function would have done must be performed by your program before or instead of calling **DialogSelect**.

Assembly-Language Information

Trap macros:

(Pascal) Routine name	(Assembly) Trap macro	Trap word
IsDialogEvent	**_IsDialogEvent**	**$A97F**
DialogSelect	**_DialogSelect**	**$A980**

7.4.5 Filter Functions

Definitions

```
function YourFilterFunction
        (theDialog    : DialogPtr;      {Pointer to dialog affected}
    var theEvent    : EventRecord;    {Event to be handled}
    var itemNumber : INTEGER)        {Returns item number to report}
        : BOOLEAN;                    {Report item immediately?}
```

Notes

1. The function heading shown above is a model for the filter function you pass to the alert routines [7.4.2] or **ModalDialog** [7.4.3]. There is no Toolbox routine named **YourFilterFunction**.

2. The alert and **ModalDialog** routines pass every event they receive to the filter function before processing it. The filter function can do any of the following:

   • Respond to the event itself
   • Convert it into the equivalent of a mouse click in a specified item
   • Modify it and pass it back for processing
   • Leave it unchanged

3. A function result of **TRUE** causes the event to be treated as a mouse click in the item identified by variable parameter **itemNumber**. That is, both the alert routines and **ModalDialog** will return the given item number as if the mouse had been clicked in that item; the alert routines will also dismiss and dispose of the alert box.

4. A function result of **FALSE** causes the event to be processed normally. Since **theEvent** is a variable parameter, the filter function can modify the fields of the event record before passing it back for processing.

5. The standard filter function, used if you pass **NIL** for the **filter** parameter, just converts a press of the return or enter key into a click of the alert's or dialog's default button. If you write your own filter function, it should also perform this same conversion.

6. For modal dialogs, the default button is always item number **1** (**OK**); for alerts, you can get the item number of the default button from the **aDefItem** field of the dialog record [7.1.1].

7. Since the alert routines and **ModalDialog** mask out disk-inserted events, your filter function has to check for them itself if you want to respond to them. You can do this by calling **GetNextEvent** [2.2.1] with a **mask** parameter of **DiskMask** [2.1.3].

8. Filter functions are also commonly used for responding to command-key combinations typed from the keyboard, since the alert routines and **ModalDialog** ignore the command key.

9. Another use of filter functions is to track the mouse when it's pressed in a user item (item type **UserItem** [7.1.2]) or a resource-based control item (**CtrlItem + ResCtrl**).

7.4.6 Text Substitution

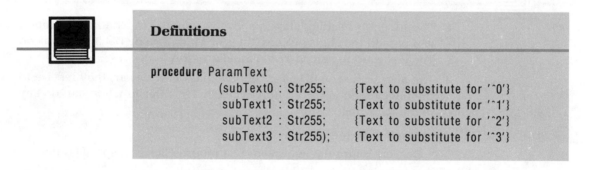

Definitions

```
procedure ParamText
            (subText0 : Str255;      {Text to substitute for '^0'}
             subText1 : Str255;      {Text to substitute for '^1'}
             subText2 : Str255;      {Text to substitute for '^2'}
             subText3 : Str255);     {Text to substitute for '^3'}
```

Notes

1. **ParamText** defines as many as four text strings to be substituted into a dialog's static text items when it's displayed on the screen.

2. The four substitution strings are represented in the actual text of the items by the placeholders ^**0**, ^**1**, ^**2**, and ^**3**.

3. The four strings passed to **ParamText** will be substituted into all static text items in all subsequent dialogs and alerts until changed by another **ParamText** call. The substitution is performed at the time the dialog is displayed.

4. Handles to the four current substitution strings are kept in consecutive locations in memory beginning at the assembly-language global variable **DAStrings**.

Assembly-Language Information

Trap macro:

(Pascal) Routine name	(Assembly) Trap macro	Trap word
ParamText	**_ParamText**	**$A98B**

Assembly-language global variable:

Name	Address	Meaning
DAStrings	**$AA0**	Handles to four text substitution strings

7.4.7 Editing in Text Boxes

Definitions

```
procedure DlgCut
          (theDialog : DialogPtr);     {Pointer to the dialog}
procedure DlgCopy
          (theDialog : DialogPtr);     {Pointer to the dialog}
procedure DlgPaste
          (theDialog : DialogPtr);     {Pointer to the dialog}
procedure DlgDelete
          (theDialog : DialogPtr);     {Pointer to the dialog}
```

Notes

1. These routines perform the standard cut-and-paste editing operations in an editable text box.

2. The operations apply to the current selection or insertion point in the dialog's current text box. If the dialog doesn't include any text boxes, nothing happens.

3. These routines are part of the Pascal Toolbox interface, not part of the Toolbox itself. They don't reside in ROM and can't be called from assembly language via the trap mechanism.

4. In assembly language, get the edit record handle for the current text box from the **textH** field of the dialog record [7.1.1] and pass it directly to the Toolbox routines **TECut**, **TECopy**, **TEPaste**, and **TEDelete** [5.5.2, 5.5.3].

7.5 Nuts and Bolts

7.5.1 Text Font and Error Sounds

Definitions

```
procedure SetDAFont
        (fontNumber : INTEGER);      {Font number for dialogs and alerts}

procedure ErrorSound
        (soundProc  : ProcPtr);      {Pointer to sound procedure}
```

Notes

1. **SetDAFont** sets the typeface for all subsequent dialog and alert boxes displayed on the screen.

2. The typeface is identified by a font number [I:8.2.1].

3. The text is always displayed in a standard type size of **12** points. If a font in that size doesn't exist for the given typeface, a suitable existing size will be scaled.

4. The default typeface for dialog and alert text is the system font (**Chicago,** font number **0**).

5. The typeface setting affects static text and editable text boxes only. Titles of control items are always displayed in the system font.

6. **SetDAFont** is part of the Pascal Toolbox interface, not part of the Toolbox itself. It doesn't reside in ROM and can't be called from assembly language via the trap mechanism.

7. In assembly language, you can control the font number for dialogs and alerts by storing into the global variable **DlgFont**.

8. **ErrorSound** sets the sound procedure for use in alerts.

9. The sound procedure should be of the form

   procedure SoundProc (soundNumber : INTEGER);

   The argument selects the desired sound with a *sound number* from **0** to **3**; the sound procedure emits the corresponding sound. See the *Inside Macintosh* manual for information on how to emit sounds from the Macintosh speaker.

10. The standard sound procedure simply emits a number of short beeps, from none to three, as specified by to the sound number. If the user has set the speaker volume to **0** with the Control Panel desk accessory, the procedure flashes the menu bar instead of beeping the speaker.

11. Passing **NIL** for the **soundProc** parameter results in no sound or blinking of the menu bar at all.

12. A pointer to the current sound procedure is kept in the assembly-language global variable **DABeeper**.

Assembly-Language Information

Trap macro:

(Pascal) Routine name	(Assembly) Trap macro	Trap word
ErrorSound	**_ErrorSound**	**$A98C**

Assembly-language global variables:

Name	Address	Meaning
DlgFont	**$AFA**	Current font number for dialogs and alerts
DABeeper	**$A9C**	Pointer to current sound procedure

7.5.2 Alert Stages

Definitions

function GetAlrtStage
            : INTEGER;   {Stage of last alert minus 1}

procedure ResetAlrtStage;

Notes

1. **GetAlrtStage** tells the stage number at which the last alert occurred; **ResetAlrtStage** resets the alert stage so that the next alert will occur at stage 1.

2. The result returned by **GetAlrtStage** is *one less than* the stage number of the last alert (**0** to **3** instead of **1** to **4**).

3. These routines are part of the Pascal Toolbox interface, not part of the Toolbox itself. They don't reside in ROM and can't be called from assembly language via the trap mechanism.

4. In assembly language, the stage number of the last alert is kept in the global variable **ACount** and its resource ID in **ANumber**. To reset to stage 1, store −1 into **ACount**.

Assembly-Language Information

Assembly-language global variables:

Name	Address	Meaning
ANumber	**$A98**	Resource ID of last alert
ACount	**$A9A**	Stage of last alert minus 1

7.5.3 Preloading Dialog Resources

Definitions

procedure CouldAlert
        (alertID : INTEGER);   {Resource ID of alert}

procedure CouldDialog
        (dialogID : INTEGER);   {Resource ID of dialog}

procedure FreeAlert
        (alertID : INTEGER);   {Resource ID of alert}

procedure FreeDialog
        (dialogID : INTEGER);   {Resource ID of dialog}

Notes

1. **CouldAlert** and **CouldDialog** read all resources associated with a given alert or dialog into the heap and make them unpurgeable.

2. Before any operation that involves ejecting or swapping disks, call these routines to read in the resources of any alerts or dialogs that may occur during the operation. This guarantees that the resources will be available even when the disk they reside on is not in the disk drive.

3. When the resources are no longer needed in memory, call **FreeAlert** and **FreeDialog** to allow them to be purged from the heap.

Assembly-Language Information

Trap macros:

(Pascal) Routine name	(Assembly) Trap macro	Trap word
CouldAlert	**_CouldAlert**	**$A989**
CouldDialog	**_CouldDialog**	**$A979**
FreeAlert	**_FreeAlert**	**$A98A**
FreeDialog	**_FreeDialog**	**$A97A**

7.6 Dialog-Related Resources

7.6.1 Resource Type 'ALRT'

Definitions

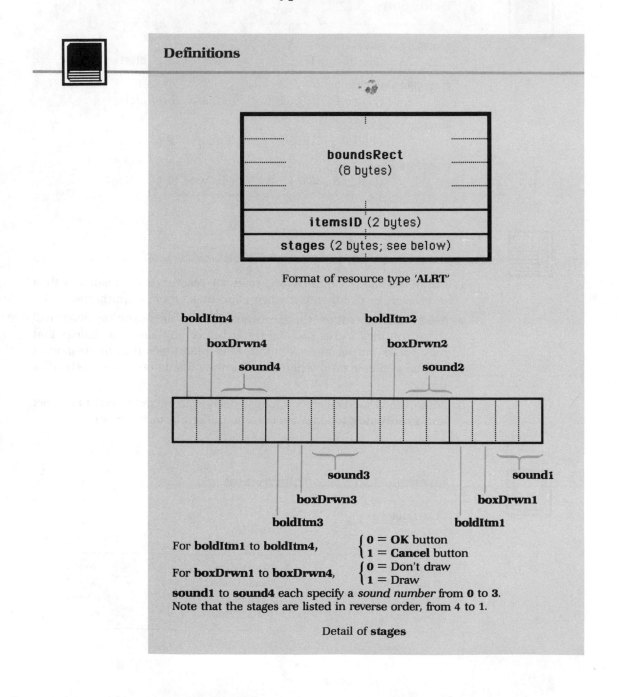

Format of resource type **'ALRT'**

For **boldItm1** to **boldItm4**, $\begin{cases} 0 = \textbf{OK} \text{ button} \\ 1 = \textbf{Cancel} \text{ button} \end{cases}$

For **boxDrwn1** to **boxDrwn4**, $\begin{cases} 0 = \text{Don't draw} \\ 1 = \text{Draw} \end{cases}$

sound1 to **sound4** each specify a *sound number* from **0** to **3**.
Note that the stages are listed in reverse order, from 4 to 1.

Detail of **stages**

Notes

1. A resource of type **'ALRT'** contains an alert template.

2. The structure of the resource is the same as that of an **AlertTemplate** record [7.1.3].

3. The resource type of the item list is **'DITL'** [7.6.3].

4. The stage list consists of four 4-bit fields packed into a single word. The stages are given in *reverse order*: the first 4-bit field defines stage 4, the last defines stage 1.

5. In each field of the stage list:

   • The first bit designates the default button at that stage of the alert: **0** for the **OK** button (item number **1**), **1** for the **Cancel** button (item number **2**).

   • The second bit tells whether the alert box is to be drawn on the screen: **1** if it is, **0** if it isn't.

   • The last two bits designate the sound number to be emitted (**0** to **3**).

6. To create an alert from an alert template, call one of the alert routines [7.4.2] with the template's resource ID.

7.6.2 Resource Type 'DLOG'

boundsRect (8 bytes)
procID (2 bytes)
visible / (unused)
goAwayflag / (unused)
refCon (4 bytes)
itemsID (2 bytes)
Length of **title**
title (indefinite length)

Format of resource type **'DLOG'**

Notes

1. A resource of type 'DLOG' contains a dialog template.

2. The structure of the resource is the same as that of a **DialogTemplate** record [7.1.4]. All of its fields are in the same form as the corresponding parameters to **NewWindow** [3.2.2] or **NewDialog** [7.2.2].

3. The resource type of the item list is 'DITL' [7.6.3].

4. The dialog title is in Pascal string form, with a 1-byte length count followed by the characters of the title. The overall size of the dialog template depends on the length of the title string.

5. To create a dialog from a dialog template, call **GetNewDialog** [7.2.2] with the template's resource ID.

7.6.3 Resource Type 'DITL'

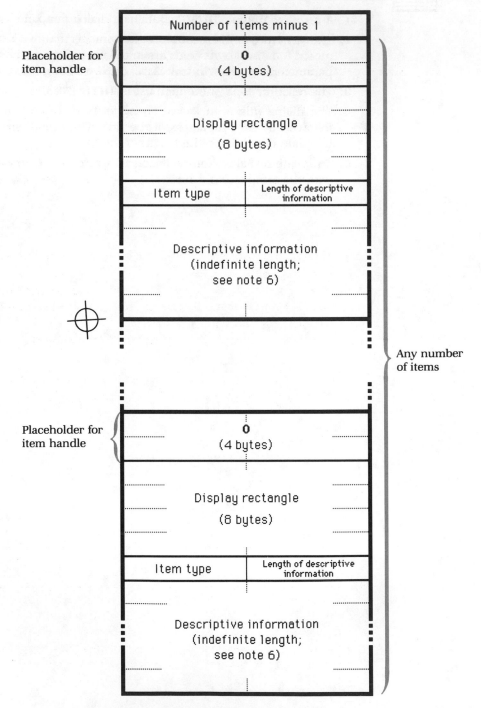

Format of resource type **'DITL'**

Notes

1. A resource of type 'DITL' contains an item list for an alert or dialog.

2. The first word of the resource is an integer that's *one less than* the number of items in the list. This is followed by the entries representing the items themselves, in the format shown.

3. The first 4 bytes of each item entry are reserved as a placeholder for the item handle.

4. The item's display rectangle is given in the local (window) coordinates of the alert or dialog box.

5. The length of the additional descriptive information in each entry, and hence of the list entry itself, is variable. The byte following the item type gives the length of the descriptive information in bytes, which must be even.

6. The descriptive information is as follows:

   - For icon and picture items, the resource ID of the icon or picture (resource type 'ICON' [I:5.5.3] or 'PICT' [I:5.5.5])

   - For resource-based control items (item type **CtrlItem + ResCtrl** [7.1.2]), the resource ID of a control template (resource type 'CNTL' [6.5.1])

   - For any other control item, the title of the control

   - For static text items, the text of the item

   - For editable text boxes, the text of the box's initial contents

   - For user items, no descriptive information at all (length **0**)

Assembly-Language Information

Offset within an item list:

Name	Offset in bytes	Meaning
DlgMaxIndex	0	Number of items minus 1

Offsets within each item:

Name	Offset in bytes	Meaning
ItmHndl	0	Item handle
ItmRect	4	Display rectangle
ItmType	12	Item type
ItmData	14	Additional descriptive information

CHAPTER

8

Files at Your Fingertips

The last topic we have left to cover is input/output. In this chapter you'll learn about the Macintosh's built-in disk drive and how to create and use files stored on it. You'll also learn how to use two of the standard packages in the system resource file, the Standard File Package (often called the MiniFinder) and the Disk Initialization Package. And we'll fill in the last remaining routines of our **MiniEdit** application program, those that handle the **File** menu commands for reading and writing files.

Disk Format

The Sony disk drive built into the Macintosh stores 400 kilobytes of information on one side of a plastic-encased, 3-1/2-inch "minidisk." The disk's recording surface consists of 80 concentric *tracks*, numbered **0** to **79** from the outside in; these in turn are divided into *sectors* of 512 bytes each (see Figure 8-1). Information is always physically transferred to and from the disk in whole 512-byte sectors.

The outer tracks, being longer, can hold more information than the inner ones. To make the most efficient possible use of the available disk space, the 80 tracks are divided into five groups of 16 each, with the outermost group (tracks **0–15**) holding twelve sectors per track, the next group (**16–31**) eleven sectors, and so on to only eight sectors each for tracks **64–79**, the innermost group. This makes an average of ten sectors per track over the entire disk; for 80 tracks, this comes to 800 sectors of half a kilobyte each, or 400 kilobytes altogether. (There may someday be a double-sided Sony drive with twice the capacity, 1600 sectors or 800 kilo-

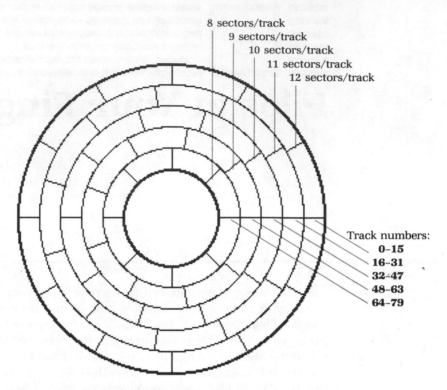

8 sectors/track
9 sectors/track
10 sectors/track
11 sectors/track
12 sectors/track

Track numbers:
0–15
16–31
32–47
48–63
64–79

Each sector holds 512 bytes of information.

Figure 8-1 Tracks and sectors

bytes.) To keep the bit transfer rate constant, the disk drive runs its motor at any of five different speeds, depending on which group of tracks it is addressing; this is why the Macintosh "sings" when the disk drive is running.

> Actually, each sector holds 524 bytes: 512 bytes of data and an extra 12-byte *tag*. The tag contains identifying information about the sector, such as what file it belongs to, its sequential position within the file, and the date and time it was written. In case of damage to the disk, a "scavenger" program can use this tag information to salvage all or most of the files on it.

In addition to the *internal disk drive* built into the Macintosh, one *external drive* can be attached through the disk drive connector on the back of the machine. The two drives are designated by *drive numbers*, **1** for the internal drive and **2** for the external. Any other external storage device connected through one of the Macintosh's serial ports, such as a large-capacity hard disk, will have a drive number of **3** or above.

The lowest-level software that communicates directly with the disk is the *disk driver*, one of three standard device drivers built directly into the Macintosh ROM. (The others are the serial communications driver and the sound driver.) The disk driver's name is **.Sony** and its driver reference number is **−5**. Different disk drives or other mass-storage devices have to provide their own device drivers to replace the standard Sony driver. These replacement drivers are RAM-based, installed in the system resource file and loaded into RAM when the system is started up.

> Most of the information in this chapter should hold true no matter what disk drive you're using, but the author makes no warranties, express or implied, with respect to any but the standard Sony disk.

The File System

You don't normally have to deal with the disk driver directly. That job is handled for you by a part of the Toolbox called the File Manager (or simply the *file system*), which allows you to view the disk as a collection of *files*. A file is just a linear sequence of bytes of any length, limited only by the capacity of the disk. You can read or write any number of bytes you need in a single file operation; the file system will convert your requests into the appropriate whole-sector data transfers and carry them out via the disk driver.

Every file has a *file name* that you use to refer to it; the file system translates the file name into the corresponding physical track and sector locations on the disk. File names can include embedded spaces and punctuation marks—any character except a colon (**:**), which as we'll see is used as a separator for volume names. The file system doesn't distinguish between upper- and lowercase letters, so the names

```
ODDS AND ENDS
Odds and Ends
odds and ends
oDdS aNd eNdS
```

are all equivalent.

File names can theoretically be as long as 255 characters, but certain parts of the Macintosh software (notably the Finder and MiniFinder) limit them to no more than 63 characters. To be on the safe side, you should always keep your file names within this limit.

Actually there are two separate file systems, a high-level and a low-level one. The low-level file system gives you the greatest possible control over your filing operations—more, in fact, than you'll ordinarily need. It's generally more convenient to use the high-level file system, which sacrifices some of that fine control in favor of simplicity and ease of use. The high-level routines are designed to perform the most common filing operations in the most straightforward way; they call the corresponding low-level routines for you, which in turn call the disk driver, which communicates directly with the disk (see Figure 8-2).

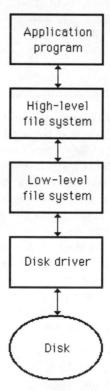

Figure 8-2 File system hierarchy

The low-level file system is technically part of the Macintosh Operating System rather than the Toolbox. It's meant to be called from assembly language, and communicates via the 68000 processor's registers. All the pertinent information about a file and the operation to be performed on it is collected into a complex data structure in memory known as a *parameter block*; a pointer to the parameter block is passed in one of the registers (register **A0**, if you must know).

The interface unit for calling the Operating System from a high-level language such as Pascal includes a set of *interface routines* (often called "glue routines" or, more whimsically, "gluons") to the low-level file system. Since all of these low-level interface routines accept a pointer to a parameter block as one of their arguments, their names all begin with the letters **PB**: **PBOpen**, **PBWrite**, and so on. Most of the high-level routines begin with **FS**, for "file system." In this chapter we'll discuss only the high-level file system; if your needs are more exotic, you'll have to look in the *Inside Macintosh* manual for details on the low-level system.

> If you're writing in assembly language, only the low-level routines are available.

Error Reporting

All file system routines, low level (**PB**) or high (**FS**), are functions that return an integer result code of type **OSErr** [I:3.1.2]; any other information they have to pass back is passed through a variable parameter. As usual, a zero result code (**NoErr**) means that all is well and the requested operation was carried out successfully; any nonzero result code (always negative) reports an error of some kind that prevented successful completion. Result codes relating to files are listed in [8.2.8].

Program 8-1 shows our **MiniEdit** program's error-handling routine, **IOCheck**. Every time we use a file system routine, we'll pass the result code it returns to **IOCheck** to check for input/output errors and respond to them as appropriate. In the normal case, when the result code it receives is **0** (**NoErr**), **IOCheck** just does nothing and returns; if it receives a nonzero error code, it notifies the user with an alert, then cancels the operation that caused the error.

```
{ Global variables }

var
   Quitting  : BOOLEAN;                              {Quit command in effect?}
   ErrorFlag : BOOLEAN;                              {I/O error flag}


procedure IOCheck (resultCode : OSErr);

   { Check for I/O error. }

   const
      opWrID = 1005;                                 {Resource ID for Already Open alert}
      ioErrID = 1006;                                {Resource ID for I/O Error alert}

   var
      alertID    : INTEGER;                          {Resource ID of alert}
      errorString : Str255;                          {Error code in string form [I:2.1.1]}
      ignore     : INTEGER;                          {Item code returned by alert}

   begin {IOCheck}

      if resultCode = NoErr then                     {Just return if no error}
         EXIT (IOCheck);

      case resultCode of

         OpWrErr:
            alertID := opWrID;                        {Use Already Open alert}

         {Insert code here to handle any other specific errors}

         otherwise
            begin
               alertID := ioErrID;                    {Use general I/O Error alert}
               NumToString (resultCode, errorString); {Convert error code to a string [I:2.3.4]}
               ParamText   (errorString, '', '', '')  {Substitute into text of alert [7.4.6]}
            end

      end; {case}
```

Program 8-1 Check for I/O error

```
    InitCursor;                          {Restore normal cursor [2.5.2]}
    ignore := StopAlert (alertID, NIL);  {Post alert [7.4.2]}

    Quitting := FALSE;                   {Cancel Quit command, if any}
    ErrorFlag := TRUE                    {Force exit to main event loop}

  end;  {IOCheck}
```

Program 8-1 (*continued*)

For most unanticipated errors, we just post a general-purpose alert message like

```
I/O Error −49
```

using **NumToString** [I:2.3.4] to convert the numerical error code into a string of digits and **ParamText** [7.4.6] to substitute it into the text of the alert. This type of message won't mean much to the average user, though. It's generally more helpful if the program can anticipate the most common types of I/O error and offer a precise description of the problem. To illustrate, we've built one such specific error check into our **IOCheck** routine: if the user tries to open a second window onto a file that's already open, we display the more helpful message

```
Sorry, can't open the same file twice.
```

In a serious application program, you would want to provide this kind of specific alert message for other errors as well.

Before posting the alert, **IOCheck** calls **InitCursor** [2.5.2] to restore the cursor to its normal arrow shape. This is necessary because some of the input/output routines that call **IOCheck** use a wristwatch cursor to signal a delay for disk activity, and we don't want the wristwatch to remain when our error alert appears on the screen. After the user dismisses the alert, we want to cancel whatever operation gave rise to the error and return to the program's main event loop to process the next event. Ideally we could do this directly with the statement

```
EXIT (DoEvent)
```

but unfortunately Apple's Pascal system doesn't allow this type of "nonlocal exit." So to achieve the same effect, we have to introduce a global Boolean flag named **ErrorFlag**, which we will set to **FALSE** on each pass of the program's **DoEvent** routine and to **TRUE** when an error is detected. After each call to **IOCheck**, the calling routine must test this flag and exit immediately if it's **TRUE**; we've already seen an example of this in our **CloseAppWindow** routine in the last chapter (Program 7-2). Then the routine that called *that* routine must do the same, and so on back up the call chain to **DoEvent**. The next time through the main loop, **DoEvent** will reinitialize **ErrorFlag** to **FALSE** in preparation for the next error check.

Volumes

The file system groups files logically into larger collections known as *volumes*. Conceptually, a volume corresponds to a physical unit of information storage; on the standard Sony disk drive, for instance, each disk is a separate volume. However, this correspondence doesn't necessarily hold for all devices. A hard disk, for instance, might be partitioned into several logical volumes sharing the one physical disk; or a "RAM disk" driver might treat an area of central memory as a volume to be accessed as if it were an external disk.

Every volume has a *volume name* of up to 27 characters, ending with a colon (:). As in file names, upper- and lowercase letters are considered equivalent. Any file name can be prefixed by a volume name:

    Humpty:Dumpty

Normally, however, you'll just give the file name itself and identify the volume by reference number. In any case, the use of prefixed volume names should be kept hidden; don't ever ask the user to supply a file name in this form.

At any given time, there's always a *current volume* that's used automatically for all file names that aren't prefixed with a volume name of their own. When the Macintosh is started up, the disk it's started from becomes the current volume. You can change the current volume with **SetVol** or find out what volume is current with **GetVol** [8.1.2].

Every volume has a *file directory* and a *block map* containing information about the files it contains and where they are on the disk. (This information is of interest mainly to the file system itself; you don't need to know its exact internal structure to do straightforward input and output.) Whenever a disk is inserted in a disk drive, its directory and block map are read into memory for use by the file system. This is called *mounting* the volume, and the Toolbox does it for you automatically; by the time you receive a disk-inserted event, the corresponding volume will already have been mounted.

The event message [2.1.4] for a disk-inserted event contains the result code returned by the mounting operation in its high-order word, along with the drive number of the disk drive involved in the low-order word. A nonzero result code means that an error has prevented the volume from being successfully mounted—for instance, the user may have inserted an uninitialized or unreadable disk. In this case you should normally pass the event message to the routine **DIBadMount** [8.4.1] (part of the Disk Initialization Package) to give the user a chance to correct the problem by initializing or ejecting the disk.

At the time a volume is mounted, it's assigned a *volume reference number* for identification. Different volumes will always have different reference numbers, even though their names may happen to be the same; to avoid ambiguity, you should use the reference number rather than the volume name whenever possible. The Toolbox routine **GetVInfo** [8.1.1] accepts a drive number identifying a physical disk drive and returns the name and reference number of the volume currently in that drive, as well as the amount of free space available on the volume.

Mounting a volume also allocates space in memory for a *volume buffer* to hold information being transferred to or from the files on the volume. The volume buffer holds one or more whole disk sectors of information. When you ask to read from a file, the sector containing the needed information is read into the volume buffer (if it isn't already there); then only the bytes you actually requested are transferred from the buffer to your program. When you write to a file, the information is just copied into the volume buffer and held there until a whole sector's worth has accumulated, at which point the entire sector is written out to the disk at once.

The file system handles all buffering for you automatically, so you should never have to concern yourself with this level of detail. However, you can explicitly "flush" the contents of the volume buffer to the disk if necessary with **FlushVol** [8.1.3]. It's generally a good idea to do this from time to time (such as every time you close a file), to avoid losing the information in the buffer in case of a power failure, meteorite impact, or similar unforeseen catastrophe.

When a disk is ejected from the disk drive, the memory space occupied by its volume buffer and block map is released. The volume is now said to be *off-line*. An off-line volume remains mounted, however, and a small amount of identifying information (94 bytes, to be exact) remains in memory so that the volume remains known to the file system. (In the Finder, for instance, the icon representing an ejected volume remains visible on the screen, but becomes "dimmed" to show that the volume is off-line.) If the user reinserts the disk in the disk drive, its block map will be read back in and a new volume buffer allocated, placing the volume back *on-line*.

The information on a volume is immediately accessible only when the volume is on-line. If you try to access a file on a volume that's off-line, the file system will eject the disk currently in the drive and display the "disk-switch" alert shown in Figure 8-3, asking the user to insert the needed volume. The only way for the user to dismiss this alert is to insert the requested disk in the disk drive, after which the file system will proceed to carry out the operation.

Figure 8-3 Disk-switch alert

When you're completely through with a volume, call **UnmountVol** [8.1.3] to *unmount* it. This completely removes all information about the volume from memory. Once it's unmounted, the volume is no longer known to the file system and its contents are no longer accessible.

Files

Files are, of course, the basic unit of information storage on a disk. Disk space for a file is allocated in fixed units called *allocation blocks*, which are always some whole number of 512-byte disk sectors. The number of sectors per allocation block is determined at the time the disk is initialized; for the standard Sony disk, each allocation block is normally two sectors, or 1024 bytes. The file system automatically adds and deletes allocation blocks as a file grows and shrinks.

The length of a file is essentially unlimited. (Actually there's a limit of 16 megabytes—2^{24} bytes—but in practice it's unlikely you'll ever need a file that long.) Byte positions within the file are numbered sequentially, starting from **0**. Like points on the QuickDraw coordinate grid or character positions in an edit record, these represent positions *between* the bytes of the file. Byte position **0** is at the beginning of the file, before the first byte; position **24** is between the 24th and 25th bytes; and so on.

A file's length is defined by two such byte positions, marking the *physical* and the *logical end-of-file*, or *EOF* (see Figure 8-4). The physical end-of-file is the byte position at the end of the file's last allocation block; it's equivalent to the number of bytes physically allocated to the file on the disk, and is always a multiple of the allocation block size. The logical end-of-file marks the end of the file's meaningful contents, and tells how many of the physically allocated bytes actually "count" as part of the file. The logical end-of-file can never be greater than the physical end-of-file.

The physical end-of-file is manipulated entirely by the file system, and is ordinarily of no concern to your program. The term "end-of-file," without a qualifier, is always understood to refer to the logical rather than the physical EOF. The routines **GetEOF** and **SetEOF** [8.2.5] respectively return and change the position of the logical end-of-file. When you set the logical EOF, the file system automatically adjusts the physical EOF accordingly, adding new allocation blocks to the end of the file if you lengthen it or releasing unneeded blocks if you shorten it.

It's also possible to explicitly add allocation blocks to a file with the file system routine **Allocate** [8.2.5]. This is sometimes useful for preallocating space when you know you're going to be lengthening a file, to avoid fragmentation on the disk. Notice that you specify the amount of space to be added to the file in *bytes*, not blocks.

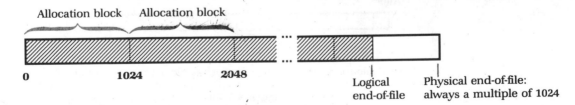

On the Sony disk drive, each allocation block is 2 sectors, or 1024 bytes.

Figure 8-4 Physical and logical end-of-file

Another important byte position within a file is the *file mark*, which designates the point where the next reading or writing operation will take place. The file system routine **GetFPos** [8.2.4] returns the current mark position. The next byte to be transferred is always the byte following the mark; the mark is then moved forward one position, so that it advances sequentially through the file as bytes are read or written (see Figure 8-5).

You can also manipulate the mark explicitly with **SetFPos** [8.2.4], to control the position of the next reading or writing operation on the file. You express the new mark position as a positive or negative offset in bytes from a specified base position, which may be either the beginning of the file (**FSFromStart**), the logical end-of-file (**FSFromLEOF**), or the current mark position (**FSFromMark**). If the resulting byte position falls before the beginning of the file or after its logical end, **SetFPos** positions the mark at the beginning or end of the file and returns an error code of **PosErr** or **EOFErr** [8.2.8], respectively.

There's also a fourth base constant, **FSAtMark**, which refers unconditionally to the current mark position, ignoring any offset. This amounts to saying "set the mark at the current position of the mark," an operation whose usefulness is not readily apparent. If you're wondering why this constant is defined and what's it's good for, you're not alone.

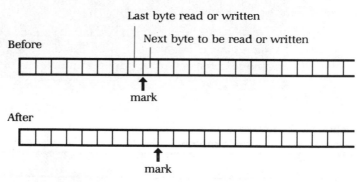

File mark advances byte by byte as file is read or written.

Figure 8-5 File mark

Working with Files

In order to read from or write to a file, you must first *open* it with **FSOpen** [8.2.2]. This makes the file known to the file system and creates the internal data structures needed to work with it. You identify the file by name and volume and get back a *file reference number* that you use from then on to refer to it. Most file system routines expect a file reference number as one of their parameters.

Of course, you can't open a file that doesn't exist. If you want to write a brand-new file to the disk, you have to create it first. The **Create** routine [8.2.1] accepts a file name and volume reference number and creates a file with that name on that volume. (You also have to supply a file type and creator signature for use by the Finder.) Notice, however, that **Create** doesn't open the file for you; you still have to call **FSOpen** to get a reference number for the file.

Once you've opened a file and gotten a reference number for it, you can proceed to read and write it with **FSRead** and **FSWrite** [8.2.3]. You give the file's reference number, the number of bytes to transfer, and a pointer to either the information to be written or the place in memory where the information to be read should go. The information will be transferred between consecutive memory locations, beginning at the address designated by the pointer, and consecutive bytes of the file, beginning at the current mark position. (You can, of course, set the mark wherever you want with **SetFPos** [8.2.4] before beginning the read or write operation.)

As the information is transferred, the mark advances sequentially through the file. If it reaches the logical end-of-file while reading, the operation terminates immediately, returning an error code of **EOFErr** [8.2.8] along with the number of bytes actually read in the **byteCount** parameter. If the mark encounters the end-of-file while writing, the end-of-file "sticks" to the mark and begins advancing along with it, lengthening the file as it goes. When the physical end-of-file is reached, a new allocation block is automatically appended to the file and the writing operation continues.

When you're finished with a file, you *close* it with **FSClose** [8.2.2], after which the reference number is no longer valid and the file can no longer be read or written. If the file was open for writing, any unwritten data that has accumulated in the volume buffer is written out to the disk. The file's entry in the volume directory is also updated and "time-stamped" with the current date and time on the built-in clock chip. However, the new directory entry is *not* automatically written out to the disk until the volume is ejected or unmounted. To keep the directory information on the disk up-to-date, you should always follow **FSClose** with a call to **FlushVol** [8.1.3].

Besides reading and writing, there are a number of auxiliary operations that you can perform on a file even when it's closed. The routines that perform these operations accept a file name and volume number instead of a file reference number. Operations in this category include deleting a file from a volume or changing its name [8.2.7], locking or unlocking it [8.2.6], and accessing or changing its Finder information [I:7.3.3]. Locking a file prevents it from being written to, deleted, or renamed.

Notice that the routines for locking and unlocking a file are not named **FSLock** and **FSUnlock**, as you might expect, but **SetFLock** ("set file lock") and **RstFLock** ("reset file lock").

Program 8-2 (**DoSave**) is our **MiniEdit** routine to handle the **Save** menu command. All it does is examine the **fileNumber** field in the window data record of the currently active window. If the window already has a file associated with it, we'll find the file's reference number in this field and we can go ahead and write the contents of the window to the file. If the **fileNumber** field is **0**, we have to ask the user with a dialog box what file to write to. This makes the **Save** command equivalent to **Save As...**, so we just call our **DoSaveAs** routine, which we'll be looking at later as Program 8-8.

The actual task of writing out a window's contents to a file is handled by the **WriteFile** routine shown in Program 8-3. (We've isolated this as a separate routine so that it can be shared by both **DoSave** and **DoSaveAs**.) The reference numbers of the file and its volume are passed in as parameters. Since writing to the disk entails a perceptible delay, we begin the **WriteFile** routine by displaying a wristwatch cursor; it will be set back to an arrow (or an I-beam) on the next pass through the main event loop. Then we get the text handle and length from the active window's edit record, which we've been keeping in the global variable **TheText**.

Our first operation on the file itself is to reposition its file mark to the beginning with **SetFPos** [8.2.4], using a base of **FSFromStart** and an offset of **0**. Next we pass the result code we get back to our **IOCheck** routine (Program 8-1) to check for errors. If **IOCheck** sets the global error flag, we skip the rest of the routine and exit immediately to the main event loop. We have to do this same dance after each and every input/output operation that returns a result code; from now on, we won't bother to mention it every time.

```
{ Global variable }

var
   TheWindow : WindowPtr;                          {Pointer to currently active window [3.1.1]}



procedure DoSave;

   { Handle Save command. }



   var
      theData    : WDHandle;                       {Handle to window's data record [Prog. 5-1]}
      dataHandle : Handle;                         {Untyped handle for locking data record [I:3.1.1]}



   begin {DoSave}

      dataHandle := Handle(GetWRefCon(TheWindow));  {Get window data [3.2.4]}

      HLock (dataHandle);                          {Lock data record [I:3.2.4]}

         theData := WDHandle(dataHandle);          {Convert to typed handle [Prog. 5-1]}
         with theData^^ do
            if fileNumber = 0 then                 {Is window associated with a file? [Prog. 5-1]}
               DoSaveAs                            {Get file name from user [Prog. 8-8]}
            else
               WriteFile (fileNumber, volNumber);  {Write to window's file [Prog. 8-3]}

      HUnlock (dataHandle)                         {Unlock data record [I:3.2.4]}

   end; {DoSave}
```

Program 8-2 Handle **Save** command

Assuming no error was detected, we're now ready to write the window's text to the file with **FSWrite** [8.2.3]. Notice that, since this routine
expects a simple pointer to the text instead of a handle, we have to pass it
the master pointer **textHandle^** instead of the text handle itself. (Of
course, we have to be careful to lock the text handle before dereferencing
it and unlock it again afterward.) After the writing operation is complete,
we call **SetEOF** [8.2.5] to trim the file to the correct length, in case there
was an earlier version longer than the one we've just written. Finally, we
flush the volume buffer with **FlushVol** [8.1.3] (to update the file's directory
information on the disk), mark the window as clean, and return.

```
{ Global variables }

var
   TheText   : TEHandle;                          {Handle to active window's edit record [5.1.1]}
   Watch     : CursHandle;                        {Handle to wristwatch cursor [2.5.1]}
   ErrorFlag : BOOLEAN;                           {I/O error flag}


procedure WriteFile (theFile : INTEGER; volNum : INTEGER);

   { Write window contents to a file. }

   var
      textHandle : Handle;                         {Handle to text of file [I:3.1.1]}
      textLength : LONGINT;                        {Length of text in bytes}
      resultCode : OSErr;                          {I/O error code [I:3.1.2]}

   begin {WriteFile}

      SetCursor (Watch^^);                         {Indicate delay [2.5.2]}

      HLock (Handle(TheText));                      {Lock edit record [I:3.2.4]}
         with TheText^^ do
            begin
               textHandle := hText;                 {Get text handle and current length}
               textLength := teLength              {  from edit record [5.1.1]       }
            end; {with}
      HUnlock (Handle(TheText));                    {Unlock edit record [I:3.2.4]}

      resultCode := SetFPos (theFile, FSFromStart, 0);  {Reset mark to beginning of file [8.2.4]}
      IOCheck (resultCode);                        {Check for error [Prog. 8-1]}
      if ErrorFlag then EXIT (WriteFile);          {On error, exit to main event loop}

      HLock (textHandle);                          {Lock text [I:3.2.4]}
         resultCode := FSWrite (theFile, textLength, textHandle^);  {Write text to file [8.2.3]}
      HUnlock (textHandle);                        {Unlock text [I:3.2.4]}
      IOCheck (resultCode);                        {Check for error [Prog. 8-1]}
      if ErrorFlag then EXIT (WriteFile);          {On error, exit to main event loop}

      resultCode := SetEOF (theFile, textLength);  {Set length of file [8.2.5]}
      IOCheck (resultCode);                        {Check for error [Prog. 8-1]}
      if ErrorFlag then EXIT (WriteFile);          {On error, exit to main event loop}
```

Program 8-3 Write window contents to a file

```
resultCode := FlushVol (NIL, volNum);          {Flush volume buffer [8.1.3]}
IOCheck (resultCode);                          {Check for error [Prog. 8-1]}
if ErrorFlag then EXIT (WriteFile);            {On error, exit to main event loop}

WindowDirty (FALSE)                            {Mark window as clean [Prog. 5-7]}

end;  {WriteFile}
```

Program 8-3 (*continued*)

Program 8-4 (**DoRevert**) handles the **Revert to Saved** command and shows how to read from a file. We begin by examining the **dirty** flag in the window data record. If this flag is **TRUE**, the window contains editing changes that will be lost if we revert to the last-saved version of the file. So before proceeding with the operation we post an alert with the message

Revert to most recently saved version of file "Flapdoodle"?

to confirm that this is really what the user wants to do. If the user clicks the alert's **Cancel** button, we'll cancel the **Revert** operation by setting the global error flag and taking an immediate exit. (Notice that since we're exiting from the middle of a *with* statement, we have to be careful to unlock the window data record before exiting.)

Assuming that the user has confirmed the **Revert** command by clicking the **OK** button in the alert box, we can now go ahead and read in the active window's file from the disk. We can safely assume that the window already has a file associated with it: if it didn't, our **DoActivate** routine (Program 5-14) would have disabled the **Revert** command on the menu the last time the window was activated, and we could never have gotten to where we are now. As we'll see later in Program 8-6, the file will already have been opened when it was first read into the window, so there's no need to open it now. We can just find out its length with **GetEOF** [8.2.5], move the mark to the beginning with **SetFPos** [8.2.4], set the text handle in the current edit record to the length of the file with **SetHandleSize** [I:3.2.3], and proceed to read the file with **FSRead** [8.2.3]. Then there are some housekeeping details to take care of, such as wrapping the text to the boundaries of the window, readjusting the window's scroll bar, and positioning the TextEdit insertion point at the beginning of the text. To get the window's contents redrawn on the screen, we call **InvalRect** [3.4.2] to force an update event. Then all that's left is to mark the window as clean and return.

```
{ Global variables }

var
   TheWindow : WindowPtr;                           {Pointer to currently active window [3.1.1]}
   TheText   : TEHandle;                            {Handle to active window's edit record [5.1.1]}
   Watch     : CursHandle;                          {Handle to wristwatch cursor [2.5.1]}
   ErrorFlag : BOOLEAN;                             {I/O error flag}


procedure DoRevert;

   { Handle Revert to Saved command. }

   const
      revertID = 1002;                              {Resource ID for Revert alert}

   var
      theData    : WDHandle;                        {Handle to window's data record [Prog. 5-1]}
      dataHandle : Handle;                          {Untyped handle for locking data record [I:3.1.1]}
      fileName   : Str255;                          {Title of window [I:2.1.1]}
      textLength : LONGINT;                         {Length of file in bytes}
      theItem    : INTEGER;                         {Item number for Revert alert}
      resultCode : OSErr;                           {I/O error code [I:3.1.2]}

begin {DoRevert}

   dataHandle := Handle(GetWRefCon(TheWindow));     {Get window data [3.2.4]}
   HLock (dataHandle);                              {Lock data record [I:3.2.4]}

      theData := WDHandle(dataHandle);              {Convert to typed handle}
      with theData^^ do
         begin

            if dirty then                           {Have window contents been changed?}
               begin
                  GetWTitle (TheWindow, fileName);  {Get file name from window title [3.2.4]}
                  ParamText (fileName, '', '', '');  {Substitute into text of alert [7.4.6]}

                  theItem := CautionAlert (revertID, NIL);  {Post alert [7.4.2]}
                  if theItem = Cancel then          {Did user cancel? [7.1.1]}
                     begin
                        HUnlock (dataHandle);       {Unlock data record [I:3.2.4]}
                        ErrorFlag := TRUE;          {Force exit to main event loop}
                        EXIT (DoRevert)             {Skip rest of operation}
                     end {if}
               end; {if}

            SetCursor (Watch^^);                    {Indicate delay [2.5.2]}
```

Program 8-4 Handle **Revert to Saved** command

```
    resultCode := GetEOF (fileNumber, textLength);   {Get length of file [8.2.5]}
    IOCheck (resultCode);                  {Check for error [Prog. 8-1]}
    if ErrorFlag then                      {Error detected?}
       begin
          HUnlock (dataHandle);            {Unlock data record [I:3.2.4]}
          EXIT (DoRevert)                  {Exit to main event loop}
       end; {if}

    resultCode := SetFPos (fileNumber, FSFromStart, 0);   {Set mark at beginning of file [8.2.4]}
    IOCheck (resultCode);                  {Check for error [Prog. 8-1]}
    if ErrorFlag then                      {Error detected?}
       begin
          HUnlock (dataHandle);            {Unlock data record [I:3.2.4]}
          EXIT (DoRevert)                  {Exit to main event loop}
       end; {if}

    HLock (Handle(TheText));               {Lock edit record [I:3.2.4]}
       with TheText^^ do
          begin

             SetHandleSize (hText, textLength);  {Adjust text to length of file [I:3.2.3, 5.1.1]}
             teLength := textLength;        {Set text length [5.1.1]}

             HLock (hText);                 {Lock the handle [I:3.2.4]}
                resultCode := FSRead (fileNumber, textLength, hText^);
                                            {Read text of file into handle [8.2.3]}
                IOCheck (resultCode);       {Check for error [Prog. 8-1]}
             HUnlock (hText)                {Unlock the handle [I:3.2.4]}

          end; {with}
    HUnlock (Handle(TheText));             {Unlock edit record [I:3.2.4]}

    if ErrorFlag then                      {Error detected during read?}
       begin
          HUnlock (dataHandle);            {Unlock data record [I:3.2.4]}
          EXIT (DoRevert)                  {Exit to main event loop}
       end  {if}

    h}
```

Program 8-4 (*continued*)

```
HUnlock (dataHandle);                        {Unlock data record [I:3.2.4]}

TECalText (TheText);                         {Wrap text to window [5.3.1]}
AdjustScrollBar;                             {Adjust scroll bar to length of text [Prog. 6-5]}
TESetSelect (0, 0, TheText);                 {Set insertion point at beginning of text [5.4.2]}

InvalRect (TheWindow^.portRect);             {Force update to redraw text [3.4.2]}
WindowDirty (FALSE)                          {Mark window as clean [Prog. 5-7]}

end;   {DoRevert}
```

Program 8-4 (*continued*)

The MiniFinder

Often, before you can carry out a filing operation, you need to ask the user what file to operate on. The easiest way to do this is with a set of standard routines known as the MiniFinder. The MiniFinder is not really part of the Toolbox but a separate package, officially named the Standard File Package. As we learned in Volume One, Chapter 7, a *package* is a collection of routines that is stored as a resource in a resource file and can be read into memory when needed. Standard packages such as the MiniFinder and its sidekick, the Disk Initialization Package, are included in the **System** file supplied on Macintosh software disks.

The Standard File Package and the Disk Initialization Package have package numbers **3** and **2**, respectively. The trap macros for using their routines from assembly language expand to call the "package traps" _Pack3 and _Pack2 [I:7.2.1], after first pushing an integer *routine selector* onto the stack to identify the desired routine within the package. The selectors for the various package routines are given in the assembly-language information boxes at the ends of the relevant reference sections.

The MiniFinder consists of two main routines: **SFGetFile** [8.3.2] to select an existing file to be read from the disk, and **SFPutFile** [8.3.3] to specify a file name to be written. Both routines obtain the needed information from the user by displaying a dialog box on the screen. All you do is call the routine, passing a *reply record* [8.3.1] to be filled in with the file name and other identifying information. The MiniFinder will keep control and handle all events until the dialog is dismissed. It takes care of all the needed processing to allow the user to select with the mouse from a scrollable list of available files, type or edit a file name, swap disks, switch disk drives, and so forth. When the dialog is finally dismissed, the Mini-Finder will fill in the fields of the reply record you supplied and return control to your program. You can then use the information in the reply record in whatever way you need.

> Although the standard dialogs described here are all you'll ordinarily need, it's possible to alter their behavior for your own purposes or replace them with "custom" dialogs of your own. You do this by providing a "dialog hook" function as a parameter to **SFGetFile** or **SFPutFile**, or by using a pair of alternate MiniFinder routines named **SFPGetFile** and **SFPPutFile** instead. See the *Inside Macintosh* manual for details.

File to Read From

Figure 8-6 shows the standard dialog box displayed by **SFGetFile**. You specify where on the screen the dialog box should appear and supply a list of up to four file types to be included in the file list. You can either list all files on the disk of the specified types, or provide a *filter function* to decide which ones to list and suppress the rest. In any case, the specified files will be listed in alphabetical order. If the list is too long to be displayed on the screen all at once, the MiniFinder will activate the list's scroll bar and handle all scrolling for you automatically; if the list is short enough to be displayed in its entirety, the scroll bar will be made inactive.

The user can select a file either by clicking it with the mouse and then clicking the **Open** button, or simply by double-clicking the file name. Either of these actions dismisses the dialog box; the MiniFinder will fill in the file name, volume reference number, and other information in the reply record, set the record's **good** field to **TRUE** to show that the file choice was confirmed, and return control to your program. If the user dismisses the dialog with the **Cancel** button, the **good** field will be set to **FALSE** to tell you to ignore the remaining fields and cancel the operation.

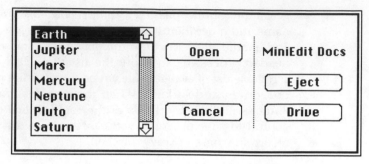

Figure 8-6 Standard Get File dialog

The **Eject** button in the dialog box allows the user to eject one disk from the drive and insert another. As disks are ejected and inserted, the MiniFinder keeps track of which disk is in the drive and displays its volume name above the **Eject** button; when the drive is empty, the **Eject** button becomes inactive. The **Drive** button switches the MiniFinder's attention from one disk drive to the other, or among the volumes on a hard disk or other multiple-volume device. (If there isn't an external disk drive connected to the Macintosh, the **Drive** button doesn't appear in the dialog box at all.)

Each time the user inserts a disk, the MiniFinder attempts to mount the new volume. If the attempt fails because of an error, it calls the Disk Initialization Package routine **DIBadMount** [8.4.1] to deal with the problem. For errors that can be corrected by initializing the disk, **DIBadMount** will post an alert such as the one shown in Figure 8-7, with the error message

This disk is unreadable

or

This disk is damaged

or

This is not a Macintosh disk

and will proceed to initialize or eject the disk, as instructed by the user. After successfully initializing a disk, it will ask the user to supply a volume name with the dialog box shown in Figure 8-8. For problems that can't be corrected by initializing the disk, **DIBadMount** will just eject it and return to the MiniFinder to wait for the user to insert another.

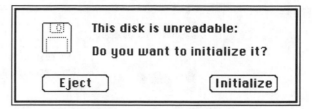

Figure 8-7 Disk initialization alert

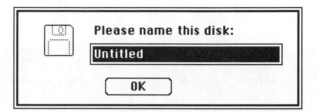

Figure 8-8 Volume name dialog

Program 8-5 (**DoOpen**) shows how our **MiniEdit** program uses **SFGetFile** to handle the **Open...** command on its **File** menu. Since **MiniEdit** operates only on plain text files, we just pass the single file type 'TEXT' in the type list, asking **SFGetFile** to list all text files on the disk. If the **good** field of the reply record comes back **FALSE**, then the user has canceled the **Open...** command and there's nothing further to do. If it's **TRUE**, we pass the file name and volume number from the reply record to another **MiniEdit** routine, **OpenFile** (Program 8-6), to open the selected file and read it into a new window on the screen.

OpenFile is factored out as a separate routine so that we can use it at the beginning of the program, to read in files the user has selected and opened from the Finder, as well as in response to the **Open...** command within **MiniEdit** itself. First we open the selected file with **FSOpen** [8.2.2], passing the file name and volume number and getting back a reference number for the file. Next we create a window for the file by calling our **DoNew** routine (Program 5-2), just as if the user had chosen the **New** command from the menu. After storing the volume and file reference numbers into the new window's data record and setting its title to the file name, we proceed to read the file's text into the window with the **DoRevert** routine we looked at earlier (Program 8-4).

```
{  Global constants  }

const
    DlgTop  = 100;                            {Top edge of dialog box for Get and Put dialogs}
    DlgLeft =  85;                            {Left edge of dialog box for Get and Put dialogs}


procedure DoOpen;

    {  Handle Open... command.  }


    var
        dlgOrigin   : Point;                  {Top-left corner of dialog box [I:4.1.1]}
        theTypeList : SFTypeList;             {List of file types to display [8.3.2]}
        theReply    : SFReply;                {Data returned by Get dialog [8.3.1]}


    begin {DoOpen}

        SetPt (dlgOrigin, DlgLeft, DlgTop);   {Set up dialog origin [I:4.1.1]}
        theTypeList [0] := 'TEXT';            {Display text files only [8.3.2]}

        SFGetFile (dlgOrigin, '', NIL, 1, theTypeList, NIL, theReply);  {Get file name from user [8.3.2]}

        with theReply do
            if good then                      {Did user confirm file selection? [8.3.1]}
                OpenFile (fName, vRefNum)     {Open file and read into window [Prog. 8-6]}

    end;  {DoOpen}
```

Program 8-5 Handle **Open...** command

```
{ Global variables }

var
   TheWindow : WindowPtr;                          {Pointer to currently active window [3.1.1]}
   ErrorFlag : BOOLEAN;                            {I/O error flag}


procedure OpenFile (fileName : Str255; vNum : INTEGER);

   { Open document file. }


   var
      theData    : WDHandle;                       {Handle to window's data record [Prog. 5-1]}
      dataHandle : Handle;                         {Untyped handle for locking data record [I:3.1.1]}
      theFile    : INTEGER;                        {Reference number of file}
      resultCode : OSErr;                          {I/O error code [I:3.1.2]}


   begin {OpenFile}
      resultCode := FSOpen (fileName, vNum, theFile);   {Open the file [8.2.2]}
      IOCheck (resultCode);                        {Check for error [Prog. 8-1]}
      if ErrorFlag then EXIT (OpenFile);           {On error, exit to main event loop}

      DoNew;                                       {Open a new window [Prog. 5-2]}

      dataHandle := Handle(GetWRefCon(TheWindow));  {Get window data [3.2.4]}
      HLock (dataHandle);                          {Lock data record [I:3.2.4]}

         theData := WDHandle(dataHandle);          {Convert to typed handle [Prog. 5-1]}
         with theData^^ do
            begin
               volNumber  := vNum;                 {Save volume and file number in  }
               fileNumber := theFile;              {   window data record [Prog. 5-1]}
               SetWTitle (TheWindow, fileName)     {File name becomes window title [3.2.4]}
            end; {with}

      HUnlock (dataHandle);                        {Unlock data record [I:3.2.4]}

      DoRevert                                     {Read file into window [Prog. 8-4]}

   end; {OpenFile}
```

Program 8-6 Open document file

We saw in Volume One, Chapter 7, how the Finder tells which document files to open at the start of the program by passing a table of *startup information*, located by way of a *startup handle* in the program's application global space. Program 8-7 (**DoStartup**) is called from the one-time **Initialize** routine at the very start of the **MiniEdit** program, to process the startup information and open the requested document files. First we call **CountAppFiles** [I:7.3.4] to find out how many documents the user selected (if any). **CountAppFiles** also returns a "message" telling whether the files were opened with the Finder's **Open** or **Print** command. Unfortunately, there isn't room in this book to talk about printing; so if the **Print** command was chosen, we just post an alert with the message

Sorry, MiniEdit doesn't support printing.

and exit back to the Finder.

If the user started up the **MiniEdit** program by selecting its icon directly, rather than by opening a document, then the number of documents you get back from **CountAppFiles** will be **0**: in this case, we just call our **DoNew** routine (Program 5-2) to open an empty window on the screen. If the number of documents is nonzero, we call **GetAppFiles** [I:7.3.4] once for each, receiving back an **AppFile** record [I:7.3.4] containing identifying information about the document file. Before opening the file, we first check to make sure it's a text file; if it isn't, we just post an alert message like

Sorry, file "Xanadu" is not a text file.

and loop back for the next document. If the file is a text file, we call **OpenFile** (Program 8-6) to open it and read it into a window. Finally we call **ClrAppFiles** [I:7.3.4] to notify the Finder that the file has been processed.

```
procedure DoStartup;

    { Process Finder startup information. }

    const
        cantPrintID = 1003;              {Resource ID for Can't Print alert}
        wrongTypeID = 1004;             {Resource ID for Wrong Type alert}


    var
        theMessage : INTEGER;           {Open or print? [I:7.3.4]}
        nDocs     : INTEGER;            {Number of documents selected in Finder}
        thisDoc   : INTEGER;            {Index number of document}
        docInfo   : AppFile;            {Startup information about one document [I:7.3.4]}
        ignore    : INTEGER;            {Item code returned by alert}
```

Program 8-7 Process Finder startup information

```
begin {DoStartup}

    CountAppFiles (theMessage, nDocs);              {Get number of documents and startup message [I:7.3.4]}

    if theMessage = AppPrint then                   {Did user choose Print in Finder? [I:7.3.4]}
        begin
            ignore := StopAlert (cantPrintID, NIL); {Post alert [7.4.2]}
            ExitToShell                             {Return to Finder [I:7.1.3]}
        end {if}

    else if nDocs = 0 then                          {If no documents selected, just    }
        DoNew                                       {   open an empty window [Prog. 5-2]}

    else
        for thisDoc := 1 to nDocs do                {Otherwise loop through documents}
            begin

                GetAppFiles (thisDoc, docInfo);     {Get startup information [I:7.3.4]}
                with docInfo do

                    if fType = 'TEXT' then           {Is it a text file?}
                        begin
                            OpenFile (fName, vRefNum);   {Read it into a window [Prog. 8-6]}
                            ClrAppFiles (thisDoc)        {Tell Finder it's been processed [I:7.3.4]}
                        end {then}

                    else
                        begin
                            ParamText (fName, '', '', '');  {Substitute file name into text of alert [7.4.6]}
                            ignore := StopAlert (wrongTypeID, NIL)  {Post alert [7.4.2]}
                        end {else}

            end {for}

end; {DoStartup}
```

Program 8-7 (*continued*)

File to Write To

The MiniFinder routine **SFPutFile** [8.3.3] displays the dialog box shown in Figure 8-9, asking for the name of a file to be written. The prompting string that appears above the dialog's text box is a parameter you supply when you call the routine. The **Eject** and **Drive** buttons work the same way as in the Get File dialog. The user can do the usual selection and typing in the text box, then confirm the file name with the **Save** button (or the return or enter key) or cancel the operation with the **Cancel** button. **SFPutFile** will then return a reply record containing the specified file name and volume number, with the **good** field set to **TRUE** if the dialog was confirmed, **FALSE** if it was canceled.

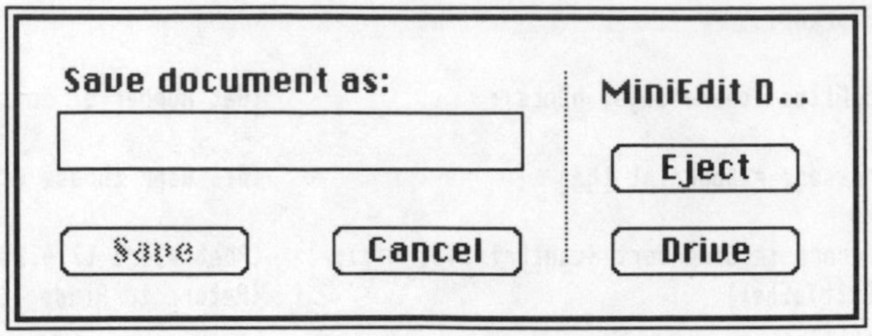

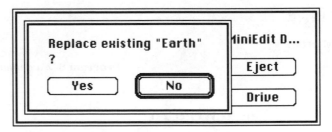

Figure 8-9 Standard Put File dialog

If the user specifies a file name that already exists on the disk, **SFPutFile** will display the alert shown in Figure 8-10. If the user clicks the **No** button, the Put File dialog will remain on the screen so the user can change the file name and try again; if **Yes**, the Put File dialog will be dismissed and the specified file name returned to you in the reply record. Even so, however, the recommended policy is *not* to replace the existing file unless it's of an appropriate file type for your own program. Don't let the user destroy other programs or their files by saving a document named, say, **MacPaint** or **Finder** or **System**.

Program 8-8 (**DoSaveAs**) illustrates this last point. In response to the **Save As...** command, we begin by calling **SFPutFile** to get a file name from the user. If the resulting reply record has its **good** field set to **FALSE**, then the user has canceled the command: we just set the global error flag, clear the **Quitting** flag in case we've reached this routine as part of a **Quit** sequence, and exit. If the **good** field is **TRUE**, our next step is to ask for the designated file's Finder information with **GetFInfo** [I:7.3.3].

Figure 8-10 Existing file alert

```
{ Global declarations }

const
   DlgTop = 100;                                   {Top edge of dialog box for Get and Put dialogs}
   DlgLeft = 85;                                   {Left edge of dialog box for Get and Put dialogs}

var
   TheWindow : WindowPtr;                          {Pointer to currently active window [3.1.1]}
   Watch     : CursHandle;                         {Handle to wristwatch cursor [2.5.1]}
   Quitting  : BOOLEAN;                            {Quit command in effect?}
   ErrorFlag : BOOLEAN;                            {I/O error flag}


procedure DoSaveAs;

   { Handle Save As... command.  }

   const
      wrongTypeID = 1004;                          {Resource ID for Wrong File Type alert}
      noTitleID   = 1000;                          {Resource ID of title string for empty window}

   var
      dlgOrigin  : Point;                          {Top-left corner of dialog box [I:4.1.1]}
      theReply   : SFReply;                        {Data returned by Put dialog [8.3.1]}
      theInfo    : FInfo;                          {File's Finder information [I:7.3.2]}
      theFile    : INTEGER;                        {Reference number of file}
      theData    : WDHandle;                       {Handle to window's data record [Prog. 5-1]}
      dataHandle : Handle;                         {Untyped handle for locking data record [I:3.1.1]}
      strHandle  : StringHandle;                   {Handle to title string for empty window [I:8.1.2]}
      untitled   : Str255;                         {Title string for empty window [I:2.1.1]}
      ignore     : INTEGER;                        {Item code returned by alert}
      resultCode : OSErr;                          {I/O error code [I:3.1.2]}

   begin {DoSaveAs}

      SetPt     (dlgOrigin, DlgLeft, DlgTop);      {Set up dialog origin [I:4.1.1]}
      SFPutFile (dlgOrigin, 'Save under what file name?', '', NIL, theReply);
                                                   {Get file name from user [8.3.3]}

      with theReply do
         begin
            if not good then                       {Did user confirm file selection? [8.3.1]}
               begin
                  Quitting  := FALSE;              {Cancel Quit command, if any}
                  ErrorFlag := TRUE;               {Force exit to main event loop}
                  EXIT (DoSaveAs)                  {Skip rest of operation}
               end; {if}
```

Program 8-8 Handle **Save As...** command

```
resultCode := GetFInfo (fName, vRefNum, theInfo);   {Get Finder info [I:7.3.3]}
case resultCode of

   NoErr:                                 {File already exists [8.2.8]}
      if theInfo.fdType <> 'TEXT' then    {Not a text file? [I:7.3.2]}
         begin
            ParamText (fName, '', '', '');  {Substitute file name into text of alert [7.4.6]}
            ignore := StopAlert (wrongTypeID, NIL);  {Post alert [7.4.2]}

            ErrorFlag := TRUE;            {Force exit to main event loop}
            EXIT (DoSaveAs)              {Skip rest of operation}
         end; {if}

   FNFErr:                                {File not found [8.2.8]}
      begin
         resultCode := Create (fName, vRefNum, 'MEDT', 'TEXT');  {Create the file [8.2.1]}
         IOCheck (resultCode);           {Check for error [Prog. 8-1]}
         if ErrorFlag then EXIT (DoSaveAs)  {On error, exit to main event loop}
      end;

   otherwise                             {Unanticipated error}
      begin
         IOCheck (resultCode);           {Post error alert [Prog. 8.1]}
         EXIT (DoSaveAs)                 {Exit to main event loop}
      end

   end; {case}

dataHandle := Handle(GetWRefCon(TheWindow));  {Get window data [3.2.4]}
HLock (dataHandle);                      {Lock data record [I:3.2.4]}

   theData := WDHandle(dataHandle);      {Convert to typed handle}
   with theData^^ do
      begin

         SetCursor (Watch^^);            {Indicate delay [2.5.2]}
```

Program 8-8 (continued)

```
if fileNumber <> 0 then              {Does window already have a file? [Prog. 5-1]}
    begin
        resultCode := FSClose (fileNumber);  {Close old file [8.2.2]}
        IOCheck (resultCode);        {Check for error [Prog. 8-1]}
        if ErrorFlag then            {Error detected during close?}
            begin
                HUnlock (dataHandle);  {Unlock data record [I:3.2.4]}
                EXIT (DoSaveAs)      {Exit to main event loop}
            end {if}
    end; {if}

resultCode := FSOpen (fName, vRefNum, theFile);  {Open new file [8.2.2]}
IOCheck (resultCode);                {Check for error [Prog. 8-1]}
if ErrorFlag then                    {Error detected during open?}
    begin
        volNumber  := 0;                     {Window is left with no file:  clear volume and}
        fileNumber := 0;                     {   file numbers in window data [Prog. 5-1]    }

        strHandle := GetString (noTitleID);  {Get string from resource file [I:8.1.2]}
        untitled  := strHandle^^;            {Convert from handle}
        SetWTitle (TheWindow, untitled)      {Set new window title [3.2.4]}
    end {then}

else
    begin
        volNumber  := vRefNum;       {Save new volume and file numbers }
        fileNumber := theFile;       {   in window data [Prog. 5-1]     }
        SetWTitle (TheWindow, fName);  {File name becomes new window title [3.2.4]}

        WriteFile (theFile, vRefNum)  {Write window's contents to file [Prog. 8-3]}
    end {else}

        end; {with}

    HUnlock (dataHandle)                      {Unlock data record [I:3.2.4]}

end {with}

end; {DoSaveAs}
```

Program 8-8 (*continued*)

A result code of **NoErr** from **GetFInfo** means that the file already exists. We want to go ahead and write to it only if it's a text file; if the file type in the Finder information record is anything other than 'TEXT', we'll post an alert with the message

Sorry, file "Frumble" is not a text file.

and exit. If there *isn't* a previously existing file with the given name, **GetFInfo** will return a result code of **FNFErr** ("file not found"); in this case, we just create a new file with the given name—giving it a file type of 'TEXT' and a creator signature of 'MEDT' (for "MiniEdit")—and proceed. On any other result code, we call **IOCheck** (Program 8-1) to post an error alert, then exit to the main event loop.

Assuming we have a valid file name to write to, our next step is to check whether the active window already has an existing file associated with it; if so, we call **FSClose** [8.2.2] to close that file before opening the new one. Then we open the new file with **FSOpen** [8.2.2], store its volume and file reference numbers into the active window's data record and its file name as the window's title, and call our earlier **WriteFile** routine (Program 8-3) to write the window's contents to the file. (If an error occurs while opening the file, the active window will be left without a file—so we set its volume and file numbers to **0** and its title to **untitled**, the same as a brand-new window created by our **DoNew** routine. Notice that, following recommended Macintosh practice, we define this standard title string as a resource and use **GetString** [I:8.1.2] to read it in. The window template used by **DoNew** contains this same string in its title field.)

Nuts and Bolts

Recall from Volume One, Chapter 6, that every file actually consists of two separate parts, or "forks": a *data fork* and a *resource fork*. The **FSOpen** routine just opens the file's data fork, which is normally what you want. There's also a routine named **OpenRF** [8.2.2] for opening the resource fork. This allows you to access the resource fork directly as a stream of "raw" bytes, with no notion of its internal structure as a collection of resources. The Toolbox itself uses this routine to read and write resources; you'll ordinarily want to use **OpenResFile** [I:6.2.1] instead, to access the resource fork at the resource level rather than the byte level.

Associated with every file is *permission* information about the kind of access that's allowed to the file: read-only, write-only, or read/write. Read-only files can actually be opened more than once, creating any number of separate *access paths* to the same file. Each access path has its own reference number and its own independent file mark; what we've been calling the file reference number is technically a "path reference number." A file with write permission, however, can only be opened once: if you try to open a second access path to the file, you'll get back the same reference number as the first time, along with the error code **OpWrErr** ("already open for writing").

When you use the low-level file system, you can specify the kind of access permission you want for each access path independently, provided that the file's own permission information allows the type of access requested. (If it doesn't, you'll get back the "permission violation" error code, **PermErr**, when you try to open the path.) You're allowed to have any number of access paths for reading the same file, but not more than one for writing to it. This degree of flexibility isn't possible with the high-level file system: the high-level routine **FSOpen** always gives every access path the same permission, whatever the file itself allows. Since there's no way to open a read-only path to a read/write file, you can't have more than one path altogether for such a file.

REFERENCE

8.1 Volume Operations

8.1.1 Volume Information

Definitions

```
function GetVInfo
    (drive         : INTEGER;      {Drive number}
     vName         : StringPtr;    {Volume name}
 var vRefNum       : INTEGER;      {Returns volume reference number}
 var freeBytes     : LONGINT)      {Returns number of free bytes on volume}
     : OSErr;                      {Result code}
```

Notes

1. **GetVInfo** returns identifying information for the volume in a specified disk drive.

2. The **drive** parameter identifies the disk drive: **1** for the internal (built-in) drive, **2** for the external drive, if any. Drive numbers greater than **2** refer to additional disk drives or other storage devices connected through a serial port.

3. The name of the volume in the specified drive is returned via parameter **vName** and its volume reference number via **vRefNum**.

4. Parameter **freeBytes** returns the number of bytes of free space available on the volume.

5. This routine is part of the high-level file system and is not directly available from assembly language. The trap macro calls the low-level routine **PBGetVInfo**; see *Inside Macintosh* for details.

6. The trap macro is spelled **_GetVolInfo**.

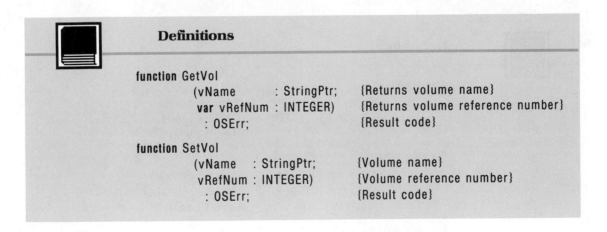

Assembly-Language Information

Trap macro:

(Pascal) Routine name	(Assembly) Trap macro	Trap word
PBGetVInfo	**_GetVolInfo**	**$A007**

8.1.2 Current Volume

Definitions

```
function GetVol
        (vName       : StringPtr;       {Returns volume name}
        var vRefNum : INTEGER)          {Returns volume reference number}
        : OSErr;                        {Result code}

function SetVol
        (vName     : StringPtr;         {Volume name}
        vRefNum : INTEGER)              {Volume reference number}
        : OSErr;                        {Result code}
```

Notes

1. **GetVol** returns the name and volume reference number of the current volume; **SetVol** makes a designated volume the current volume.

2. The volume to be made current can be identified either by name or by reference number. The **vRefNum** parameter to **SetVol** is ignored unless **vName** is **NIL**.

3. The volume designated by **vName** or **vRefNum** must be a mounted volume.

4. These routines are part of the high-level file system and are not directly available from assembly language. The trap macros call the low-level routines **PBGetVol** and **PBSetVol**; see *Inside Macintosh* for details.

Assembly-Language Information

Trap macros:

(Pascal) Routine name	(Assembly) Trap macro	Trap word
PBGetVol	**_GetVol**	**$A014**
PBSetVol	**_SetVol**	**$A015**

8.1.3 Flushing, Ejecting, and Unmounting

Definitions

```
function FlushVol
        (vName    : StringPtr;      {Volume name}
         vRefNum  : INTEGER)        {Volume reference number}
         : OSErr;                   {Result code}

function Eject
        (vName    : StringPtr;      {Volume name}
         vRefNum  : INTEGER)        {Volume reference number}
         : OSErr;                   {Result code}

function UnmountVol
        (vName    : StringPtr;      {Volume name}
         vRefNum  : INTEGER)        {Volume reference number}
         : OSErr;                   {Result code}
```

Notes

1. **FlushVol** writes out the contents of a volume buffer from memory to the disk; **Eject** places a volume logically off-line and physically ejects it from the disk drive; **UnmountVol** unmounts a volume, removing all trace of it from the file system.

2. In each case, the volume to be operated on can be identified either by name or by reference number. The **vRefNum** parameter is ignored unless **vName** is **NIL**.

3. The volume designated by **vName** or **vRefNum** must be a mounted volume.

4. There is no high-level routine for explicitly mounting a volume, since the Toolbox handles this task automatically whenever a disk is inserted.

5. In addition to the contents of the volume buffer, **FlushVol** also writes out the directory information describing the volume's contents if it has changed since the volume was last mounted or flushed.

6. Before physically ejecting the volume, **Eject** flushes the volume buffer and directory information and releases most of the memory space they occupy. A small amount of directory information (94 bytes) is retained in memory, so that the volume and its contents remain known to the file system.

7. **UnmountVol** removes all information pertaining to a volume from memory and releases the space it occupies. All open files on the volume are closed, its volume buffer and directory information are flushed, and the volume is physically ejected from the disk drive. The volume and its contents become unknown to the file system.

8. The startup volume should never be unmounted; it contains important system information that must remain accessible at all times, such as the Finder and the system resource file.

9. These routines are part of the high-level file system and are not directly available from assembly language. The trap macros call the low-level routines **PBFlushVol**, **PBEject** and **PBUnmountVol**; there are also low-level routines named **PBOffLine**, for placing a volume off-line without physically ejecting it, and **PBMountVol**, for explicitly mounting a volume. See *Inside Macintosh* for details.

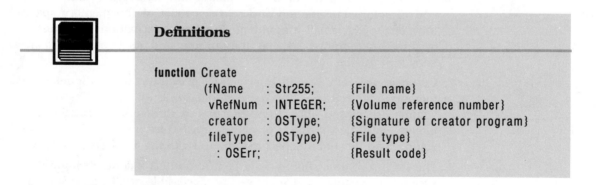

Assembly-Language Information

Trap macros:

(Pascal) Routine name	(Assembly) Trap macro	Trap word
PBFlushVol	_FlushVol	$A013
PBEject	_Eject	$A017
PBOffLine	_OffLine	$A035
PBMountVol	_MountVol	$A00F
PBUnmountVol	_UnmountVol	$A00E

8.2 File Operations

8.2.1 Creating Files

Definitions

```
function Create
        (fName    : Str255;      {File name}
         vRefNum  : INTEGER;     {Volume reference number}
         creator  : OSType;      {Signature of creator program}
         fileType : OSType)      {File type}
         : OSErr;                {Result code}
```

Notes

1. This routine creates a new file with a given name on a specified volume.

2. The new file is initially unlocked and empty.

3. The file's creation and modification dates are set from the built-in clock chip.

4. The parameters **creator** and **fileType** give the new file's creator signature and file type [I:7.3.1] for use by the Finder.

5. The new file is not opened and is not assigned a file reference number. Call **FSOpen** [8.2.2] after **Create** to open the file for writing.

6. If the volume already contains a file with the given name, the error code **DupFNErr** ("duplicate file name") [8.2.8] is returned and no new file is created.

7. This routine is part of the high-level file system and is not directly available from assembly language. The trap macro calls the low-level routine **PBCreate**; see *Inside Macintosh* for details.

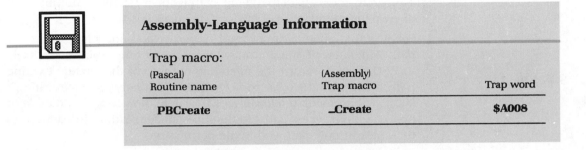

Assembly-Language Information

Trap macro:

(Pascal) Routine name	(Assembly) Trap macro	Trap word
PBCreate	_Create	**$A008**

8.2.2 Opening and Closing Files

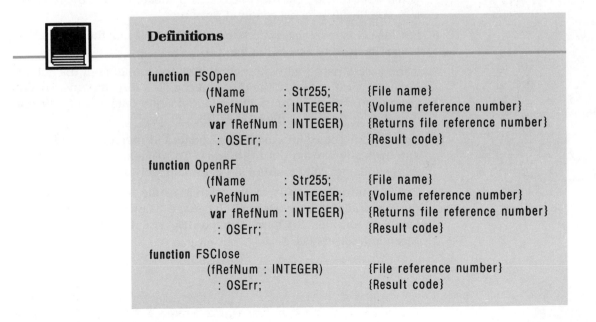

Definitions

```
function FSOpen
        (fName       : Str255;        {File name}
         vRefNum     : INTEGER;       {Volume reference number}
         var fRefNum : INTEGER)       {Returns file reference number}
         : OSErr;                     {Result code}

function OpenRF
        (fName       : Str255;        {File name}
         vRefNum     : INTEGER;       {Volume reference number}
         var fRefNum : INTEGER)       {Returns file reference number}
         : OSErr;                     {Result code}

function FSClose
        (fRefNum : INTEGER)           {File reference number}
         : OSErr;                     {Result code}
```

Notes

1. **FSOpen** opens an existing file for reading or writing.

2. The file is identified by name and volume reference number.

3. The file is assigned a file reference number, returned via the variable parameter **fRefNum**. You then use this number to identify the file for all further operations.

4. For files that allow read permission only, each call to **FSOpen** creates a separate *access path* to the file, with its own reference number and its own independent read position, or *mark* [8.2.4].

5. For files that allow write or read/write permission, only one access path with such permission may be open at a time. Subsequent calls to **FSOpen** will return the reference number of the already existing path, along with the error code **OpWrErr** ("already open for writing") [8.2.8]. (When using the low-level file system, however, it's possible to open multiple access paths to the same file for reading, in addition to the one and only path with write permission.)

6. **OpenRF** opens a file's resource fork instead of its data fork.

7. **OpenRF** is used by the Toolbox itself, to access the contents of the resource fork directly at the "raw" byte level. For most purposes you'll want to use **OpenResFile** [I:6.2.1] instead, to treat the resource fork specifically as a collection of resources.

8. **FSClose** closes an access path to a file. Once closed, the path can no longer be used to access the file.

9. If the access path had write permission, the contents of the volume buffer are written out to the disk and the file's directory information is updated. In particular, the file's modification date is set to the current date and time on the built-in clock chip.

10. The file's directory information is updated in memory only; it is *not* automatically written out to the disk. To make sure the disk is correctly updated, call **FlushVol** [8.1.3] immediately after closing the file.

11. These routines are part of the high-level file system and are not directly available from assembly language. The trap macros call the low-level routines **PBOpen**, **PBOpenRF**, and **PBClose**; see *Inside Macintosh* for details.

Assembly-Language Information

Trap macros:

(Pascal) Routine name	(Assembly) Trap macro	Trap word
PBOpen	_Open	**$A000**
PBOpenRF	_OpenRF	**$A00A**
PBClose	_Close	**$A001**

8.2.3 Reading and Writing

Definitions

```
function FSRead
        (fRefNum      : INTEGER;      {File reference number}
        var byteCount : LONGINT;      {Number of bytes to read}
        toAddr        : Ptr)          {Address to read to}
         : OSErr;                     {Result code}

function FSWrite
        (fRefNum      : INTEGER;      {File reference number}
        var byteCount : LONGINT;      {Number of bytes to write}
        fromAddr      : Ptr)          {Address to write from}
         : OSErr;                     {Result code}
```

Notes

1. These routines transfer information to or from a file.

2. The number of bytes specified by **byteCount** are read to or written from consecutive locations in memory, beginning at the address designated by the pointer **toAddr** or **fromAddr**.

3. The transfer begins at the current position of the file's mark; as the transfer proceeds, the mark is advanced to consecutive positions within the file.

4. If the mark reaches the logical end-of-file during a write, the logical end-of-file begins to advance in step with the mark, lengthening the file as it goes. New allocation blocks are added to the file as needed, advancing the physical end-of-file accordingly.

5. If the mark reaches the logical end-of-file during a read, the operation terminates and the error code **EOFErr** [8.2.8] is returned. The mark is left positioned at the logical end-of-file.

6. On completion of either a read or a write, the **byteCount** parameter returns the number of bytes actually transferred.

7. These routines are part of the high-level file system and are not directly available from assembly language. The trap macros call the low-level routines **PBRead** and **PBWrite**; see *Inside Macintosh* for details.

Assembly-Language Information

Trap macros:

(Pascal) Routine name	(Assembly) Trap macro	Trap word
PBRead	**_Read**	**$A002**
PBWrite	**_Write**	**$A003**

8.2.4 File Mark

Definitions

```
function GetFPos
        (fRefNum   : INTEGER;        {File reference number}
         var markPos : LONGINT)       {Returns current mark position in bytes}
         : OSErr;                      {Result code}

function SetFPos
        (fRefNum   : INTEGER;        {File reference number}
         markBase  : INTEGER;        {Base to set mark from}
         markOffset : LONGINT)        {Offset in bytes relative to base}
         : OSErr;                      {Result code}

const
  FSAtMark    = 0;                   {Position at current mark}
  FSFromStart = 1;                   {Position relative to start of file}
  FSFromLEOF  = 2;                   {Position relative to logical end-of-file}
  FSFromMark  = 3;                   {Position relative to current mark}
```

Notes

1. **GetFPos** returns the current byte position of a file's mark in the variable parameter **markPos**; **SetFPos** sets the position of the mark.

2. All reading and writing takes place at the mark.

3. The new position of the mark is given as an offset relative to a specified base position within the file.

4. The offset (**markOffset**) may be positive (toward the end of the file) or negative (toward the beginning).

5. The base position (**markBase**) may be the beginning of the file (**FSFromStart**), the logical end-of-file (**FSFromLEOF**), or the current mark position (**FSFromMark**).

6. A base position of **FSAtMark** refers unconditionally to the current mark position; the offset is ignored. Thus a call to **SetFPos** with **markBase** equal to **FSAtMark** has no effect at all.

7. If the specified position is beyond the logical end-of-file, the mark is positioned at the logical end-of-file and the error code **EOFErr** [8.2.8] is returned.

8. If the specified position is negative (before the beginning of the file), the mark is positioned at the beginning of the file and the error code **PosErr** ("position error") [8.2.8] is returned.

9. These routines are part of the high-level file system and are not directly available from assembly language. The trap macros call the low-level routines **PBGetFPos** and **PBSetFPos**; see *Inside Macintosh* for details.

Assembly-Language Information

Trap macros:

(Pascal) Routine name	(Assembly) Trap macro	Trap word
PBGetFPos	**_GetFPos**	**$A018**
PBSetFPos	**_SetFPos**	**$A044**

8.2.5 End-of-File

Definitions

```
function GetEOF
        (fRefNum      : INTEGER;        {File reference number}
    var logicalEOF : LONGINT)       {Returns current logical end-of-file in bytes}
        : OSErr;                    {Result code}

function SetEOF
        (fRefNum    : INTEGER;          {File reference number}
    logicalEOF : LONGINT)           {New logical end-of-file in bytes}
        : OSErr;                    {Result code}

function Allocate
        (fRefNum       : INTEGER;       {File reference number}
    var byteCount : LONGINT)        {Number of bytes to allocate}
        : OSErr;                    {Result code}
```

Notes

1. **GetEOF** returns the current byte position of a file's logical end-of-file; **SetEOF** sets it.

2. If the logical end-of-file is set beyond the current physical end-of-file, the file is lengthened by adding new allocation blocks at the end.

3. If the logical end-of-file is set more than one full allocation block short of the physical end-of-file, the file is shortened by releasing unneeded allocation blocks from the end.

4. Setting the logical end-of-file to **0** releases all disk space associated with the file.

5. **Allocate** adds enough new allocation blocks to the end of a file to lengthen it physically by at least a specified number of bytes.

6. Notice that the amount of disk space to be added to the file is expressed in *bytes*, not in allocation blocks or disk sectors. The value given for **byteCount** will be rounded upward to the next whole number of allocation blocks.

7. The actual number of bytes added to the file is returned via this same **byteCount** parameter.

8. **Allocate** has no effect on the logical end-of-file.

9. If there isn't enough free space on the volume to lengthen the file as requested, both **SetEOF** and **Allocate** return the error code **DskFul-Err** ("disk full") [8.2.8]. In this case, **SetEOF** doesn't allocate any additional space to the file and leaves its logical end-of-file unchanged; **Allocate** allocates all available space on the volume.

10. These routines are part of the high-level file system and are not directly available from assembly language. The trap macros call the low-level routines **PBGetEOF**, **PBSetEOF** and **PBAllocate**; see *Inside Macintosh* for details.

Assembly-Language Information

Trap macros:

(Pascal) Routine name	(Assembly) Trap macro	Trap word
PBGetEOF	**_GetEOF**	**$A011**
PBSetEOF	**_SetEOF**	**$A012**
PBAllocate	**_Allocate**	**$A010**

8.2.6 Locking and Unlocking Files

Definitions

```
function SetFLock
        (fName    : Str255;      {File name}
         vRefNum : INTEGER)      {Volume reference number}
         : OSErr;                {Result code}

function RstFLock
        (fName    : Str255;      {File name}
         vRefNum : INTEGER)      {Volume reference number}
         : OSErr;                {Result code}
```

Notes

1. **SetFLock** locks a file; **RstFLock** ("reset file lock") unlocks it.

2. A locked file can't be opened for writing; it also can't be deleted or renamed.

3. Locking or unlocking a file only affects subsequent attempts to open an access path to the file for writing; it has no effect on existing access paths.

4. Since the file is identified by volume and file name rather than by reference number, it needn't be open in order to lock or unlock it.

5. These routines are part of the high-level file system and are not directly available from assembly language. The trap macros call the low-level routines **PBSetFLock** and **PBRstFLock**; see *Inside Macintosh* for details.

6. The trap macros are spelled **_SetFilLock** and **_RstFilLock**.

Assembly-Language Information

Trap macros:

(Pascal) Routine name	(Assembly) Trap macro	Trap word
PBSetFLock	**_SetFilLock**	**$A041**
PBRstFLock	**_RstFilLock**	**$A042**

8.2.7 Deleting and Renaming Files

Definitions

```
function FSDelete
        (fName    : Str255;      {File name}
         vRefNum  : INTEGER)     {Volume reference number}
         : OSErr;                {Result code}

function Rename
        (oldName  : Str255;      {Old file name}
         vRefNum  : INTEGER;     {Volume reference number}
         newName  : Str255)      {New file name}
         : OSErr;                {Result code}
```

Notes

1. **FSDelete** removes a file from its volume; **Rename** changes its name.

2. Deleting a file removes both its data and resource forks.

3. A file must be closed in order to delete it. If there are any access paths open to the file, the error code **FBsyErr** ("file busy") [8.2.8] is returned and the file is not deleted.

4. A file can be renamed whether it's open or closed. Existing access paths are not affected.

5. If **oldName** is the name of a volume rather than a file, the volume will be renamed.

6. A locked file cannot be deleted or renamed.

7. These routines are part of the high-level file system and are not directly available from assembly language. The trap macros call the low-level routines **PBDelete** and **PBRename**; see *Inside Macintosh* for details.

Assembly-Language Information

Trap macros:

(Pascal) Routine name	(Assembly) Trap macro	Trap word
PBDelete	_Delete	$A009
PBRename	_Rename	$A00B

8.2.8 Error Reporting

Definitions

```
const
  NoErr        =    0;    {No error}

  DirFulErr    = −33;     {Directory full}
  DskFulErr    = −34;     {Disk full}
  NSVErr       = −35;     {No such volume}
  IOErr        = −36;     {Disk I/O error}
  BdNamErr     = −37;     {Bad name}
  FNOpnErr     = −38;     {File not open}
  EOFErr       = −39;     {Attempt to read past end-of-file}
  PosErr       = −40;     {Attempt to position before start of file}
  MFulErr      = −41;     {Memory (system heap) full}
  TMFOErr      = −42;     {Too many files open (more than 12)}
  FNFErr       = −43;     {File not found}
  WPrErr       = −44;     {Disk is write-protected}
  FLckdErr     = −45;     {File locked}
  VLckdErr     = −46;     {Volume locked}
  FBsyErr      = −47;     {File busy}
  DupFNErr     = −48;     {Duplicate file name}
  OpWrErr      = −49;     {File already open for writing}
  ParamErr     = −50;     {Invalid parameter list}
  RfNumErr     = −51;     {Invalid reference number}
  GFPErr       = −52;     {Error during GetFPos}
  VolOffLinErr = −53;     {Volume off-line}
  PermErr      = −54;     {Permission violation}
  VolOnLinErr  = −55;     {Volume already on-line}
  NSDrvErr     = −56;     {No such drive}
  NoMacDskErr  = −57;     {Non-Macintosh disk}
  ExtFSErr     = −58;     {External file system}
  FSRnErr      = −59;     {Unable to rename file}
  BadMDBErr    = −60;     {Bad master directory block}
  WrPermErr    = −61;     {No write permission}

  FirstDskErr  = −84;     {Low-level disk error}
  LastDskErr   = −64;     {Low-level disk error}
```

Notes

1. A result code of **0** (**NoErr**) signals that an operation was completed successfully.

2. Any result code between **FirstDskErr** and **LastDskErr**, inclusive, denotes a low-level disk error of some sort. See Appendix E for a complete listing of these low-level error codes.

3. In assembly language, the result code is returned in the low-order word of register **D0**.

4. The assembly-language constants for the various result codes have the same names and values listed above.

8.3 The MiniFinder

8.3.1 Reply Records

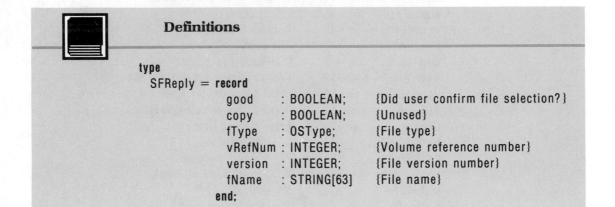

Definitions

```
type
  SFReply = record
              good     : BOOLEAN;      {Did user confirm file selection?}
              copy     : BOOLEAN;      {Unused}
              fType    : OSType;       {File type}
              vRefNum  : INTEGER;      {Volume reference number}
              version  : INTEGER;      {File version number}
              fName    : STRING[63]    {File name}
            end;
```

Notes

1. A reply record is the data structure through which the MiniFinder returns information about a file selected by the user to be read or written.

2. The **good** field tells whether the user confirmed or canceled the file selection. It will be **TRUE** if the selection was confirmed with the **Open** or **Save** button (or their equivalents), **FALSE** if the selection was canceled with the **Cancel** button.

3. **fType** is the Finder file type [I:7.3.1] of the selected file. The contents of this field are meaningful only for a file to be read [8.3.2], not for one to be written [8.3.3].

4. **vRefNum** is the volume reference number of the volume containing the selected file.

5. The current MiniFinder does not support file version numbers; the **version** field of the reply record is always set to **0**.

6. **fName** is the name of the selected file.

7. The **fName** field, and hence the overall reply record, is actually of variable length, just long enough to hold the specified file name. The field is in Pascal string format, with a 1-byte length count followed by the actual characters of the file name.

8. Notice that the MiniFinder limits the length of file names to not more than 63 characters, even though the file system itself will accept file names of up to 255 characters.

9. Reply records are part of the Standard File Package, and are defined in the interface file **PackIntf**. See Volume One, Chapter 7, for further information on the package mechanism.

Assembly-Language Information

Field offsets in a reply record:

(Pascal) Field name	(Assembly) Offset name	Offset in bytes
good	**rGood**	**0**
fType	**rType**	**2**
vRefNum	**rVolume**	**6**
version	**rVersion**	**8**
fName	**rName**	**10**

8.3.2 File to Read From

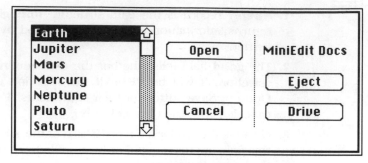

Get File dialog

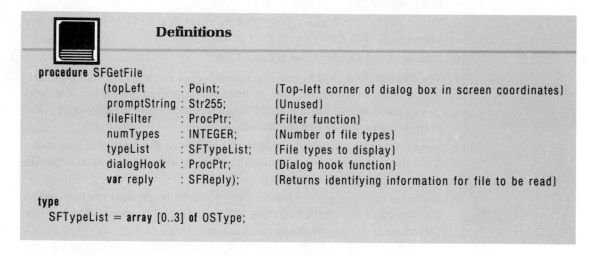

Definitions

```
procedure SFGetFile
          (topLeft       : Point;         {Top-left corner of dialog box in screen coordinates}
           promptString  : Str255;        {Unused}
           fileFilter    : ProcPtr;       {Filter function}
           numTypes      : INTEGER;       {Number of file types}
           typeList      : SFTypeList;    {File types to display}
           dialogHook    : ProcPtr;       {Dialog hook function}
       var reply         : SFReply);      {Returns identifying information for file to be read}

type
  SFTypeList = array [0..3] of OSType;
```

Notes

1. **SFGetFile** displays the dialog box shown in the figure, allowing the user to select a file to be read from the disk.

2. You supply an existing reply record [8.3.1] as the **reply** parameter; **SFGetFile** will fill in the fields of this record with identifying information about the selected file.

3. **SFGetFile** handles all events until the user dismisses the dialog box, either by clicking the **Open** or **Cancel** button or by double-clicking a file name.

4. The **topLeft** parameter gives the location of the dialog box in *global* (*screen*) *coordinates*. The dialog box is 348 pixels wide by 136 high.

5. The user selects a file by clicking the file name with the mouse and clicking the **Open** button, or just by double-clicking the file name. **SFGetFile** will then set the **good** field of the reply record to **TRUE** and the **fName**, **vRefNum**, and **fType** fields to refer to the file selected.

6. The **version** field is always set to **0**.

7. If the user dismisses the dialog with the **Cancel** button, the **good** field is set to **FALSE** and the remaining fields are undefined.

8. Scrolling of the file list is handled automatically when the user manipulates the scroll bar with the mouse. If the file list is short enough to be displayed all at once, the scroll bar is deactivated.

9. If the user types a character on the keyboard, the first file name beginning with that character is automatically selected as if it had been clicked with the mouse. If there are no file names beginning with that character, the first one starting with a higher character code [I:8.1.1] is selected.

10. The **Open** button is automatically deactivated when no file is selected in the file list.

11. The **Eject** button ejects the disk currently in the disk drive; when no disk is in the drive, this button is deactivated.

12. The **Drive** button switches attention between the internal and external disk drives, or among the available volumes on a multiple-volume device such as a hard disk. If only one volume is on-line (for instance, if there's no disk in the other drive), this button is deactivated; if no external disk drive is connected, the button is not displayed.

13. All disk-inserted events are handled automatically. The volume name of the disk currently in the drive is displayed above the **Eject** button in the dialog box.

14. If an uninitialized or otherwise unreadable disk is inserted, **DIBadMount** [8.4.1] is called to allow the user to initialize it.

15. **typeList** is a list of up to four file types [I:7.3.1]; **numTypes** tells how many. Only files of the specified types will be displayed in the dialog box for selection.

16. Even files that are flagged as invisible on the Finder desktop [I:7.3.2] will be displayed in the file list.

17. If **numTypes** $= -1$, all files on the disk will be displayed, regardless of type.

18. **fileFilter** is a pointer to an optional *filter function* that you can use to selectively omit files of the specified types from the file list. This function accepts one parameter, a pointer to a parameter block of the kind used by the low-level file system (see *Inside Macintosh*). It returns a Boolean result of **TRUE** if the file should be omitted from the displayed file list, **FALSE** if it should be included. If the **fileFilter** parameter is **NIL**, no extra filtering will be performed.

19. The **dialogHook** parameter is used for replacing the standard dialog box with a nonstandard one of your own, or for handling the standard one in a nonstandard way; see *Inside Macintosh* for details. Pass **NIL** for this parameter to use the standard dialog as described above.

20. The **promptString** parameter is a vestige of earlier versions of the MiniFinder, and is no longer used.

21. **SFGetFile** is part of the Standard File Package, and is defined in the interface file **PackIntf**. See Volume One, Chapter 7, for further information on the package mechanism.

22. The trap macro for this routine expands to call **_Pack3** [I:7.2.1] with the routine selector given below.

Assembly-Language Information

Trap macro and routine selector:

(Pascal) Routine name	(Assembly) Trap macro	Trap word	Routine selector
SFGetFile	**_SFGetFile**	**$A9EA**	**2**

8.3.3 File to Write To

Put File dialog

Definitions

procedure SFPutFile
     (topLeft   : Point;   {Top-left corner of dialog box in screen coordinates}
     promptString : Str255;   {Prompting string}
     initText   : Str255;   {Initial contents of text box}
     dialogHook   : ProcPtr;   {Dialog hook function}
     var reply   : SFReply);   {Returns identifying information for file to be written}

Notes

1. **SFPutFile** displays the dialog box shown in the figure, allowing the user to supply a file name for writing to the disk.

2. You supply an existing reply record [8.3.1] as the **reply** parameter; **SFPutFile** will fill in the fields of this record with the identifying information supplied by the user.

3. **SFPutFile** handles all events until the user dismisses the dialog box, either by clicking the **Save** or **Cancel** button or by pressing the return or enter key.

4. The **topLeft** parameter gives the location of the dialog box in *global (screen) coordinates*. The dialog box is 304 pixels wide by 104 high.

5. The user supplies a file name by typing it into the dialog's text box and either clicking the **Save** button or pressing the return or enter key. **SFPutFile** will then set the **good** field of the reply record to **TRUE** and the **fName** and **vRefNum** fields to the specified file name and volume reference number.

6. The **fType** field is unused and should be ignored; the **version** field is always set to **0**.

7. If the user dismisses the dialog with the **Cancel** button, the **good** field is set to **FALSE** and the remaining fields are undefined.

8. The text box supports standard text selection with the mouse (including extended selection with the shift key and double-click word selection), text insertion and replacement from the keyboard, and deletion with the backspace key.

9. The command key is ignored; if you want to support command-key combinations, you have to handle them yourself with a dialog hook function (see note 19).

10. If the user supplies a file name that already exists on the disk, an alert box is displayed asking whether to replace the existing file of that name. If the user answers **Yes**, the dialog is dismissed and the file name is returned to the calling program in the reply record; if **No**, the dialog remains displayed, allowing the user to change the file name and try again.

11. The **initText** parameter specifies the initial contents of the text box when the dialog is first displayed. The entire contents of the box are initially selected, so that the user can replace them just by typing from the keyboard.

12. The **promptString** parameter is displayed as a static text item above the text box.

13. The **Save** button is automatically deactivated when the text box is empty.

14. The **Eject** button ejects the disk currently in the disk drive; when no disk is in the drive, this button is deactivated.

15. The **Drive** button switches attention between the internal and external disk drives, or among the available volumes on a multiple-volume device such as a hard disk. If only one volume is on-line (for instance, if there's no disk in the other drive), this button is deactivated; if no external disk drive is connected, the button is not displayed.

16. All disk-inserted events are handled automatically. The volume name of the disk currently in the drive is displayed above the **Eject** button in the dialog box.

17. If an uninitialized or otherwise unreadable disk is inserted, **DIBad-Mount** [8.4.1] is called to allow the user to initialize it.

18. If a write-protected disk is inserted, the user is so informed with an alert box.

19. The **dialogHook** parameter is used for replacing the standard dialog box with a nonstandard one of your own, or for handling the standard one in a nonstandard way; see *Inside Macintosh* for details. Pass **NIL** for this parameter to use the standard dialog as described above.

20. **SFPutFile** is part of the Standard File Package, and is defined in the interface file **PackIntf**. See Volume One, Chapter 7, for further information on the package mechanism.

21. The trap macro for this routine expands to call **_Pack3** [I:7.2.1] with the routine selector given below.

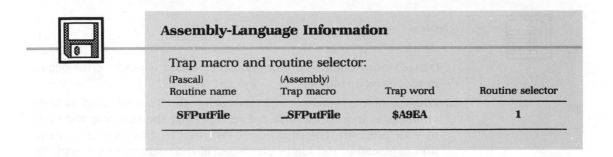

Assembly-Language Information

Trap macro and routine selector:

(Pascal) Routine name	(Assembly) Trap macro	Trap word	Routine selector
SFPutFile	**_SFPutFile**	**$A9EA**	**1**

8.4 Disk Initialization

8.4.1 Initializing a Disk

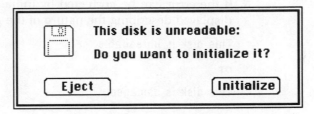

Disk initialization alert

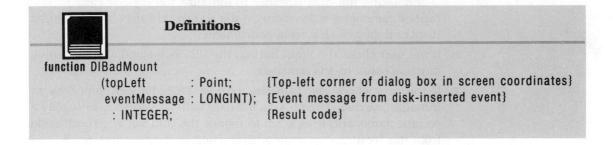

Definitions

```
function DIBadMount
        (topLeft      : Point;        {Top-left corner of dialog box in screen coordinates}
        eventMessage  : LONGINT);     {Event message from disk-inserted event}
        : INTEGER;                    {Result code}
```

Notes

1. **DIBadMount** takes whatever action is needed when an error occurs in mounting a volume.

2. When a disk is inserted in a disk drive, the Toolbox automatically attempts to mount the disk before reporting the disk-inserted event to your program. The result code returned by this mounting operation is placed in the high-order word of the event message, with the drive number in the low-order word.

3. On receiving a disk-inserted event with a nonzero result code, pass the event message to **DIBadMount** to handle the error.

4. If the error cannot be corrected by initializing the disk, **DIBadMount** ejects the disk and returns the error code from the event message as its function result.

5. If the error can be corrected by initializing the disk, an alert box is displayed describing the nature of the problem—

   This disk is unreadable

   or

   This disk is damaged

   or

   This is not a Macintosh disk

   —and asking the user whether to initialize the disk or eject it. The **topLeft** parameter tells where on the screen this alert box should be displayed, in *global (screen) coordinates*.

6. If the user clicks the **Eject** button, the disk is ejected and a positive function result of **1** is returned.

7. If the user clicks the **Initialize** button, **DIBadMount** proceeds to initialize the disk. Then it asks the user with a dialog box to supply a volume name, and tries again to mount the volume. The result code from this mounting operation is returned as the function result.

8. While the disk is being initialized, an alert box is displayed with the message

   Initializing disk. . .

9. In the event of an error during initialization, another alert appears with the message

Initialization failed!

After the user dismisses this alert, **DIBadMount** returns the error code from the initialization attempt as its function result. This will be a low-level disk error between **FirstDskErr** and **LastDskErr** [8.2.8]; see Appendix E for a complete listing of these low-level error codes.

10. **DIBadMount** is part of the Disk Initialization Package, and is defined in the interface file **PackIntf**. See Volume One, Chapter 7, for further information on the package mechanism.

11. If the Disk Initialization Package and its resources aren't available in memory when an uninitialized disk is inserted, the user will be asked to switch disks so they can be loaded from the system resource file. This in turn makes the disk to be initialized unavailable when needed; **DIBadMount** will simply return with a positive function result of **2**. You can avoid this anomaly by preloading the Disk Initialization Package with **DILoad** [8.4.3] before any operation that may eject the system disk.

12. The trap macro for this routine expands to call **_Pack2** [I:7.2.1] with the routine selector given below.

Assembly-Language Information

Trap macro and routine selector:

(Pascal) Routine name	(Assembly) Trap macro	Trap word	Routine selector
DIBadMount	**_DIBadMount**	**$A9E9**	**0**

8.4.2 Initialization Stages

Definitions

```
function DIFormat
        (drive : INTEGER)          {Drive number}
        : OSErr;                   {Result code}

function DIVerify
        (drive : INTEGER)          {Drive number}
        : OSErr;                   {Result code}

function DIZero
        (drive   : INTEGER;        {Drive number}
         vName : Str255)           {Volume name}
        : OSErr;                   {Result code}
```

Notes

1. These routines perform the three stages of disk initialization as separate operations. You don't normally call them yourself; they're called for you by **DIBadMount** [8.4.1].

2. **DIFormat** formats the disk into sectors; **DIVerify** verifies the formatting; **DIZero** writes volume information, a block map, and a file directory representing an empty volume (one containing no files).

3. **DIZero** permanently destroys any files the disk may previously have contained.

4. **DIFormat** and **DIVerify** return result codes for their respective operations. If the operation is successful, the result will be **0** (**NoErr**); otherwise it will be a low-level disk error between **FirstDskErr** and **LastDskErr** [8.2.8]. See Appendix E for a complete listing of these low-level error codes.

5. **DIZero** returns a low-level disk error if the zeroing operation fails; otherwise it proceeds to mount the new volume and returns the result code from the mounting operation.

6. These routines are part of the Disk Initialization Package, and are defined in the interface file **PackIntf**. See Volume One, Chapter 7, for further information on the package mechanism.

7. The trap macros for these routines expand to call **_Pack2** [I:7.2.1] with the routine selectors given below.

Assembly-Language Information

Trap macros and routine selectors:

(Pascal) Routine name	(Assembly) Trap macro	Trap word	Routine selector
DIFormat	**_DIFormat**	**$A9E9**	**6**
DIVerify	**_DIVerify**	**$A9E9**	**8**
DIZero	**_DIZero**	**$A9E9**	**10**

8.4.3 Preloading the Disk Initialization Code

Definitions

procedure DILoad;

procedure DIUnload;

Notes

1. **DILoad** preloads the Disk Initialization Package and its resources from the system resource file and makes them unpurgeable from the heap; **DIUnload** makes them purgeable again, so that the space they occupy can be reused.

2. Call **DILoad** before ejecting the system disk from the disk drive, or before any operation that may cause it to be ejected. This ensures that the Disk Initialization Package will be available in memory if needed, and prevents the anomalous situation described in [8.4.1, note 11].

3. Call **DIUnload** when the Disk Initialization Package is no longer needed in memory (for instance, when the system disk is reinserted in the disk drive).

4. The MiniFinder routines **SFGetFile** [8.3.2] and **SFPutFile** [8.3.3] automatically call **DILoad** and **DIUnload** for you, so there's no need to call them yourself when using the MiniFinder.

5. These routines are part of the Disk Initialization Package, and are defined in the interface file **PackIntf**. See Volume One, Chapter 7, for further information on the package mechanism.

6. The trap macros for these routines expand to call **_Pack2** [I:7.2.1] with the routine selectors given below.

Assembly-Language Information

Trap macros and routine selectors:

(Pascal) Routine name	(Assembly) Trap macro	Trap word	Routine selector
DILoad	**_DILoad**	**$A9E9**	**2**
DIUnload	**_DIUnload**	**$A9E9**	**4**

APPENDIX

A

Toolbox Summary

Chapter 2 Events

2.1 Internal Representation of Events

2.1.1 Event Records

```
type
  EventRecord = record
              what     : INTEGER;     {Event type}
              message  : LONGINT;     {Type-dependent information}
              when     : LONGINT;     {Time of event on system clock}
              where    : Point;       {Mouse position in global (screen) coordinates}
              modifiers : INTEGER     {State of modifier keys and mouse button}
            end;
```

2.1.2 Event Types

const

```
NullEvent    = 0;    {Nothing happened}
MouseDown    = 1;    {Mouse button pressed}
MouseUp      = 2;    {Mouse button released}
KeyDown      = 3;    {Key pressed}
KeyUp        = 4;    {Key released}
AutoKey      = 5;    {Automatic keyboard repeat}
UpdateEvt    = 6;    {Window must be redrawn}
DiskEvt      = 7;    {Disk inserted}
ActivateEvt  = 8;    {Window activated or deactivated}
NetworkEvt   = 10;   {Network event (reserved for system use)}
DriverEvt    = 11;   {I/O driver event (reserved for system use)}
App1Evt      = 12;   {Available for application use}
App2Evt      = 13;   {Available for application use}
App3Evt      = 14;   {Available for application use}
App4Evt      = 15;   {Available for application use}
```

2.1.3 Event Masks

const

```
MDownMask     = $0002;   {Mouse-down event}
MUpMask       = $0004;   {Mouse-up event}
KeyDownMask   = $0008;   {Key-down event}
KeyUpMask     = $0010;   {Key-up event}
AutoKeyMask   = $0020;   {Auto-key event}
UpdateMask    = $0040;   {Update event}
DiskMask      = $0080;   {Disk-inserted event}
ActivMask     = $0100;   {Activate/deactivate event}
NetworkMask   = $0400;   {Network event (reserved for system use)}
DriverMask    = $0800;   {I/O driver event (reserved for system use)}
App1Mask      = $1000;   {Application-defined event}
App2Mask      = $2000;   {Application-defined event}
App3Mask      = $4000;   {Application-defined event}
App4Mask      = $8000;   {Application-defined event}
EveryEvent    = $FFFF;   {Any event}
```

2.1.4 Event Messages

const

```
KeyCodeMask  = $0000FF00;   {Mask for extracting key code from keyboard event}
CharCodeMask = $000000FF;   {Mask for extracting character code from keyboard event}
```

2.1.5 Event Modifiers

const

OptionKey	= $0800;	{Option key}
AlphaLock	= $0400;	{Caps lock key}
ShiftKey	= $0200;	{Shift key}
CmdKey	= $0100;	{Command key}
BtnState	= $0080;	{Mouse button}
ActiveFlag	= $0001;	{Activate or deactivate event?}

2.2 Event Reporting

2.2.1 Retrieving Events

function GetNextEvent

(mask	: INTEGER;	{Mask designating event types of interest}
var theEvent	: EventRecord)	{Returns information about event}
	: BOOLEAN;	{Should application respond to event?}

function EventAvail

(mask	: INTEGER;	{Mask designating event types of interest}
var theEvent	: EventRecord)	{Returns information about event}
	: BOOLEAN;	{Should application respond to event?}

2.3 Posting and Removing Events

2.3.1 Emptying the Event Queue

procedure FlushEvents

(whichMask	: INTEGER;	{Event types to be flushed}
stopMask	: INTEGER);	{Event types on which to stop}

2.3.2 Posting Events

function PostEvent

(eventType	: INTEGER;	{Type of event}
message	: LONGINT)	{Event message}
	: OSErr;	{Result code}

procedure SetEventMask

(newMask	: INTEGER);	{New setting of system event mask}

2.4 The Mouse

2.4.1 Reading the Mouse Position

procedure GetMouse
        (**var** mouseLoc : Point);   {Returns mouse location in local (window) coordinates}

2.4.2 Reading the Mouse Button

function Button
      : BOOLEAN;   {Is mouse button down?}

function StillDown
      : BOOLEAN;   {Is mouse button still down from previous press?}

function WaitMouseUp
      : BOOLEAN;   {Is mouse button still down from previous press?}

2.5 The Cursor

2.5.1 Cursor Records

```
type
  CursHandle = ^CursPtr;
  CursPtr    = ^Cursor;

  Cursor     = record
                 data    : Bits16;   {Cursor image}
                 mask    : Bits16;   {Transfer mask}
                 hotSpot : Point     {Point coinciding with mouse}
               end;

Bits16 = array [0..15] of INTEGER;    {16 rows of 16 bits each}
```

2.5.2 Setting the Cursor

```
procedure InitCursor;

procedure SetCursor
          (newCursor : Cursor)   {Cursor to be made current}

function   GetCursor
          (cursorID : INTEGER)   {Resource ID of desired cursor}
            : CursHandle;        {Handle to cursor in memory}

var
  Arrow : Cursor;                {Standard arrow cursor (for general use)}

const
  IBeamCursor = 1;               {Resource ID for I-beam cursor (for text selection)}
  CrossCursor  = 2;              {Resource ID for cross cursor (for graphics selection)}
  PlusCursor   = 3;              {Resource ID for plus-sign cursor (for "structured selection")}
  WatchCursor = 4;               {Resource ID for wristwatch cursor ("wait a minute")}
```

2.5.3 Showing and Hiding the Cursor

```
procedure HideCursor;

procedure ShowCursor;
```

2.5.4 Obscuring and Shielding the Cursor

```
procedure ObscureCursor;

procedure ShieldCursor;
          (shieldRect   : Rect;   {Shield rectangle}
           globalOrigin : Point); {Origin of coordinate system in global (screen) coordinates}
```

2.6 The Keyboard

2.6.1 Reading the Keyboard

```
procedure GetKeys
          (var keys : KeyMap);     {Returns current state of keyboard}

  type
    KeyMap = packed array [0..127] of BOOLEAN;
```

2.7 The System Clock

2.7.1 Reading the System Clock

```
function  TickCount
              : LONGINT;                    {Current time on system clock}

procedure Delay
          (duration    : LONGINT;     {Length of delay in ticks}
           var endTime : LONGINT);     {Returns time on system clock at end of delay}
```

2.7.2 Performing Periodic Tasks

```
procedure SystemTask;
```

2.8 The Speaker

2.8.1 Beeping the Speaker

```
procedure SysBeep
          (duration : INTEGER);      {Length of beep in seconds}
```

Chapter 3 Windows

3.1 Internal Representation of Windows

3.1.1 Window Records

```
type
  WindowPtr  = GrafPtr;                              {For drawing into window}
  WindowPeek = ^WindowRecord;                        {For accessing window-specific fields}

  WindowRecord = record
                   port          : GrafPort;         {Graphics port for this window}
                   windowKind    : INTEGER;          {Window class}
                   visible       : BOOLEAN;          {Is window visible?}
                   hilited       : BOOLEAN;          {Is window highlighted?}
                   goAwayFlag    : BOOLEAN;          {Does window have close region?}
                   spareFlag     : BOOLEAN;          {Reserved for future use}
                   strucRgn      : RgnHandle;        {Handle to structure region}
                   contRgn       : RgnHandle;        {Handle to content region}
                   updateRgn     : RgnHandle;        {Handle to update region}
                   windowDefProc : Handle;           {Handle to window definition function}
                   dataHandle    : Handle;           {Handle to definition function's data}
                   titleHandle   : StringHandle;     {Handle to window's title}
                   titleWidth    : INTEGER;          {Private}
                   controlList   : ControlHandle;    {Handle to start of control list}
                   nextWindow    : WindowPeek;       {Pointer to next window in window list}
                   windowPic     : PicHandle;        {Handle to QuickDraw picture      }
                                                     {  representing window's contents}
                   refCon        : LONGINT           {Reference constant}
                 end;

const
  DialogKind = 2;                                    {Window class for dialog and alert boxes}
  UserKind   = 8;                                    {Window class for application-created windows}
```

3.2 Creating and Destroying Windows

3.2.1 Initializing the Toolbox for Windows

procedure InitWindows;

3.2.2 Creating Windows

function NewWindow

(wStorage	: Ptr;	{Storage for window record}
windowRect	: Rect;	{Window's port rectangle in screen coordinates}
title	: Str255;	{Window's title}
visible	: BOOLEAN;	{Is window initially visible?}
windowType	: INTEGER;	{Window definition ID}
behindWindow	: WindowPtr;	{Window in front of this one}
hasClose	: BOOLEAN;	{Does window have a close region?}
refCon	: LONGINT)	{Window's reference constant}
: WindowPtr;		{Pointer to new window}

function GetNewWindow

(templateID	: INTEGER;	{Resource ID of window template}
wStorage	: Ptr;	{Storage for window record}
behindWindow	: WindowPtr)	{Window in front of this one}
: WindowPtr;		{Pointer to new window}

const   {Standard window definition IDs: }

DocumentProc	= 0;	{Standard document window}
DBoxProc	= 1;	{Standard dialog or alert box}
PlainDBoxProc	= 2;	{Dialog or alert box with plain border}
AltDBoxProc	= 3;	{Dialog or alert box with "shadow"}
NoGrowDocProc	= 4;	{Document window with no size box}
RDocProc	= 16;	{Accessory window}

3.2.3 Destroying Windows

procedure CloseWindow

(theWindow : WindowPtr);		{Window to destroy}

procedure DisposeWindow

(theWindow : WindowPtr);		{Window to destroy}

3.2.4 Setting Window Properties

```
procedure SetWTitle
        (theWindow : WindowPtr;      {Pointer to the window}
         newTitle   : Str255);       {New title}

procedure GetWTitle
        (theWindow : WindowPtr;      {Pointer to the window}
         var theTitle : Str255);     {Returns current title}

procedure SetWRefCon
        (theWindow : WindowPtr;      {Pointer to the window}
         newRefCon : LONGINT);       {New reference constant}

function  GetWRefCon
        (theWindow : WindowPtr)      {Pointer to the window}
          : LONGINT;                 {Returns current reference constant}
```

3.3 Window Display

3.3.1 Showing and Hiding Windows

```
procedure HideWindow
        (theWindow : WindowPtr);     {Window to hide}

procedure ShowWindow
        (theWindow : WindowPtr);     {Window to show}

procedure ShowHide
        (theWindow : WindowPtr;      {Window to show or hide}
         showFlag   : BOOLEAN);      {Show or hide?}
```

3.3.2 Moving and Sizing Windows

```
procedure MoveWindow
        (theWindow : WindowPtr;      {Pointer to the window}
         hGlobal    : INTEGER:       {New horizontal position in screen coordinates}
         vGlobal    : INTEGER;       {New vertical position in screen coordinates}
         activate   : BOOLEAN);      {Activate the window?}

procedure SizeWindow
        (theWindow : WindowPtr;      {Pointer to the window}
         newWidth   : INTEGER;       {New width}
         newHeight  : INTEGER;       {New height}
         update     : BOOLEAN);      {Update the window?}
```

3.3.3 Front-to-Back Ordering

function FrontWindow
         : WindowPtr;   {The currently active window}

procedure BringToFront
       (theWindow   : WindowPtr);   {Window to bring to front}

procedure SendBehind
       (theWindow   : WindowPtr;   {Window to demote}
        behindWindow : WindowPtr);   {Window to send it behind}

3.3.4 Window Highlighting

procedure HiliteWindow
       (theWindow : WindowPtr;   {Window to highlight}
        onOrOff   : BOOLEAN);   {Highlight or unhighlight?}

procedure DrawGrowIcon
       (theWindow : WindowPtr);   {Window to draw size region for}

3.4 Updating Windows

3.4.1 Update Processing

procedure BeginUpdate
       (theWindow : WindowPtr);   {Window being updated}

procedure EndUpdate
       (theWindow : WindowPtr);   {Window being updated}

3.4.2 Manipulating the Update Region

procedure InvalRect
       (badRect   : Rect);   {Rectangle to add to update region}

procedure InvalRgn
       (badRegion : RgnHandle);   {Region to add to update region}

procedure ValidRect
       (goodRect   : Rect);   {Rectangle to remove from update region}

procedure ValidRgn
       (goodRegion : RgnHandle);   {Region to remove from update region}

3.4.3 Window Pictures

procedure SetWindowPic
        (theWindow : WindowPtr;   {Pointer to the window}
       thePicture : PicHandle);   {Handle to its new window picture}

function   GetWindowPic
        (theWindow : WindowPtr)   {Pointer to the window}
        : PicHandle;   {Handle to its current window picture}

3.5 Responding to the Mouse

3.5.1 Locating Mouse Clicks

function FindWindow
        (mousePoint   : Point;   {Point where mouse was pressed, in screen coordinates}
       var theWindow : WindowPtr; {Returns window the mouse was pressed in}
       : INTEGER;   {Part of the window where mouse was pressed}

const
   InDesk   = 0;   {In desktop (screen background)}
   InMenuBar   = 1;   {In menu bar}
   InSysWindow = 2;   {In a system window}
   InContent   = 3;   {In content region of an application window}
   InDrag   = 4;   {In drag region of an application window}
   InGrow   = 5;   {In size region of an application window}
   InGoAway   = 6;   {In close region of an application window}

3.5.2 Window Selection

procedure SelectWindow
        (theWindow : WindowPtr);   {Window to activate}

3.5.3 Click in a System Window

procedure SystemClick
        (theEvent   : EventRecord;   {Event to be processed}
       theWindow : WindowPtr);   {System window affected}

3.5.4 Drag, Size, and Close Regions

procedure DragWindow
       (theWindow : WindowPtr;   {Pointer to the window}
     startPoint : Point;   {Point where mouse was pressed, in screen coordinates}
     limitRect   : Rect);   {Rectangle limiting movement of window}

function GrowWindow
       (theWindow : WindowPtr;   {Pointer to the window}
     startPoint : Point;   {Point where mouse was pressed, in screen coordinates}
     sizeRect   : Rect);   {Rectangle limiting dimensions of window}
      : LONGINT;   {New dimensions of window}

function TrackGoAway
       (theWindow : WindowPtr;   {Pointer to the window}
     startPoint : Point)   {Point where mouse was pressed, in screen coordinates}
      : BOOLEAN;   {Close the window?}

3.6 Nuts and Bolts

3.6.1 Nuts and Bolts

procedure GetWMgrPort
       (**var** wMgrPort : GrafPtr);   {Returns pointer to Window Manager port}

Chapter 4 Menus

4.1 Internal Representation of Menus

4.1.1 Menu Records

```
type
  MenuHandle = ^MenuPtr;
  MenuPtr    = ^MenuInfo;

  MenuInfo   = record
                 menuID     : INTEGER;   {Menu ID number}
                 menuWidth  : INTEGER;   {Width of menu in pixels}
                 menuHeight : INTEGER;   {Height of menu in pixels}
                 menuProc   : Handle;    {Handle to menu definition procedure}
                 enableFlags : LONGINT;  {Which items are enabled?}
                 menuData   : Str255     {Menu title and contents}
               end;
```

4.2 Creating and Destroying Menus

4.2.1 Initializing the Toolbox for Menus

```
procedure InitMenus;
```

4.2.2 Creating Menus

```
function NewMenu
          (menuID    : INTEGER;   {Menu ID}
           menuTitle : Str255)    {Menu title}
           : MenuHandle;          {Handle to new menu}

function GetMenu
          (menuID : INTEGER)      {Resource ID of desired menu}
           : MenuHandle;          {Handle to menu in memory}
```

4.2.3 Destroying Menus

procedure DisposeMenu
        (theMenu : MenuHandle);   {Menu to destroy}

4.3 Building Menus

4.3.1 Adding Menu Items

procedure AppendMenu
        (theMenu : MenuHandle;   {Handle to the menu}
       defString : Str255);   {String defining item(s) to append}

4.3.3 Adding Resource Names to a Menu

procedure AddResMenu
        (theMenu : MenuHandle;   {Handle to the menu}
       rsrcType : ResType);   {Resource type to be added}

procedure InsertResMenu
        (theMenu : MenuHandle;   {Handle to the menu}
       rsrcType : ResType;   {Resource type to be added}
       afterItem : INTEGER);   {Number of item to insert after}

4.3.4 Counting Menu Items

function CountMItems
        (theMenu : MenuHandle)   {Handle to the menu}
       : INTEGER;   {Number of items in the menu}

4.4 Building the Menu Bar

4.4.1 Adding and Removing Menus

procedure ClearMenuBar;

procedure InsertMenu
       (theMenu : MenuHandle;   {Menu to insert}
        beforeID : INTEGER);   {ID of menu to insert it before}

procedure DeleteMenu
       (menuID : INTEGER);   {Menu to delete}

4.4.2 Reading Menu Bars as Resources

function GetNewMBar
     (menuBarID : INTEGER)   {Resource ID of desired menu bar}
      : Handle;   {Handle to menu bar in memory}

4.4.3 Drawing the Menu Bar

procedure DrawMenuBar;

4.4.4 Changing Menu Bars

function   GetMenuBar
        : Handle;   {Handle to copy of menu bar}

procedure SetMenuBar
       (menuBar : Handle);   {Handle to menu bar to be made current}

4.4.5 Getting Menus from the Menu Bar

function GetMHandle
     (menuID : INTEGER)   {Menu ID}
      : MenuHandle;   {Handle to the menu}

4.5 Responding to the Mouse and Keyboard

4.5.1 Choosing Menu Items

function MenuSelect
          (startPoint : Point)   {Point where mouse was pressed, in screen coordinates}
                : LONGINT;   {Menu item chosen}

function MenuKey
          (ch : CHAR)   {Character typed with command key}
                : LONGINT;   {Menu item chosen}

4.5.2 Opening and Closing Desk Accessories

function   OpenDeskAcc
          (accName : Str255)   {Name of desk accessory to open}
                : INTEGER;   {Reference number of desk accessory}

procedure CloseDeskAcc
          (refNum : INTEGER)   {Reference number of desk accessory to close}

4.5.3 Editing in Desk Accessories

function SystemEdit
          (editCmd : INTEGER)   {Command to relay}
                : BOOLEAN;   {Handled by desk accessory?}

const
   UndoCmd = 0;   {Edit code for Undo command}
   CutCmd   = 2;   {Edit code for Cut command}
   CopyCmd = 3;   {Edit code for Copy command}
   PasteCmd = 4;   {Edit code for Paste command}
   ClearCmd = 5;   {Edit code for Clear command}

4.5.4 Highlighting Menu Titles

procedure HiliteMenu
          (menuID : INTEGER);   {ID number of menu to highlight}

4.6 Controlling Menu Items

4.6.1 Text of an Item

procedure SetItem
    (theMenu   : MenuHandle;   {Handle to the menu}
     theItem   : INTEGER;   {Item number within the menu}
     itemString : Str255);   {New text of item}

procedure GetItem
    (theMenu   : MenuHandle;   {Handle to the menu}
     theItem   : INTEGER;   {Item number within the menu}
     var itemString : Str255);   {Returns current text of item}

4.6.2 Enabling and Disabling Items

procedure DisableItem
    (theMenu : MenuHandle;   {Handle to the menu}
     theItem : INTEGER);   {Item number within the menu}

procedure EnableItem
    (theMenu : MenuHandle;   {Handle to the menu}
     theItem : INTEGER);   {Item number within the menu}

4.6.3 Character Style of Menu Items

procedure SetItemStyle
    (theMenu : MenuHandle;   {Handle to the menu}
     theItem : INTEGER;   {Item number within the menu}
     theStyle : Style);   {New character style}

procedure GetItemStyle
    (theMenu   : MenuHandle;   {Handle to the menu}
     theItem   : INTEGER;   {Item number within the menu}
     var theStyle : Style);   {Returns current character style}

4.6.4 Marking Items

procedure CheckItem
        (theMenu : MenuHandle;   {Handle to the menu}
         theItem : INTEGER;   {Item number within the menu}
         checked : BOOLEAN);   {Check or uncheck?}

procedure SetItemMark
        (theMenu : MenuHandle;   {Handle to the menu}
         theItem   : INTEGER;   {Item number within the menu}
         markChar : CHAR);   {Character to mark item with}

procedure GetItemMark
        (theMenu   : MenuHandle;   {Handle to the menu}
         theItem   : INTEGER;   {Item number within the menu}
         var markChar : CHAR);   {Returns character item is currently marked with}

const
  NoMark = 0;   {Item is unmarked}

4.6.5 Item Icons

procedure SetItemIcon
        (theMenu : MenuHandle;   {Handle to the menu}
         theItem : INTEGER;   {Item number within the menu}
         iconNum : Byte);   {New icon number}

procedure GetItemIcon
        (theMenu   : MenuHandle;   {Handle to the menu}
         theItem   : INTEGER;   {Item number within the menu}
         var iconNum : Byte);   {Returns current icon number}

4.7 Nuts and Bolts

4.7.1 Menu Dimensions

procedure CalcMenuSize
        (theMenu : MenuHandle);   {Handle to the menu}

4.7.2 Flashing Menu Items

procedure SetMenuFlash
        (flashCount : INTEGER);   {Number of flashes when menu item chosen}

procedure FlashMenuBar
        (menuID : INTEGER);   {Handle to the menu}

4.8 Menu-Related Resources

4.8.1 Resource Type 'MENU'

const
  TextMenuProc = 0;   {Resource ID of standard menu definition procedure}

Chapter 5 Text Editing

5.1 The Editing Environment

5.1.1 Edit Records

type
  TEHandle = ^TEPtr;
  TEPtr   = ^TERec;

  TERec = **record**
        destRect   : Rect;   {Destination (wrapping) rectangle}
        viewRect   : Rect;   {View (clipping) rectangle}
        selRect   : Rect;   {Private}
        lineHeight : INTEGER; {Line height in pixels}
        fontAscent : INTEGER; {First baseline}

```
    selPoint   : Point;           {Private}
    selStart   : INTEGER;         {Start of selection (character position)}
    selEnd     : INTEGER:         {End of selection (character position)}
    active     : INTEGER;         {Private}
    wordBreak  : ProcPtr;         {Pointer to word-break routine}
    clikLoop   : ProcPtr;         {Pointer to click-loop routine}
    clickTime  : LONGINT;         {Private}
    clickLoc   : INTEGER;         {Private}
    caretTime  : LONGINT;         {Private}
    caretState : INTEGER;         {Private}
    just       : INTEGER;         {Justification}
    teLength   : INTEGER;         {Length of text in characters}
    hText      : Handle;          {Handle to text}
    recalBack  : INTEGER;         {Private}
    recalLines : INTEGER;         {Private}
    clikStuff  : INTEGER;         {Private}
    crOnly     : INTEGER;         {Break line at carriage returns only?}
    txFont     : INTEGER;         {Font number of typeface}
    txFace     : Style;           {Character style}
    txMode     : INTEGER;         {Transfer mode for text}
    txSize     : INTEGER;         {Type size in points}
    inPort     : GrafPtr;         {Pointer to graphics port}
    highHook   : ProcPtr;         {Pointer to "custom" highlighting routine}
    caretHook  : ProcPtr;         {Pointer to "custom" insertion point routine}
    nLines     : INTEGER;         {Number of lines of text}
    lineStarts : array [0..16000] of INTEGER
                                  {Character positions of line starts}
  end;

const
  TEJustLeft   =  0;              {Left justification}
  TEJustCenter =  1;              {Center justification}
  TEJustRight  = −1;              {Right justification}
```

5.1.2 Text Representation

type
    CharsHandle = ^CharsPtr;
    CharsPtr   = ^Chars;

    Chars   = **packed array** [0..32000] **of** CHAR;

5.2 Preparation for Text Editing

5.2.1 Initializing the Toolbox for Text Editing

procedure TEInit;

5.2.2 Creating and Destroying Edit Records

function TENew
                (destRect : Rect;   {Destination (wrapping) rectangle}
                 viewRect : Rect)   {View (clipping) rectangle}
                   : TEHandle);   {Handle to new edit record}

procedure TEDispose
                (editRec : TEHandle);   {Handle to edit record}

5.2.3 Text to Be Edited

procedure TESetText
                (textPtr   : Ptr;   {Pointer to text}
                 textLength : LONGINT;   {Length of text in characters}
                 editRec   : TEHandle); {Handle to edit record}

function TEGetText
                (editRec : TEHandle);   {Handle to edit record}
                   : CharsHandle;   {Handle to text}

5.3 Text Display

5.3.1 Wrapping and Justification

procedure TECalText
        (editRec : TEHandle);   {Handle to edit record}

procedure TESetJust
        (just   : INTEGER;   {Justification}
        editRec : TEHandle);   {Handle to edit record}

5.3.2 Displaying Text on the Screen

procedure TEUpdate
        (updRect : Rect;   {Update rectangle in window coordinates}
        editRec : TEHandle);   {Handle to edit record}

procedure TextBox
        (textPtr : Ptr;   {Pointer to text}
        length   : LONGINT;   {Length of text in characters}
        textRect : Rect;   {Display rectangle in local coordinates}
        just   : INTEGER);   {Justification}

5.3.3 Scrolling

procedure TEScroll
        (horiz   : INTEGER;   {Horizontal scroll distance in pixels}
        vert   : INTEGER;   {Vertical scroll distance in pixels}
        editRec : TEHandle);   {Handle to edit record}

5.4 Text Selection

5.4.1 Selection with the Mouse

procedure TEClick
        (startPoint : Point;   {Point where mouse was pressed, in window coordinates}
        extend   : BOOLEAN;   {Extend existing selection?}
        editRec   : TEHandle);   {Handle to edit record}

function   GetDblTime
         : LONGINT;   {Current double-click interval in ticks}

5.4.2 Selection Control

procedure TESetSelect
        (selStart : LONGINT;   {Start of selection (character position)}
         selEnd   : LONGINT;   {End of selection (character position)}
         editRec : TEHandle);   {Handle to edit record}

5.4.3 Selection Display

procedure TEActivate
        (editRec : TEHandle);   {Handle to edit record}

procedure TEDeactivate
        (editRec : TEHandle);   {Handle to edit record}

procedure TEIdle
        (editRec : TEHandle);   {Handle to edit record}

function GetCaretTime
        : LONGINT;   {Current blink interval in ticks}

5.5 Editing Operations

5.5.1 Keyboard Input

procedure TEKey
        (ch   : CHAR;   {Character typed}
         editRec : TEHandle);   {Handle to edit record}

5.5.2 Cutting and Pasting

procedure TECut
        (editRec : TEHandle);   {Handle to edit record}

procedure TECopy
        (editRec : TEHandle);   {Handle to edit record}

procedure TEPaste
        (editRec : TEHandle);   {Handle to edit record}

5.5.3 Scrapless Editing

procedure TEDelete
       (editRec : TEHandle);   {Handle to edit record}

procedure TEInsert
       (textPtr   : Ptr;   {Pointer to insertion text}
        textLength : LONGINT;   {Length of insertion text in characters}
        editRec   : TEHandle); {Handle to edit record}

5.5.4 Scrap Access

function   TEScrapHandle
        : Handle;   {Handle to Toolbox scrap}

function   TEGetScrapLen
        : LONGINT;   {Current length of Toolbox scrap in characters}

procedure TESetScrapLen
       (newLength : LONGINT);   {New length of Toolbox scrap in characters}

5.5.5 Scrap Transfer

function TEFromScrap
       : OSErr;   {Result code}

function TEToScrap
       : OSErr;   {Result code}

5.5.6 Search and Replace

function Munger
       (textHandle   : Handle;   {Handle to destination text}
        startAt   : LONGINT;   {Character position at which to start search}
        targetText   : Ptr;   {Pointer to target text}
        targetLength : LONGINT;   {Length of target text}
        replaceText   : Ptr;   {Pointer to replacement text}
        replaceLength : LONGINT)   {Length of replacement text}
        : LONGINT;   {Character position at end of operation}

5.6 Nuts and Bolts

5.6.1 Click-Loop Routine

```
procedure SetClikLoop
        (clikLoop : ProcPtr;        {Pointer to click-loop routine}
         editRec  : TEHandle);      {Handle to edit record}

function   YourClikLoop
           : BOOLEAN;              {Continue tracking?}
```

5.6.2 Word-Break Routine

```
procedure SetWordBreak
        (wordBreak : ProcPtr;       {Pointer to word-break routine}
         editRec   : TEHandle);     {Handle to edit record}

function   YourWordBreak
        (theText  : Ptr;            {Pointer to text}
         charPos  : INTEGER)        {Character position within text}
         : BOOLEAN;                 {Is there a word break at that position?}
```

Chapter 6 Controls

6.1 Internal Representation of Controls

6.1.1 Control Records

```
type
  ControlHandle = ^ControlPtr;
  ControlPtr    = ^ControlRecord;

  ControlRecord = packed record
                    nextControl  : ControlHandle;    {Handle to next control in window's control list}
                    contrlOwner  : WindowPtr;        {Pointer to window this control belongs to}
                    contrlRect   : Rect;             {Location of control within window}
                    contrlVis    : Byte;             {Is control visible?}
                    contrlHilite : Byte;             {Highlighting state}
                    contrlValue  : INTEGER;          {Current setting}
                    contrlMin    : INTEGER;          {Minimum setting}
                    contrlMax    : INTEGER;          {Maximum setting}
                    contrlDefProc : Handle;          {Handle to control definition function}
                    contrlData   : Handle;           {Handle to definition function's data}
                    contrlAction : ProcPtr;          {Pointer to default action procedure}
                    contrlRfCon  : LONGINT;          {Reference "constant" for application use}
                    contrlTitle  : Str255            {Title of control}
                  end;
```

6.2 Creating and Destroying Controls

6.2.1 Creating Controls

function NewControl

(owningWindow	: WindowPtr;	{Pointer to window the new control belongs to}
controlRect	: Rect;	{Location of control within window}
title	: Str255;	{Title of control}
visible	: BOOLEAN;	{Is control initially visible?}
initialValue	: INTEGER;	{Initial setting}
minValue	: INTEGER;	{Minimum setting}
maxValue	: INTEGER;	{Maximum setting}
controlType	: INTEGER;	{Control definition ID}
refCon	: LONGINT);	{Initial reference constant}
: ControlHandle;		{Handle to new control}

function GetNewControl

(templateID	: INTEGER;	{Resource ID of control template}
owningWindow	: WindowPtr)	{Pointer to window the new control belongs to}
: ControlHandle;		{Handle to new control}

const   {Standard control definition IDs: }

PushButProc	= 0;	{Pushbutton}
CheckBoxProc	= 1;	{Checkbox}
RadioButProc	= 2;	{Radio button}
ScrollBarProc	= 16;	{Standard scroll bar}
UseWFont	= 8;	{Use window's font for control title}

6.2.2 Destroying Controls

procedure DisposeControl

(theControl : ControlHandle);	{Control to be destroyed}

procedure KillControls

(theWindow : WindowPtr);	{Window whose controls are to be destroyed}

6.2.3 Setting Control Properties

procedure SetCTitle
       (theControl : ControlHandle;   {Handle to the control}
       newTitle   : Str255);   {New title}

procedure GetCTitle
       (theControl : ControlHandle;   {Handle to the control}
       var theTitle : Str255);   {Returns current title}

procedure SetCRefCon
       (theControl : ControlHandle;   {Handle to the control}
       newRefCon : LONGINT);   {New reference constant}

function   GetCRefCon
       (theControl : ControlHandle)   {Handle to the control}
       : LONGINT;   {Current reference constant}

6.2.4 Control Setting and Range

procedure SetCtlValue
       (theControl : ControlHandle;   {Handle to the control}
       newValue : INTEGER);   {New setting}

function   GetCtlValue
       (theControl : ControlHandle)   {Handle to the control}
       : INTEGER   {Current setting}

procedure SetCtlMin
       (theControl : ControlHandle;   {Handle to the control}
       newMin   : INTEGER);   {New minimum setting}

function   GetCtlMin
       (theControl : ControlHandle)   {Handle to the control}
       : INTEGER   {Current minimum setting}

procedure SetCtlMax
       (theControl : ControlHandle;   {Handle to the control}
       newMax   : INTEGER);   {New maximum setting}

function   GetCtlMax
       (theControl : ControlHandle)   {Handle to the control}
       : INTEGER   {Current maximum setting}

6.3 Control Display

6.3.1 Showing and Hiding Controls

procedure HideControl
   (theControl : ControlHandle); {Handle to the control}

procedure ShowControl
   (theControl : ControlHandle); {Handle to the control}

procedure DrawControls
   (theWindow : WindowPtr);   {Pointer to the window}

6.3.2 Moving and Sizing Controls

procedure MoveControl
   (theControl : ControlHandle; {Handle to the control}
    hLocal : INTEGER; {New horizontal coordinate}
    vLocal : INTEGER); {New vertical coordinate}

procedure SizeControl
   (theControl : ControlHandle; {Handle to the control}
    newWidth : INTEGER; {New width}
    newHeight : INTEGER); {New height}

6.3.3 Control Highlighting

procedure HiliteControl
   (theControl : ControlHandle; {Handle to the control}
    hiliteState : INTEGER); {Part of the control to be highlighted}

6.4 Responding to the Mouse

6.4.1 Locating Mouse Clicks

```
function FindControl
        (mousePoint  : Point;          {Point where mouse was pressed, in window coordinates}
         theWindow   : WindowPtr;      {Window the mouse was pressed in}
     var theControl : ControlHandle)  {Returns control the mouse was pressed in}
        : INTEGER;                     {Part of the control where mouse was pressed}

function TestControl
        (theControl  : ControlHandle;  {Control to be tested}
         mousePoint : Point)           {Point where mouse was pressed, in window coordinates}
        : INTEGER;                     {Part of the control where mouse was pressed}

const
  InButton      = 10;                  {In a pushbutton}
  InCheckbox    = 11;                  {In a checkbox or radio button}

  InUpButton    = 20;                  {In up arrow of a scroll bar}
  InDownButton  = 21;                  {In down arrow of a scroll bar}
  InPageUp      = 22;                  {In page-up region of a scroll bar}
  InPageDown    = 23;                  {In page-down region of a scroll bar}

  InThumb       = 129;                 {In scroll box of a scroll bar}
```

6.4.2 Tracking the Mouse

```
function   TrackControl
        (theControl : ControlHandle;   {Handle to the control}
         startPoint : Point;           {Point where mouse was pressed, in window coordinates}
         actionProc : ProcPtr)         {Repeated action while tracking}
        : INTEGER;                     {Part of control affected}

procedure SetCtlAction
        (theControl : ControlHandle;   {Handle to the control}
         newAction : ProcPtr);         {New action procedure}

function   GetCtlAction
        (theControl : ControlHandle)   {Handle to the control}
        : ProcPtr;                     {Current action procedure}
```

6.4.3 Dragging a Control

```
procedure DragControl
          (theControl : ControlHandle;      {Handle to the control}
           startPoint : Point;              {Point where mouse was pressed}
           limitRect  : Rect;               {Rectangle limiting movement}
           trackRect  : Rect;               {Rectangle limiting tracking}
           axis       : INTEGER);           {Axis constraint}

const
   BothAxes  = 0;                           {Both axes}
   HAxisOnly = 1;                           {Horizontal only}
   VAxisOnly = 2;                           {Vertical only}
```

Chapter 7 Dialogs

7.1 Internal Representation of Dialogs

7.1.1 Dialog Records

```
type
   DialogPtr     = WindowPtr;               {For treating as a window}
   DialogPeek    = ^DialogRecord;           {For accessing dialog-specific fields}

   DialogRecord = record
                     window   : WindowRecord;   {Dialog window}
                     items    : Handle;         {Handle to item list}
                     textH    : TEHandle;       {Handle to edit record for current text box}
                     editField : INTEGER;       {Item number of current text box minus 1}
                     editOpen  : INTEGER;       {Private}
                     aDefItem  : INTEGER        {Item number of default button}
                  end;

const
   OK     = 1;                              {Item number of OK button}
   Cancel = 2;                              {Item number of Cancel button}
```

7.1.2 Item Types

```
const
  UserItem      =   0;        {Application-defined item}
  CtrlItem      =   4;        {Control}
    BtnCtrl     =       0;        {Pushbutton}
    ChkCtrl     =       1;        {Checkbox}
    RadCtrl     =       2;        {Radio button}
    ResCtrl     =       3;        {Other, defined by control template resource}
  StatText      =   8;        {Static text}
  EditText      =  16;        {Editable text box}
  IconItem      =  32;        {Icon}
  PicItem       =  64;        {Picture}

  ItemDisable = 128;          {Item is disabled}
```

7.1.3 Alert Templates

```
type
  AlertTHndle = ^AlertTPtr;
  AlertTPtr   = ^AlertTemplate;

  AlertTemplate = record
                    boundsRect : Rect;       {Alert window's port rectangle in screen coordinates}
                    itemsID    : INTEGER;    {Resource ID of item list}
                    stages     : StageList   {Stage list}
                  end;

  StageList = packed record
                    boldItm4    : 0..1;       {Stage 4: item number of default button minus 1}
                    boxDrwn4    : BOOLEAN;    {Stage 4: draw alert box on screen?}
                    sound4      : 0..3;       {Stage 4: sound number to emit}

                    boldItm3    : 0..1;       {Stage 3: item number of default button minus 1}
                    boxDrwn3    : BOOLEAN;    {Stage 3: draw alert box on screen?}
                    sound3      : 0..3;       {Stage 3: sound number to emit}

                    boldItm2    : 0..1;       {Stage 2: item number of default button minus 1}
                    boxDrwn2    : BOOLEAN;    {Stage 2: draw alert box on screen?}
                    sound2      : 0..3;       {Stage 2: sound number to emit}

                    boldItm1    : 0..1;       {Stage 1: item number of default button minus 1}
                    boxDrwn1    : BOOLEAN;    {Stage 1: draw alert box on screen?}
                    sound1      : 0..3;       {Stage 1: sound number to emit}
                  end;
```

7.1.4 Dialog Templates

type
  DialogTHndle = ^DialogTPtr;
  DialogTPtr   = ^DialogTemplate;

  DialogTemplate = **record**

boundsRect	: Rect;	{Dialog window's port rectangle in screen coordinates}
procID	: INTEGER;	{Dialog window's definition ID}
visible	: BOOLEAN;	{Is dialog window visible?}
filler1	: BOOLEAN;	{Padding}
goAwayFlag	: BOOLEAN;	{Does dialog window have a close box?}
filler2	: BOOLEAN;	{Padding}
refCon	: LONGINT;	{Dialog window's reference constant}
itemsID	: INTEGER;	{Resource ID of item list}
title	: Str255	{Title of dialog window}

       end:

7.2 Creating and Destroying Dialogs

7.2.1 Initializing the Toolbox for Dialogs

procedure InitDialogs
    (restartProc : ProcPtr);   {Pointer to restart procedure}

7.2.2 Creating Dialogs

function NewDialog

(dStorage	: Ptr;	{Storage for dialog record}
windowRect	: Rect;	{Dialog window's port rectangle in screen coordinates}
title	: Str255;	{Title of dialog window}
visible	: BOOLEAN;	{Is dialog window initially visible?}
windowType	: INTEGER;	{Dialog window's definition ID}
behindWindow	: WindowPtr;	{Window in front of this one}
goAwayFlag	: BOOLEAN;	{Does dialog window have a close box?}
refCon	: LONGINT;	{Dialog window's reference constant}
itemList	: Handle)	{Handle to item list}
: DialogPtr;		{Pointer to new dialog record}

function GetNewDialog

(templateID	: INTEGER;	{Resource ID of dialog template}
dStorage	: Ptr;	{Storage for dialog record}
behindWindow	: WindowPtr)	{Window in front of this one}
: DialogPtr;		{Pointer to new dialog record}

7.2.3 Destroying Dialogs

procedure CloseDialog
          (theDialog : DialogPtr);   {Dialog to destroy}

procedure DisposDialog
          (theDialog : DialogPtr);   {Dialog to destroy}

7.3 Manipulating Items

7.3.1 Access to Items

procedure SetDItem
          (theDialog   : DialogPtr;   {Pointer to the dialog}
          itemNumber: INTEGER;   {Item number}
          itemType   : INTEGER;   {New item type}
          itemHandle : Handle;   {New item handle}
          dispRect   : Rect);   {New display rectangle}

procedure GetDItem
          (theDialog   : DialogPtr;   {Pointer to the dialog}
          itemNumber   : INTEGER;   {Item number}
          var itemType   : INTEGER;   {Returns item type}
          var itemHandle : Handle;   {Returns item handle}
          var dispRect   : Rect);   {Returns display rectangle}

7.3.2 Text of an Item

procedure SetIText
          (itemHandle : Handle;   {Handle to text item}
          theText   : Str255);   {New text}

procedure GetIText
          (itemHandle : Handle;   {Handle to text item}
          var theText : Str255);   {Returns current text}

procedure SelIText
          (theDialog   : DialogPtr;   {Pointer to dialog}
          itemNumber : INTEGER;   {Item number}
          selStart   : INTEGER;   {Start of selection (character position)}
          selEnd   : INTEGER);   {End of selection (character position)}

7.4 Using Alerts and Dialogs

7.4.1 Static Display

procedure DrawDialog
        (theDialog : DialogPtr);   {Dialog to be drawn}

7.4.2 Using Alerts

function Alert
        (alertID : INTEGER;   {Resource ID of alert template}
        filter   : ProcPtr)   {Pointer to filter function}
        : INTEGER;   {Item number that dismissed alert}

function NoteAlert
        (alertID : INTEGER;   {Resource ID of alert template}
        filter   : ProcPtr)   {Pointer to filter function}
        : INTEGER;   {Item number that dismissed alert}

function CautionAlert
        (alertID : INTEGER;   {Resource ID of alert template}
        filter   : ProcPtr)   {Pointer to filter function}
        : INTEGER;   {Item number that dismissed alert}

function StopAlert
        (alertID : INTEGER;   {Resource ID of alert template}
        filter   : ProcPtr)   {Pointer to filter function}
        : INTEGER;   {Item number that dismissed alert}

const
  NoteIcon   = 1;   {Resource ID of Note standard icon}
  CautionIcon = 2;   {Resource ID of standard Caution icon}
  StopIcon   = 0;   {Resource ID of standard Stop icon}

7.4.3 Using Modal Dialogs

procedure ModalDialog
        (filter   : ProcPtr;   {Pointer to filter function}
        var itemNumber : INTEGER);   {Returns item number of reported item}

7.4.4 Using Modeless Dialogs

```
function   IsDialogEvent
             (theEvent : EventRecord)          {Event to be handled}
               : BOOLEAN;                       {Is event dialog-related?}

function   DialogSelect
             (theEvent      : EventRecord;      {Event to be handled}
              var theDialog    : DialogPtr;     {Returns pointer to dialog affected}
              var itemNumber : INTEGER)         {Returns item number of reported item}
               : BOOLEAN;                        {Response needed?}
```

7.4.5 Filter Functions

```
function   YourFilterFunction
             (theDialog      : DialogPtr;       {Pointer to dialog affected}
              var theEvent   : EventRecord;     {Event to be handled}
              var itemNumber : INTEGER)         {Returns item number to report}
               : BOOLEAN;                        {Report item immediately?}
```

7.4.6 Text Substitution

```
procedure ParamText
             (subText0 : Str255;                {Text to substitute for '^0'}
              subText1 : Str255;                {Text to substitute for '^1'}
              subText2 : Str255;                {Text to substitute for '^2'}
              subText3 : Str255);               {Text to substitute for '^3'}
```

7.4.7 Editing in Text Boxes

```
procedure DlgCut
             (theDialog : DialogPtr);           {Pointer to the dialog}

procedure DlgCopy
             (theDialog : DialogPtr);           {Pointer to the dialog}

procedure DlgPaste
             (theDialog : DialogPtr);           {Pointer to the dialog}

procedure DlgDelete
             (theDialog : DialogPtr);           {Pointer to the dialog}
```

7.5 Nuts and Bolts

7.5.1 Text Font and Error Sounds

procedure SetDAFont
        (fontNumber : INTEGER);   {Font number for dialogs and alerts}

procedure ErrorSound
        (soundProc : ProcPtr);   {Pointer to sound procedure}

7.5.2 Alert Stages

function   GetAlrtStage
            : INTEGER;   {Stage of last alert minus 1}

procedure ResetAlrtStage;

7.5.3 Preloading Dialog Resources

procedure CouldAlert
        (alertID : INTEGER);   {Resource ID of alert}

procedure CouldDialog
        (dialogID : INTEGER);   {Resource ID of dialog}

procedure FreeAlert
        (alertID : INTEGER);   {Resource ID of alert}

procedure FreeDialog
        (dialogID : INTEGER);   {Resource ID of dialog}

Chapter 8 Files

8.1 Volume Operations

8.1.1 Volume Information

```
function GetVInfo
        (drive        : INTEGER;      {Drive number}
        vName         : StringPtr;    {Volume name}
        var vRefNum   : INTEGER;      {Returns volume reference number}
        var freeBytes : LONGINT)      {Returns number of free bytes on volume}
        : OSErr;                      {Result code}
```

8.1.2 Current Volume

```
function GetVol
        (vName       : StringPtr;     {Returns volume name}
        var vRefNum  : INTEGER)       {Returns volume reference number}
        : OSErr;                      {Result code}
```

```
function SetVol
        (vName    : StringPtr;        {Volume name}
        vRefNum   : INTEGER)          {Volume reference number}
        : OSErr;                      {Result code}
```

8.1.3 Flushing, Ejecting, and Unmounting

```
function FlushVol
        (vName   : StringPtr;         {Volume name}
        vRefNum  : INTEGER)           {Volume reference number}
        : OSErr;                      {Result code}
```

```
function Eject
        (vName   : StringPtr;         {Volume name}
        vRefNum  : INTEGER)           {Volume reference number}
        : OSErr;                      {Result code}
```

```
function UnmountVol
        (vName   : StringPtr;         {Volume name}
        vRefNum  : INTEGER)           {Volume reference number}
        : OSErr;                      {Result code}
```

8.2 File Operations

8.2.1 Creating Files

```
function Create
        (fName    : Str255;          {File name}
         vRefNum  : INTEGER;         {Volume reference number}
         creator  : OSType;          {Signature of creator program}
         fileType : OSType)          {File type}
         : OSErr;                    {Result code}
```

8.2.2 Opening and Closing Files

```
function FSOpen
        (fName        : Str255;      {File name}
         vRefNum      : INTEGER;     {Volume reference number}
         var fRefNum  : INTEGER)     {Returns file reference number}
         : OSErr;                    {Result code}

function OpenRF
        (fName        : Str255;      {File name}
         vRefNum      : INTEGER;     {Volume reference number}
         var fRefNum  : INTEGER)     {Returns file reference number}
         : OSErr;                    {Result code}

function FSClose
        (fRefNum : INTEGER)          {File reference number}
         : OSErr;                    {Result code}
```

8.2.3 Reading and Writing

```
function FSRead
        (fRefNum       : INTEGER;    {File reference number}
         var byteCount : LONGINT;    {Number of bytes to read}
         toAddr        : Ptr)        {Address to read to}
         : OSErr;                    {Result code}

function FSWrite
        (fRefNum       : INTEGER;    {File reference number}
         var byteCount : LONGINT;    {Number of bytes to write}
         fromAddr      : Ptr)        {Address to write from}
         : OSErr;                    {Result code}
```

8.2.4 File Mark

```
function GetFPos
        (fRefNum    : INTEGER;        {File reference number}
         var markPos : LONGINT)       {Returns current mark position in bytes}
         : OSErr;                     {Result code}

function SetFPos
        (fRefNum    : INTEGER;        {File reference number}
         markBase   : INTEGER;        {Base to set mark from}
         markOffset : LONGINT)        {Offset in bytes relative to base}
         : OSErr;                     {Result code}

const
   FSAtMark   = 0;                    {Position at current mark}
   FSFromStart = 1;                   {Position relative to start of file}
   FSFromLEOF = 2;                    {Position relative to logical end-of-file}
   FSFromMark = 3;                    {Position relative to current mark}
```

8.2.5 End-of-File

```
function GetEOF
        (fRefNum    : INTEGER;        {File reference number}
         var logicalEOF : LONGINT)    {Returns current logical end-of-file in bytes}
         : OSErr;                     {Result code}

function SetEOF
        (fRefNum    : INTEGER;        {File reference number}
         logicalEOF : LONGINT)        {New logical end-of-file in bytes}
         : OSErr;                     {Result code}

function Allocate
        (fRefNum    : INTEGER;        {File reference number}
         var byteCount : LONGINT)     {Number of bytes to allocate}
         : OSErr;                     {Result code}
```

8.2.6 Locking and Unlocking Files

```
function SetFLock
        (fName    : Str255;        {File name}
         vRefNum : INTEGER)        {Volume reference number}
         : OSErr;                  {Result code}

function RstFLock
        (fName    : Str255;        {File name}
         vRefNum : INTEGER)        {Volume reference number}
         : OSErr;                  {Result code}
```

8.2.7 Deleting and Renaming Files

```
function FSDelete
        (fName    : Str255;        {File name}
         vRefNum : INTEGER)        {Volume reference number}
         : OSErr;                  {Result code}

function Rename
        (oldName  : Str255;        {Old file name}
         vRefNum  : INTEGER;       {Volume reference number}
         newName : Str255)         {New file name}
         : OSErr;                  {Result code}
```

8.2.8 Error Reporting

const

NoErr	=	0;	{No error}
DirFulErr	=	−33;	{Directory full}
DskFulErr	=	−34;	{Disk full}
NSVErr	=	−35;	{No such volume}
IOErr	=	−36;	{Disk I/O error}
BdNamErr	=	−37;	{Bad name}
FNOpnErr	=	−38;	{File not open}
EOFErr	=	−39;	{Attempt to read past end-of-file}
PosErr	=	−40;	{Attempt to position before start of file}
MFulErr	=	−41;	{Memory (system heap) full}
TMFOErr	=	−42;	{Too many files open (more than 12)}
FNFErr	=	−43;	{File not found}
WPrErr	=	−44;	{Disk is write-protected}
FLckdErr	=	−45;	{File locked}
VLckdErr	=	−46;	{Volume locked}
FBsyErr	=	−47;	{File busy}
DupFNErr	=	−48;	{Duplicate file name}
OpWrErr	=	−49;	{File already open for writing}
ParamErr	=	−50;	{Invalid parameter list}
RfNumErr	=	−51;	{Invalid reference number}
GFPErr	=	−52;	{Error during GetFPos}
VolOffLinErr	=	−53;	{Volume off-line}
PermErr	=	−54;	{Permission violation}
VolOnLinErr	=	−55;	{Volume already on-line}
NSDrvErr	=	−56;	{No such drive}
NoMacDskErr	=	−57;	{Non-Macintosh disk}
ExtFSErr	=	−58;	{External file system}
FSRnErr	=	−59;	{Unable to rename file}
BadMDBErr	=	−60;	{Bad master directory block}
WrPermErr	=	−61;	{No write permission}
FirstDskErr	=	−84;	{Low-level disk error}
LastDskErr	=	−64;	{Low-level disk error}

8.3 The MiniFinder

8.3.1 Reply Records

type
```
  SFReply = record
            good     : BOOLEAN;        {Did user confirm file selection?}
            copy     : BOOLEAN;        {Unused}
            fType    : OSType;         {File type}
            vRefNum  : INTEGER;        {Volume reference number}
            version  : INTEGER;        {File version number}
            fName    : STRING[63]      {File name}
          end;
```

8.3.2 File to Read From

procedure SFGetFile
```
            (topLeft      : Point;      {Top-left corner of dialog box in screen coordinates}
            promptString : Str255;     {Unused}
            fileFilter   : ProcPtr;    {Filter function}
            numTypes     : INTEGER;    {Number of file types}
            typeList     : SFTypeList; {File types to display}
            dialogHook   : ProcPtr;    {Dialog hook function}
            var reply    : SFReply);   {Returns identifying information for file to be read}
```

type
```
  SFTypeList = array [0..3] of OSType;
```

8.3.3 File to Write To

procedure SFPutFile
```
            (topLeft     : Point;       {Top-left corner of dialog box in screen coordinates}
            promptString : Str255;      {Prompting string}
            initText     : Str255;      {Initial contents of text box}
            dialogHook   : ProcPtr;     {Dialog hook function}
            var reply    : SFReply);    {Returns identifying information for file to be written}
```

8.4 Disk Initialization

8.4.1 Initializing a Disk

```
function DIBadMount
        (topLeft        : Point;          {Top-left corner of dialog box in screen coordinates}
         eventMessage : LONGINT);         {Event message from disk-inserted event}
          : INTEGER;                      {Result code}
```

8.4.2 Initialization Stages

```
function DIFormat
        (drive : INTEGER)       {Drive number}
          : OSErr;              {Result code}

function DIVerify
        (drive : INTEGER)       {Drive number}
          : OSErr;              {Result code}

function DIZero
        (drive   : INTEGER;     {Drive number}
         vName : Str255)        {Volume name}
          : OSErr;              {Result code}
```

8.4.3 Preloading the Disk Initialization Code

procedure DILoad;

procedure DIUnload;

Resource Type 'ALRT'

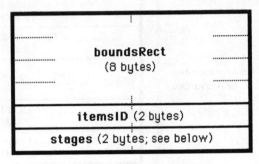

Format of resource type **'ALRT'**

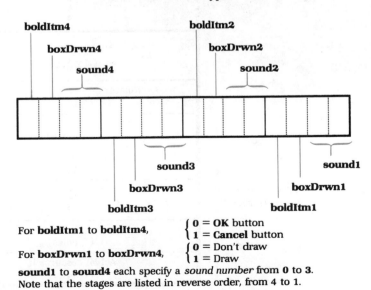

For **boldItm1** to **boldItm4**, $\begin{cases} \textbf{0} = \textbf{OK} \text{ button} \\ \textbf{1} = \textbf{Cancel} \text{ button} \end{cases}$

For **boxDrwn1** to **boxDrwn4**, $\begin{cases} \textbf{0} = \text{Don't draw} \\ \textbf{1} = \text{Draw} \end{cases}$

sound1 to **sound4** each specify a *sound number* from **0** to **3**.
Note that the stages are listed in reverse order, from 4 to 1.

Resource Type 'BNDL'

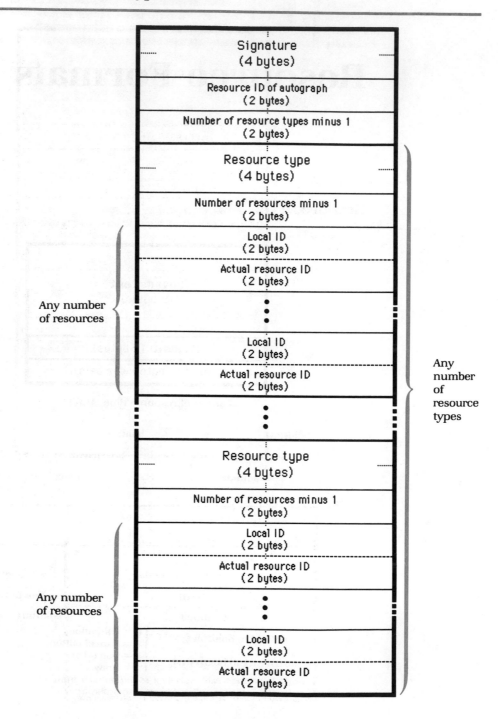

Resource Type 'CNTL'

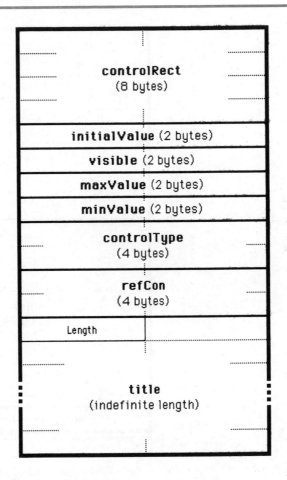

Resource Type 'CODE'

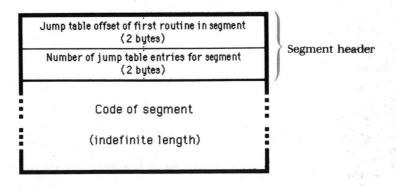

Resource Type 'CURS'

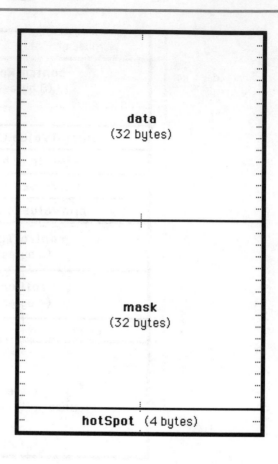

Resource Type 'DITL'

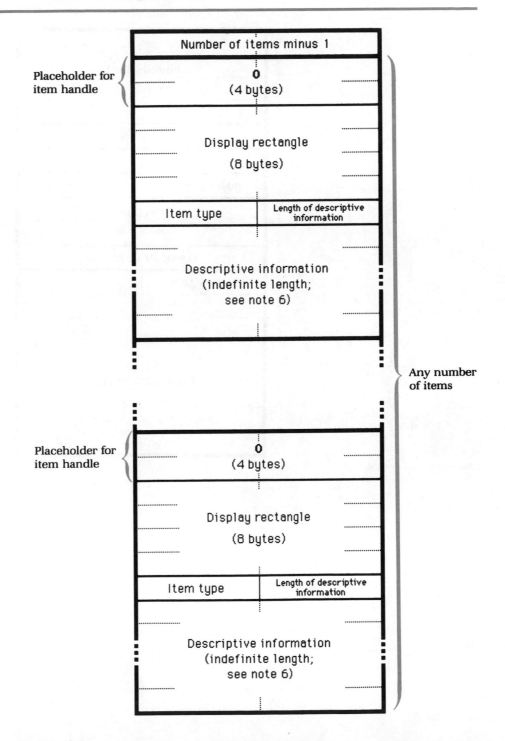

Resource Type 'DLOG'

boundsRect (8 bytes)	
procID (2 bytes)	
visible	(unused)
goAwayflag	(unused)
refCon (4 bytes)	
itemsID (2 bytes)	
Length of title	
title (indefinite length)	

Resource Type 'FONT'

fontType (2 bytes)
firstChar (2 bytes)
lastChar (2 bytes)
widMax (2 bytes)
kernMax (2 bytes)
nDescent (2 bytes)
fRectWid (2 bytes)
chHeight (2 bytes)
owTloc (2 bytes)
ascent (2 bytes)
descent (2 bytes)
leading (2 bytes)
rowWords (2 bytes)
bitImage (indefinite length)
locTable (indefinite length)
owTable (indefinite length)

Resource Type 'FREF'

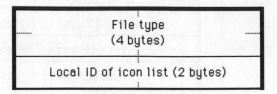

File type (4 bytes)
Local ID of icon list (2 bytes)

Resource Type 'FWID'

fontType (2 bytes)
firstChar (2 bytes)
lastChar (2 bytes)
widMax (2 bytes)
kernMax (2 bytes)
nDescent (2 bytes)
fRectWid (2 bytes)
chHeight (2 bytes)
owTloc (2 bytes)
ascent (2 bytes)
descent (2 bytes)
leading (2 bytes)
owTable (indefinite length)

Resource Type 'ICN#'

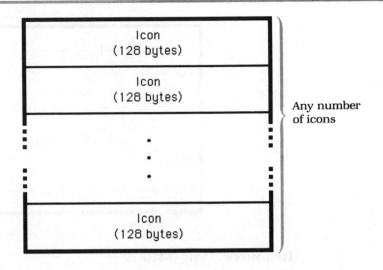

Resource Type 'ICON'

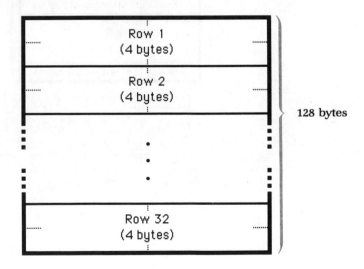

Resource Type 'INIT'

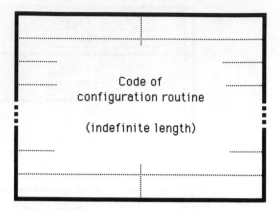

Resource Type 'MBAR'

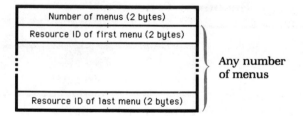

Resource Type 'MENU'

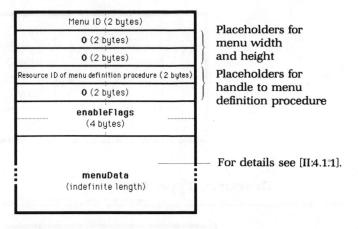

Placeholders for menu width and height

Placeholders for handle to menu definition procedure

For details see [II:4.1.1].

Resource Type 'PACK'

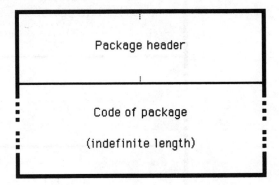

Resource Type 'PAT '

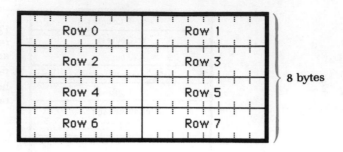

Resource Type 'PAT#'

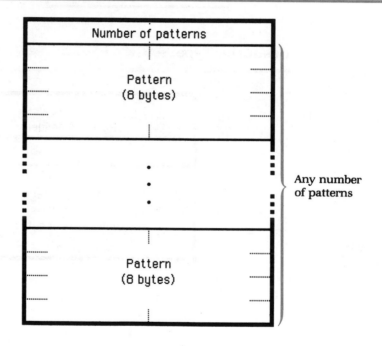

Resource Type 'PICT'

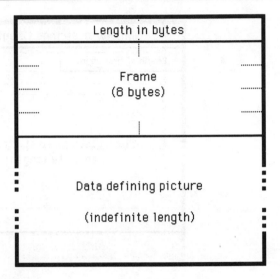

Resource Type 'STR '

The maximum length of a '**STR** ' resource is 255 characters.

Resource Type 'STR#'

Resource Type 'TEXT'

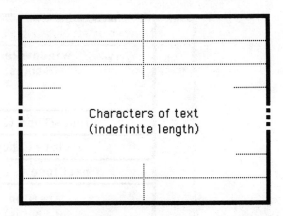

Characters of text
(indefinite length)

A 'TEXT' resource does *not* begin with a length byte.

Resource Type 'WIND'

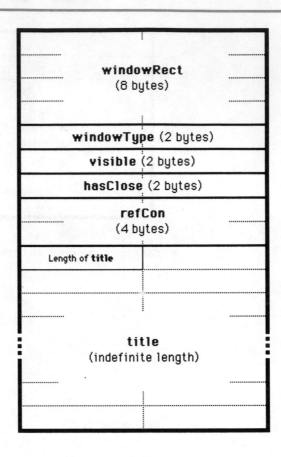

APPENDIX

C

Memory Layouts

128K Macintosh

128K
Macintosh

$00	Trap Vectors
$100	System Globals
$400	Dispatch Table
$800	System Globals
$B00	System Heap
$4E00	Application Heap
	Stack
	Application Global Space
$1A700	Main Screen Buffer
$1FC7F	
$1FD00	Main Sound Buffer
$1FFE3	
$1FFFF	

KEY

  System Use

↑ Arrows show direction of
growth of stack and
application heap.

Memory layout for 128K Macintosh

512K "Fat Mac"

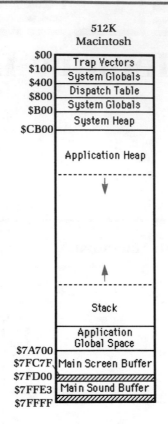

Memory layout for 512K "Fat Mac"

512K Macintosh XL (Lisa)

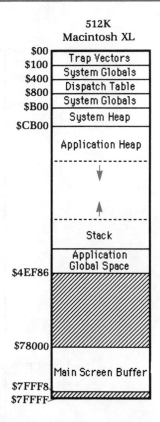

Memory layout for 512K Macintosh XL

1M Macintosh XL (Lisa)

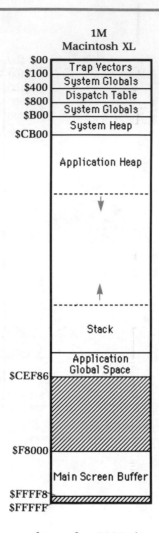

Memory layout for 1M Macintosh XL

Key Codes and Character Codes

Key Codes

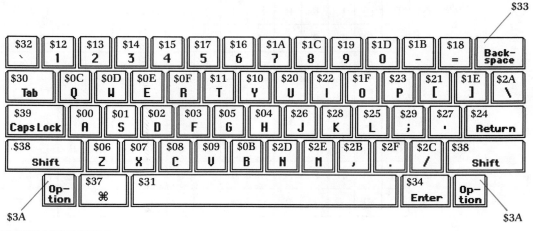

Small hexadecimal numbers are key codes.

Key codes

Character codes

First hex digit

		$0	$1	$2	$3	$4	$5	$6	$7	$8	$9	$A	$B	$C	$D	$E	$F
	$0	NUL	□	Space	0	@	P	`	p	Ä	ê	†	∞	¿	–	□	□
	$1	□	⌘	!	1	A	Q	a	q	Å	ë	°	±	¡	—	□	□
	$2	□	✓	"	2	B	R	b	r	Ç	í	¢	≤	¬	"	□	□
	$3	□	◆	#	3	C	S	c	s	É	ì	£	≥	√	"	□	□
	$4	□		$	4	D	T	d	t	Ñ	î	§	¥	ƒ	'	□	□
	$5	□	□	%	5	E	U	e	u	Ö	ï	•	µ	≈	'	□	□
	$6	□	□	&	6	F	V	f	v	Ü	ñ	¶	∂	∆	÷	□	□
Second hex digit	$7	□	□	'	7	G	W	g	w	á	ó	ß	Σ	«	◊	□	□
	$8	□	□	(	8	H	X	h	x	à	ò	®	∏	»	ÿ	□	□
	$9	TAB	□	)	9	I	Y	i	y	â	ô	©	π	…	□	□	□
	$A	□	□	*	:	J	Z	j	z	ä	ö	™	∫	non-break space	□	□	□
	$B	□	□	+	;	K	[	k	{	ã	õ	´	ª	À	□	□	□
	$C	□	□	,	<	L	\	l	|	å	ú	¨	º	Ã	□	□	□
	$D	CR	□	–	=	M	]	m	}	ç	ù	≠	Ω	Õ	□	□	
	$E	□	□	.	>	N	^	n	~	é	û	Æ	æ	Œ	□	□	
	$F	□	□	/	?	O	_	o		è	ü	Ø	ø	œ	□	□	□

Characters with shading are typed
as two-character combinations.

Character codes

APPENDIX

Error Codes

Operating System Errors

The following is a complete list of Operating System error codes. Not all are covered in this book, and some of the meanings may be obscure. (I don't know what a bit-slip nybble is either.) For the errors you're most likely to encounter, see reference sections [I:3.1.2, I:6.6.1, II:8.2.8].

Number	Name	Meaning
0	**NoErr**	No error; all is well
−1	**QErr**	Queue element not found during deletion
−2	**VTypErr**	Invalid queue element
−3	**CorErr**	Trap ("core routine") number out of range
−4	**UnimpErr**	Unimplemented trap
−17	**ControlErr**	Driver error during Control operation
−18	**StatusErr**	Driver error during Status operation
−19	**ReadErr**	Driver error during Read operation
−20	**WritErr**	Driver error during Write operation
−21	**BadUnitErr**	Bad unit number
−22	**UnitEmptyErr**	No such entry in unit table
−23	**OpenErr**	Driver error during Open operation
−24	**CloseErr**	Driver error during Close operation
−25	**DRemovErr**	Attempt to remove an open driver
−26	**DInstErr**	Attempt to install nonexistent driver
−27	**AbortErr**	Driver operation aborted
−28	**NotOpenErr**	Driver not open
−33	**DirFulErr**	Directory full
−34	**DskFulErr**	Disk full
−35	**NSVErr**	No such volume

Number	Name	Meaning
−36	**IOErr**	Disk I/O error
−37	**BdNamErr**	Bad name
−38	**FNOpnErr**	File not open
−39	**EOFErr**	Attempt to read past end-of-file
−40	**PosErr**	Attempt to position before start of file
−41	**MFulErr**	Memory (system heap) full
−42	**TMFOErr**	Too many files open (more than 12)
−43	**FNFErr**	File not found
−44	**WPrErr**	Disk is write-protected
−45	**FLckdErr**	File locked
−46	**VLckdErr**	Volume locked
−47	**FBsyErr**	File busy
−48	**DupFNErr**	Duplicate file name
−49	**OpWrErr**	File already open for writing
−50	**ParamErr**	Invalid parameter list
−51	**RfNumErr**	Invalid reference number
−52	**GFPErr**	Error during **GetFPos**
−53	**VolOffLinErr**	Volume off-line
−54	**PermErr**	Permission violation
−55	**VolOnLinErr**	Volume already on-line
−56	**NSDrvErr**	No such drive
−57	**NoMacDskErr**	Non-Macintosh disk
−58	**ExtFSErr**	External file system
−59	**FSRnErr**	Unable to rename file
−60	**BadMDBErr**	Bad master directory block
−61	**WrPermErr**	No write permission
−64	**NoDriveErr**	No such drive
−65	**OffLinErr**	Drive off-line
−66	**NoNybErr**	Can't find 5 nybbles
−67	**NoAdrMkErr**	No address mark
−68	**DataVerErr**	Data read doesn't verify
−69	**BadCksmErr**	Bad checksum (address mark)
−70	**BadBtSlpErr**	Bad bit-slip nybbles (address mark)
−71	**NoDtaMkErr**	No data mark
−72	**BadDCksumErr**	Bad checksum (data mark)
−73	**BadDBtSlpErr**	Bad bit-slip nybbles (data mark)
−74	**WrUnderrun**	Write underrun
−75	**CantStepErr**	Can't step disk drive
−76	**Tk0BadErr**	Track 0 bad
−77	**InitIWMErr**	Can't initialize disk chip ("Integrated Wozniak Machine")
−78	**TwoSideErr**	Two-sided operation on one-sided drive
−79	**SpdAdjErr**	Can't adjust disk speed
−80	**SeekErr**	Seek to wrong track
−81	**SectNFErr**	Sector not found
−85	**ClkRdErr**	Error reading clock
−86	**ClkWrErr**	Error writing clock
−87	**PRWrErr**	Error writing parameter RAM
−88	**PRInitErr**	Parameter RAM uninitialized

Number	Name	Meaning
−89	**RcvrErr**	Receiver error (serial communications)
−90	**BreakRecd**	Break received (serial communications)
−100	**NoScrapErr**	No desk scrap
−102	**NoTypeErr**	No item in scrap of requested type
−108	**MemFullErr**	No room; heap is full
−109	**NilHandleErr**	Illegal operation on empty handle
−110	**MemAdrErr**	Bad memory address
−111	**MemWZErr**	Illegal operation on free block
−112	**MemPurErr**	Illegal operation on locked block
−113	**MemAZErr**	Address not in heap zone
−114	**MemPCErr**	Pointer check failed
−115	**MemBCErr**	Block check failed
−116	**MemSCErr**	Size check failed
−192	**ResNotFound**	Resource not found
−193	**ResFNotFound**	Resource file not found
−194	**AddResFailed**	**AddResource** failed
−195	**AddRefFailed**	**AddReference** failed
−196	**RmvResFailed**	**RmveResource** failed
−197	**RmvRefFailed**	**RmveReference** failed

"Dire Straits" Errors

The following errors are reported directly to the user—not to the running program—by the "Dire Straits" Manager (officially called the System Error Handler). Errors in this category are considered so serious that recovery is impossible: the Toolbox simply displays a "dire straits" alert box (the one with the bomb icon) on the screen, forcing the user to restart the system. Some people insist that **DS** really stands for "deep spaghetti," but most Macintosh programmers prefer a more colorful term.

Number	Name	Meaning
1	**DSBusErr**	Bus error
2	**DSAddressErr**	Address error
3	**DSIllInstErr**	Illegal instruction
4	**DSZeroDivErr**	Attempt to divide by zero
5	**DSChkErr**	Check trap
6	**DSOvflowErr**	Overflow trap
7	**DSPrivErr**	Privilege violation
8	**DSTraceErr**	Trace trap
9	**DSLineAErr**	"A emulator" trap
10	**DSLineFErr**	"F emulator" trap
11	**DSMiscErr**	Miscellaneous hardware exception
12	**DSCoreErr**	Unimplemented core routine
13	**DSIRQErr**	Uninstalled interrupt
14	**DSIOCoreErr**	I/O core error
15	**DSLoadErr**	Segment Loader error
16	**DSFPErr**	Floating-point error

Number	Name	Meaning
17	**DSNoPackErr**	Package 0 not present
18	**DSNoPk1**	Package 1 not present
19	**DSNoPk2**	Package 2 not present
20	**DSNoPk3**	Package 3 not present
21	**DSNoPk4**	Package 4 not present
22	**DSNoPk5**	Package 5 not present
23	**DSNoPk6**	Package 6 not present
24	**DSNoPk7**	Package 7 not present
25	**DSMemFullErr**	Out of memory
26	**DSBadLaunch**	Can't launch program
27	**DSFSErr**	File system error
28	**DSStkNHeap**	Stack/heap collision
30	**DSReinsert**	Ask user to reinsert disk
31	**DSNotTheOne**	Wrong disk inserted

A P P E N D I X

Summary of Trap Macros and Trap Words

Trap Macros

The following is an alphabetical list of assembly-language trap macros covered in both volumes of this book, with their corresponding trap words. For routines belonging to the standard packages, the trap word shown is one of the eight package traps (_**Pack0** to _**Pack7**) and is followed by a routine selector in parentheses.

Trap macro name	Trap word	Reference section
_**AddPt**	**$A87E**	[I:4.4.1]
_**AddResMenu**	**$A94D**	[II:4.3.3]
_**AddResource**	**$A9AB**	[I:6.5.3]
_**Alert**	**$A985**	[II:7.4.2]
_**Allocate**	**$A010**	[II:8.2.5]
_**AppendMenu**	**$A933**	[II:4.3.1]
_**BackPat**	**$A87C**	[I:5.1.1]
_**BeginUpdate**	**$A922**	[II:3.4.1]
_**BitAnd**	**$A858**	[I:2.2.2]
_**BitClr**	**$A85F**	[I:2.2.1]
_**BitNot**	**$A85A**	[I:2.2.2]
_**BitOr**	**$A85B**	[I:2.2.2]
_**BitSet**	**$A85E**	[I:2.2.1]
_**BitShift**	**$A85C**	[I:2.2.2]
_**BitTst**	**$A85D**	[I:2.2.1]
_**BitXOr**	**$A859**	[I:2.2.2]
_**BlockMove**	**$A02E**	[I:3.2.5]
_**BringToFront**	**$A920**	[II:3.3.3]
_**Button**	**$A974**	[II:2.4.2]

Trap macro name	Trap word	Reference section
_CalcMenuSize	$A948	[II:4.7.1]
_CautionAlert	$A988	[II:7.4.2]
_Chain	$A9F3	[I:7.1.1]
_ChangedResource	$A9AA	[I:6.5.2]
_CharWidth	$A88D	[I:8.3.4]
_CheckItem	$A945	[II:4.6.4]
_ClearMenuBar	$A934	[II:4.4.1]
_ClipRect	$A87B	[I:4.3.6]
_Close	$A001	[II:8.2.2]
_CloseDeskAcc	$A9B7	[II:4.5.2]
_CloseDialog	$A982	[II:7.2.3]
_ClosePgon	$A8CC	[I:4.1.4]
_ClosePicture	$A8F4	[I:5.4.2]
_ClosePort	$A87D	[I:4.3.2]
_CloseResFile	$A99A	[I:6.2.1]
_CloseRgn	$A8DB	[I:4.1.6]
_CloseWindow	$A92D	[II:3.2.3]
_CmpString	$A03C	[I:2.1.2]
_CompactMem	$A04C	[I:3.3.2]
_CopyBits	$A8EC	[I:5.1.2]
_CopyRgn	$A8DC	[I:4.1.7]
_CouldAlert	$A989	[II:7.5.3]
_CouldDialog	$A979	[II:7.5.3]
_CountMItems	$A950	[II:4.3.4]
_CountResources	$A99C	[I:6.3.3]
_CountTypes	$A99E	[I:6.3.3]
_Create	$A008	[II:8.2.1]
_CreateResFile	$A9B1	[I:6.5.1]
_CurResFile	$A994	[I:6.2.2]
_Date2Secs	$A9C7	[I:2.4.3]
_Delay	$A03B	[II:2.7.1]
_Delete	$A009	[II:8.2.7]
_DeleteMenu	$A936	[II:4.4.1]
_DetachResource	$A992	[I:6.3.2]
_DialogSelect	$A980	[II:7.4.4]
_DIBadMount	$A9E9 (0)	[II:8.4.1]
_DiffRgn	$A8E6	[I:4.4.8]
_DIFormat	$A9E9 (6)	[II:8.4.2]
_DILoad	$A9E9 (2)	[II:8.4.3]
_DisableItem	$A93A	[II:4.6.2]
_DisposControl	$A955	[II:6.2.2]
_DisposDialog	$A983	[II:7.2.3]
_DisposHandle	$A023	[I:3.2.2]
_DisposMenu	$A932	[II:4.2.3]
_DisposPtr	$A01F	[I:3.2.2]
_DisposRgn	$A8D9	[I:4.1.6]
_DisposWindow	$A914	[II:3.2.3]
_DIUnload	$A9E9 (4)	[II:8.4.3]
_DIVerify	$A9E9 (8)	[II:8.4.2]
_DIZero	$A9E9 (10)	[II:8.4.2]

Trap macro name	Trap word	Reference section
_DragControl	$A967	[II:6.4.3]
_DragWindow	$A925	[II:3.5.4]
_DrawChar	$A883	[I:8.3.3]
_DrawControls	$A969	[II:6.3.1]
_DrawDialog	$A981	[II:7.4.1]
_DrawGrowIcon	$A904	[II:3.3.4]
_DrawMenuBar	$A937	[II:4.4.3]
_DrawPicture	$A8F6	[I:5.4.3]
_DrawString	$A884	[I:8.3.3]
_DrawText	$A885	[I:8.3.3]
_Eject	$A017	[II:8.1.3]
_EmptyHandle	$A02B	[I:3.3.3]
_EmptyRect	$A8AE	[I:4.4.4]
_EmptyRgn	$A8E2	[I:4.4.7]
_EnableItem	$A939	[II:4.6.2]
_EndUpdate	$A923	[II:3.4.1]
_EqualPt	$A881	[I:4.4.1]
_EqualRect	$A8A6	[I:4.4.5]
_EqualRgn	$A8E3	[I:4.4.8]
_EraseArc	$A8C0	[I:5.3.5]
_EraseOval	$A8B9	[I:5.3.4]
_ErasePoly	$A8C8	[I:5.3.6]
_EraseRect	$A8A3	[I:5.3.2]
_EraseRgn	$A8D4	[I:5.3.7]
_EraseRoundRect	$A8B2	[I:5.3.3]
_ErrorSound	$A98C	[II:7.5.1]
_EventAvail	$A971	[II:2.2.1]
_ExitToShell	$A9F4	[I:7.1.3]
_FillArc	$A8C2	[I:5.3.5]
_FillOval	$A8BB	[I:5.3.4]
_FillPoly	$A8CA	[I:5.3.6]
_FillRect	$A8A5	[I:5.3.2]
_FillRgn	$A8D6	[I:5.3.7]
_FillRoundRect	$A8B4	[I:5.3.3]
_FindControl	$A96C	[II:6.4.1]
_FindWindow	$A92C	[II:3.5.1]
_FixMul	$A868	[I:2.3.2]
_FixRatio	$A869	[I:2.3.2]
_FixRound	$A86C	[I:2.3.1]
_FlashMenuBar	$A94C	[II:4.7.2]
_FlushEvents	$A032	[II:2.3.1]
_FlushVol	$A013	[II:8.1.3]
_FrameArc	$A8BE	[I:5.3.5]
_FrameOval	$A8B7	[I:5.3.4]
_FramePoly	$A8C6	[I:5.3.6]
_FrameRect	$A8A1	[I:5.3.2]
_FrameRgn	$A8D2	[I:5.3.7]
_FrameRoundRect	$A8B0	[I:5.3.3]
_FreeAlert	$A98A	[II:7.5.3]
_FreeDialog	$A97A	[II:7.5.3]

Trap macro name	Trap word	Reference section
_FreeMem	$A01C	[I:3.3.1]
_FrontWindow	$A924	[II:3.3.3]
_GetAppParms	$A9F5	[I:7.3.4]
_GetClip	$A87A	[I:4.3.6]
_GetCRefCon	$A95A	[II:6.2.3]
_GetCTitle	$A95E	[II:6.2.3]
_GetCtlAction	$A96A	[II:6.4.2]
_GetCtlValue	$A960	[II:6.2.4]
_GetCursor	$A9B9	[II:2.5.2]
_GetDItem	$A98D	[II:7.3.1]
_GetEOF	$A011	[II:8.2.5]
_GetFileInfo	$A00C	[I:7.3.3]
_GetFName	$A8FF	[I:8.2.5]
_GetFNum	$A900	[I:8.2.5]
_GetFontInfo	$A88B	[I:8.2.6]
_GetFPos	$A018	[II:8.2.4]
_GetHandleSize	$A025	[I:3.2.3]
_GetIndResource	$A99D	[I:6.3.3]
_GetIndType	$A99F	[I:6.3.3]
_GetItem	$A946	[II:4.6.1]
_GetIText	$A990	[II:7.3.2]
_GetItmIcon	$A93F	[II:4.6.5]
_GetItmMark	$A943	[II:4.6.4]
_GetItmStyle	$A941	[II:4.6.3]
_GetKeys	$A976	[II:2.6.1]
_GetMaxCtl	$A962	[II:6.2.4]
_GetMenuBar	$A93B	[II:4.4.4]
_GetMHandle	$A949	[II:4.4.5]
_GetMinCtl	$A961	[II:6.2.4]
_GetMouse	$A972	[II:2.4.1]
_GetNamedResource	$A9A1	[I:6.3.1]
_GetNewControl	$A9BE	[II:6.2.1]
_GetNewDialog	$A97C	[II:7.2.2]
_GetNewMBar	$A9C0	[II:4.4.2]
_GetNewWindow	$A9BD	[II:3.2.2]
_GetNextEvent	$A970	[II:2.2.1]
_GetPattern	$A9B8	[I:5.1.1]
_GetPen	$A89A	[I:5.2.4]
_GetPenState	$A898	[I:5.2.1]
_GetPicture	$A9BC	[I:5.4.2]
_GetPixel	$A865	[I:4.2.3]
_GetPort	$A874	[I:4.3.3]
_GetPtrSize	$A021	[I:3.2.3]
_GetResAttrs	$A9A6	[I:6.4.2]
_GetResFileAttrs	$A9F6	[I:6.6.2]
_GetResInfo	$A9A8	[I:6.4.1]
_GetResource	$A9A0	[I:6.3.1]
_GetRMenu	$A9BF	[II:4.2.2]
_GetScrap	$A9FD	[I:7.4.3]
_GetString	$A9BA	[I:8.1.2]

Trap macro name	Trap word	Reference section
_GetVol	$A014	[II:8.1.2]
_GetVolInfo	$A007	[II:8.1.1]
_GetWindowPic	$A92F	[II:3.4.3]
_GetWMgrPort	$A910	[II:3.6.1]
_GetWRefCon	$A917	[II:3.2.4]
_GetWTitle	$A919	[II:3.2.4]
_GlobalToLocal	$A871	[I:4.4.2]
_GrafDevice	$A872	[I:8.3.2]
_GrowWindow	$A92B	[II:3.5.4]
_HandAndHand	$A9E4	[I:3.2.6]
_HandToHand	$A9E1	[I:3.2.5]
_HideControl	$A958	[II:6.3.1]
_HideCursor	$A852	[II:2.5.3]
_HidePen	$A896	[I:5.2.3]
_HideWindow	$A916	[II:3.3.1]
_HiliteControl	$A95D	[II:6.3.3]
_HiliteMenu	$A938	[II:4.5.4]
_HiliteWindow	$A91C	[II:3.3.4]
_HiWord	$A86A	[I:2.2.3]
_HLock	$A029	[I:3.2.4]
_HNoPurge	$A04A	[I:3.2.4]
_HomeResFile	$A9A4	[I:6.4.3]
_HPurge	$A049	[I:3.2.4]
_HUnlock	$A02A	[I:3.2.4]
_InfoScrap	$A9F9	[I:7.4.2]
_InitAllPacks	$A9E6	[I:7.2.2]
_InitCursor	$A850	[II:2.5.2]
_InitDialogs	$A97B	[II:7.2.1]
_InitFonts	$A8FE	[I:8.2.4]
_InitGraf	$A86E	[I:4.3.1]
_InitMenus	$A930	[II:4.2.1]
_InitPack	$A9E5	[I:7.2.2]
_InitPort	$A86D	[I:4.3.2]
_InitWindows	$A912	[II:3.2.1]
_InsertMenu	$A935	[II:4.4.1]
_InsertResMenu	$A951	[II:4.3.3]
_InsetRect	$A8A9	[I:4.4.4]
_InsetRgn	$A8E1	[I:4.4.7]
_InvalRect	$A928	[II:3.4.2]
_InvalRgn	$A927	[II:3.4.2]
_InverRect	$A8A4	[I:5.3.2]
_InverRgn	$A8D5	[I:5.3.7]
_InverRoundRect	$A8B3	[I:5.3.3]
_InvertArc	$A8C1	[I:5.3.5]
_InvertOval	$A8BA	[I:5.3.4]
_InvertPoly	$A8C9	[I:5.3.6]
_IsDialogEvent	$A97F	[II:7.4.4]
_IUDateString	$A9ED (0)	[I:2.4.4]
_IUTimeString	$A9ED (2)	[I:2.4.4]

Trap macro name	Trap word	Reference section
_KillControls	$A956	[II:6.2.2]
_KillPicture	$A8F5	[I:5.4.2]
_KillPoly	$A8CD	[I:4.1.4]
_Launch	$A9F2	[I:7.1.1]
_Line	$A892	[I:5.2.4]
_LineTo	$A891	[I:5.2.4]
_LoadSeg	$A9F0	[I:7.1.2]
_LocalToGlobal	$A870	[I:4.4.2]
_LodeScrap	$A9FB	[I:7.4.4]
_LongMul	$A867	[I:2.3.3]
_LoWord	$A86B	[I:2.2.3]
_MapPoly	$A8FC	[I:4.4.9]
_MapPt	$A8F9	[I:4.4.9]
_MapRect	$A8FA	[I:4.4.9]
_MapRgn	$A8FB	[I:4.4.9]
_MaxMem	$A11D	[I:3.3.1]
_MenuKey	$A93E	[II:4.5.1]
_MenuSelect	$A93D	[II:4.5.1]
_ModalDialog	$A991	[II:7.4.3]
_MountVol	$A00F	[II:8.1.3]
_Move	$A894	[I:5.2.4]
_MoveControl	$A959	[II:6.3.2]
_MovePortTo	$A877	[I:4.3.5]
_MoveTo	$A893	[I:5.2.4]
_MoveWindow	$A91B	[II:3.3.2]
_Munger	$A9E0	[II:5.5.6]
_NewControl	$A954	[II:6.2.1]
_NewDialog	$A97D	[II:7.2.2]
_NewHandle	$A122	[I:3.2.1]
_NewMenu	$A931	[II:4.2.2]
_NewPtr	$A11E	[I:3.2.1]
_NewRgn	$A8D8	[I:4.1.6]
_NewString	$A906	[I:8.1.2]
_NewWindow	$A913	[II:3.2.2]
_NoteAlert	$A987	[II:7.4.2]
_NumToString	$A9EE (0)	[I:2.3.4]
_ObscureCursor	$A856	[II:2.5.4]
_OffLine	$A035	[II:8.1.3]
_OffsetPoly	$A8CE	[I:4.4.6]
_OffsetRect	$A8A8	[I:4.4.4]
_OfsetRgn	$A8E0	[I:4.4.7]
_Open	$A000	[II:8.2.2]
_OpenDeskAcc	$A9B6	[II:4.5.2]
_OpenPicture	$A8F3	[I:5.4.2]
_OpenPoly	$A8CB	[I:4.1.4]
_OpenPort	$A86F	[I:4.3.2]
_OpenResFile	$A997	[I:6.2.1]
_OpenRF	$A00A	[II:8.2.2]
_OpenRgn	$A8DA	[I:4.1.6]

Trap macro name	Trap word	Reference section
_Pack0	$A9E7	[I:7.2.1]
_Pack1	$A9E8	[I:7.2.1]
_Pack2	$A9E9	[I:7.2.1]
_Pack3	$A9EA	[I:7.2.1]
_Pack4	$A9EB	[I:7.2.1]
_Pack5	$A9EC	[I:7.2.1]
_Pack6	$A9ED	[I:7.2.1]
_Pack7	$A9EE	[I:7.2.1]
_PaintArc	$A8BF	[I:5.3.5]
_PaintOval	$A8B8	[I:5.3.4]
_PaintPoly	$A8C7	[I:5.3.6]
_PaintRect	$A8A2	[I:5.3.2]
_PaintRgn	$A8D3	[I:5.3.7]
_PaintRoundRect	$A8B1	[I:5.3.3]
_ParamText	$A98B	[II:7.4.6]
_PenMode	$A89C	[I:5.2.2]
_PenNormal	$A89E	[I:5.2.2]
_PenPat	$A89D	[I:5.2.2]
_PenSize	$A89B	[I:5.2.2]
_PinRect	$A94E	[I:4.4.3]
_PortSize	$A876	[I:4.3.5]
_PostEvent	$A02F	[II:2.3.2]
_Pt2Rect	$A8AC	[I:4.1.2]
_PtInRect	$A8AD	[I:4.4.3]
_PtInRgn	$A8E8	[I:4.4.3]
_PtrAndHand	$A9EF	[I:3.2.6]
_PtrToHand	$A9E3	[I:3.2.5]
_PtrToXHand	$A9E2	[I:3.2.5]
_PtToAngle	$A8C3	[I:5.3.5]
_PurgeMem	$A04D	[I:3.3.3]
_PutScrap	$A9FE	[I:7.4.3]
_Random	$A861	[I:2.3.5]
_Read	$A002	[II:8.2.3]
_RealFont	$A902	[I:8.2.5]
_ReallocHandle	$A027	[I:3.3.3]
_RecoverHandle	$A128	[I:3.2.1]
_RectInRgn	$A8E9	[I:4.4.3]
_RectRgn	$A8DF	[I:4.1.7]
_ReleaseResource	$A9A3	[I:6.3.2]
_Rename	$A00B	[II:8.2.7]
_ResError	$A9AF	[I:6.6.1]
_ResrvMem	$A040	[I:3.2.1]
_RmveResource	$A9AD	[I:6.5.3]
_RstFilLock	$A042	[II:8.2.6]
_ScalePt	$A8F8	[I:4.4.9]
_ScrollRect	$A8EF	[I:5.1.5]
_Secs2Date	$A9C6	[I:2.4.3]
_SectRect	$A8AA	[I:4.4.5]
_SectRgn	$A8E4	[I:4.4.8]
_SelectWindow	$A91F	[II:3.5.2]

Trap macro name	Trap word	Reference section
_SelIText	$A97E	[II:7.3.2]
_SendBehind	$A921	[II:3.3.3]
_SetApplLimit	$A02D	[I:3.3.4]
_SetClip	$A879	[I:4.3.6]
_SetCRefCon	$A95B	[II:6.2.3]
_SetCTitle	$A95F	[II:6.2.3]
_SetCtlAction	$A96B	[II:6.4.2]
_SetCtlValue	$A963	[II:6.2.4]
_SetCursor	$A851	[II:2.5.2]
_SetDateTime	$A03A	[I:2.4.1]
_SetDItem	$A98E	[II:7.3.1]
_SetEmptyRgn	$A8DD	[I:4.1.7]
_SetEOF	$A012	[II:8.2.5]
_SetFileInfo	$A00D	[I:7.3.3]
_SetFilLock	$A041	[II:8.2.6]
_SetFontLock	$A903	[I:8.2.7]
_SetFPos	$A044	[II:8.2.4]
_SetHandleSize	$A024	[I:3.2.3]
_SetItem	$A947	[II:4.6.1]
_SetIText	$A98F	[II:7.3.2]
_SetItmIcon	$A940	[II:4.6.5]
_SetItmMark	$A944	[II:4.6.4]
_SetItmStyle	$A942	[II:4.6.3]
_SetMaxCtl	$A965	[II:6.2.4]
_SetMenuBar	$A93C	[II:4.4.4]
_SetMFlash	$A94A	[II:4.7.2]
_SetMinCtl	$A964	[II:6.2.4]
_SetOrigin	$A878	[I:4.3.4]
_SetPBits	$A875	[I:4.3.4]
_SetPenState	$A899	[I:5.2.1]
_SetPort	$A873	[I:4.3.3]
_SetPt	$A880	[I:4.1.1]
_SetPtrSize	$A020	[I:3.2.3]
_SetRecRgn	$A8DE	[I:4.1.7]
_SetRect	$A8A7	[I:4.1.2]
_SetResAttrs	$A9A7	[I:6.4.2]
_SetResFileAttrs	$A9F7	[I:6.6.2]
_SetResInfo	$A9A9	[I:6.4.1]
_SetResPurge	$A993	[I:6.5.5]
_SetString	$A907	[I:8.1.2]
_SetVol	$A015	[II:8.1.2]
_SetWindowPic	$A92E	[II:3.4.3]
_SetWRefCon	$A918	[II:3.2.4]
_SetWTitle	$A91A	[II:3.2.4]
_SFGetFile	$A9EA (2)	[II:8.3.2]
_SFPutFile	$A9EA (1)	[II:8.3.3]
_ShieldCursor	$A855	[II:2.5.4]
_ShowControl	$A957	[II:6.3.1]
_ShowCursor	$A853	[II:2.5.3]
_ShowHide	$A908	[II:3.3.1]

Trap macro name	Trap word	Reference section
_ShowPen	$A897	[I:5.2.3]
_ShowWindow	$A915	[II:3.3.1]
_SizeControl	$A95C	[II:6.3.2]
_SizeRsrc	$A9A5	[I:6.4.3]
_SizeWindow	$A91D	[II:3.3.2]
_SpaceExtra	$A88E	[I:8.3.2]
_StillDown	$A973	[II:2.4.2]
_StopAlert	$A986	[II:7.4.2]
_StringToNum	$A9EE (1)	[I:2.3.4]
_StringWidth	$A88C	[I:8.3.4]
_StuffHex	$A866	[I:2.2.4]
_SubPt	$A87F	[I:4.4.1]
_SysBeep	$A9C8	[II:2.8.1]
_SysEdit	$A9C2	[II:4.5.3]
_SystemClick	$A9B3	[II:3.5.3]
_SystemTask	$A9B4	[II:2.7.2]
_TEActivate	$A9D8	[II:5.4.3]
_TECalText	$A9D0	[II:5.3.1]
_TEClick	$A9D4	[II:5.4.1]
_TECopy	$A9D5	[II:5.5.2]
_TECut	$A9D6	[II:5.5.2]
_TEDeactivate	$A9D9	[II:5.4.3]
_TEDelete	$A9D7	[II:5.5.3]
_TEDispose	$A9CD	[II:5.2.2]
_TEGetText	$A9CB	[II:5.2.3]
_TEIdle	$A9DA	[II:5.4.3]
_TEInit	$A9CC	[II:5.2.1]
_TEInsert	$A9DE	[II:5.5.3]
_TEKey	$A9DC	[II:5.5.1]
_TENew	$A9D2	[II:5.2.2]
_TEPaste	$A9DB	[II:5.5.2]
_TEScroll	$A9DD	[II:5.3.3]
_TESetJust	$A9DF	[II:5.3.1]
_TESetSelect	$A9D1	[II:5.4.2]
_TESetText	$A9CF	[II:5.2.3]
_TestControl	$A966	[II:6.4.1]
_TEUpdate	$A9D3	[II:5.3.2]
_TextBox	$A9CE	[II:5.3.2]
_TextFace	$A888	[I:8.3.2]
_TextFont	$A887	[I:8.3.2]
_TextMode	$A889	[I:8.3.2]
_TextSize	$A88A	[I:8.3.2]
_TextWidth	$A886	[I:8.3.4]
_TickCount	$A975	[II:2.7.1]
_TrackControl	$A968	[II:6.4.2]
_TrackGoAway	$A91E	[II:3.5.4]
_UnionRect	$A8AB	[I:4.4.5]
_UnionRgn	$A8E5	[I:4.4.8]
_UniqueID	$A9C1	[I:6.5.3]
_UnloadSeg	$A9F1	[I:7.1.2]

Trap macro name	Trap word	Reference section
_UnlodeScrap	$A9FA	[I:7.4.4]
_UnmountVol	$A00E	[II:8.1.3]
_UpdateResFile	$A999	[I:6.5.4]
_UprString	$A854	[I:2.1.2]
_UseResFile	$A998	[I:6.2.2]
_ValidRect	$A92A	[II:3.4.2]
_ValidRgn	$A929	[II:3.4.2]
_WaitMouseUp	$A977	[II:2.4.2]
_Write	$A003	[II:8.2.3]
_WriteResource	$A9B0	[I:6.5.4]
_XOrRgn	$A8E7	[I:4.4.8]
_ZeroScrap	$A9FC	[I:7.4.3]

Trap Words

Here is the same list sorted numerically by trap word. Again, routine selectors are given in parentheses following the trap word for routines belonging to the standard packages.

Trap word	Trap macro name	Reference section
$A000	_Open	[II:8.2.2]
$A001	_Close	[II:8.2.2]
$A002	_Read	[II:8.2.3]
$A003	_Write	[II:8.2.3]
$A007	_GetVolInfo	[II:8.1.1]
$A008	_Create	[II:8.2.1]
$A009	_Delete	[II:8.2.7]
$A00A	_OpenRF	[II:8.2.2]
$A00B	_Rename	[II:8.2.7]
$A00C	_GetFileInfo	[I:7.3.3]
$A00D	_SetFileInfo	[I:7.3.3]
$A00E	_UnmountVol	[II:8.1.3]
$A00F	_MountVol	[II:8.1.3]
$A010	_Allocate	[II:8.2.5]
$A011	_GetEOF	[II:8.2.5]
$A012	_SetEOF	[II:8.2.5]
$A013	_FlushVol	[II:8.1.3]
$A014	_GetVol	[II:8.1.2]
$A015	_SetVol	[II:8.1.2]
$A017	_Eject	[II:8.1.3]
$A018	_GetFPos	[II:8.2.4]
$A01C	_FreeMem	[I:3.3.1]
$A01F	_DisposPtr	[I:3.2.2]

Trap word	Trap macro name	Reference section
$A020	_SetPtrSize	[I:3.2.3]
$A021	_GetPtrSize	[I:3.2.3]
$A023	_DisposHandle	[I:3.2.2]
$A024	_SetHandleSize	[I:3.2.3]
$A025	_GetHandleSize	[I:3.2.3]
$A027	_ReallocHandle	[I:3.3.3]
$A029	_HLock	[I:3.2.4]
$A02A	_HUnlock	[I:3.2.4]
$A02B	_EmptyHandle	[I:3.3.3]
$A02D	_SetApplLimit	[I:3.3.4]
$A02E	_BlockMove	[I:3.2.5]
$A02F	_PostEvent	[II:2.3.2]
$A032	_FlushEvents	[II:2.3.1]
$A035	_OffLine	[II:8.1.3]
$A03A	_SetDateTime	[I:2.4.1]
$A03B	_Delay	[II:2.7.1]
$A03C	_CmpString	[I:2.1.2]
$A040	_ResrvMem	[I:3.2.1]
$A041	_SetFilLock	[II:8.2.6]
$A042	_RstFilLock	[II:8.2.6]
$A044	_SetFPos	[II:8.2.4]
$A049	_HPurge	[I:3.2.4]
$A04A	_HNoPurge	[I:3.2.4]
$A04C	_CompactMem	[I:3.3.2]
$A04D	_PurgeMem	[I:3.3.3]
$A11D	_MaxMem	[I:3.3.1]
$A11E	_NewPtr	[I:3.2.1]
$A122	_NewHandle	[I:3.2.1]
$A128	_RecoverHandle	[I:3.2.1]
$A850	_InitCursor	[II:2.5.2]
$A851	_SetCursor	[II:2.5.2]
$A852	_HideCursor	[II:2.5.3]
$A853	_ShowCursor	[II:2.5.3]
$A854	_UprString	[I:2.1.2]
$A855	_ShieldCursor	[II:2.5.4]
$A856	_ObscureCursor	[II:2.5.4]
$A858	_BitAnd	[I:2.2.2]
$A859	_BitXOr	[I:2.2.2]
$A85A	_BitNot	[I:2.2.2]
$A85B	_BitOr	[I:2.2.2]
$A85C	_BitShift	[I:2.2.2]
$A85D	_BitTst	[I:2.2.1]
$A85E	_BitSet	[I:2.2.1]
$A85F	_BitClr	[I:2.2.1]
$A861	_Random	[I:2.3.5]
$A865	_GetPixel	[I:4.2.3]
$A866	_StuffHex	[I:2.2.4]
$A867	_LongMul	[I:2.3.3]
$A868	_FixMul	[I:2.3.2]

Trap word	Trap macro name	Reference section
$A869	_FixRatio	[I:2.3.2]
$A86A	_HiWord	[I:2.2.3]
$A86B	_LoWord	[I:2.2.3]
$A86C	_FixRound	[I:2.3.1]
$A86D	_InitPort	[I:4.3.2]
$A86E	_InitGraf	[I:4.3.1]
$A86F	_OpenPort	[I:4.3.2]
$A870	_LocalToGlobal	[I:4.4.2]
$A871	_GlobalToLocal	[I:4.4.2]
$A872	_GrafDevice	[I:8.3.2]
$A873	_SetPort	[I:4.3.3]
$A874	_GetPort	[I:4.3.3]
$A875	_SetPBits	[I:4.3.4]
$A876	_PortSize	[I:4.3.5]
$A877	_MovePortTo	[I:4.3.5]
$A878	_SetOrigin	[I:4.3.4]
$A879	_SetClip	[I:4.3.6]
$A87A	_GetClip	[I:4.3.6]
$A87B	_ClipRect	[I:4.3.6]
$A87C	_BackPat	[I:5.1.1]
$A87D	_ClosePort	[I:4.3.2]
$A87E	_AddPt	[I:4.4.1]
$A87F	_SubPt	[I:4.4.1]
$A880	_SetPt	[I:4.1.1]
$A881	_EqualPt	[I:4.4.1]
$A883	_DrawChar	[I:8.3.3]
$A884	_DrawString	[I:8.3.3]
$A885	_DrawText	[I:8.3.3]
$A886	_TextWidth	[I:8.3.4]
$A887	_TextFont	[I:8.3.2]
$A888	_TextFace	[I:8.3.2]
$A889	_TextMode	[I:8.3.2]
$A88A	_TextSize	[I:8.3.2]
$A88B	_GetFontInfo	[I:8.2.6]
$A88C	_StringWidth	[I:8.3.4]
$A88D	_CharWidth	[I:8.3.4]
$A88E	_SpaceExtra	[I:8.3.2]
$A891	_LineTo	[I:5.2.4]
$A892	_Line	[I:5.2.4]
$A893	_MoveTo	[I:5.2.4]
$A894	_Move	[I:5.2.4]
$A896	_HidePen	[I:5.2.3]
$A897	_ShowPen	[I:5.2.3]
$A898	_GetPenState	[I:5.2.1]
$A899	_SetPenState	[I:5.2.1]
$A89A	_GetPen	[I:5.2.4]
$A89B	_PenSize	[I:5.2.2]
$A89C	_PenMode	[I:5.2.2]
$A89D	_PenPat	[I:5.2.2]
$A89E	_PenNormal	[I:5.2.2]

Trap word	Trap macro name	Reference section
$A8A1	_FrameRect	[I:5.3.2]
$A8A2	_PaintRect	[I:5.3.2]
$A8A3	_EraseRect	[I:5.3.2]
$A8A4	_InverRect	[I:5.3.2]
$A8A5	_FillRect	[I:5.3.2]
$A8A6	_EqualRect	[I:4.4.5]
$A8A7	_SetRect	[I:4.1.2]
$A8A8	_OffsetRect	[I:4.4.4]
$A8A9	_InsetRect	[I:4.4.4]
$A8AA	_SectRect	[I:4.4.5]
$A8AB	_UnionRect	[I:4.4.5]
$A8AC	_Pt2Rect	[I:4.1.2]
$A8AD	_PtInRect	[I:4.4.3]
$A8AE	_EmptyRect	[I:4.4.4]
$A8B0	_FrameRoundRect	[I:5.3.3]
$A8B1	_PaintRoundRect	[I:5.3.3]
$A8B2	_EraseRoundRect	[I:5.3.3]
$A8B3	_InverRoundRect	[I:5.3.3]
$A8B4	_FillRoundRect	[I:5.3.3]
$A8B7	_FrameOval	[I:5.3.4]
$A8B8	_PaintOval	[I:5.3.4]
$A8B9	_EraseOval	[I:5.3.4]
$A8BA	_InvertOval	[I:5.3.4]
$A8BB	_FillOval	[I:5.3.4]
$A8BE	_FrameArc	[I:5.3.5]
$A8BF	_PaintArc	[I:5.3.5]
$A8C0	_EraseArc	[I:5.3.5]
$A8C1	_InvertArc	[I:5.3.5]
$A8C2	_FillArc	[I:5.3.5]
$A8C3	_PtToAngle	[I:5.3.5]
$A8C6	_FramePoly	[I:5.3.6]
$A8C7	_PaintPoly	[I:5.3.6]
$A8C8	_ErasePoly	[I:5.3.6]
$A8C9	_InvertPoly	[I:5.3.6]
$A8CA	_FillPoly	[I:5.3.6]
$A8CB	_OpenPoly	[I:4.1.4]
$A8CC	_ClosePgon	[I:4.1.4]
$A8CD	_KillPoly	[I:4.1.4]
$A8CE	_OffsetPoly	[I:4.4.6]
$A8D2	_FrameRgn	[I:5.3.7]
$A8D3	_PaintRgn	[I:5.3.7]
$A8D4	_EraseRgn	[I:5.3.7]
$A8D5	_InverRgn	[I:5.3.7]
$A8D6	_FillRgn	[I:5.3.7]
$A8D8	_NewRgn	[I:4.1.6]
$A8D9	_DisposRgn	[I:4.1.6]
$A8DA	_OpenRgn	[I:4.1.6]
$A8DB	_CloseRgn	[I:4.1.6]
$A8DC	_CopyRgn	[I:4.1.7]

Trap word	Trap macro name	Reference section
$A8DD	_SetEmptyRgn	[I:4.1.7]
$A8DE	_SetRecRgn	[I:4.1.7]
$A8DF	_RectRgn	[I:4.1.7]
$A8E0	_OfsetRgn	[I:4.4.7]
$A8E1	_InsetRgn	[I:4.4.7]
$A8E2	_EmptyRgn	[I:4.4.7]
$A8E3	_EqualRgn	[I:4.4.8]
$A8E4	_SectRgn	[I:4.4.8]
$A8E5	_UnionRgn	[I:4.4.8]
$A8E6	_DiffRgn	[I:4.4.8]
$A8E7	_XOrRgn	[I:4.4.8]
$A8E8	_PtInRgn	[I:4.4.3]
$A8E9	_RectInRgn	[I:4.4.3]
$A8EC	_CopyBits	[I:5.1.2]
$A8EF	_ScrollRect	[I:5.1.5]
$A8F3	_OpenPicture	[I:5.4.2]
$A8F4	_ClosePicture	[I:5.4.2]
$A8F5	_KillPicture	[I:5.4.2]
$A8F6	_DrawPicture	[I:5.4.3]
$A8F8	_ScalePt	[I:4.4.9]
$A8F9	_MapPt	[I:4.4.9]
$A8FA	_MapRect	[I:4.4.9]
$A8FB	_MapRgn	[I:4.4.9]
$A8FC	_MapPoly	[I:4.4.9]
$A8FE	_InitFonts	[I:8.2.4]
$A8FF	_GetFName	[I:8.2.5]
$A900	_GetFNum	[I:8.2.5]
$A902	_RealFont	[I:8.2.5]
$A903	_SetFontLock	[I:8.2.7]
$A904	_DrawGrowIcon	[II:3.3.4]
$A906	_NewString	[I:8.1.2]
$A907	_SetString	[I:8.1.2]
$A908	_ShowHide	[II:3.3.1]
$A910	_GetWMgrPort	[II:3.6.1]
$A912	_InitWindows	[II:3.2.1]
$A913	_NewWindow	[II:3.2.2]
$A914	_DisposWindow	[II:3.2.3]
$A915	_ShowWindow	[II:3.3.1]
$A916	_HideWindow	[II:3.3.1]
$A917	_GetWRefCon	[II:3.2.4]
$A918	_SetWRefCon	[II:3.2.4]
$A919	_GetWTitle	[II:3.2.4]
$A91A	_SetWTitle	[II:3.2.4]
$A91B	_MoveWindow	[II:3.3.2]
$A91C	_HiliteWindow	[II:3.3.4]
$A91D	_SizeWindow	[II:3.3.2]
$A91E	_TrackGoAway	[II:3.5.4]
$A91F	_SelectWindow	[II:3.5.2]

Trap word	Trap macro name	Reference section
$A920	_BringToFront	[II:3.3.3]
$A921	_SendBehind	[II:3.3.3]
$A922	_BeginUpdate	[II:3.4.1]
$A923	_EndUpdate	[II:3.4.1]
$A924	_FrontWindow	[II:3.3.3]
$A925	_DragWindow	[II:3.5.4]
$A927	_InvalRgn	[II:3.4.2]
$A928	_InvalRect	[II:3.4.2]
$A929	_ValidRgn	[II:3.4.2]
$A92A	_ValidRect	[II:3.4.2]
$A92B	_GrowWindow	[II:3.5.4]
$A92C	_FindWindow	[II:3.5.1]
$A92D	_CloseWindow	[II:3.2.3]
$A92E	_SetWindowPic	[II:3.4.3]
$A92F	_GetWindowPic	[II:3.4.3]
$A930	_InitMenus	[II:4.2.1]
$A931	_NewMenu	[II:4.2.2]
$A932	_DisposMenu	[II:4.2.3]
$A933	_AppendMenu	[II:4.3.1]
$A934	_ClearMenuBar	[II:4.4.1]
$A935	_InsertMenu	[II:4.4.1]
$A936	_DeleteMenu	[II:4.4.1]
$A937	_DrawMenuBar	[II:4.4.3]
$A938	_HiliteMenu	[II:4.5.4]
$A939	_EnableItem	[II:4.6.2]
$A93A	_DisableItem	[II:4.6.2]
$A93B	_GetMenuBar	[II:4.4.4]
$A93C	_SetMenuBar	[II:4.4.4]
$A93D	_MenuSelect	[II:4.5.1]
$A93E	_MenuKey	[II:4.5.1]
$A93F	_GetItmIcon	[II:4.6.5]
$A940	_SetItmIcon	[II:4.6.5]
$A941	_GetItmStyle	[II:4.6.3]
$A942	_SetItmStyle	[II:4.6.3]
$A943	_GetItmMark	[II:4.6.4]
$A944	_SetItmMark	[II:4.6.4]
$A945	_CheckItem	[II:4.6.4]
$A946	_GetItem	[II:4.6.1]
$A947	_SetItem	[II:4.6.1]
$A948	_CalcMenuSize	[II:4.7.1]
$A949	_GetMHandle	[II:4.4.5]
$A94A	_SetMFlash	[II:4.7.2]
$A94C	_FlashMenuBar	[II:4.7.2]
$A94D	_AddResMenu	[II:4.3.3]
$A94E	_PinRect	[I:4.4.3]
$A950	_CountMItems	[II:4.3.4]
$A951	_InsertResMenu	[II:4.3.3]
$A954	_NewControl	[II:6.2.1]
$A955	_DisposControl	[II:6.2.2]
$A956	_KillControls	[II:6.2.2]

Trap word	Trap macro name	Reference section
$A957	_ShowControl	[II:6.3.1]
$A958	_HideControl	[II:6.3.1]
$A959	_MoveControl	[II:6.3.2]
$A95A	_GetCRefCon	[II:6.2.3]
$A95B	_SetCRefCon	[II:6.2.3]
$A95C	_SizeControl	[II:6.3.2]
$A95D	_HiliteControl	[II:6.3.3]
$A95E	_GetCTitle	[II:6.2.3]
$A95F	_SetCTitle	[II:6.2.3]
$A960	_GetCtlValue	[II:6.2.4]
$A961	_GetMinCtl	[II:6.2.4]
$A962	_GetMaxCtl	[II:6.2.4]
$A963	_SetCtlValue	[II:6.2.4]
$A964	_SetMinCtl	[II:6.2.4]
$A965	_SetMaxCtl	[II:6.2.4]
$A966	_TestControl	[II:6.4.1]
$A967	_DragControl	[II:6.4.3]
$A968	_TrackControl	[II:6.4.2]
$A969	_DrawControls	[II:6.3.1]
$A96A	_GetCtlAction	[II:6.4.2]
$A96B	_SetCtlAction	[II:6.4.2]
$A96C	_FindControl	[II:6.4.1]
$A970	_GetNextEvent	[II:2.2.1]
$A971	_EventAvail	[II:2.2.1]
$A972	_GetMouse	[II:2.4.1]
$A973	_StillDown	[II:2.4.2]
$A974	_Button	[II:2.4.2]
$A975	_TickCount	[II:2.7.1]
$A976	_GetKeys	[II:2.6.1]
$A977	_WaitMouseUp	[II:2.4.2]
$A979	_CouldDialog	[II:7.5.3]
$A97A	_FreeDialog	[II:7.5.3]
$A97B	_InitDialogs	[II:7.2.1]
$A97C	_GetNewDialog	[II:7.2.2]
$A97D	_NewDialog	[II:7.2.2]
$A97E	_SelIText	[II:7.3.2]
$A97F	_IsDialogEvent	[II:7.4.4]
$A980	_DialogSelect	[II:7.4.4]
$A981	_DrawDialog	[II:7.4.1]
$A982	_CloseDialog	[II:7.2.3]
$A983	_DisposDialog	[II:7.2.3]
$A985	_Alert	[II:7.4.2]
$A986	_StopAlert	[II:7.4.2]
$A987	_NoteAlert	[II:7.4.2]
$A988	_CautionAlert	[II:7.4.2]
$A989	_CouldAlert	[II:7.5.3]
$A98A	_FreeAlert	[II:7.5.3]
$A98B	_ParamText	[II:7.4.6]
$A98C	_ErrorSound	[II:7.5.1]

Trap word	Trap macro name	Reference section
$A98D	_GetDItem	[II:7.3.1]
$A98E	_SetDItem	[II:7.3.1]
$A98F	_SetIText	[II:7.3.2]
$A990	_GetIText	[II:7.3.2]
$A991	_ModalDialog	[II:7.4.3]
$A992	_DetachResource	[I:6.3.2]
$A993	_SetResPurge	[I:6.5.5]
$A994	_CurResFile	[I:6.2.2]
$A997	_OpenResFile	[I:6.2.1]
$A998	_UseResFile	[I:6.2.2]
$A999	_UpdateResFile	[I:6.5.4]
$A99A	_CloseResFile	[I:6.2.1]
$A99C	_CountResources	[I:6.3.3]
$A99D	_GetIndResource	[I:6.3.3]
$A99E	_CountTypes	[I:6.3.3]
$A99F	_GetIndType	[I:6.3.3]
$A9A0	_GetResource	[I:6.3.1]
$A9A1	_GetNamedResource	[I:6.3.1]
$A9A3	_ReleaseResource	[I:6.3.2]
$A9A4	_HomeResFile	[I:6.4.3]
$A9A5	_SizeRsrc	[I:6.4.3]
$A9A6	_GetResAttrs	[I:6.4.2]
$A9A7	_SetResAttrs	[I:6.4.2]
$A9A8	_GetResInfo	[I:6.4.1]
$A9A9	_SetResInfo	[I:6.4.1]
$A9AA	_ChangedResource	[I:6.5.2]
$A9AB	_AddResource	[I:6.5.3]
$A9AD	_RmveResource	[I:6.5.3]
$A9AF	_ResError	[I:6.6.1]
$A9B0	_WriteResource	[I:6.5.4]
$A9B1	_CreateResFile	[I:6.5.1]
$A9B3	_SystemClick	[II:3.5.3]
$A9B4	_SystemTask	[II:2.7.2]
$A9B6	_OpenDeskAcc	[II:4.5.2]
$A9B7	_CloseDeskAcc	[II:4.5.2]
$A9B8	_GetPattern	[I:5.1.1]
$A9B9	_GetCursor	[II:2.5.2]
$A9BA	_GetString	[I:8.1.2]
$A9BC	_GetPicture	[I:5.4.2]
$A9BD	_GetNewWindow	[II:3.2.2]
$A9BE	_GetNewControl	[II:6.2.1]
$A9BF	_GetRMenu	[II:4.2.2]
$A9C0	_GetNewMBar	[II:4.4.2]
$A9C1	_UniqueID	[I:6.5.3]
$A9C2	_SysEdit	[II:4.5.3]
$A9C6	_Secs2Date	[I:2.4.3]
$A9C7	_Date2Secs	[I:2.4.3]
$A9C8	_SysBeep	[II:2.8.1]
$A9CB	_TEGetText	[II:5.2.3]

Trap word	Trap macro name	Reference section
$A9CC	_TEInit	[II:5.2.1]
$A9CD	_TEDispose	[II:5.2.2]
$A9CE	_TextBox	[II:5.3.2]
$A9CF	_TESetText	[II:5.2.3]
$A9D0	_TECalText	[II:5.3.1]
$A9D1	_TESetSelect	[II:5.4.2]
$A9D2	_TENew	[II:5.2.2]
$A9D3	_TEUpdate	[II:5.3.2]
$A9D4	_TEClick	[II:5.4.1]
$A9D5	_TECopy	[II:5.5.2]
$A9D6	_TECut	[II:5.5.2]
$A9D7	_TEDelete	[II:5.5.3]
$A9D8	_TEActivate	[II:5.4.3]
$A9D9	_TEDeactivate	[II:5.4.3]
$A9DA	_TEIdle	[II:5.4.3]
$A9DB	_TEPaste	[II:5.5.2]
$A9DC	_TEKey	[II:5.5.1]
$A9DD	_TEScroll	[II:5.3.3]
$A9DE	_TEInsert	[II:5.5.3]
$A9DF	_TESetJust	[II:5.3.1]
$A9E0	_Munger	[II:5.5.6]
$A9E1	_HandToHand	[I:3.2.5]
$A9E2	_PtrToXHand	[I:3.2.5]
$A9E3	_PtrToHand	[I:3.2.5]
$A9E4	_HandAndHand	[I:3.2.6]
$A9E5	_InitPack	[I:7.2.2]
$A9E6	_InitAllPacks	[I:7.2.2]
$A9E7	_Pack0	[I:7.2.1]
$A9E8	_Pack1	[I:7.2.1]
$A9E9	_Pack2	[I:7.2.1]
$A9E9 (0)	_DIBadMount	[II:8.4.1]
$A9E9 (2)	_DILoad	[II:8.4.3]
$A9E9 (4)	_DIUnload	[II:8.4.3]
$A9E9 (6)	_DIFormat	[II:8.4.2]
$A9E9 (8)	_DIVerify	[II:8.4.2]
$A9E9 (10)	_DIZero	[II:8.4.2]
$A9EA	_Pack3	[I:7.2.1]
$A9EA (1)	_SFPutFile	[II:8.3.3]
$A9EA (2)	_SFGetFile	[II:8.3.2]
$A9EB	_Pack4	[I:7.2.1]
$A9EC	_Pack5	[I:7.2.1]
$A9ED	_Pack6	[I:7.2.1]
$A9ED (0)	_IUDateString	[I:2.4.4]
$A9ED (2)	_IUTimeString	[I:2.4.4]
$A9EE	_Pack7	[I:7.2.1]
$A9EE (0)	_NumToString	[I:2.3.4]
$A9EE (1)	_StringToNum	[I:2.3.4]
$A9EF	_PtrAndHand	[I:3.2.6]

Trap word	Trap macro name	Reference section
$A9F0	**_LoadSeg**	[I:7.1.2]
$A9F1	**_UnloadSeg**	[I:7.1.2]
$A9F2	**_Launch**	[I:7.1.1]
$A9F3	**_Chain**	[I:7.1.1]
$A9F4	**_ExitToShell**	[I:7.1.3]
$A9F5	**_GetAppParms**	[I:7.3.4]
$A9F6	**_GetResFileAttrs**	[I:6.6.2]
$A9F7	**_SetResFileAttrs**	[I:6.6.2]
$A9F9	**_InfoScrap**	[I:7.4.2]
$A9FA	**_UnlodeScrap**	[I:7.4.4]
$A9FB	**_LodeScrap**	[I:7.4.4]
$A9FC	**_ZeroScrap**	[I:7.4.3]
$A9FD	**_GetScrap**	[I:7.4.3]
$A9FE	**_PutScrap**	[I:7.4.3]

APPENDIX

G

Summary of Assembly-Language Variables

System Globals

Listed below are all assembly-language global variables covered in this book, with their hexadecimal addresses. *Warning:* The addresses given may be subject to change in future versions of the Toolbox; always refer to these variables by name instead of using the addresses directly.

Variable name	Address	Reference section	Meaning
ACount	**$A9A**	[7.5.2]	Stage of last alert minus 1
ANumber	**$A98**	[7.5.2]	Resource ID of last alert
CaretTime	**$2F4**	[5.4.3]	Current blink interval in ticks
CurActivate	**$A64**	[3.4.3]	Pointer to window awaiting activate event
CurDeactivate	**$A68**	[3.4.3]	Pointer to window awaiting deactivate event
DABeeper	**$A9C**	[7.5.1]	Pointer to current sound procedure
DAStrings	**$AA0**	[7.4.6]	Handles to four text substitution strings
DeskPort	**$9E2**	[3.6.1]	Pointer to general-purpose full-screen port
DlgFont	**$AFA**	[7.5.1]	Current font number for dialogs and alerts
DoubleTime	**$2F0**	[5.4.1]	Current double-click interval in ticks
GrayRgn	**$9EE**	[3.6.1]	Handle to region defining gray desktop
KeyMap	**$174**	[2.6.1]	System keyboard map

Variable name	Address	Reference section	Meaning
KeypadMap	**$17C**	[2.6.1]	System keypad map
MBState	**$172**	[2.4.2]	State of mouse button
MenuFlash	**$A24**	[4.7.2]	Current flash count for menu items
MenuList	**$A1C**	[4.4.4]	Handle to current menu bar
RestProc	**$A8C**	[7.2.1]	Pointer to restart procedure
SysEvtMask	**$144**	[2.3.2]	System event mask
TEScrpHandle	**$AB4**	[5.5.4]	Handle to text scrap
TEScrpLength	**$AB0**	[5.5.4]	Length of text scrap in characters
TheCrsr	**$844**	[2.5.2]	Current cursor record
TheMenu	**$A26**	[4.5.4]	Menu ID of currently highlighted menu
Ticks	**$16A**	[2.7.1]	System clock
WindowList	**$9D6**	[3.1.1]	Pointer to first window in window list
WMgrPort	**$9DE**	[3.6.1]	Pointer to Window Manager port

QuickDraw Globals

The QuickDraw global variable listed below is located at the given offset relative to the QuickDraw globals pointer, which in turn is pointed to by address register **A5**.

Variable name	Offset in bytes	Reference section	Meaning
Arrow	**−108**	[2.5.2]	Standard arrow cursor

APPENDIX H

MiniEdit Source Listing

Following is a complete listing of the source code for the **MiniEdit** example application program developed in this volume.

```pascal
program MiniEdit;

    { Example program to illustrate event-driven structure [Prog. II:2-1].  }

    uses {$U-}
        {$U Obj/MemTypes } MemTypes,
        {$U Obj/QuickDraw} QuickDraw,
        {$U Obj/OSIntf    } OSIntf,
        {$U Obj/ToolIntf } ToolIntf,
        {$U Obj/PackIntf } PackIntf;

    const

        ScreenWidth    = 512;               {Width of screen in pixels}
        ScreenHeight   = 342;               {Height of screen in pixels}
        MenuBarHeight  = 20;                {Height of menu bar in pixels}
        TitleBarHeight = 18;                {Height of window title bar in pixels}
        ScreenMargin   = 4;                 {Width of "safety margin" around edge of screen}

        MinWidth   = 80;                    {Minimum width of window in pixels}
        MinHeight  = 80;                    {Minimum height of window in pixels}
        SBarWidth  = 16;                    {Width of scroll bars in pixels}
        TextMargin = 4;                     {Inset from window to text rectangle}

        DlgTop  = 100;                      {Top edge of dialog box for Get and Put dialogs}
        DlgLeft = 85;                       {Left edge of dialog box for Get and Put dialogs}

        AppleID = 1;                        {Menu ID for Apple menu}
```

533

```
         AboutItem = 1;                          {Item number for About... command}

    FileID = 2;                                  {Menu ID for File menu}
        NewItem   = 1;                           {Item number for New command}
        OpenItem  = 2;                           {Item number for Open... command}
        CloseItem = 3;                           {Item number for Close command}
        SaveItem  = 5;                           {Item number for Save command}
        SaveAsItem = 6;                          {Item number for Save As... command}
        RevertItem = 7;                          {Item number for Revert to Saved command}
        QuitItem  = 9;                           {Item number for Quit command}

    EditID = 3;                                  {Menu ID for Edit menu}
        UndoItem  = 1;                           {Item number for Undo command}
        CutItem   = 3;                           {Item number for Cut command}
        CopyItem  = 4;                           {Item number for Copy command}
        PasteItem = 5;                           {Item number for Paste command}
        ClearItem = 7;                           {Item number for Clear command}

    AboutID     = 1000;                          {Resource ID for About alert}
    SaveID      = 1001;                          {Resource ID for Save alert}
    RevertID    = 1002;                          {Resource ID for Revert alert}
    CantPrintID = 1003;                          {Resource ID for Can't Print alert}
    WrongTypeID = 1004;                          {Resource ID for Wrong Type alert}
    OpWrID      = 1005;                          {Resource ID for Already Open alert}
    IOErrID     = 1006;                          {Resource ID for I/O Error alert}

    NoTitleID = 1000;                            {Resource ID of title string for empty window}

type
    WDHandle   = ^WDPtr;
    WDPtr      = ^WindowData;
    WindowData = record
                    editRec    : TEHandle;       {Handle to edit record [II:5.1.1]}
                    scrollBar  : ControlHandle;  {Handle to scroll bar [II:6.1.1]}
                    dirty      : BOOLEAN;         {Document changed since last saved?}
                    padding    : Byte;           {Extra byte for padding [I:3.1.1]}
                    volNumber  : INTEGER;         {Volume reference number}
                    fileNumber : INTEGER          {File reference number}
                 end;


var

    TheEvent : EventRecord;                      {Current event [II:2.1.1]}

    TheWindow    : WindowPtr;                     {Pointer to currently active window [II:3.1.1]}
    TheScrollBar : ControlHandle;                 {Handle to active window's scroll bar [II:6.1.1]}
    TheText      : TEHandle;                       {Handle to active window's edit record [II:5.1.1]}
```

```
    AppleMenu : MenuHandle;              {Handle to Apple menu [II:4.1.1]}
    FileMenu  : MenuHandle;              {Handle to File menu [II:4.1.1]}
    EditMenu  : MenuHandle;              {Handle to Edit menu [II:4.1.1]}

    IBeam : CursHandle;                  {Handle to I-beam cursor [9.5.1]}

    Watch : CursHandle;                  {Handle to wristwatch cursor [9.5.1]}

    WindowCount  : INTEGER;              {Total number of windows opened}
    ScrapCompare : INTEGER;              {Previous scrap count for comparison [I:7.4.2]}
    ScrapDirty   : BOOLEAN;              {Has scrap been changed?}

    Quitting  : BOOLEAN;                 {Closing up shop?}
    Finished  : BOOLEAN;                 {All closed?}
    ErrorFlag : BOOLEAN;                 {I/O error flag}


{-----------------------------------------------------------------------------}


{Forward Declarations}

procedure Initialize; forward;
      { One-time-only initialization. }
  procedure SetUpMenus; forward;
        { Set up menus. }
  procedure SetUpCursors; forward;
        { Set up cursors. }
  procedure DoStartup; forward;
        { Process Finder startup information. }
procedure MainLoop; forward;
      { Execute one pass of main program loop. }
  procedure FixCursor; forward;
        { Adjust cursor for region of screen. }
  procedure DoEvent; forward;
        { Get and process one event. }
    procedure DoMouseDown; forward;
          { Handle mouse-down event. }
      procedure DoMenuClick; forward;
            { Handle mouse-down event in menu bar. }
        procedure DoMenuChoice (menuChoice : LONGINT); forward;
              { Handle user's menu choice. }
          procedure DoAppleChoice (theItem : INTEGER); forward;
                { Handle choice from Apple menu. }
            procedure DoAbout; forward;
                  { Handle About MiniEdit... command. }
          procedure DoFileChoice (theItem : INTEGER); forward;
                { Handle choice from File menu. }
            procedure DoNew; forward;
                  { Handle New command. }
```

```
    procedure OffsetWindow (whichWindow : WindowPtr); forward;
        { Offset location of new window. }
  procedure DoOpen; forward;
        { Handle Open... command. }
    procedure OpenFile (fileName : Str255; vNum : INTEGER); forward;
        { Open document file. }
  procedure DoClose; forward;
        { Handle Close command. }
    procedure CloseAppWindow; forward;
        { Close application window. }
    procedure CloseSysWindow; forward;
        { Close system window. }
  procedure DoSave; forward;
        { Handle Save command. }
  procedure DoSaveAs; forward;
        { Handle Save As... command. }
    procedure WriteFile (theFile : INTEGER; volNum : INTEGER); forward;
        { Write window contents to a file. }
  procedure DoRevert; forward;
        { Handle Revert to Saved command. }
  procedure DoQuit; forward;
        { Handle Quit command. }
procedure DoEditChoice (theItem : INTEGER); forward;
        { Handle choice from Edit menu. }
  procedure DoUndo; forward;
        { Handle Undo command. }
  procedure DoCut; forward;
        { Handle Cut command. }
  procedure DoCopy; forward;
        { Handle Copy command. }
  procedure DoPaste; forward;
        { Handle Paste command. }
  procedure DoClear; forward;
        { Handle Clear command. }
procedure DoContent (whichWindow : WindowPtr); forward;
    { Handle mouse-down event in content region. }
  procedure DoScroll (thePart : INTEGER; thePoint : Point); forward;
      { Handle mouse-down event in scroll bar. }
    procedure ScrollText (theControl: ControlHandle; thePart : INTEGER); forward;
        { Scroll text within window. }
    procedure AdjustText; forward;
        { Adjust text within window to match scroll bar setting. }
    function AutoScroll : BOOLEAN; forward;
        { Handle automatic scrolling during text selection. }
  procedure DoSelect (thePoint : Point); forward;
        { Handle mouse-down event in text rectangle. }
  procedure FixEditMenu; forward;
        { Enable/disable editing commands. }
```

```
        procedure DoDrag (whichWindow : WindowPtr); forward;
            { Handle mouse-down event in drag region.  }
        procedure DoGrow (whichWindow : WindowPtr); forward;
            { Handle mouse-down event in size region.  }
          procedure FixScrollBar; forward;
               { Resize window's scroll bar.  }
          procedure FixText; forward;
               { Resize window's text rectangle.  }
        procedure DoGoAway (whichWindow : WindowPtr); forward;
            { Handle mouse-down event in close region.  }
      procedure DoKeystroke; forward;
          { Handle keystroke.  }
        procedure DoTyping (ch : CHAR); forward;
            { Handle character typed from keyboard.  }
      procedure DoUpdate; forward;
          { Handle update event.  }
      procedure DoActivate; forward;
          { Handle activate and deactivate events.  }
  procedure WindowDirty (isDirty : BOOLEAN); forward;
      { Mark window dirty or clean.  }
  procedure AdjustScrollBar; forward;
      { Adjust scroll bar to length of document.  }
  procedure ScrollToSelection; forward;
      { Scroll current selection into view.  }
  procedure ScrollCharacter (theCharacter : INTEGER; toBottom : BOOLEAN); forward;
      { Scroll character into view.  }
  procedure ReadDeskScrap; forward;
      { Copy desk scrap to Toolbox scrap.  }
  procedure WriteDeskScrap; forward;
      { Copy Toolbox scrap to desk scrap.  }
  procedure IOCheck (resultCode : OSErr); forward;
      { Check for I/O error.  }


{------------------------------------------------------------------------------}


procedure Initialize;

   { Do one-time-only initialization [Prog. II:2-6].  }

   var
      theMask : INTEGER;                           {New value for system event mask [II:2.1.3]}
```

```
begin {Initialize}

    InitGraf (@ThePort);                         {Initialize QuickDraw [I:4.3.1]}
    InitFonts;                                   {Initialize fonts [I:8.2.4]}
    InitWindows;                                 {Initialize windows [II:3.2.1]}
    InitMenus;                                   {Initialize menus [II:4.2.1]}
    TEInit;                                      {Initialize text editing [II:5.2.1]}
    InitDialogs (NIL);                           {Initialize dialogs [II:7.2.1]}

    theMask := EveryEvent - KeyUpMask - MUpMask; {Disable key-up and mouse-up events [II:2.1.3]}
    SetEventMask (theMask);                       {Set the mask [II:2.3.2]}
    FlushEvents  (EveryEvent, 0);                 {Clear out event queue [II:2.3.1]}

    SetUpMenus;                                   {Create program's menus}
    SetUpCursors;                                 {Get standard cursors}

    TheText      := NIL;                          {Clear global pointers/handles}
    TheWindow    := NIL;
    TheScrollBar := NIL;

    WindowCount := 0;                             {Initialize window count}
    DoStartup;                                    {Process Finder startup information}

    ScrapDirty   := FALSE;                        {Toolbox and desk scraps initially agree}
    ScrapCompare := InfoScrap^.scrapCount + 1;    {Force scrap transfer [I:7.4.2]}
    ReadDeskScrap;                                {Read desk scrap into Toolbox scrap}

    Quitting := FALSE;                            {Initialize quitting flags}
    Finished := FALSE

end;  {Initialize}
```

{--}

```
procedure SetUpMenus;

    { Set up menus [Prog. II:4-2].  }

    begin {SetUpMenus}

        AppleMenu := GetMenu (AppleID);           {Get Apple menu from resource file [II:4.2.2]}
        AddResMenu (AppleMenu, 'DRVR');           {Add names of available desk accessories [II:4.3.3]}
        InsertMenu (AppleMenu, 0);                {Install at end of menu bar [II:4.4.1]}

        FileMenu := GetMenu (FileID);             {Get File menu from resource file [II:4.2.2]}
        InsertMenu (FileMenu, 0);                 {Install at end of menu bar [II:4.4.1]}
```

```
    EditMenu := GetMenu (EditID);              {Get Edit menu from resource file [II:4.2.2]}
    InsertMenu (EditMenu, 0);                  {Install at end of menu bar [II:4.4.1]}

    DrawMenuBar                                {Show new menu bar on screen [II:4.4.3]}

  end;  {SetUpMenus}
```

{--}

```
procedure SetUpCursors;

  { Set up cursors [Prog. II:2-7].  }

  begin {SetUpCursors}

    IBeam := GetCursor (IBeamCursor);          {Get cursors from system resource file [II:2.5.2]}
    Watch := GetCursor (WatchCursor);

    InitCursor                                 {Set standard arrow cursor [II:2.5.2]}

  end;  {SetUpCursors}
```

{--}

```
procedure DoStartup;

  { Process Finder startup information [Prog. II:8-7].  }

  var
    theMessage : INTEGER;                      {Open or print? [I:7.3.4]}
    nDocs      : INTEGER;                      {Number of documents selected in Finder}
    thisDoc    : INTEGER;                      {Index number of document}
    docInfo    : AppFile;                      {Startup information about one document [I:7.3.4]}
    ignore     : INTEGER;                      {Item code returned by alert}

  begin {DoStartup}

    CountAppFiles (theMessage, nDocs);         {Get number of documents and startup message [I:7.3.4]}

    if theMessage = AppPrint then              {Did user choose Print in Finder? [I:7.4.3]}
      begin
        ignore := StopAlert (CantPrintID, NIL);  {Post alert [II:7.4.2]}
        ExitToShell                            {Return to Finder [I:7.1.3]}
      end {if}

    else if nDocs = 0 then                     {If no documents selected,  }
      DoNew                                    {  just open an empty window}
```

```
        else
          for thisDoc := 1 to nDocs do            {Otherwise loop through documents}
             begin

                GetAppFiles (thisDoc, docInfo);    {Get startup information [I:7.3.4]}
                with docInfo do

                   if fType = 'TEXT' then          {Is it a text file?}
                      begin
                         OpenFile (fName, vRefNum);  {Read it into a window}
                         ClrAppFiles (thisDoc)      {Tell Finder it's been processed [I:7.3.4]}
                      end {then}

                   else
                      begin
                         ParamText (fName, '', '', '');  {Substitute file name into text of alert [II:7.4.6]}
                         ignore := StopAlert (WrongTypeID, NIL)  {Post alert [II:7.4.2]}
                      end {else}

             end {for}

   end; {DoStartup}


{-------------------------------------------------------------------------------}


procedure MainLoop;

   { Execute one pass of main program loop [Prog. II:2-2].  }

   begin {MainLoop}

      if FrontWindow = NIL then begin             {Is the desktop empty? [II:3.3.3]}

         DisableItem (EditMenu, UndoItem);        {Disable inapplicable menu commands [II:4.6.2]}
         DisableItem (EditMenu, CutItem);
         DisableItem (EditMenu, CopyItem);
         DisableItem (EditMenu, PasteItem);
         DisableItem (EditMenu, ClearItem);

         DisableItem (FileMenu, CloseItem);
         DisableItem (FileMenu, SaveItem);
         DisableItem (FileMenu, SaveAsItem);
         DisableItem (FileMenu, RevertItem)
```

```
      end; {then}

         FixCursor;                              {Adjust cursor for region of screen}
         SystemTask;                             {Do system idle processing [II:2.7.2]}

         if TheText <> NIL then
            TEIdle (TheText);                     {Blink cursor [II:5.4.3]}

         DoEvent                                 {Get and process one event}

      end;  {MainLoop}

{----------------------------------------------------------------------------}


procedure FixCursor;

   {  Adjust cursor for region of screen [Prog. II:2-8].  }

   var
      mousePoint : Point;                        {Current mouse position in window coordinates [I:4.1.1]}
      textRect   : Rect;                         {Active window's text rectangle [I:4.1.2]

   begin {FixCursor}

      if Quitting then                           {Skip cursor adjustment during quit sequence}
         EXIT (FixCursor);

      if FrontWindow = NIL then                  {Screen empty? [II:3.3.3]}
         InitCursor                              {Set arrow cursor [II:2.5.2]}

      else if FrontWindow = TheWindow then       {Is one of our windows active? [II:3.3.3]}
         begin

            GetMouse (mousePoint);               {Get mouse position [II:2.4.1]}
            textRect := TheText^^.viewRect;      {Get window's text rectangle [II:5.1.1]}

            if PtInRect (mousePoint, textRect) then  {Is mouse in text rectangle? [I:4.4.3]}
               SetCursor (IBeam^^)               {Set I-beam cursor [II:2.5.2]}
            else
               InitCursor                        {Set arrow cursor [II:2.5.2]}

         end {if}

      else                                       {A system window is active:      }
         {Do nothing}                            {   let desk accessory set cursor}

   end; {FixCursor}

{----------------------------------------------------------------------------}
```

```
procedure DoEvent;

   { Get and process one event [Prog. II:2-5].  }

   begin {DoEvent}

      ErrorFlag := FALSE;                              {Clear I/O error flag}

      if GetNextEvent (EveryEvent, TheEvent) then      {Get next event [II:2.2.1]}

         case TheEvent.what of

            MouseDown:
               if not Quitting then
                  DoMouseDown;                          {Handle mouse-down event}

            KeyDown, AutoKey:
               if not Quitting then
                  DoKeystroke;                          {Handle keystroke}

            UpdateEvt:
               DoUpdate;                                {Handle update event}

            ActivateEvt:
               DoActivate;                              {Handle activate/deactivate event}

            otherwise
               {Do nothing}

            end {case}

      else if Quitting and (TheEvent.what = NullEvent) then  {Closing up shop after a Quit command?}
         begin
            if FrontWindow <> NIL then                  {Any windows on the screen? [II:3.3.3]}
               DoClose                                  {Close the frontmost}
            else
               Finished := TRUE                         {Signal end of program}
         end {if}

   end; {DoEvent}

{-------------------------------------------------------------------------------}

procedure DoMouseDown;

   { Handle mouse-down event [Prog. II:3-7].  }

   var
      whichWindow : WindowPtr;                          {Window that mouse was pressed in [II:3.1.1]}
      thePart     : INTEGER;                            {Part of screen where mouse was pressed [II:3.5.1]}
```

```
begin {DoMouseDown}

    thePart := FindWindow (TheEvent.where, whichWindow);    {Where on the screen was mouse pressed? [II:3.5.1]}

    case thePart of

        InDesk:
            {Do nothing};

        InMenuBar:
            DoMenuClick;                                    {Handle click in menu bar}

        InSysWindow:
            SystemClick (TheEvent, whichWindow);            {Handle click in system window [II:3.5.3]}

        InContent:
            DoContent (whichWindow);                        {Handle click in content region}

        InDrag:
            DoDrag (whichWindow);                           {Handle click in drag region}

        InGrow:
            DoGrow (whichWindow);                           {Handle click in size region}

        InGoAway:
            DoGoAway (whichWindow)                          {Handle click in close region}

        end {case}

    end; {DoMouseDown}

{-----------------------------------------------------------------------------}

procedure DoMenuClick;

    { Handle mouse-down event in menu bar [Prog. II:4-3]. }

    var
        menuChoice : LONGINT;                               {Menu ID and item number}

    begin {DoMenuClick}

        menuChoice := MenuSelect (TheEvent.where);          {Track mouse [II:4.5.1]}
        DoMenuChoice (menuChoice)                           {Handle user's menu choice}

    end; {DoMenuClick}

{-----------------------------------------------------------------------------}
```

```
procedure DoMenuChoice ((menuChoice : LONGINT)};

   { Handle user's menu choice [Prog. II:4-5].  }

   var
      theMenu : INTEGER;                        {Menu ID of selected menu}
      theItem : INTEGER;                        {Item number of selected item}

   begin {DoMenuChoice}

      if menuChoice <> 0 then                   {Nothing to do if 0}

         begin

            theMenu := HiWord(menuChoice);      {Get menu ID [I:2.2.3]}
            theItem := LoWord(menuChoice);      {Get item number [I:2.2.3]}

            case theMenu of

               AppleID:
                  DoAppleChoice (theItem);      {Handle choice from Apple menu}

               FileID:
                  DoFileChoice  (theItem);      {Handle choice from File menu}

               EditID:
                  DoEditChoice  (theItem)       {Handle choice from Edit menu}

               end; {case}

            HiliteMenu(0)                       {Unhighlight menu title [II:4.5.4]}

         end {if}

   end; {DoMenuChoice}

{----------------------------------------------------------------------------------}

procedure DoAppleChoice ((theItem : INTEGER)};

   { Handle choice from Apple menu [Prog. II:4-6].  }

   var
      accName   : Str255;                       {Name of desk accessory [I:2.1.1]}
      accNumber : INTEGER;                      {Reference number of desk accessory}

   begin {DoAppleChoice}
```

```
        case theItem of

            AboutItem:
                DoAbout;                              {Handle About MiniEdit... command}

            otherwise
                begin

                    if FrontWindow = NIL then         {Is the desktop empty? [II:3.3.3]}
                        begin

                            EnableItem (FileMenu, CloseItem);  {Enable Close command [II:4.6.2]}

                            EnableItem (EditMenu, UndoItem);   {Enable standard editing commands}
                            EnableItem (EditMenu, CutItem);    {   for desk accessory [II:4.6.2]}
                            EnableItem (EditMenu, CopyItem);
                            EnableItem (EditMenu, PasteItem);
                            EnableItem (EditMenu, ClearItem)

                        end;

                    GetItem (AppleMenu, theItem, accName);  {Get accessory name [II:4.6.1]}
                    accNumber := OpenDeskAcc (accName)      {Open desk accessory [II:4.5.2]}

                end

        end {case}

    end; {DoAppleChoice}

{---------------------------------------------------------------------------}


procedure DoAbout;

    { Handle About MiniEdit... command [Prog. II:7-1]. }

    var
        ignore : INTEGER;                            {Item number for About alert}

    begin {DoAbout}

        ignore := Alert (AboutID, NIL)               {Post alert [II:7.4.2]}

    end; {DoAbout}

{---------------------------------------------------------------------------}
```

```
procedure DoFileChoice ((theItem : INTEGER)};

   { Handle choice from File menu [Prog. II:4-8].  }

   begin {DoFileChoice}

      case theItem of

         NewItem:
            DoNew;                              {Handle New command}

         OpenItem:
            DoOpen;                             {Handle Open... command}

         CloseItem:
            DoClose;                            {Handle Close command}

         SaveItem:
            DoSave;                             {Handle Save command}

         SaveAsItem:
            DoSaveAs;                           {Handle Save As... command}

         RevertItem:
            DoRevert;                           {Handle Revert to Saved command}

         QuitItem:
            DoQuit                              {Handle Quit command}

         end {case}

   end;  {DoFileChoice}


{--------------------------------------------------------------------------------}

procedure DoNew;

   { Handle New command [Prog. II:5-2].  }

   const
      windowID = 1000;                          {Resource ID for window template [II:3.7.1]}
      scrollID = 1000;                          {Resource ID for scroll bar template [II:6.5.1]}

   var
      theData    : WDHandle;                    {Handle to window's data record}
      dataHandle : Handle;                      {Untyped handle for creating data record [I:3.1.1]}
      destRect   : Rect;                        {Wrapping rectangle for window's text [I:4.1.2]}
      viewRect   : Rect;                        {Clipping rectangle for window's text [I:4.1.2]}
```

```
begin {DoNew}

   TheWindow := GetNewWindow (windowID, NIL, WindowPtr(-1));  {Make new window from template [II:3.2.2]}

   OffsetWindow {TheWindow};                     {Offset from location of previous window}
   ShowWindow   {TheWindow};                     {Make window visible [II:3.3.1]}

   SetPort  (TheWindow);                         {Get into the window's port [I:4.3.3]}
   TextFont (Geneva);                            {Set text font [I:8.3.2, I:8.2.1]}

   with TheWindow^.portRect do                   {Set up clipping rectangle [I:4.2.2]}
      SetRect (viewRect, 0, 0, right - (SBarWidth - 1), bottom - (SBarWidth - 1));
   destRect := viewRect;
   InsetRect (destRect, TextMargin, TextMargin); {Inset wrapping rectangle by text margin [I:4.4.4]}

   dataHandle := NewHandle (SIZEOF(WindowData)); {Allocate window data record [I:3.2.1]}
   SetWRefCon (TheWindow, LONGINT(dataHandle));  {Store as reference constant [II:3.2.4]}

   HLock (dataHandle);                           {Lock data record [I:3.2.4]}

      theData := WDHandle(dataHandle);           {Convert to typed handle}
      with theData^^ do
         begin
            editRec    := TENew (destRect, viewRect);    {Make edit record [II:5.2.2]}
            scrollBar  := GetNewControl (scrollID, TheWindow);  {Make scroll bar [II:6.2.1]}
            dirty      := FALSE;                  {Document is initially clean}
            fileNumber := 0;                      {Window has no associated file}
            volNumber  := 0;                      {  or volume              }

            SetClikLoop (@AutoScroll, editRec);   {Install auto-scroll routine [II:5.6.1]}

            TheScrollBar := scrollBar;            {Set global handles}
            TheText      := editRec
         end; {with}

   HUnlock (dataHandle);                         {Unlock data record [I:3.2.4]}

   EnableItem (FileMenu, CloseItem)              {Enable Close command on menu [II:4.6.2]}

end;  {DoNew}

{----------------------------------------------------------------------------}


procedure OffsetWindow ((whichWindow : WindowPtr)};

   { Offset location of new window [Prog. II:3-11].  }

   const
      hOffset = 20;                              {Horizontal offset from previous window, in pixels}
      vOffset = 20;                              {Vertical offset from previous window, in pixels}
```

```
var
   windowWidth  : INTEGER;                              {Width of window in pixels}
   windowHeight : INTEGER;                              {Height of window in pixels}
   hExtra       : INTEGER;                              {Excess screen width in pixels}
   vExtra       : INTEGER;                              {Excess screen height in pixels}
   hMax         : INTEGER;                              {Maximum number of windows horizontally}
   vMax         : INTEGER;                              {Maximum number of windows vertically}
   windowLeft   : INTEGER;                              {Left edge of window in global coordinates}
   windowTop    : INTEGER;                              {Top edge of window in global coordinates}

begin {OffsetWindow}

   with whichWindow^.portRect do
      begin
         windowWidth  := right  - left;                 {Get window dimensions from }
         windowHeight := bottom - top;                  {  port rectangle [I:4.2.2]}
         windowHeight := windowHeight + TitleBarHeight  {Adjust for title bar}
      end;

   hExtra := ScreenWidth  -  windowWidth;               {Find excess screen width}
   vExtra := ScreenHeight - (windowHeight + MenuBarHeight);  {  and height          }

   hMax := (hExtra div hOffset) + 1;                    {Find maximum number of windows horizontally}
   vMax := (vExtra div vOffset) + 1;                    {  and vertically                          }

   WindowCount :=  WindowCount + 1;                     {Increment window count}
   windowLeft  := (WindowCount mod hMax) * hOffset;     {Calculate offsets}
   windowTop   := (WindowCount mod vMax) * vOffset;
   windowTop   :=  windowTop + TitleBarHeight + MenuBarHeight;  {Adjust for title bar and menu bar}

   MoveWindow (whichWindow, windowLeft, windowTop, FALSE)   {Move window to new location [II:3.3.2]}

   end; {OffsetWindow}


{------------------------------------------------------------------------------}


procedure DoOpen;

   { Handle Open... command [Prog. II:8-5].  }

   var
      dlgOrigin   : Point;                              {Top-left corner of dialog box [I:4.1.1]}
      theTypeList : SFTypeList;                         {List of file types to display [II:8.3.2]}
      theReply    : SFReply;                            {Data returned by Get dialog [II:8.3.1]}
```

```
    begin {DoOpen}

        SetPt (dlgOrigin, DlgLeft, DlgTop);          {Set up dialog origin [I:4.1.1]}
        theTypeList [0] := 'TEXT';                   {Display text files only [II:8.3.2]}

        SFGetFile (dlgOrigin, '', NIL, 1, theTypeList, NIL, theReply);   {Get file name from user [II:8.3.2]}

        with theReply do
          if good then                               {Did user confirm file selection? [II:8.3.1]}
            OpenFile (fName, vRefNum)                 {Open file and read into window}

    end; {DoOpen}

{-------------------------------------------------------------------------------}


procedure OpenFile ((fileName : Str255; vNum : INTEGER));

    { Open document file [Prog. II:8-6]. }


    var
        theData    : WDHandle;                       {Handle to window's data record}
        dataHandle : Handle;                         {Untyped handle for locking data record [I:3.1.1]}
        theFile    : INTEGER;                        {Reference number of file}
        resultCode : OSErr;                          {I/O error code [I:3.1.2]}


    begin {OpenFile}

        resultCode := FSOpen (fileName, vNum, theFile);    {Open the file [II:8.2.2]}
        IOCheck (resultCode);                        {Check for error}
        if ErrorFlag then EXIT (OpenFile);           {On error, exit to main event loop}

        DoNew;                                       {Open a new window}

        dataHandle := Handle(GetWRefCon(TheWindow));  {Get window data [II:3.2.4]}
        HLock (dataHandle);                          {Lock data record [I:3.2.4]}

          theData := WDHandle(dataHandle);           {Convert to typed handle}
          with theData^^ do
            begin
              volNumber  := vNum;                    {Save volume and file number}

                fileNumber := theFile;               {   in window data record   }
                SetWTitle (TheWindow, fileName)      {File name becomes window title [II:3.2.4]}
            end; {with}
```

```
      HUnlock (dataHandle);                    {Unlock data record [I:3.2.4]}

      DoRevert                                 {Read file into window}

   end;  {OpenFile}

{-----------------------------------------------------------------------------}

procedure DoClose;

   {  Handle Close command [Prog. II:3-3].  }

   begin {DoClose}

      if FrontWindow = TheWindow then          {Is the active window one of ours? [II:3.3.3]}
         CloseAppWindow                        {Close application window}
      else
         CloseSysWindow                        {Close system window}

   end;  {DoClose}

{-----------------------------------------------------------------------------}

procedure CloseAppWindow;

   {  Close application window [Prog. II:7-2].  }

   const
      saveItem    = 1;                         {Item number for Save button}
      discardItem = 2;                         {Item number for Discard button}
      cancelItem  = 3;                         {Item number for Cancel button}

   var
      theData    : WDHandle;                   {Handle to window's data record}
      dataHandle : Handle;                     {Untyped handle for destroying data record [I:3.1.1]}
      theTitle   : Str255;                     {Title of window [I:2.1.1]}
      theItem    : INTEGER;                    {Item number for Save alert}
      resultCode : OSErr;                      {I/O error code [I:3.1.2]}
      thisWindow : WindowPtr;                  {Pointer to window being closed [II:3.1.1]}

   begin {CloseAppWindow}

      dataHandle := Handle(GetWRefCon(TheWindow));  {Get window data [II:3.2.4]}
      HLock (dataHandle);                      {Lock data record [I:3.2.4]}

      theData := WDHandle(dataHandle);         {Convert to typed handle}
      with theData^^ do
         begin

            if dirty then                      {Have window contents been changed?}
```

```
begin

    GetWTitle (TheWindow, theTitle);   {Get window title [II:3.2.4]}
    ParamText (theTitle, '', '', '');   {Substitute into alert text [II:7.4.6]}

    theItem := CautionAlert (SaveID, NIL);   {Post alert [II:7.4.2]}
    case theItem of

        saveItem:
            begin
                DoSave;                    {Save window contents to disk}
                if ErrorFlag then          {Check for I/O error}
                    begin
                        HUnlock (dataHandle);   {Unlock data record [I:3.2.4]}
                        EXIT (CloseAppWindow)   {Exit to main event loop}
                    end {if}
            end;

        discardItem:
            {Do nothing};

        cancelItem:
            begin
                Quitting := FALSE;         {Cancel Quit command, if any}
                HUnlock (dataHandle);      {Unlock data record [I:3.2.4]}
                EXIT (CloseAppWindow)      {Exit to main event loop}
            end

        end {case}

    end; {if}

if fileNumber <> 0 then                   {Is window associated with a file?}
    begin
        resultCode := FSClose (fileNumber);   {Close file [II:8.2.2]}
        IOCheck (resultCode);              {Check for error}
        if ErrorFlag then                  {Error detected?}
            begin
                HUnlock (dataHandle);      {Unlock data record [I:3.2.4]}
                EXIT (CloseAppWindow)      {Exit to main event loop}
            end {if}
    end; {if}

TEDispose (editRec);                       {Dispose of edit record [II:5.2.2]}

TheScrollBar := NIL;                       {Clear global handles}
TheText      := NIL

end; {with}
```

```
    HUnlock (dataHandle);                          {Unlock data record [I:3.2.4]}

    thisWindow := TheWindow;                       {Save window pointer (DoActivate will change TheWindow)}
    HideWindow (TheWindow);                        {Force deactivate event [II:3.3.1]}

    if GetNextEvent (ActivateEvt, TheEvent) then   {Get deactivate event [II:2.2.1, II:2.1.2]}
      DoActivate;                                  {   and handle it                 }
    if GetNextEvent (ActivateEvt, TheEvent) then   {Get activate event [II:2.2.1, II:2.1.2]}
      DoActivate;                                  {   and handle it                 }

    DisposHandle  (dataHandle);                    {Dispose of window data record [I:3.2.2]}
    DisposeWindow (thisWindow)                     {Dispose of window [II:3.2.3]}

  end;  {CloseAppWindow}

{-------------------------------------------------------------------------------}


procedure CloseSysWindow;

  { Close system window [Prog. II:4-7]. }

  var
    whichWindow : WindowPeek;                      {Pointer for access to window's fields [II:3.1.1]}
    accNumber   : INTEGER;                         {Reference number of desk accessory [I:7.5.5]}

  begin {CloseSysWindow}

    whichWindow := WindowPeek(FrontWindow);        {Convert to a WindowPeek [II:3.1.1, II:3.3.3]}

    accNumber := whichWindow^.windowKind;          {Get reference number of desk accessory [II:3.1.1]}
    CloseDeskAcc (accNumber)                       {Close desk accessory [II:4.5.2]}

  end;  {CloseSysWindow}

{-------------------------------------------------------------------------------}


procedure DoSave;

  { Handle Save command [Prog. II:8-2]. }

  var
    theData    : WDHandle;                         {Handle to window's data record}
    dataHandle : Handle;                           {Untyped handle for locking data record [I:3.1.1]}
```

```
begin {DoSave}

   dataHandle := Handle(GetWRefCon(TheWindow));      {Get window data [II:3.2.4]}

   HLock (dataHandle);                               {Lock data record [I:3.2.4]}

      theData := WDHandle(dataHandle);               {Convert to typed handle}
      with theData^^ do
         if fileNumber = 0 then                      {Is window associated with a file?}
            DoSaveAs                                  {Get file name from user}
         else
            WriteFile (fileNumber, volNumber);       {Write to window's file}

   HUnlock (dataHandle)                              {Unlock data record [I:3.2.4]}

end;  {DoSave}
```

```
{----------------------------------------------------------------------------------}
```

```
procedure DoSaveAs;

   { Handle Save As... command [Prog. II:8-8]. }

   var
      dlgOrigin  : Point;           {Top-left corner of dialog box [I:4.1.1]}
      theReply   : SFReply;         {Data returned by Put dialog [II:8.3.1]}
      theInfo    : FInfo;           {File's Finder information [I:7.3.2]}
      theFile    : INTEGER;         {Reference number of file}
      theData    : WDHandle;        {Handle to window's data record}
      dataHandle : Handle;          {Untyped handle for locking data record [I:3.1.1]}
      strHandle  : StringHandle;    {Handle to title string for empty window [II:8.1.2]}
      untitled   : Str255;          {Title string for empty window [I:2.1.1]}
      ignore     : INTEGER;         {Item code returned by alert}
      resultCode : OSErr;           {I/O error code [I:3.1.2]}

   begin {DoSaveAs}

      SetPt     (dlgOrigin, DlgLeft, DlgTop);        {Set up dialog origin [I:4.1.1]}
      SFPutFile (dlgOrigin, 'Save under what file name?', '', NIL, theReply);
                                                     {Get file name from user [II:8.3.3]}
      with theReply do
         begin
            if not good then                         {Did user confirm file selection? [II:8.3.1]}
               begin
                  Quitting  := FALSE;                {Cancel Quit command, if any}
                  ErrorFlag := TRUE;                 {Force exit to main event loop}
                  EXIT (DoSaveAs)                    {Skip rest of operation}
               end; {if}
```

```
resultCode := GetFInfo (fName, vRefNum, theInfo);  {Get Finder info [I:7.3.3]}
case resultCode of

    NoErr:                                {File already exists [II:8.2.8]}
      if theInfo.fdType <> 'TEXT' then    {Not a text file? [I:7.3.2]}
        begin
          ParamText (fName, '', '', '');  {Substitute file name into text of alert [II:7.4.6]}
          ignore := StopAlert (wrongTypeID, NIL);  {Post alert [II:7.4.2]}

          ErrorFlag := TRUE;              {Force exit to main event loop}
          EXIT (DoSaveAs)                 {Skip rest of operation}
        end; {if}

    FNFErr:                               {File not found [II:8.2.8]}
      begin
        resultCode := Create (fName, vRefNum, 'MEDT', 'TEXT');  {Create the file [II:8.2.1]}
        IOCheck (resultCode);             {Check for error}
        if ErrorFlag then EXIT (DoSaveAs) {On error, exit to main event loop}
      end;

    otherwise                            {Unanticipated error}
      begin
        IOCheck (resultCode);            {Post error alert}
        EXIT (DoSaveAs)                  {Exit to main event loop}
      end

  end; {case}

dataHandle := Handle(GetWRefCon(TheWindow));  {Get window data [II:3.2.4]}
HLock (dataHandle);                      {Lock data record [I:3.2.4]}

  theData := WDHandle(dataHandle);       {Convert to typed handle}
  with theData^^ do
    begin

      SetCursor (Watch^^);               {Indicate delay [II:2.5.2]}

      if fileNumber <> 0 then            {Does window already have a file?}
        begin
          resultCode := FSClose (fileNumber);  {Close old file [II:8.2.2]}
          IOCheck (resultCode);          {Check for error}
          if ErrorFlag then              {Error detected during close?}
            begin
              HUnlock (dataHandle);      {Unlock data record [I:3.2.4]}
              EXIT (DoSaveAs)            {Exit to main event loop}
            end {if}
        end; {if}
```

```
            resultCode := FSOpen (fName, vRefNum, theFile);   {Open new file [II:8.2.2]}
            IOCheck (resultCode);              {Check for error}
            if ErrorFlag then                  {Error detected during open?}
                begin
                    volNumber  := 0;                   {Window is left with no file:  clear volume}
                    fileNumber := 0;                   {    and file numbers in window data        }

                    strHandle := GetString (noTitleID);  {Get string from resource file [I:8.1.2]}
                    untitled  := strHandle^^;            {Convert from handle}
                    SetWTitle (TheWindow, untitled)      {Set new window title [II:3.2.4]}
                end {then}

            else
                begin
                    volNumber  := vRefNum;       {Save new volume and file }
                    fileNumber := theFile;       {   numbers in window data}
                    SetWTitle (TheWindow, fName);  {File name becomes new window title [II:3.2.4]}

                    WriteFile (theFile, vRefNum)  {Write window's contents to file}
                end {else}

        end; {with}

    HUnlock (dataHandle)                        {Unlock data record [I:3.2.4]}

  end {with}

end;  {DoSaveAs}

{-----------------------------------------------------------------------------}


procedure WriteFile ((theFile : INTEGER; volNum : INTEGER));

  { Write window contents to a file [Prog. II:8-3]. }

  var
     textHandle : Handle;                       {Handle to text of file [I:3.1.1]}
     textLength : LONGINT;                       {Length of text in bytes}
     resultCode : OSErr;                         {I/O error code [I:3.1.2]}

  begin {WriteFile}

     SetCursor (Watch^^);                        {Indicate delay [II:2.5.2]}

     HLock (Handle(TheText));                    {Lock edit record [I:3.2.4]}
        with TheText^^ do
           begin
              textHandle := hText;              {Get text handle and current length}
              textLength := teLength             {  from edit record [II:5.1.1]    }
           end; {with}
     HUnlock (Handle(TheText));                  {Unlock edit record [I:3.2.4]}
```

```
      resultCode := SetFPos (theFile, FSFromStart, 0);   {Reset mark to beginning of file [II:8.2.4]}
      IOCheck (resultCode);                              {Check for error}
      if ErrorFlag then EXIT (WriteFile);                {On error, exit to main event loop}

      HLock (textHandle);                                {Lock text [I:3.2.4]}
         resultCode := FSWrite (theFile, textLength, textHandle^); {Write text to file [II:8.2.3]}
      HUnlock (textHandle);                              {Unlock text [I:3.2.4]}
      IOCheck (resultCode);                              {Check for error}
      if ErrorFlag then EXIT (WriteFile);                {On error, exit to main event loop}

      resultCode := SetEOF (theFile, textLength);        {Set length of file [II:8.2.5]}
      IOCheck (resultCode);                              {Check for error}
      if ErrorFlag then EXIT (WriteFile);                {On error, exit to main event loop}

      resultCode := FlushVol (NIL, volNum);              {Flush volume buffer [II:8.1.3]}
      IOCheck (resultCode);                              {Check for error}
      if ErrorFlag then EXIT (WriteFile);                {On error, exit to main event loop}

      WindowDirty (FALSE)                                {Mark window as clean}

   end;  {WriteFile}


{---------------------------------------------------------------------------------}


procedure DoRevert;

   ( Handle Revert to Saved command [Prog. II:8-4]. }

   var
      theData    : WDHandle;                             {Handle to window's data record}
      dataHandle : Handle;                               {Untyped handle for locking data record [I:3.1.1]}
      fileName   : Str255;                               {Title of window [I:2.1.1]}
      textLength : LONGINT;                              {Length of file in bytes}
      theItem    : INTEGER;                              {Item number for Revert alert}
      resultCode : OSErr;                                {I/O error code [I:3.1.2]}

   begin {DoRevert}

      dataHandle := Handle(GetWRefCon(TheWindow));       {Get window data [II:3.2.4]}
      HLock (dataHandle);                                {Lock data record [I:3.2.4]}

         theData := WDHandle(dataHandle);                {Convert to typed handle}
         with theData^^ do
            begin

               if dirty then                             {Have window contents been changed?}
                  begin
                     GetWTitle (TheWindow, fileName);    {Get file name from window title [II:3.2.4]}
                     ParamText (fileName, '', '', '');   {Substitute into text of alert [II:7.4.6]}
```

```
          theItem := CautionAlert (RevertID, NIL);   {Post alert [II:7.4.2]}
          if theItem = Cancel then              {Did user cancel? [II:7.1.1]}
             begin
                HUnlock (dataHandle);           {Unlock data record [I:3.2.4]}
                ErrorFlag := TRUE;              {Force exit to main event loop}
                EXIT (DoRevert)                 {Skip rest of operation}
             end {if}
       end; {if}


   SetCursor (Watch^^);                         {Indicate delay [II:2.5.2]}

   resultCode := GetEOF (fileNumber, textLength);   {Get length of file [II:8.2.5]}
   IOCheck (resultCode);                        {Check for error}
   if ErrorFlag then                            {Error detected?}
      begin
         HUnlock (dataHandle);                  {Unlock data record [I:3.2.4]}
         EXIT (DoRevert)                        {Exit to main event loop}
      end; {if}


   resultCode := SetFPos (fileNumber, FSFromStart, 0);   {Set mark at beginning of file [II:8.2.4]}
   IOCheck (resultCode);                        {Check for error}
   if ErrorFlag then                            {Error detected?}
      begin
         HUnlock (dataHandle);                  {Unlock data record [I:3.2.4]}
         EXIT (DoRevert)                        {Exit to main event loop}
      end; {if}

   HLock (Handle(TheText));                     {Lock edit record [I:3.2.4]}
      with TheText^^ do
         begin

            SetHandleSize (hText, textLength);  {Adjust text to length of file [I:3.2.3, II:5.1.1]}
            teLength := textLength;             {Set text length [II:5.1.1]}

            HLock (hText);                      {Lock the handle [I:3.2.4]}
               resultCode := FSRead (fileNumber, textLength, hText^);
                                                {Read text of file into handle [II:8.2.3]}
            IOCheck (resultCode);               {Check for error}
            HUnlock (hText)                     {Unlock the handle [I:3.2.4]}

         end; {with}
   HUnlock (Handle(TheText));                   {Unlock edit record [I:3.2.4]}

   if ErrorFlag then                            {Error detected during read?}
      begin
         HUnlock (dataHandle);                  {Unlock data record [I:3.2.4]}
         EXIT (DoRevert)                        {Exit to main event loop}
      end {if}
```

```
      end; {with}

    HUnlock (dataHandle);                     {Unlock data record [I:3.2.4]}


    TECalText (TheText);                       {Wrap text to window [II:5.3.1]}
    AdjustScrollBar;                           {Adjust scroll bar to length of text}
    TESetSelect (0, 0, TheText);               {Set insertion point at beginning of text [II:5.4.2]}

    InvalRect (TheWindow^.portRect);           {Force update to redraw text [II:3.4.2]}
    WindowDirty (FALSE)                        {Mark window as clean}

  end;  {DoRevert}

{-----------------------------------------------------------------------}

procedure DoQuit;

  { Handle Quit command [Prog. II:2-4].  }

  begin {DoQuit}

    Quitting := TRUE                           {Start closing down windows}

  end;  {DoQuit}

{-----------------------------------------------------------------------}

procedure DoEditChoice ((theItem : INTEGER)};

  { Handle choice from Edit menu [Prog. II:4-9].  }

  const
    undoCmd  = 0;                              {Constant representing Undo command [II:4.5.3]}
    cutCmd   = 2;                              {Constant representing Cut command [II:4.5.3]}
    copyCmd  = 3;                              {Constant representing Copy command [II:4.5.3]}

    pasteCmd = 4;                              {Constant representing Paste command [II:4.5.3]}
    clearCmd = 5;                              {Constant representing Clear command [II:4.5.3]}

  begin {DoEditChoice}

    case theItem of

      UndoItem:
        if not SystemEdit (undoCmd) then
          DoUndo;                              {Handle Undo command}
```

```
        CutItem:
          if not SystemEdit (cutCmd) then
            DoCut;                              {Handle Cut command}

        CopyItem:
          if not SystemEdit (copyCmd) then
            DoCopy;                             {Handle Copy command}

        PasteItem:
          if not SystemEdit (pasteCmd) then
            DoPaste;                            {Handle Paste command}

        ClearItem:
          if not SystemEdit (clearCmd) then
            DoClear                             {Handle Clear command}

        end {case}

  end; {DoEditChoice}
```

{---}

```
procedure DoUndo;

  { Handle Undo command.  }

  begin {DoUndo}

    SysBeep(1)                                  {Undo command not implemented [II:2.8.1]}

  end; {DoUndo}
```

{---}

```
procedure DoCut;

  { Handle Cut command [Prog. II:5-8].  }

  begin {DoCut}

    ScrollToSelection;                          {Make sure selection is visible}

    TECut (TheText);                            {Cut the selection [II:5.5.2]}

    AdjustScrollBar;                            {Adjust scroll bar to length of text}
    AdjustText;                                 {Adjust text to match scroll bar}
    ScrollToSelection;                          {Keep insertion point visible}
```

```
        DisableItem (EditMenu, CutItem);             {Disable menu items that operate on}
        DisableItem (EditMenu, CopyItem);            {   a nonempty selection [II:4.6.2]}
        DisableItem (EditMenu, ClearItem);

        EnableItem  (EditMenu, PasteItem);           {Enable Paste command [II:4.6.2]}

        ScrapDirty := TRUE;                          {Mark scrap as dirty}
        WindowDirty (TRUE)                           {Mark window as dirty}

    end;  {DoCut}

{-----------------------------------------------------------------------------------}


procedure DoCopy;

    { Handle Copy command [Prog. II:5-9].  }

    begin {DoCopy}

        ScrollToSelection;                           {Make sure selection is visible}

        TECopy (TheText);                            {Copy the selection [II:5.5.2]}

        EnableItem (EditMenu, PasteItem);            {Enable Paste command [II:4.6.2]}

        ScrapDirty := TRUE                           {Mark scrap as dirty}

    end;  {DoCopy}

{-----------------------------------------------------------------------------------}


procedure DoPaste;

    { Handle Paste command [Prog. II:5-10].  }

    begin {DoPaste}

        ScrollToSelection;                           {Make sure selection is visible}

        TEPaste (TheText);                           {Paste the scrap [II:5.5.2]}

        AdjustScrollBar;                             {Adjust scroll bar to length of text}
        AdjustText;                                  {Adjust text to match scroll bar}
        ScrollToSelection;                           {Keep selection visible}

        DisableItem (EditMenu, CutItem);             {Disable menu items that operate on}
        DisableItem (EditMenu, CopyItem);            {   a nonempty selection [II:4.6.2]}
        DisableItem (EditMenu, ClearItem);
```

```
      WindowDirty (TRUE)                        {Mark window as dirty}

   end;  {DoPaste}
```

{--}

```
procedure DoClear;

   {  Handle Clear command [Prog. II:5-11].  }

   begin {DoClear}

      ScrollToSelection;                        {Make sure selection is visible}

      TEDelete (TheText);                       {Delete the selection [II:5.5.3]}

      AdjustScrollBar;                          {Adjust scroll bar to length of text}
      AdjustText;                               {Adjust text to match scroll bar}
      ScrollToSelection;                        {Keep insertion point visible}

      DisableItem (EditMenu, CutItem);          {Disable menu items that operate on}
      DisableItem (EditMenu, CopyItem);         {   a nonempty selection [II:4.6.2]}
      DisableItem (EditMenu, ClearItem);

      WindowDirty (TRUE)                        {Mark window as dirty}

   end;  {DoClear}
```

{--}

```
procedure DoContent ((whichWindow : WindowPtr));

   {  Handle mouse-down event in content region of active window [Prog. II:6-1].  }

   var
      thePoint   : Point;                       {Location of mouse click in window coordinates [I:4.1.1]}
      theControl : ControlHandle;               {Handle to control [II:6.1.1]}
      thePart    : INTEGER;                     {Part of control where mouse was pressed [II:6.4.1]}

   begin {DoContent}

      if whichWindow <> FrontWindow then        {Is it an inactive window? [II:3.3.3]}
         SelectWindow (whichWindow)             {If so, just activate it [II:3.5.2]}
```

```
      else
        begin

            thePoint := TheEvent.where;              {Get point in screen coordinates [II:2.1.1]}
            GlobalToLocal (thePoint);                {Convert to window coordinates [I:4.4.2]}

            thePart := FindControl (thePoint, whichWindow, theControl);
                                                     {Was mouse pressed in a control? [II:6.4.1]}

            if theControl = TheScrollBar then        {Was it in the scroll bar?}

                DoScroll (thePart, thePoint)         {Go scroll the window}

              else if theControl = NIL then          {Not in a control?}

                if PtInRect (thePoint, TheText^^.viewRect) then  {Was it in the text rectangle? [I:4.4.3]}
                  DoSelect (thePoint)                {Go handle text selection}

        end {else}

    end; {DoContent}

{--------------------------------------------------------------------------------}


procedure DoScroll ((thePart : INTEGER; thePoint : Point));

    { Handle mouse-down event in scroll bar [Prog. II:6-6]. }

    begin {DoScroll}

      if thePart = InThumb then                      {Dragging the indicator? [II:6.4.1]}

        begin
            thePart := TrackControl (TheScrollBar, thePoint, NIL);
                                                     {Track mouse with no action procedure [II:6.4.2]}
            AdjustText                               {Adjust text to new setting}
        end {then}

      else

        thePart := TrackControl (TheScrollBar, thePoint, @ScrollText)
                                                     {Track mouse with continuous scroll [II:6.4.2]}

    end; {DoScroll}

{--------------------------------------------------------------------------------}
```

```
procedure ScrollText ((theControl: ControlHandle; thePart : INTEGER));

   { Scroll text within window [Prog. II:6-8].  }

   var
      delta    : INTEGER;                      {Amount to scroll by, in lines}
      oldValue : INTEGER;                      {Previous setting of scroll bar}

   begin {ScrollText}

      case thePart of

         inUpButton:
            delta := -1;                       {Scroll up one line at a time}

         inDownButton:
            delta := +1;                       {Scroll down one line at a time}

         inPageUp:
            with TheText^^, viewRect do
               delta := (top - bottom) div lineHeight + 1;  {Scroll up by height of text rectangle [II:5.1.1]}

         inPageDown:
            with TheText^^, viewRect do
               delta := (bottom - top) div lineHeight - 1;  {Scroll down by height of text rectangle [II:5.1.1]}

         otherwise
            {Do nothing}

         end; {case}

      if thePart <> 0 then                     {Is mouse still in the original part?}
         begin
            oldValue := GetCtlValue (theControl);    {Get old setting [II:6.2.4]}
            SetCtlValue (theControl, oldValue + delta); {Adjust by scroll amount [II:6.2.4]}

            AdjustText                          {Scroll text to match new setting}
         end

   end;  {ScrollText}

{-----------------------------------------------------------------------------}

procedure AdjustText;

   { Adjust text within window to match scroll bar setting [Prog. II:6-7].  }
```

```
var
    oldScroll : INTEGER;                        {Old text offset in pixels}
    newScroll : INTEGER;                        {New text offset in pixels}


begin {AdjustText}

    HLock (Handle(TheText));                     {Lock edit record [I:3.2.4]}
        with TheText^^ do
            begin

                oldScroll := viewRect.top - destRect.top;        {Get current offset [II:5.1.1]}
                newScroll := GetCtlValue (TheScrollBar) * lineHeight;  {Scroll bar gives new offset [II:6.2.4]}

                TEScroll (0, (oldScroll - newScroll), TheText)   {Scroll by difference [II:5.3.3]}

            end; {with}
        HUnlock (Handle(TheText))                 {Unlock edit record [I:3.2.4]}

end;  {AdjustText}


{----------------------------------------------------------------------------------}


function AutoScroll( : BOOLEAN};

    { Handle automatic scrolling during text selection [Prog. II:6-9].  }


var
    mousePoint : Point;                         {Mouse location in local (window) coordinates [I:4.1.1]}
    textRect   : Rect;                          {Active window's text rectangle [I:4.1.2]}
    saveClip   : RgnHandle;                     {Original clipping region on entry [I:4.1.5]}


begin {AutoScroll}

    saveClip := NewRgn;                         {Create temporary region [I:4.1.6]}
    GetClip  (saveClip);                        {Set it to existing clipping region [I:4.3.6]}
    ClipRect (TheWindow^.portRect);             {Clip to entire port rectangle [I:4.3.6, I:4.2.2]}

        GetMouse (mousePoint);                  {Find mouse location [II:2.4.1]}
        textRect := TheText^^.viewRect;         {Get text rectangle [II:5.1.1]}

        if mousePoint.v < textRect.top then     {Above top of rectangle? [I:4.1.1, I:4.1.2]}
            ScrollText (TheScrollBar, InUpButton)   {Scroll up one line [II:6.4.1]}

        else if mousePoint.v > textRect.bottom then  {Below bottom of rectangle? [I:4.1.1, I:4.1.2]}
            ScrollText (TheScrollBar, InDownButton)  {Scroll down one line [II:6.4.1]}

        {else do nothing};
```

```
      SetClip   (saveClip);                     {Restore original clipping region [I:4.3.6]}
      DisposeRgn (saveClip);                    {Dispose of temporary region [I:4.1.6]}

      AutoScroll := TRUE                         {Continue tracking mouse [II:5.6.1]}

   end;  {AutoScroll}

{------------------------------------------------------------------------}

procedure DoSelect ((thePoint : Point)};

   { Handle mouse-down event in text rectangle [Prog. II:5-4].  }

   var
      extend : BOOLEAN;                          {Extend existing selection (Shift-click)?}

   begin {DoSelect}

      with TheEvent do
         extend := (BitAnd(modifiers, ShiftKey) <> 0);  {Shift key down? [I:2.2.2, II:2.1.5]}

      TEClick (thePoint, extend, TheText);       {Do text selection [II:5.4.1]}

      FixEditMenu                                {Enable/disable menu items}

   end;  {DoSelect}

{------------------------------------------------------------------------}

procedure FixEditMenu;

   { Enable/disable editing commands [Prog. II:5-5].  }

   begin {FixEditMenu}

      DisableItem (EditMenu, UndoItem);          {Disable Undo command [II:4.6.2]}

      HLock (Handle(TheText));                   {Lock edit record [I:3.2.4]}
         with TheText^^ do
            if selStart = selEnd then            {Is selection empty? [II:5.1.1]}
               begin
                  DisableItem (EditMenu, CutItem);      {Disable menu items that operate on}
                  DisableItem (EditMenu, CopyItem);     {  a nonempty selection [II:4.6.2]}
                  DisableItem (EditMenu, ClearItem)
               end  {then}
```

```
        else
            begin
                EnableItem (EditMenu, CutItem);         {Enable menu items that operate on }
                EnableItem (EditMenu, CopyItem);        {   a nonempty selection [II:4.6.2]}
                EnableItem (EditMenu, ClearItem)
            end; {else}
        HUnlock (Handle(TheText));                       {Unlock edit record [I:3.2.4]}

        if TEGetScrapLen = 0 then                        {Is scrap empty? [II:5.5.4]}
            DisableItem (EditMenu, PasteItem)            {Disable Paste command [II:4.6.2]}
        else
            EnableItem  (EditMenu, PasteItem)            {Enable Paste command [II:4.6.2]}

    end; {FixEditMenu}

{--------------------------------------------------------------------------------}


procedure DoDrag ((whichWindow : WindowPtr));

    { Handle mouse-down event in drag region [Prog. II:3-8]. }

    var
        limitRect : Rect;                               {Limit rectangle for dragging [I:4.1.2]}

    begin {DoDrag}

        SetRect    (limitRect, 0, MenuBarHeight, ScreenWidth, ScreenHeight);
                                                        {Set limit rectangle [I:4.1.2]}
        InsetRect  (limitRect, ScreenMargin, ScreenMargin); {Inset by screen margin [I:4.4.4]}

        DragWindow (whichWindow, TheEvent.where, limitRect) {Let user drag the window [II:3.5.4]}

    end; {DoDrag}

{--------------------------------------------------------------------------------}


procedure DoGrow ((whichWindow : WindowPtr));

    { Handle mouse-down event in size region [Prog. II:3-9]. }

    var
        sizeRect  : Rect;                               {Minimum and maximum dimensions of window [I:4.1.2]}
        newSize   : LONGINT;                            {Coded representation of new dimensions}
        newWidth  : INTEGER;                            {New width of window}
        newHeight : INTEGER;                            {New height of window}

    begin {DoGrow}

        if whichWindow <> FrontWindow then              {Is it an inactive window? [II:3.3.3]}
            SelectWindow (whichWindow)                  {If so, just activate it [II:3.5.2]}
```

```
        else
          begin

              SetRect (sizeRect, MinWidth, MinHeight, ScreenWidth, (ScreenHeight - MenuBarHeight) );
                                                    {Set size rectangle [I:4.1.2]}
              newSize := GrowWindow (whichWindow, TheEvent.where, sizeRect);
                                                    {Let user drag size region [II:3.5.4]}

              if newSize <> 0 then                  {Was size changed?}
                begin

                    EraseRect (whichWindow^.portRect);    {Clear window to white [I:5.3.2]}

                    newWidth  := LoWord(newSize);    {Extract width from low word [I:2.2.3]}
                    newHeight := HiWord(newSize);    {Extract height from high word [I:2.2.3]}
                    SizeWindow (whichWindow, newWidth, newHeight, TRUE);
                                                    {Adjust size of window [II:3.3.2]}

                    InvalRect (whichWindow^.portRect);   {Force update of window's contents [II:3.4.2]}

                    FixScrollBar;                    {Resize scroll bar}
                    FixText                          {Resize text rectangle}

                end {if}

          end {else}

    end; {DoGrow}

{-------------------------------------------------------------------------------}

procedure FixScrollBar;

    { Resize window's scroll bar [Prog. II:6-10]. }

    begin {FixScrollBar}

        HideControl (TheScrollBar);                  {Hide scroll bar [II:6.3.1]}

        with TheWindow^.portRect do
          begin

              MoveControl (TheScrollBar,             {Move top-left corner [II:6.3.2]}

                          right - (SBarWidth - 1),   {Allow for 1-pixel overlap at right}
                          -1);                       {Overlap window top by 1 pixel}
```

```
          SizeControl (TheScrollBar,              {Adjust bottom-right corner [II:6.3.2]}
                       SBarWidth,
                       (bottom + 1) - (top - 1) - (SBarWidth - 1) )
                                                  {Allow room for size box}

      end; {with}

    ShowControl (TheScrollBar);                   {Redisplay scroll bar [II:6.3.1]}

    ValidRect (TheScrollBar^^.contrlRect)         {Avoid updating again [II:3.4.2]}

  end;  {FixScrollBar}


{--------------------------------------------------------------------------------}


procedure FixText;

   {  Resize window's text rectangle [Prog. II:6-11].  }


  var
     topLine     : INTEGER;                        {First line visible in window}
     firstChar   : INTEGER;                        {Character position of first character in window}
     maxTop      : INTEGER;                        {Maximum value for top line in window}


  begin {FixText}

    SetCursor (Watch^^);                           {Indicate delay [II:2.5.2]}

    HLock (Handle(TheText));                        {Lock edit record [I:3.2.4]}
      with TheText^^ do
        begin

            topLine   := GetCtlValue (TheScrollBar); {Get previous first line [II:6.2.4]}
            firstChar := lineStarts[topLine];       {Find first character previously visible [II:5.1.1]}

            viewRect := TheWindow^.portRect;        {Display text in window's port rectangle [II:3.1.1]}
            with viewRect do
              begin
                right  := right - (SBarWidth - 1); {Exclude scroll bar, allowing for 1-pixel overlap}
                bottom := bottom - (SBarWidth - 1); {Leave space for scroll bar at bottom}
                bottom := (bottom div lineHeight) * lineHeight
                                                    {Truncate to a whole number of lines [II:5.1.1]}
              end;

            destRect := viewRect;                   {Wrap to same rectangle [II:5.1.1]}
            InsetRect (destRect, TextMargin, TextMargin);  {Inset by text margin [I:4.4.4]}

            TECalText (TheText);                    {Recalibrate line starts [II:5.3.1]}
            AdjustScrollBar;                        {Adjust scroll bar to new length}

            ScrollCharacter (firstChar, FALSE)      {Scroll same character to top of window}
```

```
                  end; {with}
            HUnlock (Handle(TheText))                      {Unlock edit record [I:3.2.4]}

      end; {FixText}

{-----------------------------------------------------------------------}

procedure DoGoAway ((whichWindow : WindowPtr)};

   { Handle mouse-down event in close region [Prog. II:3-10].  }

      begin {DoGoAway}

         if whichWindow <> FrontWindow then           {Is it an inactive window? [II:3.3.3]}
            SelectWindow (whichWindow)                 {If so, just activate it [II:3.5.2]}

         else if TrackGoAway (whichWindow, TheEvent.where) then {Otherwise, track mouse in close region [II:3.5.4]}
            DoClose                                    {   and close window                            }

      end; {DoGoAway}

{-----------------------------------------------------------------------}

procedure DoKeystroke;

   { Handle keystroke [Prog. II:4-4].  }

      var
         chCode     : INTEGER;                         {Character code from event message [8.1.1]}
         ch         : CHAR;                            {Character that was typed}
         menuChoice : LONGINT;                         {Menu ID and item number for keyboard alias}

      begin {DoKeystroke}

         with TheEvent do
            begin

               chCode := BitAnd (message, CharCodeMask); {Extract character code [I:2.2.2, II:2.1.4]}
               ch := CHR(chCode);                        {Convert to a character}

               if BitAnd (modifiers, CmdKey) <> 0 then  {Command key down? [I:2.2.2, II:2.1.5]}
                  begin
                     if what <> AutoKey then             {Ignore repeats [II:2.1.1, II:2.1.2]}
                        begin
                           menuChoice := MenuKey (ch);   {Get menu equivalent [II:4.5.1]}
                           DoMenuChoice (menuChoice)     {Handle as menu choice}
                        end
                  end
```

```
        else
            DoTyping (ch)                          {Handle as normal character}

        end {with}

    end; {DoKeystroke}

{------------------------------------------------------------------------------}

procedure DoTyping ((ch : CHAR)};

    { Handle character typed from keyboard [Prog. II:5-6]. }

    begin {DoTyping}

        ScrollToSelection;                         {Make sure insertion point is visible}

        TEKey (ch, TheText);                       {Process character [II:5.5.1]}

        AdjustScrollBar;                           {Adjust scroll bar to length of text}
        AdjustText;                                {Adjust text to match scroll bar}
        ScrollToSelection;                         {Keep insertion point visible}

        DisableItem (EditMenu, CutItem);           {Disable menu items that operate on}
        DisableItem (EditMenu, CopyItem);          {  a nonempty selection [II:4.6.2]}
        DisableItem (EditMenu, ClearItem);

        WindowDirty (TRUE)                         {Mark window as dirty}

    end; {DoTyping}

{------------------------------------------------------------------------------}

procedure DoUpdate;

    { Handle update event [Prog. II:5-3]. }

    var
        savePort    : GrafPtr;                     {Pointer to previous current port [I:4.2.2]}
        whichWindow : WindowPtr;                   {Pointer to window to be updated [II:3.1.1]}
        theData     : WDHandle;                    {Handle to window's data record}
        dataHandle  : Handle;                      {Untyped handle for locking data record [I:3.1.1]}

    begin {DoUpdate}

        GetPort (savePort);                        {Save previous port [I:4.3.3]}

            whichWindow := WindowPtr(TheEvent.message);  {Convert long integer to pointer [II:3.1.1]}
            SetPort (whichWindow);                 {Make window the current port [I:4.3.3]}
```

```
        BeginUpdate (whichWindow);                      {Restrict visible region to update region [II:3.4.1]}

          EraseRect (whichWindow^.portRect);            {Clear update region [I:5.3.2]}

          DrawGrowIcon (whichWindow);                   {Redraw size box [II:3.3.4]}
          DrawControls (whichWindow);                   {Redraw scroll bar [II:6.3.1]}

          dataHandle := Handle(GetWRefCon(whichWindow));  {Get window data [II:3.2.4]}
          HLock (dataHandle);                           {Lock data record [I:3.2.4]}
             theData := WDHandle(dataHandle);           {Convert to typed handle}

             with theData^^ do
                TEUpdate (editRec^^.viewRect, editRec); {Redraw the text [II:5.3.2]}
          HUnlock (dataHandle);                         {Unlock data record [I:3.2.4]}

        EndUpdate (whichWindow);                        {Restore original visible region [II:3.4.1]}

      SetPort (savePort)                                {Restore original port [I:4.3.3]}

    end;  {DoUpdate}

{------------------------------------------------------------------------------------}


procedure DoActivate;

   { Handle activate (or deactivate) event [Prog. II:5-14].  }

   const
      active  =   0;                                    {Highlighting code for active scroll bar [II:6.3.3]}
      inactive = 255;                                   {Highlighting code for inactive scroll bar [II:6.3.3]}

      changeFlag = $0002;                               {Mask for extracting "change bit" from event modifiers}

   var
      whichWindow : WindowPtr;                          {Pointer to the window [II:3.1.1]}
      theData     : WDHandle;                           {Handle to window's data record}
      dataHandle  : Handle;                             {Untyped handle for locking data record [I:3.1.1]}

   begin {DoActivate}

      with TheEvent do
         begin

            whichWindow := WindowPtr(message);          {Convert long integer to pointer [II:3.1.1]}
            SetPort (whichWindow);                      {Make window the current port [I:4.3.3]}

            DrawGrowIcon (whichWindow);                 {Highlight or unhighlight size box [II:3.3.4]}

            dataHandle := Handle(GetWRefCon(whichWindow));  {Get window data [II:3.2.4]}
            HLock (dataHandle);                         {Lock data record [I:3.2.4]}
```

```
theData := WDHandle(dataHandle);        {Convert to typed handle}
with theData^^ do
   if BitAnd(modifiers, ActiveFlag) <> 0 then {Test activate/deactivate bit [I:2.2.2, II:2.1.5]}

      begin

         TheWindow    := whichWindow;        {Set global pointers/handles}
         TheScrollBar := scrollBar;
         TheText      := editRec;

         HiliteControl (scrollBar, active);  {Activate scroll bar [II:6.3.3]}
         TEActivate (editRec);               {Highlight selection [II:5.4.3]}

         if BitAnd(modifiers, changeFlag) <> 0 then

                                             {Coming from a system window? [I:2.2.2, II:2.1.5]}
            ReadDeskScrap;                   {Copy desk scrap to Toolbox scrap}

         FixEditMenu;                        {Enable/disable editing commands}

         EnableItem (FileMenu, SaveAsItem);  {Enable Save As... command [II:4.6.2]}
         if dirty then                       {Is document dirty?}
            EnableItem (FileMenu, SaveItem); {Enable Save command [II:4.6.2]}
         if dirty and (fileNumber <> 0) then {Is there a file to revert to?}
            EnableItem (FileMenu, RevertItem) {Enable Revert command [II:4.6.2]}

      end {then}

   else

      begin

         TheWindow    := NIL;                {Clear global pointers/handles}
         TheScrollBar := NIL;
         TheText      := NIL;

         TEDeactivate (editRec);             {Unhighlight selection [II:5.4.3]}
         HiliteControl (scrollBar, inactive); {Deactivate scroll bar [II:6.3.3]}

         if BitAnd(modifiers, changeFlag) <> 0 then
                                             {Exiting to a system window? [I:2.2.2, II:2.1.5]}
            begin
               WriteDeskScrap;              {Copy Toolbox scrap to desk scrap}

               EnableItem (EditMenu, UndoItem); {Enable standard editing commands}
               EnableItem (EditMenu, CutItem); {    for desk accessory [II:4.6.2]  }
               EnableItem (EditMenu, CopyItem);
               EnableItem (EditMenu, PasteItem);
               EnableItem (EditMenu, ClearItem)
            end; {if}
```

```
                    DisableItem (FileMenu, SaveItem);    {Disable filing commands for desk     }
                    DisableItem (FileMenu, SaveAsItem);  {   accessory or empty desk [II:4.6.2]}
                    DisableItem (FileMenu, RevertItem)

            end; {else}

        HUnlock (dataHandle)                        {Unlock data record [I:3.2.4]}

    end {with}

  end; {DoActivate}

{----------------------------------------------------------------------------------}

procedure WindowDirty ((isDirty : BOOLEAN)};

  { Mark window dirty or clean [Prog. II:5-7]. }

  var
      theData    : WDHandle;                        {Handle to window's data record}
      dataHandle : Handle;                          {Untyped handle for locking data record [I:3.1.1]}

  begin {WindowDirty}

      dataHandle := Handle(GetWRefCon(TheWindow));  {Get window data [II:3.2.4]}
      HLock (dataHandle);                           {Lock data record [I:3.2.4]}

        theData := WDHandle(dataHandle);            {Convert to typed handle}
        with theData^^ do
          begin

            dirty := isDirty;                       {Set flag in data record}

            if isDirty then                         {Is window becoming dirty or clean?}
              begin
                  EnableItem (FileMenu, SaveItem);  {Enable Save command [II:4.6.2]}
                  if fileNumber <> 0 then           {Is window associated with a file?}
                    EnableItem (FileMenu, RevertItem)  {Enable Revert command [II:4.6.2]}
              end {then}

            else
              begin
                  DisableItem (FileMenu, SaveItem);  {Disable menu items [II:4.6.2]}
                  DisableItem (FileMenu, RevertItem)
              end {else}
```

```
        end; {with}

    HUnlock (dataHandle)                    {Unlock data record [I:3.2.4]}

  end; {WindowDirty}

{-----------------------------------------------------------------------------}

procedure AdjustScrollBar;

  { Adjust scroll bar to length of document [Prog. II:6-5]. }

  const
    active   =   0;                        {Highlighting code for active scroll bar [II:6.3.3]}
    inactive = 255;                        {Highlighting code for inactive scroll bar [II:6.3.3]}

  var
    windowHeight : INTEGER;                {Height of text rectangle in lines}
    maxTop       : INTEGER;                {Maximum value for top line in window}

  begin {AdjustScrollBar}

    with TheText^^, viewRect do
      begin
        windowHeight := (bottom - top) div lineHeight; {Get window height [II:5.1.1]}
        maxTop       := nLines - windowHeight       {Avoid white space at bottom [II:5.1.1]}

      end; {with}

    if maxTop <= 0 then                     {Is text smaller than window?}
      begin
        maxTop := 0;                        {Show all of text}
        HiliteControl (TheScrollBar, inactive)  {Disable scroll bar [II:6.3.3]}
      end {then}
    else
      HiliteControl (TheScrollBar, active);     {Enable scroll bar [II:6.3.3]}

    SetCtlMax (TheScrollBar, maxTop)        {Adjust range of scroll bar [II:6.2.4]}

  end; {AdjustScrollBar}

{-----------------------------------------------------------------------------}

procedure ScrollToSelection;

  { Scroll current selection into view [Prog. II:6-13]. }
```

```
var
   topLine     : INTEGER;                        {First line visible in window}
   bottomLine  : INTEGER;                        {First line beyond bottom of window}
   windowHeight : INTEGER;                       {Height of text rectangle in lines}

begin {ScrollToSelection}

   HLock (Handle(TheText));                       {Lock edit record [I:3.2.4]}
      with TheText^^, viewRect do
         begin

            topLine      := GetCtlValue (TheScrollBar);   {Get current top line [II:6.2.4]}
            windowHeight := (bottom - top) div lineHeight; {Get window height [II:5.1.1]}
            bottomLine   := topLine + windowHeight;        {Find line beyond bottom}

            if GetCtlMax (TheScrollBar) = 0 then  {Not enough text to fill the window? [II:6.2.4]}
               AdjustText                          {Start of text to top of window}

            else if selEnd < lineStarts[topLine] then   {Whole selection above window top? [II:5.1.1]}
               ScrollCharacter (selStart, FALSE)        {Start of selection to top of window}

            else if selStart >= lineStarts[bottomLine] then {Whole selection below window bottom? [II:5.1.1]}
               ScrollCharacter (selEnd, TRUE)           {End of selection to bottom of window}

         end; {with}
      HUnlock (Handle(TheText))                    {Unlock edit record [I:3.2.4]}

   end; {ScrollToSelection}

{---------------------------------------------------------------------------}


procedure ScrollCharacter ((theCharacter : INTEGER; toBottom : BOOLEAN));

   { Scroll character into view [Prog. II:6-12]. }

   var
      theLine      : INTEGER;                     {Number of line containing character}
      windowHeight : INTEGER;                     {Height of text rectangle in lines}

   begin {ScrollCharacter}

      HLock (Handle(TheText));                     {Lock edit record [I:3.2.4]}
         with TheText^^ do
            begin

               theLine := 0;                       {Start search at first line}
               while lineStarts[theLine+1] <= theCharacter do
                  theLine := theLine + 1;           {Find line containing character [II:5.1.1]}
```

```
        if toBottom then                   {Scrolling to bottom of window?}
          begin
            with viewRect do
                windowHeight := (bottom - top) div lineHeight;   {Get window height}
              theLine := theLine - (windowHeight - 1)        {Offset for window height}
          end; {if}

          SetCtlValue (TheScrollBar, theLine);   {Adjust setting of scroll bar [II:6.2.4]}
          AdjustText                              {Scroll text to match new setting}

        end; {with}
      HUnlock (Handle(TheText))                  {Unlock edit record [I:3.2.4]}

   end;  {ScrollCharacter}


{--------------------------------------------------------------------}

procedure ReadDeskScrap;

   { Read desk scrap into Toolbox scrap [Prog. II:5-12].  }

   var
      scrapLength : LONGINT;                {Length of desk text scrap in bytes}
      ignore      : LONGINT;                {Dummy variable for scrap offset}
      result      : OSErr;                  {Result code from scrap transfer [I:3.1.2]}

   begin {ReadDeskScrap}
      if ScrapCompare <> InfoScrap^.scrapCount then  {Has scrap count changed? [I:7.4.2]}
        begin

          scrapLength := GetScrap (NIL, 'TEXT', ignore);  {Check desk scrap for a text item [I:7.4.3]}

          if scrapLength >= 0 then              {Is there a text item?}
            begin
              result := TEFromScrap;            {Transfer desk scrap to Toolbox scrap [II:5.5.5]}
              if result <> NoErr then           {Was there an error? [I:3.1.2]}
                scrapLength := result            {Make sure scrap length is negative}
            end; {if}

          if scrapLength > 0 then              {Was scrap nonempty?}
            EnableItem (EditMenu, PasteItem)   {Enable Paste command [II:4.6.2]}
          else
            begin
              TESetScrapLen (0);               {Mark Toolbox scrap as empty [II:5.5.4]}
              DisableItem (EditMenu, PasteItem) {Disable Paste command [II:4.6.2]}
            end; {else}
```

```
            ScrapCompare := InfoScrap^.scrapCount        {Save scrap count for later comparison [I:7.4.2]}

        end {if}

    end;  {ReadDeskScrap}

{-----------------------------------------------------------------------------}

procedure WriteDeskScrap;

    { Write Toolbox scrap to desk scrap [Prog. II:5-13].  }

    var
        result : OSErr;                          {Result code from scrap transfer [I:3.1.2]}

    begin {WriteDeskScrap}

        if ScrapDirty then                       {Has scrap changed since last read?}
            begin

                ScrapCompare := ZeroScrap;       {Change scrap count, save for comparison [I:7.4.3]}

                result := TEToScrap;             {Transfer Toolbox scrap to desk scrap [II:5.5.5]}

                ScrapDirty := FALSE              {Toolbox and desk scraps now agree}

            end {if}

    end;  {WriteDeskScrap}

{-----------------------------------------------------------------------------}

procedure IOCheck ((resultCode : OSErr));

    { Check for I/O error [Prog. II:8-1].  }

    var
        alertID    : INTEGER;                    {Resource ID of alert}
        errorString : Str255;                    {Error code in string form [I:2.1.1]}
        ignore     : INTEGER;                    {Item code returned by alert}

    begin {IOCheck}

        if resultCode = NoErr then               {Just return if no error}
            EXIT (IOCheck);
```

```
    case resultCode of

      OpWrErr:
        alertID := OpWrID;                      {Use Already Open alert}

      {Insert code here to handle any other specific errors}

      otherwise
        begin
          alertID := IOErrID;                   {Use general I/O Error alert}
          NumToString (resultCode, errorString); {Convert error code to a string [I:2.3.4]}
          ParamText   (errorString, '', '', '')  {Substitute into text of alert [II:7.4.6]}
        end

      end; {case}

    InitCursor;                                 {Restore normal cursor [II:2.5.2]}
    ignore := StopAlert (alertID, NIL);         {Post alert [II:7.4.2]}

    Quitting  := FALSE;                         {Cancel Quit command, if any}
    ErrorFlag := TRUE                           {Force exit to main event loop}

  end; {IOCheck}


{----------------------------------------------------------------------------------}


  { Main program [Prog. II:2-1]. }

  begin {MiniEdit}

    Initialize;                                 {Do one-time-only initialization}

    repeat
      MainLoop                                  {Execute one pass of main loop}
    until Finished;

    WriteDeskScrap                              {Copy Toolbox scrap to desk scrap}

  end. {MiniEdit}
```

Glossary

The following is a comprehensive glossary for Volumes One and Two. *Note:* Terms shown in *italic* are defined elsewhere in this glossary.

A5 *world:* Another name for a program's *application global space*, located by means of a *base address* kept in processor register **A5**.

"above A5" *size:* The number of bytes needed between the *base address* in register **A5** and the end of the *application global space*, to hold a program's *application parameters* and *jump table*.

access *path:* An independent channel of communication for reading or writing a *file*.

access *permission:* The form of communication allowed for a particular *file* or *access path*, such as read-only, write-only, or read/write.

accessory *window:* A *window* with rounded corners, used for displaying a *desk accessory* on the screen.

action *procedure:* A routine that is called repeatedly for as long as the mouse button is held down after it is pressed in a *control*.

activate *event:* A *window event* generated by the Toolbox to signal that a given window has become the *active window*.

active *control:* A *control* that will respond to the mouse in the normal way; compare *inactive control*.

active *menu:* A *menu* that is currently included in the *menu bar*, making its contents available to be *chosen* with the mouse.

active *window:* The frontmost *window* on the screen, to which the user's mouse and keyboard actions are directed.

alert: Short for *alert box*.

alert box: A form of *dialog box* that prevents the user from interacting with any other window for as long as the alert remains on the screen, and in which the only meaningful action is to *dismiss* the alert by clicking a *pushbutton*; compare *modal dialog box, modeless dialog box.*

alert icons: A set of standard *icons* kept in the *system resource file* and used in *alert boxes* to indicate the severity of the alert; see *note alert, caution alert, stop alert.*

allocate: To set aside a *block* of memory from the *heap* for a particular use.

allocation block: The unit in which space is allocated on a given storage device, always equal to a multiple of 512 bytes; normally 1024 bytes on the standard Sony disk drive.

and: A bit-level operation in which each bit of the result is a **1** if both operands have **1**s at the corresponding bit position, or **0** if either or both have **0**s.

Apple mark: A special *control character* (character code **$14**) that appears on the Macintosh screen as a small Apple symbol; used for the title of the menu of *desk accessories.*

Apple menu: A *menu* listing the available *desk accessories*, conventionally placed first in the *menu bar* with the *Apple mark* as its title.

application event: Any of the four *event types* that are reserved for the running application program to use in any way it wishes.

application file: A *file* containing the executable code of an application program, with a *file type* of **'APPL'** and the program's own signature as its *creator signature.*

application font: The standard *typeface* used by an application program; normally **Geneva**, but can be changed to some other typeface if desired.

application global space: The area of memory containing a program's *application globals, application parameters*, and *jump table*, normally situated just before the *screen buffer* in memory and located by means of a *base address* kept in processor register **A5**.

application globals: Global variables belonging to the running application program, which reside in the *application global space* and are located at negative offsets from the *base address* in register **A5**.

application heap: The portion of the *heap* that's available for use by the running application program.

application heap limit: The memory address marking the farthest point to which the *heap* can expand, to prevent it from colliding with the *stack.*

application parameters: Descriptive information about the running program, located in the *application global space* at positive offsets from the *base address* in register **A5**. The application parameters are a vestige of the Lisa software environment, and most are unused on the Macintosh; the only ones still in use are the *QuickDraw globals pointer* and the *startup handle*.

application resource file: The *resource fork* of a program's *application file*, containing *resources* belonging to the program itself.

application window: A *window* used by the running program itself; compare *system window*.

arc: A part of an *oval*, defined by a given *starting angle* and *arc angle*.

arc angle: The angle defining the extent of an *arc* or *wedge*.

arrow cursor: The standard, general-purpose *cursor*, an arrow pointing upward at an angle of "eleven o'clock."

ascent: (1) For a text character, the height of the character above the *baseline*, in pixels. (2) For a *font*, the maximum ascent of any character in the font.

ascent line: The line marking a font's maximum *ascent* above the *baseline*.

ASCII: American Standard Code for Information Interchange, the industry-standard 7-bit character set on which the Macintosh's 8-bit *character codes* are based.

@ operator: An operator provided by Apple's Pascal compiler, which accepts a variable or routine name as an operand and produces a *blind pointer* to that variable or routine in memory.

attribute byte: The byte in a *resource map* entry that holds the *resource attributes*.

autograph: A *Finder resource* whose *resource type* is the same as a program's *signature*, and which serves as the program's representative in the *desktop file*; also called a *version data* resource.

auto-key event: An *event* reporting that the user held down a key on the keyboard or keypad, causing it to repeat automatically.

automatic scrolling: The *scrolling* of a window's contents when the user *drags* the mouse outside the window while making a *selection*.

background pattern: The *pattern* used for *erasing* shapes in a given *graphics port*.

base address: In general, any memory address used as a reference point from which to locate desired data in memory. Specifically, (1) the address of the *bit image* belonging to a given *bit map*; (2) the address of a program's *application parameters*, kept in processor register **A5** and used to locate the contents of the program's *application global space*.

base of stack: The end of the *stack* that remains fixed in memory and is not affected when items are added and removed; compare *top of stack.*

base type: In Pascal, the data type to which a given pointer type is declared to point: for example, the pointer type ^**INTEGER** has the base type **INTEGER**.

baseline: The reference line used for defining the *character images* in a *font,* and along which the *graphics pen* travels as text is drawn.

"below A5" size: The number of bytes needed between the beginning of the *application global space* and the *base address* in register **A5**, to hold a program's *application globals.*

binary point: The binary equivalent of a decimal point, separating the integer and fractional parts of a *fixed-point number.*

Binary/Decimal Conversion Package: A standard *package,* provided in the *system resource file,* that converts numbers between their internal binary format and their external representation as strings of decimal digits.

bit image: An array of bits in memory representing the *pixels* of a graphical image.

bit map: The combination of a *bit image* with a *boundary rectangle.* The bit image provides the bit map's content; the boundary rectangle defines its extent and gives it a system of coordinates.

bit-mapped display: A video display screen on which each *pixel* can be individually controlled.

blind pointer: A Pascal pointer whose *base type* is unspecified, and which can consequently be assigned to a variable of any pointer type. The standard Pascal constant **NIL** is a blind pointer; two nonstandard features of Apple's Pascal compiler, the **POINTER** function and the @ *operator,* also produce blind pointers as their results.

block: An area of contiguous memory within the *heap,* either allocated or free.

block map: A table containing information needed by the *file system* about the usage of all *allocation blocks* on a given *volume.*

bottleneck procedure: A specialized procedure for performing a low-level drawing operation in a given *graphics port,* used for *customizing* Quick-Draw operations.

boundary rectangle: (1) For a *bit map,* the *rectangle* that defines the bit map's extent and determines its system of coordinates. (2) For a *graphics port,* the boundary rectangle of the port's bit map.

bounding box: The smallest *rectangle* completely enclosing a *polygon* or *region* on the coordinate grid.

bundle: A *Finder resource* that identifies all of a program's other Finder resources, so that they can be installed in the *desktop file* when the program is copied to a new disk.

bundle bit: A flag that tells whether a program has any *Finder resources* that must accompany it when it is copied to a new disk.

button: A *control* with two possible settings, on (**1**) and off (**0**); compare *dial*.

byte: An independently addressable group of 8 bits in memory.

caps lock key: A *modifier key* on the Macintosh keyboard, used to convert lowercase letters to uppercase while leaving all nonalphabetic keys unaffected.

caret: The graphical symbol used on the screen to represent an *insertion point* in text; normally a blinking vertical bar rather than an actual proofreader's caret mark.

caution alert: A form of *alert box*, intermediate in severity between a *note alert* and a *stop alert*, that reports a moderately serious error or anomaly or asks the user for additional instructions about how to proceed with an operation.

centered: A method of text *justification* in which each line of text is positioned midway between the left and right margins; compare *flush left, flush right, full justification*.

chain: To start up a new program after reinitializing the *stack* and *application global space*, but not the *application heap*; compare *launch*.

character code: An 8-bit integer representing a text character; compare *key code*.

character height: The overall height of a font's *font rectangle*, from *ascent line* to *descent line*.

character image: A *bit image* that defines the graphical representation of a text character in a given *typeface* and *type size*.

character key: A key on the keyboard or keypad that produces a character when pressed; compare *modifier key*.

character offset: The horizontal distance, in pixels, from the left edge of the *font rectangle* to that of the *character image* for a given character; equal to the difference between the character's leftward *kern* and the maximum leftward kern in the font.

character origin: The location within a *character image* marking the position of the *graphics pen* when the character is drawn.

character position: An integer marking a point between characters in a *file* or other collection of text, from **0** (the very beginning of the text, before the first character) to the length of the text (the very end, after the last character).

character style: See *type style.*

character width: The distance in pixels by which the *graphics pen* advances after drawing a character; compare *image width.*

check mark: A special *control character* (character code **$12**) that appears on the Macintosh screen as a small check symbol; used for *marking* items on a menu.

checkbox: A *button* that retains an independent on/off setting to control the way some future action will occur; compare *pushbutton, radio buttons.*

choose: To designate a *menu item* by pointing with the mouse.

click-loop routine: A routine, associated with an *edit record,* that is called repeatedly for as long as the mouse button is held down after being pressed in the record's *view rectangle.*

clip: To confine a drawing operation within a specified boundary, suppressing any drawing that falls outside the boundary.

Clipboard: The term used in Macintosh user's manuals to refer to the *scrap.*

clipping boundaries: The boundaries to which all drawing in a given *graphics port* is confined, consisting of the port's *boundary rectangle, port rectangle, clipping region,* and *visible region.*

clipping rectangle: See *view rectangle.*

clipping region: A general-purpose *clipping boundary* associated with a *graphics port,* provided for the application program's use.

clock chip: A component of the Macintosh, powered independently by a battery, that keeps track of the current date and time even when the machine's main power is turned off.

close: To destroy an *access path* to a *file.*

close box: The small box near the left end of the *title bar,* by which a *document window* can be closed with the mouse.

close region: The area of a *window* by which it can be closed with the mouse; also called the "go-away region." In a *document window,* the close region is the *close box.*

code segment: A *resource* containing all or part of a program's executable machine code.

command key: A *modifier key* on the Macintosh keyboard, used in combination with *character keys* to type *keyboard aliases* for *menu items.*

command mark: A special *control character* (character code **$11**) that appears on the Macintosh screen as a "cloverleaf" symbol; used for displaying *command-key* equivalents of items on a menu.

compaction: The process of moving together all of the *relocatable blocks* in the *heap,* in order to coalesce the available free space.

complement: A bit-level operation that reverses the bits of a given operand, changing each **0** to a **1** and vice versa.

content: The information displayed in a *window.*

content region: The area of a *window* in which information is displayed, and which a program must draw for itself; compare *window frame.*

control: An object on the Macintosh screen that the user can manipulate with the *mouse* to operate on the contents of a *window* or to control the way they're presented.

control character: An ASCII text character with a character code from **$00** to **$1F** (as well as the character **$7F**). Most control characters have no special meaning and no visual representation on the Macintosh, but a few are defined as special-purpose symbols for use on the screen: see *apple mark, check mark, command mark, diamond mark.*

control definition function: A routine, stored as a *resource,* that defines the appearance and behavior of a particular type of *control.*

control definition ID: A coded integer representing a *control type,* which includes the *resource ID* of the *control definition function* along with additional modifying information.

control handle: A handle to a *control record.*

control list: A linked list of all the *controls* belonging to a given *window,* beginning in a field of the *window record* and chained together through a field of their *control records.*

control record: A data structure containing all the information associated with a given *control.*

control template: A *resource* containing all the information needed to create a *control.*

control type: A category of *control,* identified by a *control definition ID,* whose appearance and behavior are determined by a *control definition function.*

covered: Describes a window, control, or other object that is obscured from view by other overlapping objects. A covered object is never displayed on the screen, even if *visible;* compare *exposed.*

creator signature: A four-character string identifying the application program to which a given *file* belongs, and which should be started up when the user opens the file in the *Finder.*

cross cursor: A standard *cursor* included in the *system resource file* for use in graphics selection.

current port: The *graphics port* in use at any given time, to which most *QuickDraw* operations implicitly apply.

current resource file: The *resource file* that will be searched first in looking for a requested resource, and to which certain *resource*-related operations implicitly apply.

current text box: The *text box* in a *dialog box* that displays a *selection* or *insertion point*, and to which characters typed on the keyboard are considered to be directed.

current volume: The *volume* under consideration at any given time, to which many *file system* operations implicitly apply.

cursor: A small (16-by-16-bit) *bit image* whose movements can be controlled with the *mouse* to designate positions on the Macintosh screen.

cursor level: An integer that controls whether the *cursor* is visible on the screen.

cursor record: A data structure defining the form and appearance of a *cursor* on the screen.

customize: To redefine an aspect of the Toolbox's operation to meet the specialized needs of a particular program.

cut and paste: The standard method of editing used on the Macintosh, in which text, graphics, or other information is transferred from one place to another by way of an intermediate *scrap* or *Clipboard*.

dangling pointer: An invalid pointer to an object that no longer exists at the designated address.

data fork: The *fork* of a *file* that contains the file's data, such as the text of a document; compare *resource fork*.

date and time record: A data structure representing a calendar date and clock time, with fields for the year, month, day of the month, day of the week, hour, minute, and second; used for reading or setting the Macintosh's built-in *clock chip*.

deactivate event: A *window event* generated by the Toolbox to signal that a given window is no longer the *active window*.

dead character: (1) A text character with a zero *character width*, which doesn't advance the *graphics pen* when drawn. (2) A character (such as a foreign-language accent) that combines with the character following it to produce a single result character (such as an accented letter).

default button: The *pushbutton* displayed with a heavy black double border in an *alert* or *dialog box*; pressing the return or enter key is considered equivalent to clicking the default button with the mouse.

defining string: A string of characters specifying the title and attributes of one or more *menu items*.

definition file: An assembly-language file containing definitions of Toolbox constants and global variables, to be incorporated into an assembly-language program with an **.INCLUDE** directive.

demote: To send a *window* behind another window on the screen.

dereference: (1) In general, to convert any pointer to the value it points to. (2) Specifically, to convert a *handle* to the corresponding *master pointer*.

descent: (1) For a text character, the distance the character extends below the *baseline*, in pixels. (2) For a *font*, the maximum descent of any character in the font.

descent line: The line marking a font's maximum *descent* below the *baseline*.

desk accessory: A type of *device driver* that operates as a "mini-application" and can coexist on the screen with any other program.

desk scrap: The *scrap* maintained by the Toolbox to hold information being *cut and pasted* from one application program or *desk accessory* to another.

desktop: (1) The gray background area of the Macintosh screen, outside of any window. (2) The arrangement of windows, icons, and other objects on the screen, particularly in the **Finder**.

desktop file: A file containing *Finder*-related information about the files on a disk, including their *file types*, *creator signatures*, and locations on the Finder *desktop*.

destination rectangle: The boundary to which text is *wrapped* in an *edit record*, determining the placement of the *line breaks*; also called the "wrapping rectangle."

destination text: The text to be operated on by a search or replacement operation; compare *target text*, *replacement text*.

detach: To decouple a *resource* from its *resource file*, so that the resource will remain in memory when the file is closed.

device code: An integer identifying the output device a *graphics port* draws on, used in selecting the appropriate *fonts* for drawing text.

device driver: The low-level software through which the Toolbox communicates with an input/output device; an important special category of device drivers are *desk accessories*.

dial: A *control* that can take on any of a range of possible settings, depending on the position of a moving *indicator* that can be manipulated with the mouse; compare *button*.

dialog: Short for *dialog box*.

dialog box: A *window* used for requesting information or instructions from the user.

dialog hook: A pointer to a routine supplied to the *Standard File Package* by an application program, to replace the standard dialog box with a nonstandard one or to handle the standard one in a nonstandard way.

dialog item: A single element displayed in an *alert* or *dialog box*, such as a piece of text, an *icon*, a *control*, or a *text box*.

dialog pointer: A pointer to a *dialog record*.

dialog record: A data structure containing all the information associated with a given *alert* or *dialog box*.

dialog window: See *dialog box*.

diamond mark: A special *control character* (character code **$11**) that appears on the Macintosh screen as a small diamond symbol. This symbol is a vestige of earlier versions of the Macintosh user interface and no longer has any specific use.

dimmed: Describes an object, such as a *menu item* or a *file icon*, that is displayed in gray instead of black to show that it is not currently active or available.

dirty: Describes a *document* or *window* whose contents have been changed since they were last read from or written to the disk.

disabled dialog item: A *dialog item* that doesn't *dismiss* its *alert* or *dialog box* when clicked with the mouse or typed into from the keyboard.

disabled menu item: A *menu item* that cannot currently be *chosen* with the mouse; normally displayed in *dimmed* form on the screen.

disk driver: The *device driver* built into ROM for communicating with the Macintosh's built-in Sony disk drive.

Disk Initialization Package: A standard *package*, provided in the *system resource file*, that takes corrective action when an unreadable disk is inserted into the disk drive, usually by initializing the disk.

disk-inserted event: An *event* reporting that the user inserted a disk into a disk drive.

dismiss: To remove an *alert* or *dialog box* from the screen, typically by clicking a *pushbutton*.

dispatch table: A table in memory, used by the *Trap Dispatcher* to locate Toolbox routines in ROM.

display rectangle: The rectangle that defines the location and extent of a *dialog item* within an *alert* or *dialog box*.

document: A coherent unit or collection of information to be operated on by a particular application program.

document file: A *file* containing a *document*.

document window: The standard type of *window* used by application programs to display information on the screen.

double click: Two presses of the *mouse* button in quick succession, considered as a single action by the user.

down arrow: The arrow at the bottom or right end of a *scroll bar*, which causes it to scroll down or to the right a line at a time when clicked with the mouse.

drag: (1) To roll the mouse while holding down the button. (2) To move a window, icon, or other object to a new location on the screen by dragging with the mouse.

drag region: The area of a *window* by which it can be *dragged* to a new location with the mouse. In a *document window*, the drag region consists of the *title bar* minus the *close box*.

drive number: An integer designating a disk drive: **1** for the *internal disk drive*, **2** for the *external disk drive* (if any), **3** or greater for any other external storage device, such as a hard disk connected through one of the *serial ports*.

driver reference number: An integer between **−1** and **−32**, used to refer to a particular *device driver*; derived from the driver's *unit number* by the formula **refNum = −(unitNum + 1)**.

edit record: A complete text editing environment containing all the information needed for *TextEdit* operations.

eject: To remove a disk *volume* physically from a disk drive, placing the volume *off-line*.

empty handle: A *handle* that points to a **NIL** *master pointer*, indicating that the underlying *block* has been *purged* from the heap.

empty rectangle: A *rectangle* that encloses no pixels on the coordinate grid.

empty region: A *region* that encloses no pixels on the coordinate grid.

emulator trap: A form of *trap* that occurs when the *MC68000* processor attempts to execute an *unimplemented instruction*; used to "emulate" the effects of such an instruction with software instead of hardware.

enabled dialog item: A *dialog item* that *dismisses* its *alert* or *dialog box* when clicked with the mouse or typed into from the keyboard.

enabled menu item: A *menu item* that is currently available and can be *chosen* with the mouse.

enclosing rectangle: (1) The *rectangle* within which an *oval* is inscribed. (2) The rectangle that defines the location and extent of a *control* within its *owning window*.

end-of-file: The *character position* following the last byte of meaningful information included in a *file* (the *logical end-of-file*) or the last byte of physical storage space allocated to it (the *physical end-of-file*).

EOF: See *end-of-file*.

erase: To fill a *shape* with the *background pattern* of the *current port*.

error code: A nonzero *result code*, reporting an error of some kind detected by an *Operating System* routine.

error sound: A sound emitted from the Macintosh speaker by an *alert*.

event: An occurrence reported by the Toolbox for a program to respond to, such as the user's pressing the mouse button or typing on the keyboard.

event-driven: Describes a program that is structured to respond to *events* reported by the Toolbox.

event mask: A coded integer specifying the *event types* to which a given operation applies.

event message: A field of the *event record* containing information that varies depending on the *event type*.

event queue: The data structure in which *events* are recorded for later processing.

event record: A data structure containing all the information about a given *event*.

event type: An integer code that identifies the kind of occurrence reported by an *event*.

exception: See *trap*.

exclusive or: A bit-level operation in which each bit of the result is a **1** if the corresponding bits of the two operands are different, or **0** if they're the same.

exposed: Describes a window, control, or other object that is not obscured from view by other overlapping objects. An exposed object is displayed on the screen if *visible*; compare *covered*.

external disk drive: A disk drive separate from the Macintosh itself and connected to it via the disk drive connector on the back of the machine.

external reference: A reference from one *code segment* to a routine contained in another segment.

Fat Mac: A model of *Macintosh* with a memory capacity of 512 kilobytes.

field: One of the components of a Pascal record.

FIFO: First in, first out; the order in which items are added to and removed from a queue such as the *event queue*.

file: A collection of information stored as a named unit on a disk.

file directory: A table containing information needed by the *file system* about all of the *files* on a given *volume*.

file icon: The *icon* used by the *Finder* to represent a *file* on the screen.

file mark: The *character position* at which the next byte will be read from or written to a *file*.

file name: A string of text characters identifying a particular *file*.

file reference: A *Finder resource* that establishes the connection between a *file type* and its *file icon*.

file reference number: An identifying number assigned by the *file system* to stand for a given *file*.

file system: The part of the Toolbox that deals with *files* on a disk or other mass storage device.

file type: A four-character string that characterizes the kind of information a *file* contains, assigned by the program that created the file.

fill: To color a *shape* with a specified *pattern*.

fill pattern: A *pattern* associated with a *graphics port*, used privately by *QuickDraw* for *filling* shapes.

filter function: (1) A function supplied by an application program to process *events* in an *alert* or *dialog box* before they're acted upon by the Toolbox. (2) A function supplied to the *Standard File Package* by an application program, to selectively omit files from the list offered to the user.

Finder: The Macintosh program with which the user can manipulate files and start up applications; normally the first program to be run when the Macintosh is turned on.

Finder information record: A data structure summarizing the *Finder*-related properties of a *file*, including its *file type*, *creator signature*, and location on the Finder *desktop*.

Finder resources: The *resources* associated with a program that tell the *Finder* how to represent the program's *files* on the screen and which files to transfer when moving the program to another disk. Finder resources include *autographs*, *icon lists*, *file references*, and *bundles*.

Finder startup handle: See *startup handle*.

fixed-point number: A binary number with a fixed number of bits before and after the *binary point*; specifically, a value of the Toolbox data type **Fixed**, consisting of a 16-bit integer part and a 16-bit fraction.

Floating-Point Arithmetic Package: A standard *package*, provided in the *system resource file*, that performs arithmetic on *floating-point numbers* in accordance with the *IEEE standard*, using the Standard Apple Numeric Environment (*SANE*).

floating-point number: A binary number in which the *binary point* can "float" to any required position; the number's internal representation includes a binary exponent, or order of magnitude, that determines the position of the binary point.

flush: To write out information associated with a *volume* or *file* (such as a volume's *file directory* or the contents of its *volume buffer*) from memory to an external storage medium such as a disk.

flush left: A method of text *justification* in which the left margin is straight and the right margin is "ragged"; compare *flush right, centered, full justification.*

flush right: A method of text *justification* in which the right margin is straight and the left margin is "ragged"; compare *flush left, centered, full justification.*

folder: An object in a disk's *desktop file,* represented by an icon or a window on the screen, that can contain files or other folders; used for organizing the files on the disk.

folder number: The integer used by the *Finder* to identify a particular *folder.*

font: (1) A *resource* containing all of the *character images* and other information needed to draw text characters in a given *typeface* and *type size.* (2) Sometimes used loosely (and incorrectly) as a synonym for *typeface,* as in the terms *font number* and *text font.*

font image: A *bit image* consisting of all the individual *character images* in a given *font,* arranged consecutively in a single horizontal row; also called a *strike* of the font.

font number: An integer denoting a particular *typeface.*

font record: A data structure containing all the information associated with a given *font.*

font rectangle: The smallest rectangle, relative to the *baseline* and *character origin,* that would completely enclose all of the *character images* in a *font* if they were superimposed with their origins coinciding.

font width table: A *resource* containing all of the information on the *character widths* in a given *font,* but without the *character images* themselves; used for measuring the width of text without actually drawing it.

fork: One of the two parts of which every *file* is composed: the *data fork* or the *resource fork.*

frame: (1) To draw the outline of a *shape,* using the *pen size, pen pattern,* and *pen mode* of the *current port.* (2) See *window frame.*

free block: A contiguous *block* of space available for allocation within the *heap.*

full justification: A method of text *justification* (not supported by *TextEdit*) in which both the left and right margins are straight, with the spaces between words adjusted accordingly; compare *flush left, centered, flush right.*

global coordinate system: The coordinate system associated with a given *bit image,* in which the top-left corner of the image has coordinates (**0, 0**); the global coordinate system is independent of the *boundary rectangle* of any *bit map* or *graphics port* based on the image.

glue routine: See *interface routine.*

go-away region: See *close region.*

graphics pen: The imaginary drawing tool used for drawing lines in a *graphics port.*

graphics port: A complete drawing environment containing all the information needed for *QuickDraw* drawing operations.

grow icon: The visual representation of a window's *size region* on the screen; for a standard *document window,* a pair of small overlapping squares in the bottom-right corner of the window.

grow region: See *size region.*

handle: A pointer to a *master pointer,* used to refer to a *relocatable block.*

heap: The area of memory in which space is allocated and deallocated at the explicit request of a running program; compare *stack.*

heap zone: An independently maintained area of the *heap,* such as the *application heap* or the *system heap.*

hide: To make a window, control, or other object *invisible.*

high-level file system: A collection of *file system* routines that sacrifice detailed control over input/output operations in exchange for simplicity and ease of use; compare *low-level file system.*

highlight: To display a window, control, menu item, or other object in some distinctive way as a visual signal to the user, often (but not necessarily) by *inverting* white and black pixels.

hot spot: The point in a *cursor* that coincides with the mouse position on the screen.

I-beam cursor: A standard *cursor* included in the *system resource file* for use in text selection.

I/O driver event: A type of *event* used internally by the Toolbox to handle communication with peripheral devices.

icon: A *bit image* of a standard size (32 pixels by 32), used on the Macintosh screen to represent an object such as a disk or file.

icon list: A *resource* containing any number of *icons;* commonly used to hold a *file icon* and its mask for use by the Finder.

icon number: An integer used to identify an *icon* to be displayed on a *menu,* equal to the icon's *resource ID* plus **256**.

identifying information: The properties of a *resource* that uniquely identify it: its *resource type, resource ID,* and (optional) *resource name.*

IEEE standard: A set of standards and conventions for *floating-point* arithmetic, published by the Institute of Electrical and Electronic Engineers.

image width: The horizontal extent of a *character image*; the width in pixels of a character's graphical representation. Compare *character width*.

inactive control: A *control* that will not currently respond to the mouse, usually displayed in some distinctive way on the screen.

inactive menu: A *menu* that is not currently included in the *menu bar*, making its contents unavailable to be *chosen* with the mouse.

indicator: The moving part of a *dial* that can be manipulated with the mouse to control the dial's setting.

initial delay: The time interval before a key begins to repeat when held down; measured in *ticks* from the initial *key-down event* until the first *auto-key event*.

insertion point: An empty *selection* in a text document, denoted by a *selection range* that begins and ends at the same *character position*.

Inside Macintosh: The comprehensive manual on the Macintosh *Toolbox*, to be published by Apple Computer, Inc.

interactive item: A *dialog item*, such as a *control* or *text box*, that accepts information from the user via the mouse and keyboard; compare *static item*.

intercepted event: An *event* that is handled automatically by the Toolbox before being reported to the running program.

interface: A set of rules and conventions by which one part of an organized system communicates with another.

interface file: A text file that contains the declarations belonging to an *interface unit* in source-language form, to be incorporated into a Pascal program with a **uses** *declaration*.

interface routine: A routine, part of an *interface unit*, that mediates between the *stack-based* parameter-passing conventions of a Pascal calling program and those of a *register-based* Toolbox routine; also called a "glue routine."

interface unit: A precompiled *unit* containing declarations for Toolbox routines and data structures, making them available for use in Pascal programs.

internal disk drive: The 3-1/2-inch Sony disk drive built into the Macintosh.

International Utilities Package: A standard *package*, provided in the *system resource file*, that helps programs conform to the prevailing conventions of different countries in such matters as formatting of numbers, dates, times, and currency; use of metric units; and alphabetization of foreign-language accents, diacriticals, and ligatures.

interrupt: A signal to the *MC68000* processor from a peripheral device or other outside source, causing it to suspend normal program execution temporarily and execute an *interrupt handler* routine in response.

interrupt handler: The routine executed by the *MC68000* processor to respond to a particular type of *interrupt.*

invalid region: An area of a window's *content region* whose contents are not accurately displayed on the screen, and which must therefore be *updated.*

invert: (1) Generally, to reverse the colors of *pixels* in a graphical image, changing white to black and vice versa. (2) Specifically, to reverse the colors of all pixels inside the boundary of a given *shape.*

invisible: Describes a window, control, or other object that is logically hidden from view. An invisible object is never displayed on the screen, even if *exposed*; compare *visible.*

invisible bit: A flag that marks a file as invisible, so that the *Finder* will not display it on the screen.

item handle: A handle to a *dialog item*, kept in its dialog's *item list.*

item list: A data structure defining all of the *dialog items* associated with an *alert* or *dialog box*, located via a handle in the *dialog record.*

item number: The sequential position of a *menu item* within its menu or of a *dialog item* within its dialog's *item list*; used as an identifying number to refer to the item.

item type: An integer code denoting a kind of *dialog item.*

jump table: A table used to direct *external references* from one *code segment* to another to the proper addresses in memory; located in the *application global space*, at positive offsets from the *base address* kept in register **A5.**

justification: The way in which text in an *edit record* is aligned to the left and right edges of the *destination rectangle*; see *flush left, centered, flush right.*

K: See *kilobyte.*

kern: The amount by which a *character image* extends leftward beyond the *character origin* or rightward beyond the *character width.*

key code: An 8-bit integer representing a key on the Macintosh keyboard or keypad; compare *character code.*

key-down event: An *event* reporting that the user pressed a key on the keyboard or keypad.

key map: An array of bits in memory representing the state of the keys on the keyboard and keypad.

key-up event: An *event* reporting that the user released a key on the keyboard or keypad.

keyboard alias: A character that can be typed in combination with the *command key* to stand for a particular *menu item*.

keyboard configuration: The correspondence between keys on the Macintosh keyboard or keypad and the characters they produce when pressed.

keyboard event: An *event* that reports an action by the user with the keyboard or keypad; see *key-down event, key-up event, auto-key event*.

kilobyte: A unit of memory capacity equal to 2^{10} (1,024) bytes.

launch: To start up a new program after reinitializing the *stack, application global space*, and *application heap*; compare *chain*.

leading: The amount of extra vertical space between lines of text, measured in pixels from the *descent line* of one to the *ascent line* of the next. Although every *font* specifies a recommended leading value, the recommendation need not be followed when drawing text in a *graphics port*.

length byte: The first byte of a *Pascal-format string*, which gives the number of characters in the string, from **0** to **255**.

LIFO: Last in, first out; the order in which items are added to and removed from the *stack*.

ligature: A text character that combines two or more separate characters into a single symbol, such as **æ**.

limit pointer: A pointer that marks the end of an area of memory by pointing to the address following the last byte.

limit rectangle: A rectangle that limits the movement of a window or control when *dragged* with the mouse.

line breaks: The *character positions* marking the beginning of each new line when text is *wrapped* to a boundary.

line drawing: Drawing in a *graphics port* by moving the *graphics pen*, using the QuickDraw routines **Move, MoveTo, Line**, and **LineTo**.

Lisa: A personal computer manufactured and marketed by Apple Computer, Inc.; the first reasonably priced personal computer to feature a high-resolution *bit-mapped display* and a hand-held *mouse* pointing device. Now called *Macintosh XL*.

load: To read an object, such as a *resource* or the *desk scrap*, into memory from a disk file.

local coordinate system: The coordinate system associated with a given *graphics port*, determined by the *boundary rectangle* of the port's *bit map*.

local ID: The identifying number by which a *Finder resource* is referred to by other resources in the same *bundle*; not necessarily the same as its true *resource ID*.

localize: To tailor a program's behavior for use in a particular country.

location table: A table giving the horizontal position of each *character image* in a *font*, measured in pixels from the beginning of the *font image*.

lock: To temporarily prevent a *relocatable block* from being *purged* or moved within the heap during *compaction*.

logical end-of-file: The *character position* following the last byte of meaningful information included in a *file*.

logical shift: A bit-level operation that shifts the bits of a given operand left or right by a specified number of positions, with bits shifted out at one end being lost and **0**s shifted in at the other end.

long integer: A data type provided by Apple's Pascal compiler, consisting of double-length integers: 32 bits including sign, covering the range **±2147483647**.

long word: A group of 32 bits (2 *words*, or 4 *bytes*) beginning at a *word boundary* in memory.

low-level file system: A collection of *file system* routines that provide the greatest possible control over input/output operations, but are consequently complex and difficult to use; compare *high-level file system*.

Macintosh: A personal computer manufactured and marketed by Apple Computer, Inc., featuring a high-resolution *bit-mapped display* and a hand-held *mouse* pointing device.

Macintosh Operating System: The body of machine code built into the Macintosh *ROM* to handle low-level tasks such as memory management, disk input/output, and serial communications.

Macintosh Software Supplement: A set of software tools for developing Macintosh software on a *Lisa* computer.

Macintosh XL: The largest model of *Macintosh*, with a memory capacity of 512 kilobytes or 1 megabyte and a larger display screen than the standard Macintosh; formerly called *Lisa*.

main entry point: The point in a program's code where execution begins when the program is first started up.

main event loop: The central control structure of an *event-driven* program, which requests *events* one at a time from the Toolbox and responds to them as appropriate.

main segment: The *code segment* containing a program's *main entry point*.

mark: To affix a *mark character* to a *menu item*, indicating that the item is in the "on" or active state.

mark character: The character (usually a *check mark*) used to *mark* a *menu item*.

master pointer: A pointer to a *relocatable block*, kept at a known, fixed location in the *heap* and updated automatically by the Toolbox whenever the underlying block is moved during *compaction*. A pointer to the master pointer is called a *handle* to the block.

MC68000: The 32-bit microprocessor used in the Macintosh, manufactured by Motorola, Inc.; usually called "68000" for short.

megabyte: A unit of memory capacity equal to 2^{20} (1,048,576) bytes.

menu: A list of choices or options from which the user can choose with the mouse.

menu bar: The horizontal strip across the top of the screen from which *menus* can be "pulled down" with the mouse.

menu definition procedure: A routine, stored as a *resource*, that defines the appearance and behavior of a particular type of *menu*.

menu handle: A *handle* to a *menu record*.

menu ID: An identifying integer designating a particular *menu*; commonly the *resource ID* under which the menu is stored in a resource file.

menu item: One of the choices or options listed on a *menu*.

menu list: A data structure maintained by the Toolbox, containing handles to all currently *active menus*.

menu record: A data structure containing all the information associated with a given *menu*.

menu type: A category of *menu* whose appearance and behavior are determined by a *menu definition procedure*.

MiniEdit: The extensive example program developed in this book.

MiniFinder: See *Standard File Package*.

missing character: A character for which no *character image* is defined in a given *font*; represented graphically by the font's *missing symbol*.

missing symbol: The graphical representation used for drawing *missing characters* in a given *font*.

modal dialog box: A form of *dialog box* that prevents the user from interacting with any other window for as long as the dialog remains on the screen, but which allows actions beyond merely *dismissing* the dialog by clicking a *pushbutton*; compare *alert box*, *modeless dialog box*.

mode: A state of the system that determines its response to the user's actions with the mouse and keyboard.

modeless dialog box: A form of *dialog box* that allows the user to interact with other windows while the dialog remains on the screen; compare *alert box*, *modal dialog box*.

modifier character: A character included in the *defining string* for a *menu item* to define an attribute or property of the item.

modifier key: A key on the Macintosh keyboard that doesn't generate a character of its own, but may affect the meaning of any *character key* pressed at the same time; see *shift key, caps lock key, option key, command key.*

mount: To make a *volume* known to the file system by reading its *file directory* and *block map* into memory.

mouse: A hand-held pointing device for controlling the movements of the *cursor* to designate positions on the Macintosh screen.

mouse-down event: An *event* reporting that the user pressed the mouse button.

mouse event: An *event* that reports an action by the user with the mouse; see *mouse-down event, mouse-up event.*

mouse-up event: An *event* reporting that the user released the mouse button.

network event: A type of *event* used internally by the Toolbox to handle communication with other computers over a network.

nonrelocatable block: A *block* that can't be moved within the heap during *compaction,* referred to by single indirection with a simple pointer; compare *relocatable block.*

note alert: A form of *alert box,* less severe than either a *caution alert* or *stop alert,* that calls some possibly useful information to the user's attention.

null event: An *event* generated by the Toolbox when you request an event and there are no others to report.

object module: The file containing the compiled code of a Pascal *unit,* to be linked with that of an application program after compilation.

obscure: To remove the *cursor* temporarily from the screen until the next time the *mouse* is moved.

off-line: Describes a *volume* (such as a disk that has been *ejected* from a disk drive) for which only a minimal amount of the descriptive information needed by the *file system* is immediately available in memory; compare *on-line.*

offset/width table: A table giving the *character offset* and *character width* for each character in a given *font.*

on-line: Describes a *volume* (such as a disk currently in a disk drive) for which all of the descriptive information needed by the *file system* is immediately available in memory; compare *off-line.*

open: To create an *access path* to a *file.*

Operating System: See *Macintosh Operating System.*

option key: A *modifier key* on the Macintosh keyboard, used to type special characters such as foreign letters and accents.

or: A bit-level operation in which each bit of the result is a **1** if either or both operands have **1**s at the corresponding bit position, or **0** if both have **0**s.

ORD: A standard Pascal function for converting any scalar value to a corresponding integer (for instance, a character to its equivalent integer character code); on the Macintosh, **ORD** will also accept a pointer and return the equivalent long-integer address.

origin: (1) The top-left corner of a *rectangle.* (2) For a *bit map* or *graphics port*, the top-left corner of the *boundary rectangle*, whose coordinates determine the *local coordinate system.*

oval: A graphical figure, circular or elliptical in shape; defined by an *enclosing rectangle.*

owning window: The *window* with which a given *control* is associated.

package: A *resource*, usually residing in the *system resource file*, containing a collection of general-purpose routines that can be loaded into memory when needed; used to supplement the Toolbox with additional facilities that either require too much code or are not used frequently enough to justify taking up space in *ROM.*

package number: The *resource ID* of a *package*; must be between **0** and **7.**

package trap: One of the eight Toolbox *traps*, named **_Pack0** to **_Pack7**, used at the machine-language level to call a routine belong to a *package.*

page-down region: The area of a scroll bar's *shaft* below or to the right of the *scroll box*, which causes it to scroll down or to the right a windowful ("page") at a time when clicked with the mouse.

page-up region: The area of a scroll bar's *shaft* above or to the left of the *scroll box*, which causes it to scroll up or to the left a windowful ("page") at a time when clicked with the mouse.

paint: To fill a *shape* with the *pen pattern* of the *current port.*

parameter block: A complex data structure describing an operation to be performed by the *low-level file system.*

part code: An integer denoting the part of the screen, or of a window or control, in which the mouse was pressed.

Pascal-format string: A sequence of text characters represented in the internal format used by Apple's Pascal compiler, consisting of a *length byte* followed by from 0 to 255 bytes of *character codes.*

path reference number: An identifying number assigned by the *file system* to stand for a given *access path* to a *file.*

pattern: A small *bit image* (8 pixels by 8) that can be repeated indefinitely to fill an area, like identical floor tiles laid end to end.

pattern list: A *resource* consisting of any number of patterns.

pattern transfer modes: A set of *transfer modes* used for drawing lines or shapes or filling areas with a *pattern*.

pen: See *graphics pen.*

pen level: An integer associated with a *graphics port* that determines the visibility of the port's *graphics pen*. The pen is visible if the pen level is zero or positive, hidden if it's negative.

pen location: The coordinates of the *graphics pen* in a given *graphics port*.

pen mode: The *transfer mode* with which a *graphics port* draws lines and frames or paints shapes; should be one of the *pattern transfer modes*.

pen pattern: The *pattern* in which a *graphics port* draws lines and frames or paints shapes.

pen size: The width and height of the *graphics pen* belonging to a *graphics port*.

pen state: The characteristics of the *graphics pen* belonging to a *graphics port*, including its *pen location, pen size, pen mode,* and *pen pattern*.

physical end-of-file: The *character position* following the last byte of physical storage space allocated to a *file*.

picture: A recorded sequence of *QuickDraw* operations that can be repeated on demand to reproduce a graphical image.

picture frame: The reference *rectangle* within which a *picture* is defined, and which can be mapped to coincide with any other specified rectangle when the picture is drawn.

pixel: A single dot forming part of a graphical image; short for "picture element."

plane: A *window*'s front-to-back position relative to other windows on the screen.

plus-sign cursor: A standard *cursor* included in the *system resource file* for use in "structured selection."

point: (1) A position on the *QuickDraw* coordinate grid, specified by a pair of horizontal and vertical coordinates. (2) A unit used by printers to measure type sizes, equal to approximately 1/72 of an inch.

point size: See *type size.*

POINTER: A function provided by Apple's Pascal compiler, which accepts a *long integer* representing a memory address and returns a *blind pointer* to that address.

polygon: A graphical figure defined by any closed series of connected straight lines.

pop: To remove a data item from the top of a *stack.*

port: (1) A connector on the back of the Macintosh for serial communication with a peripheral device, such as a printer or modem. (2) Short for *graphics port.*

port rectangle: The rectangle that defines the portion of a *bit map* that a *graphics port* can draw into.

post: To record an *event* in the *event queue* for later processing.

printer driver: The *device driver* that communicates with a printer through one of the Macintosh's built-in serial ports.

pseudo-random numbers: Numbers that seem to be random but can be reproduced in exactly the same sequence if desired.

pull down: To display a *menu* on the screen by pressing the *mouse* inside its title in the *menu bar.*

purge: To remove a *relocatable block* from the heap to make room for other blocks. The purged block's *master pointer* remains allocated, but is set to **NIL** to show that the block no longer exists in the heap; all existing *handles* to the block become *empty handles.*

purgeable block: A *relocatable block* that can be *purged* from the heap to make room for other blocks.

push: To add a data item to the top of a *stack.*

pushbutton: A *button* that causes some immediate action to occur, either instantaneously when clicked with the mouse or continuously for as long as the mouse button is held down; compare *checkbox, radio buttons.*

pushdown stack: See *stack.*

QuickDraw: The extensive collection of graphics routines built into the Macintosh *ROM.*

QuickDraw globals pointer: A pointer to the global variables used by *QuickDraw,* kept at address **0(A5)** in the *application global space* and initialized with the **InitGraf** routine.

radio buttons: A group of two or more related *buttons,* exactly one of which can be on at any given time; turning on any button in the group turns off all the others. Compare *pushbutton, checkbox.*

RAM: See *random-access memory.*

RAM disk: An area of *read/write memory* that is treated as if it were an external disk.

random-access memory: A common but misleading term for *read/write memory.*

read-only memory: Memory that can be read but not written; usually called *ROM.* The Macintosh has 64K of ROM containing the built-in machine code of the *Macintosh Operating System, QuickDraw,* and the *User Interface Toolbox.*

read/write memory: Memory that can be both read and written; commonly known by the misleading term *random-access memory,* or *RAM.* The standard Macintosh has 128K of read/write memory, the *Fat Mac* has 512K, and the *Macintosh XL* has 512K or 1 megabyte.

reallocate: To allocate fresh space for a *relocatable block* that has been *purged,* updating the block's *master pointer* to point to its new location. Only the space is reallocated; the block's former contents are not restored.

recalibrate: To recalculate the *line breaks* in an *edit record* after any change in its text, *text characteristics,* or *destination rectangle.*

rectangle: A four-sided graphical figure defined by two *points* specifying its top-left and bottom-right corners, or by four integers specifying its top, left, bottom, and right edges.

reference constant: A 4-byte field included in every *window record* or *control record* for the application program to use in any way it wishes.

region: A graphical figure that can be of any arbitrary shape. It can have curved as well as straight edges, and can even have holes in it or consist of two or more separate pieces.

register-based: Describes a Toolbox routine that accepts its parameters and returns its results directly in the processor's registers; compare *stack-based.*

release: To deallocate a *block* of memory that's no longer needed, allowing the space to be reused for another purpose.

relocatable block: A *block* that can be moved within the heap during *compaction,* referred to by double indirection with a *handle;* compare *nonrelocatable block.*

repeat interval: The time interval between successive repeats when a key is held down; measured in *ticks* from one *auto-key event* to the next.

replacement text: The text to be substituted for the *target text* in a replacement operation; compare *destination text, target text.*

reply record: A data structure used by the *Standard File Package* to return identifying information about a *file* designated by the user for reading or writing.

resource: A unit or collection of information kept in a *resource file* on a disk and *loaded* into memory when needed.

resource attributes: A set of flags describing various properties of a *resource,* kept in the *attribute byte* of its *resource map* entry.

resource compiler: A utility program that constructs *resources* according to a coded definition read from a text file.

resource data: The information a *resource* contains.

resource editor: A utility program with which *resources* can be defined or modified directly on the Macintosh screen with the mouse and keyboard.

resource file: A collection of *resources* stored together as a unit on a disk; technically not a *file* as such, but merely the *resource fork* of a particular file.

resource file attributes: A set of flags describing various properties of a *resource file*.

resource fork: The *fork* of a *file* that contains the file's *resources*; usually called a *resource file*. Compare *data fork*.

resource ID: An integer that uniquely identifies a particular *resource* within its *resource type*.

resource map: The table that summarizes the contents of a *resource file*, stored as part of the file itself and read into memory when the file is opened.

resource name: An optional string of text characters that uniquely identifies a particular *resource* within its *resource type*, and by which the resource can be listed on a *menu*.

resource specification: The combination of a *resource type* and *resource ID*, or a *resource type* and *resource name*, which uniquely identifies a particular resource.

resource type: A four-character string that identifies the kind of information a *resource* contains.

result code: An integer code returned by an *Operating System* routine to signal successful completion or report an error.

return link: The address of the instruction following a routine call, to which control is to return on completion of the routine.

ROM: See *read-only memory*.

rounded rectangle: A graphical figure consisting of a *rectangle* with rounded corners; defined by the rectangle itself and the dimensions of the *ovals* forming the corners.

routine selector: An integer used to identify a particular routine within a *package*.

row width: The number of bytes in each row of a *bit image*.

SANE: The Standard Apple Numeric Environment, a set of routines for performing arithmetic on *floating-point numbers* in accordance with the *IEEE standard*; available on the Macintosh through the *Floating-Point Arithmetic Package*.

scrap: The intermediate vehicle by which information is *cut and pasted* from one place to another.

scrap count: An integer maintained by the Toolbox that tells when the contents of the *desk scrap* have been changed by a *desk accessory*.

scrap handle: A *handle* to the contents of the *desk scrap*, kept by the Toolbox in a *system global*.

scrap information record: A data structure summarizing the contents and status of the *desk scrap*.

screen buffer: The area of memory reserved to hold the *screen image*.

screen image: The *bit image* that defines what is displayed on the Macintosh screen.

screen map: The *bit map* representing the Macintosh screen, kept in the QuickDraw global variable **ScreenBits**. Its *bit image* is the *screen image*; its *boundary rectangle* has the same dimensions as the screen, with the *origin* at coordinates (**0**, **0**).

scroll: To move the contents of a *window* with respect to the window itself, changing the portion of a document or other information that's visible within the window.

scroll bar: A *control* associated with a *window* that allows the user to *scroll* the window's contents.

scroll box: The *indicator* of a *scroll bar*, a small white box that can be *dragged* to any desired position within the scroll bar's *shaft*; also called the "thumb."

sector: A portion of a *track* on a disk, holding 512 bytes of information along with a 12-byte *tag*.

seed: The starting value used in generating a sequence of *pseudo-random numbers*.

segment header: Information at the beginning of a *code segment* identifying which entries in the program's *jump table* belong to this segment.

segment number: The *resource ID* of a *code segment*.

segment 0: A special *code segment* containing the information needed to initialize a program's *application global space*.

selection: An object or part of a document designated by the user to be acted on by subsequent commands or operations.

selection range: A pair of *character positions* defining the beginning and end of the *selection* in an *edit record*.

serial driver: The *device driver* built into ROM for communicating with peripheral devices through the Macintosh's built-in *serial ports*.

serial port: A connector on the back of the Macintosh for communicating with peripheral devices such as a hard disk, printer, or modem.

setting: An integer specifying the current state or value of a *control.*

shaft: The vertical or horizontal body of a *scroll bar,* within which the *scroll box* slides.

shape: Any of the figures that can be drawn with QuickDraw *shape-drawing* operations, including *rectangles, rounded rectangles, ovals, arcs* and *wedges, polygons,* and *regions.*

shape drawing: Drawing *shapes* in a *graphics port,* using the operations *frame, paint, fill, erase,* and *invert.*

shield: To hide the *cursor* if any part of it lies within a specified *shield* rectangle.

shield rectangle: The rectangle within which the *cursor* will be hidden when *shielded.*

shift key: A *modifier key* on the Macintosh keyboard, used to convert lowercase letters to uppercase or to produce the upper character on a nonalphabetic key.

show: To make a window, control, or other object *visible.*

signature: A four-character string that identifies a particular application program, used as a *creator signature* on files belonging to the program and as the *resource type* of the program's *autograph* resource.

68000: See *MC68000.*

size box: The small box at the bottom-right corner of a *document window,* with which it can be resized by dragging with the mouse.

size region: The area of a *window* with which it can be resized by dragging with the mouse; also called the "grow region." In a *document window,* the size region is the *size box.*

SIZEOF: A function provided by Apple's Pascal compiler, which accepts a variable or type name as a parameter and returns the number of bytes of memory occupied by that variable or by values of that type.

sound buffer: The area of memory whose contents determine the sounds to be emitted by the Macintosh speaker.

sound driver: The *device driver* built into ROM for controlling the sounds emitted by the Macintosh speaker.

sound number: An integer identifying the *error sound* to be emitted by an *alert.*

sound procedure: A procedure that defines the *error sounds* to be emitted by *alerts.*

source transfer modes: A set of *transfer modes* used for transferring pixels from one *bit map* to another or for drawing text characters into a bit map.

stack: (1) Generally, a data structure in which items can be added (*pushed*) and removed (*popped*) in *LIFO* order: the last item added is always the first to be removed. (2) Specifically, the area of Macintosh *RAM* that holds parameters, local variables, return addresses, and other temporary storage associated with a program's procedures and functions; compare *heap*. One end of the stack (the *base*) remains fixed in memory, while items are added or removed at the other end (the *top*); the *stack pointer* always points to the current top of the stack.

stack-based: Describes a Toolbox routine that accepts its parameters and returns its results on the *stack*, according to Pascal conventions; compare *register-based*.

stack pointer: The address of the current top of the *stack*, kept in processor register **A7**.

stage list: A data structure that defines the behavior of a *staged alert* at each consecutive occurrence.

staged alert: An *alert* that behaves differently at consecutive occurrences.

Standard File Package: A standard *package*, provided in the *system resource file*, that provides a convenient, standard way for the user to supply file names for input/output operations; also called the **MiniFinder**.

standard fill tones: A set of five *patterns* representing a range of homogeneous tones from solid white to solid black, provided as global variables by the *QuickDraw* graphics routines.

standard patterns: The 38 *patterns* included on the standard MacPaint pattern palette, available as a *pattern list* resource in the *system resource file*.

starting angle: The angle defining the beginning of an *arc* or *wedge*.

startup handle: A *handle* to a program's *startup information*, passed to the program by the *Finder* as an *application parameter*.

startup information: A list of *document files* selected by the user to be opened on starting up an application program.

static item: A *dialog item*, such as a piece of text, an *icon*, or a *picture*, that conveys information to the user without accepting any in return; compare *interactive item*.

sticky space: A text character (character code **$CA**) that looks like a space but isn't considered a *word break* when text is *wrapped* or *selected*.

stop alert: A form of *alert box*, more severe than either a *note alert* or *caution alert*, that reports a serious error or problem making it impossible to complete the requested operation, or that warns the user of potentially dangerous or irrevocable consequences.

strike: See *font image*.

string list: A *resource* consisting of any number of *Pascal-format strings*.

structure region: The total area occupied by a *window*, including both its *window frame* and *content region*.

system clock: The clock that records the elapsed time in *ticks* since the system was last started up.

system event mask: A global *event mask* maintained by the Toolbox that controls which types of *event* can be *posted* into the *event queue*.

system font: The *typeface* (**Chicago**) used by the Toolbox for displaying its own text on the screen, such as window titles and menu items.

system globals: Fixed memory locations reserved for use by the Toolbox.

system heap: The portion of the *heap* reserved for the private use of the Macintosh Operating System and Toolbox.

system resource file: The *resource fork* of the file **System**, containing shared resources that are available to all programs.

system window: A window in which a *desk accessory* is displayed on the screen; compare *application window*.

tag: Twelve bytes of identifying information associated with a *sector* on a disk for use by the *file system*.

target text: The text to be found by a search or replacement operation; compare *destination text*, *replacement text*.

text box: A *dialog item* consisting of a box into which the user can type text from the keyboard.

text characteristics: The properties of a *graphics port* that determine the way it draws text characters, including its *text face*, *text size*, *text style*, and *text mode*.

text face: The *typeface* in which a *graphics port* draws text characters.

text file: A file of file type 'TEXT', containing pure text characters with no additional formatting or other information.

text font: Term sometimes used loosely (and incorrectly) as a synonym for *text face*.

text handle: A *handle* to a sequence of text characters in memory.

text menu: The standard *menu type* used by the Toolbox, consisting of a vertical list of item titles.

text mode: The *transfer mode* with which a *graphics port* draws text characters.

text scrap: The private *scrap* maintained by the *TextEdit* routines to hold text being *cut and pasted* from one place to another.

text size: The *type size* in which a *graphics port* draws text characters.

text style: The *type style* in which a *graphics port* draws text characters.

TextEdit: The collection of text-editing routines included in the *User Interface Toolbox.*

thumb: See *scroll box.*

tick: One sixtieth of a second, the interval between successive occurrences of the *vertical retrace interrupt*; the basic unit of time on the *system clock.*

title bar: The area at the top of a *document window* that displays the window's title, and by which the window can be *dragged* to a new location on the screen.

Toolbox: (1) The *User Interface Toolbox.* (2) Loosely, the entire contents of the Macintosh *ROM*, including the *Macintosh Operating System* and *QuickDraw* in addition to the *User Interface Toolbox* proper.

top of stack: The end of the *stack* at which items are added and removed; compare *base of stack.*

track: (1) To follow the movements of the *mouse* while the user *drags* it, taking some continuous action (such as providing visual feedback on the screen) until the button is released. (2) One of the concentric rings in which information is recorded on the surface of a disk.

tracking rectangle: A rectangle that limits the *tracking* of the mouse when the user *drags* a *control.*

Transcendental Functions Package: A standard *package*, provided in the *system resource file*, that calculates various transcendental functions on *floating-point numbers*, such as logarithms, exponentials, trigonometric functions, compound interest, and discounted value.

transfer mode: A method of combining *pixels* being transferred to a *bit map* with those already there.

translate: To move a *point* or graphical figure a given distance horizontally and vertically.

trap: An error or abnormal condition that causes the *MC68000* processor to suspend normal program execution temporarily and execute a *trap handler* routine to respond to the problem; also called an *exception.*

Trap Dispatcher: The *trap handler* routine for responding to the *emulator trap*, which examines the contents of the *trap word* and jumps to the corresponding Toolbox routine in ROM.

trap handler: The routine executed by the *MC68000* processor to respond to a particular type of *trap.*

trap macro: A macroinstruction used to call a Toolbox routine from an assembly-language program; when assembled, it produces the appropriate *trap word* for the desired routine. Trap macros are defined in the assembly-language interface to the Toolbox and always begin with an underscore character (_).

trap number: The last 8 or 9 bits of a *trap word*, which identify the particular Toolbox routine to be executed; used as an index into the *dispatch table* to find the address of the routine in ROM.

trap vector: The address of the *trap handler* routine for a particular type of *trap*, kept in the *vector table* in memory.

trap word: An *unimplemented instruction* used to stand for a particular Toolbox operation in a machine-language program. The trap word includes a *trap number* identifying the Toolbox operation to be performed; when executed, it causes an *emulator trap* that will execute the corresponding Toolbox routine in ROM.

type size: The size in which text characters are drawn, measured in printer's *points* and sometimes referred to as a "point size."

type style: Variations on the basic form in which text characters are drawn, such as bold, italic, underline, outline, or shadow.

typecasting: A feature of Apple's Pascal compiler that allows data items to be converted from one data type to another with the same underlying representation (for example, from one pointer type to another).

typeface: The overall form or design in which text characters are drawn, independent of size or style. Macintosh typefaces are conventionally named after world cities, such as **New York**, **Geneva**, or **Athens**.

unimplemented instruction: A machine-language instruction whose effects are not defined by the *MC68000* processor. Attempting to execute such an instruction causes an *emulator trap* to occur, allowing the effects of the instruction to be "emulated" with software instead of hardware.

unit: A collection of precompiled declarations that can be incorporated wholesale into any Pascal program.

unit number: The *resource ID* of a *device driver*; an integer between **0** and **31**, related to the *driver reference number* by the formula **refNum = −(unitNum + 1)**.

unload: To remove an object, such as a *code segment* or the *desk scrap*, from memory, often (though not necessarily) by writing it out to a disk file.

unlock: To undo the effects of *locking* a *relocatable block*, again allowing it to be moved within the heap during *compaction*.

unmount: To make a *volume* unknown to the file system by releasing the memory space occupied by its *file directory* and *block map*.

unpurgeable block: A *relocatable block* that can't be *purged* from the heap to make room for other blocks.

up arrow: The arrow at the top or left end of a *scroll bar*, which causes it to scroll up or to the left a line at a time when clicked with the mouse.

update: (1) To write a new version of a *resource file* to the disk, incorporating all changes made in the file's resources in memory. (2) To redraw all or part of a window's *content region* on the screen, usually because it has become *exposed* as a result of the user's manipulations with the mouse.

update event: A *window event* generated by the Toolbox to signal that all or part of a given window has become *exposed* and must be *updated* (redrawn).

update rectangle: The rectangle within which text is to be redrawn when an *edit record* is *updated.*

update region: The *region* defining the portion of a *window* that must be redrawn when *updating* the window.

user: The human operator of a computer.

user interface: The set of rules and conventions by which a human *user* communicates with a computer system or program.

User Interface Guidelines: An Apple document (part of the *Inside Macintosh* documentation) that defines the standard *user interface* conventions to be followed by all Macintosh application programs.

User Interface Toolbox: The body of machine code built into the Macintosh *ROM* to implement the features of the standard *user interface.*

uses declaration: A declaration that incorporates the code of a precompiled *unit* into a Pascal program.

valid region: An area of a window's *content region* whose contents are accurately displayed on the screen, and which therefore need not be *updated.*

VBL interrupt: Short for "vertical blanking interrupt"; see *vertical retrace interrupt.*

vector table: A table of *trap vectors* kept in the first kilobyte of RAM, used by the *MC68000* processor to locate the *trap handler* routine to execute when a *trap* occurs.

version data: Another name for a program's *autograph* resource, so called because its *resource data* typically holds a string identifying the version and date of the program.

vertical blanking interrupt: See *vertical retrace interrupt.*

vertical retrace interrupt: An *interrupt* generated by the Macintosh's video display circuitry when the display tube's electron beam reaches the bottom of the screen and returns to the top to begin the next frame. This interrupt, recurring regularly at intervals of one **tick** (sixty times per second), forms the "heartbeat" of the Macintosh system.

view rectangle: The boundary to which text is *clipped* when displayed in an *edit record;* also called the "clipping rectangle."

visible: Describes a window, control, or other object that is logically in view on the screen. A visible object is actually displayed only if *exposed*; compare *invisible*.

visible region: A *clipping boundary* that defines, for a *graphics port* associated with a *window*, the portion of the *port rectangle* that's exposed to view on the screen.

volume: A collection of *files* grouped together as a logical unit on a given storage device.

volume buffer: The area of memory set aside to hold information being transferred to or from a given *volume*.

volume name: A string of text characters identifying a particular *volume*.

volume reference number: An identifying number assigned by the *file system* to stand for a given *volume*.

wedge: A graphical figure bounded by a given *arc* and the lines joining its endpoints to the center of its *oval*.

wide-open region: A rectangular *region* extending from coordinates (**−32768, −32768**) to (**32767, 32767**), encompassing the entire QuickDraw coordinate plane.

window: An area of the Macintosh screen in which information is displayed, and which can overlap and hide or be hidden by other windows.

window class: An integer code that identifies the origin and general purpose of a *window*, as opposed to its appearance and behavior; compare *window type*.

window data record: A data structure maintained by an application program (not by the Toolbox!) that contains auxiliary information about a *window* and is accessed via a *handle* stored as the window's *reference constant*.

window definition function: A routine, stored as a *resource*, that defines the appearance and behavior of a particular type of *window*.

window definition ID: A coded integer representing a *window type*, which includes the *resource ID* of the *window definition function* along with additional modifying information.

window event: An *event* generated by the Toolbox to coordinate the display of *windows* on the screen; see *activate event*, *deactivate event*, *update event*.

window frame: The part of a *window* that's independent of the information it displays, and which is drawn automatically by the Toolbox; compare *content region*.

window list: A linked list of all *windows* in existence at any given time, chained together through a field of their *window records*.

Window Manager port: The *graphics port* in which the Toolbox draws all *window frames*.

window picture: A QuickDraw *picture* used in place of *update events* to redraw the contents of a *window*.

window pointer: A pointer to a *window record*.

window record: A data structure containing all the information associated with a given *window*.

window template: A *resource* containing all the information needed to create a *window*.

window type: A category of *window*, identified by a *window definition ID*, whose appearance and behavior are determined by a *window definition function*; compare *window class*.

word: A group of 16 bits (2 *bytes*) beginning at a *word boundary* in memory.

word boundary: Any even-numbered memory address. Every *word* or *long word* in memory must begin at a word boundary.

word break: A *character position* marking the beginning or end of a word.

word-break routine: A function associated with an *edit record* that determines the locations of the *word breaks* in the record's text.

word wrap: A method of *wrapping* text in which an entire word is carried forward when beginning a new line, so that no word is ever broken between lines.

wrap: To format text or other information against a boundary by beginning a new line whenever the edge of the boundary is reached.

wrapping rectangle: See *destination rectangle*.

wristwatch cursor: A standard *cursor* included in the *system resource file* for use in signalling processing delays.

Index

===

This is a cumulative index, incorporating page references to *Macintosh Revealed*, Volumes I and II.

615

The Software Featured in MACINTOSH REVEALED Available on Disk

*If you want to produce programs with that professional Macintosh look, you'll want a copy of the **MiniEdit** source disk that is now available directly from Hayden.*

MiniEdit is a simple interactive text editor that shows you how to use the User Interface Toolbox in an actual application program. It is specifically designed to illustrate as many features as possible of the standard Macintosh user interface, including windows, menus, scroll bars, desk accessories, text editing, dialog boxes, and filing.

The disk contains the complete source code of the *MiniEdit* program as listed in Appendix H of this book. The program already includes all the Toolbox calls you need to implement the standard user interface features. By using it as a "shell" within which to develop your own Macintosh applications, you can avoid "reinventing the wheel" for every program you write.

Complete the order form and return it along with $19.95, plus $2.50 to cover postage and handling, to order a disk copy of *MiniEdit*, the example program featured in this volume.